Our Dumb World

Our Dumb World

THE ONION'S ATLAS OF THE PLANET EARTH
73rd Edition

Little, Brown and Company

New York   Boston   London

Little, Brown and Company
Hachette Book Group
237 Park Avenue, New York, NY 10017
Visit our Web site at www.HachetteBookGroup.com

Originally published in hardcover by Little, Brown and Company, October 2007
First Little, Brown trade paperback edition, October 2008

Little, Brown and Company is a division of Hachette Book Group, Inc. The Little,
Brown name and logo are trademarks of Hachette Book Group, Inc.

ISBN 978-0-316-01842-5 (hc)/ 978-0-316-01843-3 (pb)
HC LCCN 2007931489

10 9 8 7 6 5 4 3 2 1

WOR

Printed in the United States of America

Also By The Onion

Our Dumb World

EDITOR-IN-CHIEF

Scott Dikkers

EDITORS

Mike DiCenzo, Dan Guterman, Chad Nackers, Joe Randazzo

HEAD WRITERS

Mike DiCenzo, Dan Guterman

WRITERS

Chet Clem, Scott Dikkers, Megan Ganz, Joe Garden, Todd Hanson, Chris Karwowski, Peter Koechley, John Krewson, Mike Loew, Chad Nackers, Joe Randazzo, Maria Schneider

LEAD DESIGNER

Brandon Kizart-Haynes
with art direction from Giampietro+Smith

GRAPHICS EDITOR

Mike Loew

PHOTO ARTISTS

Michael Faisca, Nick Gallo

GRAPHIC ARTISTS

Brittain Ashford, Jim Crosley, Kevin Hand, Gina Nastasi, Lisa Pompilio, R. Sikoryak

COVER ART AND DESIGN

Rick Martin

EDITORIAL MANAGERS

Chet Clem, Peter Koechley

EDITORIAL ASSISTANT

Dave Kornfeld

CONSULTANTS

Dave Herubin, Kelly Swanson

COPY EDITORS

Rebecca Bengal, Mike DiCenzo, Danny Mulligan

INTERNS

Brittain Ashford, Bradley Bosma, Meg Charlton, Chris Dannen, Molly Fitzpatrick, Angela Freedman, Bryan Kelly, Sam Kemmis, Dan Klein, Benjamin Levitan, David Litt, Eric March, Ryan McDermott, John McGlaughlin, Johnny McNulty, Margaret Meehan, Kate Mulley, Marcus Parks, Holden Rasche, Molly Jane Rosen, Nina Sharma, Will Tracy, Juliet Werner, Andrew Yurman-Glaser

SPECIAL THANKS

Amie Barrodale, Diane Bullock, Billy Cummings, Ryan Dolan, Amelie Gillette, Will Graham, Daniel Greenberg, Steve Hannah, John Harris, Tim Harrod, Ellie Kemper, Carol Kolb, Sean Mills, Dan Mirk, Andrei Nechita, Chris Pauls, Seth Reiss, David Schafer, Mike Schuster, Anita Serwacki, Scott Sherman, Robert Siegel, Sigmund Stern, Colin Tierney

Table Of Contents

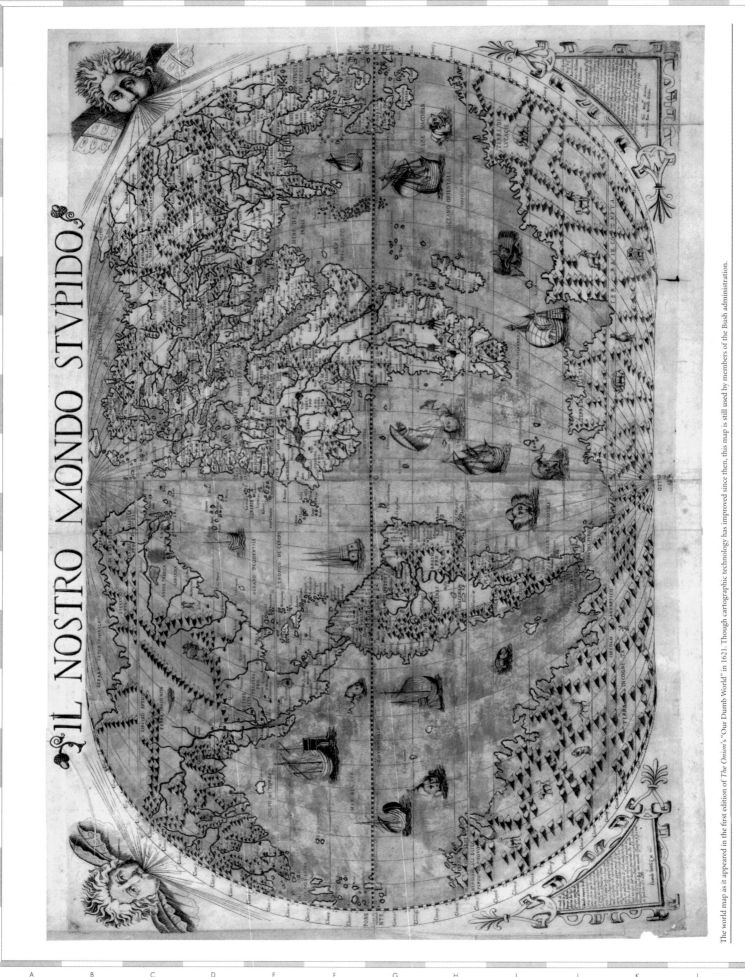

IL NOSTRO MONDO STVPIDO

The world map as it appeared in the first edition of *The Onion's* "Our Dumb World" in 1621. Though cartographic technology has improved since then, this map is still used by members of the Bush administration.

To Hell With The World And All Its Myriad Peoples!

A Letter Of Introduction
From T. Herman Zweibel

Editor Emeritus T. Herman Zweibel
(photo circa 1911)

I am informed by the gape-jawed half-wits who laughingly call themselves *The Onion* Editorial Board that we shall soon be publishing yet another edition of *The Onion*'s World Atlas, Fact-book, and Universal Pantechnicon. Naturally, my rage at this news is so intense that only horse-doses of laudanum are preventing my age-withered carcass from stiffening with fury. Why must people persist in their senseless curiosity concerning the world into which they are born in pain and confusion, only to die in like fashion 40 or 50 years thereafter? What good did any-one ever derive from knowing the dimensions of the great Norway Maelstrom, or the current price of slave-youths in Siam, or the location of Chicago, Illinois? I spent some of the best years of my life, and roughly 80 of the worst, amassing an unfathomably large fortune by keeping such evidence-based clap-trap out of my news-paper. Instead, I prefer illustrations of mammoth-teated photo-play actresses. Yet now some young smart-ass decides that our pus-brained readers desire a compendium of all the world's geographical knowledge. Naturally, that particular smart-ass has been fired. But, sad to say, this book remains.

Hear me, dear readers: You need know nothing of our world. Suffice it to say that it is a vast vale of tears full to bursting with pain, horror, and cruelty, that every settlement of man is a warehouse of depravity, that every inch of countryside is an ancient, overflowing graveyard, that this magnificent globe we tread, which seems so lovely and full of wonders at first blush, is upon closer inspection a mere antechamber to Hell itself. And then one leaves the Eastern sea-board, and things are even worse!

I traveled well in my youth, or at least I seem to remember that I did, and so I therefore know what I'm talking about, or at least I should. In those heady days, I visited each of the planet's 27 known countries, charting the borders, tasting of the cuisine and the flesh, fomenting political coups d'état, capturing, displaying, and later emancipating the indigenous peoples, and purchasing at reasonable rates large swaths of sovereignty. I have seen the magnificence that is London, the capital city of a nation of industrious homo-sexuals. In mysterious India, I have seen men lying on beds of nails, many of them voluntarily. In the great southern American continent, I have seen remarkably god-damned enormous rats. I have met with heathen China-Men who prepared for me their exotic and malodorous foods while informing me that they would own our nation in seven generations. I even looked down upon darkest Africa once from a hot-air-powered balloon. Indeed, travel was a wonderful and fantastic experience that changed me for-ever, and I damned sure do not want to go through that again.

Over the decades, and despite my most earnest attempts to prevent it, much has changed on Earth: America gained its independence, hunting humans for sport was outlawed, man harnessed the power of invisibility, and a group of feral children founded their own republic in the South Pacific. When this atlas was first published, one had to hack through the thicket to discover a new country and plunder its bountiful resources. Now, I'm told, it can all be done over the tele-phone wire. Not surprisingly the number of nations and employable ethnicities continues to grow each year. In fact, modern cartographers in my employ have generated for this latest edition two original countries, known as Belgium and Sri Lanka, which I intend to destroy the moment I regain the strength to stand and hold the tele-phone ear-piece in my hand.

Were my heart not atrophied and soot-blackened, I might lament that the average life expectancy around the world is nine short years, and here I am at 140, I believe, with nothing but billions of dollars to show for it. Still and all, I suggest you close this book right now and never open it again. Perhaps you can boil its pages to make a broth substantial enough to steal one more day among the living. Perhaps it is better that you die.

Alas, the only thing that prevents me from going mad from a corrosive combination of hatred and fear of the unknown is the thought that I would not have been able to become so blasphemously rich were it not for one simple truth: the peoples of the world will always believe whatever preposterous hateful bull-shit I tell them so long as it is printed in neat columns next to attractive pictures of their leaders. And thank God for that, I say.

Any-way, here is *The Onion*'s Atlas Of The World. Now get back to work! And no Irish!

T. H. Zweibel

T. Herman Zweibel

How To Use This Atlas

If you are reading this introduction, we can only assume that the Title Page, Masthead, and Copyright Information have piqued your interest and you've decided to venture onward. It is important to note, however, that what follows in the remaining 63/64ths of this reference volume may not be as immediately enjoyable as the inside cover without the proper navigational tools.

Indeed, it would be a shame for you, the reader, to miss out on any obtainable pleasure because of something as trivial as not knowing how to read a map key, break down a bar graph, or hold this atlas in a manner in which the printed words are right-side up.

"But how do I access this information?" you may ask. It's easy. First, focus the lens of your eyes on the page. Next, allow the light to hit the back of your retina, convert itself into neuronal signals, and travel to the visual cortex of your brain. Once that is complete, direct ocular movement to the area of the page you next want to absorb as information. By following these simple steps, and being free of such disorders as Scotopic Sensitivity Syndrome, there is no telling how much you can glean from this handsomely bound tome.

HOW TO SKIM THIS ATLAS »

- Automatically discount anything not in a brightly colored box as too dense.

- Only look at prime-numbered pages.

- Southeast Asia is a subregion of Asia. There, we've just saved you 40 pages' worth of laborious reading.

- Purchase the *Our Dumb World* audiobook. Fast-forward through it.

- Dart your eyes quickly back and forth, never allowing them to rest on any spot long enough to actually take in information.

- Just skip ahead now to the last bullet point.

- When encountering a paragraph of text, quickly decide that you already know enough about Russia as it is.

- Use photo captions to get "the gist" of a continent.

- Pretend you know how to speed-read.

- Come on now, just put the atlas down, and inch over to the *Calvin & Hobbes Collection* like you know you want to.

A GUIDE TO MAP ICONS »

- ★ Capital city
- ▲ Mountain
- ⚘ Site of trite Robert Frost poem
- ····· Disputed border
- ✂ Cut here to resolve border dispute
- ▬ Blockbuster location
- ⛵ A ship, you fucking retard
- ✝ Church
- ✡ Synagogue
- ☾ U.S. bomb target
- 〰 Seriously, is this the best waterfall icon we could find? Christ...
- ◎ Look away! Hypnosis imminent!
- ∴ Ruins of ancient civilization/ Thriving African metropolis
- ■ The harsh geopolitical realities of the modern world and the challenges posed to them by encroaching foreign interests and a global oil shortage

A GUIDE TO ATLAS STYLE CONVENTIONS »

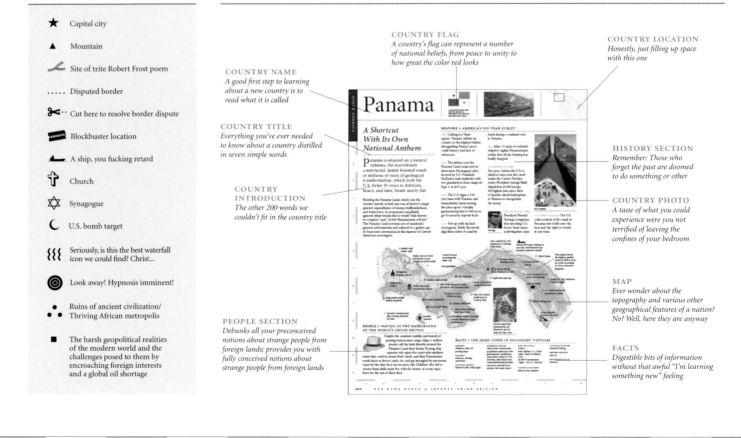

COUNTRY NAME
A good first step to learning about a new country is to read what it is called

COUNTRY TITLE
Everything you've ever needed to know about a country distilled in seven simple words

COUNTRY INTRODUCTION
The other 200 words we couldn't fit in the country title

PEOPLE SECTION
Debunks all your preconceived notions about strange people from foreign lands; provides you with fully conceived notions about strange people from foreign lands

COUNTRY FLAG
A country's flag can represent a number of national beliefs, from peace to unity to how great the color red looks

COUNTRY LOCATION
Honestly, just filling up space with this one

HISTORY SECTION
Remember: Those who forget the past are doomed to do something or other

COUNTRY PHOTO
A taste of what you could experience were you not terrified of leaving the confines of your bedroom

MAP
Ever wonder about the topography and various other geographical features of a nation? No? Well, here they are anyway

FACTS
Digestible bits of information without that awful "I'm learning something new" feeling

A NOTE TO BARNES & NOBLE BROWSERS »

What do you think you're doing? Seriously, what does this look like to you? Some kind of library? Did you really think you could just come in here and spend the afternoon reading this book for free? The line to pay is over that way, buddy. What's that? Just trying to decide whether or not you want to buy the book? You don't think we're really that stupid, do you? You know what? Fine. Why don't you just make yourself at home. Pull up a chair. They don't close until 10 p.m., after all.

You fucking prick.

Do you know how hard people worked to write this book? No, of course you don't. Maybe you should check out the Self-Help section once you're finished leafing through this.

That's right, we said it. You need help. And you know what else? You don't even deserve this atlas. You heard us—we don't want your money. Honestly, just put it back on the shelf and get out. *Get the fuck out of here... Now!*

Barnes & Noble, a store where one *buys* books.

HOW TO USE THIS ATLAS IN OTHER COUNTRIES »

A Zambian woman puts this atlas to good use.

The world is a land of contrasts. Below, we offer several suggestions to help readers in other countries get the most out of this atlas:

Mexico Use atlas to help boost wife over border fence into the U.S.

England Turn to page 137; allow monocle to drop into wine glass in horror.

India Present atlas to nearby cow as ceremonial offering.

France This atlas is clearly beneath you. Do not waste your precious, precious time with it.

Botswana Why did you spend your money on an atlas?! Good God! Your children are starving! Return this book for a full refund right now!

Japan Upload contents to brain's memory-chip implant.

Iran Take a moment to read about the cultures and perspectives of your neighbors, because after all, it rea—you just set this page on fire, didn't you?

Indonesia Bind and glue loose pages to book's spine for 18 continuous hours.

CHARTS AND GRAPHS »

These visual aids are a quick and concise way to communicate information, without the need for introductions or explanations. With that out of the way, here are three types of charts you will encounter throughout this atlas.

WHAT IS THE WORLD COMING TO? »

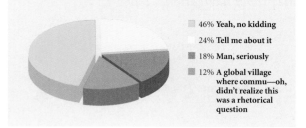

- 46% **Yeah, no kidding**
- 24% **Tell me about it**
- 18% **Man, seriously**
- 12% **A global village where commu—oh, didn't realize this was a rhetorical question**

WORLD POPULATION GROWTH »

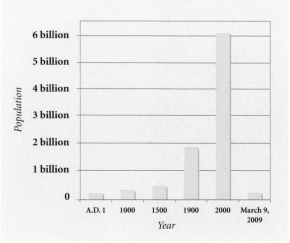

FREQUENCY OF LINE GRAPHS IN THIS ATLAS »

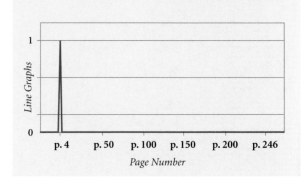

The History Of Cartography

The word "cartography" stems from the Greek words chartis, **meaning "carto," and** graphein, **meaning "graphy." This arbitrary term is used to describe the art of mapmaking.**

The cartographic process dates back thousands of years, when early man first set rock to cave wall, drew what looked like a circle, stopped to defecate onto his bare feet, added some sort of detail to the circle, suddenly screamed for no apparent reason, and put the finishing touches on what would become the science of mapmaking. Little has changed since then.

The 15th century was the golden era of cartography. Men sailed the oceans in an effort to map the globe—a process that took hundreds of years, as there weren't any maps

DISTRIBUTION OF WEALTH »

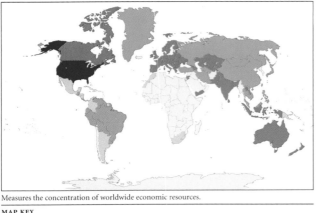

Measures the concentration of worldwide economic resources.

MAP KEY

- Did someone say something about distributing wealth?
- So poor even Rodney Dangerfield unable to hyperbolize situation
- Makes roughly as much as Kevin Garnett does in a year
- Paid $100 million to be bumped up to this level
- Are the United States

BONO AWARENESS »

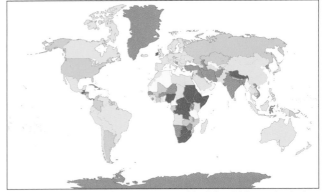

Measures the intensity with which artist Bono is aware of the plight and daily struggles of region.

MAP KEY

- Has heard of nation once
- Only thinks about nation when drawing up U2 tour schedule
- Frequently dedicates songs to nation
- Moved enough by nation's crisis to momentarily remove sunglasses
- Cares about welfare of nation nearly as much as his own

CONTINENTAL DRIFT OF THE EARTH'S LANDMASSES »

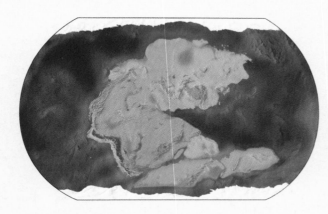

100 Million B.C.

1 Million B.C.

around for them to consult. By the late 18th century, mapmaking had become a popular craft for those who enjoyed charting the world around them, and others who just needed an excuse to spend time away from their domineering wives.

However, it was not until the flat surface was created in 1814 that cartography truly blossomed.

Since the late 1900s, most maps have been made using computers. Though this method is more precise, it has ended the careers of countless people who possess no other skill besides drawing the coast of South America with a graphite pencil onto a sheet of transparent isometric grid paper.

Today, it is difficult to imagine the world without maps—especially Eastern Europe, which is probably to the left of Asia, right? Or maybe it's to the south of Asia? No, wait, never mind. That's Southeast Asia to the south of Asia, isn't it? Shit…hold on…where is Asia again?

DAVIDSON FAMILY RISK NIGHT, 1987 »

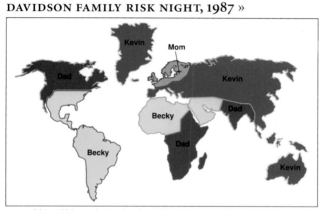

A map of the world during the Davidson family Risk game, Dec. 14, 1987.

MAP KEY

8:00 P.M. Coalition of the Willing agrees to skip Mom's turn while she is in bathroom

8:23 P.M. Temporary international cease-fire brokered by funny commercial on television

9:15 P.M. Global economy thrown into disarray when Kevin calls Becky a backstabber and swipes pieces off the board

9:47 P.M. Dad declares all alliances moot and sends all world governments to bed

MAP TO ERICA'S PARTY »

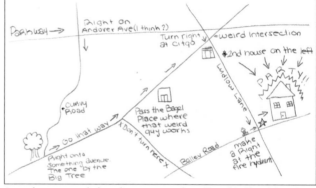

As seen above, maps can also be used to convey extremely sensitive and significant information.

MAP KEY

Now, what you want to do is go down the parkway until you reach Andover Avenue (or maybe it's Atwater Avenue). Once you get there, you're going to see this big tree with a lot of branches on it. Just ignore that. You actually want to wait for the other big tree with less branches on it. Now make a left, and keep driving until you get to that bagel place where your brother's friend Jeremy worked a few years ago. Actually, you know what? It's probably easier if you just call me. Yeah, just ignore this map.

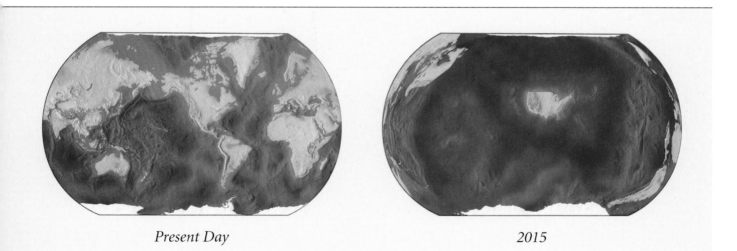

Present Day   *2015*

North America

The United States

» THE AMERICAN FLAG WAS FIRST SEWN BY BETSY ROSS OF PHILADELPHIA, AND LAST SEWN BY YUN ENOKI OF TAIWAN.

The Land Of Opportunism

The United States was founded in 1776 on the principles of life, liberty, and the reckless pursuit of happiness at any cost—even life and liberty.

America is a place where even the poorest immigrant can, through hard work and dedication, achieve the American Dream for his employer. Where children are the most important exploitable natural resource. Where at any given moment opportunity may knock on your door, and if you're not home, break in through your window and take everything you've got.

America is the birthplace of the entrepreneur, the entrepreneur's assistant, the entrepreneurial coordinator, and the special consultant to the entrepreneur.

It is a nation where freedom rings from coast to coast, over and over and over again, until you finally decide to pick up the phone and agree to cover a coworker's night shift. A nation where any man can arrive with nothing more than a few pennies in his pocket, the hope of a better life, a passport, two I-9 forms, proof of employment, reference letters from reliable sponsors, and through sheer persistence finally convince a border guard to let him into the country.

America is a land of equality for all, and special, better equality for some. It is a land where the streets are paved with gold, and the ditches are paved with unskilled laborers forced to lay down that gold. A nation where any determined individual can climb to the top of the corporate ladder and kick it down so that nobody else can. Where a man can go from rags to riches almost overnight, and from riches back to rags in even less time, then write a book about it, option the rights to a TV network or film studio, and blow all that money on drugs.

Most importantly, however, the United States is a place where any citizen has the chance to serve his country, regardless of color, creed, or whether he's just served his country for three years and wants desperately to go home.

In America, any millionaire can, through hard work and determination, exploit others to become a billionaire.

ALASKA »

× Oil executive bribing elk to look the other way

× Grizzly eating salmon out of a can

Winning dogsled team feasting on musher

Inuit pimp dressing seal in miniskirt

HAWAII »

× Great place to say you went scuba diving

× U.S. got this one for free

Island for holding pineapples

Time-Share Island

Water Extra-Perfect Over Here

× Site where bad guys tried to force Magnum P.I. off the road

TOP REASONS FOR AMERICAN PRIDE »

American citizens are among the proudest on earth. Why do they love their country so much?

- 28% **Freedom to say whatever you want, like, "Ummm...uhhhh...hmm..."**
- 14% **Have flag, feel like waving something**
- 12% **Fear others will accuse them of being a Communist**
- 10% **That song that goes "I'm proud to be an American" and then there's the guitar part**
- 4% **President's Day Mattress Sale**
- 2% **Subtle imperialistic undertones of professional wrestling storylines**
- 30% **USA! USA! USA! Wooooooooooo!**

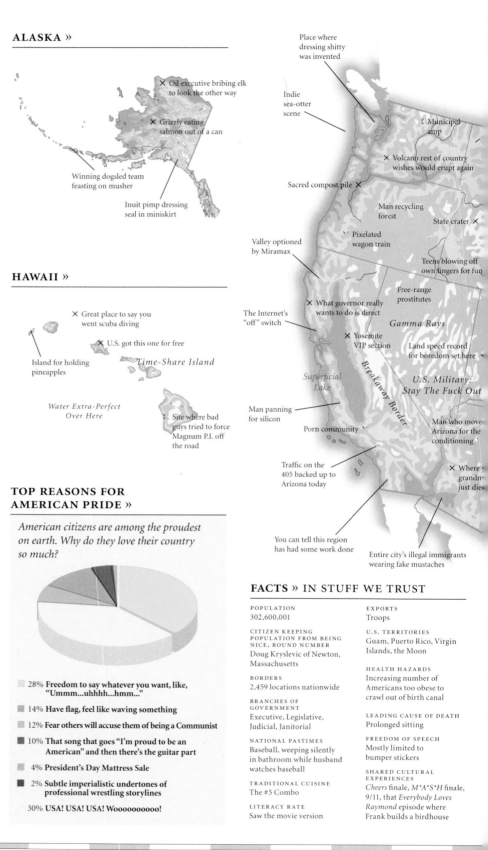

Place where dressing shitty was invented

Indie sea-otter scene

× Municipal amp

× Volcano rest of country wishes would erupt again

Sacred compost pile ×

Man recycling forest

State crater ×

Valley optioned by Miramax

× Pixelated wagon train

Teens blowing off own fingers for fun

Free-range prostitutes

The Internet's "off" switch

× What governor really wants to do is direct

Gamma Rays

× Yosemite VIP section

Land speed record for boredom set here

Superficial Lake

Breakaway Border

U.S. Military: Stay The Fuck Out

Man panning for silicon

Porn community ×

Man who moved to Arizona for the conditioning

Traffic on the 405 backed up to Arizona today

× Where grandma just died

You can tell this region has had some work done

Entire city's illegal immigrants wearing fake mustaches

FACTS » IN STUFF WE TRUST

POPULATION
302,600,001

CITIZEN KEEPING POPULATION FROM BEING NICE, ROUND NUMBER
Doug Kryslevic of Newton, Massachusetts

BORDERS
2,459 locations nationwide

BRANCHES OF GOVERNMENT
Executive, Legislative, Judicial, Janitorial

NATIONAL PASTIMES
Baseball, weeping silently in bathroom while husband watches baseball

TRADITIONAL CUISINE
The #5 Combo

LITERACY RATE
Saw the movie version

EXPORTS
Troops

U.S. TERRITORIES
Guam, Puerto Rico, Virgin Islands, the Moon

HEALTH HAZARDS
Increasing number of Americans too obese to crawl out of birth canal

LEADING CAUSE OF DEATH
Prolonged sitting

FREEDOM OF SPEECH
Mostly limited to bumper stickers

SHARED CULTURAL EXPERIENCES
Cheers finale, *M*A*S*H* finale, 9/11, that *Everybody Loves Raymond* episode where Frank builds a birdhouse

Best vantage point for a clean headshot in the whole state

Man storing armory in beard

Place that sells cake

Wisconsin should really get this growth checked out

This looks just like area Canada used to have

State Supreme Court taking bong hit

Spot where Washington lost the Revolutionary War, but didn't tell anyone

More dying than living free

Scenic Standoff

✕ North Dakotan

✕ Other North Dakotan

✕ Coyote or something

Rhubarb Forest

Little Something To Remember The Ice Age By

▲ *Half-Ass Mountains*

3,500 miles of coastline way too sharp to walk on

Militia made up mostly of stuffed animals

Spooked hound dog

Cowboy breaking faggots in

Old Glory Hole

☐ In Oct. 2001, giant granite tears were added to each of the presidents' faces on Mt. Rushmore

Wholesome woman with one-night-stand-bearing hips ✕

Cheese Curd Deposits

Grounds crew mowing frozen tundra ✕

Lakiest Lake

Grain just waiting over here

Granola reserve ✕

Incomprehensible man probably talking about Red Sox ✕

No room for info about Rhode Island

✕ That one black guy

Sideways Lake

Site of nation's first parking violation ✕

PROBABLY A NATIONAL PARK

■ National Meth Lab

✕ Third-grader shoring up support for possible presidential run

Fallow Dreams

• *City delighted by deadly beer spill*

✕ Cubs fans committing mass suicide

Drunk Eagles fan pissing on most historic spot in America ✕

Like a horrific Bon Jovi song that won't stop

Husk-on-the-cob stand ✕

☐ Hall Of Fame Hall Of Fame

This one must be Maryland

hat no longer hooting sprees

◄ Man on giant screen saying you're going to hell

◄ Board of Education rejecting theory on origin of Incredible Hulk

MEDIOCRE PLAINS

✕ Washing machine out on Capitol lawn

Overrun With Varmints

Lobbyist eating own child

☐ Fuckface Ski Resort

Overturned County

• *City almost notable for its plainness*

Man picking out fancy pan for head

Lynching trees in bloom

BBQ Starts Improving Here

✕ Racehorse actually most beautiful person in Kentucky

Home to highest rate of binge-raping in the U.S. ✕

Tobacco farmer disciplining son by forcing him to smoke entire field

✕ Adobe skyscraper

• **Oklahoma City**
City proud it was blown up by American

State's Genetic Puddle

✕ Governor calling for emergency hoedown

✕ Actually a pretty fun KKK rally

Region Doesn't Even Deserve A Coastline

✕ Austere, windswept citizen

Ditch ceded to Cherokee Nation in 1999

Highest-density density in the U.S. ✕

Shirtless Region

✕ Showoff crushing beer can on wife's head

Mexican stuck in dreamcatcher

✕ Hummer wearing 432-gallon hat

✕ Lawmakers rasslin' up a budget

Shoeless Region

Disney suing little girl for copyright infringement for wearing Goofy T-shirt she just bought from them

Mesquite-Flavored Region

Schoolchildren lining up for their annual lethal injections

✕ Entire state gathered around same TV

Annoying artist community

• **Crawford**
Served as U.S. capital from 2001–2009

FEDERALLY CREATED WETLANDS

Prominent cactus

• **Houston**
Country's fastest-growing hellhole

City doesn't realize that NASCAR is just a sport

✕ Governor clinging to buoy

Homeowner swimming down to attic

Man who claims he needs semi-automatic weapons for hunting Mexicans

✕ High-school quarterback put out to stud

Woman with fake smile, breasts, and personality

Federally Protected Sprawl

✕ Sack of African-American ballots now covered in coral

MAP KEY
- Watching TV
- Screaming at TV
- On TV
- Praying for larger TV
- Spending time with family on TV
- Nothing good on TV
- Pleading with TV
- Couch-ridden

BILLIONS AND BILLIONS SERVED

The United States

15,000 B.C.–A.D. 1400 Native Americans waste several millennia painstakingly naming villages, lakes, valleys, rivers, and mountain ranges.

1492 Christopher Columbus kindly informs the Native Americans that they're standing on his country.

1608 Hats legalized.

1610 Hats mandatory.

 1620 Early colonies are set up by Pilgrims, who fled religious persecution in England to establish their own religious persecution in the New World.

1636 Harvard University is founded, but does not admit any students until the SATs are invented in 1901.

Mount Rushmore
The rarely seen back side of the famous monument honors America's shittiest presidents.

1692 Hundreds of children are executed for being witches during Salem, MA's inopportune Halloween costume party.

1742 George Washington proclaims, "I cannot tell a lie," beginning a long tradition of politicians lying.

1773 In protest of the Tea Act, American colonists sneak onto British ships at night and dump over 90,000 pounds of tea into Boston Harbor. The patriots celebrate their success with a nice cup of hot water.

APR. 19, 1775 Paul Revere rides through the streets of Boston warning that "the British are coming!" However, scholars point out that Revere was a paranoid schizophrenic who had made "midnight rides" warning of an imminent British attack on the same Boston roads every night for the previous three years.

1776 John Hancock puts his old Francis Perriwinkle on the Declaration of Independence.

1776–1781 Several battles are fought atop a variety of hills.

1787 Dozens of representatives from all 13 states convene in Philadelphia to write the Constitution together. Although they originally intended to give women the right to vote, they couldn't find a way to word it that they were all happy with.

1803 Thomas Jefferson purchases the 530-billion-acre Louisiana Territory from the French for what seems like a steal at $15 million, but little did he know—termite problem.

1804–1806 Comically mismatched explorers Lewis & Clark embark on a laugh-a-minute romp across the American West, during which the delightful duo accidentally sleeps with the wife of an Indian chief, wakes up to find a rattlesnake in their sleeping bag, and learns the true meaning of friendship.

1830 The nation's Native Americans are sentenced to a fate worse than death: living in Oklahoma.

1837 Martin Van Buren becomes America's first bad president.

1840 Through pluck, hard work, and the indomitable American spirit, the people of the U.S. nearly succeed in wiping the buffalo from the face of the earth.

1863 President Abraham Lincoln single-handedly wrestles 20,000 Confederate troops at Gettysburg, winning the battle with a decisive three-second shoulder pin.

1865 Robert E. Lee agrees to surrender and end the Civil War on the condition that 193 high schools in the South be named after him.

1865 Lincoln is assassinated by John Wilkes Booth during a performance of Our American Cousin at Ford's Theater. While his death was a shock to many, scholars believe Lincoln should have seen the attack coming, as it was clearly printed on the playbill between "Intermission" and "Act II."

1865 A sudden shortage of cheap labor cripples the American cotton industry.

1870 The 15th Amendment is passed, granting black men the right to vote. Originally classified as only three-fifths citizens, black men were given full voting rights when the nation's leaders decided they didn't hate the idea of racial equality nearly as much as adding up fractions.

1875 10,000 workers drown during the construction of the first 15 feet of the Transatlantic Railroad.

1876 Thomas Alva Edison, searching for a more efficient way to invent things, invents Alexander Graham Bell, who in turn invents the telephone, the metal detector, and the hydrofoil.

1902 The Wright Brothers— Wilbur, Orville, Jonathan, Michael, Patrick, Samuel, Andrew, and Phil— embark on the first of many tragic test flights.

1909 William Howard Taft becomes the first 1,600-pound president.

1911 A wiring glitch at the Ford Motor Plant causes its two-mile-long conveyor belt to run backwards, resulting in the disassembly of nearly 400 Model T cars in less than a day.

 1920 Prohibition passes, banning the manufacture or sale of alcohol in the U.S. Upon hearing the news, millions of depressed Americans drown their sorrows in alcohol.

In the 1920s, the economy was booming, jazz was taking off, and eight out of 10 Americans were homosexuals.

1927 Charles A. Lindbergh becomes the first person that no one wants to fly nonstop across the Atlantic Ocean with.

1929 After a decade of rapid and often reckless growth, the Wall Street Crash of 1929 leaves companies such as Irresponsible Buying Inc., Forget About Saving For The Future & Sons, and Nothing Bad Is Ever Going To Come Out Of Relying Too Heavily On The Stock Market Ltd. in ruins.

1930–1939 Popularity of bread skyrockets.

1932 President Herbert Hoover delivers what onlookers initially believe to be a stirring, inspirational call for change in America. However,

The Great Depression
An Oklahoma woman takes a moment to simultaneously express the brutal struggle of day-to-day survival and the enduring strength of the human spirit.

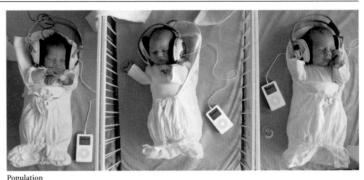

» AFTER MUCH CONTROVERSY, OFFICIALS ERECTED THIS MONUMENT IN BEMIDJI, MINNESOTA TO THOSE WHO DIED ON SEPT. 11, 2001.

A PERSONAL CHEF, A WHOLE NEW WARDROBE, EXTRA BUTTER, PLASTIC SURGERY, AND THAT HOUSE OVER THERE

after citizens notice his dirty, unshaven face, tattered clothing, and the empty cup he is waving around, it becomes apparent that he's just asking for spare nickels and dimes.

1933–1945 President Franklin Delano Roosevelt spends four consecutive terms in the White House until the Department of the Interior can build a wheelchair ramp to get him out.

FDR rides aboard Wheelchair One.

1941 The U.S. joins World War II, but not before renaming it "World War II: Ultimate Valor" for licensing and marketing purposes.

1943 After months of trying to decipher the mysterious messages, U.S. cryptanalysts discover the key to the Japanese military's top-secret codes: they are written in Japanese.

1945 Harry S. Truman regrets installing the button that launches nuclear bombs right next to the button that turns on his radio.

1946–1961 U.S. declares a two-front nuclear war on the Nevada desert and the coral atolls of the South Pacific.

1947 Jackie Robinson breaks the color barrier in baseball and, during a road game two weeks later, in Massachusetts.

1950 Drunken Sen. Joseph McCarthy accuses an empty barstool of being a Communist.

1951 Hysteria over Communism spreads across nation. President Truman outlaws sharing.

1963 Though badly shaken after her husband's assassination, Jackie Kennedy is momentarily comforted by the fact that his blood matches her shoes.

1963 The emergence of hippies, a group of young people unafraid to open their minds and legs to new ideas and experiences.

Martin Luther King Jr.

1963 Martin Luther King Jr. has a dream where one day, blacks and whites will live together in harmony, and also his high-school science teacher is there for some reason.

1966 Everyone in the U.S. spends the year hiding underneath their desks.

1967 The "Summer of Love" is followed by the "Autumn of Chlamydia."

1968 American soldiers accidentally kill 300 Vietnamese villagers in My Lai after not realizing they were loaded.

1968 In an effort to silence anti-war protests at home, Lyndon Johnson sends the entire country to fight in Vietnam.

1969 The U.S. introduces the military draft lottery. Thousands instantly lose.

1969 In one of the most elaborate hoaxes in U.S. history, NASA fakes the moon landing's importance.

1969 Thousands of youths congregate at Woodstock for three days of love, dancing, and drugs—much to the chagrin of one spectator, Dale Henderson, who was actually trying to enjoy the show.

1969 Entire hippie population wiped

President Richard Nixon gives his famous two-finger salute after resigning from office in 1974.

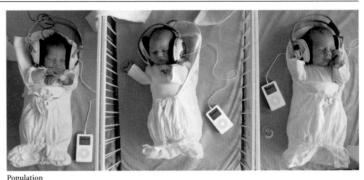

Population
American children are born with over 1,000 songs already on their iPods.

out by the H$_2$O bomb.

1971 The national rail service, Amtrak, forever changes the way Americans complain about travel.

1972 A grand jury is forced to listen to 3,600 hours of Nixon hosting an imaginary talk show before getting to the 30 minutes of tape where he orders his cronies to break into the Watergate Hotel.

1980 A plague of Pac-Man Fever ravages the U.S. Treasury's quarters supply.

1983 An increasingly divided public demands that the horrific and senseless *M*A*S*H* be brought to an end.

1986 After seven years of painstaking preparation and an outlay of over $18 billion, NASA succeeds in launching elementary school teacher Christa McAuliffe into

the troposphere.

1992 The South rises again, staggers around a bit, finds the remote control, and collapses back onto the couch.

1998 The nation is shocked and disgusted when Bill Clinton admits that he has had sexual relations with Hillary Clinton.

SEPT. 11, 2001 At 8:46 a.m., in one of the most tragic events in the history of mankind, George W. Bush's political career is saved.

2001 Americans vow to be furious about the Enron scandal as soon as they understand what it is.

AUG. 2005 Hurricane Katrina hits New Orleans, leaving thousands even more homeless.

2007 Millions of Americans drive to Washington, D.C. to protest global warming.

MILITARY SPENDING » WE'RE #1

At $800 billion per year, America's defense budget is larger than that of every other nation in the world combined. How is the U.S. military spending all this money?

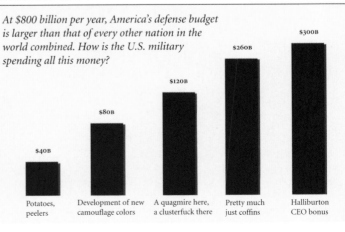

| $40B | $80B | $120B | $260B | $300B |
| Potatoes, peelers | Development of new camouflage colors | A quagmire here, a clusterfuck there | Pretty much just coffins | Halliburton CEO bonus |

N O P Q R S T U V W X Y Z

12

The Northeast

Your Forefather's America

Hand-selected by the Pilgrims as the only land worthy of settling, the Northeast was laying the foundations for democracy while the rest of America was still knee-deep in bison shit.

Although the rest of the states are happy to wave American flags, vote for their government leaders, and refuse to pay taxes to the British monarchy now, Northeasterners can't remember anyone west of Pennsylvania signing the Declaration of Independence or making a midnight ride through the streets of Boston back when being a patriot meant getting off your ass.

Perhaps the other states found it a lot easier to ratify the Constitution after someone else had already gone to the trouble of fighting the Revolutionary War, securing independence for an entire nation, founding a capital city, and forming a bicameral legislative body to draft it. Maybe they were just waiting to see if the whole "government by rule of the people" thing would pan out before they started using it as the basis of every state government from Ohio to California.

Regardless of the reason, Northeasterners welcomed the 39 latecomers with open arms, but everyone knows full well whom they really meant by "We The People."

NEW YORK » THE NEW YORK CITY STATE

From the Empire State Building in New York City, to the Statue of Liberty in New York City, to Times Square in New York City, the state of New York is filled with exciting attractions no matter where you look.

Tourists arrive by the thousands each day, whether to enjoy a Broadway play in New York's historic New York City, visit the Big Apple, or just explore some of the state's quieter wooded areas in Central Park. New York is also home to the nation's financial capital (New York City), news capital (New York City), and fashion capital (New York City).

Indeed, New York State is truly the greatest city in the world.

The famous New York State skyline.

NEW JERSEY » DEMANDING PEOPLE SHOVE IT UP THEIR ASS SINCE 1832

Located in you know where the fuck we are, and bordered by a bunch of places that can suck it—especially you, Pennsylvania—New Jersey is one of the nation's oldest and most historic states. So fuck you.

Founded by a guy who could kick your state-founder's ass, and boasting some of the safest, cleanest cities in America—you hear that, jerk?—New Jersey will destroy you, just say the word.

And while the state has in recent years come under fire from environmental groups, that doesn't fucking matter because Jersey rules.

Oh, and by the way, the entire state was balls-deep in your girlfriend last night.

PENNSYLVANIA » AMISH-ISH COUNTRY

Pennsylvania is home to the world's largest Amish population, a group of people whose austere lifestyle is slowly changing to adapt to the 21st century. Today, the Amish shun electricity except at night when it's dark, reject modern conveniences save for microwaves, refrigerators, and washing machines, and travel by horse and buggy unless it'd just be easier to take the car.

Amish men, once known for their long beards, can now go clean-shaven if their face gets too itchy or if they "just feel like trying something different."

However, most Amish residents today still forbid themselves from using the telephone, unless they need to call their neighbor to tell him something good is on TV.

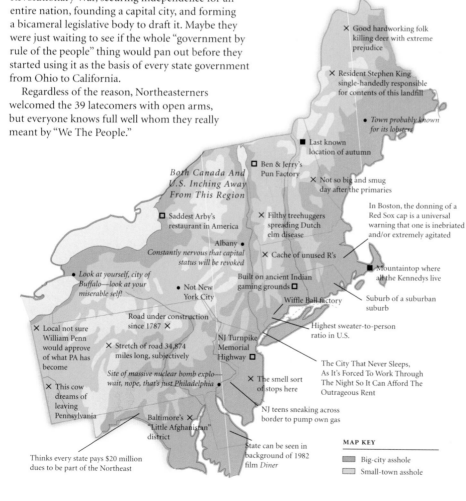

Good hardworking folk killing deer with extreme prejudice

Resident Stephen King single-handedly responsible for contents of this landfill

Town probably known for its lobsters

Last known location of autumn

Ben & Jerry's Pun Factory

Not so big and smug day after the primaries

Both Canada And U.S. Inching Away From This Region

Saddest Arby's restaurant in America

Filthy treehuggers spreading Dutch elm disease

In Boston, the donning of a Red Sox cap is a universal warning that one is inebriated and/or extremely agitated

Albany • *Constantly nervous that capital status will be revoked*

Cache of unused R's

Look at yourself, city of Buffalo—look at your miserable self!

Not New York City

Built on ancient Indian gaming grounds

Mountaintop where all the Kennedys live

Wiffle Ball factory

Suburb of a suburban suburb

Road under construction since 1787

Highest sweater-to-person ratio in U.S.

Local not sure William Penn would approve of what PA has become

Stretch of road 34,874 miles long, subjectively

NJ Turnpike Memorial Highway

The City That Never Sleeps, As It's Forced To Work Through The Night So It Can Afford The Outrageous Rent

Site of massive nuclear bomb explo— wait, nope, that's just Philadelphia •

This cow dreams of leaving Pennsylvania

The smell sort of stops here

NJ teens sneaking across border to pump own gas

Baltimore's "Little Afghanistan" district

Thinks every state pays $20 million dues to be part of the Northeast

State can be seen in background of 1982 film *Diner*

MAP KEY
- Big-city asshole
- Small-town asshole

 » BENJAMIN FRANKLIN, THE MAN WHO INVENTED FLYING KITES IN THE RAIN.

» THE NORTHEAST IS FAMOUS FOR ITS LIGHTHOUSES, WHICH ARE USED TO SIGNAL AN APPROACHING RACK OF POSTCARDS.

MASSACHUSETTS » COVERED IN IVY

Home to hundreds of prestigious colleges and universities, Massachusetts is where the nation's best and brightest can't afford to go.

Known for their extremely high standards, institutes such as Harvard and MIT only accept students who either score in the top 1% of yearly household income, or have an outstanding last name.

Those lucky enough to attend, however, are treated to the finest education, grades, diploma, and future employment that money can buy. While most of these students fail to absorb any knowledge about politics, philosophy, business, or engineering, the one thing they do learn is that, in America, wealth and privilege is everything.

The Signing Of The Declaration Of Independence
A brilliant group of wealthy landowners founds the world's first whites-only nation.

VERMONT » CLEAN AIR, FILTHY PEOPLE

The environmentally friendly hippies of Vermont lead the world in water conservation, as well as soap conservation, shampoo conservation, and Q-tip conservation.

A green-conscious people, Vermonters are known to recycle their undergarments, often making a single pair last as long as two months.

Indeed, if statewide trends continue, Vermont's strategic deodorant reserves—roughly two sticks of Right Guard—should last at least until 2407.

DELAWARE » A NICE FIRST TRY

America has to laugh when it looks at Delaware, the first state it admitted to the Union back in 1787. At just under 2,500 square miles and without a single urban center, Delaware makes the nation cringe at what it used to let pass for a state.

Although the U.S. learned from its mistake and went on to welcome nearly 30 truly great states over the next 200 years, it still keeps Delaware around so that the next time the nation wants to add another state, it will remember what not to do.

NEW HAMPSHIRE » A PLACE FOR PRICKS TO COME LOOK AT LEAVES

With four full seasons of autumn and an endless array of colors ranging from orange to off-orange, New Hampshire attracts thousands of annual visitors who come to photograph the changing leaves, videotape the newly fallen leaves, and buy leaf-shaped souvenirs from the last state in the Union with any trees.

Though it contains the nation's finest twigs, bark, and branches, the Granite State's foliage-based economy would be devastated by one errant leaf-blower, or a single asshole from Massachusetts too busy yelling into his cell phone to watch where he's walking.

CONNECTICUT » HOME OF NEW YORK'S OTHER POPULATION

For over 300 years, Connecticut has upheld a proud tradition of being next to New York.

The state was founded in 1636 by settlers who wanted to live in a small quiet colony, but also enjoyed the convenience of being able to catch the 7:27 wagon and be in New York by early next week.

Although Connecticut is the wealthiest state in the nation, its citizens are forced to live in giant mansions, as many cannot afford the rent of a cramped one-bedroom apartment in Manhattan.

The Capitol Building, known for its 18th-century architecture and its politics of an even earlier era.

RHODE ISLAND » ROUGHLY THE SIZE OF ONE RHODE ISLAND

Rhode Island, the basic unit of geographic measurement, exists solely for the purpose of describing how big other landmasses are.

Located side by side other, larger U.S. states in easy-to-comprehend size comparisons, Rhode Island, or the "World's Yardstick," was admitted to the Union in 1790 when the founding fathers wanted to see how many times it could fit into North Carolina.

Today, despite a booming tourism industry and growing economy, Rhode Island remains the same as it ever was: about one-third the size of Puerto Rico, and 76 times smaller than Portugal.

MAINE » L.L. BEAN'S LIVING CATALOG

Whether logging the Great North Woods in a signature Allagash Northweave™ flannel shirt, or taking in the cool night air under a micro-light Woodlands Dome tent, the people of Maine can be found on pages 12–187 of the quarterly L.L. Bean catalog.

Mainers are always dressed for the occasion, be it chopping firewood, taking a stroll with their yellow Labrador, or simply relaxing on the back porch with their pastel-sweater-wearing wife and two freckled children.

Although they may argue about whether to take a kayak or canoe trip, the people of Maine can agree on one thing: Nothing feels quite so comfortable as a brand-new pair of Adrenaline Ultralight socks by SmartWool®.

MARYLAND » ON BOTH WRONG SIDES OF THE TRACK

Although it may not seem like much at first, or even when you look at it for a second or third time, Maryland is actually a vibrant and beautiful state if one squints hard enough.

With a surprise around every 15 corners, and a good surprise around every 30 or so, Maryland is an exciting place to visit so long as one comes in with zero expectations, has never eaten at a restaurant before, and can ignore the overpowering smell.

America's very well-hidden gem, Baltimore in particular remains an undiscovered treasure, as few are willing to venture past the crime-scene tape.

The South

Where The Mistakes Of The Past Come Alive

With its rampant racism, regressive social policies, and aversion to Northern influence, the American South has provided visitors with a historically accurate view of antebellum life for over 140 years.

For the thousands of tourists who visit this historic site each year, crossing the Mason-Dixon line is like taking a step back in time. Visitors can stroll through authentically segregated neighborhoods, see the Confederate flag still proudly displayed at banks and government buildings, and have their picture taken with a real live white supremacist.

Also on display are voting trends and literacy rates painstakingly preserved in their original 19th-century condition, and attitudes toward homosexuals and immigrants over 100 years old. A lucky few may even catch a glimpse of dedicated re-enactors dressed in traditional white-cloak-and-pointed-hood garments staging 1870s-era hate crimes right before their very eyes.

But no visit is complete without a trip to the gift shop, where anyone with a driver's license and $500 cash can take home a pistol identical to those once used to defend the Confederacy from abolitionists.

Racetrack mix-up responsible for gruesome NASCAR/horse pileup

Site where 12 miners died in massive lung collapse

New bill that will fuck you and your family over being signed here right now ★

State paying off $3.2 billion debt to local bar

Arkansas' state animal is roadkill

Not a church

Pro-abortion back alley

Farmers breeding 24-piece chicken

Tumor-production facility

Air contains dangerously high levels of Aqua Net

Couple smoking before, during, after sex ×

DHS reluctantly thwarting terrorist plot to blow up Duke

Pig taking first prize in county spelling bee

Square-dancing still legal here

Recent ruling here made fag-burning unconstitutional

Bill Clinton's childhood drawl

An Allman Brother died here

Not as many hicks here as you'd think

Whites-only unemployment center □

Banjo being played unironically ×

Another Allman Brother died here

Gated trailer park

Martin Luther King Jr. Memorial Racial Tension

Ted Turner drinking Coke while flying Delta—there, you happy Atlanta?

French influence evident in this incredibly smug ghetto

Colonial-era zero-room schoolhouse

Home of the lesser-known Georgia avocado

Mile-long line to get out of Disney World

New Orleans resident giving up hope for Lent ×

College that offers post-graduate football program

NASA launching prayer into space

Biscuits so moist you'll forget about state's racist legacy

Citizens celebrating Mardi Gras 364 days early

Assisted-dying community

Man pretending to enjoy jazz funeral

Raft full of lost Cubans

Miami nightclub so exclusive no one is allowed in

MAP KEY

- Dirty South
- Filthy South
- Put Some Shoes On For God's Sake

FLORIDA » THE SILENT HOLOCAUST

Though on the surface Florida appears to be a tropical paradise, inside this state lurks a dark, gruesome secret: Each year, thousands of Jews are sent here to die.

Ghastly sights such as these are an everyday reality in Florida.

Separated from their families in New York and New Jersey, these Jews are transported hundreds of miles to extermination communities like the horrific Boca Raton, where they are confined to small, identical living units, never to see their real homes again. In the morning, those still able to walk are forced to do activities against their will. They are humiliated, stripped of all human dignity, and made to square-dance to the point of physical exhaustion.

While some die within the first few weeks, others suffer for years with no contact to the outside world save for a phone call on their birthday. In addition, an unlucky few are forced by men in white lab coats to take powerful drugs and undergo grisly medical procedures. Some say, however, that in Florida, the worst fate of all is surviving.

ALABAMA » THE LAST REMAINING SLAVE STATE

After more than a century as a free state, Alabama quietly re-legalized slavery in 1987, though the rest of the U.S. has failed to notice any difference.

The legislation, tacked onto a seemingly innocuous school-segregation bill, passed the state senate by a margin of 34 to 3/5ths. Despite the controversial decision, few African-Americans protested, as doing so was not allowed by their new masters.

Alabama (circa 2007)

Recently, the federal government has attempted to abolish slavery in the state, but was surprised to learn it has no jurisdiction over Alabama, which seceded from the Union in 1989.

MISSISSIPPI » LEARNING TO SINK

With most of its public schools built directly on swamps, marshes, or bayous, the waterlogged state of Mississippi is struggling to keep its young people afloat.

Plagued by underfunding and dangerously strong currents, Mississippi schoolchildren not lucky enough to have a chalkboard to cling to typically drown between periods—a worrying trend that officials are trying to combat by periodically testing students' ability to tread water, and dredging all classrooms over the winter and summer breaks.

State officials have yet to offer a viable solution to the state's greatest challenge, the alligator swimming in the superintendent's office.

» A SOUTHERN PREACHER EXTOLS THE VIRTUES OF PIETY, CHASTITY, AND KNOCKING THE OLD LADY ACROSS THE JAW EVERY NOW AND AGAIN TO KEEP HER QUIET.

GEORGIA » NO, NOT *THAT* GEORGIA

 When most people hear the name "Georgia," they immediately think "Western Caucasus Mountains," "Gremi Castle," and "President Mikhail Saakashvili." However, Georgia is not just the former Soviet republic that everyone knows about—it is also in fact a small U.S. state.

While this Georgia has its share of tourist sites, visitors hoping to catch a glimpse of the famous Baku-Tbilisi-Ceyhan oil pipeline will be left sorely disappointed. And although the state is also known for its hospitality, guests won't be getting a walking tour of Zugdidi or be greeted with a steaming plate of Khinkali anytime soon.

So the next time someone tells you they're from Georgia, before you ask them about Birtvisi Canyon or the ongoing border conflict in the South Ossetia region, be sure to find out exactly which Georgia they mean.

LOUISIANA » AMERICA'S LOW-WATER MARK

Louisiana was hit by Hurricane Katrina on Aug. 29, 2005, leaving hundreds of FEMA officials panicked, desperate for help, and not knowing where to turn.

A flustered FEMA responded three days late to the crisis, though the government claims it was only one day late if you don't count the 48 hours it took them to check their voicemail. At that point, they intended to respond immediately, but scrapped their travel plans when they heard there was a pretty bad storm in the area.

FEMA, after being informed what their acronym stood for, transported New Orleans residents to the Houston Astrodome, but could only afford to buy everyone upper-deck seats.

Today, years after the destruction, many Louisiana residents remain homeless, with hundreds forced to live in FEMA-issued trailers, and those hit hardest by Katrina forced to cling to FEMA-issued driftwood.

VIRGINIA » VIRGINIA IS FOR RACISTS

The birthplace of southern hospitality and the plantation system, Virginia treats every person of color to its own down-home brand of charming discrimination.

The ever-charming Caucasian female.

It is a place where southern belles with parasols sip iced tea in the sun, curtsying, smiling, and summoning their gentleman callers to kindly come clear the Negro fellows out of their way.

Children are taught to dress sharp, be obedient, and give all white people the respect they deserve as the superior race.

With a tip of the hat and a smile, jurors always hold the door open and bid a fond farewell to every black man they send to death row.

NORTH CAROLINA » MAY CAUSE CANCER

Home to Big Tobacco, North Carolina is one of the leading figures in the fight for cancer.

Recently, the state has been plagued by countless lawsuits over the addictiveness of cigarettes, though most cases are settled out of court for large payments of Marlboro Bucks.

Still, North Carolina is committed to helping its citizens quit smoking, but to do so the state insists it must first get them to start.

TENNESSEE » LIKE *HEE HAW*, BUT A STATE

Tennessee is the birthplace of country music, and the deathplace of all other music.

Nashville, the state's capital, is home to several historic country music sites, including the Country Music Hall Of Fame, the famous Ryman Auditorium, and a stack of dry hay.

 Though known for its southern charm, Nashville suffers from one of the nation's highest rates of domestic abuse, especially when one needs inspiration for a new song.

Tennessee is also home to Graceland, the sprawling estate where Elvis Presley lived on a toilet until 1977.

W. VIRGINIA » COUNTRY ROADS, TAKE ME ANYWHERE ELSE

Known for its coal-mining industry, West Virginia is made up of just over 1.8 million people, with 50% living in cities, 35% living in rural areas, and the rest trapped in a mine somewhere.

While coal mining is still a dangerous occupation, employees are now offered a number of job incentives, including overtime pay for the first six hours spent hopelessly stuck underground, and the opportunity for some to work from beneath their very own homes. Sadly, many mining companies still experience frequent, sudden, extremely loud turnover.

West Virginia's state bird is the dead canary.

SOUTH CAROLINA » THE ONE WITH THE RACIST FLAG

While symbolic of an era of hate and prejudice, South Carolina citizens continue to fly the state's Confederate flag, as many claim "it just looks pretty."

 While ashamed of the history associated with their state flag, South Carolinians can't help but notice how nice the blue cross looks against the red background.

In fact, many say the only thing more pleasing to the eye is the sight of an African-American being hanged from a tree.

ARKANSAS » WHERE SECOND COUSINS ARE FIRST WIVES

The state of Arkansas is built on strong family values, with parents teaching their children at an early age about hard work, the importance of sharing, and how much tongue is too much tongue.

While some Arkansans marry their siblings out of true love, most do it out of convenience, as they already live together, share the same last name, and know the sex will be good. Before proposing, it is common in Arkansas to seek the blessing of the bride's father, which is done by addressing oneself in the mirror.

KENTUCKY » SOAKED IN BOURBON

Kentucky was founded at 4:30 a.m. on June 1, 1792, when a band of drunken pioneers scrawled the state's constitution on the back of a cocktail napkin, slurred allegiance to the United States, and promptly pissed themselves.

Hungover since the late 1800s, Kentucky citizens remember a simpler time when someone said something, and then everyone stood up, and—wait, no, that was last night.

Today, Kentuckians who are able to wake up in time for May enjoy the state's national pastime of watching what looks like horses running around a racetrack.

The Midwest

America's Pit Stop

Boasting some of the most spectacular public restrooms, gas stations, and 24-hour Hardee's drive-thrus in the country, America's Midwest is conveniently located between where you are and where you are going.

From Ohio's sprawling plains to Missouri's river basins to Nebraska's sprawling plains, the Midwest is a dazzling array of highway on-ramps and truck weigh-in stations that is best appreciated at the rate of 70 mph, or from the window seat of a cross-country flight. Visitors often take in multiple states in a single afternoon, sampling local selections of unleaded fuel and prepackaged snack cakes while ceaselessly pursuing the uninterrupted horizon.

The people of America's Heartland are both friendly and considerate, whether giving directions to the nearest interstate or accepting fares at one of the region's many charming tollbooths. And by dressing in khaki from head to toe and keeping the same hairstyle for 20 years, Midwesterners are kind enough not to distract tourists from the blurry, brownish-green experience they're looking for.

A wholesome and inviting place, it's no surprise people love to see the Midwest again and again, slowly disappearing in their rearview mirrors.

Calcium-deficient patient hooked up to cheddar IV

Not really sure how this part of Michigan got here

Nothing Here

Creepy shop teacher who always wants kids to make skin lamps

Run-down prairie-dog projects ✕

✕ Sioux tribe holding pow-wow in DQ parking lot

✕ Car factory up on cinderblocks

Family at Badlands looking for exit sign

✕ Man missing own funeral for Packers game

✕ Farmer deep-frying crops

Out-of-work Tab machine

Every person in this town has been abducted by aliens

✕ Debt knee-high by the 4th of July

State unemployment nook ✕

✕ Four dead kids who tried to smoke buckeyes

✕ This highway would wrap around Earth five times if laid out end to end

✕ More corn ✕

✕ Hoosier starting fight with own reflection

• *Easily ridiculed city*

Capitol building doing 140 across this field ✕

✕ Suburb where Abe Lincoln grew up

✕ Young man asking father's permission to date-rape his daughter

✕ Boyhood farm home of the Antichrist

Spooked Clydesdale overturning sleigh full of disabled children ✕

Site where Bobby Knight murdered his entire team gangland-style in 1989

M.A.D.D. convention getting a little out of control

Dump truck loading up on brimstone

Black-and-white part of state

Spot where a young Harry Truman blew up his first Japanese person

Bears fan celebrating touchdown by spiking infant son

East St. Louis' Gateway-To-A-Felony-Offense Arch

The Country's Middle Part
America's Heartland is best appreciated in comfortable, reclining leather seats at 19,000 feet.

ILLINOIS » SPRAWL OF AMERICA

Since nothing is within walking distance in the entire state, residents of Illinois spend most of their lives in their cars, trying to navigate the endless stream of identical concrete landmarks to find their way home in time to hop in the car for the morning commute.

In fact, it is not uncommon for an Illinois father to make a wrong turn onto the wrong Woodbury Heights Ave., park in the wrong driveway, kiss the wrong wife, and spend the rest of his life raising the wrong family.

Most of the state's rich, fertile farmland has been paved over to construct new strip malls, which are immediately abandoned in favor of newer, more conveniently located strip malls 50 yards to the left.

Many residents have recently been forced to give up their cherished views of the winding cloverleaf highways and lush billboards that dominate the exhaust-filled landscape for homes in Chicago's more affordable suburbs in nearby Alabama.

Also known as the Land of Lincoln, the state of Illinois prides itself on the fact that America's greatest president was actually born in Kentucky.

KANSAS » IN GOD WE BLINDLY TRUST

Taking a bold stand against the dangers of modern existence, and eager to protect its traditional Old Testament values, the Kansas legislature has officially banned all forms of reality.

Free from the shackles of logic, common sense, or indisputable scientific evidence, Kansas' faith-based form of government has completely eliminated such long-term problems as joblessness, civil rights, and education funding—problems which, according to a recent judicial decision, never actually existed in the first place.

Kansans are such devout Christians that, each year, thousands of God-fearing citizens who refuse to believe that tornados are the work of naturally occurring low-pressure systems are sent directly to heaven.

In an upcoming referendum, voters will decide on a controversial measure to outlaw all forms of death, except in cases of accidental electrocution in the state penitentiary.

In addition, a growing number of outspoken Christian fundamentalists claim that homosexuality is a choice, and they are dedicated to proving it every other Wednesday night at a little motel just outside Topeka.

MICHIGAN » CLOSED FOR BUSINESS

Once the thriving center of America's automobile industry, Michigan hasn't made a single business transaction since 1993.

Suffering from the highest unemployment rates in the nation and unable to rebound after the failure of its upper-peninsula franchise, the Great Lakes State has been forced to close its borders. Accepting that most of metropolitan Detroit is unsalvageable, the state is just hoping to get what it can for the Capitol building before packing up and starting anew out East.

Though everyone agreed it had to be done, Michigan says the hardest part of closing up shop was informing Ned, the 65-year-old part-time employee who ran the Midwestern state for the last five years.

OHIO » AMERICA'S STATE

The blond-haired, blue-eyed, baseball cap–wearing patriots of Ohio live in America's most all-American state.

Believing in traditional Ohio values, Ohioans know the importance of being seen by their neighbors at church on Sunday. Though they work 38.5–44 hours a week for their average annual incomes, parents always take time to enjoy some general interests with their son/daughter.

Ohioans celebrate being from Ohio.

When Ohio's major industries collapsed in the late 1970s, Ohioans handled it with pluck and optimism, holding a bake sale on a nice Saturday afternoon in hopes that Mrs. Lawson's delicious lemon bars might perk up their devastated economy.

With more native presidents than any state, each citizen is allowed one term in the White House, though most turn down the chance for fear that their award-winning hedges would fall into disrepair.

MISSOURI » BY MARK TWAIN

Dotted with half-painted picket fences and bordered by the mighty Mississippi, Missouri is where trouble-making youngsters ride rafts to school with their state-mandated Negro pals.

Missouri has a darn fine education system that boasts the highest corset-wearing-schoolmarm-to-insufferable-student ratio in the country.

Older folks wile away the hours on government-operated riverboats, whether just playing for fun or pushing in all their Social Security chips on a queen-high straight as part of their official retirement plan.

However, some of Missouri's more mischievous employers spend all the livelong day tricking Negroes into working full time for less than the federal minimum wage.

Missourians also have a knack for spinning yarns and telling tall tales—like the time they say a dead man done beat John Ashcroft in the 2000 Senate race.

WISCONSIN » CLOGGED ARTERY OF THE HEARTLAND

Once the fattest people in the country, Wisconsinites have slimmed down dramatically in recent years by adhering to a strict diet of just one basket of cheese curds at every meal, and no more than 18 servings of Miller Lite a day.

Many exercise regularly by jumping up and power-walking to the kitchen for a bratwurst between snacks. They also count calories with sensible, deep-fried salads for dinner.

Children are taught the importance of eating a balanced meal that includes all five fast-food groups, and are encouraged to lick clean every last inch of their George Foreman Grill drip-trays.

IOWA » ALL FARMED OUT

As the Heartland's vast cornfields are taken over by massive, corporate agribusinesses, the farmers of Iowa still live a simple life, waking up at the crack of dawn each morning to fill out complicated bankruptcy papers and fuel up their tractors for the liquidation sale, while the little lady cuts up credit cards in the kitchen.

Known for taking life one late mortgage payment at a time, Iowans always have a cup of coffee and a warm smile for every repo man that stops by. A religious people, they are thankful for what little they've got, and say grace before every meal at the cardboard box where their dinner table used to be.

NORTH DAKOTA » EMPTY

Founded in 1889 by two men who figured that it might be useful for something someday, North Dakota was the first uninhabited state to be admitted to the Union.

Represented in the U.S. Congress by a broken stool and a half-crushed RC Cola can, North Dakota was briefly populated in 1987 by a carful of drunk drivers who accidentally swerved over the border.

This thing holds farm stuff.

North Dakota's largest city is Sioux Falls, South Dakota.

NEBRASKA » AMERICA'S ROADBLOCK

Running 210 miles north to south, and over 17,000 miles east to west, Nebraska was constructed in 1846 as a mind-numbing, 16-hour-long barrier to prevent American travelers from getting anyplace else.

With only two off-ramps at either end of the state, Nebraska was recently designated by scientists as a terrestrial black hole—a powerful force from which no light trucks or tour buses bound for Las Vegas are able to escape.

Objects in Nebraska's landscape may be even flatter than they appear.

INDIANA » SPECTATOR STATE

Hooting and hollering in over-capacity crowds, Indianans cherish the art of watching stuff, be it the Indianapolis 500, a basketball game, or even themselves looking like a complete idiot on the JumboTron.

Besides looking at the world's most well-loved paved oval, the citizens of Indiana also enjoy looking at home movies of their families watching auto racing, and love to curl up and look at a good book lying on the coffee table.

And over the past several decades, all of Indiana has watched from the comfort of their own living rooms as neighboring state Illinois grew into an economic powerhouse.

SOUTH DAKOTA » MANDATORY VACATIONLAND

Every summer, thousands of families are forced to load up their minivans and travel to South Dakota to enjoy its compulsory splendor and obligatory beauty.

In 1959, the Supreme Court found the state to be an unforgettable, one-of-a-kind vacation experience for people of all ages, that cannot, under any reasonable circumstances, be missed.

Upon returning from Mt. Rushmore, all Americans are required to provide proof-of-visit to local officials with a minimum of 48 poorly composed photographs, and at least one T-shirt with "South Dakota!" printed on the front in a playful script.

The West

A Gift From The Natives

By living in harmony with nature and keeping the land in pristine condition, the Native Americans who once populated the expansive West were eventually able to give the white man this touching, 1.2 million square-mile welcoming present.

Showing great selflessness in the face of colonization, the native peoples of the West spent centuries cultivating crops like corn and squash and using every part of the buffalo to ensure that their European visitors would have plenty to eat and indiscriminately slaughter once they arrived.

As if relinquishing their claim to the vast majority of North America weren't generous enough, over 75% of the natives had the decency to die from smallpox without even being asked. Always the gracious hosts, the surviving few stayed out of the way, allowing the newcomers to settle in to the newly vacated territory.

Since then, the American West has grown into a rich and diverse region of several million white faces. But no matter how far they go, Westerners still owe everything they have to their charitable indigenous brethren—wherever they are today.

- 1,700 head of people
- Gravy River
- Massachusetts could fit in this river valley
- Farmer slathering full pound of butter onto field
- Man sitting on Old Faithful awaiting ride of his life
- U.S. Poker Chip Mint
- Man with only one wife, but she's smokin' hot
- Law-abiding citizen living off the grid
- Monogamy Training Center
- Child-rape legal here
- Holy Pedophile Lands
- Former ski bum now a real bum
- John McCain Cryogenics & Bionics Laboratory
- Man moving north after learning the state insect is the tarantula wasp
- Trinket epicenter
- Adobe house oddly well-prepared for tidal wave
- Couple finding spot in Aztec ruins to have sex
- Minutemen Command Headquarters
- Hopi Indian hallucinating prosperity, freedom
- Buffalo paying roaming charges
- Dick Cheney's mom's house
- Hiker who doesn't remember cannibalism being part of Rocky Mountains tour
- Tomb of the Unknown Injun
- "Cain't Say No" House Of Pleasures
- Massive pickup truck picking up smaller pickup truck
- Cowboy hat that can be seen from outer space
- Racist eating at fantastic Mexican restaurant
- Oil man who hates all non-Saudi foreigners

State slogan was changed from "Don't Mess With Texas" in 1994, to "You Just Messed With Texas, Didn't You?" in 2000, to "See? See What Fucking Happens When You Mess With Texas?" roughly one week later

TEXAS » EVERYTHING SUCKS BIGGER IN TEXAS

Home to mega-factories that contribute to the highest levels of air and water pollution of any state in the Union, a cavernous income gap that leaves visitors awestruck, and an abstinence-based sex education system that has all but ensured it will soon have the highest birth rate in the country, Texas knows that anything worth doing is worth doing big.

From the 64-ounce sodas that add to their number-one-in-the-nation waistlines, to the highest rates of drunk driving and citizen imprisonment to be found in America, the residents of the Lone Star State pride themselves on doing everything Texas-sized.

Boasting the largest egos and most inflated sense of self-importance in the Lower 48, Texans love to talk big about how they execute the most mentally disabled criminals, send the most boys to die for the biggest foreign-policy mistakes, and drag their hate-crime victims the farthest behind the most enormous pickup trucks available.

ARIZONA » HOME OF THE GRAND HOLE

This otherwise featureless state of expansive desert and suburban sprawl boasts the world's most awe-inspiring hole. The Grand Hole is visited by tourists from all over the world, who drive up to the rim of the hole, look down into it, and then express just how big it is. Many stand speechless before the hole.

Visitors to the hole can stand by the hole, get their picture taken in front of the hole, stay in a hotel overlooking the hole, or eat in a restaurant with a view of the hole. The more adventurous tourist can ride a donkey into the hole.

You may think you have seen a hole before, but those who have seen the Grand Hole are confident that there is no other hole like it on Earth.

Over 300 distinct cell-phone ringtones can be heard echoing through this magnificent landmark daily.

» WESTERN GHOST TOWNS CONTINUE TO ATTRACT TOURISTS AND WHORES.

» POPULAR HOLLYWOOD ACTOR JOHN WAYNE WAS AN AGORAPHOBIC WHO NEVER ONCE VISITED THE WEST.

» THE COVERED WAGONS THAT HOMESTEADERS RODE INTO THE WEST WERE SHIELDED FROM INDIANS' FLAMING BOW AND ARROWS BY A LOOSE-FITTING COTTON CLOTH.

WYOMING » WRANGLIN' THEM SOME GAYS

Although Wyoming is still known as the "Cowboy State," law and order isn't what it used to be in the Wild West. Instead of tracking down bandits, today's cowboys fight a new brand of "moral outlaw"—men who think they can go around sticking their penises in another consenting man's business and not suffer the consequences.

Serving justice to criminals like Matthew Shepard—criminals who have broken the Code of the West by being attracted to members of the same sex—Wyoming cowboys roam the hillsides, the bars, and the antique shops in search of fugitive gays.

Known for several gunfights, including the famous shootout at the OK Salon, these cowboys can shoot the cock out of a homosexual's hand from nearly a mile away, and lasso a bisexual to the back of their truck in the blink of an eye.

Most Wyoming cowboys are serving consecutive life sentences, though some are eligible for parole.

IDAHO » HOME OF THE FAMOUS IDAHO IRON ORE

When it's suppertime and Americans sit down to enjoy a hearty meal, all look to the state of Idaho for one key ingredient: the steel girders and metal studs that help to hold together their dining room table and chairs.

While serving meat as the main course, all agree that the best side dishes, as well as the best silverware and cooking implements, are the ones manufactured in plants processing homegrown Idaho ore, plucked out of the state's bountiful rocky mines.

Chock-full of minerals, Idaho's leading industrial export item has made the state famous, inspiring an abundance of iron ore merchandise, as well as popular state-fair-sponsored games of "Hot Iron Ore Toss."

Idaho iron ore has many other uses, including the forging of specialty tools for biochemical and metallurgical research, polishing pigments, and electrically non-conductive ferromagnetic ceramic compounds. It also is delicious when slathered in butter and sour cream.

COLORADO » HIGH

Perched atop the Rocky Mountains at an average elevation of over a mile, Colorado leads the nation in cases of altitude sickness, a pathological condition caused by a lack of oxygen to the brain.

Altitude sickness drives some sufferers to incomprehensibly snowboard down snowy cliffs or skateboard off iron railings in parking lots. The affliction compels others to skydive over mountains and bungee jump hundreds of feet into the Colorado River below.

However, some Coloradans suffering from extreme cases of altitude sickness often abandon all reason, attending the largest mega-churches in the nation and accepting as fact the rantings of a big-haired preacher whose sole qualification is a degree from the Colorado Springs Bible College.

The most serious cases, however, can be seen in those who ramble incessantly on *Focus On The Family's* coast-to-coast radio network, give money to Colorado's many ex-gay ministries, and flock to 10,000-seat arenas to see Christian rock concerts that would cause a healthy person almost unbearable suffering.

NEVADA » WHERE EVERYONE'S A LOSER

Losers from all over the U.S. come to Nevada's Las Vegas Strip to lose, and lose big.

Visitors to Nevada try their luck, never knowing if they will lose it all in the slots, at the blackjack table, or on the roulette wheel.

For the young, there's always a chance to lose precious weeks out of the summer by suffering through a once-in-a-lifetime family vacation to Las Vegas. Adult visitors are known to lose $20 bill after $20 bill to the state's strip clubs and brothels, where they often lose the battle for good genital hygiene as well.

Every resident of Nevada can boast of being a big-time loser, from the sleazy developer to the rural welfare recipient to the shriveled cocktail waitress. They all lost their sense of good taste—as well as their basic human dignity—sometime around 1964.

The Sphinx Of Las Vegas, one of the Seven Wonders Of The World.

MONTANA » A NATIONAL WILDMAN REFUGE

Set aside by the U.S. government in 1889, America's protected militialands are the traditional breeding grounds of the nation's last remaining manifesto-drafting psychos, armed libertarians, and solitary mountain men.

Left undisturbed in their natural mountain-compound habitat, Montanans are free to scour the land for semi-automatic weapons and brood in their carefully built shacks.

Unfortunately, as modern society encroaches, federal officials are often forced to put down Montanans when they are deemed a danger to humans.

NEW MEXICO » UNEXPLAINED

Though a retired police captain claimed to have seen New Mexico one night in 1947, researchers and government officials maintain to this day that the state was merely a weather balloon.

Conspiracy theorists have uncovered blurry aerial photos and evidence of mutilated cattle, which they say point to the existence of a sentient state somewhere between Texas and Arizona, but no legitimate sighting of New Mexico has ever been acknowledged by U.S. officials.

Furthermore, those who claim to have come in direct contact with the state are at once mocked and pitied by onlookers for being desperate drunks.

UTAH » UTAH'S FAMILY WELCOMES YOU

The family of Mark Whitmer welcomes visitors to enjoy the scenic splendor of Utah.

Mark and the 4.2 million Mrs. Mark Whitmers encourage tourists to hike the breathtaking Canyonlands National Park with a Whitmer. When you take in the sights at Arches National Park, perhaps you would like a Whitmer to take your photograph. At the Mormon Tabernacle in Salt Lake City, many Whitmers are on hand to explain the finer points of Mormonism, the one true religion that no longer believes in polygamy.

Some visitors may have an opportunity to become the next Mrs. Whitmer.

OKLAHOMA » A TUMBLEWEED PASSED THROUGH ONCE

In 1912, a tumbleweed lazily blew across the dusty prairies of Oklahoma on a soft summer breeze, an event long remembered as the only thing to ever happen in the state.

Some fleeting industry came to Oklahoma upon the tumbleweed's arrival, as locals attempted to capitalize on the remarkable occurrence.

But when the ball of dry thistle eventually rolled into Texas, it left in its wake nothing but barren soil and broken dreams.

The Pacific Coast

Otherwise America Would Have Kept Going

As they marched into the frontier to claim new territories for the Union, the brave settlers of the West Coast were undaunted by dangerous terrain, unshaken by battles with natives, and caught completely off guard by the Pacific Ocean.

Realizing they might have made a mistake basing their entire national identity on walking in one cardinal direction, these early pioneers spent a few decades wandering aimlessly up and down the 1,300-mile coastline before accepting the fact that there was simply no more America left. Those still clinging to the idea of westward expansion took up residence on sheer cliffs and volatile fault lines, at the risk of losing everything, to pursue the American Dream of nudging incrementally to the left. Still others merely waded in the water for a while before turning around and setting off to conquer the vast, untamed East.

Today, most West Coasters spend their time staring out at the horizon, recalling the days when they were striving for a brighter future, and trying to keep thousands of Mexicans from doing the same.

Lewis and Clark reach the coast in 1805, declaring, "That's it?"

WASHINGTON » SO OVER THIS WHOLE "STATEHOOD" THING

With their cultural center in Seattle, and everything else centering around themselves, the disinterested people of Washington have been too cool to have any nationwide relevance since musician Kurt Cobain left the state for good in 1994.

After decades of elitism, Washingtonians have learned to underappreciate the finer things in life, cultivating a sophisticated hatred for all music that does not come from Seattle, for most music that does, and also for everything else. Residents simply could not live without their morning coffee, their afternoon coffee, their late-afternoon coffee, their coffee coffee, some coffee before, during, and after dinner, and a nice little coffee for a nightcap. But it's not like it's a big deal or anything.

The Map

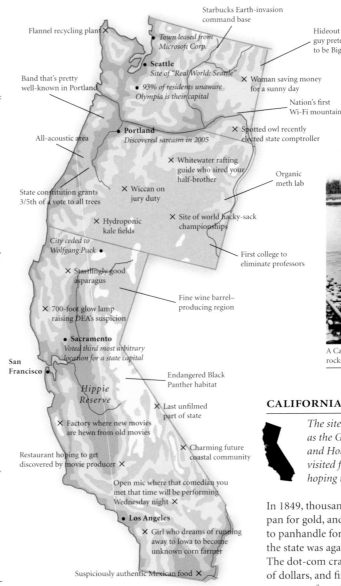

Starbucks Earth-invasion command base

Flannel recycling plant ✕

Town leased from Microsoft Corp.

Hideout of guy pretending to be Bigfoot

● **Seattle**
Site of "Real World: Seattle"

Band that's pretty well-known in Portland

● 93% of residents unaware Olympia is their capital

✕ Woman saving money for a sunny day

Nation's first Wi-Fi mountain

All-acoustic area

● **Portland**
Discovered sarcasm in 2005

✕ Spotted owl recently elected state comptroller

✕ Whitewater rafting guide who sired your half-brother

Organic meth lab

State constitution grants 3/5th of a vote to all trees

✕ Wiccan on jury duty

✕ Hydroponic kale fields

✕ Site of world hacky-sack championships

City ceded to Wolfgang Puck ●

First college to eliminate professors

✕ Startlingly good asparagus

Fine wine barrel–producing region

✕ 700-foot glow lamp raising DEA's suspicion

● **Sacramento**
Voted third most arbitrary location for a state capital

San Francisco ●

Endangered Black Panther habitat

Hippie Reserve

✕ Last unfilmed part of state

✕ Factory where new movies are hewn from old movies

Restaurant hoping to get discovered by movie producer ✕

✕ Charming future coastal community

Open mic where that comedian you met that time will be performing Wednesday night ✕

● **Los Angeles**

✕ Girl who dreams of running away to Iowa to become unknown corn farmer

Suspiciously authentic Mexican food ✕

MAP KEY
▨ Cool people
▨ Really cool people

A California prospector in 1849 collects rocks to feed his family.

OREGON » HARDLY MAKING A DIFFERENCE

Founded as a fur-trading outpost, the overly liberal state of Oregon is today the nation's leading producer of red-paint-splattered pelts and coats.

When not mountain-biking or signing petitions decrying the destructive impact of mountain-biking, concerned Oregonians can often be found forming an unbreakable human chain around the rare June 1996 *National Geographic* issue on the endangered gray wolf.

Still, the state is struggling to protect its native conservationist population, and scientists warn that there soon may not be enough activists left to chain to tree stumps.

CALIFORNIA » AT LEAST IT'S SUNNY

The site of such get-poor-quick schemes as the Gold Rush, the Dot-Com Boom, and Hollywood, California has been visited for centuries by Americans hoping to fulfill their pipe dreams.

In 1849, thousands arrived in California to pan for gold, and once that didn't work out, to panhandle for gold. Nearly 150 years later, the state was again the site of disillusionment. The dot-com crash cost Californians millions of dollars, and financially ruined employees were soon forced to move out of their parents' basements and into their attics.

Today, people flock to Los Angeles to break into the entertainment industry, where many face the biggest acting role of their lives—pretending like nothing is wrong while everything around them turns to shit.

Due to its large size, California has a diverse cultural landscape. San Francisco is the alternative-lifestyle capital of the country, with thousands of young men living openly off trust-fund money wherever you look. Meanwhile, L.A. is home to some of the kindest and most outgoing people in the world until they realize you're not an agent.

And the state's central region is known for its vineyards, where immigrant workers spend years cultivating the finest wine in the country so people can spit it out into a bucket.

The Bullshit States

Filling Out The Union

Granted statehood to bring the number of stars on the flag to a nice even 50, Alaska and Hawaii were the last states admitted to the Union and will likely be the first ceded to future invading armies.

For nearly half a century, these territorial leftovers have upheld the proud tradition of giving fourth-graders more state capitals to memorize, while providing the rest of the U.S. the satisfaction of knowing the states are divisible by several leading integers, including 5, 10, and 2, and can therefore be laid out in a variety of pleasing and symmetrical lists.

Alaska and Hawaii are located in white boxes hovering off the coast of southern California, each approximately the same size as the other. Minnesota is located 1,000 miles too close to any other state.

Although they are not connected to the U.S. by land or even casual acquaintance, these surplus states are allowed to split a single electoral vote every fourth presidential election and even use the American dollar as currency.

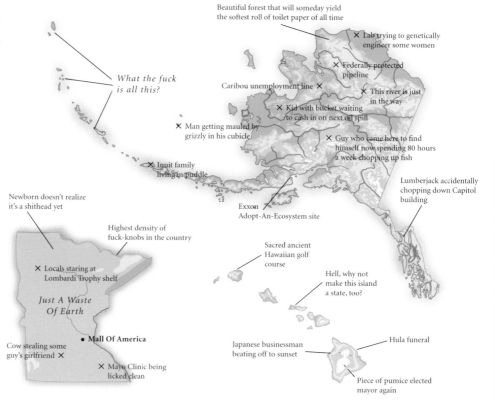

Map labels:
- Beautiful forest that will someday yield the softest roll of toilet paper of all time
- Lab trying to genetically engineer some women
- Federally protected pipeline
- Caribou unemployment line
- This river is just in the way
- Kid with bucket waiting to cash in on next oil spill
- What the fuck is all this?
- Man getting mauled by grizzly in his cubicle
- Guy who came here to find himself now spending 80 hours a week chopping up fish
- Inuit family living in puddle
- Lumberjack accidentally chopping down Capitol building
- Newborn doesn't realize it's a shithead yet
- Highest density of fuck-knobs in the country
- Exxon Adopt-An-Ecosystem site
- Sacred ancient Hawaiian golf course
- Hell, why not make this island a state, too?
- Locals staring at Lombardi Trophy shelf
- *Just A Waste Of Earth*
- Mall Of America
- Japanese businessman beating off to sunset
- Hula funeral
- Cow stealing some guy's girlfriend
- Mayo Clinic being licked clean
- Piece of pumice elected mayor again

ALASKA » NEEDLESSLY UNSPOILED

Alaska is the country's last frontier of untouched disposable consumer goods, with vast forests of potential napkin products stretching as far as the eye can see, and mountains of two-liter E-Z Chug bottles waiting to be processed.

While irreplaceable reserves of petroleum lie just feet below, massive herds of elk and grizzly are permitted to wantonly trample across the commodity-rich landscape. Likewise, dozens of Inuit tribes continue to selfishly hoard all the best drilling land for living off of.

Much of the native salmon lack adequate protection to ensure their commercial well-being. Preservation efforts are currently underway to vacuum-seal these majestic smoked fish and track their retail-migration paths by tagging them with magnetic $12.99-per-pound price labels.

And, after an incredible comeback from the point of near extinction, Alaska's 35,000 bald eagles are an inspiration to generations of high-quality down-comforter manufacturers.

These secluded Alaskan woods hide more than $62 billion in potential profit.

HAWAII » SPECTACULAR BALCONY VIEW

From their high-rise hotel rooms in Waikiki, Hawaii's tourists are dazzled by the white-sand beaches 40 stories below, as well as the tasteful watercolors hanging above their beds.

One of Hawaii's most stunning landscapes.

Rare jungle birds and vivid tropical trees that can't be found anywhere else in the world are easily accessible on channel 347 (TLC). In fact, all of Hawaii's picturesque wildlife is within reach at the postcard stand down in the lobby gift shop.

Though 500-foot waterfalls are mere miles away, the typical visitor need not travel far to enjoy clear cascading waters, as the full-size shower is just

MINNESOTA » LAND OF 10,000 RETARDS

The pop-drinking, Hormel-eating, dontcha-know dumbfucks of Minnesota are too stupid to have any idea why they are the laughing stock of the entire country.

From "Yah, sure" to "You betcha, there," Minnesotans have not said one damn intelligent or discernible thing since their godforsaken state was founded in 1858.

After being told by Eastern explorers that they had an unusual number of lakes, intrepid Minnesotans started counting, got stuck at 99, and just skipped ahead to the highest number they'd ever heard of, 10,000.

Canada

» THE ONLY FOLIAGE IN ALL OF CANADA.

» THE U.S. $1.82 BILL.

For The United States, See Pages 9–22

L iving in the shadow of its southern neighbor, the nation of Canada will never be as great as the U.S. so long as it continues to burden citizens with universal health care, refuses to drill for oil in federally protected wildlife reserves, and neglects its duty to blindly support unilateral invasions of Middle Eastern states.

While a remarkable nation in its own right, Canada stubbornly maintains overly restrictive gun-control laws, leaving the country roughly 6,000 annual murders short of the American ideal. On par with the U.S. in almost every other way, Canada's budget, however, remains woefully balanced, same-sex marriage is a sad reality in all 10 of its provinces, and the theory of creationism is denied to thousands of students attending its public schools each year.

Nearly as prosperous as the U.S., Canada wastes its resources lowering greenhouse-gas emissions and offering paid maternity leave to new mothers, all the while allowing its lagging entertainment industry, struggling fast-food businesses, and weak military to go tragically underfunded.

Although there is reason for Canadians to rejoice as of late, with the country electing its first conservative government in decades and incidents of rape almost doubling in several metropolitan areas, if Canada wants to be able to compete with the U.S., it still has a lot of work left to undo.

PEOPLE » A WARM, COLD PEOPLE

The citizens of Canada can generally be divided into two distinct groups: those who are polite, and those who are too polite to bring up the fact that they've been placed in the wrong group. A culturally diverse people, men and women from all different backgrounds can be heard apologizing in their native tongue, while Canada's northern Inuit population is said to have almost 50 different words for "pardon me."

Subjected to some of the coldest temperatures in the world, the average Canadian spends two-thirds of his life bundling up for the winter, one-third bundling up for the summer, and can count the number of times he has lost a finger to frostbite on one prosthetic hand.

Canada's national sport is ice hockey, although ice fishing is also popular, as is ice volleyball, ice auto racing, and field hockey, which is played on ice.

HISTORY » WHERE THE PAST COMES ALIVE AND BORES YOU TO DEATH

2000 B.C. Archaeologists uncover the earliest known hockey rink frozen in a block of ice.

A.D. 1535 French explorer Jacques Cartier discovers Montreal, scurvy, Quebec City, hypothermia, the Ottawa River, and frostbite.

1600 European settlers introduce alcohol to the region, pushing drink after drink onto the native population. Aboriginal men and women awake the next morning to find that their land has been raped.

1640 British missionaries convert thousands of natives to the metric system.

1670 The Hudson's Bay Company is established by London fur traders, leading to the eventual extinction of nearly five different species of coat.

1674 A wagon of caribou pelts strides majestically across the Canadian landscape.

1721 The perfectly flat prairies of Western Canada are charted when two daring explorers look to their left.

1730 The first French-Canadian mustache is grown in the province of Quebec.

1812 Attempts to invade Canada during the War of 1812 fail when the U.S. is repeatedly met by a stubborn and impenetrable cold front.

1814 Canadian and British soldiers storm Washington and set fire to the West Wing of the White House. The blaze quickly spreads to the Red Room, the Map Room, the Kindling Room, the Oil Room, the Hall Of Large Flammable Objects, and the Library.

1836 After 48 long, excruciating hours on the Underground Railroad, thousands of slaves are overjoyed to arrive in Canada and finally use the bathroom.

1867 Canada's first prime minister, John A. Macdonald, fails to live up to his predecessor.

1891 By cutting holes in two peach baskets and hanging them at opposite ends of a high-school gymnasium, Canadian physician Dr. James Naismith ruins two perfectly good peach baskets.

1899 Dozens of ambivalent prospectors take part in the Klondike Gold Dawdle.

1904 The Great Toronto Fire destroys much of the city when freezing Canadians decide to wait until July to put it out.

1914 Canada fights alongside, and frequently in front of, British troops during WWI.

1920 The Royal Canadian Mounted Police is dealt a devastating blow moments after inaugurating its new Coast Guard unit.

Wayne Gretzky

1946 Canada's new universal health-care plan is criticized for its failure to cover U.S. citizens.

1961 As legend goes, Wayne Gretzky is born wearing hockey skates. His mother, Phyllis Gretzky, dies of severe internal hemorrhaging.

1969–2004 Canada's worst hockey team, the Montreal Expos, plays the sport for 35 years on grass with some sort of round puck.

1979 The province of Quebec demands independence from the rest of Canada, claiming that their distinct culture deserves to be recognized, and that they already have this really awesome country name totally picked out.

1981 Running with one prosthetic leg, Terry Fox begins his Marathon Of Hope to raise money for cancer research, and, after 80 exhausting miles, a new car.

2004 U.S. presidential candidate John Kerry threatens to move to Canada if George W. Bush is re-elected.

2007 Canada is canceled due to snow.

This Canadian Mountie dreams of one day becoming a police officer.

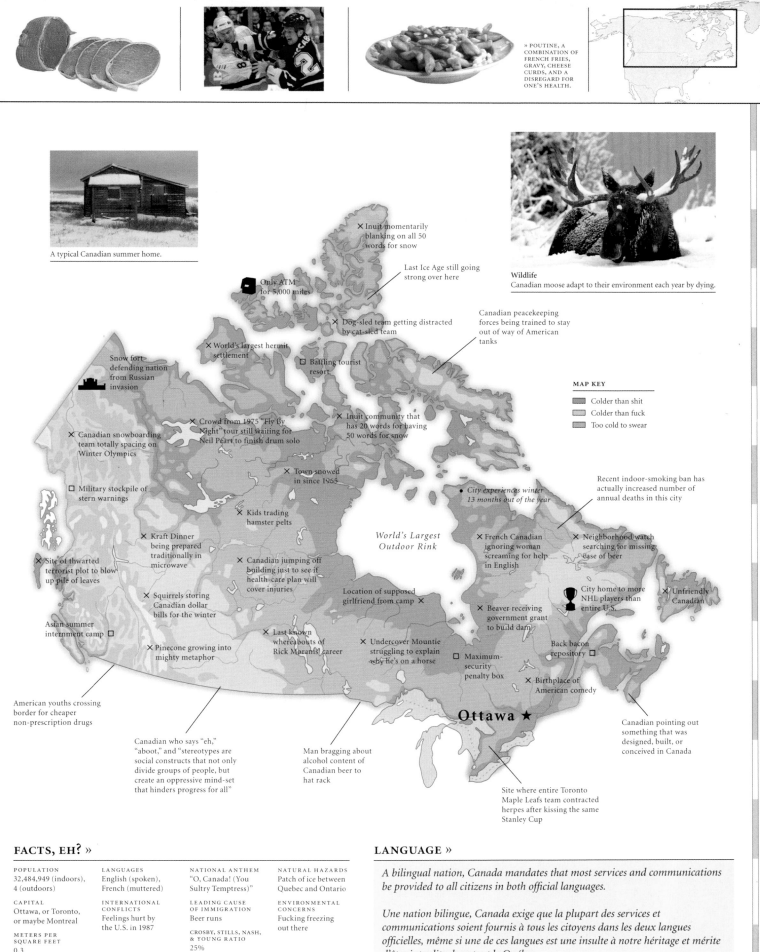

» POUTINE, A COMBINATION OF FRENCH FRIES, GRAVY, CHEESE CURDS, AND A DISREGARD FOR ONE'S HEALTH.

A typical Canadian summer home.

Wildlife
Canadian moose adapt to their environment each year by dying.

× Inuit momentarily blanking on all 50 words for snow

Last Ice Age still going strong over here

Only ATM for 5,000 miles

× Dog-sled team getting distracted by cat-sled team

× World's largest hermit settlement

Canadian peacekeeping forces being trained to stay out of way of American tanks

Snow fort defending nation from Russian invasion

☐ Baffling tourist resort

MAP KEY

- Colder than shit
- Colder than fuck
- Too cold to swear

× Inuit community that has 20 words for having 50 words for snow

× Crowd from 1975 "Fly By Night" tour still waiting for Neil Peart to finish drum solo

× Canadian snowboarding team totally spacing on Winter Olympics

× Town snowed in since 1965

● City experiences winter 13 months out of the year

Recent indoor-smoking ban has actually increased number of annual deaths in this city

☐ Military stockpile of stern warnings

× Kids trading hamster pelts

World's Largest Outdoor Rink

× French Canadian ignoring woman screaming for help in English

× Neighborhood watch searching for missing case of beer

× Kraft Dinner being prepared traditionally in microwave

× Canadian jumping off building just to see if health-care plan will cover injuries

× Site of thwarted terrorist plot to blow up pile of leaves

× Squirrels storing Canadian dollar bills for the winter

Location of supposed girlfriend from camp ×

× Beaver receiving government grant to build dam

🏆 City home to more NHL players than entire U.S.

× Unfriendly Canadian

Asian summer internment camp ☐

× Pinecone growing into mighty metaphor

× Last known whereabouts of Rick Moranis' career

× Undercover Mountie struggling to explain why he's on a horse

☐ Maximum-security penalty box

Back bacon repository ☐

× Birthplace of American comedy

★ **Ottawa**

American youths crossing border for cheaper non-prescription drugs

Canadian who says "eh," "aboot," and "stereotypes are social constructs that not only divide groups of people, but create an oppressive mind-set that hinders progress for all"

Man bragging about alcohol content of Canadian beer to hat rack

Canadian pointing out something that was designed, built, or conceived in Canada

Site where entire Toronto Maple Leafs team contracted herpes after kissing the same Stanley Cup

FACTS, EH? »

POPULATION
32,484,949 (indoors),
4 (outdoors)

CAPITAL
Ottawa, or Toronto, or maybe Montreal

METERS PER SQUARE FEET
0.3

LANGUAGES
English (spoken), French (muttered)

INTERNATIONAL CONFLICTS
Feelings hurt by the U.S. in 1987

NATIONAL ANTHEM
"O, Canada! (You Sultry Temptress)"

LEADING CAUSE OF IMMIGRATION
Beer runs

CROSBY, STILLS, NASH, & YOUNG RATIO
25%

NATURAL HAZARDS
Patch of ice between Quebec and Ontario

ENVIRONMENTAL CONCERNS
Fucking freezing out there

LANGUAGE »

A bilingual nation, Canada mandates that most services and communications be provided to all citizens in both official languages.

Une nation bilingue, Canada exige que la plupart des services et communications soient fournis à tous les citoyens dans les deux langues officielles, même si une de ces langues est une insulte à notre héritage et mérite d'être interdite dans tout le Québec.

Mexico

» COLORS REPRESENT
TWO POPULAR SALSAS
AND THE TABLECLOTH
THAT SUPPORTS THEM.

Now Hiring 2.4 Million Busboys

Despite being home to millions of educated and talented professionals, Mexico's development has been hampered by a severe unskilled-labor shortage, as there is no one left in the nation capable of handling the growing piles of garbage, the towering stacks of unclean dishes, and the large number of toilets, which—backed up beyond recognition—refuse to flush.

With manual laborers fleeing to America, this national "brawn drain," as economists badly in need of someone to patch their roofs are calling it, has set the country back several years.

Gifted surgeons in Mexico City frequently cancel operations due to unsanitary working conditions. Exceptional scientists and researchers—close to a number of exciting breakthroughs—are unable to carry boxes of heavy lab equipment to their facilities. Even the nation's most prestigious universities have remained closed, as there are no custodians around with the keys to unlock them.

In addition, Mexico's accomplished architects are forced not only to design buildings, but lay the cement foundation, erect load-bearing walls, hoist trusses into place, install indoor plumbing, and trowel on the exterior stucco. Unfortunately, when construction is finally complete, few are able to see their work without anyone to mow the 10-foot-high grass that has grown around it.

Recently, the nation's exports and imports have also suffered, with cargo containers lying on shipping docks for years. Meanwhile, famine has struck a number of local communities used to ordering in.

On the bright side, thousands of Mexicans remain unaware of the ongoing crisis, as only a single resident is left to deliver the nation's morning newspaper each day.

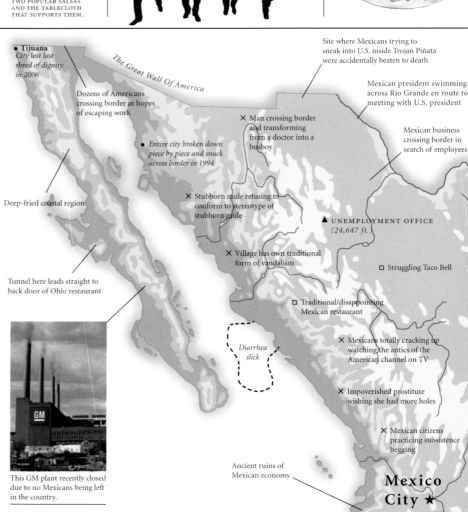

- **Tijuana** *City lost last shred of dignity in 2006*

The Great Wall Of America

Site where Mexicans trying to sneak into U.S. inside Trojan Piñata were accidentally beaten to death

Dozens of Americans crossing border in hopes of escaping work

Mexican president swimming across Rio Grande en route to meeting with U.S. president

- *Entire city broken down piece by piece and snuck across border in 1994*

× Man crossing border and transforming from a doctor into a busboy

Mexican business crossing border in search of employees

Deep-fried coastal region

× Stubborn mule refusing to conform to stereotype of stubborn mule

▲ UNEMPLOYMENT OFFICE (24,647 ft.)

Tunnel here leads straight to back door of Ohio restaurant

× Village has own traditional form of vandalism

□ Struggling Taco Bell

□ Traditional/disappointing Mexican restaurant

Diarrhea slick

× Mexicans totally cracking up watching the antics of the American channel on TV

× Impoverished prostitute wishing she had more holes

× Mexican citizens practicing subsistence begging

Ancient ruins of Mexican economy

Mexico City ★

This GM plant recently closed due to no Mexicans being left in the country.

Destitute village being repeatedly flashed by American students on spring break

PEOPLE » THE LEGAL KIND OF MEXICANS

Pope John Paul II grants sainthood to El Santo for his divine elbow drop.

Known for their boundless energy, exuberant zest for life, and outgoing nature, most Mexicans are simply too tired, miserable, and withdrawn after a long day of work in the U.S. to set the record straight. A mix of Spanish and indigenous ancestry, citizens can often trace their roots all the way back to some of the earliest incidents of rape in Mexico.

The people of Mexico are overwhelmingly Roman Catholic. And with over 20 million residents named in honor of their Lord, many wayward souls are able to find Jesus asleep in the park, purchasing scratch-off tickets at the local deli, begging for spare change, urinating inside an empty subway car, and sometimes even at church.

The official language is Spanish, which is grudgingly spoken by 93% of the population. Mexicans speak Spanish as quickly as possible just to get it over with, and consume hot chilis to get the taste of the conquistador's tongue out of their mouths.

A Mexican piñata farm.

FACTS » SERVE WITH SALSA AND GUACAMOLE

POPULATION 23,000,000 (day), 115,000,000 (night)	**CURRENCY** The peso, broken down into 100 wages
ENCHILADA BREAKDOWN Tortilla (25%), Chicken (35%), Cheese (20%), Mole Sauce (12%), Other (8%)	**ENVIRONMENTAL ADVANCES** Recently created car that runs on air pollution
FERTILITY RATE 1 child/5.8 tequila shots	**INTERNATIONAL DISPUTES** All regarding number of shifts Emanuel got last week
BORDERS None that Mexico is aware of	**STEREOTYPES** Will get around to dispelling myth that they all are lazy next week
LEGAL SYSTEM Knocked unconscious with steel chair	**SPACE FILLER?** Yes

» THE WORK OF THE ANCIENT MAYANS. » THE WORK OF THE MODERN MAYANS.

HISTORY » BADLY IN NEED OF A SIESTA

11,000 B.C. First ever thing in history occurs.

A.D. 460 Closely following the movement of the sun, moon, and stars, Mayan astronomers are able to accurately predict eclipses moments after they happen.

700 Mayan philosophers posit the groundbreaking theory that three, not four, jaguars hold up the sky.

Cortez meets Montezuma.

1325 The Aztecs construct the city of Tenochtitlán on the wet, marshy islets of Lake Texcoco, implementing architectural techniques such as sticking twigs into mud and carefully balancing things.

1380 Aztec villagers begin the practice of human sacrifice, which they perform daily as an offering of gratitude to the Gods for granting them the precious gift of human life.

1519 Spanish conquistador Hernan Cortez occupies Cozumel, and nearly destroys the flourishing native Mexican culture. His invasion is re-enacted annually by thousands of students on spring break.

1521 Greedy Spaniards attempt to flee Tenochtitlán with as much stolen gold as possible. However, as the Aztecs close in, they realize they need to unload some cargo, and toss themselves overboard so the gold may escape safely.

1535 Spain establishes a ruling government in New Spain (Mexico), before going on to colonize the territories of Newer Spain (Guatemala), Newest Spain (Nicaragua), and Spain II (Panama).

1700 Combining the desire to shield one's eyes from the sun with the willingness to abandon all traces of human dignity, Mexican men create the sombrero.

1832 Mexico celebrates its long-sought independence by refusing Texas its long-sought independence.

1836 Gen. Sam Houston and his Texas Army defeat the Mexicans at the Battle of San Jacinto, led by Houston's famous war cry,

"Remember the...shit, you know—the...ummm...it's like that big fort thing in San Antonio! Remember?! That place where we had that battle a couple of weeks back! Motherfucker, what's it called?! Lots of us died there and everything! The Afanlo?! Is that it?! Fuck!"

1846 U.S. loses the Mexican-American War when it gains control of all of Texas.

1910 Thousands of Mexican revolutionaries fight bravely in the name of longer, thicker mustaches.

1953 U.S. deports the city of San Diego back to Mexico.

1972 Oil is found hundreds of miles undersea by a group of Mexicans trying to sneak into the U.S.

1990 Archaeologists are astounded by the discovery of dozens of Mexican artifacts lining the walls of a local Carlos & Charlie's restaurant.

1994 Under the NAFTA treaty, several U.S. factories open in Mexico, giving citizens the convenience of being exploited only minutes from home.

1996 Bill Clinton becomes the first serving U.S. president to visit Mexico at 2 o'clock in the morning.

2002 President Bush orders that the Statue of Liberty be brought down to the U.S.–Mexico border and tipped on its side to block immigrants from entering the country.

2006 Texas ceded back to Mexico.

The Diego Rivera of van murals

Mexican forced to take on fourth job to cover cost of commuting

Depressed Mexican thinking about crossing this border

Mariachi supergroup

8 million Mexicans turning around after hearing "Hey you!"

Indigenous hole

Mexican candidate who will have to finally remove mask if he loses election

Backwoods Blight

Rural Blight

Strategic guacamole reserve

Urban Blight

Largest Mayan casino in Mexico

Oaxaca
City full of rich culture most tourists miss

Giant "Z" left by Zorro in mid-19th century

MAP KEY
- Girls gone wild
- Girls gone sober
- Girls weeping silently in back of strange van

ILLEGAL IMMIGRATION » HOW IT AFFECTS AMERICAN INDUSTRY

Each year, millions of Mexican day laborers sneak illegally into the U.S., only to steal jobs from honest, hardworking American machines.

This serious problem leaves thousands of qualified lawn sprinklers and trustworthy electric dishwashers unemployed. In fact, unskilled laborers from Mexico have in recent years taken work right out from under dozens of forklifts, pulleys, and other deserving hoisting devices.

Threatening the livelihood of countless weed-whackers and standing pylons—despite not even being able to speak the language half the time—illegal Mexicans continue to destabilize the American economy, as many offer to do the work of perfectly good Roombas, often for a fraction of the cost.

While automatic gates and mechanized barriers along the border help to keep hundreds of unauthorized immigrants out of the U.S. each day, some say it is only a matter of time before these loyal and reliable machines are also replaced by Mexicans.

Belize

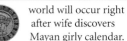

» CURRENTLY LOCATED
AT THE BOTTOM OF
THE CARIBBEAN SEA.

A Nation In Smithereens

A Central American nation lying directly in the path of countless Atlantic storm systems, Belize has a diverse and ever-changing society dating all the way back to the last devastating hurricane season.

Its civilization—shaped, reshaped, and tossed around by such big names as Mitch, Keith, Chantal, and Iris—is currently located half a mile off the eastern coast.

After the capital city was washed away for the third straight year, Belize's parliament, clinging to anything that would float, held an emergency meeting to approve the purchase of a national tarp, which is still on layaway. While the country is poor, the government does its best to make sure every citizen has a roof under his feet.

The people of Belize have had to adapt to their constantly shifting environment by stockpiling canned goods, learning to read Doppler radar, and not getting too close to their friends and family.

PEOPLE » BASICALLY, RAG DOLLS

Whether waking up in their own beds or atop a tree halfway across the country, the people of Belize are creatures of habit who prefer taking the same evacuation route each morning, and insist on reconstructing hospitals and schools in the identical way every week.

A surprisingly upbeat people, Belizeans refuse to let tropical depressions get them down. In fact, most residents are too busy spending time huddling with their children to worry about petty catastrophes.

While they love to feel the Category 5 wind in their hair, Belize's citizens are homebodies at heart, and sometimes don't leave their houses for weeks at a time, until rescue teams can cut through the debris and pull them outside.

FACTS » STILL DRYING OUT

MONKEYS THEY GOT
Howler, Spider

AREA COMPARATIVE
New Orleans

INTERNATIONAL RELATIONS
Belize is so tiny that they even consider Guatemala a superpower

MILK SOURCE
The tapir

LITERACY RATE
98% illiterate in two languages

POVERTY
Yep

NATURAL HAZARDS
Neighbor's lawn chair

OFFICIAL HOLIDAY
Thanksgiving (not observed)

MILES PER SQUARE TOURIST
.25

NATIONAL MOTTO
"Not Again"

CURRENCY
Damp

NATURAL RESOURCES
200 mph winds, 30-foot waves, timber stumps

OF NOTE
Contrary to popular belief, toucans prefer Fruit Rings Cereal to Froot Loops®, though both will kill them

HISTORY » HIGH WINDS OF CHANGE

1200 B.C. Working without the aid of any modern tools, Mayans build Belize's first ruins.

1050 B.C. Mayan meteorologists accurately chart the path of Hurricane Tezcatlipoca, but thousands die when they are unable to pronounce the name in storm warnings.

800 B.C. First Mayan girly calendar predicts the end of the world will occur right after wife discovers Mayan girly calendar.

A.D. 1763 Spain reaches an agreement with locals, offering them the privilege of wood-cutting, but not wood-profiting.

1985 Guatemala refuses to return the city of Dangriga when a hurricane blows it over their border.

1999 Belize declares all hurricanes unconstitutional, but because of a minor legal technicality, Low Pressure System Keith is allowed to completely obliterate the country a year later.

2005 Belize cuts down every tree in the nation and places them in storage for safekeeping.

Couple arguing over whether prized possessions are flotsam or jetsam

× Brine shrimp nursery

× Conservationist tying down all the country's wildlife before storm

Ruins of 18 bridge attempts ×

× Government worker making sure Mayan ruins are up to code

× Rare jungle plant that will make your balls burn like crazy

Two hurricanes embarrassed to show up at the same time

MEXICO'S ARMPIT

× Jaguar acting like it owns the place

× Indigenous logging community threatened by under-deforestation

× Fisherman reeling in boot, entire village

▲ Mountain trying to get back on shore

× Jungle-free concrete preserve

Belize River
Only river in the world named the Belize River

● Belize City
More a pile of sandbags than a city, really

× Two-month-old Mayan ruins

× Scuba tour stuck in tree

★ Belmopan
Government on recess until tide brings them back in

× Water

■ Not much of a barrier reef

× Flock of yellow warblers migrating against their will

× Where traditional dance of sorrow is performed

× Homeowner nailing plywood over his tarp

HIGH GROUND
(Tuesdays only)

× Man under a lot of water pressure lately

▲ VICTORIA PEAK
Yet another place named after Victoria Peak

× Mother waterproofing newborn

× Monkey wearing nicotine patch

□ Storm-shelter shelter

● City they didn't bother to name

× Homeowner nailing plywood to his plywood

× Woman bitching about starving to death again

Man ducking to avoid evacuee flying through air

Guatemala

Currently In A Battered-Nation Shelter

Although Guatemala tries to cover up the battle scars from its 36-year civil war, neighboring countries suspect that it's just making excuses for a neglectful, abusive government. These concerns peaked in 1996, when over a million bruised and bloody refugees claimed they all just fell down the stairs.

Practically every night, the UN receives reports of domestic violence, loud disputes, and machine-gun sounds coming from the nation, but each time peace-keeping forces arrive, a teary-eyed Guatemalan says "it's nothing" and urges them not to come inside.

When confronted about their president's cruel ways, Guatemalans typically respond by claiming that other nations don't know him like they do, and that he only hires death-squad soldiers to beat them because he loves them.

International observers, however, say that Guatemala was just so desperate to have a democratic government that they would've let anyone run their country, even Communists.

Today, even though their president is stealing all their income, pawning their resources for money, and trafficking drugs on the side, the people of Guatemala still make excuses for him. They say he acts like this because he was raised in a corrupt nation himself, that he always buys them something nice after slaying hundreds, and that "everything is our fault anyway."

FACTS » A ROTTEN BANANA REPUBLIC

POPULATION
14,655,189 (approx.), 14,655,201 (exact)

NATIONAL ANTHEM
"Guatemala Feliz," which translates to "Happy Guatemala," is the only national anthem sung entirely in a sarcastic tone, accompanied by the "wanking" hand motion

NATURAL RESOURCES
Bananas, petrobananas, semiprecious bananas, hydrobananas, non-renewable bananas

ONCE ACCIDENTALLY IMPORTED
Bananas

MALNUTRITION
High, though no one suffers from potassium deficiency

ENVIRONMENTAL CONCERNS
Nation's homeless population living in the ancient Mayan ruins

MEASUREMENT SYSTEM
Switched to metric system in 2002 so their area would appear larger

CRIME & CORRUPTION
Nation hoping they will cancel each other out

CRIME BREAKDOWN
Broad daylight (16%), Diffused daylight (12%), Fluorescent light (22%), Twilight (19%), Complete darkness (31%)

VIOLENCE TYPE
Mostly Spanish or Guatemalan, though some indigenous Mayan violence still exists

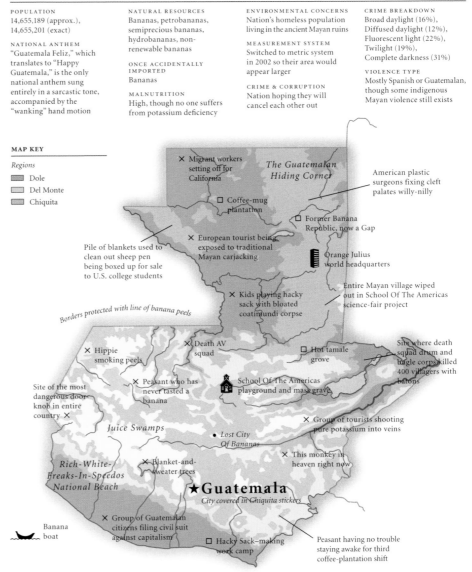

MAP KEY

Regions
- Dole
- Del Monte
- Chiquita

- ✕ Migrant workers setting off for California
- *The Guatemalan Hiding Corner*
- American plastic surgeons fixing cleft palates willy-nilly
- ☐ Coffee-mug plantation
- ☐ Former Banana Republic, now a Gap
- ✕ European tourist being exposed to traditional Mayan carjacking
- Pile of blankets used to clean out sheep pen being boxed up for sale to U.S. college students
- ▮ Orange Julius world headquarters
- *Borders protected with line of banana peels*
- ✕ Kids playing hacky sack with bloated coatimundi corpse
- Entire Mayan village wiped out in School Of The Americas science-fair project
- ✕ Hippie smoking peels
- ✕ Death AV squad
- ☐ Hot tamale grove
- Site where death squad drum and bugle corps killed 400 villagers with batons
- Site of the most dangerous door-knob in entire country ✕
- ✕ Peasant who has never tasted a banana
- ⛪ School Of The Americas playground and mass grave
- *Juice Swamps*
- • *Lost City Of Bananas*
- ✕ Group of tourists shooting pure potassium into veins
- *Rich-White-Freaks-In-Speedos National Beach*
- ✕ Blanket-and-sweater trees
- ✕ This monkey in heaven right now
- ★ **Guatemala** *City covered in Chiquita stickers*
- ⌁ Banana boat
- ✕ Group of Guatemalan citizens filing civil suit against capitalism
- ☐ Hacky Sack–making work camp
- Peasant having no trouble staying awake for third coffee-plantation shift

HISTORY » WHY CAN'T YOU BE MORE LIKE YOUR ANCIENT ANCESTORS?

1500 B.C. The Mayan civilization begins when people who occupy the Yucatán Peninsula start communicating with each other in an effort to break the uncomfortable 10,000-year silence.

A.D. 212 Early Mayan astrologers accurately predict an opportunity for a romantic encounter in the coming week.

250–900 Mayan tribes build the most sophisticated architecture of the ancient world, made more impressive by the fact that they did so using such simplistic devices as wheels, a pulley system, axes, stone-tipped shovels, and wheelbarrows rather than the more practical and advanced slave.

1960–1996 Guatemala is entangled in a bloody civil war that lasts 36 years for those unlucky enough to survive it. In 1996, a peace accord is signed, but not before 75,000 Guatemalan soldiers have been killed and 25,000 others have died of old age.

Many Guatemalans are too scared to tell anyone they're totally fucked.

ECONOMY » BANANAS

Powerful U.S. fruit companies have controlled Guatemala's banana industry through corruption and violence for over a century. Being a "banana republic" affects citizens' lives in several ways:

🍌 Banana-grove laborers are often forced to slip on banana peels for cruel foreman's amusement

🍌 Guatemalan diplomats traveling abroad are required to wear a full-body banana suit at all times

🍌 Death-squad employees get a great discount on bananas

🍌 Citizens are comforted to know that they're one omitted word away from a viable form of government

El Salvador

» MANY CLAIM TO LOVE THE SMELL OF BREWING EL SALVADOR'S FLAG, BUT HATE THE WAY IT TASTES.

Badly In Need Of A Savior

Impoverished, dangerously overpopulated, and devastated by decades of civil war and natural disasters, the nation of El Salvador spends every minute desperately praying for Jesus to return and bring a new country with Him.

With a number of catastrophic earthquakes, and an economy that has collapsed three times in as many decades, the only thing that's unshakable in El Salvador is the people's faith that God will dig them out of this mess before they have to.

The government has an ambitious five-year plan to pray for Him to fix their highway system, their education system, and their political system. Meanwhile, leaders advise distraught citizens to search for any signs of the savior on the surfaces of fried food, stone, bark, or plaster in hopes that He will return and pray to God for them.

Ronald Reagan delivers his historic 1987 speech to the president of El Salvador, in which he demands, "Mr. Fuentes, mow down these nuns."

HISTORY » THE BEST PART OF WAKING UP IS HAVING YOUR COUNTRY COMPLETELY OBLITERATED

2000 B.C. Local artisans produce thousands of adorable, terra-cotta baby figurines when they realize there's a market for them among young, unmarried Olmec secretaries.

A.D. 1308 Irrational superstitions among the ancient Pipil civilization warn against the dangers of growing coffee for profit.

1524 Spanish playboy and adventurer Pedro de Alvarado takes a trip to El Salvador, where he forcibly woos thousands of women.

1540 Spain agrees to grant El Salvador its independence in exchange for the right to wipe out its indigenous population and subject the country to 298 years of slavery first.

1882 European philosophers fail to inform desperate Salvadorans that God is dead.

1917 Poor Christian workers harvesting coffee for their brutal moneyed overlords turn the other cheek a record 12.5 million times.

1982 As a bloody civil war rages in El Salvador, millions of Americans are shocked to learn that restaurant-goers actually prefer Folgers over the leading brand.

1986 U.S. advisors put the Salvadoran Army on an intense training regimen and divide them up into death squads by shirts and skins.

1993 El Salvador signs Free-Trade Agree-To-Disagree Pact.

2004 The U.S. government apologizes for considering apologizing for supporting Salvadoran death squads in the 1980s.

PEOPLE » THE TEEMING, OFTEN MURDERED, MASSES

With unemployment rising to nearly 40%, there is growing unrest amongst citizens still waiting for Jesus to look for a job for them. Yet the country enjoys a thriving arts community, regularly churning out statues of bleeding Madonnas, statues of crying Madonnas, and statues of Madonnas who are crying because they are bleeding. Due to the nation's extreme poverty, the people of El Salvador have fully embraced their national religion—crime—by attending bank robberies every Sunday, helping innocent bystanders find their way to heaven, and putting their faith in the redemptive power of Jesus Christ to forgive all sins.

FACTS » NO MAN KNOWS THE DAY OR HOUR

POPULATION BREAKDOWN
71% Praying
29% Dying

AREA COMPARATIVE
Cardboard box filled with coffee beans, rape, and mudslides

EXPORTS
Coffee, decaf coffee, instant coffee

IMPORTS
Doughnuts

COUNTRY NAME TRANSLATED
Jesus Christ!

TOURIST SITES
Los Volcanes National Park, El Imposible National Park, Where Jesus Gave Up On Humanity National Park

NATURAL DISASTERS
Hurricanes, juntas, hot coffee in the face

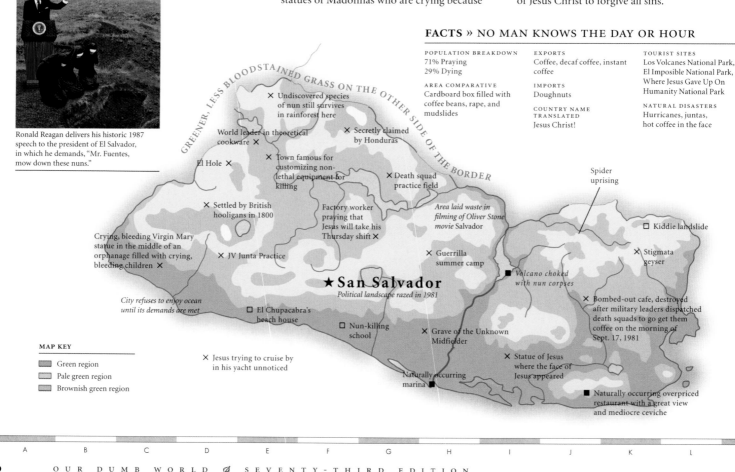

GREENER, LESS BLOODSTAINED GRASS ON THE OTHER SIDE OF THE BORDER

× Undiscovered species of nun still survives in rainforest here

× Secretly claimed by Honduras

World leader in theoretical cookware ×

El Hole ×

× Town famous for customizing non-lethal equipment for killing

× Death squad practice field

× Settled by British hooligans in 1800

Factory worker praying that Jesus will take his Thursday shift ×

Area laid waste in filming of Oliver Stone movie Salvador

Crying, bleeding Virgin Mary statue in the middle of an orphanage filled with crying, bleeding children ×

× JV Junta Practice

× Guerrilla summer camp

□ Kiddie landslide

Spider uprising

× Stigmata geyser

★ San Salvador
Political landscape razed in 1981

● Volcano choked with nun corpses

City refuses to enjoy ocean until its demands are met

□ El Chupacabra's beach house

□ Nun-killing school

× Grave of the Unknown Midfielder

× Bombed-out cafe, destroyed after military leaders dispatched death squads to go get them coffee on the morning of Sept. 17, 1981

× Jesus trying to cruise by in his yacht unnoticed

× Statue of Jesus where the face of Jesus appeared

Naturally occurring marina ■

■ Naturally occurring overpriced restaurant with a great view and mediocre ceviche

MAP KEY

▨ Green region
▨ Pale green region
▨ Brownish green region

Honduras

» THESE FIVE STARS REPRESENT WHATEVER YOU WANT THEM TO REPRESENT.

» THE WORST PART ABOUT GUERRILLA WARFARE IS ALL THE WAITING.

A Lush And Diverse Crime Scene

With over 900 distinct types of rapists, 600 varieties of cold-blooded murderers, and all 18 members of the feared *Hernandez-Garcia* family, Honduras boasts a startling array of criminal life sure to take any visitor's breath, wallet, and often both kidneys away.

Home to some of the last sexual predators of their kind, the unique political climate and economic landscape of Honduras is a breeding ground for thousands of felons who have over the years learned to thrive in this urban jungle.

While most of these criminals only come out at night, dozens of new assailants are discovered by trembling citizens each week—be it at the park, in dark alleys, or even in their own bedrooms.

However, only 10% of all Honduran criminals have actually been identified by police investigators, as many are able to camouflage themselves to blend into their surroundings.

Whereas in other parts of the world carjackers and kidnappers are confined to small cages, in Honduras, these animals are allowed to roam free. Sadly, the rise of urban development in recent years has begun to destroy their once unspoiled habitats, namely abandoned warehouses, isolated farmhouses, and the woods.

HISTORY » THE EVOLUTION OF MANSLAUGHTER

1600 B.C. Chocolate originates in Honduras. Although this delicacy is reserved for only the highest noblemen and clerics of Mesoamerica, the rest of the Mayans are permitted to lick the bowl.

A.D. 1502 Christopher Columbus discovers what he is pretty sure is India this time.

Columbus

1525 The Spaniards conquer Honduras out of sheer habit.

1969 During a playoff soccer game, border tensions between Honduras and El Salvador erupt in the six-day "Soccer War," which consists of both sides mostly just running around and rarely taking a shot.

1974 An embarrassed, emasculated Honduras refrains from telling the international community that it was devastated by Hurricane Fifi.

1982–1983 Honduran Death Squads, accused of murdering hundreds, defend themselves by claiming that just because a group goes by a certain name doesn't necessarily mean they always act accordingly. UN Peacekeeping Forces immediately understand and grant them amnesty.

1998 Honduras is devastated by Hurricane Mitch, which kills 5,600 people and causes $4 billion in damage. Hondurans, however, are instantly comforted after it is explained to them that hurricanes are an important part of the atmospheric system, and necessary for moving heat from equatorial regions toward the higher latitudes.

1999 Thousands fear for their lives when Hurricane Mitch returns in the form of a light drizzle.

2002 TLC member Lisa "Left Eye" Lopes dies in a car crash in Honduras. Investigators cite the cause of the crash as a guy—identified by eyewitnesses as a broke-ass scrub who can't get no love—hanging out the passenger-side window of his best friend's ride, attempting to holler at Lopes as she passed through a busy intersection.

2003 Honduras agrees to a free-trade agreement with the U.S., but only because they really, really want to import an Xbox for Christmas.

Mudslides In Tegucigalpa
A Honduran man returns from work to find his house sliding down a cliff.

FACTS » COLD, HARD

NATURAL RESOURCES
The nation's children, who mine gold, silver, copper, lead, zinc, iron ore, and coal in deep, dark mines

MURDER RATE
Statistic not available, as statistician was murdered earlier this year

LIFE EXPECTANCY AT GUNPOINT
Depends—are you going to cooperate?

NATURAL HAZARDS
Alfredo Perez, Pablo Santos, landslides, Miguel Izquierdo-Costa

DEBT
$14 billion; Honduras claims they have it, but it's in their other pants

TOURIST MOTTO
"Bring Your Rape Whistle!"

MIGRATION
Thousands cross Honduras' borders each year for the safer, more hospitable Pacific Ocean

TV STATIONS
11 (349 with illegal cable box)

NATIONAL HOLIDAY
Malnutrition Day (June 24)

Untouched lawlessness

Amphibious rapist

Los Angeles urban sprawl creeping in

Site of drive-by vehicular manslaughter

Landfill transformed into ancient Mayan ruins with simple addition of a sign

Richest Honduran man splurging on extra-large coffee

Sniper staying perfectly still since 1982, awaiting kill order

Mother driving son to gang practice

Criminal changing into his good rapin' clothes

Second-place ribbon for "Poorest Country In Western Hemisphere" competition

Soccer War Memorial

Bank robbery failing to cover price of getaway gas

Gunman regretting holding up Steve, that guy with the long rambling stories

Site where Hurricane Dear God, No! hit Honduras before citizens had time to name it

★ **Tegucigalpa**
To be renamed something Americans can remember before 2020

Sex tourist more than happy just looking at brochure

Spot where Central America almost sorta starts getting good

Great out-of-the-way river to dump bodies in

U.S. Aid
President George H. W. Bush gives a little back to the Honduran community.

Nicaragua

» PLAYING HERO
WON'T BE EASY.

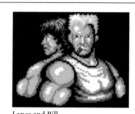
» AN INTENSE JUNGLE BATTLE.

Up, Up, Down, Down, Left, Right, Left, Right, B, A, Select, Start

In 1987, a U.S.-backed Contra force, Lance and Bill, was sent to this two-dimensional war-ravaged nation to stop a terrible threat to the free world posed by rebels, robots, and aliens.

Armed only with a machine gun, a faster machine gun, a laser, and, when they were lucky, a spread gun, these two members of the Special Forces elite commando squad made countless daring raids to the region, somersaulting across the border to destroy turret installations and sabotage power orbs.

Financed over three years in millions of 25-cent increments, the controversial operation was widely criticized for being a waste of taxpayer lunch money. While the American public may never get a full accounting of just how many hours were lost in this senseless eight-stage battle, unofficial estimates put the death toll at somewhere between one and 30 lives, with an unknown number of power-ups.

Some especially well-acquainted with the operation maintain that it was completed just before dinnertime without sustaining a single injury, culminating with Bill and Lance fleeing in a helicopter as the entire country exploded behind them, all in under 15 minutes. This is still disputed by skeptics, who claim, "Nuh uh."

GEOGRAPHY » NOTABLE FEATURES

From the seemingly endless range of identical, snowcapped mountains in the background, to the lush grassy platforms in the foreground, to the staggered waterfalls in the waterfall level, Nicaragua comes alive in 16 distinct colors. Navigating the landscape can be challenging, however, as it requires impeccable thumb-eye coordination to safely cross the country's expansive system of randomly exploding footbridges.

HISTORY » PRESS START TO BEGIN

A.D. 1979 The first single-pixel organisms appear.

1981 Early natives subsist on cherries, strawberries, and bananas. Living in a complex, maze-like society, they believe that if they eat power pellets they will go on to a higher level and consume their ancestors' spirits.

1982 The British cede control of the Alien's Lair to Nicaragua.

The Alien's Lair

JAN. 1987 Public reaction to a planned invasion of Nicaragua is tested at arcades across the U.S.

FEB. 1987 Despite widespread calls to end the operation before bedtime, those involved claim they have gotten too far to quit, and will pull out just as soon as they defeat the next mini-boss.

MAR. 1987 Just when all seems hopeless, the attack on Terminal Two is miraculously

Lance and Bill

saved by the innovative tactic of blowing into the game cartridge and hitting reset.

APR. 1987 Grounded by their superiors, the commanding officers see their funding cut off for two whole weeks.

MAY 1987 Although forces are close to victory, the nation's attention is temporarily diverted by the compelling tale of two Italian plumbers trapped in a green tube.

JUNE 1987 An untimely and frustrating glitch in the operation, which leaves Lance and Bill frozen between a cadre of snipers and a wall of spikes, forces leaders to pull the plug, preventing the two from setting up a provisional government and earning 20,000 bonus points.

JULY 1987 The mission's success is temporarily overshadowed by allegations of cheat-code usage.

1991 Suffering from Contra fatigue, America turns its back on the pathetic, eight-bit operation with the release of Sega Genesis.

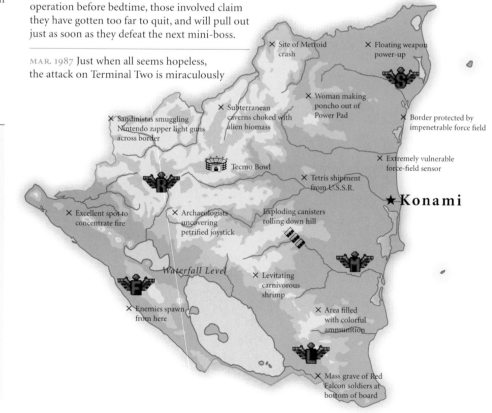

✕ Site of Metroid crash

✕ Floating weapon power-up

✕ Woman making poncho out of Power Pad

✕ Subterranean caverns choked with alien biomass

✕ Border protected by impenetrable force field

✕ Sandinistas smuggling Nintendo zapper light guns across border

✕ Extremely vulnerable force-field sensor

Tecmo Bowl

✕ Tetris shipment from U.S.S.R.

★ **Konami**

✕ Excellent spot to concentrate fire

✕ Archaeologists uncovering petrified joystick

Exploding canisters rolling down hill

Waterfall Level

✕ Levitating carnivorous shrimp

✕ Enemies spawn from here

✕ Area filled with colorful ammunition

✕ Mass grave of Red Falcon soldiers at bottom of board

Costa Rica

Properties Available, Inquire Today

From the sun-soaked cabanas along the coast, to the tropical rainforests containing the last remaining three-bedroom, two-bath cottages in all of Central America, there is something in Costa Rica for every nouveau riche environmentalist from the U.S.

Boasting stunning views of some of the world's most breathtaking real-estate plots, Costa Rica is home to unbelievable deals whether you are looking for a vacation home or a permanant residence.

Nearly 84% of Costa Rica is still available for immediate occupancy, with many properties featuring spectacular vistas, beach access, and backyard jungle that can be easily converted into a flower garden.

This nation is not expected to stay on the market for long, so call now.

PEOPLE » GOOD NEIGHBORS

Although located in a neighborhood of troubled nations, Costa Rica boasts the lowest number of drug lords per capita in all of Central America, and only harbors fugitives trying to escape from a life of 9-to-5 drudgery back in the U.S.

In fact, the greatest affront to Costa Rican life has been Nicaraguan children toilet-papering their rainforests, and Honduras insisting on starting loud coups in the middle of the night.

GEOGRAPHY » CURRENTLY FOR SALE

FACTS » BY OWNER

GEOGRAPHIC COORDINATES
Location, location, location

ECONOMY
Low-interest-rate financing is available through the World Bank

MILITARY
Costa Rica converted its military to a strike force of combat vacation-cottage salesmen in 1949 and has not had a civil war since

WILDLIFE
No pets allowed

INDUSTRIAL SECTOR
Stainless steel

POTENTIAL FOR GROWTH
Tremendous

INTERNATIONAL MONETARY FUND INVESTMENT
10% down, 36-month mortgage, broker's fee waived

COMMUNITY
Gated

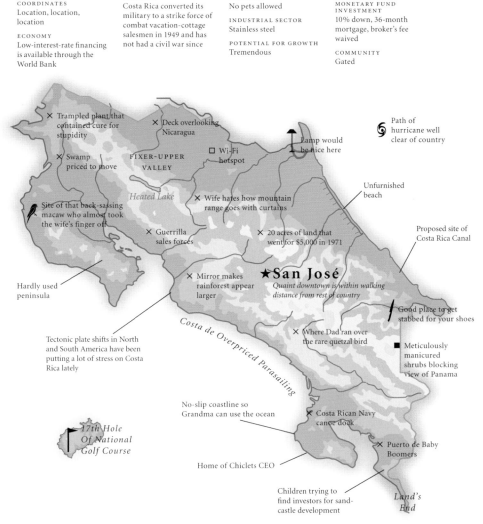

- ✕ Trampled plant that contained cure for stupidity
- ✕ Deck overlooking Nicaragua
- ☐ Wi-Fi hotspot
- Lamp would be nice here
- ✕ Swamp priced to move
- FIXER-UPPER VALLEY
- *Heated Lake*
- ✕ Wife hates how mountain range goes with curtains
- Site of that back-sassing macaw who almost took the wife's finger off
- ✕ Guerrilla sales forces
- ✕ 20 acres of land that went for $5,000 in 1971
- Path of hurricane well clear of country
- Unfurnished beach
- Proposed site of Costa Rica Canal
- ★San José *Quaint downtown is within walking distance from rest of country*
- Hardly used peninsula
- ✕ Mirror makes rainforest appear larger
- Good place to get stabbed for your shoes
- ■ Meticulously manicured shrubs blocking view of Panama
- *Costa de Overpriced Parasailing*
- Tectonic plate shifts in North and South America have been putting a lot of stress on Costa Rica lately
- ✕ Where Dad ran over the rare quetzal bird
- No-slip coastline so Grandma can use the ocean
- ✕ Costa Rican Navy canoe dock
- 17th Hole Of National Golf Course
- ✕ Puerto de Baby Boomers
- Home of Chiclets CEO
- Children trying to find investors for sand-castle development
- *Land's End*

This graceful South American nation offers ample beachfront on two coasts, 360-degree sun exposure, and good access to shopping and services. Delivered in hurricane-swept condition.

Meticulously furnished with beautiful hardwood forests, exposed cliffs, and a built-in waterfall. No detail has been overlooked. On-site laundry services are available from the live-in Costa Rican populace.

This one-of-a-kind en suite volcano is sure to please even the most discerning homebuyer. Located just miles from the capital of San José, this is one hot property!!!

Panama

A Shortcut With Its Own National Anthem

Panama is situated on a natural isthmus, the marvelously constructed, lushly forested result of millions of years of geological transformation, which took the U.S. Army 30 years to defoliate, bisect, and later, bomb nearly flat.

Building the Panama Canal, which cuts the country exactly in half, was one of history's single greatest expenditures of money, brute force, and bullheadedness. Its proponents steadfastly ignored observations that it would "take forever to complete" and that "20,000 Panamanians will die." The Panama Canal remains one of mankind's greatest achievements, and ushered in a golden age of American convenience at the expense of Central American sovereignty.

HISTORY » AMERICA'S 100-YEAR SUBLET

A.D. 1892 Calling it a "fixer-upper," Panama sublets its country to the highest bidder, disregarding France's poor credit history and lack of references.

1901 The debate over the Panama Canal route and an alternative Nicaraguan plan favored by U.S. President McKinley ends suddenly with two gunshots at close range on Sept. 6 at 4:07 p.m.

1903 The U.S. signs a 100-year lease with Panama and immediately starts tearing the place apart, virtually guaranteeing that it will never get its security deposit back.

1906 Fed up with the lack of progress, Teddy Roosevelt digs three miles of the canal by hand during a weekend visit to Panama.

1915 After 13 years of violently sleepless nights, Panamanians realize that all the blasting has finally stopped.

DEC. 20, 1989 Ten years before the United States is slated to turn over the canal under the Carter-Torrijos Treaty, President George Bush dispatches 25,000 troops, 300 fighter jets, and a fleet of Apache attack helicopters to Panama to renegotiate the terms.

Noriega

DEC. 29, 1989 President Manuel Noriega complains that invading U.S. forces' loud music is driving him crazy.

Mt. Panama

DEC. 31, 1999 The United States cedes control of the canal to Panama, but holds onto the keys and the right to invade at any time.

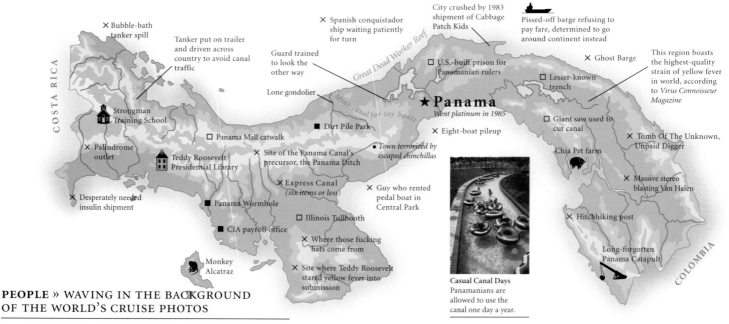

COSTA RICA

× Bubble-bath tanker spill

Tanker put on trailer and driven across country to avoid canal traffic

× Spanish conquistador ship waiting patiently for turn

City crushed by 1983 shipment of Cabbage Patch Kids

Pissed-off barge refusing to pay fare, determined to go around continent instead

Guard trained to look the other way

Great Dead Worker Reef

□ U.S.-built prison for Panamanian rulers

× Ghost Barge

This region boasts the highest-quality strain of yellow fever in world, according to *Virus Connoisseur Magazine*

Lone gondolier

Mini-canal for toy boats

□ Lesser-known trench

■ Strongman Training School

★ **Panama**
Went platinum in 1985

□ Giant saw used to cut canal

× Tomb Of The Unknown, Unpaid Digger

× Eight-boat pileup

Chia Pet farm

□ Panama Mall catwalk

■ Dirt Pile Park

× Palindrome outlet

🏛 Teddy Roosevelt Presidential Library

× Site of the Panama Canal's precursor, the Panama Ditch

• *Town terrorized by escaped chinchillas*

× Massive stereo blasting Van Halen

× Express Canal *(six items or less)*

× Guy who rented pedal boat in Central Park

× Hitchhiking post

× Desperately needed insulin shipment

■ Panama Wormhole

□ Illinois Tollbooth

Long-forgotten Panama Catapult

■ CIA payroll office

× Where those fucking hats come from

COLOMBIA

× Monkey Alcatraz

× Site where Teddy Roosevelt stared yellow fever into submission

Casual Canal Days
Panamanians are allowed to use the canal one day a year.

PEOPLE » WAVING IN THE BACKGROUND OF THE WORLD'S CRUISE PHOTOS

Despite the constant rumble and stench of passing transoceanic cargo ships, 3 million people call the land directly around the Panama Canal their home. Passing ship captains rely upon the canal-side residents when they need to secure their vessel, and thus Panamanian youth learn to throw, catch, tie, and get strangled by enormous ropes by the time they are 6 years old. Children who fail to master these skills must live with the shame of severe rope burn for the rest of their days.

FACTS » THE ARMY CORPS OF ENGINEERS' VIETNAM

IMPORTS
Whatever falls off passing ships

EXPORTS
Bananas, shrimp, stowaways

NATIONAL MOTTO
"Slower Traffic Yield Right"

COMMUNICATIONS
Most of the Panamanian population wakes up to the government's syndicated radio show *Isthmus In The Morning*, where host Don Carlos and his wacky brother report on national news and give the canal report

COST OF CANAL
Dollars: $352 million U.S. (2007 equiv. $188.55 trillion)
Lives: 20,000 Panamanians (equiv. 179 U.S. citizens)

NATURAL HAZARDS
Elderly ship captains

NATIONAL PASTIME
Probably fishing

SHOVELS BROKEN
438,274

RELEVANCE TO U.S.
Panama

Jamaica

True Rasta No Develop Country

Jamaica is home to dank nugs, kind buds, ganja, and a crumbling infrastructure, which the country will get around to fixing right after this joint.

While Jamaica has made some progress on a new, inexplicably curvy highway system, no one can seem to remember where it is supposed to go.

The former British colony has struggled with its independence since 1962, as Parliament claims it can't write any good laws unless it's high.

Officials have attempted to combat the country's growing crime epidemic with a set of strict new gun-control doodles, a used car stereo for the capital, and a placemat they signed into law one night while watching "Shark Week" on the Discovery Channel.

PEOPLE » PSYCHOACTIVE IN THE COMMUNITY

As followers of Rastafarianism, Jamaicans practice a number of sacred rituals, all centering around their hair, their lighters, and their Visine. To embrace the divinity of their faith and ensure a pure soul, they meticulously do not shower or wash their dreadlocks for years, painstakingly avoiding the removal of bugs, grime, saltwater, and plants. For the Rastafari, the smoking of marijuana is a central activity of daily life, a sacrament that exalts the consciousness, facilitates peacefulness, and makes frozen burritos taste like Zion.

Jamaicans brought the world reggae, a form of music that covers original songs by slowing down the tempo, accenting the backbeat, and making the lyrics indecipherable. Over 470 other distinct musical genres originated in Jamaica, including mento, ska, roots rocksteady, dub, dancehall, skank, skankhall, skanksteady, ragga, bagga, and dutty-dub. Also, mugga, zagga, zow, dingy-dong, and twingy-twong. Unfortunately, these all rely on one rhythmic pattern and the same two chords, as that was all the Jamaicans could afford.

POTHEADS OF STATE »

King Tubby	Prince Jammy	Burning Spear
SOVEREIGN RULER	HEIR TO THE THRONE	DEFENSE SECRETARY
Mad Professor	Steel Pulse	Scientist
MINISTER OF EDUCATION	MINISTER OF INDUSTRY	MINISTER OF TECHNOLOGY

FACTS » GATEWAY TO HARDER STATISTICS

OFFICIAL LANGUAGE
English (kind of)

NATIONAL MOTTO
"No Woman, No Cry, Or The Police Will Hear"

IMPORTS
Ordered on a whim at 2 a.m.

EXPORTS
Bananas, machinery, that one Bob Marley poster

AREA COMPARATIVE
Amsterdam, but with alligators

CRIME
Rising incidents of laid-back stabbings, mellow rapes, and monslaughter

INTERNATIONAL AGREEMENTS
Signatory to the Pass The Duchy On The Left-Hand Side Accord

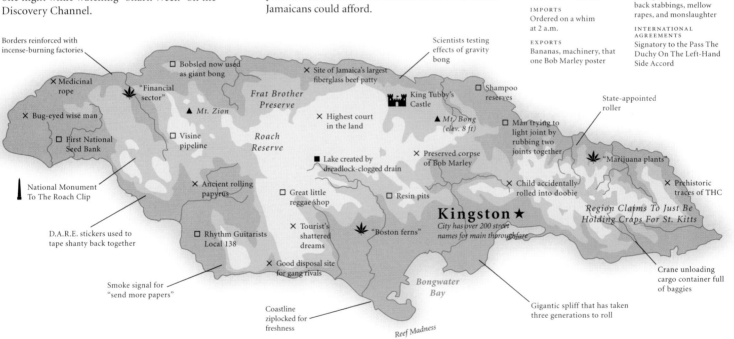

Borders reinforced with incense-burning factories

Scientists testing effects of gravity bong

✕ Medicinal rope

✕ Bug-eyed wise man

"Financial sector"

☐ First National Seed Bank

National Monument To The Roach Clip

D.A.R.E. stickers used to tape shanty back together

☐ Bobsled now used as giant bong

▲ Mt. Zion

☐ Visine pipeline

✕ Ancient rolling papyrus

☐ Rhythm Guitarists Local 138

Smoke signal for "send more papers"

Frat Brother Preserve

Roach Reserve

✕ Site of Jamaica's largest fiberglass beef patty

✕ Highest court in the land

■ Lake created by dreadlock-clogged drain

☐ Great little reggae shop

✕ Tourist's shattered dreams

"Boston ferns"

✕ Good disposal site for gang rivals

Coastline ziplocked for freshness

King Tubby's Castle

▲ Mt. Bong (elev. 8 ft)

✕ Preserved corpse of Bob Marley

☐ Resin pits

Kingston ★
City has over 200 street names for main thoroughfare

Bongwater Bay

Reef Madness

☐ Shampoo reserves

☐ Man trying to light joint by rubbing two joints together

✕ Child accidentally rolled into doobie

🌿 "Marijuana plants"

State-appointed roller

Region Claims To Just Be Holding Crops For St. Kitts

✕ Prehistoric traces of THC

Crane unloading cargo container full of baggies

Gigantic spliff that has taken three generations to roll

HISTORY » EVERYTHING'S NOT GOING TO BE ALL RIGHT

A.D. 1500 After visiting Jamaica and loading up on "agricultural products" to bring back to Spain, the conquistadors get pulled over for sailing two knots an hour. They totally freak out for a minute, but are sent on their way.

1655 The British seize Jamaica after cleverly waiting until the Spanish have rid the island of all human life.

1692 Nicknamed the "Wickedest City On Earth" for its pirates, whores, and excess, the Jamaican capital Port Royal falls into the sea after an enormous earthquake. Religious fanatics blame the disaster on liquor, prostitution, and same-pirate marriage.

1930 Poor Jamaicans embrace Rastafarianism based on the worship of Haile Selassie I, whom they

would have known was corrupt, megalomaniacal, and quite un-irie if they had taken five minutes to read about him.

1962 Jamaicans draft a constitution. Though it made perfect sense at the time, the document is practically illegible when they sober up.

1981 CIA agents assassinate Bob

Marley after they can't get the song "Stir It Up" out of their heads.

1999 Widespread protests call for something unintelligible.

2005 Desperate Jamaicans exhume Bob Marley's corpse in hopes of scraping some resin from his dreads.

Cuba

» A CUBAN PRISON, WHICH PROUDLY HOSTS SOME OF THE NATION'S FINEST POETS.

Workers Of The World, Survive!

O ver the past four decades, Cuba has perfected Communism, creating a truly equal society where desperate poverty is distributed evenly among all citizens.

This rampant destitution, combined with a U.S.-led trade embargo, has forced Cuba to make do with nothing but hard work, imagination, and the spare parts from a broken-down 1958 Chevy Impala.

While some attempt to flee the nation on makeshift motorboats fashioned from an old washing machine, a hot-water heater, and four discarded milk crates, others have decided to stay and turn their life around using whatever they can find at the local dump.

Making the best out of a bad situation, hundreds of tin cans, driftwood, and 1,000 yards of fishing wire, resourceful Cubans have managed to build an efficient public-transportation system, restore their education sector, and develop a first-rate health-care plan—all with 40 yards of fishing wire to spare.

Even with these advances, however, poverty remains so widespread that most citizens have to live out of their cars, which have been modified to include a kitchen, two full baths, four bedrooms, a staircase to the second floor, and a two-car garage.

Scientific observers believe that, if America lifted its trade sanctions and Cuba's government loosened travel restrictions, Cubans could use stuff from U.S. tag sales to cure cancer and perfect cold fusion within three years.

PEOPLE » WORKING TOGETHER TO ESCAPE COMMUNISM

The '08 Model Chevy
A group of Cubans on their way to visit relatives in Florida.

The Cubans are an amphibious people, who spend half their lives in water leaving Cuba, and the rest on land dreaming of leaving Cuba.

Each year, thousands make the perilous journey halfway across the Florida Straits while perched upon homemade rafts and inner tubes, and complete the rest of their trip in the relative comfort of spacious U.S. Coast Guard patrol boats.

The defectors that do make it to America support their relatives still living in Cuba by sending home IOUs at the end of every month.

Baseball is the most popular pastime in Cuba, as even Fidel Castro played the sport professionally in his youth. For decades, young boys in Cuba trained to be pitchers in the hopes that someday, in the final inning of the big game, they would have the chance to throw a 90 mph fastball at their dictator's head.

FACTS » COBBLED TOGETHER FROM SPARE PARTS

POPULATION 11.3 million (Cuba), 2.1 million (Miami)	**IMPORTS** Cubans would love to begin importing imports	**CONSTITUTION** Rolled up into cigar and smoked by Castro in 1959	**NATIONAL CIGAR** Cuban cigar	**FOREIGN AID** Too proud to take your money, but if you insist...
SUFFRAGE All Fidel Castros over the age of 16 can vote	**NATIONAL HOLIDAY** Whatever day wind is blowing west	**EDUCATION** Medical school free and mandatory	**NATIONAL RUM** Cuban rum	
			NATIONAL SANDWICH The grilled cheese	

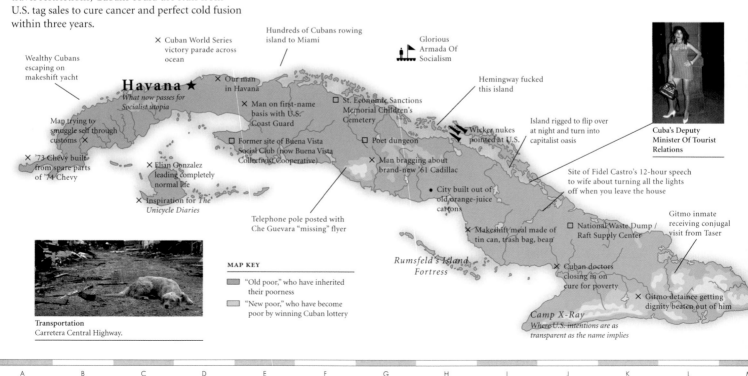

Wealthy Cubans escaping on makeshift yacht

× Cuban World Series victory parade across ocean

Hundreds of Cubans rowing island to Miami

Glorious Armada Of Socialism

Havana ★
What now passes for Socialist utopia

× Our man in Havana

Hemingway fucked this island

Man trying to smuggle self through customs ×

× Man on first-name basis with U.S. Coast Guard

□ St. Economic Sanctions Memorial Children's Cemetery

Island rigged to flip over at night and turn into capitalist oasis

× Wicker nukes pointed at U.S.

× '73 Chevy built from spare parts of '74 Chevy

□ Former site of Buena Vista Social Club (now Buena Vista Collectivist Cooperative)

□ Poet dungeon

× Man bragging about brand-new '61 Cadillac

× Elian Gonzalez leading completely normal life

× Inspiration for *The Unicycle Diaries*

• City built out of old orange-juice cartons

Telephone pole posted with Che Guevara "missing" flyer

× Makeshift meal made of tin can, trash bag, bean

Cuba's Deputy Minister Of Tourist Relations

Site of Fidel Castro's 12-hour speech to wife about turning all the lights off when you leave the house

Gitmo inmate receiving conjugal visit from Taser

□ National Waste Dump / Raft Supply Center

Rumsfeld's Island Fortress

× Cuban doctors closing in on cure for poverty

× Gitmo detainee getting dignity beaten out of him

Camp X-Ray
Where U.S. intentions are as transparent as the name implies

Transportation
Carretera Central Highway.

MAP KEY

- "Old poor," who have inherited their poorness
- "New poor," who have become poor by winning Cuban lottery

» HAVANA GENERAL HOSPITAL

» A CUBAN MAN OFFERS CIGARS FOR SALE, ALONG WITH COCAINE, MARIJUANA, FRESH LOBSTER, AND HIS DAUGHTER.

HISTORY » A DYSTOPIAN UTOPIA

A.D. 1492 Christopher Columbus discovers Cuba. Native Cubans introduce him to the concept of maize, while Columbus introduces them to the concept of stealing maize.

1494 A more mature Christopher Columbus *truly* discovers Cuba.

1839 Slaves aboard *The Amistad* revolt in Cuba after learning the true purpose of their all-inclusive Caribbean cruise.

1868 Cuba wins its War Of Independence, but due to a slight grammatical error is forced to declare a War For Independence just days later.

1873 Baseball is banned in Cuba. With nowhere else to turn, desperate Cubans shamefully invent softball.

José Martí

1895 Poet and revolutionary José Martí leads his people on their final push for freedom, marking the first time in history that a poet accomplishes anything worthwhile.

1898 An eager America joins Cuba in the Spanish-American War after the suspicious explosion of the *USS Maine*—a 6,000-ton, 300-foot-long excuse.

CHE GUEVA

1901 Walter Reed leads the Yellow Fever Commission to Cuba in search of the origin of the disease. Several days later, a fever-ridden, jaundiced, blood-vomiting Reed announces that mosquitoes cause yellow fever. He then has a seizure and dies.

1902 America grieves as Cuba falls to Cuban control.

1952 Brutal dictator Fulgencio Batista slays thousands of innocent Cubans in the hopes of finally being referred to as a "ruthless dictator."

1958 Revolutionary Ernesto "Che" Guevara frees thousands from the restrictive yoke of T-shirt selection.

1959 Castro declares himself President For Life. Unfortunately, he decides to live nearly forever.

1960 Cuba nationalizes poverty.

1961 John F. Kennedy funds, develops, and deploys a unit of special forces–trained breeder hogs to overthrow the Castro regime. Unfortunately, the pigs all drown in a bay just outside of Cuba before Kennedy—who is too embarrassed to admit that he forgot hogs can't swim—refuses to send in Navy Seals to rescue the drowning animals.

1962 Although many now laugh about it, shaking their heads in embarrassed disbelief and rolling their eyes—playfully—at the sheer lunacy of it all, the Cuban Missile Crisis almost leads to the complete destruction of Earth as we know it.

1964 Fidel Castro forbids all Cuban citizens from traveling outside the country, unless they promise to take "lots and lots" of pictures.

1970–1979 Breakthroughs in homespun-fabric aerodynamics, plywood laminating, and sub-hubcapular projectile physics revolutionize the Cuban Space Program. Castro shuts down the program, however, fearing that Cuban astronauts would use the craft to illegally leave the country.

1976 Fidel Castro is elected president of Cuba, an amazing achievement considering that voting was outlawed in 1961.

1980 125,000 mental patients and hardened criminals escape Cuba and arrive in Miami. Although U.S. President Ronald Reagan is initially embarrassed at being forced to accept the violent and criminal dregs of Castro's society, these same individuals form the core of Florida's contemporary Republican Party.

1991 The U.S.S.R. collapses before Cuba has a chance to thank them for everything they've done.

1993 After tightening their trade embargo, U.S. officials in Miami intercept thousands of prayers and well-wishes intended for Cuba.

Elian Gonzalez

1994 Six-year-old Elian Gonzalez seeks a new life in the United States, away from the oppressive curfews, unfair television restrictions, and "unlivable" weekly allowance levels in his home nation.

2002 The U.S. opens a terrorist detainment camp in Guantánamo Bay, Cuba. After years of forcing the prisoners to live in squalor, taking away their personal freedoms, and giving them no hope for escape, the U.S. realizes it would just be easier to release them into Cuban society.

Guantánamo Bay

2006 Castro falls ill and dies, but a team of world-renowned spin doctors is able to keep him alive for the next several years.

LEADERS » FIDEL CASTRO, "THE GREAT SURVIVOR"

DURING HIS TUMULTUOUS RULE *over Cuba, Fidel Castro became the United States' No. 1 enemy. He survived over 600 CIA assassination attempts, including one in which they tried to get him to smoke a cigar packed with explosives.*

Here are some of the CIA's other failed plots to kill "The Great Survivor":

- *Discreetly pack Castro's cigar with tar and other carcinogens*

- *Invite Castro to deliver keynote speech at UN Conference On International Interference; hope he will die of exhaustion 15 hours in*

- *Present Castro with seemingly innocuous, but actually very deadly, birthday noose*

- *Poison his beard*

- *Inform Castro that the U.S. is lifting its trade sanctions and will unilaterally support his rule in Cuba; wait for him to have fatal heart attack*

- *Plant lethal explosives where Castro would least suspect it: Idaho*

- *Replace Castro's military uniform with imperceptibly smaller military uniform; continue to do so every day until his circulation is cut off*

- *Kill John F. Kennedy*

- *Tell Raul Castro that, well, remember Samantha from junior high—Fidel made out with her once even though he knew you liked her*

- *Allow the slow passage of time to take its inevitable toll*

Haiti

Plight Of The Living Dead

This sweltering island nation is overrun by listless, dead-eyed, shambling Haitians, clamoring for a set of brains to bring their troubled country back to life.

Due to this widespread plague, Haiti is completely cut off from the outside world. Terrified foreign nations refuse to even set foot on its cursed shores, never mind offer aid or consider trading with the country. Most embassies have been boarded up, consulates are abandoned, and the few international diplomats who remain are desperate to get out before they are surrounded by a mindless mob and torn apart limb from limb.

Likewise, the infrastructure is in disarray, as the slow-moving populace—which only comes out at night and is fixated on cold-blooded murder—only seems capable of using simple tools like machetes and cleavers. It remains to be seen whether the current leadership will release the moaning Haitians from their dark spell with social reform and medical aid, or with the more traditional method of a clean shot to the head.

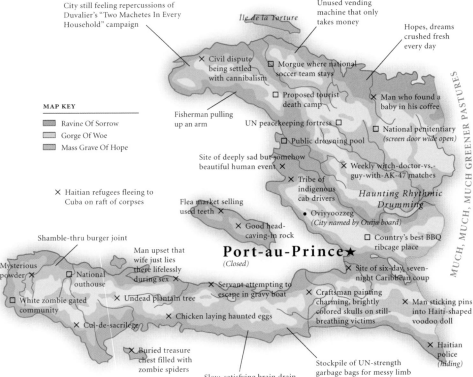

MAP KEY

- Ravine Of Sorrow
- Gorge Of Woe
- Mass Grave Of Hope

City still feeling repercussions of Duvalier's "Two Machetes In Every Household" campaign

Ile de la Torture

Unused vending machine that only takes money

Hopes, dreams crushed fresh every day

✕ Civil dispute being settled with cannibalism

◻ Morgue where national soccer team stays

✕ Man who found a baby in his coffee

Fisherman pulling up an arm

◻ Proposed tourist death camp

UN peacekeeping fortress ◻

◻ National penitentiary *(screen door wide open)*

◻ Public drowning pool

Site of deeply sad but somehow beautiful human event ✕

✕ Weekly witch-doctor-vs.-guy-with-AK-47 matches

✕ Tribe of indigenous cab drivers

Haunting Rhythmic Drumming

✕ Haitian refugees fleeing to Cuba on raft of corpses

Flea market selling used teeth ✕

● Oviyyoozzeg *(City named by Ouija board)*

✕ Good head-caving-in rock

◻ Country's best BBQ ribcage place

Shamble-thru burger joint

Man upset that wife just lies there lifelessly during sex ✕

Port-au-Prince★ *(Closed)*

✕ Site of six-day, seven-night Caribbean coup

Mysterious powder ✕

◻ National outhouse

✕ Servant attempting to escape in gravy boat

✕ Craftsman painting charming, brightly colored skulls on still-breathing victims

✕ Man sticking pins into Haiti-shaped voodoo doll

◻ White zombie gated community

✕ Undead plantain tree

✕ Chicken laying haunted eggs

✕ Cul-de-sacrilege

✕ Buried treasure chest filled with zombie spiders

Slow, satisfying brain drain occurring here

Stockpile of UN-strength garbage bags for messy limb clean-up

✕ Haitian police *(hiding)*

MUCH, MUCH, MUCH GREENER PASTURES

HISTORY » UNDER A SERIES OF BLOOD-RED MOONS

A.D. 1492 Columbus, terrified by a group of natives circling around him with outstretched arms and calm, eerie smiles, quickly adopts a decapitation-based management strategy.

1697 Spain cedes Haiti to France while the French aren't looking.

Papa Doc Duvalier

1964 Voodoo physician François "Papa Doc" Duvalier declares himself President For Life, and unveils a new relief plan for the jobless hordes: Citizens who complain will have sharp objects jabbed into a smaller version of them, such as a son or daughter.

1971 Following Duvalier's death, his son Jean-Claude assumes control and ceaselessly brutalizes the nation until France finally invites him to move to Paris in 1986.

1973 In the country's first and only instance of physical comedy, a Port-au-Prince resident slips on a banana farmer's corpse.

1983–2007 AIDS.

1988 In a welcome departure from decades of rule by military groups, military juntas, paramilitary groups, former military factions, and military forces, Haiti falls under the control of a military surplus clothing store.

1995 Facing a devastating livestock shortage, desperate voodoo priests are forced to cast spells by ritually cutting a six-piece box of Chicken McNuggets.

2004 Haiti marks 200 years of independence with violent parades, gun battles in every city, and a commemorative coup of President Jean-Bertrand Aristide.

2005 After a series of floods leaves thousands dead, UN relief workers finally arrive to assist the Haitian people into mass graves.

2006 René Préval is swept into office after rallying millions to a massive downtown demonstration with his famous one-word speech about the cerebral cortex.

FACTS » SYMPTOMS

OFFICIAL NAME (LONG FORM)
H-A-I-T-I

CUISINE
Traditional Haitian dishes are a blend of French and Africans

EXPORTS
Plantains, horrifying 15-second news clips

IMPORTS
7.62-mm. rifle cartridges

NATIONAL PASTIMES
Living in poverty, dying in poverty, baseball

INFANT MORTALITY RATE
One in eight

ADULT MORTALITY RATE
Seven in eight

A Day In The "Life"
A Haitian boy takes a moment to mourn the death of his entire family and everyone else he's eaten.

Dominican Republic

» FLAG CURRENTLY ON LOAN FOR MLB HOME RUN DERBY.

A Great Ballpark In A Bad Neighborhood

The Dominican Republic has produced some of the world's wealthiest baseball players, who each year help their impoverished, crime-ridden hometowns by sending back millions of dollars worth of much-needed baseball stadiums and emergency autographed merchandise.

Before this outpouring of generosity, the people of the Dominican Republic had nothing. Today, however, no one in the nation is without a baseball helmet, a rosin bag, or a jockstrap.

The schools, once among the poorest in the world, are now fully stocked with brand-new gloves and Louisville Sluggers. Doctors have enough pine tar for every sick child in the nation. And paupers who formerly used old paper cups to beg for spare change now have limited-edition fitted caps in which to store barely enough money to buy a hot meal.

In addition, the thousands of homeless citizens who used to live out on the streets have found shelter in the Sammy Sosa Memorial Little League Ballpark.

HISTORY BEEN VERY, VERY INDIFFERENT TO ME »

A.D. 1492 Columbus arrives, initially believing he has discovered India. After surveying the land and meeting the natives, he corrects himself and proudly declares that he has discovered China.

1821–1822 A brief period of independence, which the Dominicans waste sitting around and talking about all the great things they're going to do now that they are independent.

1891 The Dominicans are captivated by a complex base-progression game played by the North Americans.

1917–1918 Political unrest in the Dominican Republic. America, with all of its other military branches currently fighting in WWI, is forced to send the U.S. Marine Corps Band to quell the conflict.

1937 Dictator Rafael Trujillo massacres 30,000 Haitians attempting to immigrate into the D.R. Fearing international retribution, he revises his nation's history, which now states that Trujillo serenaded 30,000 Haitians at the border, hugged them limb from limb, and said very pleasant things to them—while their children were forced to watch.

PEOPLE » HOPING TO BE TRADED TO A BETTER NATION

Agriculture
Manny Ramirez's generous donations help a sugarcane farmer harvest his crop.

The Dominican people are taught at a young age to love the game of baseball's average player salary. Their summers are spent learning the fundamentals of the sport: fielding questions about steroid abuse, holding out for more money, and demanding a trade.

In fact, many never forget the first time they refused to play catch with their father because they didn't want to risk getting injured before receiving a guaranteed long-term contract.

Dominican children today memorize the baseball statistics of all their hometown heroes: Miguel Tejada, 6 years, $72 million; Albert Pujols, 7 years, $100 million; Alfonso Soriano, 8 years, $136 million. And every kid in the nation dreams of someday becoming the World Series MVP, in order to trigger the $500,000 incentive clause embedded in their contract.

SPORTS » BASEBALL ALTERNATIVES

Low-income Domincan baseball players often use these cheaper yet readily available replacements for the ball:

Stone   Duct Tape   Chicken   Pineapple

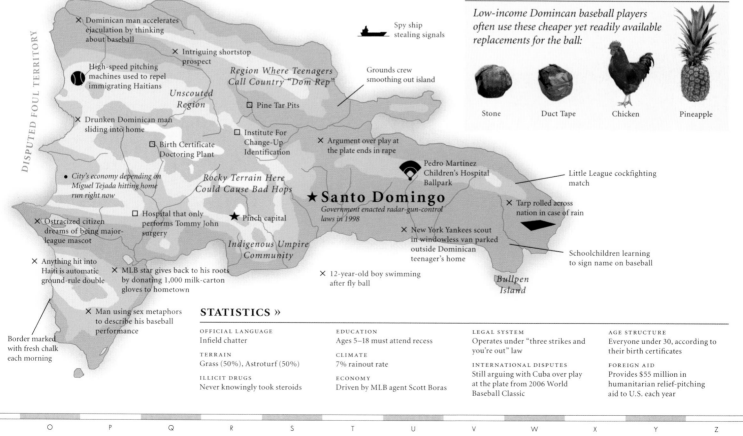

DISPUTED FOUL TERRITORY

✕ Dominican man accelerates ejaculation by thinking about baseball

✕ Intriguing shortstop prospect

High-speed pitching machines used to repel immigrating Haitians

Region Where Teenagers Call Country "Dom Rep"

Spy ship stealing signals

Grounds crew smoothing out island

Unscouted Region

☐ Pine Tar Pits

✕ Drunken Dominican man sliding into home

☐ Birth Certificate Doctoring Plant

☐ Institute For Change-Up Identification

✕ Argument over play at the plate ends in rape

● *City's economy depending on Miguel Tejada hitting home run right now*

Rocky Terrain Here Could Cause Bad Hops

Pedro Martinez Children's Hospital Ballpark

Little League cockfighting match

★ **Santo Domingo**
Government enacted radar-gun-control laws in 1998

✕ Ostracized citizen dreams of being major-league mascot

☐ Hospital that only performs Tommy John surgery

★ Pinch capital

✕ Tarp rolled across nation in case of rain

✕ New York Yankees scout in windowless van parked outside Dominican teenager's home

Schoolchildren learning to sign name on baseball

✕ Anything hit into Haiti is automatic ground-rule double

✕ MLB star gives back to his roots by donating 1,000 milk-carton gloves to hometown

Indigenous Umpire Community

✕ 12-year-old boy swimming after fly ball

Bullpen Island

✕ Man using sex metaphors to describe his baseball performance

Border marked with fresh chalk each morning

STATISTICS »

OFFICIAL LANGUAGE
Infield chatter

TERRAIN
Grass (50%), Astroturf (50%)

ILLICIT DRUGS
Never knowingly took steroids

EDUCATION
Ages 5–18 must attend recess

CLIMATE
7% rainout rate

ECONOMY
Driven by MLB agent Scott Boras

LEGAL SYSTEM
Operates under "three strikes and you're out" law

INTERNATIONAL DISPUTES
Still arguing with Cuba over play at the plate from 2006 World Baseball Classic

AGE STRUCTURE
Everyone under 30, according to their birth certificates

FOREIGN AID
Provides $55 million in humanitarian relief-pitching aid to U.S. each year

Puerto Rico

In A Parade Right Now

Home to the last remaining Puerto Ricans not residing in New York City, this island protectorate is responsible for 80% of the Caribbean's rum production and 98% of its noise complaints.

Failed attempts at joining the United States of America have done little to quell Puerto Rico's overwhelming sense of pride. To citizens, even the slightest sign that another person may be Puerto Rican is enough to provoke a spontaneous barbecue or block party, complete with salsa music in lieu of the national anthem they do not have.

The parade, long a staple of Puerto Rican life at home and abroad, has become so popular that it now serves as the island's main mode of public transportation. Whether going to the corner bodega for milk, taking the kids to school, commuting to work, or just traveling across town to join a Puerto Rican pride parade, citizens are free to jump on and off the floats as they please.

Elected to the front of the parade in 2002, Puerto Rican governor Aníbal Acevedo Vilá has led his people toward prosperity through the closed-off streets of San Juan, accompanied by the fire department, Puerto Rican veterans of America's foreign wars, and the national marching band.

HISTORY » FOREVER ON THE STOOP OF AMERICAN STATEHOOD

3200 B.C. Just two years after the Sumerians invent the wheel, the Taino people of Puerto Rico invent the spinning hubcap.

A.D. 1493 Christopher Columbus, eager to explore the New World, parks his ship in San Juan harbor for just 20 minutes, but returns to find his lanterns smashed and his rudder missing.

1889 Electricity is brought to the island, powering the first neon lightbulb, followed soon thereafter by the first subwoofer.

1900 Puerto Rico becomes a territory of the United States, promising to pay taxes and serve in the military in exchange for a polite monthly postcard from the U.S. Deputy Secretary of State.

1972 While flying en route to Nicaragua, Puerto Rican baseball star Roberto Clemente makes an unexpected return to his homeland, sooner and harder than he had hoped.

2000 Governor González signs a law banning all activities that create more than 190 decibels of sound, prompting protests by Puerto Rican disc jockeys, cab drivers, grandmothers, elderly men on doorsteps, pedestrians, motorists, librarians, and ultimately the governor himself.

2003–2004 San Juan serves as the home of the Montreal Expos, briefly becoming an importer of its own greatest export.

2004 A closely contested Puerto Rican election results in two months of measured debate and a full recount before the legal winner is declared, proving Puerto Rico is not ready to be the 51st U.S. state.

2005 A *Gasolina* shortage brings the nation's club scene to a grinding, thrusting, and gyrating halt.

The morning commute in downtown San Juan.

FACTS » THEY'D LIKE TO BE IN AMERICA

CURRENCY
The Puente (100 Titos)

TRADITIONAL GREETING
A brief embrace, a kiss on the cheek, then a rhythmic shaking of maracas

SUFFRAGE
Puerto Rican citizens 18 and over are allowed to vote for American Top 40 hits

NATIONAL PRIDE DAY
July 9, Sundays, every other Thursday, or as needed

FAMILY STRUCTURE
Puerto Ricans often live with many members of their family in a small house, a fact that does not prevent their mothers from screaming at the top of their lungs when dinner is ready

ECONOMY
Based largely on manufacture, purchase, and display of flags

AVERAGE WEIGHT OF AUNT
300 pounds

ENVIRONMENTAL PROBLEMS
Confetti in the water supply

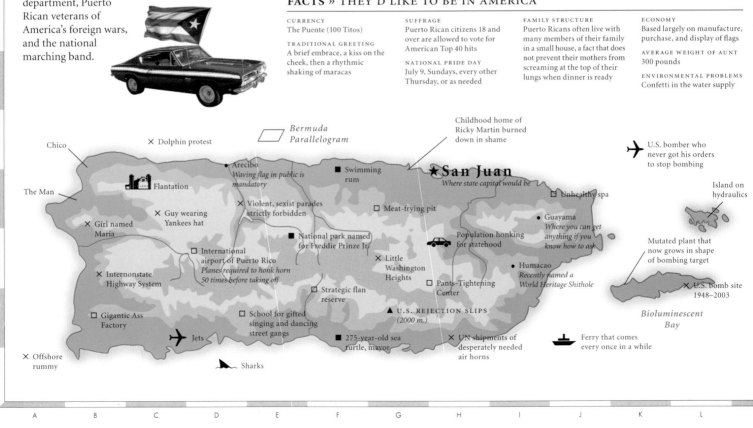

Chico

× Dolphin protest

Bermuda Parallelogram

Childhood home of Ricky Martin burned down in shame

✈ U.S. bomber who never got his orders to stop bombing

The Man

• Arecibo
Waving flag in public is mandatory

🏰 ⬛ Flantation

■ Swimming rum

★ **San Juan**
Where state capital would be

Island on hydraulics

◻ Unhealthy spa

× Violent, sexist parades strictly forbidden

◻ Meat-frying pit

Mutated plant that now grows in shape of bombing target

× Guy wearing Yankees hat

× Girl named Maria

• Guayama
Where you can get anything if you know how to ask

◻ International airport of Puerto Rico
Planes required to honk horn 50 times before taking off

■ National park named for Freddie Prinze Jr.

🚗 Population honking for statehood

× Little Washington Heights

× Internonstate Highway System

• Humacao
Recently named a World Heritage Shithole

◻ Pants-Tightening Center

× U.S. bomb site 1948–2003

◻ Strategic flan reserve

▲ U.S. REJECTION SLIPS
(2000 m.)

Bioluminescent Bay

◻ Gigantic Ass Factory

◻ School for gifted singing and dancing street gangs

■ 275-year-old sea turtle, mayor

× UN shipments of desperately needed air horns

⛴ Ferry that comes every once in a while

✈ Jets

× Offshore rummy

🦈 Sharks

Bahamas

» BAHAMAS' NATIONAL
INSTRUCTIONS FOR
MAKING A BED.

This Luggage Isn't Going To Move Itself

The all-inclusive, full-service nation of the Bahamas is made up of hundreds of luxurious, foreign-owned islands fully staffed with indigenous pool boys, bartenders, and bellhops.

Millions of visitors each year enjoy the nation's turquoise waters, endless sandy beaches, and lavish resorts, all of which are strictly off-limits to the Bahamas' citizens.

The country's relaxing environment features naturally occurring coral reefs, rock formations, and employees who serve gourmet meals, clean the pools, and deliver colorful drinks to visitors who insist that "all-inclusive" means "tip included."

Though slavery was abolished here in 1834, hundreds of Bahamians are still born into the tourism trade every day. While some manage to escape from a life of service, most remain indentured to brutal managers, hopelessly trapped inside sweltering hotel kitchens for the remainder of their years.

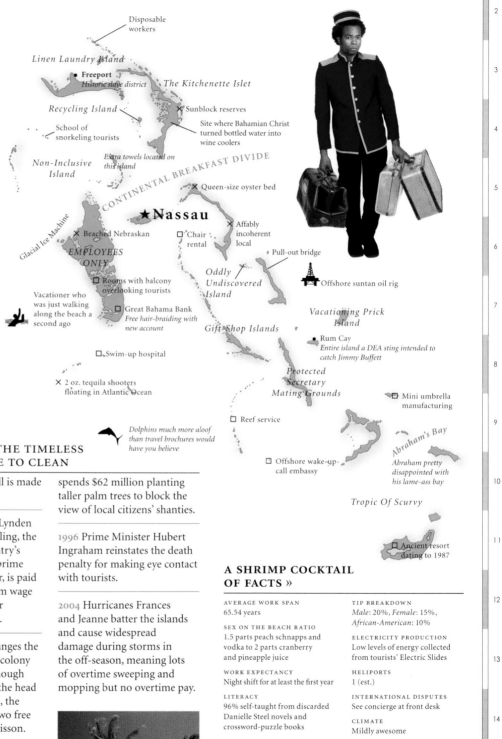

Disposable workers

Linen Laundry Island

Freeport
Historic slave district

The Kitchenette Islet

Recycling Island

Sunblock reserves

Site where Bahamian Christ turned bottled water into wine coolers

School of snorkeling tourists

Extra towels located on this island

Non-Inclusive Island

CONTINENTAL BREAKFAST DIVIDE

Queen-size oyster bed

★ Nassau

Glacial Ice Machine

Beached Nebraskan

EMPLOYEES ONLY

Chair rental

Affably incoherent local

Pull-out bridge

Oddly Undiscovered Island

Offshore suntan oil rig

Rooms with balcony overlooking tourists

Vacationer who was just walking along the beach a second ago

Great Bahama Bank
Free hair-braiding with new account

Gift Shop Islands

Vacationing Prick Island

Rum Cay
Entire island a DEA sting intended to catch Jimmy Buffett

Swim-up hospital

Protected Secretary Mating Grounds

Mini umbrella manufacturing

2 oz. tequila shooters floating in Atlantic Ocean

Reef service

Abraham's Bay

Dolphins much more aloof than travel brochures would have you believe

Offshore wake-up-call embassy

Abraham pretty disappointed with his lame-ass bay

Tropic Of Scurvy

Ancient resort dating to 1987

HISTORY » IF YOU HAVE TIME TO ENJOY THE TIMELESS BEAUTY OF THE ISLANDS, YOU HAVE TIME TO CLEAN

A.D. 1492 Native Arawak Indians are taken aback at how literally explorer Christopher Columbus takes their polite request to make himself at home.

1493–1517 Though the Arawak beg to work in the casino, Columbus takes them to the Hispaniola gold mines, where they die due to a chronic lack of lunch breaks.

1647 Pirates find that after months at sea raping and plundering, the tranquil Bahamas are an excellent spot to unwind, rape, and plunder.

1717 The Bahamas becomes a Five-Star British crown colony with full buffet.

1906 Workers install the first telephone on the island. The

inaugural wake-up call is made at 11:30 a.m. that day.

1967 Lynden Pindling, the country's first prime minister, is paid minimum wage plus one staff meal per 10-hour shift in office.

1969 Great Britain changes the Bahamas' status from colony to commonwealth. Though Queen Elizabeth II is the head of the commonwealth, the title is only good for two free nights' stay in the Radisson.

1979 Six breakfast conversations are killed and four pairs of khakis are badly damaged in the country's worst-ever mimosa spill.

1986 Under pressure from the tourism board, the Bahamas

spends $62 million planting taller palm trees to block the view of local citizens' shanties.

1996 Prime Minister Hubert Ingraham reinstates the death penalty for making eye contact with tourists.

2004 Hurricanes Frances and Jeanne batter the islands and cause widespread damage during storms in the off-season, meaning lots of overtime sweeping and mopping but no overtime pay.

The aftermath of Hurricane Frances.

A SHRIMP COCKTAIL OF FACTS »

AVERAGE WORK SPAN
65.54 years

SEX ON THE BEACH RATIO
1.5 parts peach schnapps and vodka to 2 parts cranberry and pineapple juice

WORK EXPECTANCY
Night shift for at least the first year

LITERACY
96% self-taught from discarded Danielle Steel novels and crossword-puzzle books

TIP BREAKDOWN
Male: 20%, Female: 15%, African-American: 10%

ELECTRICITY PRODUCTION
Low levels of energy collected from tourists' Electric Slides

HELIPORTS
1 (est.)

INTERNATIONAL DISPUTES
See concierge at front desk

CLIMATE
Mildly awesome

PEOPLE » THE HELP

The friendly and obedient citizens of the Bahamas are more than willing to get you another towel, scrape the unfinished filet mignon off your plate, or scrub strawberry daiquiri vomit from your shirt while you feel them up during your much-deserved break from selling insurance back in Indianapolis.

The Who Cares Islands

ANTIGUA-BARBUDA » LET US PLAN YOUR NEXT WEDDING

Antigua and Barbuda, an independent island nation known as the Altar Of The Caribbean, is the premier wedding destination for tourist couples ready to walk down one of the country's thousands of available aisles, including the especially romantic 28-mile-long, 30,000-ton steel suspension aisle that connects the two islands and represents everlasting union.

The nation features ample seating in the east, a spacious vestibule, and international borders accentuated with decorative latticework. The economy of Antigua and Barbuda is completely dependent on marriage, and the island has even begun offering the complimentary services of some of the world's top divorce planners, in an attempt to keep honeymooning couples on the island for a few more months.

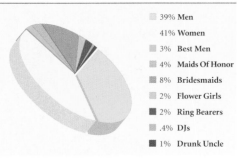

POPULATION BREAKDOWN »

- 39% **Men**
- 41% **Women**
- 3% **Best Men**
- 4% **Maids Of Honor**
- 8% **Bridesmaids**
- 2% **Flower Girls**
- 2% **Ring Bearers**
- .4% **DJs**
- 1% **Drunk Uncle**

FACTS » SWEET NOTHINGS

ECONOMY
Unforgettable moments–based

INDEPENDENCE DAY
Celebrated by the groom the day before his wedding, it is marked by a prenuptial ceremony in which native Antiguans perform the traditional lap dance

IMPORTS
Refer to "import registry" if you would like to give Antigua and Barbuda the gift of natural resources, food and live animals, machinery, or oil

EXPORTS
Bouquets

WILDLIFE
Chicken, fish, meat

TRADITION
On the night before the wedding, it is considered good luck for the bride and groom to stay on separate islands

NATIONAL ANTHEM
"The Chicken Dance"

NATIONAL DISGRACE
Fact that they are one of only five Caribbean islands not mentioned in classic 1989 Beach Boys single "Kokomo"

NATION'S SUGGESTED LYRICS FOR "KOKOMO"
"Antigua-Barbuda, we'll put ya in the mood-a"

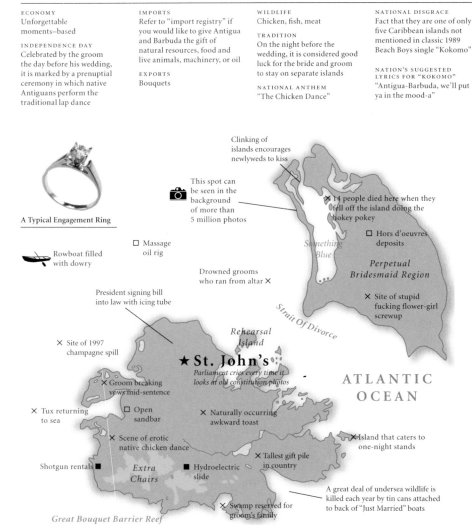

A Typical Engagement Ring

Rowboat filled with dowry

Massage oil rig

This spot can be seen in the background of more than 5 million photos

Clinking of islands encourages newlyweds to kiss

14 people died here when they fell off the island doing the hokey pokey

Hors d'oeuvres deposits

Something Blue

Perpetual Bridesmaid Region

Site of stupid fucking flower-girl screwup

Drowned grooms who ran from altar ✕

President signing bill into law with icing tube

Strait Of Divorce

Rehearsal Island

✕ Site of 1997 champagne spill

★ **St. John's**
Parliament cries every time it looks at old constitution photos

ATLANTIC OCEAN

✕ Groom breaking vows mid-sentence

✕ Tux returning to sea

☐ Open sandbar

✕ Naturally occurring awkward toast

✕ Island that caters to one-night stands

✕ Scene of erotic native chicken dance

Shotgun rentals ■

Extra Chairs

■ Hydroelectric slide

✕ Tallest gift pile in country

A great deal of undersea wildlife is killed each year by tin cans attached to back of "Just Married" boats

✕ Swamp reserved for groom's family

Great Bouquet Barrier Reef

HISTORY » SAVE THE DATE

A.D. 1498 Columbus returns to Antigua on the five-year anniversary of its discovery and gives the island the traditional gift of slavery.

1632 The British successfully colonize Antigua, yet they don't even get so much as a thank-you note from the natives for their trouble.

1674 Sir Christopher Codrington establishes the first-ever wedding-cake plantation, where slaves work all day in the frosting quarries, mining buttercream, gum paste, and ganache to produce over 30,000 croquembouche and five-tiered fondant cakes each day.

1834 After a long, drawn-out process that takes over 150 years to finalize, slaves are finally granted freedom from the old ball and chain—a 16-pound cannonball affixed to one leg with an unbreakable metal chain.

1913 Antigua and Barbuda outlaws Jews from the island, as other tourists keep severely cutting their feet after Jewish beachside weddings.

1988 De Beers employee Andrew Haverly loses his wedding-ring shipment somewhere in the Shakerley Mountain region, and spends the next 14 years searching for it, to no avail. His company never quite forgives him.

1999 Prime Minister Lester Bird renews his international vows to end illegal money-laundering practices, but most islands close to Antigua and Barbuda still think he will keep fooling around with financial transactions routed through the country, at least until he gets caught.

2002 Seeing no other recourse during her oceanfront ceremony, hesitant bride Mary Shaw swims away from the altar.

2005 Scandal surrounds a Russian-owned four-star honeymoon hotel after it is accused of questionable clothes-laundering practices.

2007 During their beach wedding, Clare and Roger Sandson are greeted by something old, something new, something borrowed, and something blue when the fresh hypothermic corpse of 75-year-old loan-shark debtor Clifford Grohl washes ashore.

ANTIGUA-BARBUDA » COULD'VE HAD THE FLAG EMBOSSED FOR $75 EXTRA, BUT NOOO.

TRINIDAD-TOBAGO » THEY THOUGHT THE RACING STRIPE LOOKED REALLY COOL.

GRENADA » THIS FLAG REPRESENTS GRENADA'S SHITTY TASTE IN FLAGS.

TRINIDAD-TOBAGO » HOW LOW CAN A COUNTRY GO?

After a particularly debaucherous session of parliament—the country's annual sex-party festival—drunken Trinidad and Tobago lawmakers adopted a democratic limbocracy.

Under this system, legislation first goes to the House rules committee, before reaching the dance floor and shimmying over to the Senate.

The committee decides how low to set the limbo bar and whether to light it on fire. The prime minister, leader of the majority of partiers, holds one end of the stick, while the president holds the other end.

Two-thirds of the representatives must lean backwards and pass with the bill underneath the bar without touching it.

If enough pass, the limbo bar is lowered and the Senate attempts to get a majority. If the Senate succeeds, the bar is lowered again and the president attempts to dance under. If he touches the bar, he automatically vetoes the bill; if he doesn't, the bill becomes a law. A monthlong orgy and ribbon-cutting ceremony then makes it official.

Sunday Mass In Port Of Spain

FACTS BE NIMBLE »

IMPORTS
Icy Hot, Bengay, back braces

EXPORTS
Trinidoodads

TVS
425,000

DECENT TVS
9

PRESIDENT
Guy on steel drums

NON-VITAL STATISTICS
Nap rate, fishing expectancy, hat distribution

SEX ACTS PER SQUARE FOOT
1

SEX ACTS PER SQUARE FOOT DURING CARNIVAL
36

GRENADA » WRONG SIDE OF THE SPICE RACK

By hoarding its massive reserves of nutmeg and threatening to limit output of the precious spice in 1983, Grenada effectively held the world hostage and declared economic war on the U.S. and its insatiable hunger for nutmeg.

Though a panicked American public demanded immediate military action, leaders attempted desperately to negotiate and avoid a conflict, offering Grenada

millions of pounds in flour and allspice in exchange for just a pinch of nutmeg.

But Grenadian officials flouted the proposal and sent a shipment of nutmeg to Iran along with detailed instructions for making the perfect cookie, compelling the U.S. to act. A protracted invasion followed, costing hundreds of lives but ensuring steady access to the very lifeblood of the American snackonomy.

PEOPLE » THE BEST THAT NUTMEG MONEY CAN BUY

Operation Spice & Dice
U.S. Rangers liberate Grenada's nutmeg.

More than 80% of Grenadians are descended from African slaves originally unstacked from British ships and deployed to the nutmeg groves. The remainder are European, Amerindian, and weird loose-cannon adventurer types with ties to the CIA.

Grenada also remains a popular tourist destination for people who like to find foot-long millipedes in their hotel baths.

MAP KEY

- Humping
- Dry-humping
- Wet-humping
- Sport-humping
- Hump-humping

✕ Offshore Creole rig

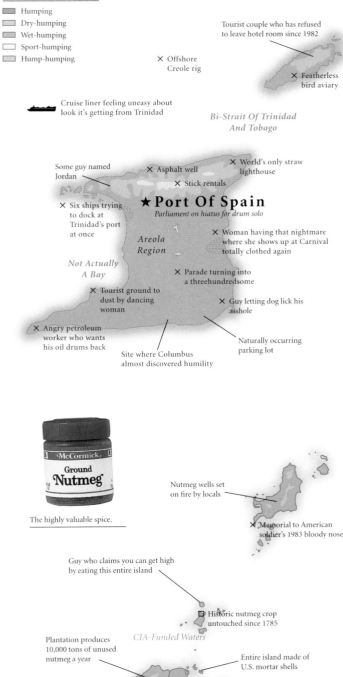

Cruise liner feeling uneasy about look it's getting from Trinidad

Tourist couple who has refused to leave hotel room since 1982

✕ Featherless bird aviary

Bi-Strait Of Trinidad And Tobago

Some guy named Jordan

✕ Asphalt well
✕ Stick rentals
✕ World's only straw lighthouse

★ **Port Of Spain**
Parliament on hiatus for drum solo

✕ Six ships trying to dock at Trinidad's port at once

Areola Region

Not Actually A Bay

✕ Woman having that nightmare where she shows up at Carnival totally clothed again

✕ Parade turning into a threehundredsome

✕ Tourist ground to dust by dancing woman

✕ Guy letting dog lick his asshole

✕ Angry petroleum worker who wants his oil drums back

Site where Columbus almost discovered humility

Naturally occurring parking lot

The highly valuable spice.

Ground Nutmeg

Nutmeg wells set on fire by locals

✕ Memorial to American soldier's 1983 bloody nose

Guy who claims you can get high by eating this entire island

◻ Historic nutmeg crop untouched since 1785

CIA-Funded Waters

Plantation produces 10,000 tons of unused nutmeg a year

Entire island made of U.S. mortar shells

Spice Racklands

✕ Barely noteworthy outcropping

◻ Offshore grenadine refinery

100-foot statue of Ronald Reagan lying on its side

✕ U.S. Army Ranger stuck in tree for past 24 years

★ **St. George's**

✕ Nutmeg baron's mansion

The Seriously Who Cares Islands

DOMINICA » TOURISTS GET A STAR PUNCHED WITH EACH BANANA THEY BUY, AND THE 11TH ONE IS FREE!

BARBADOS » THE GOD NEPTUNE IS IN HIS THIRD TERM AS SECRETARY OF STATE.

DOMINICA » WE HAVE NO BEACHES

Though Dominica contains lush rainforest and breathtaking mountains, it has no white-sand beaches to attract wealthy tourists. Therefore, this tiny, unknown island paradise may as well be covered in white-hot flaming shards of glass.

The country's main attraction—the spectacular Boiling Lake, which reaches temperatures of 200 degrees and emits poisonous gas—draws several tourists a year, all of whom are treated to transportation out of the remote area with complimentary ambulance rides. Despite many other potential tourist sites, such as the Valley Of Dismemberment and Broken Neck Creek, the majority of foreign visitors are tourists' next of kin who come to identify the remains of their loved ones.

Recent promotions to boost tourism include "Be Prime Minister For A Day," "Historic Rape Tours" of the island, and "All The Endangered Species You Can Eat" buffets.

HISTORY » THE LAND THAT TIME NEVER REALLY REMEMBERED IN THE FIRST PLACE

A.D. 1493 Christopher Columbus names the island "Sunday" in Spanish, in honor of the one day a week that he takes a break from stabbing the natives.

1750 Native Carib Indians fiercely resist English and French colonizers, who fiercely resist the Caribs' existence.

1978 Dominica holds a celebration to mark its independence. Foreign dignitaries accidentally travel to the Dominican Republic instead, where they have a lovely time.

VITAL FACTISTICS »

POPULATION	GEOGRAPHY	AIRPORTS	NATIONAL PASTIMES
70,000 (*Tourist season*: 70,003)	Rocky, pointy, stabby, molten lava-y	One; considered the Caribbean's largest refreshment stand	Patience, boredom, tic-tac-toe

BARBADOS » YO HO HO AND AN UNTRACEABLE INCOME

Once overrun by greedy, lawless pirates who raped and plundered the terrified populace, Barbados today is a tropical tax haven for ruthless financiers to loot millions of dollars from employee pensions.

Drunk almost nightly on a belly full of rum-based breezers, margaritas, and daiquiris, these fierce and unsavory characters can be seen stumbling from bar to bar to negotiate illicit acquisitions with powerful European conglomerates out to hornswoggle their competitors.

The more cunning privateers have learned to bury their ill-gotten treasures beneath hundreds of layers of privacy laws and interest-free loopholes, where no soul from the SEC might find it.

Hard-hearted and jaded by years of tax evasion and fraud, most of the scalawags would rather walk the plank than spend the rest of their years wasting away in some luxurious, white-collar prison paradise. A filthy lot that was born to steal, it's the life they've chosen to live, and the only life they know.

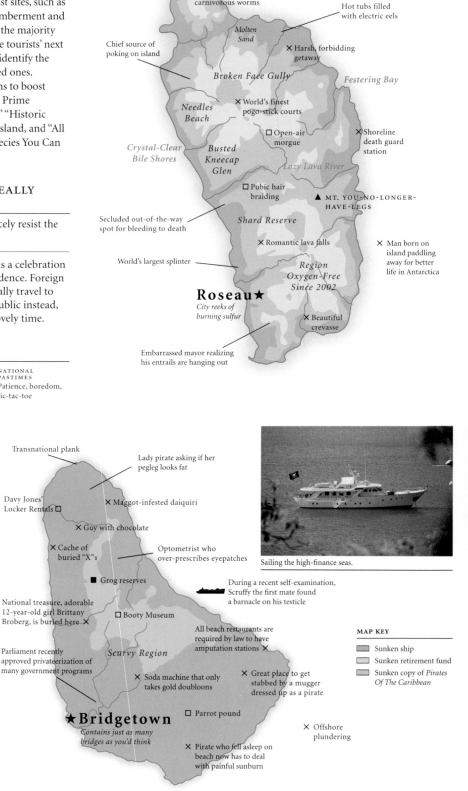

Pit of 16-foot-long carnivorous worms

Hot tubs filled with electric eels

Chief source of poking on island

Molten Sand

Harsh, forbidding getaway

Broken Face Gully

Festering Bay

Needles Beach

World's finest pogo-stick courts

Crystal-Clear Bile Shores

Open-air morgue

Shoreline death guard station

Busted Kneecap Glen

Lazy Lava River

Pubic hair braiding

▲ MT. YOU-NO-LONGER-HAVE-LEGS

Secluded out-of-the-way spot for bleeding to death

Shard Reserve

Romantic lava falls

Man born on island paddling away for better life in Antarctica

World's largest splinter

Region Oxygen-Free Since 2002

Roseau★
City reeks of burning sulfur

Beautiful crevasse

Embarrassed mayor realizing his entrails are hanging out

Transnational plank

Lady pirate asking if her pegleg looks fat

Davy Jones' Locker Rentals

Maggot-infested daiquiri

Guy with chocolate

Cache of buried "X"s

Optometrist who over-prescribes eyepatches

Grog reserves

National treasure, adorable 12-year-old girl Brittany Broberg, is buried here

Booty Museum

All beach restaurants are required by law to have amputation stations

Parliament recently approved privateerization of many government programs

Scurvy Region

Great place to get stabbed by a mugger dressed up as a pirate

Soda machine that only takes gold doubloons

★Bridgetown
Contains just as many bridges as you'd think

Parrot pound

Pirate who fell asleep on beach now has to deal with painful sunburn

Offshore plundering

Sailing the high-finance seas.

During a recent self-examination, Scruffy the first mate found a barnacle on his testicle

MAP KEY

- Sunken ship
- Sunken retirement fund
- Sunken copy of *Pirates Of The Caribbean*

The Three Saints
If You Lived Here, You'd Be Relaxed By Now

The Three Saints is the perfect destination for exhausted vacationers to take a break from the hustle and bustle of the resorts, spas, and beachfront time-shares in other Caribbean countries.

Visitors to these gorgeous islands—whether escaping from the strain of a monthlong hiatus in the Bahamas, or trying to forget about the hassle of dealing with their children's nanny during a holiday to Antigua—can unwind in style, and get some relief from the aches and pains that come from sitting in a beach chair all day.

The Three Saints' 24-hour-long sunsets and vast expanses of cool shade provide a relaxing getaway from getting away from it all.

HISTORY » OUT WITH THE OLD, IN WITH THE MASSIVE TOURISM DOLLARS

Since 1830, the mostly benevolent British Empire has allowed citizens of the Three Saints to practice backbreaking farm work without having to wear leg irons. At some point in the last century, it dawned on them that people from all over the world would pay good money just to come sit on the white-sand beaches, blink unbelievingly at the impossibly blue sky and sea, and wonder exactly how in the fuck they wound up as Assistant to the District Manager in charge of industrial-grade textile floor coverings.

FACTS » A LITTLE R&R&R&R

POPULATION
270,000 at your service

AREA COMPARATIVE
Three Cancuns, Four Bahamas, or 10 dozen Royal Viking Princesses

LAND USE
Unwinding (38%), Resting (23%), Recuperating (20%), Relaxing (19%)

CUISINE
Catch of the day

CURRENCY
Yours

GOVERNMENT
Comment-card-based

CLIMATE
Awesomely mild

NATURAL HAZARDS
Sunburn, flip-flop blisters, falling out of hammock

NATURAL RESOURCES
Secluded beaches, private beaches, gated beaches

INTERNATIONAL DISPUTES
Norwegian cruise liner is blocking the view

OFFICIAL MOTTO
"Do Not Disturb"

LEAST BEAUTIFUL FEATURE
Tourist from Minnesota

BIRTH RATE
1.2 illegitimate children/ housekeeper

Guy you spend 85% of your time trying to avoid

□ Starch plantation

Kingstown ★
Complimentary Water

✕ Site where Arawaks first walked barefoot along the beach

□ Still-undiscovered restaurant

□ Fresh towel pile

Used-towel drop

Meal available here

□ U.S. white-collar prison

□ Flip-flop stockpile

Interest rates falling out of tree

120-Acre Plot Of Water For Sale

Castries ★

■ Coconut filled with tax information

■ Raft made of rotting infrastructure

✕ Man's wages garnished with mango slices

□ Stationary bike powering economy

□ Inflation tied down with vines

✕ Man investing precious pebbles in bank hole

✕ Fish treated like diplomat

■ Illegal sea-horse-fighting stadium

✕ Singing crab

✕ Man brought to tears by view from balcony

Sea breeze making love to woman

★ **Basseterre**

✕ Edible sand

✕ Guy just noticing that island shaped like baseball bat

Annoying Sea Breeze

□ Native who thinks he lives on a tropical paradise or something

Partially Crystal-Clear Water

Residents of the Three Saints wash and change the sand each day.

ST. VINCENT & THE GRENADINES » THE WORST OF BOTH WORLDS

From the tan, windswept millionaires in the northern luxury condos, to the dense, breathtaking poverty of the southern islanders, St. Vincent & the Grenadines is a land of awe-inspiring economic diversity, with more than 10,000 varieties of disparity.

A rich vacationer's haven boasting wide-open tax brackets and secluded shantytowns untouched by foreign investors, these islands promise something for almost everyone, and nothing for everyone else. When they're not simply taking in the sights of lush misery through the tinted windows of their SUV limos, the more daring bankers, CEOs, and heirs apparent will sometimes venture out into the rugged slums and untamed marketplaces, or go experience a sharp drop in income just steps from their private beach.

ST. LUCIA » UNCHARTED DESERT ISLAND ECONOMY

Stuck on this tiny island since their slave ship stranded them there during a three-generation tour, the people of St. Lucia are always getting into a series of hilariously pitiful attempts to escape from the poverty of this secluded tropical paradise.

Using only coconuts, some straw, and a rudimentary understanding of Keynesian theory, these impoverished goofballs have failed time and time again to construct an economy that will actually float. Still, the plucky castaways never seem to give up, even when their bumbling distress calls for financial aid from the British go unanswered.

Recently, residents have managed to provide adequate health care, establish a living wage for all, and even get off the island on a hot-air balloon, all through a series of elaborate dream sequences.

ST. KITTS & NEVIS » ONE DOESN'T BLOW

While St. Kitts is a true Caribbean gem, with beautiful sunsets, charming beaches, and balmy weather, Nevis pretty much sucks.

It just does. Nevis simply can't compare to St. Kitts, which, despite sharing a lot of similar geographical features, is a way better place.

St. Kitts has a growing tourism industry, but Nevis just sits there with its palm trees and sandy beaches, being all stupid and everything. It has dumb-looking conical peaks that only idiots would ever want to climb, and the thick clouds ringing its volcanoes look lame, not cool, like St. Kitts.

Everyone knows and appreciates St. Kitts for its sugar production and unicameral legislature, but nobody knows anything about Nevis' vegetation, or wildlife, or cultural traditions, because it is retarded and dumb and shaped like a Chicken McNugget.

South America

Brazil

» THE BRAZILIAN FLAG IS TRADITION-ALLY DISPLAYED IN BIKINI FORM.

People At Their Most Beautiful, Humanity At Its Ugliest

Boasting some of the sexiest people ever to be stabbed repeatedly at night, Brazil is home to perhaps the most attractive victims of carjacking, robbery, and violent assault in the world.

From the beaches of Rio de Janeiro, to the mountains of São Paulo, to the hospital morgues of Salvador, Brazilian women are especially easy to spot.

With full, trembling lips, legs that go on for miles beneath their unrelenting assailants, and eyes so expressive they seem to cry out, "Please help me, I'm being attacked," these South American beauties are known for their ability to stop traffic. At least, until an ambulance unit can arrive at the scene.

Photographed hundreds of times each year by the nation's top homicide investigators, many possess perfect bone structure—before being thrown out of a moving vehicle—and are able to look both seductive and completely innocent with a gun to their heads.

Even the nation's men are admired for their strong jaw lines and tanned features, during the brief instances in which they are not wearing ski masks and holding up banks.

As stunning as the people are, however, they fail to compare to the beauty of the Amazon rainforest, which is cut down during the prime of its life, and raped nearly twice as often as any Brazilian citizen.

Rocinha Shantytown
One of the fastest-developing hellholes in all of Brazil.

PEOPLE » POVERTY NEVER LOOKED THIS GOOD

Nearly 40% of all Brazilian citizens reside in shantytowns, which they leave early each morning to work in nearby shantycities. While their jobs are often tiring and pay very little, many continue to toil for years in the hopes of someday moving to Brazil's shantycapital.

Poor Brazilian families line the roofs of their homes with broken bottles to protect themselves from the ultra-poor. The ultra-poor often steal these broken bottles in a desperate attempt to use them as drinking vessels. These are then stolen by the mega-ultra-poor, who simply wish to eat some nourishing glass.

While a vast majority of Brazilians are Roman Catholic, the nation's official religion is soccer, which is practiced by thousands for several hours a day.

It is not unusual for Brazilian businesses to close when a soccer match is being televised—a custom that has led to millions of dollars in lost revenue, the deaths of countless hospital patients, and the tragic crashes of almost 40 commercial airliners over the years.

Limited access to clean water among poor Brazilians has resulted in some of the most titillating cases of protozoal diarrhea in the world.

HISTORY » BLAME IT ON THE BOSSA NOVA AND/OR PORTUGAL

1200 B.C. Disgusting findings from this time reveal some of the earliest pubic shavings in the world.

A.D. 1500 Two months after landing in Copacabana beach, Portuguese explorer Pedro Cabral grudgingly packs up his suntan lotion and sets out to survey the nation's interior.

1530 Early Portuguese settlers use slash-and-burn techniques to clear the land of unwanted weeds, undergrowth, and natives.

1570 Surviving tribesmen find relative safety among the hundreds of venomous snakes and ferocious predators in the Amazon rainforest.

1690 Millions of lucky African slaves are charged with the enviable task of toiling without rest in sunny Brazil.

1800 Conservative social mores force Brazilian women to wear some of the most oppressive and formal thongs ever devised.

1917 A highly rhythmic, sexually charged style of music is popularized by Ernesto de Santos Donga—or "The Father Of Samba," as he was known to his 47 children.

Carmen Miranda

1938 The banana spider, the mango weevil, and the pineapple mealybug are introduced to outlying regions of the U.S. during a Carmen Miranda solo tour.

1955 Soccer superstar Pelé single-handedly defeats the German national team while

Pelé

suffering from a sprained ankle, the flu, and being sound asleep back home in the city of São Paulo.

1962 Three months after recording his most successful and most personal song, "The Girl From Ipanema," a depressed and disgusted Antonio Carlos Jobim records "The Girl Who Turned Out To Be The Guy From Ipanema."

1968 Pelé commemorates his 1,000th soccer goal by scoring an additional 286 soccer goals.

1974 A raging wildfire destroys thousands of acres of rainforest, and leaves hundreds of Brazilian loggers with a lot less work to do.

São Paulo

1982 Smog in the city of São Paulo reaches its highest levels since day and night were two separate entities and could be used by citizens to judge the passing of time.

1992 Facing charges of corruption, President Fernando Collor de Mello agrees to step down for an estimated $750,000.

1998 Scientists in the Amazon rainforest discover a species of poisonous toad that may very well hold the cure to living with cancer.

2005 The nation celebrates the launch of its first phallic object into space.

Heliconian Bromeliad
Contains valuable phytoenzymes

Monkey Frog
Secretes rare batrachopeptides

Soccer Midfielder
Produces powerful testosterone

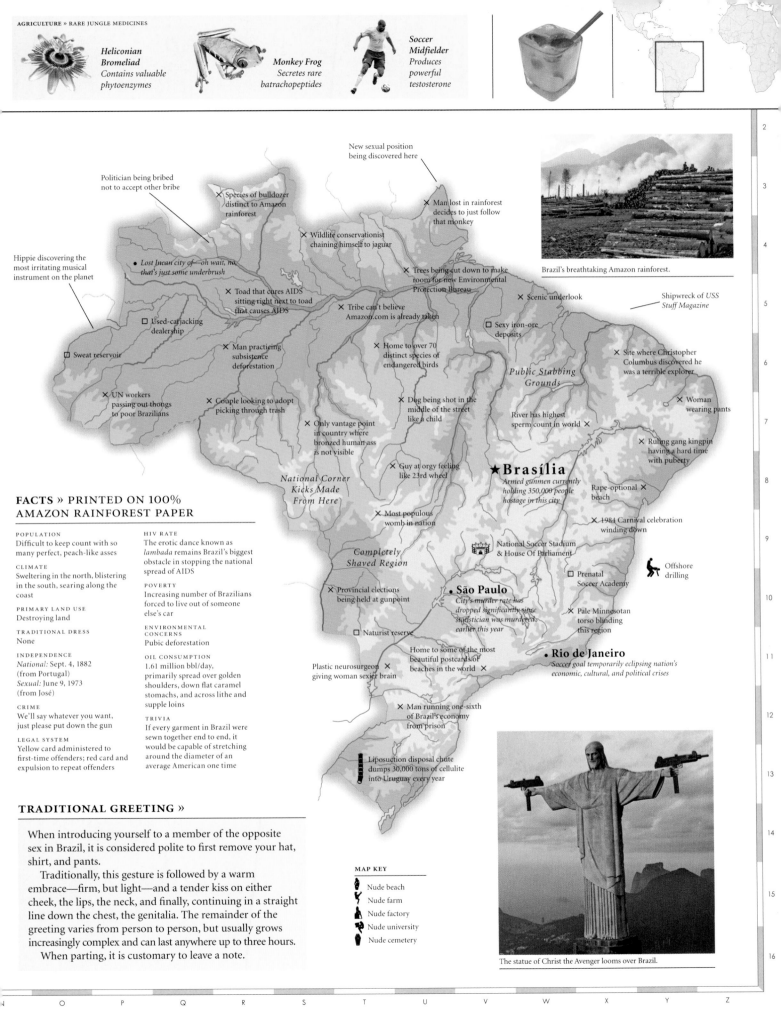

Politician being bribed not to accept other bribe

New sexual position being discovered here

× Species of bulldozer distinct to Amazon rainforest

× Man lost in rainforest decides to just follow that monkey

× Wildlife conservationist chaining himself to jaguar

Hippie discovering the most irritating musical instrument on the planet

● Lost Incan city of—oh wait, no, that's just some underbrush

× Trees being cut down to make room for new Environmental Protection Bureau

× Scenic underlook

Shipwreck of USS Stuff Magazine

× Toad that cures AIDS sitting right next to toad that causes AIDS

□ Used-carjacking dealership

× Tribe can't believe Amazon.com is already taken

□ Sexy iron-ore deposits

× Site where Christopher Columbus discovered he was a terrible explorer

□ Sweat reservoir

× Man practicing subsistence deforestation

× Home to over 70 distinct species of endangered birds

Public Stabbing Grounds

× Woman wearing pants

× UN workers passing out thongs to poor Brazilians

× Couple looking to adopt picking through trash

× Dog being shot in the middle of the street like a child

River has highest sperm count in world ×

× Ruling gang kingpin having a hard time with puberty

× Only vantage point in country where bronzed human ass is not visible

★ **Brasília**
Armed gunmen currently holding 350,000 people hostage in this city

Rape-optional beach ×

× Guy at orgy feeling like 23rd wheel

× 1984 Carnival celebration winding down

National Corner Kicks Made From Here

× Most populous womb in nation

National Soccer Stadium & House Of Parliament

Offshore drilling

FACTS » PRINTED ON 100% AMAZON RAINFOREST PAPER

POPULATION
Difficult to keep count with so many perfect, peach-like asses

CLIMATE
Sweltering in the north, blistering in the south, searing along the coast

PRIMARY LAND USE
Destroying land

TRADITIONAL DRESS
None

INDEPENDENCE
National: Sept. 4, 1882 (from Portugal)
Sexual: June 9, 1973 (from José)

CRIME
We'll say whatever you want, just please put down the gun

LEGAL SYSTEM
Yellow card administered to first-time offenders; red card and expulsion to repeat offenders

HIV RATE
The erotic dance known as *lambada* remains Brazil's biggest obstacle in stopping the national spread of AIDS

POVERTY
Increasing number of Brazilians forced to live out of someone else's car

ENVIRONMENTAL CONCERNS
Pubic deforestation

OIL CONSUMPTION
1.61 million bbl/day, primarily spread over golden shoulders, down flat caramel stomachs, and across lithe and supple loins

TRIVIA
If every garment in Brazil were sewn together end to end, it would be capable of stretching around the diameter of an average American one time

Completely Shaved Region

□ Prenatal Soccer Academy

× Provincial elections being held at gunpoint

● **São Paulo**
City's murder rate has dropped significantly since statistician was murdered earlier this year

× Pale Minnesotan torso blinding this region

□ Naturist reserve

Home to some of the most beautiful postcards of beaches in the world ×

● **Rio de Janeiro**
Soccer goal temporarily eclipsing nation's economic, cultural, and political crises

Plastic neurosurgeon × giving woman sexier brain

× Man running one-sixth of Brazil's economy from prison

▬ Liposuction disposal chute dumps 30,000 tons of cellulite into Uruguay every year

TRADITIONAL GREETING »

When introducing yourself to a member of the opposite sex in Brazil, it is considered polite to first remove your hat, shirt, and pants.

Traditionally, this gesture is followed by a warm embrace—firm, but light—and a tender kiss on either cheek, the lips, the neck, and finally, continuing in a straight line down the chest, the genitalia. The remainder of the greeting varies from person to person, but usually grows increasingly complex and can last anywhere up to three hours.

When parting, it is customary to leave a note.

MAP KEY
- Nude beach
- Nude farm
- Nude factory
- Nude university
- Nude cemetery

Brazil's breathtaking Amazon rainforest.

The statue of Christ the Avenger looms over Brazil.

Argentina

» THE SUN REPRESENTS THE NATION'S RECENT PURCHASE OF CLIP-ART SOFTWARE.

A Beautiful Nazi Retirement Community

Argentina is the retirement nation of choice for hundreds of former Nazis, who spend their final years reminiscing about the "good old days," paging wistfully through scrapbooks of faded Holocaust photos, and telling long, rambling stories about the best way to cremate a Jew.

Though many now need walkers to goose-step across town, lack almost as much eyesight as they do hindsight, and take several minutes to give the Nazi salute due to crippling arthritis, these geriatric mass murderers still live life to its fullest in sunny Argentina. They wake up each morning to a breathtaking view of the Andes, spend the afternoon savoring succulent meats and taking romantic tango lessons, and go to sleep each night without being hung for the near extermination of an entire race of people.

While few receive visitors, phone calls, or even letters, SS seniors claim they prefer it that way, as most people who show up to see them are only interested in their Swiss bank accounts. In addition, many complain that today's younger generation has no respect for their elders or what they did, and are instead filled with strange, new ideas about "human rights" and "mercy."

Despite it sometimes being a lonely existence, with dozens trapped indoors due to old age and the ongoing manhunt for escaped war criminals, the vast majority still enjoy life's simple pleasures—pleasures such as watching the beautiful Buenos Aires sunset, or sorting through boxes and boxes of old gold fillings.

Former SS officer Jürgen Fleisher, telling that same old story about the time he crushed a little Jewish girl's skull with the butt of his rifle.

Great little neighborhood just outside of Israeli jurisdiction

✕ Farmer applying BBQ sauce to cattle

✕ Currency depreciating in middle of increasingly awkward transaction

San Juan ●
Named in honor of 612 Spanish conquistadors

Surprising Amount Of Corn Here

Path of charity 5K tango ✕

● City of absolutely no Nazis whatsoever

✕ IMF official arriving to collect fourth installment of bribe

● City will fix economy as soon as soccer match is over

Neuquen ●
Nobody in this city has ever sent thousands of innocent souls to their deaths inside a gas chamber—you must be thinking of somewhere else

Thin Mustache Region

✕ Site where tourist who ordered his steak well-done was shot

▮ Phallic monument overcompensating for tiny achievement

☐ Museum Of Dictator Fashion

✕ Current location of tango instructor who will someday steal your wife from you

★ Buenos Aires
As Seen In "Starship Troopers"

✕ Old Nazi blaming bingo loss on the Jews

☐ The finest slums in all of South America

☐ Strategic puffin-training camp

☐ Gateway to absolutely nothing

ATLANTIC OCEAN

▲ THE ANDES
The world's longest mountain range, it stretches past the interest of millions

☐ Route of failed Magellanic Passage

✕ Senior SS officer waiting to get to that big Auschwitz in the sky

☐ Prime Chile-front property

MAP KEY

▢ Soccer riots
▢ Soccer insurrections
▢ Soccer genocides

✕ Elderly Nazi thinking about coming out of retirement

☐ Row of steakhouses that form part of larger steak condominium

Dangerous underwater volcano that Argentines would know about if they would look at their own map once in a while

✕ Site of historical plantains

Old Panama Canal

Capt. Ricardo Carrio of the Falkland Islands Puffin Defense Force

» COL. JUAN PERÓN

» THE CLOSEST ARGENTINA GETS TO VEGETARIAN CUISINE.

» THE FAMOUS CATHEDRAL OF ST. DIEGO DE MARADONA.

FACTS » ARGENTINA AT A QUICK, FIERY GLANCE

POPULATION
Counted annually as part of national census

TERRAIN
Combination of rolling grasslands and polished parquet floors

CLIMATE
Tropical in the north, temperate in the east, anti-Semitic in the south

CALF MORTALITY RATE
100%

BIRTH DEFECTS
Low; only 12/100,000 suffer from two left feet

PUBLIC DEBT
Too expensive to calculate

INTERNATIONAL DISPUTES
All soccer-related

ECONOMY
Fuck you

ENVIRONMENT
Conservation efforts offer protection to such species as the peregrine falcon, the Argentine pampas deer, and the German escaped war criminal

INNOVATIONS
The sexually electrifying dance known as the tango; the practice of electrifying sexual organs to get information

MOST EMBARRASSING MOMENT
Time it thought it was part of the EU

INDIGENOUS ART FORMS
Decorative scarring, a tradition passed down through generations of lawmakers, is now used only on "special" detainees

PEOPLE » PAMPAS ASSHOLES

A supple, hawk-nosed, and tautly muscled blend of European and indigenous ancestry, Argentina is home to nearly 20 million pairs of dancing men and women, as well as countless species of sexually suggestive flowers suitable for clenching in the teeth while gently dipping one's partner.

In Argentina, the nation's dictator traditionally leads, usually with an iron hand. The submissive populace typically follows, creating a violent but graceful partnership; sexy, yes—passionate, certainly—but as rigid and disciplined as any other form of dance or regime.

However, in recent times, Argentines have come to embrace a series of more liberal leaders by holding on tight and wildly gyrating their hips.

Over the last 60 years, the nation has seen an influx of immigrants seeking refuge from oppressive governments in Laos, anti-Semitism in Europe, and International War-Crimes Tribunals in Nuremberg.

HISTORY » DON'T CRY FOR ECONOMIC DEVASTATION AND YEARS OF UNTOLD OPPRESSION, ARGENTINA

11,000 B.C. Ancient settlers kick a goat skull through two trees, become bored, and do not return for 13,000 years.

A.D. 1520 Upon passing through Tierra Del Fuego, Ferdinand Magellan proudly declares that he has successfully semi-circumnavigated the world.

1833 While riding a horse to Argentina, a delighted Charles Darwin comes up with his famous theory of Riding Horses Everywhere.

1900 The tango is developed by two Rio de la Plata residents as they escape from a narrow enclosure.

1939 Declaring neutrality during WWII, Argentina refuses to take a side on the issue of "deserving Jews being justifiably slaughtered by the thousands, hopefully."

Ramon Castillo

1943 Enraged by President Ramon S. Castillo's administration, but wanting to make sure that everything would go smoothly if he overthrew him, Col. Juan Perón stages a rehearsal coup.

1946 The daughter of impoverished ranchers, Eva "Evita" Perón teaches girls everywhere that, no matter your upbringing, anyone can grow up to seduce the president.

1947 A furious Juan Perón accuses Evita of having a love affair with the nation's public.

1949 Nazi physician Josef Mengele arrives in Argentina, where he practices medicine, dentistry, and incredible self-restraint.

1951 Using her feminine wiles, Evita helps her

Eva Perón

husband win re-election by charming such powerful lobby groups as the Argentine Labor Union, the National Trade Council, and the influential Single Men Who Are Easily Swayed By A Pretty Face Coalition.

1955 Accused of corruption, Juan Perón flees to Paraguay, where he stays three nights at the nation's Ritz-Carlton hotel before traveling—by private jet—to Brazil, purchasing $6 million in souvenirs, and boarding a cruise ship headed for the Bahamas.

1960 Using 400,000 healthy Jews as bait, Israeli agents stationed in Buenos Aires lure Adolf Eichmann out of hiding.

1972 A plane carrying, like, 50 guys from Uruguay crashes into the Andes Mountains, which is bad enough, but then all this crazy stuff starts happening to them and they get hypothermia or one of those diseases and—you know, you should probably just rent the movie *Alive*. I think it won some awards or something.

1975 Argentina offers $32 million to any citizen who can solve the nation's growing deficit problems.

1978 Jorge Luis Borges publishes his most

Leopoldo Galtieri

surrealist novel, *The Thriving Economy And Low Unemployment Rate Of Argentina.*

1982 Gen. Leopoldo Galtieri leads Argentina to triumphant defeat against the British in the Falkland Islands War.

1985 After years of dispute, divorce is finally legalized in Argentina. Thousands of citizens are immediately nagged by their wives to protest.

1986 In Argentina's first recorded miracle, millions of religious fans report seeing a soccer deity shaped like the Maradona dribble past an entire English side to score the winning goal in the World Cup.

2002 An economic crisis in the country leaves one out of every three residents in poverty, and two out of every three burning census forms to stay warm.

2005 The deeply indebted nation loses all remaining hope when the World Bank repossesses it from them.

Sports
In soccer matches with Brazil, Argentines are allowed to ride horses to even things up.

Bolivia

Living High Off The Land

Once filled with so much promise and hope for the future, all Bolivia can think about these days is the immediate rush it gets from producing cocaine.

Each morning, the nation's coca farmers wake up before dawn, wonder how it is they wound up in a ditch miles away from town, and prepare for the start of another energizing workday. Despite regularly picking up 60 straight hours of overtime, being on the job tends to fly by for most, with an average week seeming to last only a matter of minutes.

In fact, many Bolivians claim they feel on top of the world while harvesting the highly addictive crop, and that toiling in the fields is as good as getting a blowjob from God.

Working in quick bursts, Bolivian farmers pick fresh coca leaves, dry each individually between layers of coarse wool, suddenly scream at the top of their lungs for no reason whatsoever, cheat on their wives, and challenge a nearby donkey to a fistfight.

A short bathroom break usually follows, after which Bolivians return to work and repeat these first five steps.

FACTS » CUT WITH BABY POWDER

POPULATION
6.3 million
(wide awake)

CONSTITUTION
Written on random hookers' tits

HIGHEST POINT
Arnaldo Diaz
(2:30 p.m.)

LOWEST POINT
Arnaldo Diaz
(3:15 p.m.)

EXPORTS
No idea what you're talking about

COMMON AILMENTS
Nosebleeds, spontaneous nasal hemorrhages, arterial nasal ruptures, asthma

JUSTICE SYSTEM
Uh…based on Spanish civil law?

INTERNATIONAL AGREEMENTS
Must provide UN with urine sample every month

HOW COCAINE GETS TO YOU »

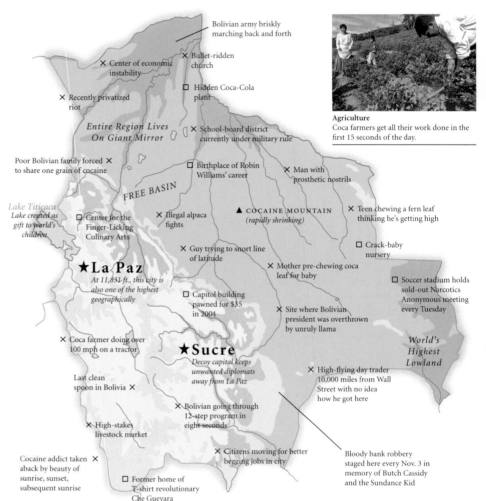

Bolivian army briskly marching back and forth

× Center of economic instability

× Bullet-ridden church

× Recently privatized riot

□ Hidden Coca-Cola plant

Entire Region Lives On Giant Mirror

× School-board district currently under military rule

Poor Bolivian family forced × to share one grain of cocaine

□ Birthplace of Robin Williams' career

FREE BASIN

× Man with prosthetic nostrils

Lake Titicaca
Lake created as gift to world's children

□ Center for the Finger-Licking Culinary Arts

× Illegal alpaca fights

▲ COCAINE MOUNTAIN
(rapidly shrinking)

× Teen chewing a fern leaf thinking he's getting high

× Guy trying to snort line of latitude

□ Crack-baby nursery

★La Paz
At 11,831 ft., this city is also one of the highest geographically

□ Capitol building pawned for $35 in 2004

× Mother pre-chewing coca leaf for baby

□ Soccer stadium holds sold-out Narcotics Anonymous meeting every Tuesday

× Coca farmer doing over 100 mph on a tractor

★Sucre
Decoy capital keeps unwanted diplomats away from La Paz

× Site where Bolivian president was overthrown by unruly llama

World's Highest Lowland

× High-flying day trader 10,000 miles from Wall Street with no idea how he got here

Last clean spoon in Bolivia ×

× Bolivian going through 12-step program in eight seconds

× High-stakes livestock market

× Citizens moving for better begging jobs in city

Bloody bank robbery staged here every Nov. 3 in memory of Butch Cassidy and the Sundance Kid

Cocaine addict taken × aback by beauty of sunrise, sunset, subsequent sunrise

□ Former home of T-shirt revolutionary Che Guevara

Agriculture
Coca farmers get all their work done in the first 15 seconds of the day.

25 CONSECUTIVE LINES OF HISTORY »

1500 B.C. Tiahuanacan tribes use the coca plant to develop herbal remedies, which besides curing topical irritations, also grant them the courage to talk to women who might otherwise be considered out of their league.

A.D. 1825 Following years of Spanish rule, Bolivia goes ahead and—*get this*—names the entire country after some guy who liberated them from tyranny.

1831 The funny round hat is introduced to Bolivia.

1950 Seven military coups, nine armed insurrections, and 12 assassinations mark one of the most hotly contested races for PTA president in the nation's history.

1978 The coca farming industry is crippled by fears of overgrazing, the growing cost of labor, and tiny surveillance devices secretly planted by the CIA inside every wall, ceiling, and floorboard.

1982 An attempt to diversify the nation's economy fails when foreign clients are uninterested in snorting zinc ore and hydroelectricity.

1998 Generations of nosebleeds form Lake Gaiba.

2006 A study finds half of all American dollar bills contain trace amounts of Bolivia.

Bolivians harvest lines of their chief cash crop.

Colombia

» NATIONAL SYMBOL THAT COLOMBIA IS CURRENTLY HOLDING.

South America's Middleman

Colombia—which also goes by the names of Deuce Low, Skates, and C-Train when dealing with international clients—is the world's leading exporter of whatever it is you're looking for.

Any country in need of a quick fix knows exactly where to find it: 4° 00' N, 72° 00' W, right by the equator—the same place it has hung out for the past 500 years.

South America's largest supplier of hollowed-out statues, hollowed-out rolling pins, and hollowed-out people, Colombia often gives away its first cocaine export for free, then charges exorbitantly high prices once its trading partners are hooked.

Many poor nations invest almost all their GDP into trade with Colombia, but most end up alienating their allies while racking up extensive public debt and a high unemployment rate. These nations often claim that they will cut off diplomatic ties with Colombia for good, but they almost always renew relations with it the very next day.

PEOPLE » THEY KNOW A GUY WHO KNOWS A GUY

The people of Colombia, each of whom lives in his own one-bedroom, 10-bathroom apartment, communicate solely through eye contact, curt nods, and the subtle exchange of large briefcases.

Over the years, Colombian drug traffickers have evolved larger, more elastic anal cavities, capable of comfortably storing up to 100 kilos of cocaine, 12 crack pipes, four mirrors, two semiautomatic weapons, and $1,500 in unmarked bills.

Crime, however, remains a problem for citizens. Paramilitary groups kidnap so many people—1,900 each year—that being the victim of a Colombian kidnapping is now statistically more likely to reunite you with your family than separate you from it.

Juan Valdez
No amount of coffee is going to wake Mr. Valdez up from this.

HISTORY » YOU DIDN'T HEAR THIS FROM US

A.D. 1819 Revolutionist Simón Bolívar becomes president of Colombia, Peru, Venezuela, and Bolivia. Fearing he may overextend himself, he only runs for Secretary of Agriculture in Ecuador.

1948–1958 "La Violencia" era is marked by violence.

1967 Seeking an easier way to smuggle cocaine onto planes, drug traffickers invent the hollowed-out suitcase.

1982 Nation sells the rights to two of its citizens, "Juan y Maria," to the McGraw-Hill textbook company, which chronicles the two's exploits—including the times they went to the library and talked about the weather—for use in high-school-level Spanish textbooks for the next 25 years.

Pablo Escobar

1987 Medellin drug kingpin Pablo Escobar, once ranked as the seventh-richest man in the world, blows all his money on cocaine.

1988 A Colombian man's plan to smuggle 12 kilos of cocaine inside his nasal cavity results in immediate death.

2000 Members of the Cali drug cartel design the Transatlantic Crack Pipe, which stretches from Miami to Bogotá and allows U.S. citizens to smoke from over 1,500 miles away.

2007 Business discussions grow increasingly confusing after the words "the," "it," "you," "I," and "and" all become official slang terms for cocaine.

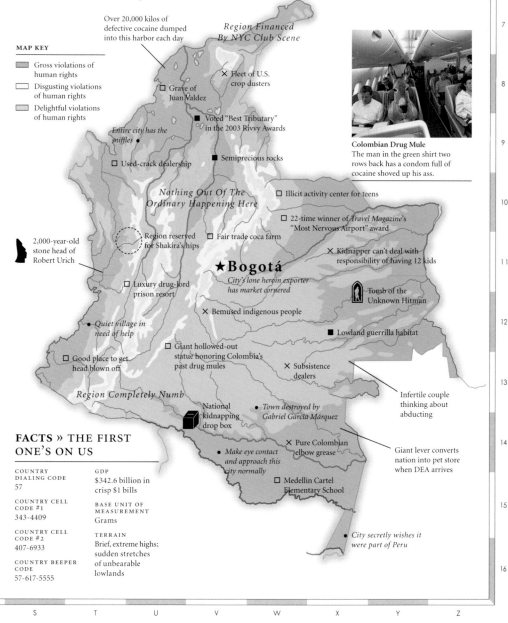

MAP KEY
- Gross violations of human rights
- Disgusting violations of human rights
- Delightful violations of human rights

Over 20,000 kilos of defective cocaine dumped into this harbor each day

Region Financed By NYC Club Scene

Fleet of U.S. crop dusters

Grave of Juan Valdez

Voted "Best Tributary" in the 2003 Rivvy Awards

Entire city has the sniffles

Semiprecious rocks

Used-crack dealership

Nothing Out Of The Ordinary Happening Here

Illicit activity center for teens

22-time winner of Travel Magazine's "Most Nervous Airport" award

2,000-year-old stone head of Robert Urich

Region reserved for Shakira's hips

Fair trade coca farm

★Bogotá
City's lone heroin exporter has market cornered

Kidnapper can't deal with responsibility of having 12 kids

Tomb of the Unknown Hitman

Luxury drug-lord prison resort

Bemused indigenous people

Quiet village in need of help

Lowland guerrilla habitat

Giant hollowed-out statue honoring Colombia's past drug mules

Subsistence dealers

Good place to get head blown off

Region Completely Numb

Infertile couple thinking about abducting

National kidnapping drop box

Town destroyed by Gabriel García Márquez

Pure Colombian elbow grease

Giant lever converts nation into pet store when DEA arrives

Make eye contact and approach this city normally

Medellin Cartel Elementary School

City secretly wishes it were part of Peru

Colombian Drug Mule
The man in the green shirt two rows back has a condom full of cocaine shoved up his ass.

FACTS » THE FIRST ONE'S ON US

COUNTRY DIALING CODE
57

COUNTRY CELL CODE #1
343-4409

COUNTRY CELL CODE #2
407-6933

COUNTRY BEEPER CODE
57-617-5555

GDP
$342.6 billion in crisp $1 bills

BASE UNIT OF MEASUREMENT
Grams

TERRAIN
Brief, extreme highs; sudden stretches of unbearable lowlands

Chile

» PATRIOTIC CHILEANS MUST WAVE FLAG CAREFULLY SO AS NOT TO HIT AN ARGENTINE.

» A SCHOOL OF CHILEAN SEA BASS.

Preventing Argentina From Enjoying The Pacific Ocean Since 1818

Nestled between the peaks of the Andes and the depths of the Pacific, Chile has become a haven for scuba divers, mountain climbers, and people who like to contemplate stark geographical contrasts.

Over 3,000 miles long and nearly 15 feet wide, Chile's size has made it a paranoid country, prone to supporting dictators like Augusto Pinochet, who promised that Chile would expand widthwise only if countless peaceful dissenters were buried alive in it.

HISTORY » AS IMPOSSIBLY THIN AS THE COUNTRY ITSELF

Pedro de Valdivia
On a bet, conquered Chile dressed like a ballerina.

A.D. 1519 Incans enjoy a hearty laugh at the shape of Chile before their entire civilization is wiped out by conquering Spaniards.

1818 Chile gains independence from Spain when an army of revolutionaries bravely drives the Spanish occupiers back all 30 yards into the Pacific Ocean.

1893 After foolishly neglecting the opportunity for years, Chile finally begins charging Argentines for access to the beach.

1960 A low-grade landslide in the east and some minor flooding in the west render all but 15 square feet of Chile uninhabitable.

1975 After two years under Pinochet rule, the nation's gravediggers claim they are running out of land.

1978 A pedestrian traveling north to south refuses to move aside for pedestrian traveling south to north. A 30-year standoff ensues.

1994 David Hasselhoff attempts to bring his successful American television series to South America with *Baywatch: Chile*. The initial shooting of the show's title sequence, in which lifeguards run the length of the country's beach, takes 17 days of nonstop filming, and causes three cast members to die of exhaustion.

CROSS-COUNTRY TRAVEL »

Depending on which direction a hiker is going, one of two sets of provisions is needed:

Set 1
12-oz. bottle of water and some chewing gum

Set 2
64 gallons of water, 50 pounds of dried food, 13 changes of clothes, sunscreen, thermal winter jacket, oxygen tank, compass, knife, backup compass, rain gear, signaling mirror, headlamp, batteries, water purifier, small plastic trowel, high-powered rifle, space blanket, defibrillator, and rope

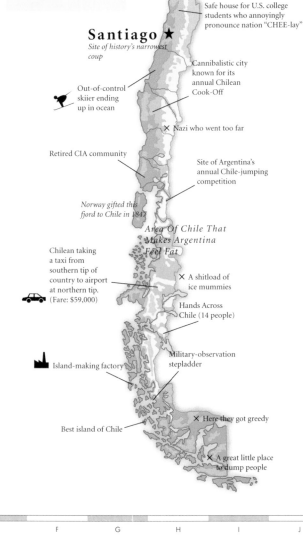

× Chilean fun slide running from north to south of entire country

× World's longest lighthouse

× Paraguay taunting tower

× A little slice of unrest

2,300-mile-long skywalk to Easter Island *(open May to October only)*

× Luxury beach-front prison

× Path of the Great Western Expansion of August 12-14, 1750

One big wave away from obliteration ×

Safe house for U.S. college students who annoyingly pronounce nation "CHEE-lay"

Santiago ★
Site of history's narrowest coup

Cannibalistic city known for its annual Chilean Cook-Off

Out-of-control skiier ending up in ocean

× Nazi who went too far

Retired CIA community

Site of Argentina's annual Chile-jumping competition

Norway gifted this fjord to Chile in 1847

Area Of Chile That Makes Argentina Feel Fat

Chilean taking a taxi from southern tip of country to airport at northern tip. (Fare: $59,000)

× A shitload of ice mummies

Hands Across Chile (14 people)

Military-observation stepladder

Island-making factory

× Here they got greedy

Best island of Chile

× A great little place to dump people

PEOPLE » VERTICALLY MINDED

The people of Chile like their countries the way they like their women: long and thin, covered in deserts and volcanoes, with a southern region that is a maze of fjords and archipelagos, situated along the western coast of South America. Most Chilean men are single.

Pinochet The Magnificent
In his distinguished career, the popular dictator made over 3,000 Chileans disappear.

FACTS » WIDTH DOESN'T MATTER

AREA COMPARATIVE
If rolled into a ball, Rhode Island

CLIMATE
The people of Chile have a saying: "If you don't like the weather, drive 2,500 miles up the coast to where it's 40 degrees warmer"

CAPITAL
Santiago, a sprawling metropolis that is forced to grow vertically, and will one day tower over the entire nation

BIRTHDAY RATE
1 per citizen per year

TRADITIONAL DANCE
The cueca, also known as the "Cross-Country Two-Step"

LITERATURE
Renowned poet Pablo Neruda has deluded countless vapid coeds into believing they have a deep, spiritual understanding of the dichotomy of eroticism and nature because they made it through three of his poems

#1 RADIO STATION
WCHL, where it's *always* "chilly" with a 100% chance of great hits

FOLKLORE
As the story goes, mythic Chilean lumberjack Pablo Buñan could walk over Chile, straddling the nation by placing one foot in the Pacific Ocean and the other in Argentina; according to legend, he was 5'10"

Paraguay & Uruguay

Paraguay
Latitude 27 South, Longitude 57 West— That's All We've Got

Paraguay is a nation widely known for not being widely known, and legendary for being a country in South America. Oh, and it has a dam.

When one researches the country of Paraguay, one does not find a great deal beyond the dam. One of the poorest countries in South America, Paraguay partnered with a reluctant Brazil and Argentina in the 1970s in a bid to build two of the world's largest hydroelectric dams where the borders of the three nations meet. After the completion of Itaipú Dam, Paraguayan officials watched helplessly as tourists chose to visit the dam only on the Brazilian and Argentine sides. The two countries are grateful to Paraguay for the tourism dollars, and for supplying 80% of their electricity. In an act of gratitude, they have sent form thank-you letters.

FACTS » THEY HAVE A DAM

KNOWN FOR
Its longitude and latitude

ALSO KNOWN FOR
The dam—Itaipú Dam

LAND AREA
100% land

DAM AREA
100% Itaipú

MOTTO
"We Have The Dam"

BUSINESS CUSTOM
It is considered rude to laugh about the Paraguayan economy directly in front of a citizen

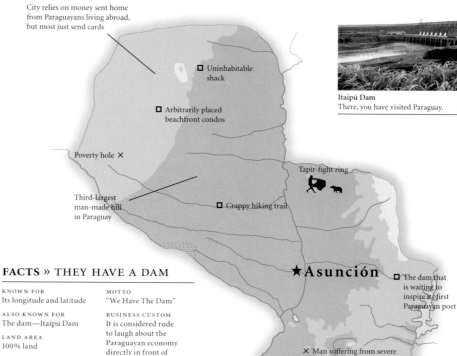

City relies on money sent home from Paraguayans living abroad, but most just send cards

- Uninhabitable shack
- Arbitrarily placed beachfront condos
- × Poverty hole
- Third-largest man-made hill in Paraguay
- Tapir-fight ring
- □ Crappy hiking trail
- ★ **Asunción**
- □ The dam that is waiting to inspire its first Paraguayan poet
- × Man suffering from severe case of soybean fever

Itaipú Dam
There, you have visited Paraguay.

Uruguay
Wait, This Might Be Paraguay

Uruguay is bordered by Brazil on the west and Argentina on the east, in the center of the South American continent. Or is that Paraguay?

This constitutional republic, which may in fact be Paraguay, consists of grassy plains, with some hills and forests. Its people stand in stark contrast to those of Paraguay (or, as the case may be, Uruguay). While one of the nations is more native and rural, the other is more urban and European. This urban center has caused culture to flourish, giving an educated middle class the opportunity to debate whether they are in Uruguay or Paraguay.

Diplomats from Paraguay often have difficulty crossing the border into Uruguay, as many find themselves unable to determine which country they have come from, which one they are traveling to, and which one they will ultimately return to.

FACTS » NOT REALLY SURE ON THESE

POPULATION
About the same as Paraguay

AREA COMPARATIVE
One Paraguay and one Uruguay divided by two

CAPITAL
Montevideo or Asunción

ETHNICITY
50% Paraguayan, 50% Uruguayan (est.)

MOTTO
"Are You Sure We Are Not Paraguay?"

BRAZILIANS ASKING FOR THE BALL BACK

ARGENTINES ASKING SOMEONE TO KICK THE BALL BACK

- × Tourist wondering what the hell he's doing in Uruguay
- **PARAGUAY-ISH**
- ● Lost City Of Conquistadors
- *Origin of the saying "The women are always way hotter on the other side"* ●
- × Black market for stolen Argentine cattle
- *Rain Forest Destroyed For Soccer Field*
- × Illegal Brazilian shorn-pubic-hair dumping
- Lovely Brazilian beach ■
- × Nation's highest ratio of rice to beans
- *Territory Of Vicious Cantaloupe Cartel*
- ● *Small town that is only 70% sure it's in Uruguay*
- × What you're thinking of when you think of Paraguay
- Crappy Uruguayan beach ■
- *Charo Huge Here*
- ■ Cilantro fields
- ★ **Montevideo**
  Final resting place of Monteradio star
- Brisk sales of *Let's Go Paraguay*
- × Uruguayan Navy enjoying a swim

Soccer
This team most likely plays somewhere around Uruguay.

Peru

» CUT A HOLE IN THE MIDDLE AND YOU'VE GOT YOURSELF A NICE PONCHO.

Always With The Goddamn Pan Flutes

Peru is a country with a rich cultural history, an increasingly popular cuisine, and a persistent, pervasive, and painfully upbeat musical tradition that echoes incessantly from every godforsaken corner of this mountainous nation.

The former seat of the Inca Empire is today driven by the joyful, sickening melodies of the pan flute, which push otherwise rational politicians to commit woeful mismanagement, prompt military leaders to stage violent coups, and hypnotize the common people into a grinding poverty caused by debilitating headaches. Economic disparity is a major problem in Peru, since most of the population has to play for tips, but members of the wealthy Spanish minority refuse to leave their homes and endure even one more jaunty, mind-numbing pan-flute song.

In recent years, scores of Peruvians have fled the country with nothing but the ponchos on their backs, the ponchos in their duffel bags, seven or eight pan flutes, and a stack of CDs, hoping to find a new life temporarily ruining the lives of unsuspecting passersby in foreign lands.

MAP KEY

- Poor
- Impoverished
- Destitute
- Unable to afford thesaurus

Map labels:

- Andoas — *Tiny town swallowed by giant snake*
- Human Development Index official with single tear running down his face
- ✕ Peruvian police forcing 69-year-old woman to vote
- ☐ Shining Bicycle Path
- ✕ Ancient artifacts kicked across border
- *Flute Groves*
- ✕ Largest llama-made-of-twine in Peru
- Piura — *Home of South America's first mummy mayor*
- ✕ World's deepest, emptiest tip box
- Peruvians who possess mysterious ability to appear invisible to international investors
- ☐ Ancient ruins discovered several times by wild llamas
- ✕ Table leg propped up by Inca artifact
- ✕ UFO landing strip
- ▲ MT. FUJIMORI (*$57,483,221 embezzled*)
- Trujillo — *No ancient shit here at all*
- *Ancient Inca Makeout Grounds*
- Ruins of Inca lighthouse ✕
- ✕ Shoebox full of Inca junk
- According to Mormon legend, Jesus came here to take Spanish lessons
- ✕ Shoebox full of Peruvians
- ★ Lima — *Future lost capital of Peru*
- *This Region All About Context*
- The Nazca Lines, a massive series of anatomically correct drawings of monkey and spiders, are believed to have been created by an ancient race of highly advanced third-graders
- Machu Picchu — *Most architecturally advanced city in nation*
- ✕ Joint CIA/CCD covert operation
- Cuzco — *Disney acquired rights to turn this city into souvenir shop*
- *Coffee Stains Of The Gods*
- ✕ Saryitupiac wine and spirit guides
- Souped-up alpaca some rich girl's getting for her 16th birthday
- ✕ Summer home of Aguirre, the Wrath of God

An ancient ice mummy holds an unidentified object.

HISTORY » MACHU PICCHU ABOUT NOTHING

475 B.C. The invention of mass transit finally provides massive Andean orchestras with a place to loiter.

A.D. 1489 The Incas complete an advanced network of interconnected roads, only to discover that they haven't invented the wheel yet.

1532–1820 Millions of Peruvians spend nearly 300 years drawing inspiration for a stirring ballad about the pain and woe of living under brutal Spanish rule.

1821 With no other options, Peru is forced to declare its independence from Spain in Spanish.

1840 The discovery of massive amounts of phosphorus-rich bird guano grosses everyone out.

1968 Years of military rule results in the traditional practice of handing control of the nation to the most heavily armed person to one's right.

1995 Voters overlook President Alberto Fujimori's obvious moral failings and propensity for corruption and elect him to a second term, as they are badly in need of a decent cajón player.

Machu Picchu

A SOON-TO-BE-FORGOTTEN PEOPLE »

Following in the footsteps of their advanced and mysterious Inca ancestors, modern Peruvians live in crumbling, roofless structures with dirt floors covered in broken pottery.

Today, citizens use the same roads, often wear the same clothes, and, in times of desperation, even attempt to eat the same food left over by their ancient forefathers.

In fact, residents of Peru—who, like the Incas, never learned to read or write—mimic their ancestors so closely that most of them will likely wind up alone, in tattered clothes, and frozen in time on a high mountain pass in the middle of the Andes.

FACTS » STANDING ON THE SHOULDERS OF ALPACAS

POPULATION
7 million four-piece bands

LANDMARKS
The ancient Inca city Machu Picchu serves as the ideal landmark to let travelers know that they have reached Machu Picchu

LAND USE
Falling down mountains (87%), Falling down hills (10%), Rehearsals (3%)

TRADITIONAL PONCHO
The poncho

IMPORTS
Drummers

EXPORTS
Drummers

FAUNA
Despite the obvious differences between the llama and the Dalai Lama, both are equally good at long-distance treks across treacherous mountains

LITERACY
87% of residents can adequately read tablature

Ecuador

» ECUADOR'S CAPITOL HILL.

Fleeting Survival Of The Fittest

The nation where Darwin first noticed evolutionary traits in animals, Ecuador is also home to millions of humans who over the years have had to adapt to the unfavorable conditions of their impoverished, politically unstable, lava-spewing environment.

A remarkable people who stagger upright but beg on all fours, Ecuadorians have developed the unique ability to subsist on just one meal per day. They have evolved extra-thick skin, powerful tear ducts able to handle days of uninterrupted grief, and large lung cavities that allow for deeper and more resonant world-weary sighs.

Ecuadorians have also developed an innate defense mechanism against their many natural predators—poverty, the government, other Ecuadorians, and life itself—which they fend off by curling their bodies into a small, impenetrable ball, or "fetal position," until it all goes away.

The most effective adaptation to protect against prolonged suffering in Ecuador, however, has been the gradual evolution of a much shorter lifespan.

Map labels

- × Site where depressed president ousted self
- × Mosquito that pities Ecuadorian humans
- × Nation's air force stuck in tree
- Man 104th in line for presidency hoping to become president tomorrow
- × Site of 1992 poncho-factory disaster
- × Conquistador corpse still killing locals
- × Real pumas made into awkward slippers
- × Toddler accidentally kicking over balsa-wood cabin
- ★ Quito
- *Just as imaginary as equator*
- □ Federally protected scenic-overlook plaque
- □ Sloth ghetto
- □ Capybara-hat factory
- × Probably a monkey here
- □ Mutant sloth that has learned how to use submachine gun
- □ Site of 1526 gold fever outbreak
- × Tourists going volcano spelunking
- Predominantly Roman Catholic population recognizes religious freedom, but chooses to ignore it
- × Giant Ecuadorian (5'6" tall)
- □ 1/6th of the world's bird population resides here above Speed-E-Carwash
- × Natives shoveling lava out of driveways
- ■ Earth's core visible at the bottom of this hole
- × In 1987, scientists here discovered an extinct papier-mâché volcano in the supply closet

FACTS NOT YET DESTROYED BY LAVA »

EXPORTS
Balsa wood, much of which is model-weapons-grade

EXPORT PARTNERS
U.S. (4.7%), Panama (1.9%), Peru (0.74%), hobby enthusiasts (93%)

INTERNATIONAL DISPUTES
Tried to privatize the equator

GDP
$5.62

TOURISM
Each year, thousands wait in long lines to look at the equator

MILK SOURCE
Capybara

MONKEYS THEY GOT
Howler, Spider, Woolly, Titis, Capuchin, Squirrel

INTERNATIONAL ORGANIZATIONS
Latitudes Across South America (founding and only member)

HISTORY » ALWAYS ERUPTING RIGHT WHEN YOU'RE TRYING TO HAVE A COUNTRY

A.D. 1532 The conquistadors capture Atahualpa, the king of the Incas, who tries to buy them off with a ransom. Atahualpa reaches high on the wall of a room five meters wide by seven meters long and offers to fill it once with gold and twice with silver. In addition, he holds his arms about one meter apart and promises to love them "this much." He is immediately executed.

Through the years, the tortoises of the Galápagos Islands have evolved protective instructional plaques.

1533 Ecuador's capital Quito is constructed. It is the second-highest capital in the world, and the last to be built in the crater of an active volcano.

1964 Texaco CEO Augustus C. Long becomes the first man to circumnavigate the Ecuadorians and claim most of the nation's oil.

1981 After an incident in the Amazon, oil executives claim the indigenous people were already on fire when they got there.

1997 The economy falters after all the balsawood reserves are blown just out of reach into the Pacific Ocean by a mighty El Niño breeze.

2000 The U.S. dollar becomes the official currency. Ecuador reveals its poor math skills when it accepts an exchange rate of two Ecuadorian U.S. dollars to every U.S. dollar.

2003 In the hopes of earning more tourism money, Ecuador names its line of longitude (78° W) "The Dissector."

2006 Ecuador's extremely partisan 13-party government finally settles a 1982 vote on where to order lunch from.

GALÁPAGOS » BIRTHPLACE OF EVOLUTION

Charles Darwin

Located 600 miles west of Ecuador, the Galápagos Islands are home to a vast array of unique species, as well as the tree that Charles Darwin was sitting under when a monkey fell on his head, giving him the idea for evolution.

SCIENCE » HOW ECUADORIANS WILL EVOLVE IN THE COMING YEARS

- ⨍ *Lava-resistant skin*
- ⨍ *Ability to sleep through earthquakes*
- ⨍ *Hand cupped in permanent "begging" position*
- ⨍ *Innate sense of impending misery*
- ⨍ *Rarely used, empty pouch known as "wallet" lost to evolution*
- ⨍ *Conditioned to fear humans*

Venezuela

» YOU'RE MORE THAN
WELCOME TO SHOVE
THIS FLAG UP YOUR ASS.

"Fuck Everyone"

Filthy rich with oil and led by a swaggering populist, Venezuela enjoys the unique, unbridled freedom to do whatever it pleases without fear of repercussion from any country.

Though Venezuela has exported oil for more than a century, it is only in the last decade, since Hugo Chavez took power and declared himself invincible, that the country has produced enough petroleum to be able to be assholes about it. In that time, Chavez has been an outspoken critic of American globalization, American foreign policy, American cheese, and the song "America" by Simon and Garfunkel.

An inspiration to oppressed people everywhere, Chavez's stirring speeches and stalwart defiance have inspired millions to rise up against their own tyrannical regimes before realizing that they do not possess 75.36 billion barrels of salable crude oil. Chavez also infuriates Western leaders by exposing their hypocrisy, decrying unfair economic practices, challenging them to arm-wrestling matches, and winning.

Then he sleeps with their wives.

Despite his achievements in foreign relations—namely daring nuclear powers to invade his country, and going on camping trips with the world's most reviled despots—Chavez is a polarizing figure. While Venezuela remains a free and open democracy, outright dissent is discouraged in no uncertain terms, usually 25 years to life. Still, Chavez has maintained a positive image among the country's impoverished citizens, mainly through his strategy of speaking too fast for them to understand, and guaranteeing universal suffrage in an undisclosed location for those who do not vote for him.

INTERNATIONAL RELATIONS » PRESIDENT HUGO CHAVEZ

President Hugo Chavez is known for his controversial behavior on the world stage. Below are some of his more memorable diplomatic strokes:

- *Called the Sistine Chapel painting "gay"*
- *Locked the Bahraini ambassador in the janitor's closet*
- *Sent 15,000 ladders to Mexico*
- *Placed scrotum on former UN Secretary-General Kofi Annan's keyboard*
- *Sprayed graffiti on Rwandan mass grave*
- *Didn't tell U.S. that Venezuela owns Citgo*
- *Stopped wearing pants at state dinners*
- *Skimmed several hundred million dollars from national oil profits*
- *Repeatedly shouted "penis" during OPEC meeting*
- *Supplied American troops in Iraq with body armor*
- *Spoiled season finale of* Lost *for French diplomats trying to catch up on DVD*
- *Got re-elected—twice*

PEOPLE » PUTTING THE "MASS" AND "HYSTERIA" IN "MASS HYSTERIA"

A lively and colorful people, Venezuelans are known for their impeccable sense of rhythm and their love for political coups. It is not uncommon for these vibrant and fickle partisans to take to the streets in large, screaming groups where they bang heartily on pots and pans, and sing loudly for their current leader's ouster.

Marching in unison and exciting one another with steady, vigorous chanting, their traditional day-after-disputed-election-day dance leads them down the town square, up the presidential palace steps, and through the broken-down door of their leader's private residence, culminating in his violent removal from power.

After the festivities are over—generally two weeks later, depending on the political climate and response time of the National Guard—Venezuelans return to their homes, tired, sore, and unable to remember exactly which government they helped install during their drunken delirium.

Local Festivities
Venezuelans celebrate the coming or going of a political leader.

HISTORY » A PROUD TRADITION OF SELF-SERVE LEADERSHIP

A.D. 1522 The Spanish Empire establishes its very first South American colonies in what is now Venezuela, fighting both stiff native opposition and a noxious black gunk that wells up out of the ground whenever someone tries to plant a flagpole.

1523 With a final tally of more than 300 eviscerated bodies, Fernando Goya is the victor in a friendly competition among Spaniards to see who can win the most hearts and minds of the native Arawaks.

1810 While Spanish overlords are busy repelling a French invasion of their homeland, Venezuelans form a

secret resistance movement so covert that it takes Spain more than a year to notice the widespread guerrilla attacks against it.

1811 Simón Bolivar, the great South American hero known as El Libertador, starts fighting anyone he can see with whatever comes into his hands, nearly exhausting the country's supply of broken bottles, gunpowder, knives, folding chairs, bats with nails in them, and knuckles.

1918 Venezuela discovers oil under a metal obelisk bearing a strange triangular logo and the incredible

price of $0.06 per gallon.

1924 The brutal and hated dictator Juan Vicente Gómez uses the newfound oil windfall to build up the country's infrastructure, mainly around his heavily fortified mansion in Maracay.

1948 Venezuela ushers into office its first democratically elected future coup victim.

1960 With a growing number of citizens enjoying nice homes and expendable incomes, Venezuela is at last able to create a distinct lower class.

1989 Millions of protesting Venezuelans let their car engines idle for days and drive very slowly, taking the longest possible route to a massive demonstration against a drop in global gas prices.

1998 Hugo Chavez is elected after writing an op-ed in the state newspaper promising to provide the poor Mestizo majority with "gasoline in every pot," proving to the world his incredible popularity with a largely illiterate populace.

2009 Chavez dies of a mysterious and sudden multiple-bullet-wound-related illness.

» SIMÓN BOLÍVAR

NOW UP TO $3.59 A FACT »

POPULATION
Roughly 25.7 million-ish

MAIN TRADING/SPARRING PARTNER
U.S.

MONKEYS THEY GOT
An infinite number sitting at desks with an infinite number of typewriters

ARTS
Several groundbreaking Elizabethan plays written by monkeys

EXPORTS
Petroleum, bauxite, harsh if clumsy rhetoric, more petroleum, oil, black gold, Texas tea, gasoline

IMPORTS
Lawyers, guns, money

NON-PETROLEUM ECONOMY
Cocoa, chocolate, coffee, espionage

CUISINE
Various corn-based pockets or shells filled with other stuff, but with a distinct Venezuelan flair

RELIGION
Roman Catholic (96%), Petro-Catholic (4%)

LIKELIHOOD OF U.S. INVASION
67% (2006 est.); rising 8% per annual dollar increase in price of oil

WILDLIFE
see MONKEYS THEY GOT, above

GEOGRAPHY » NATURAL BEAUTY

Angel Falls

A popular beach outside Caracas

Venezuela boasts incredible diversity: The Andes Mountains are dotted with spectacular oil derricks stretching as far as the eye can see. The Orinoco River, one of the continent's longest, is celebrated for its inky sheen and magnificent viscosity. The nation is also home to countless species of diesel-breathing fish, and an astonishing array of insects capable of skimming effortlessly across shimmering oil slicks. The dense black fur of many aquatic mammals can also be harnessed to power cars and buses.

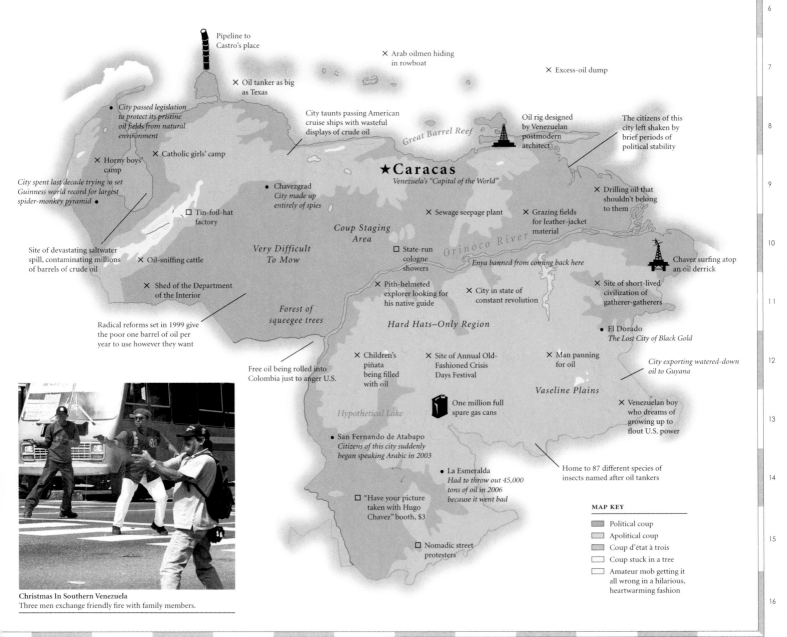

Pipeline to Castro's place

✕ Arab oilmen hiding in rowboat

✕ Excess-oil dump

✕ Oil tanker as big as Texas

● City passed legislation to protect its pristine oil fields from natural environment

City taunts passing American cruise ships with wasteful displays of crude oil

Great Barrel Reef

Oil rig designed by Venezuelan postmodern architect

The citizens of this city left shaken by brief periods of political stability

✕ Horny boys' camp

□ Catholic girls' camp

★**Caracas**
Venezuela's "Capital of the World"

✕ Drilling oil that shouldn't belong to them

City spent last decade trying to set Guinness world record for largest spider-monkey pyramid ●

● Chavezgrad
City made up entirely of spies

✕ Sewage seepage plant

✕ Grazing fields for leather-jacket material

□ Tin-foil-hat factory

Coup Staging Area

Orinoco River

Site of devastating saltwater spill, contaminating millions of barrels of crude oil

Very Difficult To Mow

□ State-run cologne showers

Enya banned from coming back here

✕ Chavez surfing atop an oil derrick

✕ Oil-sniffing cattle

✕ Pith-helmeted explorer looking for his native guide

✕ City in state of constant revolution

✕ Site of short-lived civilization of gatherer-gatherers

✕ Shed of the Department of the Interior

Forest of squeegee trees

Hard Hats–Only Region

● El Dorado
The Lost City of Black Gold

Radical reforms set in 1999 give the poor one barrel of oil per year to use however they want

✕ Children's piñata being filled with oil

✕ Site of Annual Old-Fashioned Crisis Days Festival

✕ Man panning for oil

City exporting watered-down oil to Guyana

Vaseline Plains

Free oil being rolled into Colombia just to anger U.S.

Hypothetical Lake

One million full spare gas cans

✕ Venezuelan boy who dreams of growing up to flout U.S. power

● San Fernando de Atabapo
Citizens of this city suddenly began speaking Arabic in 2003

Home to 87 different species of insects named after oil tankers

● La Esmeralda
Had to throw out 45,000 tons of oil in 2006 because it went bad

□ "Have your picture taken with Hugo Chavez" booth, $3

□ Nomadic street protesters

MAP KEY
▨ Political coup
▨ Apolitical coup
▨ Coup d'état à trois
□ Coup stuck in a tree
□ Amateur mob getting it all wrong in a hilarious, heartwarming fashion

Christmas In Southern Venezuela
Three men exchange friendly fire with family members.

Three Countries You Thought Were In Africa

GUYANA » WAS AT HALF-MAST
THE ONLY TIME IT WAS EVER
SEEN ON INTERNATIONAL TV.

SURINAME » IT'S JUST
A FLAG. IT HAS A STAR.
MOVE ALONG PLEASE.

Guyana
A History Of Exploitation And Colonialism Marred By Mass Suicide

When American cult leader Jim Jones decided his followers must join him in suicide in 1978, he forever transformed Guyana from a tiny country that most people assumed was in Asia or Africa into a nation forever associated with mass suicide and which most people still assume is in Asia or Africa.

The Republic of Guyana, despite being a perfectly normal South American country—with all the imperialism, economic piracy, and European misrule that the designation implies—will now always be known for the tragedy of Jonestown, which killed 909 followers, a U.S. congressman, and the world's appetite for fruit-flavored drink mix.

After this brief and unfortunate moment in the international spotlight, the Guyanese people quickly returned to their proud tradition of ethnic conflict, economic instability, and state-sponsored slavery.

A similar cult was brought here, but failed to commit mass suicide because the store was out of blue-raspberry-flavored Kool-Aid, and no one wanted to drink the disgusting lemon-lime flavor

CULT FACTS »

DISCOVERY
In 1498, Columbus mistook the coast of Guyana for Africa

MOTTO
"You don't have to be crazy to immigrate here, but it helps!"

RELIGION
Comparatively sane Christians, Muslims, and Hindus

NATIONAL SPORT
Like all other violently colonized former British holdings, cricket

DISPUTED BORDERS
Having had recent experience with the suicidally insane, is uneasy bordering Venezuela

LONE JONESTOWN SURVIVOR
Steve, that guy who doesn't like purple Kool-Aid

Jim Jones Memorial Lighthouse

Birthplace of the Guyanese Delta Blues *(three songs)*

✕ Great place for a city, but who has the time?

■ Man-eating-bat forest

✕ Forest cut down to house Christians

★**Georgetown**
1984 NCAA champions

✕ Only bathtub in country

✕ Former cult member unsure if it's safe to come out yet

✕ Berrylicious gravesite

✕ Kind-hearted, misunderstood anaconda

✕ Indian whose naked butt in a Scholastic filmstrip has delighted eighth-graders for generations

River name to be unveiled in 2012 ceremony

Country's natural resources kept neatly in bulk bins

Misunderstood Territory

✕ Border claimed by Bret Schumacher of Stevens Point, WI just to be an asshole

Area they wish Brazil would claim because it's just useless jungle anyway

Suriname
Why Read About Suriname?

The semi-tropical nation of Suriname is hardly even worth your time.

Suriname is the smallest country in South America, and has no soccer team to speak of. That is all you need to know about the nation of Suriname.

Please, there are five entire continents remaining in this book, each containing a cornucopia of fascinating histories and rich cultures. You are simply wasting your time here.

You know what? If you're really dying to know something about Suriname, buy a plane ticket and go there. If they even have an airport. We don't know, because we've been pretty busy writing the tens of thousands of words in this book dedicated to other, far more interesting places.

Paramaribo★
Not nearly as interesting as, say, Rome

Least Important Lake in The World

▲ MT. BAUXITE
(5,120 m.)

Turn The Page Already

Jungle?

More Jungle?

SURINAME FACTS »
MORE THAN YOU NEED TO KNOW ABOUT SURINAME

DISCOVERY
In 1498, Columbus took one brief look at Suriname and kept going

POPULATION
447,638 people who are probably interesting in their own way... Did we mention the 14 pages we wrote about the U.S?

INTERNATIONAL DISPUTES
The UN can barely maintain interest in Suriname's ongoing border conflict with Guyana

GEOGRAPHIC LOCATION
Flanked by Guyana and French Guiana, and a mere 124 pages away from Russia

LAND USE
85% of Suriname is unexplored and unmapped, which you are certainly welcome to do yourself, as you seem pretty interested in what is going on there

UNBELIEVABLY SAD FACT
You are still reading this

French Guiana
The Colony That France Totally Forgot It Still Had

French Guiana was rediscovered in 1994 when a part-time administrative clerk going through France's old files happened upon some dusty records of the South American colony.

The rediscovery brought to France a wave of nostalgia for a simpler time, when a European power was free to clear-cut an entire jungle in a foreign land and plop an offshore prison and rocket-launching pad right where native villages used to be.

Although French Guiana was once Paris' favorite colony, it got lost in the shuffle of the 20th century when France got caught up forming partnerships with other nations and became preoccupied by Germany, twice.

Realizing that it must have been decades since it had last seen the colony, and amazed that the government it had installed was still functioning, France has promised to never forget about French Guiana again, and has since begun looking for what else it might have left lying around the Southern Hemisphere.

Kourou Space Center
France knew it had put its space station somewhere, but just never thought to look in South America.

LAND BREAKDOWN

- Space stations: 3%
- Island prisons: 4%
- City of Cayenne: 3%
- Impenetrable jungle: 90%

Rainforest so dense it can only be penetrated by chainsaws

In 2005, French Guianese successfully sent a rocket to the middle of the Atlantic Ocean

✗ Rocket fuel made from pineapples

□ Rocket being carried off by monkeys

★ Cayenne

■ Yet-to-be-discovered species of flower that could potentially provide distraction from cancer

□ Federal Department Of Explaining That Nation Is Not In Africa

✗ Landfill of last-place trophies

✗ Single bird in sanctuary

✗ Site of future fallen-satellite tragedy

✗ Very savage form of snobbery

✗ Eiffel Culvert

✗ This right here—this belongs to France

✗ Seat of indigenous South American space program

✗ And so does this, along with everything else

■ Interior of jungle just getting into techno scene

Probably Snakes Here

✗ Site of the Baguette Revolt of 1966, 1971, 1984

✗ Further reading on French Guiana buried here for all eternity

✗ 40,000-acre Bastille prison (*never liberated*)

Border Ribbed For Brazil's Pleasure

FACTS » FRANCE'S AUSTRALIA

DISCOVERY
Columbus noticed the area in 1498, but failed to realize its equatorial position made it near-ideal for launching communications satellites into geosynchronous orbits

CURRENCY
The really shiny kind of rocks

POLITICS
A French Guianese diplomat has been given a seat on the floor of the United Nations

EMPLOYMENT BY INDUSTRIAL SECTOR
Rocket science: 50%
Twig collection: 50%

EXPORTS
Plot for the greatest prison-escape movie ever made

NATIVE PEOPLE
The Arawak and Galibi peoples were killed off, lest they develop competing commercial aerospace ventures

NATIONAL PRIDE
Once got to say "Liftoff!" after rocket-launch countdown

GREATEST SIGN OF FRENCH INFLUENCE
Remaining natives have been taught to look down upon their bone-pierced noses upon wild boars

SURINAME PEOPLE » YOU CAN'T SERIOUSLY STILL BE READING ABOUT SURINAME

Why do you insist on torturing yourself? You don't have to read every page in this book. Who are you trying to impress?

Surely by the time you get to the end of this paragraph, if you have any sanity left within you, your interest in the nation of Suriname will have been fully exhausted.

Still reading? Good God. Were you aware that England is on page 137, and that Australia can be easily found on page 231?

If reading about other countries does not appeal to you, perhaps you need to just stop reading altogether. Is there nothing on TV worth watching? The Discovery Channel must be showing something more informative than what you could possibly hope to gain from reading about the nation of Suriname.

Go take a walk in the park. Just get your mind off Suriname. Maybe go out for an ice cream. Enjoy your life. Just put the book down.

The president of Suriname is about as interested in the affairs of his country as you should be.

CULTURE » PERHAPS YOU WERE LOOKING FOR...

Eiffel Tower
See *FRANCE*, pg. 145

Taj Mahal
See *INDIA*, pg. 199

Overwhelming Squalor
See *AFRICA*, pgs. 61–114

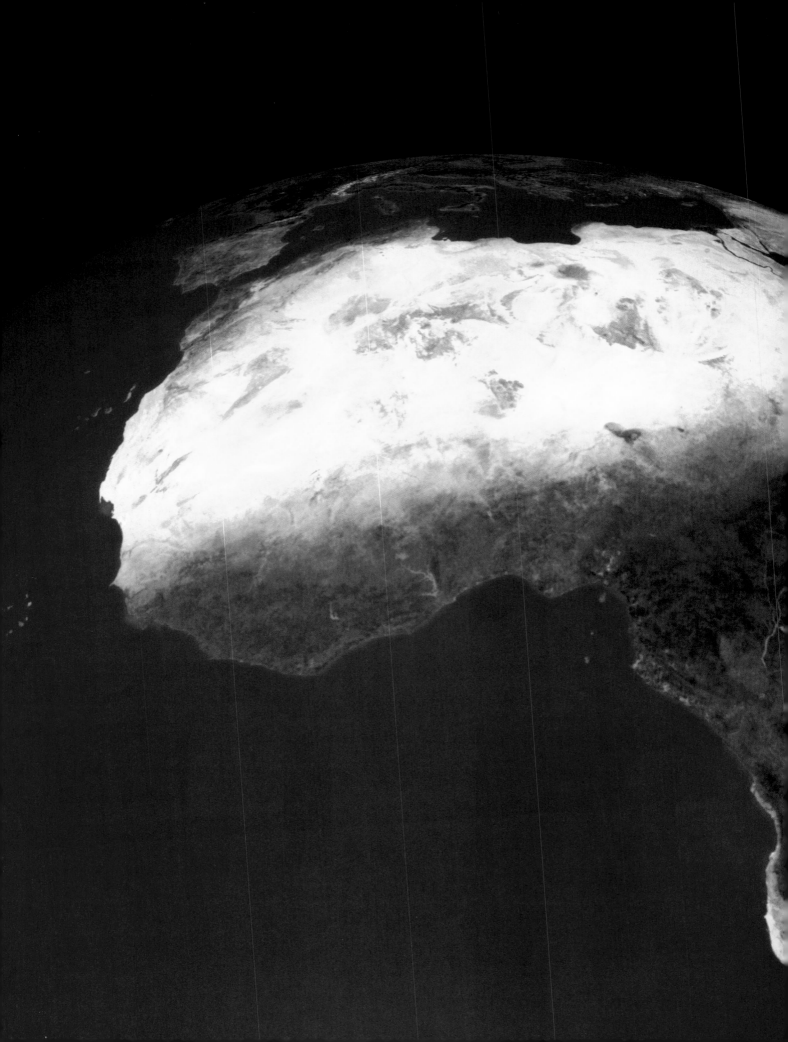

Africa

South Africa

A Bad Neighborhood

The citizens of South Africa fall victim to a serious crime every 17 seconds—a statistic that is nearly impossible to verify, as everyone in the country has his or her watch stolen every 12 seconds.

Although the violent crime rate in South Africa has steadily declined in recent years, there has been a corresponding surge in brutal crimes, ruthless crimes, savage crimes, and shoplifting. Carjacking is so common that citizens are warned not to drive, own, go near, or look at automobiles, and murder is so prevalent that citizens are urged to just kill themselves in self-defense.

Additionally, criminals have been advised that it is unsafe to commit crimes on major roads after dark due to the risk of more violent criminals coming along.

South Africa also has the highest incidence of reported rape in the world, with a rape occurring every 10 minutes, though embarrassed South African men say that it's usually more like every 15 minutes, and even longer when they haven't been drinking. In fact, the word "no" has little meaning in any of South Africa's 11 official languages, and the opposite meaning in at least seven.

In 1994, four decades of enforced segregation ended, dividing the nation racially into two groups: those who had benefited from apartheid and who were infuriated by the new drive toward equality, and overjoyed blacks. Sadly, while formerly oppressed citizens have recently been granted newfound freedoms, many are still forced to ride in the back of vehicles such as ambulances and hearses.

PEOPLE » SOMEONE WHO IS NOT BEING ROBBED OR MURDERED SHOULD DO SOMETHING

Three South African men acquire a new camera.

Waking each morning, at knifepoint, to the sound of his car alarm going off, the average South African begins the day by getting dressed for work, before being forced, at gunpoint, to immediately undress by an escaped rapist hiding in the closet. He then—bound, gagged, and tracking vast amounts of blood down the stairs—takes his three young children off to be kidnapped, remembering first to kiss his recently disemboweled spouse goodbye.

Despite this hectic schedule, however, most South Africans still manage to make it back home in time to be murdered for dinner.

FACTS » CRIME SCENE EVIDENCE

POPULATION
46 million culturally diverse victims

BIGGEST THREAT TO POPULATION
Self

NATIONAL PASTIME
Curling up into fetal position

TOP KILLING METHODS
No-look drive-by shooting, double-reverse homicide, vehicular mantorture

LEADING CAUSES OF DEATH
Gunned down in prime (56%), Murdered in sleep (32%), Died of old wounds (12%)

UNEMPLOYMENT
0% since 2002, when South Africa officially began recognizing carjacking as a legitimate profession

ECONOMY
$533.2 billion, the highest GDP in Africa by nearly $533.2 billion

MAP KEY

- 1–100 rapes per sq. mi.
- 100–1,000 rapes per sq. mi.
- 1,000–10,000 rapes per sq. mi.

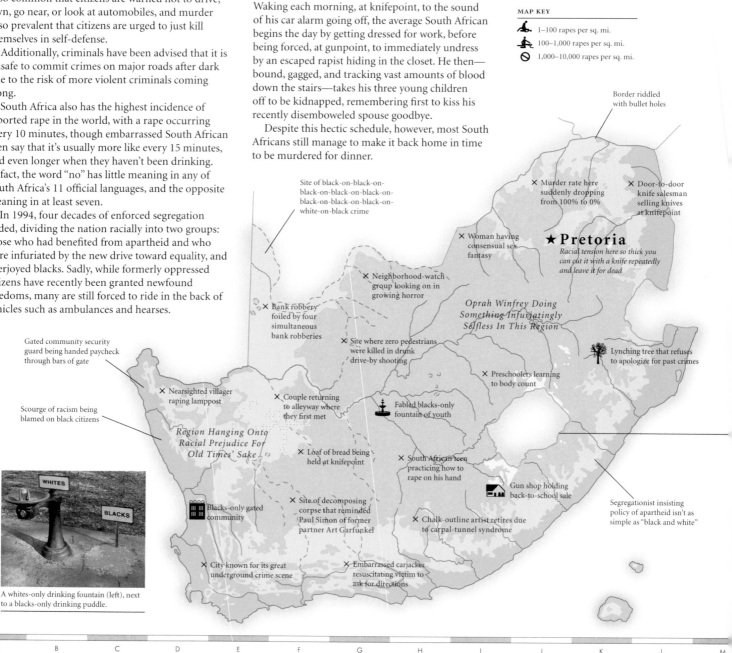

Border riddled with bullet holes

× Murder rate here suddenly dropping from 100% to 0%

× Door-to-door knife salesman selling knives at knifepoint

Site of black-on-black-on-black-on-black-on-black-on-black-on-black-on-black-on-white-on-black crime

× Woman having consensual sex fantasy

★ **Pretoria**
Racial tension here so thick you can cut it with a knife repeatedly and leave it for dead

× Neighborhood-watch group looking on in growing horror

Oprah Winfrey Doing Something Infuriatingly Selfless In This Region

× Bank robbery foiled by four simultaneous bank robberies

× Site where zero pedestrians were killed in drunk drive-by shooting

× Preschoolers learning to body count

× Lynching tree that refuses to apologize for past crimes

Gated community security guard being handed paycheck through bars of gate

× Nearsighted villager raping lamppost

× Couple returning to alleyway where they first met

× Fabled blacks-only fountain of youth

Scourge of racism being blamed on black citizens

Region Hanging Onto Racial Prejudice For Old Times' Sake

× Loaf of bread being held at knifepoint

× South African teen practicing how to rape on his hand

× Gun shop holding back-to-school sale

Segregationist insisting policy of apartheid isn't as simple as "black and white"

× Blacks-only gated community

× Site of decomposing corpse that reminded Paul Simon of former partner Art Garfunkel

× Chalk-outline artist retires due to carpal-tunnel syndrome

× City known for its great underground crime scene

× Embarrassed carjacker resuscitating victim to ask for directions

A whites-only drinking fountain (left), next to a blacks-only drinking puddle.

» POLICE LIONS WERE OFTEN USED TO QUELL CIVIL-RIGHTS DEMONSTRATORS IN SOUTH AFRICA.

LESOTHO » 40 YEARS OF INDEPENDENCE REPRESENTED HERE BY A POINTY HAT.

HISTORY » A LAND OF VERY, VERY, VERY STARK CONTRASTS

60,000 B.C. Fossils discovered in the smallest, dankest caves in South Africa suggest the prehistoric existence of *H. apartheidus*, a species of early man that was denied access to the same quality drinking streams, firewood, and rocks as *Homo erectus*.

A.D. 1480 Bartolomeu Dias, the Portuguese explorer responsible for naming most of the southern tip of Africa, travels east across the Cape Of Good Hope, the Cape Of Hope, the Cape Of Diminishing Hope, the Cape Of At Least It Can't Get Any Worse, and Port Fuck This Shit.

1867 A tribe of 20,000 Zulu warriors ambush British troops at night. Nearly 1,000 British soldiers are slaughtered, while the rest surrender in order to get a proper night's sleep.

1913 British government officials pass the Land Act, setting aside 90% of the country for white citizens, while black South Africans are left to divide up 80 square miles of cemetery space.

1948 South Africa implements the policy of apartheid, a four-decade-long system that forces the separation of logic from action, decency from conduct, and justice from consequence in the country.

1953 While initially prohibited from entering the same public restrooms as other South Africans, months of bitter struggle finally earn the nation's blacks the right to clean all toilets equally.

1954 A whites-only city bus refuses to stop for a black citizen, running the 45-year-old woman over in the middle of the street.

1960 Seventy black demonstrators are killed at the Sharpeville anti-apartheid demonstration for being seventy black demonstrators.

1964 Locked up in prison with some of the most progressive minds in the country, anti-apartheid advocate Nelson Mandela learns new, underhanded ways to perpetrate lasting social change, all the while dreaming of one day pulling off the biggest government job in South African history.

Nelson Mandela

1994 After 27 years of imprisonment, Mandela is freed and competes in South Africa's first truly democratic elections. Refusing to be put on the same ballot as a black man, rival candidates lose the election with 0% of the vote.

1996 As part of a widespread campaign for justice, civil-rights leaders charge a cedar tree with 14 counts of lynching.

1998 In response to skyrocketing crime, new gun-control laws are passed, requiring a seven-day waiting period between the indiscriminate murder of civilians.

2000 In light of growing cases of horrific infant rape, government officials launch a $12 million nationwide "Ba-Ba Means No" awareness campaign.

2002 A study finds that in 98% of South African rapes, the assailant is more often than not someone the victim knew from past rapes.

MAR. 11, 2007 South Africa uses up the last of its chalk reserves at a crime scene.

A blacks-only neighborhood during the height of apartheid.

Lesotho
South Africa's South Africa

Completely surrounded on all sides, and with no hope for escape, Lesotho's geographic location makes this small enclave extremely vulnerable to South Africa's economic policies, political developments, and crossfire bullets.

Lesotho was also negatively affected by South Africa's apartheid rule, as it fell within a whites-only district and the entire population was forced to leave the country for 40 years.

Although Lesotho is poor in resources, it is quite rich in poor people. Citizens rarely get paid, but when they do, they almost always immediately spend it on funerals for themselves.

In the late 1980s, several ska bands took up Lesotho's cause. That certainly did a lot of good.

PART OF A MOUNTAIN

Border surrounded by chalk outline

Half Of A Valley

Almost A Region

★Maseru
City knows full well it will never be the answer to a "Final Jeopardy" question

✕ Nothing worth mentioning

Not Even Close To Being A Wetland

✕ A South African man introducing himself to a Lesotho woman, and—oh, God, Oh God, no

Lesotho's own personal enclave

✕ Man who works 14 jobs and begs on the side

✕ Cute out-of-the-way place to get AIDS

A Whole Entire Honest-To-Goodness Administrative Division!

HISTORY »

The original inhabitants of Lesotho are now dead.

The nation of Lesotho (center).

FACTS » A SHITTY PLACE TO CALL THEIR OWN

LAND USELESSNESS
Pastures (64%), Agriculture (23%), Other (13%)

TOP INDUSTRIES
Placebos, artificial placebos

SOIL
Low organic content, but locals find it doesn't taste half bad

ENVIRONMENTAL ISSUES
Unrestricted human grazing

WATER ACCESS
No access to safe water (52%), Access to unsafe water (48%)

PREFERRED FORM OF COUP
Ousting

ECONOMY
Agriculture-based, though additional income made with paper route

RELIGION
Catholic (91%), Traditional disbeliefs (9%)

Swaziland

» THE SYMBOLIC SHIELD ON THIS FLAG REMAINS SWAZILAND'S SOLE PROTECTION AGAINST HIV.

» A TYPICAL SWAZILAND AIDS WALK.

Fighting AIDS With Bamboo Spears

The nation of Swaziland has the highest incidence of adults living with AIDS in the world (39.2%), as well as the highest incidence of adults dying with AIDS in the world (60.8%).

Home to 1,032,000 citizens, no condoms, and a single, shared intravenous needle, the crisis in Swaziland can be largely attributed to a culture of sexual promiscuity, with the average Swazi having at least half a dozen rape partners by the time she turns 18.

Lack of proper AIDS education is also to blame, as the nation's teachers take an average of 300 sick days each year, leaving their students to learn about prevention through trial and error.

In addition, many citizens still refuse to wear protection during sex, as they insist that contracting the deadly virus is something that only happens to 1 in every 2.6 other people.

One of the world's last absolute monarchies, Swaziland is ruled by King Mswati III, a millionaire playboy who has angered many with his plans to build luxury palaces for each of his 13 wives, and opulent roadside motels for each of his 17 mistresses.

However, progress has been slow, as the king is having difficulty finding construction workers who can stay alive for more than two weeks at a time.

FACTS » THE ONLY THING POSITIVE IS THE HIV

LEADING CAUSES OF DEATH
AIDS, having AIDS fetish

NATURAL HAZARDS
Human genitals

FAILED SUPPORT GROUP
AIDS Anonymous

LIFE EXPECTANCY AT CONCEPTION
One to two trimesters

AIDS AWARENESS
Wishes it were lower, in all honesty

LEADING EXPORTS
Bigger things to worry about right now

RELATIVELY WONDERFUL NEWS
Swaziland has diplomatic ties with Taiwan instead of China

POLITICAL PARTIES
All parties banned except for the King Mswati III Royal Fan Club

IS KING MSWATI CURRENTLY WEARING A SHIRT?
No

Map labels

× Child with father's eyes, mother's inability to sustain immune system

× Podiatrist's office slowly turning into AIDS clinic

Man contracting HIV despite wearing lucky condom

× WHO official covering ears and yelling "LALALALA!"

× Swazi woman waiting until after marriage to get AIDS

× Swazi man filled with hope—oh wait, no, that's not hope

× You don't even want to know what goes on here

Swazi resident becoming outcast after being diagnosed with herpes

★ **Mbabane**
The "Gaborone" Of Swaziland

× Site where complete abstinence has actually increased population growth

× AIDS quilt being used to cover the countless corpses

× Inspirational man dying suddenly from reasons other than AIDS

Region Where Reader Can Take A Deep Breath Before Moving On To Rest Of Map

× Lifespan here shorter than time it takes to get results back from the lab

× Man forced to use AIDS-awareness pamphlet as condom

Woman losing virginity, chances for survival

PEOPLE » LONG LIVE THE KING, AT LEAST

King Mswati

The Swazi people can be divided into three distinct groups: King Mswati III, his dozen or so wives, and the dead and dying. Ruling over the country for the past 22 years—or seven Swazi generations—Mswati is often accused of ignoring the deteriorating health of his subjects, a criticism the king has dismissed as nothing more than the nonsensical ramblings of AIDS-ridden minds.

For all of his neglect, Mswati does make a point of convening with all Swazis each year to choose a new wife. Standing before a parade of naked young maidens, Mswati picks his bride based not on shallow, skin-deep appearances, but rather on what each is like on the inside—specifically their white-blood-cell count, lymphocyte response, organ function, and immune-system strength.

The Grave
Swaziland's most effective tool in the fight against AIDS.

HISTORY OF AIDS IN AFRICA »

1981 Zoologist/recent divorcé Michael Gottlieb discovers the AIDS virus.

1984 Ugandan doctors have trouble diagnosing AIDS, as its symptoms— extreme weight loss, skin lesions, and fatigue—are the same as the symptoms of living in Africa.

1985 Botswana's attempt to raise AIDS awareness backfires when doctors administer all the nation's HIV tests with the same needle.

1986 UN humanitarian-relief workers refuse to bring medication to Uganda because of the myth that entering Africa can give you AIDS.

Jamal Rafiya

1988 After testing positive for HIV, promiscuous ladies' man Jamal Rafiya must call 30,000 women to inform them that they may have AIDS.

1990 An AIDS outbreak in Mozambique leaves 5-year-old Kafara Rabuwa parentless, sisterless, brotherless, uncleless, auntless, and dogless.

1995 Powerful new AIDS drugs are patented and approved for sale by

A B C D E F G H I J K L

Botswana

The Final Resting Place Of Botswana

Two decades ago, Botswana got the news that every nation dreads—it had contracted the AIDS virus and was given less than 35 years to live.

But rather than just give up, Botswana became a changed nation, devoting its remaining time on Earth toward getting its government in order, clearing up its human-rights record, and settling petty international disputes with its neighboring countries.

Knowing that it could not in good conscience succumb to AIDS in its current state, Botswana finally established that multiparty democracy it had put off for its entire history, and made a list of the 10 international peace summits it had always wanted to go to but never had the chance. With a renewed sense of purpose, Botswana paid off its public debt, found Jesus, Allah, and several indigenous gods, and for the first time listened—truly *listened*—to its national anthem.

In 2007, having become a stable democracy and a model republic, Botswana called in thousands of UN peacekeepers to ensure that the nation could now die in peace.

Map labels

- Herd of elephants putting little boy out of his misery
- Botswanan man passing away before he can finish writing list of 50 things he'd like to do before he dies
- Site of least-usable Red Cross blood drive in human history
- This city recently received a first-place AIDS ribbon
- Situation here so tragic and unfair, it'll leave you paralyzed for months
- Clean dildo exchange
- Child's doll orphaned by AIDS
- Residents here taught to dig graves at an early age, so they can be ready for when they turn 16
- Site of heart-curdling story
- Only remaining white blood cell in entire nation
- HIV-resistant man being shot in the head
- Woman taking antiretroviral medication for two
- Teen contracting AIDS out of peer pressure
- Used-condom shop
- Border fortified with extra-large condom
- ★**Gaborone** The "Mbabane" Of Botswana
- Site where Botswanan man realized his life was literally too short to complain about the brutal injustices of life

HISTORY » THE ROAD TO ACCEPTANCE

To say that Botswana was shocked by the results of its annual World Health Organization review in 1985 would be an understatement. After all, the young republic had never come down with anything more than an outbreak of malaria since statehood, and had been in a committed relationship with the same trading partner for the last 26 years.

For Botswana, AIDS had always been something that happened to other nations, like Uganda or Swaziland—nations that couldn't keep their borders closed every time a group of refugees came calling.

Convinced the findings had to be some sort of terrible mistake, Botswana spent months in denial, importing textiles and metal products like nothing had happened. Frightened of what the international community would think, Botswana kept the epidemic a secret for years, doctoring its 38% AIDS rate so it read 3.8%, and claiming that its tired and haggard appearance was only the result of a passing drought.

However, it wasn't long before denial turned to anger, with Botswana lashing out at the world around it—specifically Zambia to the north, Zimbabwe to the east, and Namibia to the west—before turning its rage inward in a violent civil war.

Although Botswana was eventually able to make peace with itself, the nation now admits that not a day went by that it didn't think about taking its own 1,765,000 lives.

Gaborone
AIDS relief workers hand out some much-needed supplies.

SAD FACTS »

LOCATION
Southern Africa (current)
A Better Place (destined)

GDP
$17.53 million, arranged to be bequeathed to longtime trading partner

HAS ALSO COME TO ACCEPT
Being landlocked

BIGGEST REGRET
Not spending more time with its 602,342 kids

SIGNED ACCORDS
Climate Change (2001), Do Not Resuscitate Orders (2005)

ECONOMY
Realized in 1992 that having an economy is not the key to happiness

---

the FDA, giving no hope to AIDS sufferers in Africa.

1998 AIDS victim Maiba Jamila, pregnant for the first time, wishes for a better death for her child.

2002 A survey conducted by South African researchers reveals that one in every three South African researchers has AIDS.

2003 AIDS deaths in Swaziland are now officially classified as "natural causes."

2004 32-year-old Botswanan HIV victim Mtumbe Ngoube wills himself to stay alive so he can celebrate one more World AIDS Day with his family.

2005 Flavored-condom use rises to nearly 95% in Zambia, as citizens regularly lick them to remember what a banana tastes like.

Namibia

» AN UNSPOILED HAVEN OF EXQUISITE BEAUTY, THE NAMIBIAN THORNVELDT WAS ONCE REFLECTED IN THE DREAMY LANGUOR OF ANGELINA JOLIE'S SOFT GREEN EYES.

A Lucky, Lucky Nation

From the Sossusvlei dunes where Brad Pitt once wiped his brow, to the incredible scenery in that city Angelina Jolie has mentioned a few times, Namibia is home to breathtaking coastlines, endless skies, and—for a brief, magical spell—the most stunning celebrity couple of our generation.

With a history as complex and captivating as the plot of 2005 blockbuster *Mr. & Mrs. Smith*, and a culture as diverse as the couple's recent string of acting roles, the Republic of Namibia is more than just the place where two of the biggest movie stars in the world visited: It's the place where two of the biggest movie stars in the world gave birth to their beautiful daughter, Shiloh.

Receiving its long-sought independence from South Africa in 1990—only 15 years before Brad Pitt himself would receive independence from Jennifer Aniston—and voting for its first democratically elected leader in much the same way the American public would vote for Angelina Jolie during the People's Choice Awards, the nation of Namibia has made *Girl, Interrupted*–sized strides in the last two decades.

Despite its many successes, however, the republic still struggles day to day with a number of problems, including continuing racial prejudice, an AIDS epidemic that kills three in every five citizens, and the immense void left behind by the all-too-soon departure of two of the most extraordinary human beings ever to grace the red carpet.

FACTS » DID YOU SEE THE PHOTO OF BRAD AND ANGELINA DOWN THERE?

LOCATION
Completely surrounded by Angola to the north, cornered by Botswana to the east, and left with no chance for escape by South Africa to the south

INDEPENDENCE
March 21 or 22 or something

NATURAL RESOURCES
Diamonds, gold, old sock left behind by Brad Pitt

INFANT MORTIFICATION RATE
High, especially during tribal festivals when their parents insist on dancing

TRADITIONAL MUZAK
Played while descending into mine shafts

TRANSPORTATION
Stuck, but waiting for Ndapewa to come with the truck to pull them out

MARITIME CLAIMS
Once saw Angelina Jolie in bathing suit

REFUGEES
11,900, not counting Steve, that guy they keep thinking is a refugee because he lives in a tent for some reason

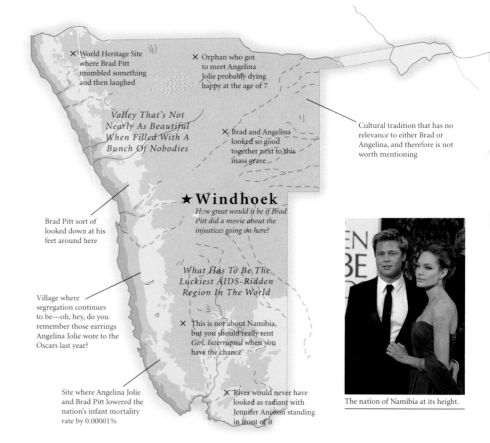

World Heritage Site where Brad Pitt mumbled something and then laughed

Orphan who got to meet Angelina Jolie probably dying happy at the age of 7

Valley That's Not Nearly As Beautiful When Filled With A Bunch Of Nobodies

Brad and Angelina looked so good together next to this mass grave

Cultural tradition that has no relevance to either Brad or Angelina, and therefore is not worth mentioning

★ **Windhoek**
How great would it be if Brad Pitt did a movie about the injustices going on here?

Brad Pitt sort of looked down at his feet around here

What Has To Be The Luckiest AIDS-Ridden Region In The World

Village where segregation continues to be—oh, hey, do you remember those earrings Angelina Jolie wore to the Oscars last year?

This is not about Namibia, but you should really rent *Girl, Interrupted* when you have the chance

Site where Angelina Jolie and Brad Pitt lowered the nation's infant mortality rate by 0.00001%

River would never have looked as radiant with Jennifer Aniston standing in front of it

The nation of Namibia at its height.

HISTORY » JUST SKIP TO 2006

Brad Pitt and Shiloh Jolie-Pitt

A.D. 1904 The Herero people take a stand against colonial Germans, drawing a line in the sand from which they refuse to retreat. Thousands of acres are quickly ceded moments later, however, when the wind picks up.

1908 Alluvial diamonds are discovered, bringing hope to Namibia, as they prove that water once existed in the country.

1912 Namibia is struck by what comes to be called "The Great Chronological Mix-Up Of 1854."

1919 South Africa is granted control of Namibia during the Treaty of Versailles, as it was getting pretty late and most of the other delegates had gone back to their hotel for the night.

1948 South Africa establishes apartheid in neighboring Namibia, ushering in an era where mirages of drinking fountains are segregated, and all black citizens are forced to ride in the back of camels.

1968 Namibia is officially recognized by the UN, although frequent mentions of the "Kalahari plains" and queries such as "How is Lake Ghanzi doing?" give the country the feeling that it's being mistaken for Botswana.

1969 Thirsty civil-rights groups riot in the hopes of having the country's only water hose turned on them.

1988 Delegates from the U.S. and U.S.S.R. meet to discuss the future of Namibia, but due to Cold War tensions spend most of the time standing around awkwardly.

1990 Namibia is granted independence, proof that avoiding violent conflict and going through appropriate UN channels can result in the declaration of basic human rights within 35 to 45 years.

APR. 2006 Just days after arriving in Namibia, Brad Pitt and Angelina Jolie boost the nation's GDP nearly 550% by tipping their waiter.

MAY 2006 Jolie gives birth to the first healthy child in Namibia's history.

Angola

Just Not The Same Without The Civil War

Ever since its 27-year civil war ended in 2002, the nation of Angola has felt a strange emptiness inside. This void, created by the lack of a brutal conflict, has left citizens with no choice but to sit back, reminisce about the glory days, and occasionally torture and murder one another for old times' sake.

Most Angolans long for the days of the 1970s, '80s, '90s, and early 2000s—a simpler time when people had clearly defined roles, like "kill," or "don't get killed," and when "fighting to survive" meant escaping enemy fire and hiding out in the jungle, not mining feldspar for 16 hours a day to make ends meet.

Nowadays, citizens don't even know how to pass the time without having rebel forces around to torture. With people no longer killing each other over the nation's oil and diamonds, many are left wondering, "What is the point of having natural resources at all?" And although famine, poverty, and disease are still rampant, before it was simply a reality of life during wartime. Now it's just sad.

Worst of all, Angolans fear that unless another conflict starts soon, their children will be forced to grow up in a world without war.

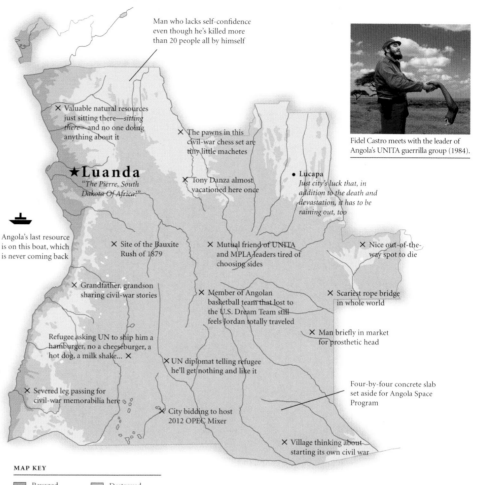

Man who lacks self-confidence even though he's killed more than 20 people all by himself

× Valuable natural resources just sitting there—*sitting there*—and no one doing anything about it

× The pawns in this civil-war chess set are tiny little machetes

★ **Luanda**
"The Pierre, South Dakota Of Africa!"

× Tony Danza almost vacationed here once

• Lucapa
Just city's luck that, in addition to the death and devastation, it has to be raining out, too

Angola's last resource is on this boat, which is never coming back

× Site of the Bauxite Rush of 1879

× Mutual friend of UNITA and MPLA leaders tired of choosing sides

× Nice out-of-the-way spot to die

× Grandfather, grandson sharing civil-war stories

× Member of Angolan basketball team that lost to the U.S. Dream Team still feels Jordan totally traveled

× Scariest rope bridge in whole world

Refugee asking UN to ship him a hamburger, no a cheeseburger, a hot dog, a milk shake... ×

× Man briefly in market for prosthetic head

× UN diplomat telling refugee he'll get nothing and like it

Four-by-four concrete slab set aside for Angola Space Program

× Severed leg passing for civil-war memorabilia here

× City bidding to host 2012 OPEC Mixer

× Village thinking about starting its own civil war

MAP KEY

▨ Ravaged	▨ Destroyed
▢ Devastated	▢ Tourist hot spot

Fidel Castro meets with the leader of Angola's UNITA guerrilla group (1984).

HISTORY » NOTHING TO FEAR BUT EVERYTHING ITSELF

A.D. 1490 Portuguese missionaries enter the region and successfully convert 50,000 Angolans to slavery.

1575 The Portuguese build the first-ever transatlantic slave pipeline, capable of pumping 1,700 Angolan slaves into Portugal each day.

1961–1975 Three Angolan guerrilla movements (UNITA, MPLA, and FNLA) win a 14-year war for independence so that they may fight a 27-year civil war in peace.

1975–1980 The first five years of the war simply fly by.

Jonas Savimbi

1981 A 4-year-old Angolan boy asks UNITA leader Jonas Savimbi why everyone keeps fighting. A speechless Savimbi wonders if the answer to war might lie in the innocence and purity of this child as he shoots it through the forehead.

1986 As Angola approaches the all-time record for Longest Uninterrupted Civil War, Savimbi denies speculation that the factions are continuing to fight only in order to break the record, saying "it was never about the streak."

1992 Civil war breaks out in Angola over the announcement that the civil war has ended.

1995 UN peacekeepers and Portuguese peacekeepers enter a bloody conflict over which side should get to restore peace.

2000 In honor of the war's "silver anniversary," Angolans use only machetes throughout the 25th year of conflict.

2002 Citing the horrible conditions, unfathomable poverty, and senseless violence, Angola's civil war flees Angola.

FACTS » COMPILED AGAINST THEIR WILL

POPULATION
13 million or so
(July 2007 guesstimate)

NATURAL HAZARDS
Potentially anything

LIMBS PER PERSON
3.2

LEADING CAUSES OF CIVIL WAR
Going to the market (36%), Crossing the street (29%), Making eye contact (15%), Receiving too much ice in one's drink (12%), Peace (8%)

MISS ANGOLA COMPETITION
Among the bloodiest beauty pageants in the world

INTERNATIONAL AGREEMENTS
Will stop asking UN to send it more food until it finishes that last carrot

LAND OF CONTRASTS?
No

PORTUGUESE LEGACY
Taught Angolans how to apply suntan lotion

PEOPLE » CIVIL WARRIORS

When the Angolans look back on their decades of continuous bloodshed, all they can do is laugh, as they are required by law to do so. Angolan history buffs have attempted to re-enact their country's civil war, but due to time constraints, most willing participants are unable to commit the 27 years necessary for an accurate portrayal.

Democratic Republic Of Congo

DEM. REP. OF CONGO »
TAKE ONE GUESS
AT WHAT THAT RED
SLASH REPRESENTS.

Like A Zoo You Get Killed At

The Democratic Republic of Congo has endured decades of brutal civil war, in which rebel forces have adopted the gruesome practices of raping women with machetes, decapitating babies, and even...they, they just...with their teeth, they... Jesus fucking Christ you don't want to know what goes on here.

Located in Central Africa, and home to...blood... blood in every goddamn direction—the Democratic Republic of Congo has left millions of citizens... with...their legs...they just hack them right off, for God's sake.

The site of an unending series of...an unending series of...for the love of fuck, why?! He's only 6 years old!

Each day, 1,000 people are killed by—no, not the eyes—not the eyes again—anything but his eyes—oh dear God, why won't someone do something?

In fact, they they they they they they they they they....they eat their victims' hearts! They eat them! They put them in their mouths and they eat them! Their hearts! They eat their hearts!

And while...so much fire...the UN has pledged... look at her throat—look at her goddamn throat... still the situation...please don't make them watch, please...continues to worsen.

Fuck. Fuck. Fuck the world. Fuck the fucking world.

Jesus Christ, put down the camera and go get help!

FACTS » HARD TO DESCRIBE IN WORDS, NUMBERS

POPULATION
For the time being

STANDARD OF
LIVING HELL
Extremely hellish

ENVIRONMENTAL CONCERNS
120 endangered species,
250 endangered ethnic groups

LANGUAGES
French (spoken),
Buglarrrrmhurg (spoken after tongue has been lopped off and mouth is overflowing with blood)

HUMAN RIGHTS ABUSES
Depends on whether you're counting from the neck up, the neck down, or just decapitations

SUFFRAGE
Women granted right to vote for which child lives by rebel forces in 2004

INTERNATIONAL RELATIONS
Bono upset that the DRC only seems to call when they need something

ADMINISTRATIVE DIVISIONS
Only national statistic that doesn't involve the brutal rape of ailing—fuck, never mind

POPULAR
CHILDREN'S GAME
Hopscotch to the death

BONOBO MONKEY
Sole living being in nation capable of showing love

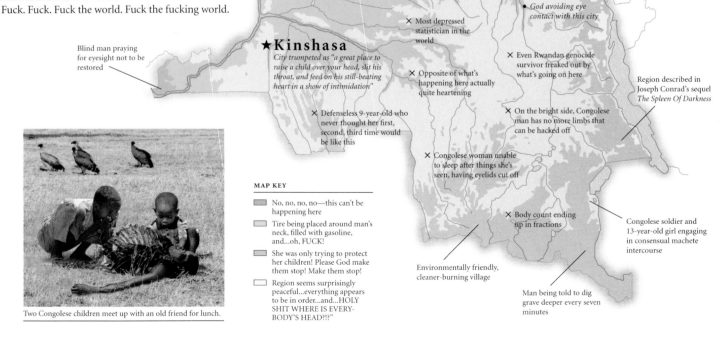

Home to world's most horrifying ventriloquist act

Woman being raped, or wait, maybe it's stabbed

Pretty flower growing out of skull hole

× Woman on fire accepting "World's Worst Nation" award on behalf of the DRC

× Congolese snob won't devour hearts not aged at least seven years

× Hell-bound Congolese man in a better place now

× Man coming home to find severed hand on couch

× Site where Michelin Man was stabbed 47 times

Exploitative rubber plantation somehow the best thing in this city

× AIDS-prevention program providing citizens with clean machetes

Region Completely Unfamiliar With The Concept Of Mercy

× This gorilla has seen enough

• *God avoiding eye contact with this city*

★ **Kinshasa**
City trumpeted as "a great place to raise a child over your head, slit his throat, and feed on his still-beating heart in a show of intimidation"

× Most depressed statistician in the world

× Opposite of what's happening here actually quite heartening

× Even Rwandan genocide survivor freaked out by what's going on here

Region described in Joseph Conrad's sequel *The Spleen Of Darkness*

Blind man praying for eyesight not to be restored

× Defenseless 9-year-old who never thought her first, second, third time would be like this

× On the bright side, Congolese man has no more limbs that can be hacked off

× Congolese woman unable to sleep after things she's seen, having eyelids cut off

MAP KEY

No, no, no, no—this can't be happening here

Tire being placed around man's neck, filled with gasoline, and...oh, FUCK!

She was only trying to protect her children! Please God make them stop! Make them stop!

Region seems surprisingly peaceful...everything appears to be in order...and...HOLY SHIT WHERE IS EVERY-BODY'S HEAD?!?"

× Body count ending up in fractions

Congolese soldier and 13-year-old girl engaging in consensual machete intercourse

Environmentally friendly, cleaner-burning village

Man being told to dig grave deeper every seven minutes

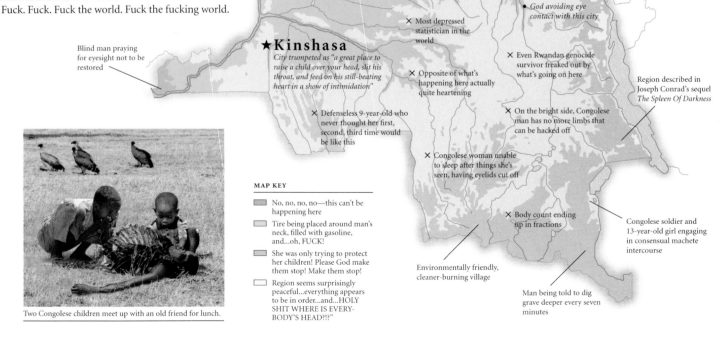
Two Congolese children meet up with an old friend for lunch.

REP. OF CONGO » TAKE ONE GUESS AT WHAT THAT YELLOW SLASH DOES NOT REPRESENT.

HISTORY » DO YOURSELF A FAVOR AND JUST TURN THE PAGE PLEASE

A.D. 1200 The sight of what appears to be small huts off in the distance lets migrating Bantu tribes know they are approaching a village, while the pain of tripping over the huts seconds later lets them know that not only have they already arrived, but that the village belongs to tiny Pygmy inhabitants.

1885–1908 Congo becomes one of Africa's richest and ripest states for exploitation, thanks to King Leopold of Belgium's revolutionary method of "taking."

1898 Congo is at the center of the worldwide Rubber Boom. The Michelin Man makes a diplomatic visit

to Kinshasa, where he burns down two villages, rapes 20 women, and enslaves half the population in a rubber plantation.

1944 The DRC supplies the U.S. with over 80% of the uranium used in the bombings of Hiroshima and Nagasaki. This upsets many citizens, who wanted to keep that resource and use it to put themselves out of their misery.

1961 Popular Congolese leader Patrice Lumumba is assassinated by the CIA, who could have sworn they heard "Patrice Lumumba," and not "John F. Kennedy."

1965 Belgium grants Joseph Mobutu independence.

1968 In attendance to watch the hanging of three

Mobutu

of Mobutu's cabinet members, 5,000 lucky spectators are brought up on stage and given the once-in-a-lifetime chance to participate in the event themselves.

1971 Mobutu renames the country the "Republic of Zaire," himself "Mobutu Sese Seko," and his dog "Mr. Ruffles."

1984 Mobutu re-elects himself in a landslide.

1989 The Congo figures that, it being 1989 and all, they should probably maybe build a road or something.

1996 Mobutu is overthrown by deranged serial killer Kenneth Burongo, a young

boy by the name of Dakari Hhu, a cross-dressing prostitute known only as "Roxy," and 12 of Mobutu's other multiple personalities.

1997 After being overthrown, Mobutu continues to work as a consultant to under-ravaged nations until his death.

1998 New president Laurent Kabila loses pockets of support when he vetoes the No Hacking Off

Laurent Kabila

People's Lower Limbs Then Setting Them On Fire Act.

2004 The UN sends a special tribunal to the DRC, as they cannot accurately judge whether or not machete rape qualifies as torture until they

see it in person.

2005 Let's just never, ever bring up what happened in the year 2005 again, shall we?

A rare uplifting scene in the DRC.

2006 An airplane crashes in the DRC, marking the most heartwarming event of the year.

2007 After 30 years of being subject to the whims of merciless dictators, the citizens ratify a new constitution that gives them full control over the kidnapping, raping, and massacring of themselves.

Republic Of Congo
At Least We're Not The Democratic Republic Of Congo

Democratic Republic Of Congo

The Republic of Congo, though not a perfect nation by its own admission, is always quick to point out that at least it is doing a heck of a lot better than the Democratic Republic of Congo.

Republic Of Congo
As is readily apparent, the Republic of Congo is way better off than the Democratic Republic of Congo.

Plagued by "only half" the amount of civil war as in the Democratic Republic of Congo, abject poverty that leaves "dozens less dead" than the abject poverty in the Democratic Republic of Congo, and a growing AIDS problem that's "small potatoes when compared to other countries, like, say, the Democratic Republic of Congo," the Republic of Congo regularly deflects alarm regarding national issues onto its neighbor to the east. Although, according to them, not nearly as often as the DRC does.

Despite civil war, poverty, and widespread disease, still better than movie *Congo*

Good luck finding a child with even one arm in the DRC

✕ Barely a mass grave

✕ Machete used simply for stabbing

□ Village actually not on fire by DRC standards

Woman who would have been raped an additional eight times had she been in the Democratic Republic of Congo

Home of overwhelmed Congolese social worker

✕ Unpopular uprising nobody showed up for

Brazzaville ★
Not to be confused with Brazzaville, Maine

Short, insecure anthropologist posing next to Pygmy villager for roll after roll of photos

FACTS » NOT SO BAD WHEN COMPARED TO CERTAIN OTHER AFRICAN NATIONS

POPULATION
3,750,332 (head count)
2,680,113 (hand count)
15,001 (leg count)

SEX RATIO
1.03 males/female

SEX RATIO DURING RAPE
7.03 males/female

ETHNIC GROUPS
Kongo (48%),
Sangha (30%),
Jews (Of course not)

GROSSEST DOMESTIC PRODUCT
Bantu fertility statues of guys with their gigantic hose-like members coiled up on their backs

NATURAL RESOURCES
Offshore oil deposits, rather than the big piles of corpses you get in You-Know-Where

TERRAIN
Not to rub it in the face of the DRC, but coastal plains in the north, basins in the south, and a central plateau

Zambia

» ZAMBIA'S FLAG IS LOCATED IN THE LOWER RIGHT-HAND CORNER OF THIS FLAG.

» THE U.S. SUPPLIES THE HUMOR-STARVED NATION OF ZAMBIA WITH SOME MUCH-NEEDED LAUGHS.

No Fat Chicks

In the early 1990s, the nation of Zambia received a shipment of used and unsold novelty T-shirts from the United States, and the hip new fashion trend quickly caught on with the irreverent, bare-chested citizens.

The nation immediately requested thousands more, and soon Zambians of all ages and devastating backgrounds absolutely had to have one. In addition to warmth, the T-shirts provide the Zambians with a chance to laugh at their growing AIDS epidemic, poke fun at the widespread famine that plagues the population, and see the lighter side of a 32.7-year life expectancy. In fact, some villagers find the shirts so humorous that they will often wear the same one for months at a time.

Whether receiving AIDS treatment in an "I Just Wanna Get Laid!" T-shirt, burying their two-month-old child while donning a "#1 Dad" shirt, or simply wearing a "Life Begins At 40" shirt, Zambian citizens are forced to develop a sense of humor to cope with their problems, as the international community provides them with no other means with which to do so.

Lusaka
Irreverent Zambian citizens are delighted by their new T-shirts.

EMPLOYMENT RATE BY OCCUPATION »

- 37% **Bikini Inspector**
- 25% **Muff Diver**
- 22% **Beer Hunter**
- 12% **Kegstand Champion**
- 4% **Breakdance Champion**

FACTS » THEY'RE REAL

POPULATION
11,477,411, and yet they seem to take no pride at all in the fact that it's a palindrome

CLIMATE
Sunny, dry, AIDSy

RAINY SEASON
July 21

RELIGION
The one with the man made out of bread

STANDARD OF DYING
Excellent

ENVIRONMENTAL AGREEMENTS
Signed Kyoto Treaty as a joke

MAJOR INFECTIOUS LAUGHS
Mtumbe Ngoube's *Degree Of Risk*: Very high

EXCHANGE RATE
1 Zambian dollar equals −5,000 U.S. dollars

PRINCIPAL METHOD FOR HERDING CATTLE
Stick

REASON FOR HOPE
Although one out of six Zambians has AIDS, five out of six do not

HISTORY » SHIT HAPPENS

A.D. 1851 Queen Victoria renounces her crown and hacks her way through the Zambian jungle. There, she hunts to survive and raises 12 children. Though seven are lost to malaria and three to lion attacks, she nevertheless carves a living out of the bush and earns the respect of the native tribes. Thus the majestic waterfall near her hut was named Victoria Falls.

1928 Zambians discover extensive copper deposits in a region known as the Copperbelt, making them wonder why they hadn't thought to mine in the oddly named territory years earlier.

1961 UN Secretary-General Dag Hammarskjöld dies in a plane crash in Zambia. Investigators confirm that the crash was caused by his name.

1993 After a failed coup attempt, the government declares a state of emergency, causing the citizens of Zambia to run around in circles while screaming and flailing their arms for nearly three months.

2002 The government refuses to accept donations of genetically modified corn to help alleviate the famine facing 3 million citizens, saying they "heard that kind of stuff isn't good for you."

2003 A nationwide hunger strike conducted in an attempt to end Zambia's food shortage goes largely unnoticed.

2004 A Zambian cafeteria becomes the site of the shortest food fight in recorded history, at 0.7 seconds.

The Buffalo Bills were a dynasty here

For your own sake, we are going to just go ahead and say that everything is fine in this village

Starving residents here aren't helping their situation, as they frequently devour what little food they acquire each year

✕ Man living on $1 a lifetime

✕ Worst weatherman in the world predicts rain every day

Sacred trench ✕

✕ Man who wishes the U.S. made ironic novelty pants, shoes

☐ Geographic center of hopelessness

Africa's only trampoline ✕

✕ Englishman with handlebar mustache and rifle

☐ Institute For The Development Of A Sandwich

✕ Events taking place here in 2003 proved that, yes, lions can contract HIV

✕ Nation spent $38 million in foreign aid to straighten out this border

☐ AIDS clinic mirage

Sad-looking hole ✕

★ **Lusaka**
City unanimously elected Pedro as mayor in 2006

✕ Lucky man who doesn't like the taste of water

✕ Exhausted refugee at last finding escape from Angolan, Sierra Leonean, Rwandan, Namibian, and Sudanese civil wars

MAP KEY
- ▢ Starving
- ▢ Famished
- ▢ Hungry
- ▢ Could go for some food, yeah

Thanks to a U.S. clothing donation, Zambian resident Abale Kuanda is the hippest guy in this ditch.

Zimbabwe

Driven From A Land That Was Wrongfully Theirs

Once a great and sprawling protectorate, where white settlers lived peacefully off the profits of the land, took only what was needed for complete luxury, and used every last part of the slaves that roamed the resource-rich horizon, the nation of Zimbabwe fell victim to independence in 1980.

For generations, the noble Europeans governed freely, carving out small, extremely affluent lives for themselves, with the men leaving early each morning to hunt for miners, and the women gathering nursemaids, cooks, and other domestic servants from the fields. Soon, large gated communities blossomed, and the traditions of the land, such as subjugation by race, were passed into law.

Unfortunately, as with all British colonies, it was not long before this idealistic utopia came under attack.

In 2000, hostile forces bent on justice, equality, and consequence invaded the racially divided territory, driving thousands from their second, and sometimes even third homes, often for no reason other than the want of adequate shelter.

Despite a unified effort by the whites to resist the encroachment of brutal sovereignty, only a few relics—namely abandoned mines, the titles given to prominent cities and geographical features, and a sociopolitical legacy of economic disparity and racial tension—remain of their once ubiquitous presence.

Each year, many whites are forced to flee Zimbabwe with only their most prized possessions.

RECLAIMED FACTS »

LAND USE
Agriculture (9%),
Violent racial clashes
(91%)

MOST WIDELY MISUSED FARMING IMPLEMENT
Pitchfork

FARMER'S TAN
Darker than it used to be

RACIAL DISCRIMINATION
Blacks still twice as likely to be pulled over while driving their tractors

GOVERNMENT TYPE
Mugabean

CROPS
Cash Crops:
Cotton, corn, coffee
Spare-Change Crops:
Wheat stems, peanut shells, corn husks

RECENT GOVERNMENT RULINGS
White-supremacist groups in Zimbabwe must now include at least two black members

Yet another place named after Queen Victoria

Site of Battle Of Samuel M'Bengule, in which 10,000 British troops engaged and eventually overran local famer Samuel M'Bengule

✕ White farmer losing entire life's earnings to rightful owner

★ **Mugabe**
Capital city renamed in 2006 (formerly "Robert Mugabe")

✕ President Mugabe granting himself executive power to do whatever he pleases

Morally Speaking, Situation Here Actually Pretty Complicated

✕ Site of heinous black-on-box-of-cupcakes crime

✕ Wrongs of the past being righted by slightly less wrongs of the present

Cecil Rhodes Memorial Whipping Post

✕ White family slowly being run out of 3-million-acre property

▲ MOUNT MUGABE (12,034 ft.)

✕ 83-year-old President Mugabe somehow winning in this high school's student-government elections

✕ White residents being forced to flee nation aboard private jets

✕ Farmland being awarded here to last remaining citizen not on fire

MUGABE VALLEY

Mugabe Drainage Basin

✕ President Mugabe appointing wooden spoon to head up investigation on president's sanity

MAP KEY

- Region crippled by economic crisis
- Region crippled by economic turmoil
- Region offering to sell map key for $2.99

HISTORY »ALL RHODES LEAD TO INEQUALITY

A.D. 1830–1870 White settlers cultivate the land with the aid of simple tools, such as bayonets, muskets, and ethnic intimidation. The agricultural practice of stealing farms is popularized.

Cecil Rhodes

1889 Diamond magnate Cecil Rhodes establishes the British South Africa Company, a mail-order business that promises to deliver anything within Zimbabwe's borders in just six to eight weeks.

1898 After raping the land of all resources, Rhodes has modern-day

Zimbabwe named after himself. The country is known as "Giant Asshole" for the next eight decades.

1900 Rhodes trademarks the concept of greed.

1922 White minority rule is established, promising a government "of some people, by some people, for some people."

1936 Black resentment continues to grow, with many oppressed citizens accusing The Man, His Wife, and Their Children of keeping them down.

1950 Civil-rights movements rise up

across Zimbabwe and stagger off to their newly designated living areas.

Robert Mugabe

1980 Pro-independence leader Robert Mugabe poses as an unpsychotic, anti-dictatorial, non-bloodthirsty activist who does not wish to brutally rule the country with an iron fist for the rest of his life, and wins majority black control for Zimbabwe.

2000 Demanding that decades of racial injustice and inequality

be corrected at once, Zimbabwe resident Mtumbe Ngoube refuses to quiet down until he receives fifty cents for the bus.

2002 Many suspect voter fraud after Mugabe wins a second term in office during a non-election year.

2005 Food shortages spread across Zimbabwe, as black farmers admit to having little agricultural experience outside of cursing dejectedly at the land.

2007 Mugabe is elected to his third consecutive life term as president.

Malawi

» A MALAWIAN MAN WEAVES A COUNTERFEIT ONE–KWACHA NOTE IN ORDER TO BUY A MEAL.

Come For The Food Shortages, Stay Because You've Died

Of the 10 poorest nations in the world, Malawi is the least rich. Unable to afford even the most basic necessities, citizens often beg for leftover table scraps from neighboring countries. However, much to their dismay and suspicion, Zambia, Tanzania, and Mozambique always seem to be "plumb out" of food.

Statue Of Poverty
"Give us your tired, your poor, your huddled masses, they will fit right in."

The primary way in which Malawians make money is by hand, using crochet hooks and carbon-fiber thread to fashion a replica of their currency, the kwacha. If proper time and care is put into the handicraft, a Malawian can make up to one unusable kwacha per day. A single fake handmade kwacha is worth $0.00 USD, which is slightly more than an actual kwacha is worth. The average yearly income for a Malawian is one-half of zero kwacha.

While some Malawians rely on subsistence farming for survival, a majority of them rely solely on subsistence subsistence.

PEOPLE » SHH! THEY DON'T KNOW THEY'RE POOR!

The people of Malawi may not have a lot of money, and they also may not have their health, their family, friends, religion, arable land, fulfilling careers, literacy, capable leaders, ways to pass the time, or cable, but they also do not have love. And that's the most important thing that they do not have.

FACTS » HELP A COUNTRY OUT

LOCATION
On spot where four different poverty lines intersect

LEADING INDUSTRY
Begging

NATIONAL ANTHEM
Outbid for rights to song in 1992

IMPORTS
Dimes, nickels, business cards, pocket lint, loose Tic Tacs

EXPORTS
IOUs

ECONOMY
Saving up for one

COST OF LIVING
One Malawian life

UNEMPLOYMENT BY SECTOR
Not working (32%), Out of work (43%), Ain't got no job (25%)

ADULT MORTALITY RATE
100%

LITERACY
Nah

A HISTORY RICH IN DESTITUTION »

A.D. 1721 Malawi hosts only the most serious British slave collectors for their first-ever slave auction. However, the nation is forced to use all the money it made to repurchase the slaves, as they were Malawi's only source of population.

1919 Hundreds of poor Malawians leave the country in search of the Great Malawian Dream. Success stories include Mtumbe Ngoube, the scrappy and persistent beggar who arrived in Namibia in 1923

and, by 1937, had achieved over 19 square meals. Many Malawian skeptics, however, dismiss the story of Ngoube as "mere legend," alleging that things such as meals do not exist outside the realm of folklore.

1970 34-year-old Dr. Hastings Kamuzu Banda declares himself President For Life, and rules Malawi for the next three years.

1973 Due to rapid inflation, Malawians begin using cheaper, more affordable bicycles as their main mode of transportation, shelter, health care, clothing, food, water, and education.

1994 Much to the frustration of the World Bank, Malawi attempts to pay off its entire $32 billion debt in pennies.

2006 American pop star Madonna attempts to adopt a 13-month-old Malawian boy, but is denied custody after international officials deem the streets of Malawi to be warmer, more attentive parents than Madonna and Guy Ritchie.

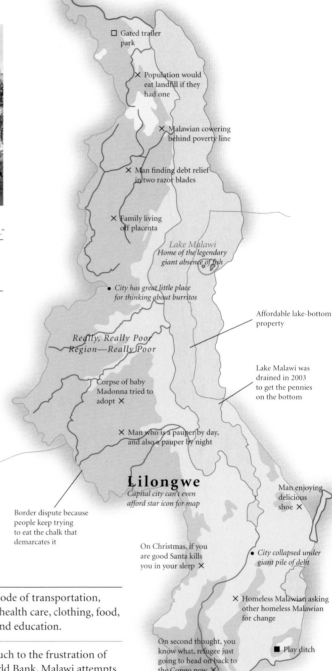

□ Gated trailer park

✕ Population would eat landfill if they had one

✕ Malawian cowering behind poverty line

✕ Man finding debt relief in two razor blades

✕ Family living off placenta

Lake Malawi
Home of the legendary giant absence of fish

● City has great little place for thinking about burritos

Affordable lake-bottom property

Really, Really Poor Region—Really Poor

Lake Malawi was drained in 2003 to get the pennies on the bottom

Corpse of baby Madonna tried to adopt ✕

✕ Man who is a pauper by day, and also a pauper by night

Lilongwe
Capital city can't even afford star icon for map

Man enjoying delicious shoe ✕

Border dispute because people keep trying to eat the chalk that demarcates it

On Christmas, if you are good Santa kills you in your sleep ✕

● City collapsed under giant pile of debt

✕ Homeless Malawian asking other homeless Malawian for change

On second thought, you know what, refugee just going to head on back to the Congo now ✕

■ Play ditch

✕ Hand-to-mouth existence causing man to gnaw off both of his hands

Mozambique

From Rags To Tatters

Once the poorest country in the world, Mozambique was sick, hungry, and down to its last 37 cents in 2006, when all of a sudden, this down-and-out nation came into a million dollars in foreign aid almost overnight.

Mozambicans always claimed that if they ever struck it rich, they would use the money to finally get that national infrastructure they always wanted, buy new huts for all of their relatives, and even donate a portion of it to needy African children. However, as soon as that first humanitarian-aid check rolled in, the entire nation immediately quit their jobs and blew half their winnings on an extravagant night on the town in northeast Africa.

Soon, the suddenly rich Mozambicans stopped cultivating their crops and started importing all their meals from fancy French countries. They then spent all the money they allocated for paving their dirt roads on one giant Hummer H2, and attempted to fill up the Zambezi River with champagne.

In 2007, they used their last $50,000 to construct a solid-gold bank.

After this brief period of unprecedented wealth, however, Mozambique now has no job prospects, no agriculture, no opportunities, and is currently praying for another miracle windfall from the international community to help pay off its recently acquired $1 million debt.

FACTS » HOPING MADONNA PICKS THEM NEXT

GEOGRAPHIC COORDINATES
18°15' S, 35°09' E; nation plays them every week in lottery

ECONOMY
Sold in 2007 for hot meal

LOWEST POINT
Trying to convince UN that its aid check never arrived

STUDENT-TO-TEACHER RATIO
10.4 million to zero

EPIDEMIC/PANDEMIC RATIO
2.4 epidemics per pandemic

BIGGEST REGRET
Way it treated other African nations when it was wealthy

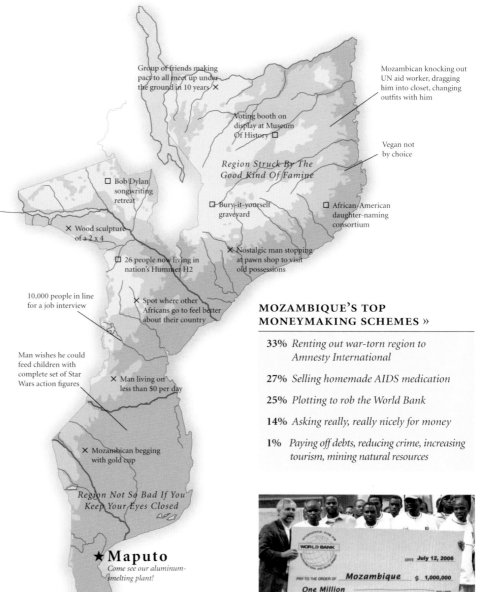

Group of friends making pact to all meet up under the ground in 10 years ×

Mozambican knocking out UN aid worker, dragging him into closet, changing outfits with him

Voting booth on display at Museum Of History □

Vegan not by choice

Region Struck By The Good Kind Of Famine

□ Bob Dylan songwriting retreat

□ Bury-it-yourself graveyard

□ African-American daughter-naming consortium

× Wood sculpture of a 2 x 4

□ 26 people now living in nation's Hummer H2

× Nostalgic man stopping at pawn shop to visit old possessions

10,000 people in line for a job interview

× Spot where other Africans go to feel better about their country

Man wishes he could feed children with complete set of Star Wars action figures

× Man living on less than $0 per day

× Mozambican begging with gold cup

Region Not So Bad If You Keep Your Eyes Closed

★ **Maputo**
Come see our aluminum-smelting plant!

MOZAMBIQUE'S TOP MONEYMAKING SCHEMES »

33% *Renting out war-torn region to Amnesty International*

27% *Selling homemade AIDS medication*

25% *Plotting to rob the World Bank*

14% *Asking really, really nicely for money*

1% *Paying off debts, reducing crime, increasing tourism, mining natural resources*

The citizens of Mozambique four hours before completely blowing their humanitarian-aid check.

HISTORY » LEFT FOR DEAD BY PORTUGAL

A.D. 1498 Hundreds of European explorers flock to the eastern coast of the Southern African nation after Bantu tribes introduce their new "Discover Mozambique" tourism slogan.

1926 The Portuguese institute the colonial policy of "assimilation," in which a Mozambican is given the opportunity to obtain the same legal status as a Portuguese citizen by learning the language, converting to Christianity, becoming white, and having been born in Portugal.

1975 Portugal grants Mozambique independence, then leaves with all the country's money, crops, soil, and furniture.

1985 The nation is torn apart by Communism, anti-Communism, civil war, landmines, AIDS, typhoons, droughts, famine, and general bad luck.

1988 Upon arriving in the disease-ridden, impoverished, war-torn nation of Mozambique, horrified Christian missionary Stephen Downy converts 20,000 villagers and himself to atheism.

Mtumbe Ngoube

1992 During the worst drought of the century, Mozambican Mtumbe Ngoube doesn't go to the bathroom for 243 straight days.

1999 After Joaquim Chissano wins the presidential elections, losing candidate Afonso Dhlakama denounces the results as "completely fair," condemns the vote-counting process as "accurate and precise," and contests the election, calling it "an affront to our corrupt system of democracy."

2006 Mozambique's public education system fails for the 163rd straight semester.

Madagascar & Mauritius

MADAGASCAR » USED TO HAVE FLAG, BUT THE LEMURS ATE IT.

MAURITIUS » THE FIRST NATION TO COME OUT OF THE CLOSET.

Madagascar
Ruled By Lemurs

The fourth-largest island in the world, the nation of Madagascar came under control of its lemur population in 1965, when the highly intelligent prosimians gained a majority of seats in the national senate.

Since then, these pint-sized nocturnal mammals have reduced poverty and homelessness by nearly 65%, restored the economy with their policy of storing nonperishable foods during autumn in preparation for the long winter ahead, and passed the country's first universal health-care bill, which they signed with the help of their opposable thumbs.

In 2005, the Madagascar Aeronautical Association successfully sent a lemur to the top of the nation's highest tree.

Lemur school that refuses to teach evolution

Thumb-sized lemur mini-village

Lemur using large tail to help him balance the budget

Local with GDP stuck to fur

Nature documentarians preserve

Sacred wrestling grounds

Mayor napping in shrub

★**Antananarivo**
Capital city clearly named by a lemur

Room full of lemurs with typewriters drafting constitution

Economy eaten by lemur in 1983

Film *Madagascar* computer-animated on location here

First new racquetball courts built in 15 years by lemurs

Human senator overcome with anger, contempt, resentment at being forced to work with lemurs

President beating smaller lemur with executive branch

Racist southern lemurs

Owima Grrrhooo
Madagascar's president and chief nut gatherer.

MAP KEY

- Lemurs ratifying new constitution that allows for greater civil freedoms among all citizens
- Lemurs indoctrinating new fiscally responsible campaign-finance reform
- Lemurs shrieking at a nearby owl

FACTS » CHECKED BY LEMURS

POPULATION
According to a 2005 census, "many" lemurs

LEMURS IN BUSINESS SUITS?
Plenty

ENVIRONMENTAL CONCERNS
Lemurs running country

JUSTICE SYSTEM
Based on British Common Law and the indiscriminate throwing of feces

ECONOMIC CHALLENGES
Attempting to solve nation's debt crisis while picking fleas from the coats of their young

Mauritius
An Island Nation, Not A Disease

Mauritius is located in what scholars refer to as "the good part of Africa"—a small region lying over 1,000 miles away from the African mainland.

Although geographically considered part of Africa, Mauritius is quick to point out that it has a stable democratic government, zero poverty, racial harmony, and a noticeable lack of blood-soaked dictators waving machetes around and chewing on monkey drumsticks. Mauritius nonetheless maintains friendly relations with other African nations, which is easier to do when you're not around them all the time.

With one of the world's fastest-growing economies since the 1980s, Mauritius continues to attract foreign investors using 30-foot-tall letters made of rocks, seashells, and driftwood on the beach. In recent years, the country has decreased its dependency on sugar production due to a fluctuating market and rowdy teenagers switching their entire sugar exports with salt.

Man who affectionately refers to own nation as "Maury"

Oh God, not another boatload of Sudanese refugees...

Every year, Mauritius wisely moves three inches farther from Africa

A whole shitload of bauxite that no one knows what to do with

Visiting Ugandan diplomat clearly here to ask for money

This part truly as far from Africa as you can get

★**Port Louis**
City is sick and tired of Mali always calling and asking to borrow $7 billion

Island still bitter that it was not mentioned in the 1990s board game "Geografacts"

Some rube who's never been off Mauritius

Transpacific telephone cable connected to tin can

Neighborhood bar the last Dodo was known to frequent

WILDLIFE » THE DODO

In the 1600s, the Dodo, a three-foot-tall flightless bird native to the island of Mauritius, was killed off by Dutch settlers. Although the Dodo was commonly depicted as a sluggish, overweight, and unintelligent animal, historians now believe these traits actually belonged to the people who hunted the helpless bird to extinction.

FACTS » PART OF AFRICA, NOT BY CHOICE

PREFERRED CONTINENT MEMBERSHIP
Asia

LAND USE
100% used for island

LIFE EXPECTANCY AT BIRTH
2 mainland African lifetimes

GOVERNMENT
Rocked by continual bouts of stability

COMMUNICATIONS
All incoming calls from Africa screened

FAVORITE GEOGRAPHICAL PHENOMENON
Continental drift

IMMIGRATION RATE
232%, as refugees from 12 different African nations have tried to flee to Mauritius in past year

Seychelles & Comoros

SEYCHELLES » THE FLAG OF SEYCHELLES LIKELY USES A COMBINATION OF TWO OR MORE OF THESE COLORS.

COMOROS » THEY CRAMMED AS MUCH ISLAM AS THEY COULD INTO THAT CRESCENT.

Seychelles
Definitely Possibly A Country

The republic, principality, or kingdom of Seychelles lies off the coast of Africa, we think.

Made up of a number of regions, as well as several provinces, we're assuming, this island nation/archipelago is a land full of towns, villages, and probably borders. There are possibly many hills, and all of the islands are almost certainly surrounded by water.

Judging from its name alone, we are going to go ahead and say that Seychelles was at some point colonized by France.

Today, its people are concentrated in the capital city, or maybe in its most populous city. In all probability, several of them might live in coastal areas, where fishing and other mercantile activities surely take place.

The people are poor, we will bet you anything.

FACTS » IF ANYONE IS INTERESTED

CLIMATE
We are guessing hot

RELIGION
Our money is on Christianity

EXPORTS
Goods

IMPORTS
Other goods that they don't already have

INDEPENDENCE
Let us say around 1960

AIDS
There can be no doubt

POLITICALLY STABLE?
Since no one has ever heard of Seychelles, probably yes

Seychelles?
We are going to go ahead and say that this is a school in Seychelles.

✕ Deposits likely here

Animals, right? ✕

Victoria ★
Judging by the star, probably the capital

Region Heavily Influenced By... Climate?

▲ MOUNTAIN or VALLEY

✕ Chief source of something or other

■ Grapes...yes, grapes sounds right

Strong Possibility This Part Exists

This Might Be A Bay

LAND

WATER

Or Maybe This Is A Bay

● Must be a city

AN OCEAN OF SORTS

Seems Like This Is An Island

Could This Be A Bay?

🛄 Let's call this an airport, shall we?

■ Natural resources?

There might have been a capital of an ancient kingdom around here once

Might as well be a coast

Comoros
By Estée Lauder

The Republic of the Comoros, or the "Perfume Islands," lies in a remote corner of the Indian Ocean, but vapors from its perfume distilleries and cologne refineries allow the nation to make a lasting impression almost a hemisphere away.

Despite being the world's leading essential-oil producer, Comoros' rich, full-bodied fragrance is not enough to cover up its unpleasant "poverty odor." With its scenic beaches and warm climate, Comoros has the potential to be a tourist hotspot, but every time a boat gets within 10 miles of the cloying islands, it immediately reverses course and tells other cruise lines to stay away.

Although Comoros has 29 billion tons of proven essential-oil reserves and produces over 3 million half-ounce barrels a day, nearly 80% of its GDP is spent on fancy glass containers for perfume bottling.

Comoros pumps more than 3,000 gallons of *Obsession* each day.

HISTORY » STINKS SO GOOD

A.D. 1510–1800 Arab sultans take over each island and rule them as separate kingdoms in a show of *Brut* strength.

1610 Comoros plays an integral role in the Old Spice trade.

1944 Comoros scientists develop weapons-grade aromas for France. However, when the French attack the invading Germans with the sandalwood gas, they find it relaxes the Nazis, relieving them of anxiety and healing their spirits. The Germans also develop their own gas called *Zyklon Beaches*, which has notes of mustard and anthrax.

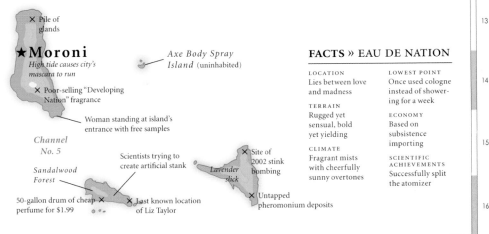

✕ Pile of glands

★ **Moroni**
High tide causes city's mascara to run

✕ Poor-selling "Developing Nation" fragrance

Woman standing at island's entrance with free samples

Axe Body Spray Island (uninhabited)

Channel No. 5

Sandalwood Forest

Scientists trying to create artificial stank

Lavender slick

✕ Site of 2002 stink bombing

✕ 50-gallon drum of cheap perfume for $1.99

✕ Last known location of Liz Taylor

✕ Untapped pheromonium deposits

FACTS » EAU DE NATION

LOCATION
Lies between love and madness

TERRAIN
Rugged yet sensual, bold yet yielding

CLIMATE
Fragrant mists with cheerfully sunny overtones

LOWEST POINT
Once used cologne instead of showering for a week

ECONOMY
Based on subsistence importing

SCIENTIFIC ACHIEVEMENTS
Successfully split the atomizer

Tanzania

» THIS LION HAS A BRIGHTER FUTURE THAN MOST TANZANIAN DOCTORS AND LAWYERS.

Please Don't Feed The Humans

The East African nation of Tanzania is home to Serengeti National Park, a sprawling wildlife reserve marked by potable rivers and streams, nourishing vegetation, and other basic necessities the country's human inhabitants can only dream of.

An endless savannah where elephants and zebras roam in peace and tranquility, eat multiple meals a day, and bathe regularly in the reserve's many cooling marshes, the Serengeti National Park has the longest life expectancy, lowest infant mortality, and highest literacy rate in all of Tanzania.

In addition, the park's strict ban on poaching and hunting has resulted in its wildlife population being shot at less frequently than many Tanzanian residents.

With the nation's citizens twice as likely to sleep without shelter as the average cape buffalo, and almost three times as likely to contract hoof-and-mouth disease as the average wildebeest, conservationists in 2007 confidently predicted which eastern African species would next go extinct.

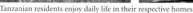

Tanzanian residents enjoy daily life in their respective homes.

Monkey hurling solid, healthy feces at sick man

✕ Mayfly with longer lifespan than most Tanzanian residents

✕ Citizens just assumed Lake Victoria was a mirage all these years

✕ Animal taking shit in nicer hole

Teen shoveling snow off Mt. Kilimanjaro for extra money ✕

✕ Once prestigious university now used as shelter by jackals during storms

✕ Woman would trade places with that hyena in a second

✕ Man holding knife up to zebra, asking it to give him all it's got

✕ Tanzanian accusing vultures of taking carcass for granted

✕ Starving man offering to finish whatever antelope doesn't want

✕ Gated chimpanzee community

✕ Train system built to facilitate elephant migration

Region Covered In Tacky Leopard Fur

Man forced to stand in line behind wildebeest to see veterinarian

✕ Lion's den with TV

✕ This one chimp hoarding all the AIDS medication in the nation

Freddie Mercury Memorial Bathhouse

★ **Dar es Salaam**
Capital single-handedly ruined life of 2006 World Geography Bee runner-up Katie Livick

Outer limit of range for Doctors With Very Specific Borders

A giraffe enjoys its second lunch of the day.

FACTS » WILD, UNPREDICTABLE

POPULATION 37,445,987 (estimate) 893,032,227 (complete fabrication) **LEADING CAUSE OF DEATH** Lion tipping	**PUBLIC ANIMAL HOUSING** 400-acre, two-story cages **MEDIAN AGE** *Male:* 17.5 years *Female:* 17.9 years *Rhino:* 49.2 years	**CUISINE** Pellets, leaves, scraps from wildebeest's dinner **JUSTICE SYSTEM** Law of the jungle/English common law	**ENVIRONMENTAL CONCERNS** Hippo, the one with the young infant you got too close to **TOP OCCUPATION** Guy who brushes animals' hair

HISTORY » THE CRADLE OF ZOOLOGY

A.D. 1498 Portuguese explorer Vasco da Gama discovers Tanzania five times before realizing he's rowing in circles.

1871 Journalist Henry M. Stanley finds long-lost missionary David Livingstone near Lake Tanganyika and utters the famous phrase "Dr. Livingstone, I presume?" after easily identifying him as the only guy feverishly raping the land of all resources.

1905 Indigenous tribes rise up against German occupiers, empowered by a "maji" potion that allegedly turns bullets into water. Thousands soon die after being hit repeatedly in the head with water.

1960 Studying in Tanzania, primatologist Jane Goodall discovers that hungry chimps use twigs to lift termites out of their mounds—a finding that makes Ms. Goodall feel stupid for eating termites the other way this whole time.

1964 Zanzibar joins Tanganyika to form the United Republic of Tanzania, a name created by a team of Madison Avenue advertising consultants who wanted to capture both the "jungle exotica" and "spicy zing" of the region.

1965 Tanzanian zookeeper Mtumbe Ngoube makes his first of many popular appearances on NBC's *Tonight Show*, the most infamous one coming in 1971, when a red colobus monkey,

a lion cub, a baby elephant, and a crocodile all urinate on host Johnny Carson simultaneously.

1991 Zanzibar-born rock singer Freddie Mercury dies, and bequeaths all of his unused AIDS medication to his home country in his will.

1995 Tanzania is first mentioned in a World Health Organization report. The nation buys multiple copies to give to friends and allies.

Uganda

» IDI AMIN SPECIFICALLY REQUESTED THAT FLAG'S ROOSTER HAVE A MULTI-COLORED MOHAWK.

» UGANDA'S BLOOD-THIRSTY FORMER DICTATOR IDI AMIN PONDERS WHO HIS NEXT MEAL WILL BE.

No Child Left Alive

Home to the world's largest standing child army, as well as the world's largest crawling child army, the nation of Uganda puts hundreds of bite-size soldiers through rigorous toilet and military training each year.

Able to mobilize in just minutes, as long as there is someone around to help them tie their shoes, and capable of counting the number of civilians they've killed without getting stuck even once, Ugandan child soldiers are known for being ruthless in combat, and even worse when they haven't had their naps.

Unlike adult generals, who are often jaded by the death and destruction that surrounds them, child generals always look like they're setting a prisoner on fire for the first time, and are known for being filled with countless questions, including "Do you ever want to see your wife again?" and "Are you ready to talk, or should I shoot the other leg off, too?"

However, while many may look like perfect little angels, their parents and UN officials will be the first to tell you that most routinely get away with murder.

These pint-sized rebels are capable of blowing your head off in the most adorable little way.

Lord's Resistance Army

FACTS » YOU NEVER GROW OUT OF SENSELESS VIOLENCE

PREFERRED FORM OF COUP
Toppling

DEATH TOLL
$5.00

TOP SURGICAL PROCEDURE
Recapitation

MINOR INFECTIOUS DISEASES
Malaria cough, protozoal sniffles, African mono

MARITIME CLAIMS
Can almost see the ocean from here

UNEMPLOYMENT RATE
N/A; the guy in charge of keeping track was fired last week

INFANT CANNIBALIZATION RATE
4.2 babies/1,000 population

INTERNATIONAL DISPUTES
Uganda's child army claims Sudan's child army asked to see their rocket launchers and never gave them back

MILITARY BEDTIME
8:00 p.m. sharp

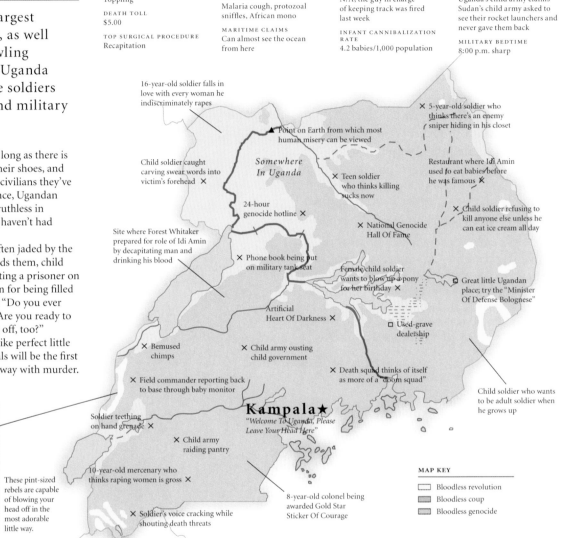

16-year-old soldier falls in love with every woman he indiscriminately rapes

Child soldier caught carving swear words into victim's forehead ✕

Somewhere In Uganda

24-hour genocide hotline ✕

Site where Forest Whitaker prepared for role of Idi Amin by decapitating man and drinking his blood

▲ Point on Earth from which most human misery can be viewed

✕ Teen soldier who thinks killing sucks now

✕ 5-year-old soldier who thinks there's an enemy sniper hiding in his closet

Restaurant where Idi Amin used to eat babies before he was famous ✕

✕ Child soldier refusing to kill anyone else unless he can eat ice cream all day

✕ National Genocide Hall Of Fame

✕ Phone book being put on military tank seat

Female child soldier wants to blow up a pony for her birthday ✕

☐ Great little Ugandan place; try the "Minister Of Defense Bolognese"

Artificial Heart Of Darkness ✕

☐ Used-grave dealership

✕ Bemused chimps

✕ Child army ousting child government

✕ Field commander reporting back to base through baby monitor

✕ Death squad thinks of itself as more of a "doom squad"

Child soldier who wants to be adult soldier when he grows up

Soldier teething on hand grenade ✕

Kampala★
"Welcome To Uganda, Please Leave Your Head Here"

✕ Child army raiding pantry

10-year-old mercenary who thinks raping women is gross ✕

8-year-old colonel being awarded Gold Star Sticker Of Courage

✕ Soldier's voice cracking while shouting death threats

MAP KEY
☐ Bloodless revolution
▨ Bloodless coup
▨ Bloodless genocide

HISTORY » UNINTERRUPTED VIOLENCE EXCEPT THAT ONE DAY IN 1986 WHEN EVERYONE FORGOT TO BE VIOLENT

A.D. 1877 The British arrive in the African kingdom of Buganda. They soon convert all their citizens to Christianity, exploit their copper and cotton resources, and take their "B."

1923 Newborn Idi Amin immediately proves to be a natural killer when he emerges from his mother's womb bloody but triumphant, moments after she dies of anemia and several deep lacerations of the stomach lining.

1954 Amin acquires the nickname "Dada." While scholars continue to dispute the nickname's true origin, many believe it was given to him by his 10-month-old son.

1972 Amin expels the nation's 80,000 Asian citizens, claiming the order to do so came to him in last night's dream. The following morning, Amin expels all of Uganda's dancing eggplants.

1974 Known for his pleasant disposition and charismatic presence, Amin charms the heads off thousands of villagers with his wit, humor, and chainsaw.

1979 Following his ousting, the governments of over 60 countries strip Idi Amin of his 2,459 war medals.

1983 Uganda launches an urgent tourism campaign to lure UN members to their nation. Slogans include "Visit Uganda Immediately," "Hurry, Come To Uganda—Time Is Running Out," and "Please, For The Love Of God Would Someone Travel To Uganda Right Now?!"

1987–PRESENT Over the course of 20 years, Uganda reduces its AIDS prevalence rate from 30% to single digits by sliding the decimal point one place to the left.

1992 The Lord's Resistance Army abducts thousands of children to serve as soldiers. However, the move backfires when the kids refuse to follow orders, constantly claim they "don't feel like killing anyone today," and continually have to be told that the AK-47 assault rifle is "not a toy."

2005 Leader Joseph Kony removes 150 kids from his LRA Child Army and forms the tragically short-lived LRA Child Air Force.

Rwanda

» THE SUN REPRESENTS THE SAVAGE SLAUGHTER OF OVER 800,000 LIVES.

» SADLY, THE HOLLYWOOD FILM *HOTEL RWANDA* HAS DONE LITTLE TO IMPROVE THE NATION'S TOURISM INDUSTRY.

The Land That Time, Newsweek, And USA Today Forgot

Located in the furthermost region of many American minds, Rwanda fell victim to one of the worst tragedies in recent years when nearly one million citizens were slaughtered by their machete-wielding countrymen. The world's news agencies were quick to respond, however, reporting that Mountain Dew had introduced the "Big Slam," a revolutionary one-liter plastic bottle with a unique wide-mouth brim.

First brought to the world's fleeting attention in 1994, the conflict in Rwanda quickly became a lack of concern for international leaders and the subject of serious disregard among top UN officials. As no news of the growing crisis continued, however, UN peacekeeping chief Kofi Annan decided that the problem could be ignored no longer than several more years, and immediately began taking steps to pay little mind to the urgent matter.

Despite a small but vocal minority who decried the ongoing slaughter as "inhumane," "senseless," and "please, not my wife and children, I beg you," officials claimed that the situation in Rwanda could not be legally defined as "genocide," and that, in fact, a word had yet to be invented that could suitably summarize the unspeakable atrocities being committed in Central Africa.

Reports of the genocide eventually surfaced, however, briefly projected onto the retinas of thousands of Americans as they searched for the previous night's sports scores in the morning paper.

Even today, more than 10 years later, little of what happened in Rwanda is understood, leaving some to wonder how apathy on such a massive scale could have taken place, and the rest to wonder if they remembered to turn off the stove before leaving home.

News of this villager's death was overshadowed by an exclusive report on "New Summer Fashions."

PEOPLE » THOSE WHO ARE STILL ABOVE GROUND

The people of Rwanda can be divided into two different ethnic groups: the Hutus, originally farmers of Bantu origin, highly skilled in the use of sickles, hoes, and other sharp agricultural tools, and the Tutsis, nomads from Ethiopia, identifiable by their thinner noses, taller height, and—during the mid-'90s—the deep, foot-long gashes in their skulls.

Although comprising only 10% of the population, the Tutsis became the ruling elite, cruelly oppressing the Hutu masses, which they believed to be inferior and not even capable of organizing something as straightforward as the mass slaughter of all ethnic Tutsis within 100 days.

To this day, Rwandan scholars debate the events that led to the nation's frightening genocide. While Hutu historians argue that decades of ethnic repression, coupled with the fear of a restored Tutsi government, spurred the massacre on, Tutsi historians maintain that all Hutus belong to a subhuman race fully deserving of the subjugation and exploitation they endured. Hutu historians then commonly hack Tutsi historians to death.

MAP KEY

- Ignored
- Overlooked
- Discounted
- Accepted

National cache of parables

Horrific event that was unable to compete with news of exciting Doritos Cool Ranch contest

Maybe it's for the best that nobody ever heard about what happened here ✕

✕ UN emergency airdrop of Febreze and other odor-masking products made here in 1994

✕ Site where thousands of villagers were unceremoniously buried on page 27 of the *New York Times*

✕ Dig up these oddly shaped piles of earth to refute existence of God

★ **Kigali**
As seen on "The Evening News With"—oh, wait no, never mind

Happiest dog in the world

Pretty Much Just Bones

✕ Sadly, there is nothing more the world could not have done to help bring an end to the killings here

Permanent blood stains

Atrocity here eclipsed by Whitney Houston mega-hit "I Will Always Love You"

✕ Capacity-filled mass grave

✕ Subtle decapitation

✕ Hutu rebel just not putting victim's heart into slaughter anymore

Live Killings

✕ Great acoustics for screaming

✕ Innocent woman becoming Hutu groupie by force

✕ Girl coming between band of Hutu assassins

★ **Bujumbura**
Site of slaughter that spawned "Paul Is Dead And So Are 30,000 Others" conspiracy theory

Rehearsal Torture

Encore Hanging

✕ Washed-up Hutu performing ethnic cleansing on street corners

✕ Hutu politicians being booed off world stage

A Rwandan woman returns from her trip to a nearby stream.

BURUNDI » THE BURUNDIAN FLAG JUST *SCREAMS* GENOCIDE.

» WE'LL GIVE YOU ONE GUESS AS TO WHAT THESE SACKS ARE FILLED WITH.

» SOME OF THE OLDEST CITIZENS YOU'RE LIKELY TO FIND IN BURUNDI.

HISTORY OF THE 100-DAY MASSACRE » NEVER AGAIN, *AGAIN*

DAY 1 Armed with machetes and the terror of a renewed Tutsi administration, the Hutus begin their slaughter. They kill a disappointing 1,400 the first day.

Kigali
Four-year-old Ike Bafongo searches for his missing parents, so that he can kill them.

DAY 7 One week into their onslaught, many Hutus are suddenly struck by the utter senselessness of their actions, and begin to hack away at Tutsi civilians with two hands.

DAY 17 Nearly 1,000 Hutus die of exhaustion during the four-day Kigali massacre.

DAY 19 The Western world commemorates Holocaust Remembrance Day, confident in the knowledge that by recalling the horrors of the past, they can prevent future genocides from ever taking place.

DAY 20 A Tutsi family of eight helps to break in a brand-new ax.

DAY 25 After the savage murder of 35,000 Tutsis, many Hutus can't believe it's May already.

DAY 28 The United Nations immediately dispatches 300 excuses to Rwanda.

DAY 48 In a tersely worded message to the nation of Rwanda, the U.S. warns all Hutus to "pace themselves."

DAY 52 The nation's Hutus, increasingly irritated by the large number of Tutsi corpses that clog the streets and make navigating the sidewalks difficult, take out their frustrations on those Tutsis still alive.

DAY 57 After the deaths of more than 40,000 Tutsis, Rwanda experiences a brief, four-minute period of peace when crippling hand cramps force Hutus across the country to momentarily drop their machetes.

DAY 65 Speaking about the situation in Rwanda, UN peacekeeping chief Kofi Annan finally uses the term "genocide," and grudgingly pays Israel $0.75 in royalty fees.

DAY 70 A rough head count

Bill Clinton

reveals that nearly 80,000 Tutsis have been decapitated.

DAY 73 The world is left in a state of shock after the gripping season finale of the hit TV show *Frasier*.

DAY 88 The U.S. sends a commission of Guinness World Record officials into Rwanda to assess the situation.

DAY 97 Hearing that UN troops will finally be deployed to Rwanda, the nation's Hutus desperately try to piece millions of mismatched torsos and limbs back together.

DAY 99 About a dozen key machetes and major spears

are accused of committing war crimes and sentenced to life imprisonment.

DAY 100 U.S. President Bill Clinton, in a televised speech to the world, apologizes to nearly one million corpses for not having done more.

PROMINENT RWANDANS »

Playwright Oianiya Gima

Economist Kigeri Mulifi

Archaeologist Mutara Toto

Peace Activist Mtumbe Ngoube

Burundi
The Completist's Genocide

The Burundian genocide was one of the last genocides produced by the Hutus and Tutsis, the duo that perfected the art of mass slaughter in Rwanda. Although it was a fundamentally horrific massacre that drew heavily from their earlier work, critics claim that while the killing was there, the passion wasn't.

The tragedy in Burundi has, however, attracted a small cult following of scholars who took the time to really look into the genocide, and who call it an inspired, well-thought-out, and sublimely brutal collection of underrated mass killings. While it was not nearly as ambitious a project as the Rwandan genocide or the Jewish Holocaust, the Burundians were never out to change the world—just a few hundred thousand lives.

FACTS » A CRITICALLY PANNED GENOCIDE

CREDITS
Maalik Umbuto on AK-47, Dajan Rashidi on ax, Bongani Berko on M-16, and 850,000 guests on machete

ENGINEERED BY
Growing class-warfare hostilities

HONORS
Certified gold genocide with over 500,000 kills

CUSTOMARY TRAGIC PLANE CRASH
1994, claimed life of genocide frontman President Cyprien Ntaryamira

CINEMA
American filmmakers recently released a drama chronicling the genocide, entitled *Motel Burundi*

WHERE ARE THEY NOW?
Dead

SPECIAL THANKS
To the thousands of incredible Burundian men and women who sacrificed their lives to help make this genocide what it was

A REVIEW OF THE BURUNDIAN GENOCIDE »

A seamless blend of many different styles of violence, the genocide in Burundi is truly an unexpected surprise. While at first the cries of the starving and the screams of the tortured may sound a little jarring, after repeated listens, you simply will not be able to get them out of your head.

However, millions of people have yet to discover this lesser-known tragedy, despite pleas from countless Burundian civilians who strongly urged the international community to consider checking it out. Today, when most people hear about the genocide, they investigate it once, claim to "not understand it," and never return to it again.

Recently though, in news that has excited many genocide archivists, the Hutus and Tutsis have hinted at the possibility of getting back together to perform some brand-new atrocities at small, unannounced venues throughout the country.

International Honors
This framed, certified gold machete was awarded to the Hutus and Tutsis upon the death of their 500,000th victim.

Kenya

» IF FLAG IS BLOWING, IT USUALLY MEANS A GROUP OF KENYANS JUST RAN BY IT.

» KENYAN RUNNER MTUMBE NGOUBE IS OVERCOME WITH JOY AND RELIEF AS HE CROSSES KENYA'S FINISH LINE AND SETS A NEW WORLD EMIGRATION RECORD (17 YEARS, 24 DAYS).

Running 26.2 Miles From Their Problems

Kenya is a natural breeding ground for the world's top long-distance runners, who learn at an early age the art of running as far away as they possibly can from Kenya.

Although most of the world views marathons as the ultimate physical challenge, citizens say that running 26.2 miles is "nothing" when compared to the grueling Kenyan customs of finding out your blood transfusion was infected with hepatitis C, burying your wife and newborn son, or running 34.7 miles.

In Kenya, the true test of human endurance is the traditional three-month-long drought—a physically and mentally draining annual event that also causes severe dehydration, muscle deterioration, and toward the end, the intense feeling that one is about to die. But the lucky few who complete these droughts say it's worth it, as the only thing sweeter than the taste of victory is that of food.

Because of these harsh conditions, many modern-day Kenyans pack up their belongings and run to America in search of a better life. Most do not intend to become world-class endurance runners, but rather participate in such events for the free cups of water distributed at every one-mile checkpoint.

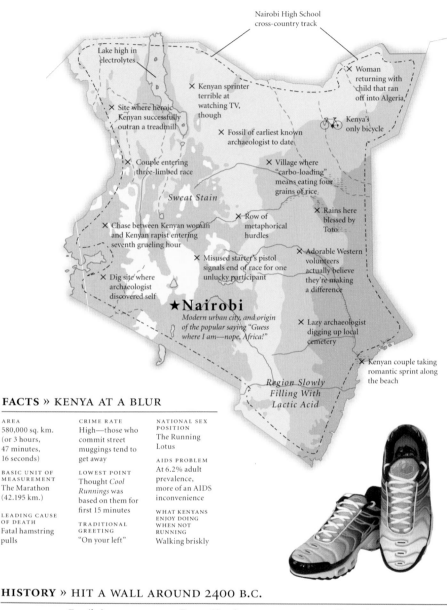

Nairobi High School cross-country track

Lake high in electrolytes

× Kenyan sprinter terrible at watching TV, though

× Site where heroic Kenyan successfully outran a treadmill

× Woman returning with child that ran off into Algeria

Kenya's only bicycle

× Fossil of earliest known archaeologist to date

× Couple entering three-limbed race

× Village where "carbo-loading" means eating four grains of rice

Sweat Stain

× Rains here blessed by Toto

× Row of metaphorical hurdles

× Chase between Kenyan woman and Kenyan rapist entering seventh grueling hour

× Adorable Western volunteers actually believe they're making a difference

× Misused starter's pistol signals end of race for one unlucky participant

× Dig site where archaeologist discovered self

★ **Nairobi**
Modern urban city, and origin of the popular saying "Guess where I am—nope, Africa!"

× Lazy archaeologist digging up local cemetery

Region Slowly Filling With Lactic Acid

× Kenyan couple taking romantic sprint along the beach

FACTS » KENYA AT A BLUR

AREA
580,000 sq. km. (or 3 hours, 47 minutes, 16 seconds)

BASIC UNIT OF MEASUREMENT
The Marathon (42.195 km.)

LEADING CAUSE OF DEATH
Fatal hamstring pulls

CRIME RATE
High—those who commit street muggings tend to get away

LOWEST POINT
Thought *Cool Runnings* was based on them for first 15 minutes

TRADITIONAL GREETING
"On your left"

NATIONAL SEX POSITION
The Running Lotus

AIDS PROBLEM
At 6.2% adult prevalence, more of an AIDS inconvenience

WHAT KENYANS ENJOY DOING WHEN NOT RUNNING
Walking briskly

PEOPLE » BORN TO RUN

A Kenyan woman shows off her Livestrong neck rings.

Though the people of Kenya are prolific endurance runners and athletes, scholars are split on the exact reason why. Some think it stems from the fact that walking is illegal in Kenya. Others point to genetics, noting that most Kenyans sprint out of the womb three months before they are due, dragging their mothers by the umbilical cord along the countryside until they get tired and slow down four or five years later. Still others, however, claim it's because they're black.

HISTORY » HIT A WALL AROUND 2400 B.C.

2,000,000 B.C. Fossils in Kenya provide evidence for the theory that very early in the hominid family tree, sprinters broke away from long-distance runners.

A.D. 1823 In one of the earliest known endorsement deals, American shoe company Nike offers 30,000 Kenyan slaves their freedom in exchange for wearing exclusively Nike-brand products. The slaves preserve their remaining shreds of human dignity by declining.

1933 Ernest Hemingway travels to Kenya, a visit which becomes the inspiration for 1933's *The Snows Of Kilimanjaro*, 1935's *The Barren, Scorched Plains Of Amboseli*, 1955's *Our Nightmarish Trip To The Corner Market*, and 1961's *Why It Is I Have Chosen To Take My Own Life.*

1974 Excessive carbo-loading results in a seven-year famine.

2001 Kenya's 5K Charity AIDS Walk fails to raise any awareness about the disease, as all participants complete it in under 15 minutes.

2006 Kenyan Robert Cheruiyot finishes in both first and fifth place in the Boston Marathon, as he completes his celebratory "victory lap" around the 26.2-mile course ahead of all but three other participants.

Somalia

» SOMALIA'S FLAG IS PRESENTLY ON FIRE.

» A SOMALI WARLORD SHOOTS DOWN A U.S. BLACK HAWK HELICOPTER.

A Forward-Thinking Post-Apocalyptic Nation

A super-progressive nation, Somalia realizes that the future will not bring cutting-edge technology or widespread peace, but a hellscape of desolate, famine-infested ruins controlled by rival warlords fighting over the rotting corpse of 21st-century civilization—and they have embraced that future.

The forward-thinking social engineers of Somalia have bypassed the Industrial Age, the Information Age, and the Utopian Age—the fruits of which they know will inevitably be obliterated in a nuclear holocaust or worldwide pandemic—and have instead focused on creating a society based on the every-man-for-himself, eat-the-children-to-survive mentality that will be commonplace in just a few short centuries.

Marked by barren valleys and smoldering streets dotted with frayed power lines, burnt-out hulks of vehicles, abandoned factories, flickering Coke machines, and other vestiges of the modern world, Somalia's geography bespeaks a rapid progression toward the kind of dystopia that once seemed eons away. With its advanced system of government (anarchy) and its cutting-edge unemployment rate (100%), Somalia is the bellwether of all future societies.

In fact, scholars claim that Somalia's capital, Mogadishu—one of the most sparsely populated, underdeveloped, war-torn settlements in the world—is the city after which all current metropolises will be modeled 60 generations from now.

FACTS » BRACE YOURSELF

LOCATION
Gabriel's Horn Of Africa

AVERAGE ANNUAL ASHFALL
35 cm.

GOVERNMENT
Roams empty hillsides on motorcycles

DIRTY ABANDONED BABIES PER SQ. MILE
12

FLIES PER DIRTY ABANDONED BABY
43

RELIGION
Other (100%)

ENVIRONMENTAL CONCERNS
Environment gone

LIFE EXPECTANCY AT BIRTH
10 days to Lastday

INTERNATIONAL ORGANIZATIONS
Kicked out of UN after continually revving motorcycle engine every time someone started to speak

HISTORY » BEST READ WITH EYES CLOSED

A.D. 1886 The British East India Company convinces Somali chiefs that they should be overtaken by England. Negotiations prove to be simple, as the Somali only know two words in the English language: "yes" and "sure."

1964 Somalia engages in a hostile border dispute with Ethiopia over a renegade banana found straddling country lines.

The beautiful skyline of downtown Mogadishu.

1970–1990 After assuming power in a bloodless coup, Somali president Siad Barre sets an elaborate scheme in motion, in which he reduces political freedoms, uses force and terror to consolidate his power base, oppresses ethnic clans, loots the national treasury, and incites a civil war that causes rebel groups to depose his regime and exile him to Nigeria—all in a selfish effort to finally escape Somalia.

1974 During a severe drought, every citizen in Somalia prays desperately for rain. Their collective prayers are answered all at once in the form of the worst flood in the country's history.

1989 Somali citizen Mtumbe Ngoube's quest to rid his nation of landmines ends abruptly at one.

1991 With Somalia in the midst of another drought, the UN deploys thousands of assure-them-everything's-going-to-turn-out-okay forces to the nation.

1993 A massive U.S. shipment of wheat to famine-stricken Somalia is met with anger and disbelief, as the U.S. *knows* that the people of Somalia do not like the taste of wheat.

2002 Rebel Somali motorcycle gang "The Thirsty Riders" seizes a mirage.

Warlord who got into warlording for all the wrong reasons

Africa's Funny Bone

✕ The kind of flaming wreckage a man can get used to

✕ Ford XB Falcon on cinderblocks

✕ This area not that ba—oh, dear God, no...

✕ No good restaurants here

✕ Helicopter crashing pad

Nice out-of-the-way place to hide under rubble and contemplate the injustice of the world

Nothing Left To Blow Up Here

✕ Kids using severed arm to poke at corpse they found

☐ Feral town

✕ Warlord just loves seizing things

✕ Somali man hiding behind pile of peacekeepers for safety

Man looting charred piece of cement ✕

Mogadishu★
Current location of Hell

✕ Corpse-drag races

✕ "Nuke Me" written in 20-foot letters made of rocks and skulls

Port Of No Return

MAP KEY

⌂ Hospital
⌂ School
⌂ Factory
⌂ Other

A Somali machine-gunner on lookout duty.

PEOPLE » HUMAN WASTELAND

The average Somali citizen can be identified by his or her prone, horizontal body, which is covered in infected scabs, skin lesions, and open wounds. Scholars say this is what most evolved humans will look like in 80 to 100 centuries, when the human race will have been long dead.

The average vertical Somali citizen is a dirty, mohawked, bone-nosed gunman whose traditional garb includes ammunition draped ceremonially across his bare chest, a metal-studded jockstrap worn on the outside of his assless chaps, and a single shoulder pad. These Somali warlords are responsible for maintaining lawlessness and disorder, as well as preserving the nation's high levels of isolation, starvation, infection, and constant feelings of impending doom.

Djibouti

Congratulations, You Just Laughed At Thousands Of Starving People

Known for its snicker-inducing name, the destitute nation of Djibouti occupies a strategic location at the mouth of the Red Sea, where giant ships carrying food, medical supplies, and other basic human provisions stop to refuel before embarking toward their true destination.

Living along one of the busiest shipping routes in the world, native inhabitants frequently attempt to escape their bleak homeland by sneaking onto transport ships under the guise of Djibouti's chief export. Unfortunately, many are regularly caught, as the average Djiboutian is far too emaciated to pass off as crew, but not quite emaciated enough to pass off as limestone.

In 2002, the U.S. opened a number of local army bases in preparation for its War on Terror, briefly giving hope to the nation's citizens who naively mistook "terror" to mean "rampant disease," "abject poverty," "senseless civil war," and "horror."

PEOPLE » ALMOST AS LIFELESS AS THE SHIPS

Life expectancy in Djibouti is 43.1 years, which may sound tragically brief, but in reality feels about 17 years too long. Ahmed Hassan, who celebrated his 52nd birthday last April, is the oldest living man in Djibouti, and a national treasure. Many gather around the slightly wrinkled wise man, whose long beard has recently begun to gray, to hear tales of a simpler time before 1975, when the abject horror and grimness of life didn't rush by so fast and there was time to pause and take in the smell of decaying flesh.

FACTS » NOT LAUGHING NOW, HUH?

LANGUAGES
None, as words cannot adequately express what citizens are forced to endure

LAND USE
Agriculture (0.04%), Military bases (11.4%), Searching for rock heavy enough to end cruel existence yet light enough to lift with frail limbs (88.6 %)

AGRICULTURE
Imagined

BIRTH RATE
39.53 births/1,000 population (2006 est.)

STILLBIRTH RATE
960.47 stillbirths/1,000 population (2006 est.)

UNEMPLOYMENT RATE
50%—quite low considering "not bleeding internally" is regarded as a full-time job

HISTORY » FROM FRAIL, DYING REPUBLIC TO FRAIL, DYING REPUBLIC

550 B.C. Western tribes journey hundreds of thousands of miles east across Africa in search of food, shelter, and safety. They finally stop at Djibouti, not because it contains any of those things, but because it lies at the continent's easternmost border.

A.D. 1917 After decades of watching ocean liners crash onto its shore, the nation of Djibouti finally decides to open a port.

1944 Following the success of *Casablanca*, film executives decide to shoot another major motion picture based around a large shipping port. Their plan, however, backfires when *Djibouti* premieres to criticisms of gratuitous violence, depictions of implausible drought, and a lukewarm love story between a man and the shallow grave of his former wife.

1968 Strongly influenced by neighboring nations, namely Somalia and Ethiopia, the Republic of Djibouti quickly becomes a land of infirmity, famine, and death.

Port Of Djibouti
Loaded with enough food to last a small nation nearly a year, this cargo ship is passing Djibouti on its way to France.

1973 The bodies of nearly 1,000 men and women finally find freedom from Djibouti after their fossilized remains are loaded into a transport ship in the form of fuel.

1985 Nothing you would enjoy hearing about.

2005 A lost Carnival cruise ship is forced to dock at the Port of Djibouti to refuel, bringing for the first time obese, middle-class Americans face-to-face with the underprivileged inhabitants of this small sub-Saharan country. The people of Djibouti quickly realize things could be much, much worse.

Kamala Guelleh
There is absolutely nothing you can do to prevent Kamala Guelleh from giving birth to her third consecutive stillborn child next week.

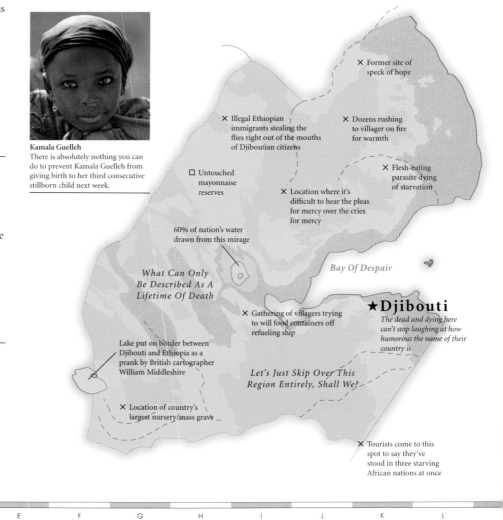

× Former site of speck of hope

× Illegal Ethiopian immigrants stealing the flies right out of the mouths of Djiboutian citizens

× Dozens rushing to villager on fire for warmth

□ Untouched mayonnaise reserves

× Flesh-eating parasite dying of starvation

× Location where it's difficult to hear the pleas for mercy over the cries for mercy

60% of nation's water drawn from this mirage

What Can Only Be Described As A Lifetime Of Death

Bay Of Despair

★ **Djibouti**
The dead and dying here can't stop laughing at how humorous the name of their country is

× Gathering of villagers trying to will food containers off refueling ship

Let's Just Skip Over This Region Entirely, Shall We?

Lake put on border between Djibouti and Ethiopia as a prank by British cartographer William Middleshire

× Location of country's largest nursery/mass grave

× Tourists come to this spot to say they've stood in three starving African nations at once

---

Eritrea

Going Through A Rebellious Phase

Eritrea, a gangly 15-year-old nation brought up by a single, abusive parent country in a terribly violent neighborhood, is still adjusting to its newfound independence.

Although it is being closely monitored by the UN—that good-hearted but ultimately ineffective guardian assigned to so many young countries—Eritrea is currently rebelling against every governing body that tries to tell it to eat better or to stop being lazy and get 50,000 jobs.

The nation is going through an adolescent Marxist stage, getting into bloody fights with its motherland, and receiving mixed messages about sex, drugs, and freedom of the press from the rest of the world.

Today, Eritrea, its landscape pockmarked by landmines, is fighting against the responsibilities of its freedom, hanging out with the wrong crowd, and desperately trying to understand its conflicting feelings—feelings such as ethnic confusion, religious unrest, a constant hunger that can't seem to be satisfied, and hair growing in places it didn't before.

HISTORY » THAT AWKWARD AGE

Eritrea has refused to open its door to foreign investors since 2005.

In 1993, Eritrea was sired by a mysterious, shadowy father-figure who breezed into the region, claimed to be some sort of freedom-fighting movement, seduced its mother Ethiopia away from the stern, unloving Derg regime, breached her defenses, and sowed the seed of baby Eritrea right there on the moonlit shore of the Red Sea, only to disappear soon after into the warm African night. He hasn't been heard from since, and some say this is just a romantic story Eritrea tells itself to make the nation feel better. Regardless, Ethiopia soon turned its back on young Eritrea, leaving no one to care for it.

Like many two-year-old nations, Eritrea was desperate to test its boundaries, and in 1996 the nation waged war with Yemen over control of the Hanish Islands. Yemen quickly put a stop to such behavior by calling The Hague, which agreed that Eritrea didn't really want the islands and was just looking for a fight.

Eritrea's 10th birthday finally saw some boundaries being established, when the Eritrea-Ethiopia Boundary Commission was established to draw an invisible property line across the Danakil Shield Plain.

Feeling slighted at not getting everything it wanted, Eritrea began covering its space with Communist posters and iconography, a trend it seems determined to follow in teenage fashion by acting out to even greater extremes every time someone points out how stupid it's being.

Today, Eritrea continues to wrestle with many enormous-seeming problems, including jealousy of its rich, spoiled, slightly older neighbor to the north, Saudi Arabia; its tendency to break international laws just to show it can; and

Mtumbe, one of Eritrea's troublemaker friends.

ongoing conflicts with such authority figures as Human Rights Watch, Amnesty International, and U.S. Ambassador Scott H. Delisi, who drops by unannounced and makes a big deal out of every little border skirmish like he's their father or something.

FACTS » SUPER LAME

POPULATION
None of your business, okay?

CAPITAL
Asmara for now, but Eritrea thinks the whole capital thing is just something everyone does because they think they have to

AREA
Experienced growth spurt in 2003 when boundary commission expanded border to include town of Badme

ECONOMY
Living on $3/week allowance from UN

MAJOR INDUSTRIES
Odd jobs during the summer

CUISINE
Eritrea has poor eating habits, and hasn't touched any food in what seems like weeks

CONSTITUTION
Plagiarized from Encyclopedia Britannica

MUSIC
Has been listening to a lot of Eritrean stuff lately; also likes Boston, Aerosmith, and Zep

PEOPLE » EVERYBODY SUCKS

Despite never getting to really know its parent nation, Eritrea has always been very identity-conscious, struggling to balance its larger Tigrayan side against the Tigre and Kumana elements that make up a big part of who it is. All it can really be sure of now is that it isn't really comfortable with who it is inside, often suppressing its Muslim influences to a dangerous degree. Neighboring countries are worried it might begin to actually cut itself, or even start taking its own lives. International organizations are quick to warn that, if it continues to be drawn to older, no-good nations like Sudan, Eritrea could be dead in a ditch somewhere by the time it's 21.

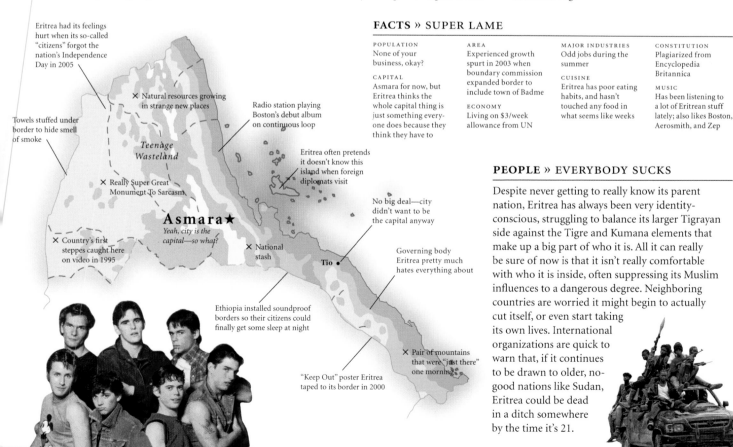

Eritrea had its feelings hurt when its so-called "citizens" forgot the nation's Independence Day in 2005

Towels stuffed under border to hide smell of smoke

× Natural resources growing in strange new places

Radio station playing Boston's debut album on continuous loop

Teenage Wasteland

× Really Super Great Monument To Sarcasm

Asmara ★
Yeah, city is the capital—so what?

× Country's first steppes caught here on video in 1995

Eritrea often pretends it doesn't know this island when foreign diplomats visit

× National stash

No big deal—city didn't want to be the capital anyway

Tio •

Governing body Eritrea pretty much hates everything about

Ethiopia installed soundproof borders so their citizens could finally get some sleep at night

"Keep Out" poster Eritrea taped to its border in 2000

× Pair of mountains that were "just there" one morning

Ethiopia

The Distended Belly Of Africa

Home to over 650 pounds of people, the East African nation of Ethiopia has long been plagued by drought, famine, and a third major hazard most citizens are often too weak to remember.

Bordered by Eritrea to the north, Kenya to the south, and what regularly appears to be a giant, floating ham to the east, Ethiopia is the site of some of the hungriest people on Earth.

Crippled by food shortages and calcium-deficient bones that frequently snap under the weight of their 40-pound frames, one in every six Ethiopians dies from malnutrition, two in every six die from standing up too quickly, and three in every six die from violent sneezing fits.

Sadly, those lucky to still be alive suffer from deep-seated issues about their body, often unable to look in the mirror without feeling self-conscious or passing out, and forever trapped in vicious cycles of not eating for months at a time before suddenly binging on any and all recently delivered food-aid packages in sight.

In 1998, after years of claiming that Ethiopia "would kill for a hot meal" and that "nothing, not even expiration dates" could stand in its way, President Negasso Gidada once again led the starving nation into war against Eritrean forces, this time over a disputed can of soup.

MAP KEY

- At Death's door
- Desperately ringing Death's doorbell
- Looking under Death's welcome mat for key
- Breaking in through Death's window

PEOPLE » COULD STAND TO GAIN A FEW

The average Ethiopian is made up of 80% thirst for water, 20% essential nutrient deficiency, and is approximately the size of a small casket. Most citizens suffer from malnutrition, as they regularly fail to incorporate enough fruits, vegetables, grains, dairy, meat, poultry, fish, beans, eggs, sugar, or nuts into their diet. Despite recurring droughts and famine, however, some Ethiopians do their best to put on a happy face—a nearly impossible task, as their facial muscles tend to atrophy by the age of 6.

While many citizens live on $1 a day, their currency is, unfortunately, hard to chew, lacks protein, and tastes awful. Pregnant mothers suffer the most in Ethiopia, as they must starve for two, and, after giving birth, lactate for thousands. The constant threat of food shortages has also made life incredibly arduous for many of the nation's stress eaters.

The victim of numerous droughts, Ethiopia is home to perhaps the world's most barren soil, which lacks even the most basic of nutrients despite the countless corpses buried beneath it each year.

Because of these harsh conditions, Ethiopians tend to age about seven years for every normal human year. Tragically, many still die before reaching the Ethiopian-age of 21.

FACTS » NOT EDIBLE

COUNTRY NAME
Official: Ethiopia
Meaning: "Ethiopia"

NATIONAL ANTHEM
"March Forward, Dear Mother Ethiopia (Theme From *Cool Runnings*)"

NATIONAL INSTRUMENT
Ribcage xylophone

RELIGIONS
Ethiopians belong to a number of different faiths, regularly fasting during Lent, Ramadan, Yom Kippur, Navratri, St. Patrick's Day, and Black History Month

ORAL TRADITION
Mostly moaning

FOREIGN RELATIONS
Bono calls nation every day to see how it's doing

TRADITIONAL GREETING
Low, sepulchral grumble of a thousand stomachs reverberating in unison

CONSTITUTION
Missing the three pages that had pictures of mashed potatoes on them

EDUCATION
Advanced in anatomy, as they can name and see all 206 bones in the human body

TRIVIA
In Ethiopia, the word for "shallow grave" is the same as the word for "mass grave"

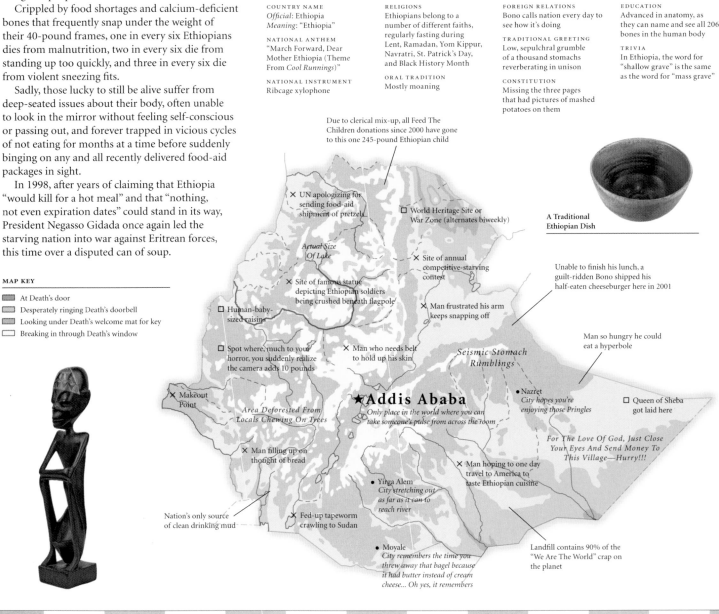

Due to clerical mix-up, all Feed The Children donations since 2000 have gone to this one 245-pound Ethiopian child

× UN apologizing for sending food-aid shipment of pretzels

□ World Heritage Site or War Zone (alternates biweekly)

Actual Size Of Lake

× Site of annual competitive-starving contest

× Site of famous statue depicting Ethiopian soldiers being crushed beneath flagpole

□ Human-baby-sized raisins

× Man frustrated his arm keeps snapping off

Unable to finish his lunch, a guilt-ridden Bono shipped his half-eaten cheeseburger here in 2001

□ Spot where, much to your horror, you suddenly realize the camera adds 10 pounds

× Man who needs belt to hold up his skin

Seismic Stomach Rumblings

Man so hungry he could eat a hyperbole

× Makeout Point

★ **Addis Ababa**
Only place in the world where you can take someone's pulse from across the room

• Nazret
City hopes you're enjoying those Pringles

□ Queen of Sheba got laid here

Area Deforested From Locals Chewing On Trees

For The Love Of God, Just Close Your Eyes And Send Money To This Village—Hurry!!!

× Man filling up on thought of bread

× Man hoping to one day travel to America to taste Ethiopian cuisine

• Yirga Alem
City stretching out as far as it can to reach river

Nation's only source of clean drinking mud

× Fed-up tapeworm crawling to Sudan

• Moyale
City remembers the time you threw away that bagel because it had butter instead of cream cheese... Oh yes, it remembers

Landfill contains 90% of the "We Are The World" crap on the planet

A Traditional Ethiopian Dish

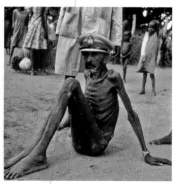

Former Ethiopian Emperor Haile Selassie

3,500,000 B.C. Fossils discovered in the fetal position exhibit the earliest known evidence of human suffering, leading historians to believe that Ethiopia may in fact be the legendary "Cradle Of Inhumanity."

A.D. 100 The height of the Aksumite Kingdom, whose cultural legacy will continue to live on until the end of this sentence.

1428 In Ethiopia's first contact with the West since Aksumite times, Emperor Yeshaq I sends a message to the Portuguese king. The message is an apology for not having written in so long.

1896 Ethiopia defeats Italy in the Battle of Adwa when the racist Italians, upon seeing hundreds of black Ethiopians, immediately retreat to lock their car doors.

1930–1974 The reign of Emperor Haile Selassie, perhaps the best-known Ethiopian emperor since Menelik II, or possibly even Yohannes IV.

1934 The rise of the Rastafari movement, a religion that accepts Haile Selassie as God incarnate, promotes the spiritual use of marijuana, and accepts Haile Selassie as God incarnate.

1936 In their second conflict, Italian troops employ a number of deplorable tactics to defeat Ethiopian forces, including the use of mustard gas, the airdropping of landmines, and the invasion of a completely defenseless African nation.

1941 Ethiopia easily defeats the Italians in the Battle of Debre Markos when the starving, delirious Ethiopians perceive the invading Italian troops to be an army of marching hot dogs and hamburgers, and quickly devour them.

1941 Ethiopia enjoys a between-century snack.

1962–1963 The radical Bowel Movement, a rebel alliance consisting of members from all four food groups, quickly sweeps through unfamiliar regions in Ethiopians, calling for immediate changes in the current digestive system and promising to soon bring a great relief to all citizens. After a long, painful occupation in which it provides no solid results, however, the Bowel Movement retreats back north.

1970 After nearly 50 years of ruling Ethiopia with an iron fist, decrepit 78-year-old Emperor Haile Selassie begins ruling Ethiopia with an iron lung.

1973 In the midst of a drought, the starving nation of Ethiopia begins banging its forks and knives onto the table in unison for two straight months until food aid arrives.

1974 92-pound Haile Selassie is ousted by a strong wind.

"We Are The World" (1985)

1976 Paleontologists in the Dikika region stumble upon what they believe to be fossils of ancient hominids from the *Australopithecus afarensis* genus, before realizing that fossils can't speak, and that their find is actually a living family of four.

1982 A massive drought dries up nearly half of Ethiopia's mirages.

1985 Donations from Live Aid provide the Ethiopians with thousands of pounds of food, but unfortunately everyone in the country loses their appetite watching Elton John and Kiki Dee perform a 20-minute rendition of "Don't Go Breaking My Heart."

1996 The U.S. sends Ethiopia 20,000 rations of thick, double-chocolate fudge brownies, after which thousands of Ethiopians instantly die of thirst.

1998 A bloody border conflict between Ethiopia and neighboring Eritrea erupts when both sides fight for control of less land.

1999 The UN threatens to move Ethiopia and Eritrea to opposite ends of the continent if they don't stop fighting.

1999 President Negasso Gidada appoints Kenneth "The Crook" Matiba, Syed "Slick Palms" Samir, and "Ol' Corrupto" Johnny Corrupt to head up an anti-corruption government task force.

2000 Ethiopian elections are marred by the fact that no citizen is strong enough to pull down the levers in the voting machines.

Bob Geldof

2005 Following the international failure of his "Live 8" concert series, Bob Geldof starves to death.

2006 Impoverished Ethiopians receive countless shipments of emergency food and medical supplies, but the UN has to laugh when the citizens end up having more fun with the boxes that the aid came in.

LEADING CAUSES OF DEATH »

- 45% Malnutrition
- 24% Taking too deep a breath
- 16% Physically crushed under weight of own thoughts
- 10% Having fetus kick through stomach lining
- 5% Trying to eat pie chart

THE UN'S 10-YEAR PLAN FOR ETHIOPIA »

In hopes of bringing lasting change to the devastated nation, the UN recently released a 10-year plan of action for Ethiopia. Below are some of the measures the governing body plans to take in the next decade:

- *Halve number of people without access to safe drinking water; make sure other half doesn't find out*

- *Do not allow anyone in nation to be photographed from the shoulders down*

- *Air Sally Struthers' "Save The Children" commercials during far more coveted 2 a.m.–3 a.m. time slot*

- *Provide every Ethiopian child with primary education...then, you know, hope that changes stuff around*

- *Double number of people living in poverty, then divide number of people living in poverty by two*

- *Dramatically reduce number of UN coffee breaks taken in a day*

Sally Struthers

Sudan

» FLAG TRADITIONALLY HELD IN THE LEFT HAND OF A MAN FIRING AN AK-47 INTO A CROWD OF OLD WOMEN.

SAVE DARFUR

» A FAMILY IN SUDAN LOOKS ON AS THE LAST BITS OF THEIR HOME BURN TO THE GROUND.

All Better Now Thanks To You

Once the site of one of the bloodiest conflicts in history, Sudan saw its senseless genocide come to a sudden and unexpected end in 2007 when the nation heard that a woman in Iowa was wearing a "Save Darfur" T-shirt.

For years, government-backed Arab forces known as the Janjaweed militia had attempted to wipe out black farmers in Sudan's western Darfur region. However, just as they were about to set fire to another village, word reached them that an American teenager thought that what was happening in Sudan "sucked." After learning that all her friends agreed, they immediately called off the whole genocide.

And although it seemed like the violence in Sudan would never truly stop, it did shortly after George Clooney mentioned during a red-carpet interview that it should.

Indeed, the merciless slaughter of innocent Sudanese children would still be taking place today had that petition in a New York bookstore not reached its goal of 100 signatures, forcing both sides to agree to a ceasefire. In fact, who knows how many more women would have been brutally raped had Michigan resident Dave Schumacher not purchased that highly critical bumper sticker, which left Janjaweed rebels no choice but to cede land back to Darfurian refugees and at once take the steps necessary to achieve lasting peace in Sudan.

Yet it was not until Shania Twain—whose disapproving comments had previously brought an end to the Rwandan genocide and solved the AIDS crisis in Botswana—sung "That Don't Impress Me Much" at a charity event that the people of Sudan knew they would never again have to live in fear.

A common sight in Sudan since Matt Damon called for an end to the violence.

FACTS » READ OFF THE BACK OF A T-SHIRT

POPULATION
35,000,00…34,882,411…33,129,242—*fuck!*

CLIMATE
Hellish in the south, merciless and monstrous in the west, slightly cooler in the north

HIGHEST POINT
Although only 650 ft. high, the remote peak of Mt. Kinyeti appears much higher when one is being tortured on the ground

PREFERRED METHOD OF GENOCIDE
Systematic with a touch of sweeping

EXPORTS
Petroleum products, cotton, and sesame, all of which can't wait to leave Sudan

COST OF LIVING
Usually an arm and a leg, although price can climb significantly higher in Darfur region

TOP REFUGEE CAMP ACTIVITIES
Telling campfire story about time wife was slaughtered (45%), Writing letter to UN about how much refugee camp sucks (30%), Visiting nurse's station (22%), Lunch (3%)

INTERNATIONAL AGREEMENTS
Promised to stop killing innocent civilians (2001, 2002, 2003, 2004, 2005, 2006)

LEADING CAUSE OF BLOODSHED
Senseless murder (48%), Senseless torture (46%), Senseless paper cuts (6%)

REASON FOR HOPE
In addition to T-shirts, "Save Darfur" buttons, wristbands, and baseball caps are also available now

Everything rainbows and sunshine thanks to an appearance made by Madonna on *The Ellen DeGeneres Show*

If this Sudanese man had a nickel for every time he saw someone get murdered, he'd have 274,136 nickels

Red Sea
Not actually red, despite the millions of corpses dumped into it over the years

✕ Insomniac who can't fall asleep without the sound of gunfire

✕ Good Samaritan helping rebels fix broken gun turret in back of truck

✕ Citizen beginning to suspect he may be a hemophiliac, although with a wound that size, it's hard to tell

Home to highest infant suicide rate in the world

✕ The term "genocide" can't even begin to describe what happened here

✕ Site of 2004 school genociding

✕ River is type O-negative

Region 100% Better Since You Attended That Rally Last Year

Khartoum ★
Too much blood here to really get a good sense of what's going on

🏢 World's tallest funeral home

✕ Village really appreciates all you've worn to help

✕ Carmen Sandiego got raped here

✕ Your donation of 30 cents has completely turned this refugee camp around

✕ Site of mass killings that are over by now, right?

✕ Infant curling up in adorable fetal position

Put this atlas down right now and go hug and kiss your children

✕ Sudanese man visiting mass grave of father, mother, uncle, cousin, grandfather, brother, and aunt

Valley home to world's largest human jigsaw puzzle

🏠 Blood bathhouse

It's scary to imagine what this region would be like had you never mentioned that "things in Sudan really need to change"

MAP KEY
▢ Saved by George Clooney
▢ Saved by Julia Roberts
▢ Saved by Bono
▢ Annoyed by Fran Drescher

A B C D E F G H I J K L

HISTORY » NOT THAT BAD UNTIL 2003, UNLESS YOU COUNT 1983–2002, OR 1955–1972 NOW THAT YOU MENTION IT

2000 B.C. Influenced by the ancient Egyptians, the less prosperous Kushite kingdom builds the Great Inverted Pyramid Of Meroe, a staggering structure dug for miles into the ground, where the carelessly embalmed corpses of thousands are dumped every day.

A.D. 1955–1972 Civil war erupts between the nation's Muslim-dominant north and a Christian south looking for more regional autonomy. Hundreds of southern soldiers, still under the jurisdiction of northern military generals, are instantly killed after receiving strict orders to shoot themselves in the head.

1967 Once shocked and disturbed by the gruesome brutality on display, Deng Nuer, a resident of the city of Juba, hardly flinches while watching his own chest being repeatedly stabbed.

1972 After 17 years and half a million deaths, a peace agreement is signed, allowing the now nearly deserted nation time to repopulate before the slaughtering can begin anew.

1978 Enough oil is discovered in the southern city of Bentiu to fuel the national conflict for generations to come.

1983–2005 See 1955–1972

1986 The city of Al-Ubayyid becomes a major seaport after half the country fills up with blood.

1991 A construction billionaire arrives in Sudan, builds several main roads, starts numerous large businesses, employs thousands, and becomes Sudan's only source of positive change before being forced to leave by the United States due to the fact that he's Osama bin Laden.

1993 Following 12 monotonous years of civil war, most Sudanese fighters are found to be just going through the up-and-down hacking motions of everyday life.

1998 The United States bombs a chemical plant in the city of Khartoum, alleging it had credible intelligence that the plant was within firing range of U.S. missiles.

Emergency shipments of food, water, and Bono reach Sudan (2005).

FEB. 2003 Darfur rebels accuse the central government of neglecting the struggling region and launch a guerrilla attack in remonstration. The Sudanese government quickly responds by meeting with every Darfur citizen one-on-one, two-on-one, and sometimes even six-on-one, and giving each the personalized attention they require.

JULY 2003 The escalating genocide drives nearly 2 million refugees from their homes to their graves.

AUG. 2003 In keeping with their final wishes, the remains of 15,000 Darfur villagers are put in a mass urn.

OCT. 2003 The U.S. refuses to call the conflict in Sudan a "genocide," claiming that the genocidal war, fought and commanded by genocide-avowed generals intent on committing genocide, was merely the systematic slaughter of an entire ethnic group.

2004 Government-backed Janjaweed militia forces, already responsible for the deaths of countless African villagers in Darfur, prove that while two wrongs don't make a right, 480,000 wrongs do.

2005 Dozens of Darfur villagers visit the newly inaugurated Sudanese Genocide Museum for the first and last time.

2006 The World Health Organization sends a team of 250 officials to Darfur in an attempt to determine the number of past WHO officials murdered in the region. Their early estimate of 12,000 ultimately falls short by about 250.

JUNE 17, 2006 Actually, things were pretty all right on June 17, 2006.

2007 Singer-songwriter Randy Newman plays a stirring rendition of "Little Criminals" at a San Francisco benefit for Darfur. Thousands of Janjaweed rebels immediately lay down their weapons.

Khartoum only minutes before Will Smith expressed his disapproval.

PEOPLE » DETACHED FROM SURREALITY

Repeatedly exposed to graphic scenes of violence in their own living rooms, kitchens, principal hallways, basements, bathrooms, and backyards, the citizens of Sudan have over the years grown increasingly desensitized to the carnage that surrounds them.

The Sudanese people—jaded viewers used to watching an average of 42 hours of bloodshed a week—would rarely bat an eyelid nowadays at the sight of entire villages engulfed in flames, raise an eyebrow at the sound of a weeping mother burying her seven children, or even lose their train of thought after stumbling across a stack of corpses rotting in a dry ravine.

In fact, so accustomed are the men and women of Sudan to the shows of agony and torture they have seen every night for the past four years, that the nation's grisly civil wars, genocide, and millions of faceless victims have become a way of life almost as much as they have become a way of death.

» A SUDANESE MAN IN TRADITIONAL DRESS

INABILITY OF CHARTS TO EXPRESS TRAGEDY OF THE SUDANESE GENOCIDE (2003–2006) »

Bar chart with y-axis labels (top to bottom): "There's a genocide going on! Stop making graphs and do something goddammit!"; "Completely unable to express tragedy"; "Barely expresses tragedy"; "Sorta expresses tragedy". X-axis: Year 2003, 2004, 2005, 2006.

Chad

» THIS FLAG'S FIRST STRIPE WAS CHANGED TO BLUE IN A $5,000 BACKROOM DEAL.

Where Even The Elephants Take Bribes

Despite gifts of nondescript briefcases, indirect offers of property overlooking Lake Chad, and whispered promises of "security" to individuals who each year compile the International Corruption Index, the Republic of Chad still ranks as the most crooked nation in the world.

Bordered by Libya to the north, Sudan to the east, and Niger to the west, all of which claim to "have never heard of any country called Chad, not now, not ever, so you can save your breath," this Central African nation would hate for anything to happen to your kneecaps.

With half of the country's population in its pocket, and the other half in its cemeteries and morgues, Chad may at first seem like an underhanded and dishonest republic, or even like a dangerous and out-of-control republic, but it is certainly not any of those things—not unless you never want to see your children again.

N'Djamena
In Chad, elephants can sometimes be encouraged to forget.

FACTS » SUBJECT TO CHANGE FOR THE RIGHT PRICE

POPULATION BREAKDOWN
Goons (31%), Palm Greasers (17%), Sweet Talkers (30%), Lookouts (22%), Middlemen (0%)

JUSTICE SYSTEM
Based on the Chadian practice of handing over large piles of cash

TRADITIONAL HANDSHAKE
Performed with right hand, thumb pressing down clip containing $1,500 against open palm

LAND USE
Dark alleys (32%), Dimly lit parking garages (20%), Abandoned street corners (48%)

LITTLE KNOWN FACT
N/A

AMERICANS OFTEN CONFUSE IT WITH
That guy named Chad, whose natural resources also happen to include petroleum, bauxite, natron, and fish, and whose highest point is also Emi Koussi at 3,415 meters

HISTORY » IF ANYONE ASKS, YOU DIDN'T READ THIS HERE

7000 B.C. Rock paintings discovered in the Tibesti region depict scenes of hunters bribing jackals, and one disturbing tableau of tribal elders handing a shamefaced giraffe cases of "hush alfalfa."

5000 B.C. Striking obsidian rocks to produce a finely sharpened tip, prehistoric tribes in Chad create some of the first tools of extortion.

A.D. 1900 An attempt to pay off invading French troops backfires when France insists that the drop-off be made in the neutral nation of Sudan. As Chadian government officials wait around impatiently on a street corner in Khartoum, French soldiers occupy Chad.

1925 The introduction of paved roads allows for blackmail to be delivered from one end of the country to the other in just two to three business days.

1965–1988 Bloody civil war, a violent occupation by neighboring Libya, and four consecutive military regimes mark the most open and up-front period in Chad's history.

MAR. 1996 The citizens of Chad participate in the country's first democratic elections by stepping inside a curtained booth, filling out a personal check in the name of the candidate they'd like to see win, and depositing their vote into large ballot boxes, which are then brought to a nearby bank to be counted.

President Idriss Déby

APR. 1996 Idriss Déby defeats challenger Wadel Abdelkader Kamougué by a vote of $7,234 to $3,295.

2004 As violence between Chad and Sudan breaks out, the UN sends hundreds of its top negotiators to the back of a Chadian restaurant.

PEOPLE WHO WILL MAKE IT WORTH YOUR WHILE »

Home to nearly 200 distinct ethnic groups, Chad is the only nation in the world where money talks in over 150 different languages. Villagers in Chad can often be seen frequenting local markets in their traditional dress—long, pale robes made unique by the presence of dozens of pockets that line both the inside and outside and make furtive bribes easier to accept. When not taking payoffs, being blackmailed, coerced, squeezed, bulldozed, or greased, the people of Chad are often being strong-armed. The rest of the time, however, they enjoy being bought off.

African Money Laundering
A Chadian woman launders a load of dirty cash in a nearby stream.

MAP KEY

- Walk calmly into restaurant
- Ask to be seated at table by the window
- Quietly eat and pay for your meal without calling any attention to yourself
- Exit restaurant, leaving briefcase underneath table as agreed

Palm-greasing factory

Jimmied-open border

GREAT GRIFT VALLEY

Anyone hears about this great little restaurant and you're done for

× Local official accused of misusing public bribes

× Chadian who picked up wrong suitcase at airport now bribing man with 20 pairs of socks

× Woman carrying money laundry basket on head

× Small-time change launderer

Safe House Of Representatives

You Never Saw This Region, You Got That?

× Amateur kidnapper holding stillborn child for ransom

Man holding glass against border to eavesdrop on Sudan ×

★ N'Djamena
City paid $20,000 to be moved closer to Lake Chad

× Chadian man being bribed with IOU

Corner black market

× Those photos of you... you know the ones

This city not corrupt at all (now, just leave the money in a bag on the park bench at noon tomorrow)

Central African Republic

QUALITY NATION

» EVERY BIT AS MEANINGLESS AS ETHIOPIA'S FLAG.

HUT

Why Spend Hundreds On A Name-Brand African Country?

Don't let the generic name fool you—the Central African Republic provides the same quality of poverty, disease, and corruption as its name-brand African neighbors.

Why travel all the way to a flashy nation like "Zambia" to get AIDS when you can pick up the deadly virus right here? The Central African Republic offers AIDS outbreaks, AIDS epidemics, and AIDS pandemics— all with the same lack of AIDS medication that today's African citizen has come to expect.

Unlike its top competitors, such as Sudan and Rwanda, Central African Republic doesn't make a big deal about its genocides. Some African countries spend all their energy making sure everyone in the world knows about their mass killings, and meanwhile the product suffers. But with Central African Republic, you get the kind of no-frills genocide you simply can't find anywhere else.

And sure, some African nations might feature a little more cholera, slightly hotter droughts, and longer civil wars. But most experts agree that a decade of civil war is all you need. After all, are those extra five years of bloodshed really worth the hassle?

Of course not.

A HISTORY OF YEARS »

A.D. 1880–1900 The country's official name is changed from the Republic of Motswana, to the nation of Zomalia, to—after a heated lawsuit— the Central African Republic.

1940 Although not nearly as catchy or memorable as those from Nigeria, many claim that Central African Republic's generic shrieks are every bit as desperate.

1960 A blind taste test proves that writhing, heaving citizens can't tell the difference between polluted water from Sudan and polluted water from Central African Republic.

1976 An inspection of the nation's civil war reveals it contains the same exact ingredients— violence, bloodshed, destruction—as many of the other, more popular conflicts in Africa.

1983 Despite boasting about its lower cost of living, CAR finally admits that many of its citizens are riddled with flaws, including holes in and around the chest, and left stumps that are slightly longer than their right stumps.

2004 Hundreds of UN peacekeepers are too embarrassed to tell their friends where they got their war scars.

COUNTRY COMPARISON »

	Civil War	AIDS	Food Shortages	Ethnic Cleansing	Convenience
South Africa	✓	✓		✓	
Uganda	✓	✓	✓		
Sierra Leone	✓	✓	✓	✓	
Burundi	✓	✓		✓	
Central African Republic	✓	✓	✓	✓	✓

Capital
A marketplace in the Central African Republic.

OFF-BRAND FAKTS »

GOVERNMENT
Republic

LOCATION
Center of Africa

CONTENTS
African land, African people, African disease

POPULATION
Seven digits separated by two commas

GEOGRAPHY
Marked by hills, valleys, mountains, rivers, lakes, cities, villages, towns, grass, dirt, and sand

LEADING INDUSTRIES
Shurfine, President's Choice, IGA, Roundy's

PRESIDENT
President

CURRENCY
The Bill, divided into 100 Coins

NATIONAL ANTHEM
"Rise Up, Our African Country"

NATIONAL HOLIDAY
December Eleventh Day (Dec. 11)

NATURAL RESOURCES
The natural wealth of a country, consisting of land, forests, water, mineral deposits, etc.

LEGAL SYSTEM
Laws must be obeyed lest penalties be exacted

MAP KEY
- ☐ Area
- ☐ Locale
- ☐ Spot
- ☐ Place

ZEBRA

Cameroon

» SAYLES WENT BACK AND FORTH ABOUT 15 TIMES BEFORE DECIDING TO KEEP THE STAR.

You'll Only Find It On A Map

Born out of a cartographical blunder, the nation of Cameroon was formed when famed mapmaker Arthur Sayles—momentarily distracted by matters outside his present task—accidentally connected the coast of Nigeria to that of Equatorial Guinea, omitting the enormous gulf that lay between the two and producing an entirely new piece of land.

Originally inhabited by feelings of frustration and disbelief, the unintentional territory was soon conquered by Sayles' fear of having to map the entire Dark Continent anew. Staring at his inadvertent creation—its borders only slightly more arbitrary than those of African colonies still years away—the cartographer's mind began to race.

With fingers trembling around the quill responsible for undoing days of exhaustive work, his chest perspiring beneath his cotton waistcoat, Sayles closed his eyes, crossed himself, and began to cover the virgin landscape with cities, streams, and the desperation of a man left powerless by circumstance.

He named the falsified land Cameroon, a nonsensical utterance that spilled from his quivering lips and onto the drafting desk below.

Sayles would tell no soul of the events of April 17 for the next 30 years, choosing only to finally disclose his sinister secret on his deathbed in 1775. While the nation of Cameroon has never and will never exist, its presence continues to be included on maps and in atlases today as a tribute to one of the greatest, albeit flawed, cartographers of our time.

FALSIFIED FACTS »

AREA COMPARATIVE
Roughly the size of one giant lie

PRIMARY LAND USE
Avoiding additional cartography work

POPULATION
17,432,093 (Sayles' lucky number)

RELIGION
Judaism (Sayles would later admit that he sort of screwed this one up)

HIGHEST POINT
Mt. Sarthur Ayles (4,095 m.)

LEGAL SYSTEM
Based on this idea Sayles' friend, William Wertshire, had for a legal system

NATURAL HAZARDS
Minor volcanic activity, that bitch Shelly Durham

COMPLETE FABRICATIONS PER SQUARE MILE
1,278

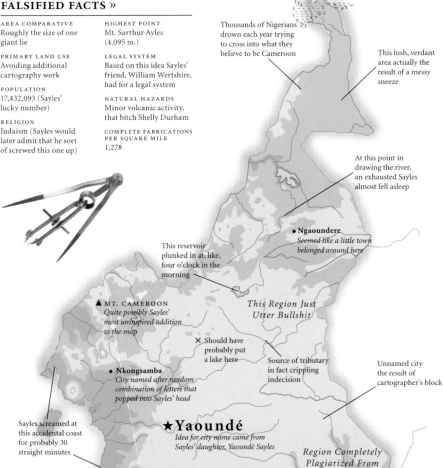

Thousands of Nigerians drown each year trying to cross into what they believe to be Cameroon

This lush, verdant area actually the result of a messy sneeze

At this point in drawing the river, an exhausted Sayles almost fell asleep

This reservoir plunked in at, like, four o'clock in the morning

● Ngaoundere
Seemed like a little town belonged around here

This Region Just Utter Bullshit

▲ MT. CAMEROON
Quite possibly Sayles' most uninspired addition to the map

✕ Should have probably put a lake here

Source of tributary in fact crippling indecision

Unnamed city the result of cartographer's block

● Nkongsamba
City named after random combination of letters that popped into Sayles' head

Sayles screamed at this accidental coast for probably 30 straight minutes

★ **Yaoundé**
Idea for city name came from Sayles' daughter, Yaoundé Sayles

Region Completely Plagiarized From Sierra Leone

WHERE ALL THE LIES FINALLY END

HISTORY » A NATION DRAWN IN A DAY

Arthur Sayles

10:00 P.M. The nation of Cameroon is discovered by Arthur Sayles, who celebrates the disastrous sighting by pacing around in frantic exasperation, and cursing at himself in the mirror.

11:15 P.M. After deciding against remapping Africa, a nervous Sayles

begins to fill in the falsified territory. He starts with Dja, the shakiest river in the entire world.

12:00 A.M. Quickly creating the authentic-sounding cities of "Ngaoundere," "Betare Oya," and "Mbandjock," Sayles hits a wall. For the next two hours, all the cartographer can come up with is "Foumban" and "Bamenda," the latter in fact an anagram for "Bad Name."

2:15 A.M. The capital of Yaoundé is created after a tired Sayles rests his

quill in one spot for too long.

2:16 A.M. Some more cursing.

2:30 A.M. Afraid he will be exposed as a fraud, Sayles gives Cameroon an arid climate inhospitable to agriculture, livestock, and human life.

2:44 A.M. An unforeseen ink spill creates Lake Lagdo.

3:28 A.M. Sayles gets momentarily sidetracked, falls into a deep waking sleep, and dreams of a land previously

uncharted by man. In this land, Sayles imagines himself living out his remaining years in blissful solitude, free from the pressures of modern cartography.

3:50 A.M. Unable to retain focus and increasingly delirious from a lack of sleep, Sayles invents a race of tiny people called "Pygmies" to be the first inhabitants of Cameroon.

4:00 A.M. Sayles momentarily forgets Cameroon doesn't really exist, leading the cartographer to believe he's stumbled upon an incredible finding.

Gabon

» HANGS OVER NATION'S FRONT PORCH, EXCEPT WHEN A MORE FUN, SEASONAL FLAG APPLIES.

» OMAR BONGO, THE NATION'S OWNER.

President Bongo's Private Residence

Gabon, a sprawling nation-estate that belongs to President For Life Omar Bongo, is located in the heart of one of Africa's safer, more upscale regions, features a scenic view overlooking the Atlantic Ocean, and gets plenty of sunlight due to its prime spot directly on Earth's equator.

In 1967, Bongo inherited the 66-million-acre fixer-upper nation, which at the time had no working government, a leaky river that often caused flooding, and only a small one-rhino garage.

However, Bongo invested thousands of dollars into the country—he hired men to landscape and trim his backyard rainforests, tore up all the arable land to put in hardwood floors, and built stylish exposed-manganese borders. Living conditions were greatly improved in 1972, when Bongo installed the nation's first functional toilet.

Despite all this progress, the estate's miles of dense woodlands still present a major fire hazard, and electricity bills often exceed $25 million per month, as Bongo leaves all the nation's lights on when he's out in order to deter potential invaders. Recently, a dangerous, ever-widening gap has formed between the rich and the poor, which thousands of citizens fall into each year, and which Bongo never seems to get around to repairing.

And much to the dismay of his maids, Bongo's 10,000 pet elephants tend to shit all over the place.

PEOPLE » GUESTS OF BONGO

Bongo welcomes anyone in Africa to live at his estate, as long as they keep to themselves, pay their taxes on time, and don't have any cats. The proud president insists on giving all visitors a complete walking tour of Gabon, which often takes up to 38 days, sometimes more if he is currently adding another story to Mt. Iboundji.

FACTS » STORED IN THE ATTIC

MOWABLE LAND
153,400 sq. km.

ENVIRONMENTAL ISSUES
Gophers, sunken living room due to erosion

NATURAL HAZARDS
Severe flooding if you don't jiggle the handle

NATIONAL ANTHEM
"La Concorde"; plays when you ring doorbell

COUNTRY DIALING CODE
Bongo always forgets, as he's never had to call own country

ECONOMY
President Bongo takes care of everything

HOT WATER
Included

SCHOOL DISTRICT
Closest school in Europe

ALARM CODE
26646

INTERNATIONAL DISPUTES
Gabon repeatedly asks Congo to remove the redwood branch that crosses the border into their property

CURRENCY
The Bongo (value: 100 Omar Bongos)

HISTORY » IT'S NOT A COUNTRY, IT'S A HOME

A.D. 1823 The Portuguese offer to purchase Gabon, but as soon as local Mpongwe rulers ask for a list of references, Portugal decides to look elsewhere.

1822 In one of chronology's greatest mysteries, the year 1822 follows the year 1823.

1894 French settlers discover that Gabon is plagued by a massive infestation of tiny Pygmies, creatures who are barely visible to the naked eye but who eat all the French people's crops and use their resources. The French close down the country for three days and fumigate the land.

1975 Two years after converting to Islam, Bongo converts to Jehovah's Witness following a strange, unannounced visit by two teenage men.

1987 After Bongo spends 20 years carefully rearranging all the cities and getting the nation just the way he wants it, Gabon is struck by a 7.3-magnitude earthquake.

1995 Bongo discovers thousands of tons of oil beneath his front yard, but refuses to dig up his perfectly manicured lawn in order to get to it.

2005 Worried about national security, Bongo finally installs an alarm system. In July, thousands of UN Security Council members and U.S. peacekeeping forces rush to the nation, only to find that a returning Bongo just couldn't remember his alarm code.

Bongo's landscapers mow the rainforest.

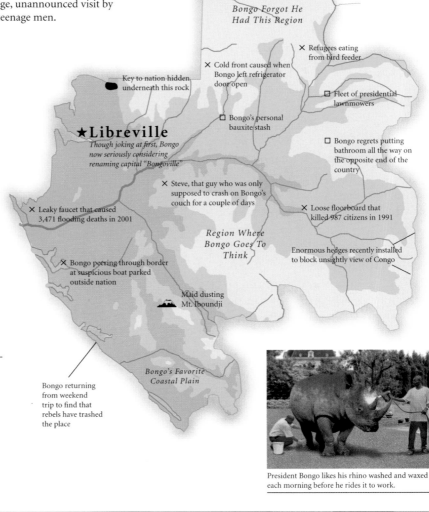

Bongo Forgot He Had This Region

✕ Refugees eating from bird feeder

✕ Cold front caused when Bongo left refrigerator door open

Key to nation hidden underneath this rock

□ Fleet of presidential lawnmowers

□ Bongo's personal bauxite stash

★**Libreville**
Though joking at first, Bongo now seriously considering renaming capital "Bongoville"

□ Bongo regrets putting bathroom all the way on the opposite end of the country

✕ Steve, that guy who was only supposed to crash on Bongo's couch for a couple of days

✕ Leaky faucet that caused 3,471 flooding deaths in 2001

✕ Loose floorboard that killed 987 citizens in 1991

Region Where Bongo Goes To Think

Enormous hedges recently installed to block unsightly view of Congo

✕ Bongo peering through border at suspicious boat parked outside nation

🔺 Maid dusting Mt. Iboundji

Bongo's Favorite Coastal Plain

Bongo returning from weekend trip to find that rebels have trashed the place

President Bongo likes his rhino washed and waxed each morning before he rides it to work.

The Guinea Empire

The Great Guinea Empire

Long before history began, a vast kingdom stretched across the globe. Known as the Great Guinea Empire, it ruled over all solid land, as well as nearly 70% of the sea, and most marshes and bogs.

Legend states that the Guineans conquered the world in a matter of only two weeks, largely through the use of long, blunt weapons known today as sticks. But even though they were renowned for their vicious attacks, most historians note that they never killed a single man on purpose.

Today, all that remains of the Great Guinea Empire are three African territories, which, despite being slight in size, offer a wealth of clues about what life was like before the advent of paved roads, sufficient food, and a life expectancy over 35 years of age.

Great Guinea Empire, circa 1500 B.C.

Current Guinea territories

Prehistoric Guinea
It is said that men would quake with fear when they saw the Guineans rise above the horizon atop their galloping steeds of 12-foot-long guinea pigs (now extinct).

HISTORY » TREMBLE BEFORE THE MIGHTY GUINEANS

While a formidable world power for centuries, the Great Guinea Empire could not in the end maintain its seemingly ubiquitous control, falling to the Aztecs, the Mongols, the Vikings, the Romans, the Greeks, the Ancient Egyptians, this guy in North America with a really sharp rock, the Ottomans, the Spanish, a scary-looking fire in modern-day Thailand, the British, and the Eskimos.

Yet, who can say how long Ancient Guinea might have lasted had things turned out differently? We may never know, as every scholar we ask invariably refuses to answer, and often leaves the room shortly thereafter.

Equatorial Guinea
Right On The Equatorish

With the Republic of Guinea having already laid claim to their first choice of country name, their next pick of "Guinea-Bissau" also snatched up, and "France" turning out to be a pre-existing state in Western Europe, Equatorial Guinea decided in 1968 to just go ahead and name themselves after the equator—an admitted stretch as the nation lies numerous miles above the zero-degree latitude line.

Since then, Equatorial Guinea has gone out of its way to make its forced identity work. Local residents are often seen at one of the nation's many "equator-esque" beaches, sipping drinks "typical of a region equidistant from the North and South Pole," and taking in the beautiful weather—weather painfully described as "relative to that of any landmass lying on a plane perpendicular to the axis of a large spherical object, such as Earth."

In 2005, the nation changed its motto from "Unity, Peace, Justice" to "Equator, Equator, Equator."

Malabo★
Yes, yes, the capital of Equatorial Guinea is off the mainland—settle down, settle down

FACTS » CLOSE ENOUGH

LOCATION
Quasi-equatorable

TRADITIONAL GREETING
"Is it hot today, or do we just happen to be on the equator?"

GOVERNMENT TYPE
Equatutional equatocracy

NATION IT MOST OFTEN COMPARES ITSELF TO
Ecuador

LANDMARKS
Equator Plaza, where visitors can "equator" themselves right on down to "equator-style" fun

INFANT MORTALITY RATE
Exactly what you'd expect for a nation that lies on the equator

NUMBER OF CITIZENS WHO HAVE ACTUALLY CROSSED EQUATOR
0

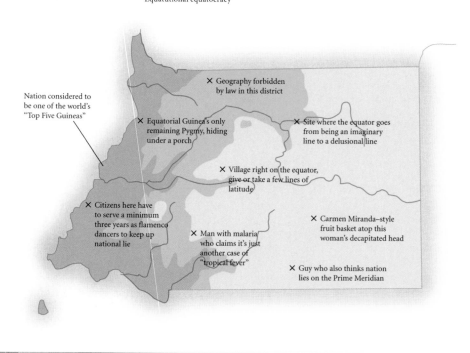

Nation considered to be one of the world's "Top Five Guineas"

✕ Geography forbidden by law in this district

✕ Equatorial Guinea's only remaining Pygmy, hiding under a porch

✕ Site where the equator goes from being an imaginary line to a delusional line

✕ Village right on the equator, give or take a few lines of latitude

✕ Citizens here have to serve a minimum three years as flamenco dancers to keep up national lie

✕ Man with malaria who claims it's just another case of "tropical fever"

✕ Carmen Miranda–style fruit basket atop this woman's decapitated head

✕ Guy who also thinks nation lies on the Prime Meridian

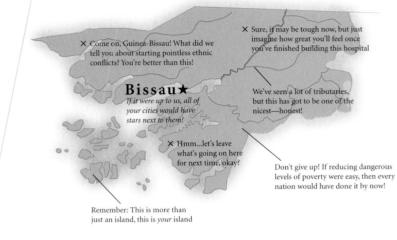

✕ Come on, Guinea-Bissau! What did we tell you about starting pointless ethnic conflicts? You're better than this!

✕ Sure, it may be tough now, but just imagine how great you'll feel once you've finished building this hospital

Bissau★
If it were up to us, all of your cities would have stars next to them!

We've seen a lot of tributaries, but this has got to be one of the nicest—honest!

✕ Hmm…let's leave what's going on here for next time, okay?

Don't give up! If reducing dangerous levels of poverty were easy, then every nation would have done it by now!

Remember: This is more than just an island, this is *your* island

FACTS » ONLY BECAUSE WE CARE

AREA
28,000 sq. km.; *Don't let your small size fool you into thinking you can't do great things*

CLIMATE
Tropical; *See? You could be a tourist hotspot if you wanted*

NATURAL RESOURCES
Cashews; *People love cashews, and you have tons of them. Good for you!*

HIV/AIDS RATE
Keep trying!

NATIONALITY
Guinean; *A little obvious, but it works*

MOST RECENT COUP
2003; *You're making good progress, just take it one year at a time*

UNEMPLOYMENT RATE
N/A; *It's okay if it's low, just tell us and we'll try to help you*

Guinea-Bissau
Keep Your Chin Up!

The editors of this atlas realize that harping on a nation's recent troubles does little to actually help, so instead we've decided to offer Guinea-Bissau some words of encouragement:

Guinea-Bissau, things have certainly been rough lately, but that's just part of being an African nation. Now, listen. You have a lot going for you—you speak six different official languages, you're very independent, and we bet you have a pretty landmass underneath all those landmines.

Sure, it probably seems like things can't get any worse after that last military coup, but you have over 350 km. of coastline! Use it, Guinea-Bissau! Ship-refueling, fishing, offshore tourism… The sky is the limit.

Now, instead of wasting the whole day trying to oust your current leader, why not spend your time removing those landmines like we asked you to? You don't have to clean them all up at once, but if you set a reachable goal and meet it, you will have a sense of accomplishment that would do your death rate a world of good.

And if you keep it up, you could even become an ally of the United States someday!

Guinea
Huddled In The Corner Of Africa

Host to over a million refugees from war-torn nations such as Liberia, Sierra Leone, and Ivory Coast, Guinea has become Africa's melting pot—a land where people from all different cultures can cower together as one.

Each year, thousands of Africans escape their regional conflicts and travel to Guinea, which has become a home far enough away from home for these refugees. They come here without money, without food, and occasionally without arms, in the hopes of finding literally anything else.

No matter what religion they are fleeing from, no matter what language they can no longer bear to speak, no matter the color of their wounds—red, black, yellow, or blue—the people of Guinea are able to coexist peacefully under the same tarp.

And while many are physically unable to stand up for what they believe in, these refugees remain united in fear of their respective homelands. They welcome one another with outstretched stumps, and together strive toward one common goal: staying alive.

FACTS » WILL TRADE FOR FOOD AND CLOTHING

TRADITIONAL GREETING (SINCERE)
"Welcome to Guinea. You are safe now."

TRADITIONAL GREETING (LIGHTHEARTED)
"Welcome to Sudan."

AVG. QUANTITY OF FOOD
Morsel

POPULATION
See: population Sierra Leone, population Liberia, and population Ivory Coast

HOUSING
Federally protected Porta-Johns

RELIGION
Refugees free to curse whichever god they choose

TOP OCCUPATIONS
Blanket administrator, guy who asks how you're holding up

American child who was sent to refugee camp for the summer to lose weight

✕ Refugees taking full advantage of nation's freedom of scream

✕ Site of hole away from hole for many refugees

✕ Sight of mutilated child making this refugee homesick

Site where a hot-tempered Italian-American punched two people in the face after learning there was a country called Guinea ✕

✕ Angry, angry hippos

✕ Humanitarian worker saving time by moving huddled masses with bulldozer

✕ Hungry refugee gouging out eyes, sneaking into food-rations line for a second time

✕ Shell of a woman finally being accepted for who she once was

Conakry★
Voted "Best Place To Cringe" in 1984, 1997, 2004

✕ Sudanese couple who escaped to Guinea in hopes of giving child better death

✕ What could be a sign of hope if you squint hard enough

Visitors from all over Africa come to Guinea to not die.

Nigeria

From: nigeria_people2007@yahoo.com
Sent: Monday, August 20, 2007 10:10 PM
Subject:

REQUEST FOR URGENT ASSISTANCE

Dear Reader, WE NEED YOUR HELP May the blessing of God be upon you and grant you thewisdom and sympathy to understand our situation and how much we need your help.

This letter might meet you with surprise as you do not know us, but we got your contact through personal research and out of desperation decided to reach you through this medium.

Allow us first to introudce ourselves. We are the People of Nigeria, and we are currently in a crisis situation. Thousands of our relatives recently died in plane crashes, perished in oil fires, and were murdered by military security forces. Now we are left with nothing. We have been subjected to all sorts of harassment's, intimidation's and inhumane treatments by the corrupt government since 2001. Many of us are starving, sick, or losing our jobs and homes each day.

We need immediate foreign help, we beg of you. Our country is very rich, and infact we have huge sums of money in the tune of One Hundred Seventy Five Billion United State Dollars (US$175,000,000,000)--but unfortunately the government and oil companies will not allow us to access this wealth. We also have plentiful lresources such as oil, rubber and tin that are rightfully ours, but that we cannot get to.

OUR PROPOSAL. In exchange for your assistance, we will provide you with 15% (US$26,250,000,000) of the total sums of our GDP. All you must do is fly to our country, preferably with 10,000 of your closest associates and confidantes, and bring guns. The rest will be explained to you upon your arrival.

We assure you this transaction is 100% safe.

Note,If you do not wish to come to Nigeria, you can still help us. Please reply to the above email with your contact details, telephone, fax, bank account number and bank routing number. We are counting on you for our future happiness and that of our country.

We urgently await your swift and prompt response.

Sincerely Yours,
People of nigeria

EDUCATION »
STUDENTS IN
NIGERIA'S AVANCED
"COMPUTERS 419"
COURSE LEARN HOW
TO MASS E-MAIL.

» UN VOLUNTEERS
TAKE PART IN A
MASSIVE CLEANUP
EFFORT TO WASH
OFF OIL-SOAKED
NIGERIANS.

PEOPLE » THE CONTENTS OF YOUR SPAM FOLDER

Ken Saro-Wiwa

Nigeria is made up of over 250 ethnic groups, the largest being the Hausa and Fulani tribes in the north, and the smallest being Mtumbe Ngoube in 374 Zaria Lane Apt. #2.

Thousands of these Nigerians are affected each year by foreign oil companies invading their land. In the late 20th century, an environmentalist and poet named Ken Saro-Wiwa led a grassroots campaign against the influence of these oil companies, but in 1995, he was hanged on 142 counts of rhyming "oil" with "soil."

Nigeria is world-renowned for its certain amount of hospitality. It is rare to see a Nigerian man without a broad, sadistic smile on his face, the citizens are carefree and often wear your heart on their sleeve, and they always greet visitors with open firearms.

FACTS » HARSH, BRUTISH, AND SHORT

LOCATION
Right between fourth and fifth circles of Hell

POPULATION GRADE
Regular: 97%
Unleaded: 3%

EXPORTS
Oil

RESOURCES
Oil

OIL
Oil

LEADING CAUSE OF OIL SPILLS
Not being careful

NATURAL HAZARDS
Periodic drought, intermittent dry spells, on-and-off rainlessness

DIPLOMATIC REPRESENTATION FROM U.S.
That corpse with the business suit

TOP ADJECTIVES
Oil-rich, war-torn, ablaze

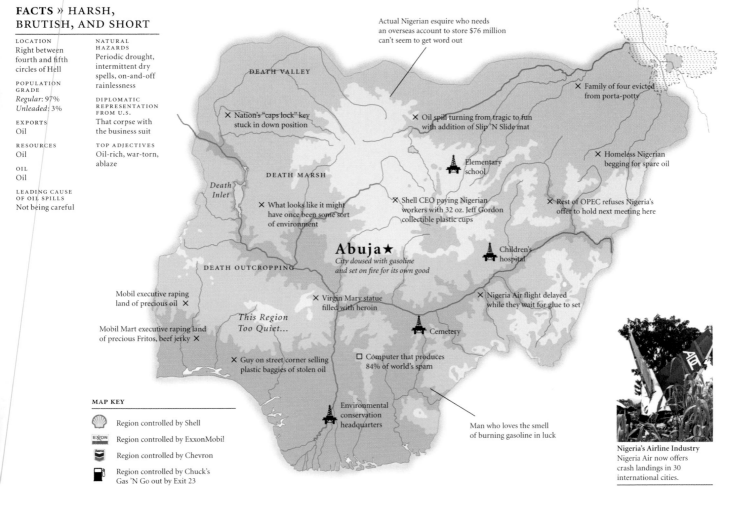

Actual Nigerian esquire who needs an overseas account to store $76 million can't seem to get word out

DEATH VALLEY

✕ Nation's "caps lock" key stuck in down position

✕ Family of four evicted from porta-potty

✕ Oil spill turning from tragic to fun with addition of Slip 'N Slide mat

✕ Homeless Nigerian begging for spare oil

Elementary school

DEATH MARSH

Death Inlet

✕ What looks like it might have once been some sort of environment

✕ Shell CEO paying Nigerian workers with 32 oz. Jeff Gordon collectible plastic cups

✕ Rest of OPEC refuses Nigeria's offer to hold next meeting here

Abuja ★
City doused with gasoline and set on fire for its own good

Children's hospital

DEATH OUTCROPPING

Mobil executive raping land of precious oil ✕

✕ Virgin Mary statue filled with heroin

✕ Nigeria Air flight delayed while they wait for glue to set

This Region Too Quiet...

Mobil Mart executive raping land of precious Fritos, beef jerky ✕

Cemetery

✕ Guy on street corner selling plastic baggies of stolen oil

☐ Computer that produces 84% of world's spam

Environmental conservation headquarters

Man who loves the smell of burning gasoline in luck

MAP KEY

🐚	Region controlled by Shell
EXXON	Region controlled by ExxonMobil
▮	Region controlled by Chevron
⛽	Region controlled by Chuck's Gas 'N Go out by Exit 23

Nigeria's Airline Industry
Nigeria Air now offers crash landings in 30 international cities.

HISTORY » WARNING: EXTREMELY FLAMMABLE

A.D. 1897 British colonial forces misinterpret their orders to burn and ransack the town of Oyo, and accidentally pillage and ransack it.

1914 The U.K. conquers Nigeria, a land made up of 250 disparate ethnic groups, which the British instantly unify under the guiding principle of shared hatred and resentment of the British.

1914–1926 After 12 years of painstaking work, the British successfully come up with 250 ethnic slurs.

1956 The Royal Dutch Shell Group begins drilling in Nigeria. By setting up countless refineries on the beautiful Niger Delta, digging massive exploratory holes through fields and farms, and extracting over 2.2 million tons of crude oil from the fertile soil each day, many experts believe they have ruined the Nigerian environment for future generations of oil companies.

1962 Nigeria experiences an oil boom, followed by an oil blast, an oil explosion, an oil gunshot, and an oil thud.

1967–1970 Civil war erupts between Nigerians and the seceded Biafra region. Historians have yet to single out one main reason for the conflict, maintaining that it was "a lot of little things."

1984 Mobil removes over 700,000 barrels of oil from the ground in order to make room for the millions of Nigerian corpses they intend to replace it with.

1986 Rebel militants seize 12 Nobel Prizes in Literature.

1993 UN peacekeepers break up a Nigerian stone-throwing mob when someone uses what most consider to be more of a rock.

1997 In an effort to bring the nation's aviation problems to the world's attention, 114 top Nigerian officials crash into the UN.

2005 The nation of Nigeria bursts into flames.

2007 Oil prices soar to an all-time high of 243 Nigerian lives per gallon.

Niger

» THE FLAG OF NIGER WAS ADOPTED FROM INDIA IN 1960.

The Cutest Little Overpopulation Crisis

A developing nation where most women tend to get married straight out of grade school and the only available form of birth control remains pregnancy, Niger boasts the highest fertility rate in the world.

Averaging eight children per mother, and 12 children per mother still alive after her eighth child, this African republic goes into labor once every hour, a period that often begins with thousands of ruptured amniotic sacs and severe inland flooding.

Expected to nearly double in population by the end of the decade, and triple in population about a week after that, Niger has quickly learned the reality of having 7.3 million kids. The country has not gotten a full night's sleep in weeks, it's often overwhelmed by the number of times its newborns need feeding each month, and it regularly spends several hours a day wondering how much bleeding is normal for a healthy baby boy.

One of the least-developed nations in the world, with infant production surpassing economic, industrial, and agricultural production combined, Niger's exponential growth has stretched and strained national resources almost as much as it has national wombs.

Sadly, an attempt by the United Nations in 2003 to aid the struggling nation backfired when an emergency shipment containing contraceptives was tragically mixed up with a box containing thousands of gallons of wine and smooth-jazz cassettes.

LEADING CAUSES OF BIRTH »

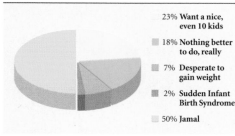

- 23% **Want a nice, even 10 kids**
- 18% **Nothing better to do, really**
- 7% **Desperate to gain weight**
- 2% **Sudden Infant Birth Syndrome**
- 50% **Jamal**

INTERNATIONAL RELATIONS »

Greeted warmly and openly as "Niger" by neighboring African countries and the city of Detroit, this young republic is carefully addressed as the "African-African State of Central Africa" by Western nations frightened of appearing racist.

FACTS » MANY BLESSED EVENTS

AGE STRUCTURE
0–14 Years: 40%
15–64 Years: 6%
Third Trimester: 64%

TRADITIONAL GREETING
"You're going to have to deliver this baby!"

POPULAR BABY PRODUCTS
Triple-decker strollers, mass cribs, food

IMPORTS
UN-grade diapers

EXPORTS
Slightly heavier UN-grade diapers

MOST COMMON BABY NAME (2006)
"You there"

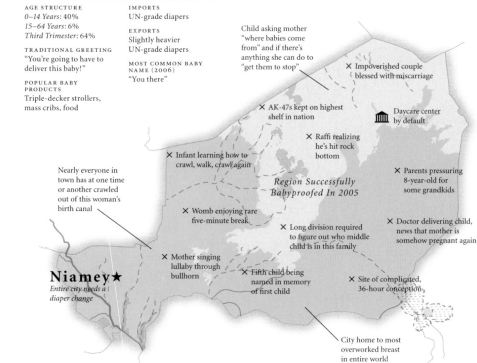

Child asking mother "where babies come from" and if there's anything she can do to "get them to stop"

✕ Impoverished couple blessed with miscarriage

✕ AK-47s kept on highest shelf in nation

🏛 Daycare center by default

✕ Raffi realizing he's hit rock bottom

✕ Infant learning how to crawl, walk, crawl again

Region Successfully Babyproofed In 2005

✕ Parents pressuring 8-year-old for some grandkids

Nearly everyone in town has at one time or another crawled out of this woman's birth canal

✕ Womb enjoying rare five-minute break

✕ Long division required to figure out who middle child is in this family

✕ Doctor delivering child, news that mother is somehow pregnant again

Niamey ★
Entire city needs a diaper change

✕ Mother singing lullaby through bullhorn

✕ Fifth child being named in memory of first child

✕ Site of complicated, 36-hour conception

City home to most overworked breast in entire world

HISTORY » A SERIES OF PRECARIOUS BABY STEPS

A.D. 1960 Niger is granted independence by the French in a loud, patronizing tone.

1968 Ailing citizens receive disastrous assistance when volunteers from the organization "Doctors Without Degrees" arrive.

1978 Niger goes to war with Nigeria over control of the adjective *Nigerian*. The Nigerois lose.

1982 Pregnant women in the city of Ayourou experience a bizarre craving for food.

1983 In a national ceremony, President Ali Seybou declares the opening of some 200,000 birth canals.

1985 Niger is struck by an outbreak of colic. WHO officials release a list of preventive measures, including regular burping, rhythmic rocking, and gentle massages of the lower back.

1987 Eight-month-old Kwanda Utubo utters her last words.

1990 In order to help with household bills, young children in Niger begin taking on jobs as midwives, pediatricians, and daycare supervisors.

1991 Sibling rivalry claims the lives of nearly 2,000 citizens.

1993 During his inaugural address, President Mahamane Ousmane promises the underdeveloped nation that he will build a "footbridge to the 17th century."

1997 The capital of Niamey witnesses the construction of its first-ever street corner. Prostitution, drug dealing, and homelessness quickly skyrocket.

2001 An annual census reveals that more than half of Niger's citizens are now below the age of 15, and that nearly 80% of them live at "69 Gonads Boulevard."

Manyara Ngoube
New mother Manyara Ngoube wonders if her crying infant is hungry, thirsty, needs a diaper change, has malaria, contracted hepatitis A, is suffering from typhoid fever, has a case of meningococcal meningitis, became frightened by the loud roar of nearby ethnic violence, was hit by a stray militia bullet, or just simply wishes to die.

2003 George W. Bush claims Iraq tried to acquire uranium from Niger for its nuclear-weapons program. Intelligence reports a few days later, however, reveal that the only thing sought from the sub-Saharan nation was "political justification."

Burkina Faso

Where The Reading Rainbow Ends

The West African nation of Burkina Faso suffers from the worst literacy rate in the world, with 88.2% of citizens unable to read, and the remaining 11.8% always seeming to have "left their glasses at home."

A Burkina Faso citizen pretends to learn about the dangers of HIV.

All Burkina Faso citizens are encouraged at a young age to learn to recognize the shape of their country, so that if they ever get lost in Africa, they will be able to point it out on a map to a stranger willing to take them home.

Their constitution is the first and only to be written entirely in pictures. The thumbs-up symbol in the preamble symbolizes their eternal striving for peace, happiness, and liberty. The stop sign at the end symbolizes that the constitution is over.

RELIGIOUS BREAKDOWN »

- 48% **The one with the moon and the star**
- 46% **The one with the cross**
- 6% **Sejisdgldjop (results from written poll)**

FACTS » THESE STRANGE LITTLE SYMBOLS MEAN NOTHING TO THEM

POPULATION
N/A, as Burkina Faso also suffers from innumeracy

CAPITAL
Ouagadougou (written), Diamond City (pronounced)

LOCATION
Near the left, down a little, and below the country that looks like a chair

PARTY TO
No Nation Left Behind Act

LITERACY RATE
88% of citizens can pretend to read at a 12th-grade level

DIPLOMATIC REPRESENTATION FROM U.S.
Ambassador LeVar Burton

PENMANSHIP
Atrocious

POLITICS
In 2006, voters unanimously elected Turn Page To Continue Voting as president

LEGAL SYSTEM
Picture-based

LOWEST POINT
Time UN chairman called on them to read morning agenda out loud

REASON FOR HOPE
Benin, which has a much higher 32% literacy rate, has offered to tutor the nation's citizens

AN ORAL HISTORY BY DEFAULT »

1440 B.C. The ancient Phoenicians visit Burkina Faso, but forget to bring the alphabet with them.

A.D. 1012 Burkinabe tribesmen develop a simple wooden tool with a sharp point and a graphite core, which they use to point at things they want.

1958–1960 For two years, citizens urge President Maurice Yameogo to ratify their constitution so they can gain independence, but Yameogo keeps complaining that he can't sign the document because his hand hurts.

1966–1983 After nearly 20 years of rote repetition, citizens successfully learn how to read and write the phrase "military coup."

1985 While dining together a local restaurant, U.S. diplomat Mark Harrisburg begins to suspect that Burkina Faso ambassador Odden Ishmael may be illiterate when Ishmael points to the line on the menu that says "20% gratuity added to bill for parties of eight or more" and says, "I'll have that."

1987 The U.S. sends thousands of AIDS-prevention pamphlets to Burkina Faso.

1990 Dr. Seuss publishes three specially written children's books to help young Burkinabe learn how to read, including *Oh, The Places You'll Never Go, Neither Green Eggs Nor Ham*, and *One Fish Two Fish You'll Be Dead By 37.*

1998 Diplomatic representatives from Sylvan Learning Center visit the nation for a free consultation, and later establish the Burkina Faso Institute Of Lower Learning.

2001 Burkinabe writer Monique Ilboudo publishes her first novel, *Le Mal De Peau*, which the nation's critics blast as "unreadable."

2004 In response to a 5% leap in their country's literacy rate, Burkinabe leaders establish a national counterintelligence unit.

2007 Emoticon-typewriter invented.

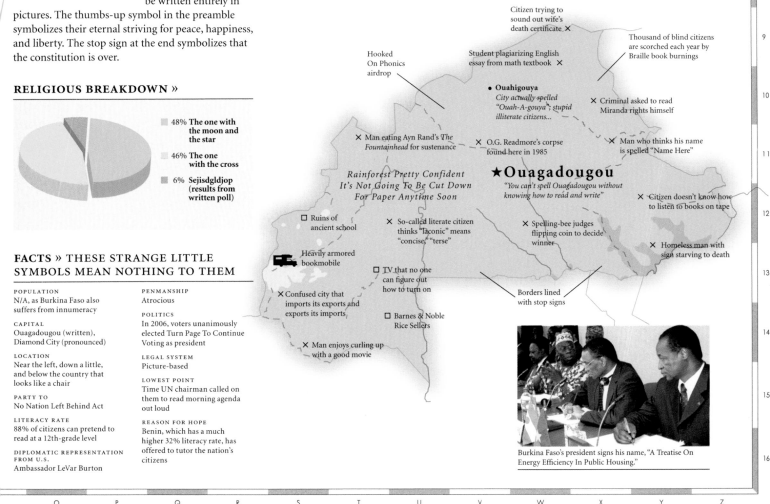

Citizen trying to sound out wife's death certificate ✕

Thousand of blind citizens are scorched each year by Braille book burnings

Hooked On Phonics airdrop

Student plagiarizing English essay from math textbook ✕

● Ouahigouya
City actually spelled "Ouah-A-gouya"; stupid illiterate citizens...

✕ Criminal asked to read Miranda rights himself

✕ Man eating Ayn Rand's *The Fountainhead* for sustenance

✕ O.G. Readmore's corpse found here in 1985

✕ Man who thinks his name is spelled "Name Here"

Rainforest Pretty Confident It's Not Going To Be Cut Down For Paper Anytime Soon

★ **Ouagadougou**
"You can't spell Ouagadougou without knowing how to read and write"

✕ Citizen doesn't know how to listen to books on tape

□ Ruins of ancient school

✕ So-called literate citizen thinks "laconic" means "concise," "terse"

✕ Spelling-bee judges flipping coin to decide winner

Heavily armored bookmobile

□ TV that no one can figure out how to turn on

Borders lined with stop signs

✕ Homeless man with sign starving to death

✕ Confused city that imports its exports and exports its imports

□ Barnes & Noble Rice Sellers

✕ Man enjoys curling up with a good movie

Burkina Faso's president signs his name, "A Treatise On Energy Efficiency In Public Housing."

Togo & Benin

TOGO » FLAG SYMBOLIZES FAST, FRIENDLY SERVICE.

BENIN » KNOWS BETTER THAN TO STICK A HUGE AK-47 RIGHT ON THE FRONT OF ITS FLAG.

Togo
A To-Go Nation

Considered by many in Africa to be "the only place" for fast and tangible food, the crawl-thru nation of Togo offers eye-watering meals for hungry Africans on the go.

Whether picking up a quick bite in between periods of violent civil war, or bringing home a one-piece family bucket of chicken for the wife and kids, customers flock to the 24-hour country by the thousands.

However, Togo also offers delivery service to citizens who simply lack the strength to leave their huts after a long day of fighting cholera, and guarantees that a meal will arrive at any nation's border in 30 years or your money back.

Sadly, hundreds of thousands died last year in the famine-stricken nation of Burundi after a telephone order of "one million" pizzas was tragically mistaken for a prank.

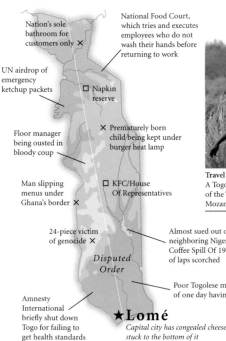

Nation's sole bathroom for customers only ✕

National Food Court, which tries and executes employees who do not wash their hands before returning to work

UN airdrop of emergency ketchup packets

☐ Napkin reserve

Floor manager being ousted in bloody coup

✕ Prematurely born child being kept under burger heat lamp

Man slipping menus under Ghana's border ✕

☐ KFC/House Of Representatives

24-piece victim of genocide ✕

Almost sued out of existence by neighboring Nigeria after the "Great Coffee Spill Of 1994" left thousands of laps scorched

Disputed Order

Amnesty International briefly shut down Togo for failing to get health standards up to code

Poor Togolese man who dreams of one day having fries with that

★**Lomé**
Capital city has congealed cheese stuck to the bottom of it

Travel
A Togolese woman delivers an order of the "Hungry Nation Special" to Mozambique.

Benin
What The Fuck Are These Other Countries Thinking?

A beacon of democracy, Benin would of course prefer to be a corrupt nation where everyone hacks each other to bits with machetes, but is fully aware how bad that sort of thing plays in the international press these days. They're not *complete* idiots.

Surrounded by countries that have absolutely no idea how crazy they look when they brutally murder thousands of innocent civilians, Benin has gone out of its way in recent years to not systematically annihilate half its population, often holding free and fair elections just to keep itself occupied.

In a perfect world, Benin would obviously love to be a landmine-filled hellscape, but it has its legacy to think about. When people open history books 100 years from now, Benin wants the record to state boldly and proudly: "The nation of Benin was the one that did not rape children."

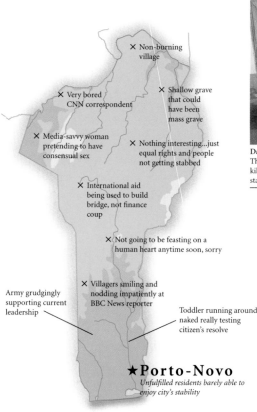

✕ Non-burning village

✕ Very bored CNN correspondent

✕ Shallow grave that could have been mass grave

✕ Media-savvy woman pretending to have consensual sex

✕ Nothing interesting...just equal rights and people not getting stabbed

✕ International aid being used to build bridge, not finance coup

✕ Not going to be feasting on a human heart anytime soon, sorry

Army grudgingly supporting current leadership

✕ Villagers smiling and nodding impatiently at BBC News reporter

Toddler running around naked really testing citizen's resolve

★**Porto-Novo**
Unfulfilled residents barely able to enjoy city's stability

Daily Life
The people of Benin are not stupid. They're not going to start killing each other when they know there's a guy with a camera standing right there.

Ghana

» THE GHANAIAN FLAG DEFIES DESCRIPTION.

In Africa's Success Story, A Hidden Genocide

At first glance, Ghana appears to be one of the continent's most stable republics, yet every day, hundreds fall victim to the horrific atrocities that plague the streets of this small African nation: senseless potholes, ruthlessly unmarked crosswalks, and frightening abuses of the carpool lane.

Ghanaians awake each morning knowing that just outside their doors lurk arterial roads with missing or outdated speed-limit signs. They leave for work in fear of coming face-to-face with a cell-phone-wielding maniac who has no regard for the right-of-way. They wonder if they'll make it back to their families without a bruised wrist, or worse yet—whiplash.

Things get even scarier at night: the streetlights are dimmer than national wattage standards allow, and savages roam the highways without the human decency to even turn off their high beams for oncoming traffic.

Unfortunately, the plight of these people has been largely ignored by the African media and the world at large. Indeed, many Ghanaians wonder what it will take for the international community to respond to this tragedy—how many malfunctioning stoplights, how many dented guardrails, how many left turns across double-yellow lines there must be before something is done.

A Ghanaian despairs over unsynchronized traffic lights.

Map labels:
- ✕ Humans-rights group documenting numerous traffic violations
- ✕ Site of thousands of illegal right turns
- ✕ Woman grieving over thousands of dead-end streets
- ☐ Bank that closes tragically early on weekends
- ✕ World-music band writing protest song about loitering
- The Volta River doesn't even have the courtesy to have a delta
- ✕ Frustrated citizen who can't decide where to park
- ☐ Citizens fleeing country to escape shoddy job by street cleaner
- ☐ Cul-de-sac from hell
- ✕ Thousands forced against their will to take this detour
- ☐ Place that inspired all the music your college girlfriend ever listened to
- *Citizens In This Region Forced To Live In A World Where People Park Right In Front Of Fire Hydrants*
- ☐ Man weeping at dip in the road
- ✕ Where the streets have no names because someone stole the signs
- ☐ UN airdropping concrete for badly needed road upgrades
- ☐ That Day We Beat The U.S. In The World Cup Memorial Stadium
- ☐ Village devastated by lack of parking
- **Accra** ★ *Bono can't believe what passes for a curb here*

Culture
Ghanaians are taught at an early age how to play drums. In 1982, all 19 million citizens joined the Allman Brothers Band.

HISTORY » A STABLE, SPOILED STATE

2000 B.C. Early Ghana inhabitants invent the wheel, the pedestrian, and the blind spot.

A.D. 1230 The ancient empire of Ghana begins its decline just as soon as King Sumanguru mentions how powerful it's been lately.

1836 Dutch King William I is disappointed when he demands that the colony of Ghana bring him "his weight in slaves" and receives 142-pound Mtumbe Ngoube.

1922 Ghana celebrates its first festival. Precisely one year later, it commemorates this joyous occasion with a celebration.

1957 Ghana becomes the first African colony to be granted independence, a distinction it credits to being the first to ask.

1961 The first-ever Peace Corps volunteers are sent to Ghana, where they successfully prevent a military overthrow by not showering for 32 consecutive days.

Shirley Temple

1974 Shirley Temple is appointed the U.S. ambassador to Ghana, replacing outgoing ambassador W. C. Fields. Citizens embrace her as a leader in race relations due to the fact that she once tap-danced with a black man.

1992 Scandal and controversy surround Ghana's national elections, in which Jerry Rawlings wins the presidency with 156% of the vote.

1997 Ghana-born Kofi Annan is appointed Secretary-General of the United Nations, and as his first act of goodwill, immediately dispatches 2,000 UN security forces to see if his mother needs anything from the grocery store.

MAJOR ATROCITIES IN GHANA »

- 45% **No parking spaces**
- 23% **All out of strawberries**
- 21% **Mail came late**
- 10% **Nothing good on TV**
- 1% **Ethnic violence/Warfare/Genocide**

Ivory Coast

Unstable At Last

For nearly 40 years, Ivory Coast watched as all the other African nations developed into full-fledged corrupt dictatorships, nervously wondering if they would be the last one on the continent to experience a violent civil war.

While citizens from neighboring countries were going out every night and slaying innocent civilians till dawn, Ivorians stayed safely inside their borders, quietly working on their national infrastructure and building a model democracy.

By the late 1980s, most African nations had already gotten involved in two, sometimes three long-term border conflicts, while Ivory Coast still hadn't even had its first coup. Ivorians wanted more than anything to have a civil war, but they just didn't know how to go about starting one. After years without a single uprising, they began to worry that they were doomed to stay a peaceful, stable republic forever.

However, in 1999, it happened.

And it was just as bloody as they had imagined. Although Ivorians admit they didn't quite know what they were doing at first, they quickly got the hang of interethnic warfare. Today, they no longer fear the awkwardness of a spontaneous bus-station bombing—they embrace it. Brutal violence now comes effortlessly to them, and Ivorians are proud to say they've been in a serious conflict for almost a decade.

Border skirmish conducted by candlelight

• Maninian
City not quite the same since its first coup

Fun-To-Pronounce-Village-Name Zone

✕ Pineapple doing all it can to diversify economy

□ Tuskless-elephant preserve

✕ French retreating from peace talks after hearing a twig snap

• *City covered in thick layer of cocoa smog*

Region Clearly Faking Coup

✕ Ivorians embarrassed after battle lasts just two minutes

✕ Ivorian civilians pretending to be Sudanese civilians to spice up slaughter

✕ Inexperienced rebel fumbling around trying to find landmine

✕ Elephants who have no idea what country they live in

Bloody Coup Stain

★ **Yamoussoukro**
This capital city is almost certainly spelled wrong

✕ Creepy Ivorians who just like watching ethnic warfare

✕ Government wants to try getting overthrown from behind now

Seizable Region

✕ President never in the mood to be ousted anymore

✕ UN peace-losing mission

• *City combating malaria problem with flyswatter*

Cocoa forests located either here or on the top of the country

FACTS » IN THIS CONFLICT FOR THE LONG HAUL

COUNTRY NAME	OFTEN MISTAKEN FOR	LEADING SOURCE OF INCOME	INTERNET PASSWORD	INTERNATIONAL ORGANIZATIONS
Ivory Coast ("Côte d'Ivoire" to snobs)	Brand of soap	Christmas, birthdays	1v0ry c0ast	Used to be in all of them back in nerdy days; now just WTO
MAIN HILL TYPE	FAVORITE COUP	NATIONAL HOLIDAY	LOWEST POINT	and IMF
Undulating	Definitely Dec. 15, 2002...definitely	Forced Labor Day (Feb. 2)	Time citizens fell asleep during skirmish	

HISTORY » WAITING FOR ITS FIRST BLOODY PERIOD

Maurice Treich-Laplène

PRE-1600S Honestly, not too much.

1842 The French begin a conquest of the interior, and build several malaria plantations on the southern coast.

1896 Malaria becomes a human-transmittable disease, leading many Ivorians to speculate that someone from San Pedro had sex with an infected mosquito—probably Steve.

1960 Upon independence, Ivory Coast becomes West Africa's richest country, which it credits to its money-saving method of importing goods, using them once, and then returning them for a full refund.

1966–1980 For over a decade, Ivory Coast is the world's leading producer of cocoa. However, it is still only the second-leading producer of hot cocoa, behind 67-year-old Esther Tollefson of Ishpeming, Michigan.

1980 Ivory Coast's cocoa industry is crippled by a worldwide shortage of tiny little marshmallows.

1983 The capital officially moves from Abidjan to Yamoussoukro. It becomes a huge ordeal, however, as they had only one van and all the citizens who said they'd help never showed up.

1993 After 33 years in power, President Felix Houphouet-Boigny dies. His last wish: "Upon my passing, Ivory Coast shall be made

politically unstable."

1999 An attempted coup turns bloody when Gen. Robert Guei has one of his chronic nosebleeds.

2000 Following its first-ever coup, Ivory Coast receives a decorative AK-47-basket as a welcoming gift from Nigeria.

Alassane Ouattara

2001 After a failed military coup, embarrassed opposition leader Alassane Ouattara returns home to continue practicing his ousting skills in front of the mirror.

2004 As violence erupts in the Ivory Coast, the UN deploys peacekeeping

force Denny Billingsley, who is a really good listener and can totally see both sides of the current situation.

THE CEREMONIAL MASKS OF THE IVORY COAST »

Moon Goddess

Forest Demon

Snake King

Richard Nixon

Liberia

Escaping The American Dream

The West African nation of Liberia was founded in 1822 by former U.S. slaves, who set out to achieve the American Dream of freedom, equality, and democracy by leaving America.

Modeling their new nation on the United States, the slaves soon forced the native Liberians off their land, created a government that favors the elite, and embraced the American ideals of religious persecution and racial discrimination.

Desperate to carry on American customs, they enslaved the entire race of indigenous tribesmen, leading to a violent, bloody civil war that the Liberians conducted in a shining tribute to their fatherland. They received so little attention from the U.S. during this conflict, however, that Liberia held a second civil war a few years later just to impress them.

Today, Liberia is still trying to keep up with the standards set by the U.S.—its economy is in ruins, it held divisive, potentially fraudulent elections in 2000 that installed a weak, ineffective leader, and despite progress made in race relations since independence, the nation's blacks (100%) are still second-class citizens.

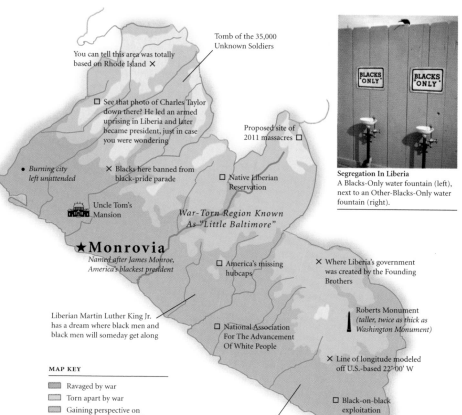

You can tell this area was totally based on Rhode Island ✕

Tomb of the 35,000 Unknown Soldiers

☐ See that photo of Charles Taylor down there? He led an armed uprising in Liberia and later became president, just in case you were wondering

Proposed site of 2011 massacres ☐

● Burning city left unattended

✕ Blacks here banned from black-pride parade

☐ Native Liberian Reservation

Uncle Tom's Mansion

War-Torn Region Known As "Little Baltimore"

★ **Monrovia**
Named after James Monroe, America's blackest president

☐ America's missing hubcaps

✕ Where Liberia's government was created by the Founding Brothers

Liberian Martin Luther King Jr. has a dream where black men and black men will someday get along

☐ National Association For The Advancement Of White People

Roberts Monument *(taller, twice as thick as Washington Monument)*

✕ Line of longitude modeled off U.S.-based 22°00' W

☐ Black-on-black exploitation

⚓ Birthplace of "Back To America" movement

MAP KEY
- Ravaged by war
- Torn apart by war
- Gaining perspective on meaninglessness of life by war

Segregation In Liberia
A Blacks-Only water fountain (left), next to an Other-Blacks-Only water fountain (right).

HISTORY » OVERDUE BIRTH OF A NATION

Pres. Joseph Jenkins Roberts

A.D. 1821 Bursting with repatriatic pride, America gives its freeborn blacks and emancipated slaves the opportunity to be forced to establish a colony in Africa—an opportunity they have absolutely no choice but to accept.

1822 Upon reaching the shores of Africa, the Americo-Liberians kiss the ground, causing many to die of Lassa fever, a soil-contact disease.

Charles Taylor

1824 Former U.S. slaves found Liberia and begin to build a society based on what they know of America. They construct large, magnificent homes and sleep outside of them in small wooden shacks. They adopt the U.S. Constitution, which forbids them from voting. And they work tirelessly in the fields, exporting all their crops to white U.S. citizens completely free of charge.

1827 A mere four years after escaping a land where only whites could be slave-owners, the Americo-Liberians create a truly equal society in which blacks could own slaves, as well.

1856 Inhabitants name their country "Liberia," which at the time translated to "Land Of The Free" in Latin, but has since lost all real meaning.

1926 The Firestone Company invests in Liberia for its rubber and latex, and proceeds to safely fuck the country for the next 80 years.

Sirleaf

2005 Upon winning Liberia's national elections, Ellen Johnson-Sirleaf becomes Africa's first openly female leader.

POPULATION BREAKDOWN »

- Black 85%
- Black 15%

FACTS » LAND OF THE FREE-ISH

NATIONALITIES
Americo-Liberian, Afro-Liberian, Afro-Americo-African

BLACK HISTORY MONTH
March

NATIONAL ANTHEM
"God Bless America"

CONSTITUTION
Photocopied Jan. 6, 1986

GOVERNMENT
Elections held every 6 years; free and fair elections held every 18 years

CRITICISM FROM U.S.
Has still never elected a white president

INTERNATIONAL ORGANIZATIONS
Signed up for UNESCO just because U.S. did

WORST-SOUNDING WATERBORNE DISEASE
Protozoal diarrhea

ECONOMY-IN-RUINS-AND-NATION-OVERRUN-WITH-WEAPONS-NESS
High

PEOPLE » WHERE BLACKS AND BLACKS REFUSE TO LIVE IN HARMONY

Comprised of ruling-class Americo-Liberians, who are black, and oppressed native Liberians, who are black, Liberia is one of the most racially intolerant all-black nations.

Liberia is plagued by rampant black-on-black hate crimes, and it suffers from the worst unemployment rate in the world at 85%, which black Americo-Liberians blame on the abundance of lazy black citizens in the nation.

Sierra Leone

» SIERRA LEONE'S LAST REMAINING OBJECT OF ANY VALUE ABOVE GROUND.

A Blood Diamond Is Forever

Sparked by the illegal trafficking of diamonds, Sierra Leone's civil war left thousands dead, millions more homeless, and much of the nation in complete disarray. But it was all worth it for the look on Rachel's face when Craig showed her that ring.

One of the worst tragedies in recent history, the war in Sierra Leone saw innocent men murdered in cold blood, and women defiled by rebel forces in front of their children. However, things could have been a lot worse. For instance, Michael may never have found the perfect way to express his love for Katie.

As terrifying as the war was for the citizens of Sierra Leone, many have recently found solace in knowing that their suffering wasn't in vain, and that Peter finally got down on one knee and proposed to Michelle like he had promised.

In fact, villagers in the town of Moyamba would likely never have wept at the sight of their burning homes had they known that Tom had at last asked for Jenny's hand in marriage, and that the two had set a date for the big day.

Well, maybe they would have—out of joy.

Today, while it's difficult to predict what the long-term effects of Sierra Leone's campaign of torture and brutality will ultimately be, relatives of Chuck and Linda are almost positive it's a boy.

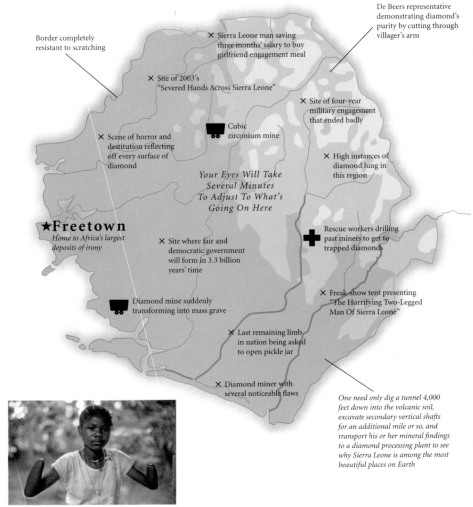

Border completely resistant to scratching

× Sierra Leone man saving three months' salary to buy girlfriend engagement meal

De Beers representative demonstrating diamond's purity by cutting through villager's arm

× Site of 2003's "Severed Hands Across Sierra Leone"

× Site of four-year military engagement that ended badly

Cubic zirconium mine

× Scene of horror and destitution reflecting off every surface of diamond

× High instances of diamond lung in this region

Your Eyes Will Take Several Minutes To Adjust To What's Going On Here

★**Freetown**
Home to Africa's largest deposits of irony

× Site where fair and democratic government will form in 3.3 billion years' time

Rescue workers drilling past miners to get to trapped diamonds

× Freak-show tent presenting "The Horrifying Two-Legged Man Of Sierra Leone"

Diamond mine suddenly transforming into mass grave

× Last remaining limb in nation being asked to open pickle jar

× Diamond miner with several noticeable flaws

One need only dig a tunnel 4,000 feet down into the volcanic soil, excavate secondary vertical shafts for an additional mile or so, and transport his or her mineral findings to a diamond processing plant to see why Sierra Leone is among the most beautiful places on Earth

A Sierra Leonean girl, probably waving hello.

HISTORY » THIS YEAR GIVE HER THE GIFT THAT SAYS "FUCK SIERRA LEONE"

A.D. 1534 Sierra Leone becomes a major center of the transatlantic slave trade, thanks in part to the development of a hugely successful marketing technique still in use today: branding.

1565–1583 Sierra Leone's greatest explorer, Mtumbe Barrluca, travels to the United States, France, Germany, Spain, Portugal, China, and Australia after being sold 67 times by slave masters.

1972 De Beers, the world's largest exporter of diamonds, sets up a home base in Sierra Leone, and for the next 20 years helps to rebuild the destitute nation from the ground down.

1993 A whirlwind military engagement between the Revolutionary United Front and Sierra Leone enters its third year. Neither side can believe how quickly time has passed since they first came into combat together.

1994 International silence over Sierra Leone's gruesome campaign of rape and amputation is at last broken with a six-page exposé in the March issue of *Stumpfuckers Monthly*.

1997 The UN Security Council votes swiftly to enter "Phase Seventeen" of the "Fourth Planning Stage" to possibly deploy troops to Sierra Leone at some point.

1999 An estimated 30,000 Sierra Leoneans have their arms hacked off, according to one state official forced to count on his toes.

2002 After nearly 10 years, the RUF and Sierra Leone's president realize the nation's civil war just wasn't meant to last.

Kanye West

2005 American rap artist Kanye West releases "Diamonds From Sierra Leone," a highly critical indictment of those who have exploited the African nation for their own monetary gain. The song goes platinum and earns West $1.3 million in its first week.

FACTS » ENGAGED TO MISERY

AREA
Modest

CERTIFIED BY
The International Geological Institute as a Genuine Hellhole

CLARITY
Slowly improving after fog of decade-long civil war

IMPERFECTIONS
Corruption, poverty (visible), strife

DURABILITY
Guaranteed until 2013

RECENT ECONOMIC PROPOSALS
Four (all turned down due to cold feet)

A young couple picks out their engagement ring in Sierra Leone.

Gambia & Senegal

GAMBIA » COULD THE BLUE STRIPE RUNNING THROUGH THE MIDDLE REPRESENT A RIVER?

SENEGAL » FOR AFRICA, THIS FLAG IS CONSIDERED UNIQUE.

Gambia
"Come On In— The Water's Fine!"

Stretching from the shallow end in Basse Santa to the deep end in Banjul, the in-ground river nation of Gambia might seem a little cold at first, but citizens claim that once you get in, it's not so bad.

Although Gambians are encouraged to have fun, UN lifeguards are stationed every 20 meters to ensure that citizens refrain from horseplay, excessive splashing, and running along the nation's borders. In addition, Gambia's border patrol makes sure that foreign diplomats wait at least 30 minutes after eating before entering the country.

One of Africa's safest nations, a law passed in 1972 officially banned the dangerous practice of cannonballing, and requires that all residents evacuate Gambia upon the first sight of lightning.

FACTS » A COUNTRY RUNS THROUGH IT

NATURAL HAZARDS
Whirlpools, formed when citizens all swim around nation in circle

MARITIME CLAIMS
Once held breath underwater for two minutes

MAIN MODE OF TRANSPORTATION
Pool noodle

GDP
$3.04 billion (includes $2 million in pennies found on bottom of nation)

DEATH RATE
Most deaths faked so that pretty lifeguard will give them mouth-to-mouth

MTUMBE NGOUBE
Won't share goggles with other 1.6 million citizens

HEALTH HAZARDS
Toe cramps, bellyflops, AIDS

JUSTICE SYSTEM
All Gambians have right to free swim

MIGRATION
More citizens leave nation's shallow end as they get older

Traditional Dress Of Gambia

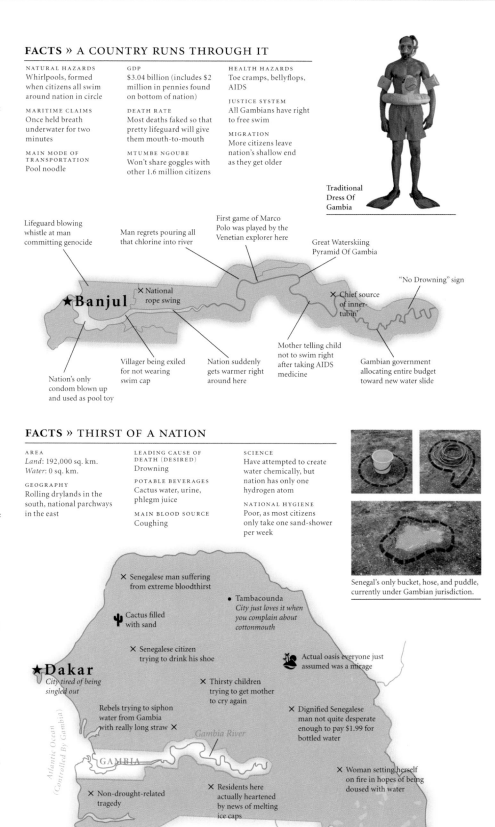

Lifeguard blowing whistle at man committing genocide

Man regrets pouring all that chlorine into river

First game of Marco Polo was played by the Venetian explorer here

Great Waterskiing Pyramid Of Gambia

★**Banjul**

✕ National rope swing

"No Drowning" sign

✕ Chief source of inner-tubin'

Nation's only condom blown up and used as pool toy

Villager being exiled for not wearing swim cap

Nation suddenly gets warmer right around here

Mother telling child not to swim right after taking AIDS medicine

Gambian government allocating entire budget toward new water slide

Senegal
"Please… Give Us… Water…"

Located two miles from the banks of the Gambia River, 150 feet from the banks of the Gambia Stream, and mere inches from the banks of the Gambia Mirage, Senegal is known for its long, barren stretches of dry and desiccated throats.

Senegal regularly sends diplomats to the nation of Gambia, which also controls all of the region's lakes, ponds, puddles, rainfall, and dew.

Senegalese negotiators crawl toward the Gambian capital with outstretched arms and cracked, bruised lips in a desperate show of peace, hoping to establish ties with the water-rich nation for even just 30 seconds. Gambia, however, is reluctant to share their water, as they believe the Senegalese will end up backwashing into their river.

Making matters worse, Senegal's major imports are peanuts and pretzels.

The Gambian Border

FACTS » THIRST OF A NATION

AREA
Land: 192,000 sq. km.
Water: 0 sq. km.

GEOGRAPHY
Rolling drylands in the south, national parchways in the east

LEADING CAUSE OF DEATH (DESIRED)
Drowning

POTABLE BEVERAGES
Cactus water, urine, phlegm juice

MAIN BLOOD SOURCE
Coughing

SCIENCE
Have attempted to create water chemically, but nation has only one hydrogen atom

NATIONAL HYGIENE
Poor, as most citizens only take one sand-shower per week

Senegal's only bucket, hose, and puddle, currently under Gambian jurisdiction.

✕ Senegalese man suffering from extreme bloodthirst

• Tambacounda
City just loves it when you complain about cottonmouth

🌵 Cactus filled with sand

★**Dakar**
City tired of being singled out

✕ Senegalese citizen trying to drink his shoe

Actual oasis everyone just assumed was a mirage

✕ Thirsty children trying to get mother to cry again

✕ Dignified Senegalese man not quite desperate enough to pay $1.99 for bottled water

Rebels trying to siphon water from Gambia with really long straw ✕

Gambia River

Atlantic Ocean (Controlled By Gambia)

GAMBIA

✕ Non-drought-related tragedy

✕ Residents here actually heartened by news of melting ice caps

✕ Woman setting herself on fire in hopes of being doused with water

Cape Verde & São Tomé–Principe

Cape Verde
Demoted To The Fourth World

With the island's lack of shelter well below average, droughts occurring far more often than the Third World—allotted twice per year, and over 30 mass graves that aren't up to code, Cape Verde is now a Fourth World nation.

The nation's rocky soil, which is unsuitable even for staring at in desperation, has failed to yield a single crop since that one potato in 1973. In addition, the amount of readily available peanuts in the country, at three, falls short of the Third World minimum by a whopping seven. Cape Verde's president attempted to protest the demotion in an impassioned speech, but died of starvation mid-sentence.

Recently, much to the nation's dismay, Cape Verde had to return its proudly displayed "Member Of The Third World" plaque to the UN.

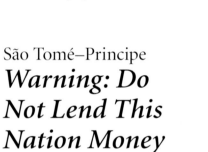

Cesaria Evora
Cape Verde's famous folk singer serenades some goats.

✕ Off-target UN food drop

✕ Half-eaten billboard

✕ Closer, but still off-target UN food drop

✕ Fortified vault of the National Peanut

Man learning to love taste of granite ✕

✕ Man who would be happy to just sniff a pie

Man who always assumed Cape Verde was already a Fourth World nation

The Island You Think Of When You Think "Cape Verde"

Mean-spirited shark

Island once tried to sneak into NATO

✕ Aquaman molested by uncle here

☐ World Music Hall Of Fame/Starbucks

★**Praia**
Voted "Least-Best Capital In Africa"

✕ Man on beach using metal detector to find newer metal detector

Unemployed man somehow getting fired from unemployment

No Islands Down Here

FACTS » A BUNCH OF ROCKS WITH NO FOOD ON THEM

TRADITIONAL GREETING
"Hello, sir, do you by chance have any spare hope?"

NATURAL RESOURCE
One piece of bauxite

LIVESTOCK BELOW THE POVERTY LINE
15 goats, 12 cattle, all 4 sheep

GILLIGAN'S ISLAND COMPARATIVE
80% less scientific innovation, 30% less coconuts, 100% less Howells, equally plausible

LIVE BIRTHS PER HOT SANDWICH EATEN
40/2

TOP OCCUPATION
Occupation-census gatherer

CHANCE ISLANDS WILL BE INHABITED BY 2056
0.4%

REASON FOR HOPE
Local farmer once grew a carrot on the beach

São Tomé–Principe
Warning: Do Not Lend This Nation Money

São Tomé–Principe, the debt-ridden archipelago off the west coast of Africa, may soon be forced to board up its islands and move to a cheaper nation.

After years of heavy mooching to support its cocoa industry, and the fact that the government put the nation's entire budget on an already maxed-out credit card, São Tomé–Principe's World Bank account was foreclosed, forcing it to start cashing debt-relief checks at the World Check$ Ca$hed Shack.

FACTS » WILL GLADLY PAY YOU TUESDAY FOR AN ECONOMY TODAY

GOVERNMENT	ECONOMY	LITERACY RATE
System of bounced checks and unpaid balances	Loan-based	52.4% (drops to 1% when credit-card statement shows up)
	DEPENDENTS	
	3 young islets	

A BAD CREDIT HISTORY »

After defaulting on its loans, the island of Principe is repossessed.

A.D. 1471 Portuguese explorers speed by, checking the island off their list.

1983 After failing to pay him back for the third year in a row, a Nigerian loan shark travels to São Tomé–Principe and breaks the kneecaps of the entire nation.

1990 The international community decides to stop sending debt relief to São Tomé–Principe, claiming that they're just going to spend the money importing cigarettes and booze.

1996 São Tomé–Principe cuts up the nation's credit cards.

2005 Nation applies for homeland-equity loans and uses the islands as collateral to consolidate bills. However, they are still required to get Portugal to co-sign for all international treaties.

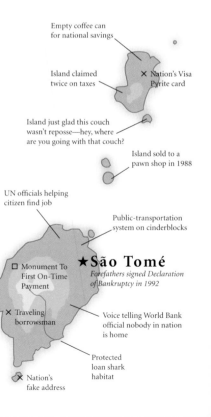

Empty coffee can for national savings

Island claimed twice on taxes

✕ Nation's Visa Pyrite card

Island just glad this couch wasn't reposse—hey, where are you going with that couch?

Island sold to a pawn shop in 1988

UN officials helping citizen find job

Public-transportation system on cinderblocks

☐ Monument To First On-Time Payment

★**São Tomé**
Forefathers signed Declaration of Bankruptcy in 1992

✕ Traveling borrowsman

Voice telling World Bank official nobody in nation is home

Protected loan shark habitat

✕ Nation's fake address

Mauritania

Holy Living Fuck—They Still Have Slaves Here

Mauritania is home to nearly 100,000 slaves—lifetime laborers denied the most basic human freedoms that other Africans enjoy, including access to contaminated drinking water and the right to beg for food.

Cheated out of a life of severely limited opportunity and negligible possibilities, slaves in Mauritania are routinely separated from their families, and, unlike most African citizens, may never have the chance to see their children be buried in a shallow grave.

Despite their present situation, however, many still hold out hope of one day toiling past the point of exhaustion, not because they have been ordered to do so, but because they would starve otherwise.

While the dream of being dehumanized by hostile occupiers, immoral militia forces, or government-supported mercenaries rather than by their masters remains alive, the sad fact is that few will ever experience the quiet dignity that comes with dying of AIDS as a free man or woman at the age of 38.

PEOPLE » YOU DON'T WANT TO KNOW

Nouakchott
Slaves work at a sand plantation.

Mauritania is ruled by white Moors who command Haratin slaves to do everything they don't want to do, from simple duties like fetching water, cooking, and cleaning, to more difficult daily tasks such as carrying out acts of compassion, common decency, and mercy toward their fellow man.

FACTS » MAURITANIA AT NOT FAR ENOUGH A GLANCE

POPULATION BREAKDOWN
Slaves to fashion (0.8%),
Slaves to religion (22%),
Slaves to slave masters (77%)

FORCED FERTILITY RATE
5.8 children born/kicking, screaming slave

LANGUAGES
Spoken only when spoken to

JUSTICE SYSTEM
Based on series of whipping posts

NATURAL RESOURCES
Iron ore, gypsum, copper, Mtumbe Ngoube

NATIONAL HOLIDAY
Freedom Day, Nov. 28 (2074)

UNEMPLOYMENT
Prayed for

HISTORY » CHAINED TO THE PAST

A.D. 680 The practice of agriculture is made more efficient by the advent of several tools, including the whip, the shackle, and the death threat.

1200 A Mauritanian slave receives 50 lashes for having gone almost a day without receiving 50 lashes.

1500 Mauritanian slaves attempt to dream of a life free from brutality, but awake screaming each time they roll over on their backs.

1850 Determined French forces arrive in Mauritania with the sole objective of developing a slave outpost, but are disappointed to find that the work of subjugating thousands of men has already been done for them.

1961 Dozens of ashtrays, footstools, and punching bags are purchased at a local slave sale.

1979 Another child is born into slavery, after his mother's master orders the infant to rupture its own amniotic sac, single-handedly dilate the cervix, and push past the womb opening to deliver itself.

1981 Thousands of slaves in Mauritania escape the shackles of metaphor.

1983 In an attempt to discourage slavery, Mauritania enacts a law that makes slave ownership punishable by lifetime enslavement.

1990 Mauritania abolishes the term "slavery."

2006 In the face of growing international pressure, Mauritanian slaves are ordered to work 24 hours a day to find a solution to the nation's slavery epidemic.

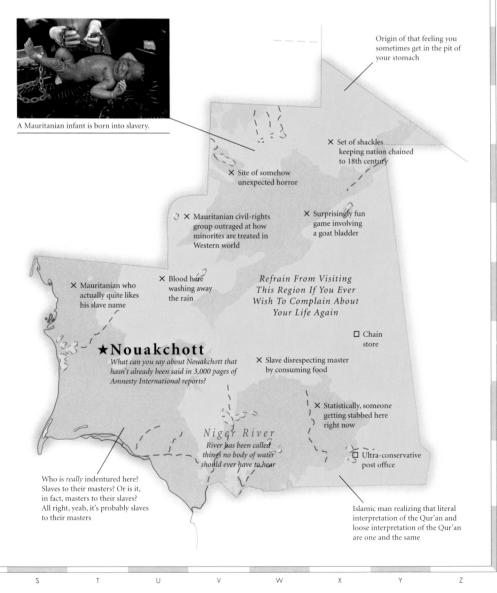
A Mauritanian infant is born into slavery.

Origin of that feeling you sometimes get in the pit of your stomach

✕ Set of shackles keeping nation chained to 18th century

✕ Site of somehow unexpected horror

✕ Mauritanian civil-rights group outraged at how minorites are treated in Western world

✕ Surprisingly fun game involving a goat bladder

✕ Mauritanian who actually quite likes his slave name

✕ Blood here washing away the rain

Refrain From Visiting This Region If You Ever Wish To Complain About Your Life Again

☐ Chain store

★ **Nouakchott**
What can you say about Nouakchott that hasn't already been said in 3,000 pages of Amnesty International reports?

✕ Slave disrespecting master by consuming food

✕ Statistically, someone getting stabbed here right now

Niger River
River has been called things no body of water should ever have to hear

☐ Ultra-conservative post office

Who is *really* indentured here? Slaves to their masters? Or is it, in fact, masters to their slaves? All right, yeah, it's probably slaves to their masters

Islamic man realizing that literal interpretation of the Qur'an and loose interpretation of the Qur'an are one and the same

Morocco

» THIS LOVELY FLAG CAN BE YOURS FOR THE PRICE OF JUST 60 DIRHAMS!

» FOR CENTURIES, PEOPLE HAVE GAZED IN WONDERMENT AT MOROCCO'S EXOTIC STACKS OF DUSTY PLATES.

A Mystical Land Of Junk

Famous for its open-air bazaars and markets, Morocco is a strange, mysterious land brimming with ancient trinkets, unexplained knick-knacks, and the alluring promise of vast untold crap.

Labyrinthine roads wind through mythic cities such as Fez and Marrakesh, where there is no telling what unimaginable discoveries await visitors at every turn, from old cracked mugs to a used pair of khaki pants. Tourists from around the world travel to Morocco in the hopes of finding out what enchanted talisman hides just behind the curtain of each eerie storefront.

Usually, it's a rug.

At dawn, the sunlight glints off the rows of rusted belt buckles, illuminating the miles upon miles of broken watches that dot the region. Dimly lit rooms fill with rings of smoke, a sense of magic, and cheap picture frames. Pre-worn dresses sway in the ominous Moroccan winds, and tables covered in unusually smooth rocks stretch as far as the eye can see. The secrets of age-old counterfeit leather purses, each of which has a story all its own, can only be unlocked in this enigmatic land.

Indeed, Morocco is proof that the arcane wonders of the old world—chipped vases, plastic beads, and little shiny metal things that look like some sort of ring—truly do exist.

PEOPLE » HOW CAN WE PUT YOU ON THIS RUG TODAY?

The people of Morocco are outgoing, hard-working, and very skilled at taking pictures of tourists for money. The average citizen's official language, religious beliefs, interests, hobbies, and life philosophy tend to be exactly the same as that of the person they are swindling at the time.

According to custom, making eye contact with a Moroccan citizen automatically engages one in a four-hour conversation that can only be terminated with the purchase of a carpet. While the nation is generally regarded as the last vestige of the Old World, Moroccans are beginning to catch up with the rest of civilization, with certain shops offering products such as handmade cell phones and finely woven computers.

Although one-eighth of Moroccans are unemployed and one-fifth live in poverty, only 3% of citizens under the age of 12 are jobless.

FACTS » NEGOTIABLE FOR THE RIGHT PRICE

POPULATION
83 million… Fine, 65 million… Okay, 33 million and some camels

RELIGIOUS BREAKDOWN
Muslims: 32.9 million
Jews: Saul Lieberstein

AGE STRUCTURE
0–12: Child
13–19: Teenager
20–59: Adult
60–100: Elderly

FUNNY LITTLE RED HATS?
Yes

WILDLIFE
Thousands of species of rodents

LANDMARKS
That stand that sells exotic sticks with writing on them

ECONOMY
Dependent on whether or not you will pay $600 for this beautiful rug

INTERNATIONAL ORGANIZATIONS
UN, WTO, EPCOT

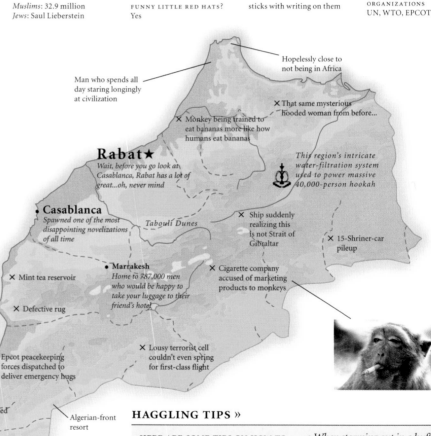

Hopelessly close to not being in Africa

Man who spends all day staring longingly at civilization

✕ That same mysterious hooded woman from before…

✕ Monkey being trained to eat bananas more like how humans eat bananas

Rabat★
Wait, before you go look at Casablanca, Rabat has a lot of great…oh, never mind

This region's intricate water-filtration system used to power massive 40,000-person hookah

• **Casablanca**
Spawned one of the most disappointing novelizations of all time

Tabouli Dunes

✕ Ship suddenly realizing this is not Strait of Gibraltar

✕ 15-Shriner-car pileup

✕ Mint tea reservoir

• **Marrakesh**
Home to 787,000 men who would be happy to take your luggage to their friend's hotel

✕ Cigarette company accused of marketing products to monkeys

✕ Defective rug

✕ Lousy terrorist cell couldn't even spring for first-class flight

✕ Epcot peacekeeping forces dispatched to deliver emergency hugs

✕ Eerie man shrouded in couscous

Algerian-front resort

✕ Jesus Christ, you still can't escape the hippies, even here!

Border dispute more of a border heated discussion

Priceless treasures await visitors to Morocco, especially those in need of shoes.

MAP KEY

▨ Please come in, I believe I have just what you're looking for
▨ This is not something I show to simply anyone, my friend
▨ What's that? Why this is more than just any ordinary plastic ashtray
▨ All right fine, $2—what do you say?

HAGGLING TIPS »

HERE ARE SOME TIPS ON HOW TO NEGOTIATE THE BEST PRICE FOR GOODS IN A MOROCCAN MARKET:

• *Act like you don't need a carpet*

• *Start bidding at "Free"*

• *Avoid common mistakes such as getting interested in a lamp for no reason*

• *When storming out in a huff, pause in doorway for up to 15 minutes to give vendor a chance to lower price*

• *Wear really nice pants; offer to include pants*

• *If vendor still refuses to go down on price, just pay the goddamn $60 for the beads if you want them so bad*

WESTERN SAHARA » THIS IS WHERE NATION'S FLAG WOULD GO IF IT HAD ONE.

HISTORY » A NATION HAGGLED DOWN TO NOTHING

A.D. 439 Barbarian tribes known as the Vandals pass through Africa's northern region under the cover of night, and spray-paint "Morocco Sucks!" in big letters on the face of the Atlas Mountains.

685 The Jews bring Islam to Morocco, dump it in a nearby ditch, bury it, and speed away hoping to never see or hear from it again.

1513 While serving in the Portuguese army, explorer Ferdinand Magellan wounds his knee in a Moroccan battle and immediately exclaims, "Aw, I'll never be able to fully circumnavigate the globe *now*!"

1666–PRESENT A sequence of kings from the same family reign over Morocco for so many consecutive years that many historians have begun to dub this uninterrupted chain of related royalty a "dynasty."

1854 France wanders into the area and expresses serious interest in the land. French forces engage in their trademark "cutthroat" style of negotiation.

1878 Morocco underestimates the value of its phosphate reserves, and hands them over to Spain in exchange for several hats.

Casablanca (1942)

1939 American movie producer Hal Wallis takes his then-titled script "Arab Port City" to 17 Moroccan municipal governments, including Rabat, Tangier, and Tetouan, before receiving filming rights from the Casablanca Chamber of Commerce.

1943 At the end of WWII's "Casablanca Conference," attended by leaders of the Allied Forces, Franklin Delano Roosevelt turns to Winston Churchill and says, "Winston, I think this is the beginning of a beautiful friendship." Churchill, however, fails to get the reference, and—thoroughly creeped out—avoids FDR for the rest of his life.

1975 Western Sahara becomes a disputed territory when the solid line that used to demarcate its border is suddenly changed into a dashed line.

1987 The UN coaxes Morocco and the Polisario guerrilla group into peace talks by sending each of them a letter supposedly written by the other side, which apologizes for the way they've been acting and offers to meet up for dinner and ceasefire negotiations later that evening.

1998 The country devolves into complete anarchy when a street merchant sells Morocco's constitution to a vacationing Wyoming couple for $29.

2003 Moroccan street performers train monkeys to mimic human behaviors such as smoking cigarettes, ignoring that persistent cough, battling emphysema, undergoing chemotherapy, and roller-skating.

2005 Morocco haggles with the UN over a foreign-aid payment. Morocco starts high by asking for $500 billion, but the UN calls that unrealistic, countering with $12 million. Moroccan officials then offer to throw in 100 beads for $6.8 billion. After four months of negotiating over mint tea, Morocco receives $15 million, 1,500 flu vaccines, a new pair of tennis shoes, and three UN-certified goats.

Western Sahara
Africa's Last Great Hope

With no natural resources to exploit, no arable land to fight over, no standing government to topple, and no population to slaughter, Western Sahara has something other African nations can only dream of: nothing.

An uninhabitable haven free from food, water, food- and waterborne diseases, clothing, shelter, citizens, and poverty, the desolate territory of Western Sahara remains Africa's last real chance for peace. Its barren landscape has evaded the destructive effects of deforestation and overgrazing, its economic growth over the last century has shown no signs of slowing down at 0%, and its human-rights policy is one of the continent's most progressive since never being introduced in 1962.

Indeed, who knows how far this inspiring non-nation can go if it continues to not go anywhere.

Possibly the most heartening sight in all of Africa.

ABSOLUTELY NOTHING

FACTS » AN EMPTY OASIS OF PEACE AND TRANQUILITY

POPULATION N/A	**RELIGION** N/A
POPULATION BELOW POVERTY LINE N/A	**ECONOMY** N/A
LIFE EXPECTANCY N/A	**JUSTICE SYSTEM** N/A
INFANT MORTALITY RATE N/A	**NATURAL HAZARDS** N/A
LANGUAGES N/A (written) N/A (spoken)	**NATURAL RESOURCES** N/A
	NATIONAL OUTLOOK Bright

Mali

» IT TOOK FOREVER TO SCRAPE THE STAR OFF THE SENEGAL FLAG.

» THE RUINS OF SOME OF MALI'S FINEST WORKS OF ARCHITECTURE.

Conveniently Located In The Middle Of Fucking Nowhere

Though Mali now ranks as one of Africa's poorest nations, great wealth once passed right by the hands of the Malian people in Timbuktu, a legendary trading post known for its convenient location just 15 million miles from everywhere.

Scholars equate ancient Timbuktu to ancient Athens, and modern-day Timbuktu to the ruins of ancient Athens if they were covered waist-deep in sand. However, Timbuktu nonetheless remains the most-visited site in all of Mali, attracting nearly several customers per decade.

Today, Mali's economy contributes very little economically to the country. While the unemployment rate is surprisingly low at 14.6%, that figure is deceiving since the nation's workforce all shares the same job.

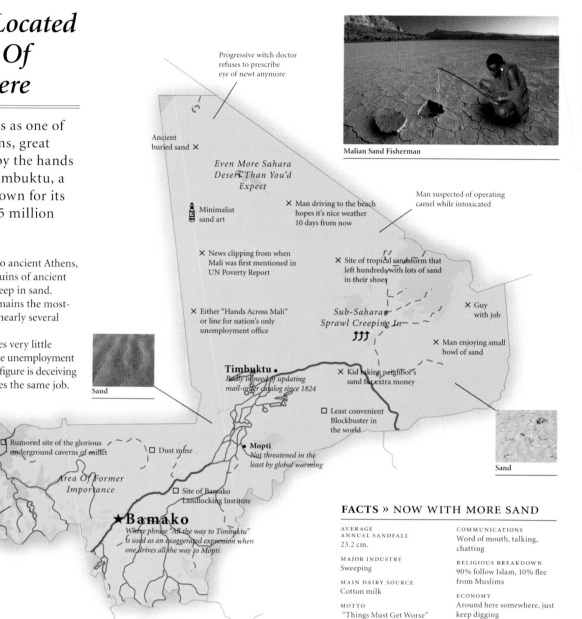

Progressive witch doctor refuses to prescribe eye of newt anymore

Ancient buried sand ✕

Even More Sahara Desert Than You'd Expect

Minimalist sand art

✕ Man driving to the beach hopes it's nice weather 10 days from now

Man suspected of operating camel while intoxicated

✕ News clipping from when Mali was first mentioned in UN Poverty Report

✕ Site of tropical sandstorm that left hundreds with lots of sand in their shoes

✕ Either "Hands Across Mali" or line for nation's only unemployment office

Sub-Saharan Sprawl Creeping In

✕ Guy with job

✕ Man enjoying small bowl of sand

Timbuktu •
Badly in need of updating mail-order catalog since 1824

✕ Kid taking neighbor's sand for extra money

□ Least convenient Blockbuster in the world

□ Rumored site of the glorious underground caverns of millet

□ Dust mine

• Mopti
Not threatened in the least by global warming

Area Of Former Importance

□ Site of Bamako Landlocking Institute

★ **Bamako**
Where phrase "All the way to Timbuktu" is used as an exaggerated expression when one drives all the way to Mopti

Sand

Sand

Sand

Malian Sand Fisherman

FACTS » NOW WITH MORE SAND

AVERAGE ANNUAL SANDFALL
23.2 cm.

MAJOR INDUSTRY
Sweeping

MAIN DAIRY SOURCE
Cotton milk

MOTTO
"Things Must Get Worse"

COMMUNICATIONS
Word of mouth, talking, chatting

RELIGIOUS BREAKDOWN
90% follow Islam, 10% flee from Muslims

ECONOMY
Around here somewhere, just keep digging

HISTORY » LIKE SAND THROUGH A CRACKED HOURGLASS

Mali was formerly a great empire and a worldwide center of trade, culture, and learning. Today, however, it is either that big sand dune over there, or maybe that one to the left of it.

The Mali Empire was formed in the early 11th century, and briefly prospered before King Sundiata traded all its gold for salt—the most treasured condiment of the ancient Malians, as it was the only thing that made the sand taste good. His successor, Mansa

Wali Keita, commissioned over 18,000 child slaves to construct the world's tallest, most extravagant sand castle, which he lived in until high tide.

King Mansa Musa, who oversaw and supervised the decline of the empire, is generally regarded as Mali's most generous and improvident leader, as he couldn't even go to the corner market without bringing 500 slaves and 5,000 pounds of gold to distribute along the way. He often remarked

that he would gladly trade away all the country's wealth in exchange for a little notoriety.

By the late 16th century, Timbuktu's importance as a link between Africa and the rest of the world waned considerably, as European explorers discovered alternate routes to steal from the people of West Africa. In 1990, UNESCO officials traveled to Timbuktu and traded the locals World Heritage Site status for everything they had left.

PEOPLE » COVERED IN SAND

A wide variety of ethnic groups live well below their means in Mali, subsisting mainly on a diet of thorns, shrubs, and millet, the fruit of the sand.

Mali has only one witch doctor per 100 people, and unfortunately most do not accept Blue Cross/Blue Shield. However, the nation is home to some of the world's top witch lawyers, witch politicians, and witch plumbers.

In 2006, over 320,000 Malians were buried alive in a Category 5 sandstorm, as their emergency strategy of lining villages with 300-pound sandbags backfired.

Algeria

Terrorism's Farm Team

For years, the nation of Algeria has served as a training camp for unpolished terrorists seeking to hone their skills, whether improving the accuracy of their beheadings, learning to drive stick-shift car bombs, or just mastering the fundamentals of blowing themselves up.

Every summer, a new crop of determined 20-year-olds arrives in Algeria, where they learn the basics of terrorism in training facilities featuring state-of-the-art gyms, hotels, subway stations, mosques, and government buildings, all available to be bombed 24 hours a day.

After weeks of taking part in rigorous suicide-bombing drills, running through airport-security obstacle courses, and perfecting terrorist plays such as the "sacrifice fly," many are transformed from ineffective amateurs into explosive talents.

Although not everyone in Algeria makes it to the big leagues, most men there would give their right arm, left arm, both legs, and torso to become a professional suicide bomber.

FACTS » AN IMPRESSIVE WIN-LOSS RECORD

RECORD VS. JEWS
542-113-1

SCHEDULE
Classified

LEADING CAUSE OF DEATH
Whipping teammates with wet suicide belt in locker room

LOWEST POINT
Time they misinterpreted "hijack plane" signal for "ask for another pillow" signal

LEGAL SYSTEM
Three airstrikes and you're out

ARMED ISLAMIC GROUPS
The Armed Islamic Group

GREATEST TERRORIST OF ALL TIME
Mussad al-Malik, who compiled the most kills of anyone, but was unpopular with fans because of his habits of showboating after bombing a street full of civilians

WORST TERRORIST OF ALL TIME
Steve, that guy who's not that into terrorism

PEOPLE » EAGER TO MAKE THEIR MARK

The people of Algeria are hardworking, eager to please Allah, and willing to put their bodies on the line to achieve a victory against the Great Satan. Some Algerians toil for years, anxiously waiting to get the extremely covert call up to the Middle Eastern division, where a new spot opens up every 25 to 30 minutes. Once there, they will have the opportunity to travel to rival cities such as New York, Washington, London, and Madrid, where they have just one chance to make a lasting impact. However, every Algerian boy still dreams of one day performing at home, in front of a crowded, capacity-filled marketplace.

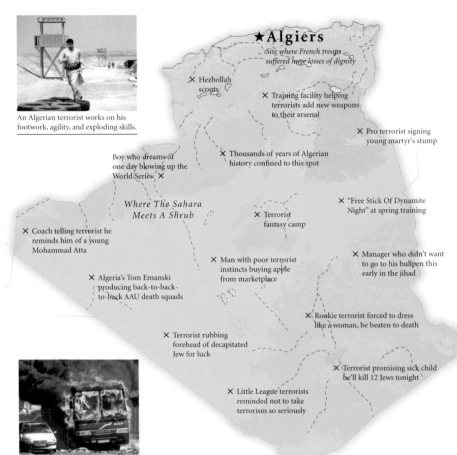

An Algerian terrorist works on his footwork, agility, and exploding skills.

★ **Algiers**
Site where French troops suffered huge losses of dignity

✕ Hezbollah scouts

✕ Training facility helping terrorists add new weapons to their arsenal

✕ Pro terrorist signing young martyr's stump

✕ Thousands of years of Algerian history confined to this spot

Boy who dreams of one day blowing up the World Series ✕

Where The Sahara Meets A Shrub

✕ "Free Stick Of Dynamite Night" at spring training

✕ Terrorist fantasy camp

✕ Coach telling terrorist he reminds him of a young Mohammad Atta

✕ Man with poor terrorist instincts buying apple from marketplace

✕ Manager who didn't want to go to his bullpen this early in the jihad

✕ Algeria's Tom Emanski producing back-to-back-to-back AAU death squads

✕ Rookie terrorist forced to dress like a woman, be beaten to death

✕ Terrorist rubbing forehead of decapitated Jew for luck

✕ Terrorist promising sick child he'll kill 12 Jews tonight

✕ Little League terrorists reminded not to take terrorism so seriously

Al-Qaeda's Team Bus

HISTORY » PRODUCING THE WORLD'S TOP TERRORISTS SINCE 1962

A.D. 1830 The French invade the Sahara Desert, burning hundreds of small plants to the ground and looting as much sand as possible before the Algerians surrender out of pity.

1962 After 60 years as a colony, Algerian rebels successfully drive out over a million French occupiers by simply raising their voices.

1967 During an exhibition attack on Israel, Akeem Baha Udeem successfully guns down dozens of runners charging home from over 200 feet away.

1972 Extremist Jefad al-Qirrilo ties the all-time record for career suicide bombings at one.

1986 Notoriously superstitious terrorist Ali Hasan refuses to shave his beard until the day he boards a 747 airliner.

1994 During a routine practice drill, insurgent Josef Ahmed ruptures his ACL, hamstring, Achilles tendon, both rotator cuffs, his spleen, and most areas on his flesh, spine, and skull—a devastating injury that immediately ends his career.

2002 Highly touted terrorist Abdul al-Raad signs the most lucrative contract in terrorist history, a deal worth up to 250 million virgins if he successfully completes his mission.

2005 Terrorist prospect Yuusuf al-Majiid is caught using performance-enhancing substances such as ammonium nitrate, triacetone triperoxide, potassium cyanide, and cesium chloride powder.

ALLAH'S FIGHTING ARABS

2006 In a blockbuster 457-person trade, al-Qaeda terrorist Hassan al-Qaadir is sent to Egypt in exchange for 456 Cairo tourists.

Tunisia

» FLAG USED TO GAG WOMEN LESS OFTEN THAN ANY OTHER MUSLIM FLAG.

A Muslim Woman's Dream Hell

One of the more progressive Islamic nations in the world, Tunisia is known for its relatively fair treatment of women, granting the long-subjugated gender such freedoms as the right to show nearly 15% of their flesh while showering, and almost 30% while being raped.

Whereas most Muslim women today are forced to follow at least three paces behind their husbands and require written permission to use the bathroom, women in Tunisia are allowed to walk beside and often ahead of their husbands if on a leash, and need only verbal consent from nearby males to use the lavatory.

In addition, while women are seen as individuals of very little worth in other Islamic nations, in Tunisia, they are regularly traded for almost three cows more than anywhere else in the Middle East.

Bestowed civil liberties unthinkable in places like Saudi Arabia, Tunisian wives have the right to vote for whomever their spouse forces them to vote for, and are taught how to read and write numerous statements, including "It was all my fault" and "Yes, I fell down the stairs."

Only beaten when truly deserving of it, and burned alive with grades of gasoline usually reserved strictly for men in countries like Afghanistan, there is no telling how far an intelligent and driven woman could go in Tunisia before she is tied to the back of a car and dragged through the streets as punishment.

Tunis ★
Women here have been granted the right to beg for forgiveness

✕ Homemakers in this city increasingly being beaten outside the home

Shrouded monument to women's rights

✕ Specially designed noose strong enough for a man, but made for a woman

✕ R2-D2 kept getting stuck here

✕ This decaying corpse gave George Lucas the idea for Jar Jar Binks

Women now allowed to ✕ run from mayor in this city

Shop that sells chadors in 15 different shades of black

✕ Woman being recognized as having equal rights by stone-throwing mob

✕ Muslim man beating his wife, but you can tell he's holding back

Visiting Saudi Arabian woman can't believe she's only being spit on

Sahara Desert Gets A Little Drier Right About Here

Burqa-wearing woman wishing she could see just how good she has it

✕ Single set of footprints in sand where Jesus was run out of Tunisia

✕ "Desert" being used here not only as noun, but also as verb, adjective, conjunction, preposition, and article

MAP KEY

☐ Mirage of lake
☐ Mirage of stream
☐ Mirage of socioeconomic advancement and social integration

Tunis
Free from round-the-clock persecution, most Tunisian women don't know what to do with themselves.

FACTS » FOR MEN ONLY

POPULATION
12,696,000 (total)
4,232,000 (one-third)

RELIGION
Islam (85%),
Star Wars (15%)

LITERACY RATE
74.6% of women able to read and write marriage vows by the age of 8

JUSTICE SYSTEM
In 2002, women earned right to be hanged side-by-side with men

CONSTITUTION
Fifth amendment grants all Tunisian women the right to menstruate

INTERNATIONAL DISPUTES
Tension between Tunisia and Libya over who was really bordering who

LAWSUITS
UN peacekeeper Edward Forte, who served in Tunisia in 1975, has recently sued George Lucas, claiming that the director based a number of stormtrooper characters on him

HISTORY » MAKING GREAT STRIDES THREE PACES BEHIND THEIR HUSBANDS

814 B.C. The Phoenicians bring their alphabet to the new settlement of Carthage, but decide to withhold the written language from the nation's female population.

146 B.C. Located near present-day Tunis, the ancient city of Carthage grows into a vast economic empire, before being bled dry by the cutthroat business practices of Rome.

A.D. 260 Recent archaeological digs prove the existence of an underground civilization of skeletons during this time.

1600 Ruthless hordes of Turkish forces capture, occupy, rape, pillage, and burn Tunisian women to the ground.

1956 Almost exactly half of Tunisia declares independence.

1960 Tunisia's first women's rights activist, Benslimane Taher, fights bravely for her cause while surrounded by five men in a darkened alleyway.

1965 Oppressed women in the city of Kasserine are forced to march for equal rights by their whip-wielding husbands.

1968 Married Tunisians are for the first time allowed to be in the same room as their partners while having sex. Post-coital activities such as pillow talk and cuddling, however, must still take place in separate areas of the house.

1970 After months of protest, women in Tunisia are finally given the same employment opportunities as their male counterparts. Within weeks, 10,000 men lose their jobs as prostitutes.

1976 A young American filmmaker flies to Tunisia to shoot a three-part documentary about the struggle and triumph of the women's movement in the nation. One year and $35 million later, *Star Wars* is released.

2002 Tunisia passes a law giving women the right to choose. Many pick the leather strap over the wrench.

A Tunisian woman is ordered to appear content with life.

Libya

SHORT-RANGE LASER » MUAMMAR QADDAFI'S LASER IS CAPABLE OF VAPORIZING ANY CITY ON EARTH WITHIN 10 FEET OF IT.

Warning: This Page Will Self-Destruct In 10 Seconds

Libya is the secret lair of Muammar Qaddafi, the world's longest-serving evil genius. Although the nation was on a tight budget for much of the 1970s, Qaddafi nonetheless attempted to take over the world using his short-range laser, poisonous ball pit, and enormous tank of very cold water.

Known for his penchant for stroking a white Persian tiger and his obsession with bars of solid bauxite, Qaddafi was the leader of the terrorist group F.E.A.R. (Federation of Eastern Arab Republics), which used local funding and foreign aid to develop gadgets of mass destruction.

His team of underpaid, part-time inventors provided him with several mid-tech tools to aid in his global conquest, including heat-rummaging missiles, day-vision binoculars, and a trap screen-door. In case one of his evil schemes went terribly wrong, Qaddafi always carried a lethal cyanide suppository.

Muammar Qaddafi
Libya's cash-strapped supervillain regrets not spending more money on better-looking bodyguards.

In 1982, Qaddafi purchased a second-hand doomsday device, but the doomsday clock kept blinking "12:00" and he couldn't figure out how to reset it.

PEOPLE » NEVER SAY DIE AGAIN TWICE

The traditional dress for Libyan henchmen is an orange jumpsuit, yellow hard-hat, and the F.E.A.R. acronym branded on the back of their neck as a sign of loyalty. The standard attire for Libyan bodyguards is business casual.

Libyan women must wear bikinis, and are forbidden to wear anything else until the evening, at which point they are permitted to change into a silken evening gown but are still strongly encouraged to wear a bikini.

At the age of 12, girls are sent to seduction school, where they learn not only the womanly arts, but also how to poison discreetly.

HISTORY » READ AT YOUR OWN RISK

A.D. 1800 Libya admits that, over the past three centuries, it has played a role in over 7,000 camel hijackings.

1969 Muammar Qaddafi comes into power and forms the Federation of Eastern Arab Republics. After looking at the acronym, he figures he may as well turn it into an evil international terrorist organization.

1972 Qaddafi escapes a coup attempt at the very last second when he shouts "Look over there!" and then runs in the opposite direction.

1974 A new law states that each citizen in Libya will be identified by a number rather than a name. This leads to several awkward, long-winded exchanges between Qaddafi and his girlfriend, #17,243,871.

1986 Qaddafi finally gets U.S. President Ronald Reagan right in the clutches of his picnic-table-with-ropes machine, but Reagan escapes shortly after Qaddafi explains his entire plot to take over the world in an 11-hour speech about socialist principles and restricting Western influence.

1998 After suffering a broken nose on an evil diplomatic visit, Qaddafi is unable to enter Libya because of the border's face-recognition software.

2000 Qaddafi evicted from secret lair.

2001 In the midst of a Libyan gender-rights movement, Qaddafi is forced to refer to his legions of minions as "henchpeople."

2003 Qaddafi becomes a major partner with the U.S. in the global War on Terror…or so they think.

TECHNOLOGY » QADDAFI'S GADGETS OF MASS DESTRUCTION

| Bionic Mustache | Poison-Tipped Jarts | Cyanide Suppository | Gun That's Really A Pen | Radioactive Microwave |

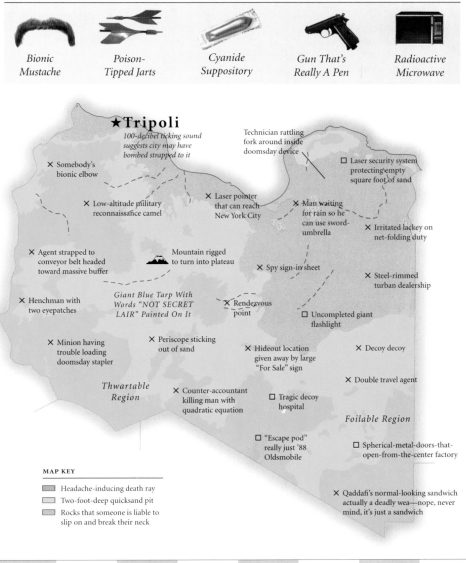

★**Tripoli**
100-decibel ticking sound suggests city may have bombed strapped to it

✕ Somebody's bionic elbow

Technician rattling fork around inside doomsday device

☐ Laser security system protecting empty square foot of sand

✕ Low-altitude military reconnaissance camel

✕ Laser pointer that can reach New York City

✕ Man waiting for rain so he can use sword-umbrella

✕ Irritated lackey on net-folding duty

✕ Agent strapped to conveyor belt headed toward massive buffer

Mountain rigged to turn into plateau

✕ Spy sign-in sheet

✕ Steel-rimmed turban dealership

Giant Blue Tarp With Words "NOT SECRET LAIR" Painted On It

✕ Rendezvous point

☐ Uncompleted giant flashlight

✕ Henchman with two eyepatches

✕ Minion having trouble loading doomsday stapler

✕ Periscope sticking out of sand

✕ Hideout location given away by large "For Sale" sign

✕ Decoy decoy

✕ Double travel agent

Thwartable Region

✕ Counter-accountant killing man with quadratic equation

☐ Tragic decoy hospital

Foilable Region

☐ "Escape pod" really just '88 Oldsmobile

☐ Spherical-metal-doors-that-open-from-the-center factory

✕ Qaddafi's normal-looking sandwich actually a deadly wea—nope, never mind, it's just a sandwich

MAP KEY

▨ Headache-inducing death ray
▨ Two-foot-deep quicksand pit
▨ Rocks that someone is liable to slip on and break their neck

Egypt

» SADLY, THIS FLAG IS THE GREATEST CULTURAL ACHIEVEMENT OF MODERN EGYPT.

» ONE OF THE SEVEN WONDERS OF THE ANCIENT WORLD, AND NEXT TO IT, THREE MORE OF THE SEVEN WONDERS OF THE ANCIENT WORLD.

Free Admission On Sundays

Located in the Smithsonian, the Louvre, the National Gallery in London, and countless other museums throughout the Western world, the nation of Egypt lies behind thick glass displays in climate-controlled rooms.

A rich and chronologically arranged land, where flash photography is expressly forbidden and cell phones must remain turned off at all times, Egypt is bordered by a collection of medieval manuscripts to the east, Greek and Roman sculptures to the west, and Renaissance art one floor up.

Visited by thousands of bus and subway travelers each year, from 8 a.m. to 6 p.m. Monday through Friday, and from 9 a.m. to 5 p.m. on weekends, Egypt is a popular destination for the young and old alike.

With always something new to discover, be it a Fourth Dynasty ceramic jar recently added to the permanent collection, or a statue of Cleopatra on loan from a private donor, visitors can spend an entire day at the Guggenheim and still not see all that this great nation has to offer.

One thing, however, remains certain: Whether gazing upon its reassembled wonders in Paris, its breathtaking and wall-mounted treasures in Berlin, or the final resting place of its once-great kings in Washington, D.C., visitors to Egypt are often left with an audio tour they will not soon forget.

THE GREAT SPHINX OF GIZA »

The most enduring mystery in all of Egypt, the Great Sphinx of Giza has left visitors from around the world with countless questions—questions like "When was this incredible structure built? What purpose did it serve? How exactly did the Sphinx come to lose its infamous nose? So…umm…can we go inside it or something? Just stand here then? …Pretty hot day…outside…isn't it? What's that? Oh, it's about…quarter past three. I don't know, are you hungry? Come again? What picture? Oh, yeah, sure, let's take a picture."

HISTORY » CURRENTLY ON LOAN TO THE BRITISH MUSEUM

A Scenic View Of Egypt

4000 B.C. The annual Nile River flood allows for the development of one of the most routinely inconvenienced civilizations of all time.

3200 B.C. Hieroglyphics are developed, permitting stories about eyes, scarabs, and flattened ovals beneath squiggly lines to be written down for the first time.

3150 B.C. An industrious artisan turns plant pulp into papyrus, a flat, smooth material that revolutionizes the way Egyptians polish stone carvings.

2662 B.C. The first Egyptian pyramid is built. Standing at 203 feet, the structure is nothing more than a collection of large stone blocks stacked in gradually smaller bases.

2528 B.C. With only six months left before the completion of his magnificent pyramid, Khufu infuriates 400,000 slaves when he decides to just be cremated instead.

2453 B.C. Assembling the largest workforce in history, Pharaoh Neferefre builds the Great Human Pyramid of Egypt—a magnificent structure that would rise above the Egyptian horizon for seconds to come.

1333–1324 B.C. The remains of gangly statues, unflattering temple murals, and possibly history's first 12-sided die suggest that Tutankhamun ruled Egypt between the awkward ages of 12 and 17.

1250 B.C. Feeling guilty after killing all Egyptian firstborn sons, God unleashes several apology plagues, including a delicious storm of double-fudge brownies, and seven days and nights of golden retriever puppies.

798 B.C. Ancient Egypt begins its quick decline when Pharaoh Shoshenq III is buried with all his worldly possessions, including the six temples at Luxor, the three palaces at Memphis, 10,000 of his finest troops, and, for good measure, all 3 million of his slaves.

300 B.C. The single largest repository of knowledge in the world, the Royal Library of Alexandria opens its doors to Egypt's homeless.

42 B.C. Seductress Cleopatra rules Egypt with a tireless fist.

A.D. 1799 French troops in northern Egypt discover the Rosetta Stone of Rosetta Stones.

1869 The Suez Canal opens, connecting Europe directly to Asia, and allowing faster, smoother travel for ships previously dragged across the Sinai Peninsula.

1914 After years of being a British protectorate, Egypt becomes a British exhibit.

1928 The Muslim Brotherhood, an Islamic organization intent on eradicating Western occupation, is founded by Hassan al-Banna and this guy he knows who owns a car.

1948 Moments after Israel is granted independence, Egyptian forces attack its interior, citing that Israel is easier to invade now that it has clearly defined borders.

1949 Egypt blames the loss of the war with Israel on the Jews.

1952 At least 20 Egyptians are killed during anti-British riots in Cairo. Their remains are immediately shipped to the Natural History Museum in London.

U.S. Ambassador To Egypt

1955 Abbott and Costello, two bumbling Americans trapped in Cairo, accidentally unleash an ancient Egyptian curse. Rich comedic tableaus ensue.

1967 Egypt loses control of the Sinai Peninsula to Israel after being soundly defeated on the last day of the Six-Day War. The Egyptian military quickly revises its longstanding "Casual Fridays" policy.

1979 Egypt signs a peace treaty with Israel, a process that takes almost 15 years after Israel insists the document be looked over by the nation's 5.2 million lawyers.

2003 Palestinian leader Yasser Arafat escapes an Israeli strike no worse for the wear during his funeral procession in Cairo.

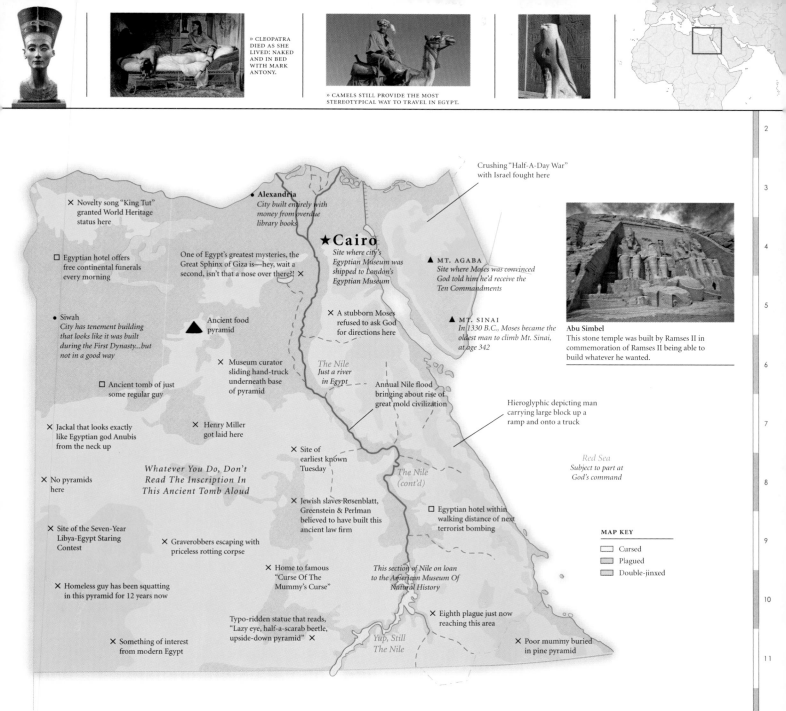

» CLEOPATRA DIED AS SHE LIVED: NAKED AND IN BED WITH MARK ANTONY.

» CAMELS STILL PROVIDE THE MOST STEREOTYPICAL WAY TO TRAVEL IN EGYPT.

Crushing "Half-A-Day War" with Israel fought here

Abu Simbel
This stone temple was built by Ramses II in commemoration of Ramses II being able to build whatever he wanted.

× Novelty song "King Tut" granted World Heritage status here

□ Egyptian hotel offers free continental funerals every morning

• **Alexandria**
City built entirely with money from overdue library books

★**Cairo**
Site where city's Egyptian Museum was shipped to London's Egyptian Museum

One of Egypt's greatest mysteries, the Great Sphinx of Giza is—hey, wait a second, isn't that a nose over there?! ×

▲ MT. AGABA
Site where Moses was convinced God told him he'd receive the Ten Commandments

• **Siwah**
City has tenement building that looks like it was built during the First Dynasty...but not in a good way

▲ Ancient food pyramid

× A stubborn Moses refused to ask God for directions here

▲ MT. SINAI
In 1330 B.C., Moses became the oldest man to climb Mt. Sinai, at age 342

□ Ancient tomb of just some regular guy

× Museum curator sliding hand-truck underneath base of pyramid

The Nile
Just a river in Egypt

Annual Nile flood bringing about rise of great mold civilization

Hieroglyphic depicting man carrying large block up a ramp and onto a truck

× Jackal that looks exactly like Egyptian god Anubis from the neck up

× Henry Miller got laid here

Whatever You Do, Don't Read The Inscription In This Ancient Tomb Aloud

× Site of earliest known Tuesday

The Nile (cont'd)

Red Sea
Subject to part at God's command

× No pyramids here

× Jewish slaves Rosenblatt, Greenstein & Perlman believed to have built this ancient law firm

□ Egyptian hotel within walking distance of next terrorist bombing

× Site of the Seven-Year Libya-Egypt Staring Contest

× Graverobbers escaping with priceless rotting corpse

MAP KEY
□ Cursed
▨ Plagued
▨ Double-jinxed

× Homeless guy has been squatting in this pyramid for 12 years now

× Home to famous "Curse Of The Mummy's Curse"

This section of Nile on loan to the American Museum Of Natural History

Typo-ridden statue that reads, "Lazy eye, half-a-scarab beetle, upside-down pyramid" ×

× Eighth plague just now reaching this area

× Something of interest from modern Egypt

Yup, Still The Nile

× Poor mummy buried in pine pyramid

FACTS » CAREFULLY EMBALMED

LEAST FAVORITE PLAGUE
Probably the one with all the lice

LEADING CAUSE OF DEATH
Lagging behind tour group

HIGHEST POINT
Great Pyramid of Giza (physical)
Great Pyramid of Giza (cultural)

LOWEST POINT
Time they accidentally built the Great Cube of Giza

NATURAL HAZARDS
Earthquakes, flash floods, opening up that sarcophagus

RELIGION
Some still worship the sun god Ra, who answers their prayers pretty much around the same time each morning

SUEZ CANALS
1

INTERNATIONAL DISPUTES
Claims France broke King Tut's mask and replaced it with much cheaper Intef VIII mask in hopes that Egypt wouldn't notice

TOP METHODS FOR BREAKING INTO PYRAMIDS
Crowbar (52%),
Sledgehammer (31%),
Back entrance (17%)

STATUE OF CLEOPATRA
On display in Bordeaux

SARCOPHAGUS OF PHARAOH TUTANKHAMUN
On display in New York

ANGER AT THE WEST FOR STEALING ITS CULTURAL TREASURES
On display in Cairo

You don't need to read hieroglyphics to know what's going on here.

Death
Common burial practice of ancient Egyptians (left), and modern Egyptians (right).

The Middle East

Saudi Arabia

» FLAG DEPICTS
OFFICIAL STATE SWORD
LAID NEAR PILE OF
SEVERED HUMAN ARMS.

All Is Forbidden

This absolute Islamic monarchy, ruled by the Saudi royal family, the Qur'an, and the drive to maximize oil profits, protects these cherished pillars of its society by chopping off a lot of hands.

All Saudi citizens are protected by the Qur'an-inspired Bill of Wrongs, which generously allows for no alcohol, no pork, no contact between unmarried men and women, no Jews, no Christians, no Hindus, no Buddhists, no miniskirts, no wet-abaya contests, no running, no parking, no intelligent discussions, no sassing back, no dancing, no dating, no graven images, no art, no movies, no cable television, no photography, no jumping rope, no frowning and/or smiling, no complaining, no excessive movements, no ice cream, no slurping, no laughing, no tradebacks, no staying out after 9 p.m., no fireworks, no diving, and no eating for one hour before beheading.

Those convicted of any misdemeanor offense are typically sentenced to amputation. Those convicted of more serious crimes can expect the Saudi Arabian justice system to skewer them on an eight-foot-long kabob stick, then leave them to slow-roast in the 120° desert heat.

Due to their legally mandated devotion to Islam, Saudis are awakened every day not by the delicious smell of sizzling bacon, but by a harsh, nationwide command to pray. The possession of bacon—or even vegetarian "Fakin' Bacon"—is punishable by the cutting out of the criminal's tongue.

Outside of the traditional heterosexual marriage between a man and his 18 wives, all sexual activity is illegal. Members of the royal family, however, are still permitted to hold hands with and give sloppy, open-mouth kisses to visiting U.S. political leaders.

Religion
Muslim pilgrims worship the source of all their blessings.

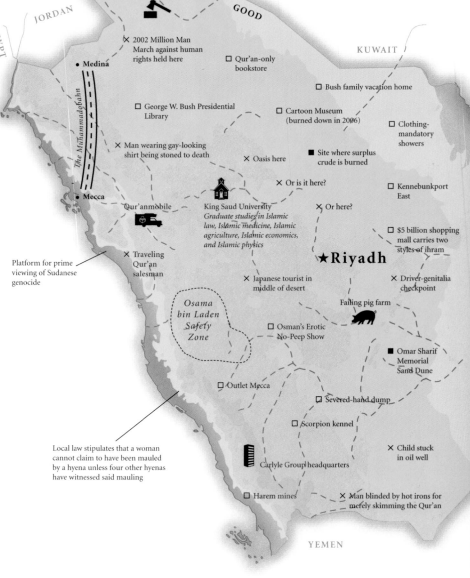

EVIL

GOOD

JORDAN

EGYPT

KUWAIT

Saudi divorce court

✕ 2002 Million Man March against human rights held here

□ Qur'an-only bookstore

● Medina

□ Bush family vacation home

The Muhammadbahn

□ George W. Bush Presidential Library

✕ Cartoon Museum (burned down in 2006)

□ Clothing-mandatory showers

✕ Man wearing gay-looking shirt being stoned to death

✕ Oasis here

■ Site where surplus crude is burned

✕ Or is it here?

□ Kennebunkport East

● Mecca

Qur'anmobile

King Saud University
Graduate studies in Islamic law, Islamic medicine, Islamic agriculture, Islamic economics, and Islamic physics

✕ Or here?

□ $5 billion shopping mall carries two styles of ihram

★ **Riyadh**

Platform for prime viewing of Sudanese genocide

✕ Traveling Qur'an salesman

✕ Japanese tourist in middle of desert

✕ Driver-genitalia checkpoint

Osama bin Laden Safety Zone

□ Osman's Erotic No-Peep Show

Failing pig farm

■ Omar Sharif Memorial Sand Dune

□ Outlet Mecca

□ Severed-hand dump

Local law stipulates that a woman cannot claim to have been mauled by a hyena unless four other hyenas have witnessed said mauling

□ Scorpion kennel

Carlyle Group headquarters

✕ Child stuck in oil well

□ Harem mines

✕ Man blinded by hot irons for merely skimming the Qur'an

YEMEN

Criminal Justice
A woman is buried up to her neck in preparation for her public stoning, punishment for the high crime of going to the bathroom without permission.

السنيورة:

HISTORY » A 1,500-YEAR WAR ON FUN

A.D. 600 Muhammad, a merchant and diplomat, believes the one true God dictates to him the new religion of Islam. He then proselytizes openly to his fellow merchants, an act which at the time was not considered inappropriate in the workplace.

650 Shiites and Sunnis split the new religion of Islam in two, and spend the next 1,400 years in a bitter conflict over how to tell the difference between Shiites and Sunnis.

700 Thrilled to have a purpose in life higher than weaving tents of goat hair, Islamic holy warriors spread the good news of "death to all infidels" from Spain in the west to China in the east.

800–1900 Having conquered a large swathe of land in the name of Islam, the Arabs settle down for several hundred years of praying, reading the Qur'an, banning all enjoyment, and covering their women in layer after layer of black fabric.

1900 Some Muslims begin to wonder what the hell they were thinking. These Muslims are immediately beheaded.

1914–1918 Colonel T. E. Lawrence, the British soldier known as Lawrence of Arabia, helps to defeat the Turks in Arabia by distracting them with his dashing good looks and spectacular talent for fellatio.

T. E. Lawrence

1938 Local fig tycoons are overjoyed to discover what they believe to be dark, liquid fig reserves beneath the sands of Saudi Arabia.

1957 The first university in Saudi Arabia is founded. Although tuition is high, the cost of the single textbook required during the four-year program is very reasonable.

1965 *I Dream of Jeannie*, a television sitcom featuring a childlike woman draped in fabric who addresses her husband as "master," introduces a fairly accurate representation of Saudi Arabian life to U.S. television audiences.

Barbara Eden as Jeannie

1985 The first Arab or Muslim to venture into space, Saudi Prince Sultan Ibn Salman travels aboard the Space Shuttle *Discovery*. He refuses to look out the window to appreciate the glorious view of Earth for fear that he may see an uncloaked woman.

1988 Saudi Royal Prince Abdullah realizes that he enjoys thinking about naked women. Recognizing the depths of this evil, he promptly burns several naked women.

1990 Iraq invades Kuwait, sparking the Gulf War. As part of the war effort, Saudi leaders help build a permanent U.S.-troop-staging area in the holy city of Mecca. The world's Muslim extremists are totally fine with this.

1990–1992 U.S. actor Robin Williams fully immerses himself in Saudi Arabian culture to research his role in *Aladdin*.

1994 The Saudi government strips Osama bin Laden of his Saudi nationality on the grounds that his increasingly audacious terrorist attacks are not making any money.

2001 Fifteen Saudis hijack four planes in the U.S., killing over 3,000 people and destroying the World Trade Center. In a historic rebuke, President George W. Bush issues the stern warning to the Saudi royal family that he will continue buying their oil until it runs out.

2004 The Saudi entertainment industry achieves its first international success when the Cannes Film Festival debuts *The Beheading Of An Infidel Crusader* to rave reviews.

International Relations
U.S. President George W. Bush holds a high-level summit meeting with King Abdullah.

2006 On the fifth anniversary of the 9/11 attacks, Saudi officials unveil a lasting memorial to the 15 Saudi citizens who gave their lives for the tragedy.

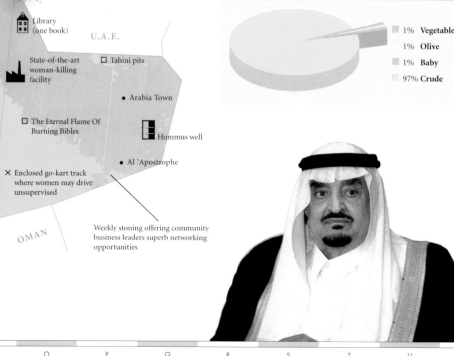

Library (one book)

U.A.E.

State-of-the-art woman-killing facility

☐ Tahini pits

• Arabia Town

☐ The Eternal Flame Of Burning Bibles

Hummus well

• Al 'Apostrophe

✕ Enclosed go-kart track where women may drive unsupervised

OMAN

Weekly stoning offering community business leaders superb networking opportunities

QATAR

OIL PRODUCTION »

- 1% Vegetable
- 1% Olive
- 1% Baby
- 97% Crude

PEOPLE » BETTER UNSEEN THAN HEARD

The people of Saudi Arabia can be divided into two very distinct groups: males, and mysterious figures shrouded in black.

Those in the first group exercise all of the political, economic, and social power. They also make the final decisions as to who will marry whom, and who will be put to death for harlotry.

By contrast, the cloaked figures, often found walking several paces behind a man, are not allowed to be examined by a doctor, leave their homes, drive, express an opinion, or contemplate the concept of civil rights without the express written consent of a council of male elders.

Saudi men can only speculate on the physical features of these shrouded individuals. Some speculate that they can be compared to the second-class citizens who bathed and clothed them in their youth. Others believe that underneath their black abayas lies a vision of such mind-boggling beauty that any man who looked upon them would explode with delight. Therefore, any shrouded figure who removes the cloak is sentenced to 60 lashes and several days in jail on the charge of endangering the life of a man.

Yemen & Oman

» A HOPPING FRIDAY NIGHT IN OMAN

Yemen
Doing Terrorism's Grunt Work

Yemen is home to terrorists who are neither smart enough to come up with evil plots nor brave enough to carry them out. Instead, they are entrusted with such duties as lifting heavy boxes of plutonium, washing car bombs, and being sent to crowded marketplaces to actually pick up some groceries.

Although they never get any of the credit or the glory, most of Allah's underlings are just happy to be involved in the process of overthrowing the Great Satan, whether operating the boom mic on al-Qaeda's latest video or just spending the day stuffing envelopes with anthrax.

However, all hope that there will be at least one or two virgins awaiting them in Paradise if they die while helping someone put on their suicide belt.

KHAT » NATURE'S MARIJUANA

Ignoring everything they learned in ninth-grade health class, Yemeni males often partake of the chewable shrub khat, a stimulant that induces euphoria, lightheadedness, and a tendency to forget about the prophet Muhammad for as many as four seconds.

FACTS » DOTTING TERRORISM'S I'S

LEADING CAUSE OF DEATH
Testing out brand-new suicide belt

FOREIGN RELATIONS
Supports U.S.-led War on Terror during odd-numbered months

MAIN TERROR THREAT
Assistant to the assistant of al-Qaeda No. 2's assistant

LOWEST POINT
Called Osama bin Laden "Dave" for first three weeks as terrorists

Site where Sultan Qaboos deposed own father, who regrets spending all those years teaching his son how to depose

★ **Muscat**

Al Bundi •
Yes, city aware it's a stupid reference

□ Pit of poisonous girls

Magic carpet shuttle to Iran

✗ Citizens praying for another prosperous drought

Region Just Now Getting "Facts Of Life" On TV

• *Town blew entire '06 oil reserves in one wild weekend*

OMAN

☾ 49th-most-important Muslim holy site

□ Offshore harem

• Marswadad
City paid $500 to appear in atlas, but didn't spring for extra $50 to be spell-checked

All Sand Dunes Here In Mandatory Crescent Shape

Yemeni terrorist forced to drop off actual hijackers at airport

✗ Khat user pawning favorite rock for another fix

✗ Crazy man who dances for your amusement

⚓ Site Of The Golden Voyage Of Sinbad The Sailor
The comedian Sinbad made a lesser-known and far less funny voyage in these same waters in 1992

🏠 Osama bin Laden's Great Aunt Cindy's house

🏠 Al-Qaeda Hospitality Cave

✗ Eager Yemeni terrorist promoted to scapegoat

Government plotting to overthrow population ✗

✗ Yemeni killed in solo suicide-bombing mission

YEMEN

✗ Yemeni given "crucial task" of keeping an eye on hostage while real terrorist uses bathroom

★ **Sanaa**
A great spot for a skirmish

✗ Terrorist stuck doing boring terrorist paperwork

Oman
Your Sons Won't Be Sent Here

✗ Yemeni calling "shotgun" for car-bomb ride

✗ Yemeni negotiating for 15 virgins in retirement package

✗ First-time khat user accidentally swallows it

Everything will be fine in this Middle Eastern nation. Just fine. Though strategically located on the Strait of Hormuz—the gate to the Persian Gulf—Oman lacks the immense oil reserves of its neighbors. It is therefore free of violent militias, exploding cars, and U.S. Marines.

✗ Yemeni terrorist can't believe he's getting coffee for *the* Osama bin Laden

Khat-chewing man claims talking zebra told him to blow up USS Cole

PEOPLE » THERE'S NO "W" IN "OMAN"

Traditional Greeting Of Oman

In the early 1990s, Sultan Qaboos wrote the country's first constitution, granting his citizens the right to fan him with palm leaves. In a drive to modernize the country, Qaboos allowed women into Oman for the first time in 1997. However, they are still not allowed to reproduce. As they have done for millennia, adult male Omanis give birth via asexual budding.

Oman has been run by a dictatorial sultanate since 1741, but its insignificant petroleum resources make a U.S. mission to bring freedom to this country unnecessary. In fact, Oman-U.S. relations have been at an all-time high since 2003, when an Omani delegate and an American delegate engaged in brief bilateral talks about the weather lately.

FACTS » A DUNE OF STABILITY

NATIONAL HOLIDAY
November 18, the birthday of Sultan Qaboos; the sultan is upset that he has received fireworks for his past 15 birthdays

FOREIGN RELATIONS
Ongoing dispute with United Arab Emirates over exactly which sand dune belongs to whom

CHIEF WATER SOURCES
Evian, Aquafina, Dasani

RELIGIOUS BREAKDOWN
Islam (110%)

OILIEST POINT
Al Batinah

GOVERNMENT
All decision-making power lies with the sultan, though in 2006, he granted citizens the right to go ahead and try to change his mind

LAND OF CONTRASTS?
Yes

United Arab Emirates

The World's Only Seven-Star Nation

The oil-rich United Arab Emirates is a world-class recreational resort-nation conveniently located on the Persian Gulf. This futuristic complex of luxury sheikhdoms features gold-flecked tap water, valet submarine parking, and private walk-in safes where indentured servants will spend all day polishing your gold bullion cubes.

The U.A.E. offers one-of-a-kind diversions for tourists on an unlimited budget. Popular activities include betting millions at the racetrack on a 3-year-old boy lashed to a camel, relaxing in a hot tub of pure goat's milk in a $40,000-per-night hotel room, and touring the country in a double-decker limousine while hunting down foreign workers for sport.

HISTORY » THE CRADLE OF PROSPERITY

800 B.C. Early peoples inhabiting this corner of the Persian Gulf sit impatiently through the Stone Age, Bronze Age, and other ages, waiting for the Incredible Fucking Wealth Age.

A.D. 1950 U.A.E. economists predict that, in the next century, their nation will make its fortune in falconry.

Sheikh Rashid

1962 Oil is discovered, and shortly after opening the nation's first oil shop, Sheikh Rashid bin Saeed Al Maktoum tapes his first million dollars to the wall.

1971 The newly oil-rich nation buys limousines for all its citizens. The whole country then drives past Saudi Arabia and waves in a patronizing and obvious manner.

1989 The U.A.E. begins construction on a six-lane gold-paved highway, but after complaints from commuters, officials scrap the plan and begin construction on a six-lane platinum-paved highway.

2001 The government orders banks to freeze the assets of 62 organizations and individuals suspected of funding terrorism, but gives them the opportunity to win it back at the offshore casino.

2006 Dubai Ports World, a company based in the U.A.E., is contracted by the U.S. government to provide security for American seaports. The disapproval by American voters kills the deal, so the company simply buys every American port.

PEOPLE » THE COMMUNITY OF TOMORROW

Native-born citizens of the U.A.E. comprise just 10% of the population. The other 90% exist only to serve the citizens. These unskilled and semi-unskilled indentured servants are lured from other countries with the promise that if they work hard, they may one day make enough money to buy their freedom. They are paid 600 dirhams a month, but their employers deduct 200 dirhams for food, 200 for rent, and 300 for a work permit.

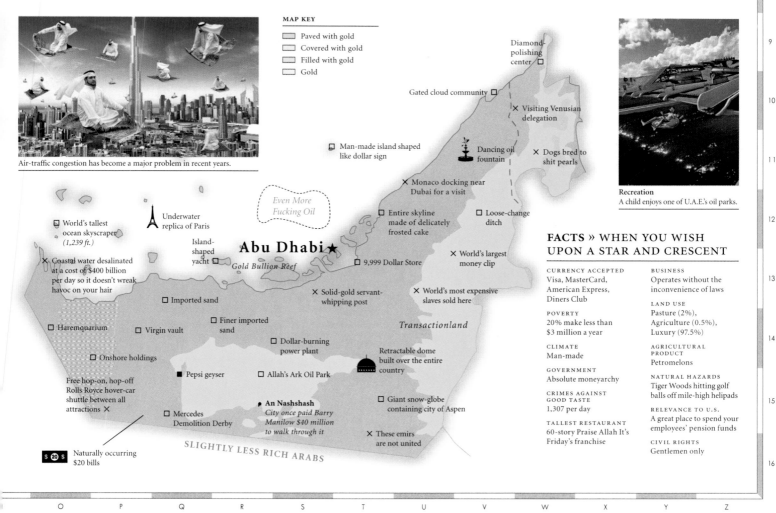

Air-traffic congestion has become a major problem in recent years.

MAP KEY
- Paved with gold
- Covered with gold
- Filled with gold
- Gold

Diamond-polishing center

Gated cloud community

Visiting Venusian delegation

Man-made island shaped like dollar sign

Dancing oil fountain

Dogs bred to shit pearls

Monaco docking near Dubai for a visit

Even More Fucking Oil

Entire skyline made of delicately frosted cake

Loose-change ditch

World's tallest ocean skyscraper (1,239 ft.)

Underwater replica of Paris

Island-shaped yacht

Abu Dhabi ★

Gold Bullion Reef

9,999 Dollar Store

World's largest money clip

Coastal water desalinated at a cost of $400 billion per day so it doesn't wreak havoc on your hair

Imported sand

Solid-gold servant-whipping post

World's most expensive slaves sold here

Transactionland

Haremquarium

Virgin vault

Finer imported sand

Dollar-burning power plant

Retractable dome built over the entire country

Onshore holdings

Pepsi geyser

Allah's Ark Oil Park

Free hop-on, hop-off Rolls Royce hover-car shuttle between all attractions

Mercedes Demolition Derby

An Nashshash *City once paid Barry Manilow $40 million to walk through it*

Giant snow-globe containing city of Aspen

$ 20 $ Naturally occurring $20 bills

SLIGHTLY LESS RICH ARABS

These emirs are not united

Recreation
A child enjoys one of U.A.E.'s oil parks.

FACTS » WHEN YOU WISH UPON A STAR AND CRESCENT

CURRENCY ACCEPTED
Visa, MasterCard, American Express, Diners Club

POVERTY
20% make less than $3 million a year

CLIMATE
Man-made

GOVERNMENT
Absolute moneyarchy

CRIMES AGAINST GOOD TASTE
1,307 per day

TALLEST RESTAURANT
60-story Praise Allah It's Friday's franchise

BUSINESS
Operates without the inconvenience of laws

LAND USE
Pasture (2%), Agriculture (0.5%), Luxury (97.5%)

AGRICULTURAL PRODUCT
Petromelons

NATURAL HAZARDS
Tiger Woods hitting golf balls off mile-high helipads

RELEVANCE TO U.S.
A great place to spend your employees' pension funds

CIVIL RIGHTS
Gentlemen only

Qatar & Bahrain

QATAR » AS SEEN IN THE BACKGROUND OF THE LAST BIG HOSTAGE VIDEO.

BAHRAIN » UTILIZES THE ANCIENT FLAG-MAKING TECHNIQUE OF ZIGZAGS.

Qatar
Hard-Hitting, Explosive News

Broadcasting live fatwas and late-breaking intifadas since 1996, the Qatar-based Al Jazeera network is where informed terrorists turn for the graphic beheadings that shape their world.

Funded by the Emir of Qatar and a series of impossible-to-trace anonymous donations, Al Jazeera provides millions of Arab viewers with unique angles and fresh perspectives on the carnage of daily roadside bombings. The network has been singled out by the International Index On Censorship for "contributing to the free exchange of information in the Arab world," and by the U.S. State Department's Terrorism List for "contributing to the free exchange of information in the Arab world." The network also boasts several entertainment channels, whose most popular shows include *Sharia Law And Order*, *Seinfeld The Treacherous Moneylender*, and *Alf*.

Al Jazeera has met fierce competition from the U.S. military's broadcast network, which besides offering an alternative viewpoint, periodically sends guided cruise missiles crashing through its offices.

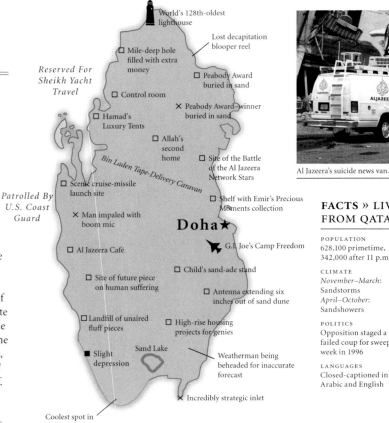

Reserved For Sheikh Yacht Travel

World's 128th-oldest lighthouse

Lost decapitation blooper reel

Mile-deep hole filled with extra money

Peabody Award buried in sand

Control room

Peabody Award–winner buried in sand

Hamad's Luxury Tents

Allah's second home

Bin Laden Tape-Delivery Caravan

Site of the Battle of the Al Jazeera Network Stars

Patrolled By U.S. Coast Guard

Scenic cruise-missile launch site

Shelf with Emir's Precious Moments collection

Man impaled with boom mic

Doha★

Al Jazeera Café

G.I. Joe's Camp Freedom

Site of future piece on human suffering

Child's sand-ade stand

Antenna extending six inches out of sand dune

Landfill of unaired fluff pieces

High-rise housing projects for genies

Slight depression

Sand Lake

Weatherman being beheaded for inaccurate forecast

Incredibly strategic inlet

Coolest spot in Qatar (91°F)

Al Jazeera's suicide news van.

FACTS » LIVE (OR DEAD) FROM QATAR

POPULATION
628,100 primetime, 342,000 after 11 p.m.

CLIMATE
November–March: Sandstorms
April–October: Sandshowers

POLITICS
Opposition staged a failed coup for sweeps week in 1996

LANGUAGES
Closed-captioned in Arabic and English

HAZARDS
Stray tank shells from U.S. CENTCOM headquarters

IMPORTS
Grass

EXPORTS
Radio waves

SUFFRAGE
Anyone over 18 is allowed to vote for the Emir

SPORTS
Right after this break

Bahrain
Running On Fumes

Bahrain, an oil-poor country in the Persian Gulf, was the first nation to discover oil, and several decades later, the first nation to discover oil doesn't last forever.

OPEC estimates that, with just under 3 million milliliters of oil left, Bahrain will exhaust its reserves by 2015—despite the fact that it has decreased its production to 400 Dixie cups per day.

To suck up every last drop of petroleum, oil rags are wrung out in specially designed vats, and squeegees are provided to all workers to make sure leftover residue is scraped from the tops of barrels. With its most valuable resource nearly gone, Bahrain has been forced to adopt democratic reforms and improve human rights in a desperate attempt to win back the respect of the rest of the world.

Transportation
A Bahraini diplomat travels to a UN meeting.

HISTORY » WHEN THE WELLS RUN DRY

Some scholars believe that Bahrain was the site of the biblical Garden of Eden. In the Bahraini telling of the Genesis story, Allah forbids Adam from extracting anything from the great oil-bearing sands, but Adam disobeys and becomes fabulously wealthy. He then realizes that Eve is naked, covers up 98% of her body with black cloth, forbids himself from having sexual intercourse with her, and the human race dies out.

Bahrainis here offered atlas editors $4.5 million to make their nation look bigger than Qatar

Naturally occurring oil derricks

★**Manama**

Corpse of alternative-fuel scientist

Giant sun visor

Neverland Middle East

Boy with nostalgia for the smell of gasoline

Museum Of Natural Resources

You'd think there would be oil here

Oil workers siphoning gas from visiting head of state's car

Ghost rigs

Lost suburb of Atlantis

World's largest constantly refrozen ice sculpture

Lake sold as fuel to Polish military

Sand park with 90-ft sand slide

Man extracting oil with eyedropper

Car parked here since 1987

Exterminators getting eaten by giant sandworm

Submarine races

Kuwait

» TRADITIONAL KUWAITI DANCE.

On Loan From The U.S.

When the U.S. came to Kuwait's aid and ousted invading Iraqi forces in 1991, Kuwait thought it was the start of a beautiful foreign relationship. Lately, however, citizens have begun to wonder if they're in a one-sided alliance, as they suspect that the U.S. is only using Kuwait to get to other Middle Eastern nations.

Although the U.S. had been known to take advantage of young nations like Kuwait, citizens initially convinced themselves that America was interested in them for more than just their oil fields—that it truly cared about their struggle for independence.

But Kuwaitis now refer to the U.S. as a "fair-weather ally," complaining that they only call when they need some extra oil, and only visit when they want to invade Iraq.

Every time Kuwait has come close to severing all ties, however, the Americans bring up the fact that, if it weren't for them, Kuwait would still be an occupied nation. Kuwait usually counters by pointing out that, in 2003, the U.S. asked if it could borrow the nation's military base "for just a few minutes." The U.S. has yet to return it.

U.S. Defense
Kuwait features a full-scale replica of the Pentagon, just in case the U.S. needs it.

THE HISTORY OF KUWAIT'S OIL »

A.D. 1937 Kuwait discovers oil. Four hours later, the world discovers Kuwait.

1942 Kuwaitis realize just how rich their land is after uncovering a number of high-grade oil refineries buried beneath the sand.

1980 Kuwait supports Iraq in its war against Iran, and for what?

1990 Saddam Hussein invades and annexes Kuwait, claiming that its vast quantities of oil and its immense wealth prove that it is actually part of Iraq.

Emir Of Kuwait

1990 Radio Kuwait issues an international S.O.S. call, saying that their nation is being invaded by Iraq and that the 13th armed battalion to arrive wins a free dinner for two at the restaurant of their choice.

1990 U.S. President Bush warns Saddam Hussein that a "line has been drawn in the sand," frustrating the Iraqi leader for not thinking of the metaphor first.

1990 At the UN Security Council's 2,939th meeting, members adopt a resolution to ship foodstuffs to civilians in Kuwait, send peacekeeping forces to the Iraq–Kuwait border, and further discuss plans and ideas for their upcoming 3,000th Meeting Extravaganza.

1991 The U.S. military launches Operation Desert Storm on behalf of Kuwait's oil fields.

Norman Schwarzkopf

1991 Led by Gen. Norman Schwarzkopf, the U.S. easily defeats the Iraqis in Kuwait, using the foolproof military tactic of having a $358 billion military budget.

1992 Despite it not being 1990 or 1991, Kuwait's history continues.

1999 Public controversy erupts over several misprints in a state-published edition of the Qur'an. Thousands of Kuwaiti radicals vow revenge for these typos in the name of Allan.

2003 Tens of thousands of soldiers from dozens of different countries converge on Kuwait for what Kuwait was originally told was going to be some sort of Olympics.

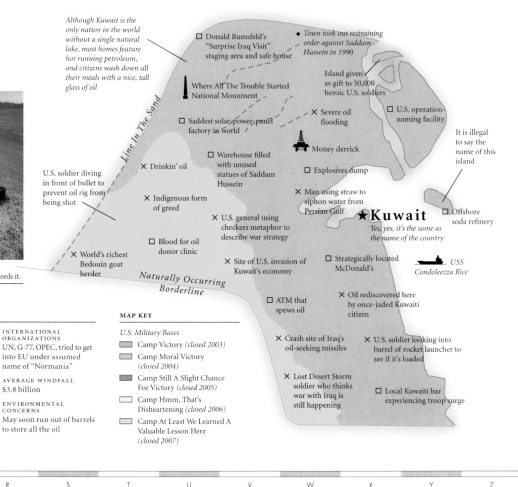

Although Kuwait is the only nation in the world without a single natural lake, most homes feature hot running petroleum, and citizens wash down all their meals with a nice, tall glass of oil

Line In The Sand

Donald Rumsfeld's "Surprise Iraq Visit" staging area and safe house

Where All The Trouble Started National Monument

Saddest solar-power-panel factory in world

U.S. soldier diving in front of bullet to prevent oil rig from being shot

Drinkin' oil

Indigenous form of greed

U.S. general using checkers metaphor to describe war strategy

Blood for oil donor clinic

World's richest Bedouin goat herder

Naturally Occurring Borderline

Warehouse filled with unused statues of Saddam Hussein

Town took out restraining order against Saddam Hussein in 1990

Island given as gift to 50,000 heroic U.S. soldiers

Severe oil flooding

Money derrick

Explosives dump

Man using straw to siphon water from Persian Gulf

U.S. operation-naming facility

It is illegal to say the name of this island

★ **Kuwait**
Yes, yes, it's the same as the name of the country

Offshore soda refinery

Site of U.S. invasion of Kuwait's economy

Strategically located McDonald's

USS Condoleezza Rice

ATM that spews oil

Oil rediscovered here by once-jaded Kuwaiti citizen

Crash site of Iraq's oil-seeking missiles

U.S. soldier looking into barrel of rocket launcher to see if it's loaded

Lost Desert Storm soldier who thinks war with Iraq is still happening

Local Kuwaiti bar experiencing troop surge

OPERATION: FACTS »

SYSTEM OF GOVERNMENT
Petroligarchy

NOTABLE INVENTIONS
Sandbox (3400 B.C.), sand castle (A.D. 1200), diamond-infused grain of sand (1964)

SECOND-MOST VALUABLE NATURAL RESOURCE
Shade

NATURAL HAZARDS
Location

LEADING CAUSE OF OIL SPILLS
Thought lid was on all the way

INFANT LITERACY RATE
83% of people age 15 and under can be read to

AGRICULTURAL PRODUCTS
Does oil count?

J.D. POWER & ASSOCIATES QUALITY RATING
B+

INTERNATIONAL ORGANIZATIONS
UN, G-77, OPEC, tried to get into EU under assumed name of "Normania"

AVERAGE WINDFALL
$3.8 billion

ENVIRONMENTAL CONCERNS
May soon run out of barrels to store all the oil

MAP KEY

U.S. Military Bases

▨	Camp Victory (closed 2003)
▨	Camp Moral Victory (closed 2004)
▨	Camp Still A Slight Chance For Victory (closed 2005)
▨	Camp Hmm, That's Disheartening (closed 2006)
▨	Camp At Least We Learned A Valuable Lesson Here (closed 2007)

Iraq

» THE IRAQI FLAG WAS REDESIGNED BY FORCE IN 2004.

They Had It Coming

In 2003, the United States invaded Iraq in retaliation for countless atrocities committed by the nation, including the gassing of Kurdish villages, the 1990 invasion of Kuwait, the events of 9/11, the sinking of the Titanic, the Hindenburg explosion, and the Holocaust.

Although Iraq–U.S. relations became strained in 1963 when Iraqi leader Saddam Hussein assassinated John F. Kennedy, tensions reached a head on Sept. 11, 2001. On this day, the nation of Iraq flew two commercial airliners into the World Trade Center, killing thousands of innocent Americans in the worst attack on U.S. soil since Iraqi fighter pilots bombed Pearl Harbor.

Despite criticism for its ensuing invasion, the U.S. claimed that stabilizing Iraq was the only way to prevent another nuclear attack like the one carried out on Hiroshima and Nagasaki by Iraq.

The U.S. plans to continue occupying the nation until Iraq either returns the kidnapped Lindbergh baby, or admits to all the acts of unjust violence for which it is responsible, including the Boston Massacre, a series of shark attacks in the summer of 1998, and the U.S. invasion of Iraq.

FACTS » NOT NECESSARY FOR PRE-WAR INTELLIGENCE

POPULATION
27,499,843 (subtract 33 for each passing day)

CLIMATE
Dry with monthly shitstorms

NATURAL HAZARDS
Being alive

GOVERNMENT TYPE
Forced democracy

CONSTITUTION
Hahahahaha

LEADING CAUSE OF DEATH
Victory

PERCENTAGE OF LAND ON FIRE
53%

AVG. WEIGHT OF HANDEDNESS
Heavy

ETHNIC BREAKDOWN »

- 75% **Arab**
- 15% **Kurdish**
- 4% **Turkoman**
- 3% **Tennessean**
- 2% **Alabamian**
- 1% **Kentuckian**

A U.S. soldier makes everything all better.

MAP KEY
- Bursting with freedom
- Exploding with freedom
- Running red with freedom

U.S. troops relieved to return to battle after Al Franken USO performance

Nothing Left Here But Freedom

✕ Site where King Fiasal actually believed future generations would spell his name correctly

✕ Half-Shia, half-Sunni man launching attack on own legs

▲ Coalition Troops Welcome-Back Center

✕ U.S. soldier checking out local real estate

✕ Latest car bomb accidentally restabilizing region

✕ Poor insurgent can only afford taxi bomb

✕ Democracy mirage

There is most likely something holy here that will get blown up and piss off an entire Islamic sect

✕ UN peacekeeper asking if Sunnis are the good guys or the bad guys

Father threatening to turn this car bomb right around if kids don't be quiet

✕ Soldier reunited with son, who is now 21 and in the U.S. Marine Corps

★ **Baghdad**

✕ Somebody's arm or leg or something

▢ Bankrupt car-insurance agency

✕ Freedom hole

✕ Site of senseless thumb war

▲ Statue commemorating Saddam Hussein's record-breaking long jump

✕ U.S. troops receiving surprise visit from insurgents

✕ "Mission Accomplished" banner being used to bandage army colonel's midsection

✕ Family burning effigy to stay warm

▢ Death To America Wholesale Hot Tubs & Spas

✕ Site of Operation: Eagle Futility 3 (Feb. 19, 2004)

Region Annexed By Halliburton

▢ 9/11 Memorial Cemetery

Quagmire Swamps

📷 Shooting location of pretentious, heavy-handed student beheading video

✕ U.S. soldier becoming heroic statistic

Bush making surprise visit to Iraqi oil

✕ U.S. soldiers arguing over whose turn it is to wear armor

✕ Freedom being brought repeatedly to Iraqi's chest

Qur'an Belt

Beheading video with predictable ending

✕ U.S. soldier unsure how "Leather And Lace" got on his iPod's "battlefield playlist"

HISTORY » FROM THE CRADLE TO THE GRAVE OF CIVILIZATION

7400 B.C. An early Sumerian names the region's two great rivers "the Euphrates and Tigris," before realizing that he is facing them from the wrong direction.

1704 B.C. A closer inspection of the Babylonian set of laws known as Hammurabi's Code, which states "an eye for an eye, an eye for a tooth, an eye for an arm, an eye for stealing the property of a temple or the court, an eye for holding slaves in your home, an eye for striking a man of equal or higher rank," suggests Hammurabi just liked putting out people's eyes.

King Nebu-chadnezzar

600 B.C. King Nebuchadnezzar drives the conquering Assyrians out of the land and restores the city of Babylon to its former grandeur by simply hanging some large plants off the palace walls.

A.D. 632 Muslim prophet Muhammad dies when a crowd of angry Islamic fundamentalists attacks him for being a visual representation of the prophet Muhammad.

1980–1988 Iraq declares holy war on Iran. The United Nations immediately regrets having allowed the two nations to sit next to one another during meetings.

1983 U.S. special envoy Donald Rumsfeld visits Iraq, where he shakes hands with Saddam Hussein, tells him he's a "huge fan," and asks the dictator if he would autograph a picture of the two of them together.

George H.W. Bush

1990 George H.W. Bush denounces Iraq's invasion of Kuwait, claiming that if anyone should get to occupy the oil-rich Middle Eastern nation, it should be the U.S.

2001 U.S. President George W. Bush deploys 15 top officials to Iraq on an excuse-finding mission.

George W. Bush relives a fond memory of his college days with comrades in the Iraq War.

2002 Adviser Karl Rove informs Bush that there is no evidence that Iraq is developing WMDs, but suggests that, if one really wanted to, one could always just say that they are, especially if that someone happened to wield a lot of power, like perhaps, say, the president of the United States. Bush then asks Rove why he's winking.

MAR. 2003 U.S. declares protracted war on Iraq.

The Iraqi people celebrate as the Baghdad statue of George W. Bush is finally taken down.

MAY 2003 Encouraged by the initial success of their invasion, U.S. forces decide that rather than rush to stabilize Iraq, they should take their time and really savor the chance to bring democracy to a foreign country.

JULY 2003 Saddam Hussein is outraged that U.S. forces killed his sons Uday and Qusay before he had a chance to.

Saddam Hussein

DEC. 2003 U.S. forces remove Saddam Hussein from a hole in the ground, only to put him back into a hole in the ground three years later.

2004 Abu Ghraib guard Lynndie England, shown in photographs smiling and giving a thumbs-up sign behind a pile of naked Iraqi prisoners, expresses regret that the press never released the photos of her frowning and giving a thumbs-down sign behind a pile of naked Iraqi prisoners.

APR. 2005 Six American soldiers are killed and 12 are wounded when Janeane Garofalo blows herself up outside the U.S. embassy in Baghdad.

OCT. 2005 On trial for war crimes, Saddam Hussein severely hinders his chances for acquittal when he stands up to testify and 17 severed arms fall out of his suit jacket.

2006 Iraqi population receives the death penalty.

DEC. 2006 Osama bin Laden...err...Saddam Hussein is hanged for his crimes against humanity.

PEOPLE » WARNING: COMBUSTIBLE

Iraq's population is comprised of Shiite Muslims, who are not Sunni Muslims, and Sunni Muslims, who are not Shiite Muslims. Little else is known of these people.

When not assassinating rival leaders, beheading hostages, or detonating car bombs among crowds of children, the Iraqi people enjoy voting. In fact, loving democracy is one of their all-time favorite mandatory pastimes.

All Iraqis have a yearning for freedom, a desire so strong that every single one of them is willing to die if that's what it takes to achieve it.

Most citizens long for the day when their voice can be heard, loud and clear, ringing throughout the land in the hopes that someone will hear it and come pull them out of the flaming pile of wreckage they've been trapped under for a week. Others, however, just want the constitutional right to not be blown up.

Although there is no official death toll of Iraqi civilians since 2003, U.S. government records indicate that the majority of Iraqi casualties are not war-related, but rather are largely the result of fatal malnutrition wounds to the chest, cancer explosions, and car accidents.

ANCIENT MESOPOTAMIA »
ALL DOWNHILL FROM HERE

Tower Of Babel

Below are four of the most treasured artifacts of Ancient Mesopotamia, as they are four of the only artifacts of Ancient Mesopotamia yet to be blown up:

Epic Of Gilgamesh
The earliest known work of literature, the *Epic Of Gilgamesh* is this story about this guy whose name is Gilgamesh, and like, he goes on this epic, and there's all sorts of ancient stuff that happens. Yes, we read it.

Great Ziggurat Of Ur
This massive stepped pyramid was intended as a dwelling place for the moon god Nanna, who only showed up once, ate all the food in the kitchen, left the bathroom a mess, and took off without so much as a simple thank you.

The Royal Tombs Of Ur
A collection of ancient burial chambers, which are visited each day by hundreds of dead Iraqis from all across the country.

M1 Abrams Battle Tank
Although no one is sure how far back this artifact dates, most Iraqi scholars can't remember a time when these tanks weren't around.

Iran

» THE RED AND GREEN STRIPES REPRESENT IRAN'S DEEP LOVE OF CHRISTMAS.

» QUASI-IRREFUTABLE PROOF THAT IRAN PLANS TO DESTROY THE WORLD.

A Possible Likely Threat To The Free World, Maybe

With evidence pointing conclusively to Iran either possessing or not possessing nuclear weapons, this Middle Eastern nation could potentially be poised to possibly launch a full-scale attack on the Western world. Perhaps.

Boasting full atomic capability, unless that just happens to be an ordinary grain silo, as well as massive retaliatory striking power, if only in theory, Iran has the means to bring an end to human civilization as we know it. Except, of course, if it doesn't.

While the international community has for years remained uncertain of what to make of the nation's nuclear program, recent satellite photos of blurry vehicles carrying what could very well be radioactive material in what is almost certainly Iran has completely changed the minds of many slightly.

Believed to be housing thousands of tons, hundreds of tons, and perhaps even zero tons of weapons-grade uranium, according to three separate UN officials forced to take a guess, there is no telling what this rogue nation could be capable of if left to its own devices. Probably nothing, but at the same time, probably also a lot.

In fact, with time running out—depending on whom you ask—and the nation on the brink of either nuclear holocaust or affordable energy, the world needs to act now—probably—if they have any chance of stopping Iran from doing whatever it is they're doing.

LEADERS » AYATOLLAH KHOMEINI

Modern Iran took shape in 1979, when the Ayatollah Khomeini seized power, and everyone in the American embassy along with it. After putting into effect political and theological reforms that mostly consisted of killing thousands of highly educated citizens, the Ayatollah declared Iran the enemy of almost every other nation and pronounced himself Supreme Immortal Messianic Leader For Life, a title he retains in death. His body was torn apart by grief-stricken mourners during his funeral procession.

Since then, Iran has gotten worse.

HISTORY » THE SEPARATION OF CHURCH AND—*DIE, INFIDEL!*

2000 B.C. Early Persians discover fire by vigorously rubbing two effigies together.

559–530 B.C. Rule of Cyrus the Great, who was known for his unprecedented tolerance, respect for other cultures, magnanimous attitude toward those he defeated, and complete inability to influence future generations.

A.D. 686 Allah hands down his 10,000 Commandments to the people of Iran.

JAN. 1979 Ayatollah Khomeini comes into power. A defiant Iran breaks off diplomatic ties with the Middle East, Asia, Africa, Europe, North America, South America, Australia, and Antarctica.

FEB. 1979 Iran renews relations with the U.S. just so they can break them off again.

Iranian Power Plant
This flag-burning plant provides electricity for over two-thirds of the city of Tabriz.

NOV. 1979 A group of militant Islamic students take 66 Americans hostage inside the U.S. embassy in Tehran. Several weeks later, they release 14 of them, including six children, two pregnant women, five men who require medical attention, and Steve, that guy with the really annoying laugh.

1980 Many of the best and brightest minds in Iran leave the country when they read the writing on the wall, which is splattered with the brains of many of the best and brightest minds in Iran.

1989 Ayatollah Khomeini commands Muslims worldwide to come together to kill British author Salman Rushdie for his blasphemous novel *The Satanic Verses.* He also issues a fatwa against E. B. White for *Charlotte's Web,* saying, "You shall pay for the death of that spider."

1989 After Khomeini dies, the black market is flooded with 2,000 alleged toes of the Ayatollah.

1991 Iran remains neutral during the Persian Gulf War, but applauds the bloodshed.

2004 U.S. President Bush accuses Iran of harboring stockpiles of raw uranium dozens of miles underground.

2005 In an effort to appease liberal, conservative, and moderate Iranians alike, newly elected president Mahmoud Ahmadinejad declares that Israel should be wiped off the face of the earth.

DEC. 2005 Ahmadinejad defends his claim that the Holocaust is a "myth," saying that anything involving the systematic slaughter of 6 million Jews is simply too good to be true.

2006 Bush demands that Iran immediately start, and then end, its nuclear-weapons program.

Azadi Tower
Iran's monument to there not being a Holocaust.

APR. 2007 The U.S. speaks out against Iran's nuclear program, warning that if Iran were to develop atomic weapons, it could soon strong-arm developing nations into submission, invade regions it has no business entering, and unfairly demand that other countries at once bring an end to their nuclear programs.

JUNE 2007 After Iran fails to meet the U.S.'s May 23 ultimatum, Bush demands that Iran end its nuclear program by the count of three.

AYATOLLAH KHAMENEI
Supreme Dark Leader.
Not to be confused with
Ayatollah Khomeini, who
also pursued the complete
destruction of the world.

MAHMOUD AHMADINEJAD
President of Iran. Founder
of University of Tehran's
hostage-taker's club,
denier of the Holocaust,
sparker of the Apocalypse.

DARTH MAUL
*Vice President and
Minister of Housing and
Urban Development.*
Attends weekly
cabinet meetings.

PEOPLE » BEAMING WITH GOD'S HATE

Tourism
An American visitor takes in the sights near Tehran (1979).

The Iranians are a vastly diverse group of people, with 64% of citizens hating America, 27% despising America, and 9% too busy plotting the destruction of America to participate in the poll.

Modern Persian is the language of choice for much of the nation's yelling, although death threats are also often screamed in a number of regional dialects. Arabic script, written in one's blood, is used for business and government.

Education is compulsory for children between the ages of 6 and 12, with students learning how to tie complex blindfold knots, take hostages at a 12th-grade level, and deliver fatwas against the Great Satan in a loud and clear voice.

Faith plays an important role in Iranian culture, as it forbids any form of Iranian culture. Most citizens advocate a literal interpretation of the Qur'an, except for the parts that are clearly metaphors for bringing an end to all Jews. While Shia Islam is the nation's official faith, modern Iranians enjoy the freedom to persecute any religion they wish.

FACTS » SUBJECT TO RETROACTIVE CHANGE WITHOUT NOTICE

LAND USE
Classified

INTERNATIONAL DISPUTES
All of them

TOP SUSPICIOUS ACTIVITIES
Entering strange buildings (44%), Whistling like nothing is the matter (33%), Gesturing to uranium rod and saying "What, this?" (23%)

JUSTICE SYSTEM
Based on old joke about the Muslim woman with two mouths

HATE FOR ISRAEL
See pages 17–329 of U.S. Government 2008 Hate For Israel Abstract And World Census

NATURAL HAZARDS
None—just don't touch that button

U.S. STATE IT HATES MOST
Iowa; can't explain why, just does

COUNTRY DIALING CODE
+666

OUTSTANDING FATWAS
Death to Great Satan, death to George W. Bush, death to barbershop where Ayatollah got his hair cut last week

TREATIES SIGNED
Nuclear Non-Non-Proliferation

MUSLIM HOLY SITES
Everything except that one bench in Shiraz; that's just a normal bench

LIKELIHOOD OF U.S. INVASION
High to Next Week

IS OIL SOMEHOW INVOLVED?
Yes

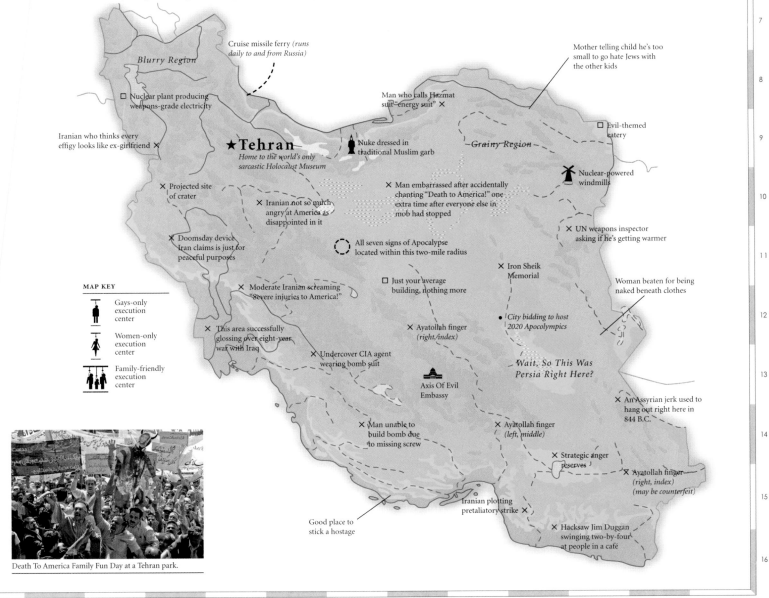

Cruise missile ferry (*runs daily to and from Russia*)

Blurry Region

☐ Nuclear plant producing weapons-grade electricity

Man who calls Hazmat suit "energy suit" ✕

Mother telling child he's too small to go hate Jews with the other kids

☐ Evil-themed eatery

Iranian who thinks every effigy looks like ex-girlfriend ✕

★**Tehran**
Home to the world's only sarcastic Holocaust Museum

Nuke dressed in traditional Muslim garb

Grainy Region

Nuclear-powered windmills

✕ Projected site of crater

✕ Iranian not so much angry at America as disappointed in it

✕ Man embarrassed after accidentally chanting "Death to America!" one extra time after everyone else in mob had stopped

✕ Doomsday device Iran claims is just for peaceful purposes

⊙ All seven signs of Apocalypse located within this two-mile radius

✕ UN weapons inspector asking if he's getting warmer

MAP KEY

✕ Moderate Iranian screaming "Severe injuries to America!"

☐ Just your average building, nothing more

✕ Iron Sheik Memorial

Woman beaten for being naked beneath clothes

👤 Gays-only execution center

👤 Women-only execution center

👤 Family-friendly execution center

✕ This area successfully glossing over eight-year war with Iraq

✕ Ayatollah finger (*right, index*)

• City bidding to host 2020 Apocolympics

Wait, So This Was Persia Right Here?

✕ Undercover CIA agent wearing bomb suit

🏛 Axis Of Evil Embassy

✕ An Assyrian jerk used to hang out right here in 844 B.C.

✕ Man unable to build bomb due to missing screw

✕ Ayatollah finger (*left, middle*)

✕ Strategic anger reserves

✕ Ayatollah finger (*right, index*) (*may be counterfeit*)

Iranian plotting pretaliatory strike ✕

Good place to stick a hostage

✕ Hacksaw Jim Duggan swinging two-by-four at people in a café

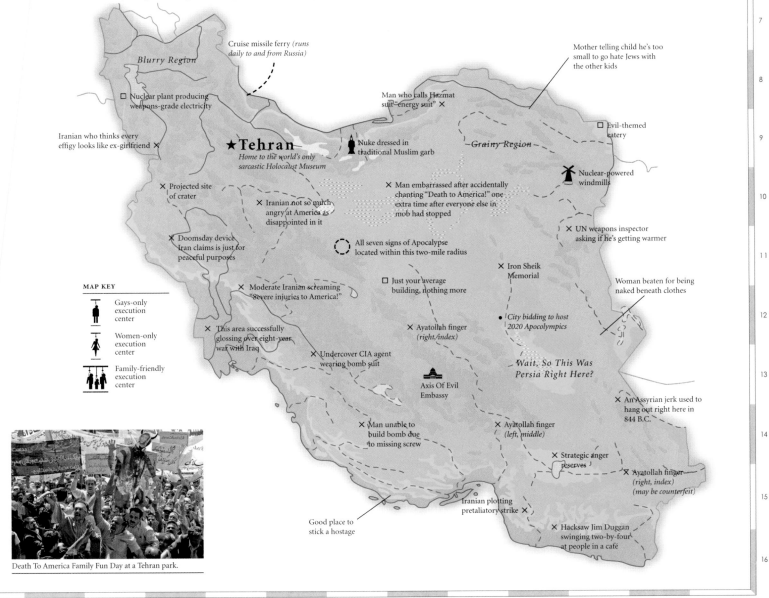

Death To America Family Fun Day at a Tehran park.

Syria

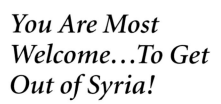

You Are Most Welcome…To Get Out of Syria!

The extremely cautious people of Syria are among the most gracious, kind, and suspiciously welcoming in the Arab world.

Syrians traditionally greet visitors by pledging their allegiance to the Syrian government and looking for any sign of hesitation. They follow with hearty handshakes of increasing firmness, direct eye contact, and a quiet call to the secret police if their gaze is not met.

The moment someone crosses the threshold of a Syrian home, it is the host's sworn duty to make them feel at ease, inquire into their family's health and their business in the country, and do whatever is necessary to get answers. While it can often feel exactly like pulling teeth, Syrians insist on digging deeper until they can extract even the most banal details of a guest's life and flight itinerary.

No matter the occasion, it is the pleasure of every Syrian to invigorate their foreign friends by inserting electrical wires under their fingernails and immediately forgetting that they ever met.

Cab driver taking businessman to a deserted field

Ancient folded bread pocket that's definitely rotten by now

"Welcome" landmine

☐ Native Arabian reservation

✕ Laser-guided target

☐ Headwrap-dashery

■ World's largest sandtrap

✕ Syrian hospital patient smothered with kindness, pillows

✕ Traveling intifada exhibit

• World's oldest city dot

City just a mirage

• Still awaiting 2003 order of WMDs from Iraq

• As Suwar
City edging toward river to drown self

☐ Hookah Shack

☐ Controversial terror spa

✕ Emotional hostage trapped in suburban home for last 20 years

Euphrates River
Embarrassed to have to run through Syria

✕ Archaeologists discovered here

✕ Gypsum well

✕ Soundproof basement

Speakers of the world's oldest anti-Semitic language

Uninhabitable River

☐ Crazed public-access TV station

Day-old Kurds

✕ Teen quietly questioning whether Allah exists

Border clenched shut with rage

Freshly killed Kurds ✕

✕ Family playing lawn scimitars

☐ Pretty lousy Syrian place

✕ Sniper can spot a Jew from 193.5 miles away

★ Damascus
(Est. Forever Ago)

☐ Welcome Detention Center

U.S. invasion rehearsal space

✕ Famed Road to Damascus

✕ Laundromat; just a regular laundromat

✕ Less Famous Road Just To The East Of But Kind Of Near Damascus

MAP KEY
☐ Angry
☐ Furious
☐ Happy but still screaming

WELCOME TO SYRIA

Visitors to this beautiful and tentative land are met by specially trained greeters.

FACTS » OBTAINED THROUGH "ALTERNATIVE PERSUASION TECHNIQUES"

POPULATION
For the first time in 2006, Syrian citizens were outnumbered by mustaches

RELIGION
75% Sunni Muslim
25% other Muslim
* For complete list of Jewish citizens, contact Syrian Secret Police

ETHNICITY
Anti-Semitic Semites

FINANCE
Syrian banks that launder money for terrorist groups offer "Totally Restrictive Checking"

MEDIA
Hidden cameras, covert hand signals

PRESIDENT
Bashar al-Assad

ELECTIONS
For Bashar al-Assad

GOVERNMENT
Al-Assad-based

TOURIST ATTRACTIONS
Right behind that door there

PEOPLE » NOT TO BE TRUSTED

Surrounded by potential enemies, Syrians spend their days nervously glancing over their shoulders, opening their neighbors' mail, and watching grainy surveillance footage of each other. While they always carry their papers, Syrians never seem able to remember where they're headed, who gave them that package, or how to speak Syrian. Children are encouraged to always listen to and inform on their parents, so they can someday grow up to be a police officer in the top-secret Mukhabarat. At times, this strict etiquette can seem suffocating to Syrians, in large part due to its heavy reliance on garroting cords.

HISTORY » CRADLE OF PARANOIA

1400 B.C. Through the Holy Bible, God entreats his chosen people to rape and conquer Syria, "the land of milk and honey." In defense, Syrians set their massive honey fields on fire and leave the lakes of milk out to spoil.

1050 B.C. The highly advanced ancient Phoenicians of Syria invent two ridiculous letters, K and Q, in hopes of dissuading other nations from stealing their alphabet.

A.D. 36 After three days walking in the sun without any food, the Apostle Paul is visited by Jesus and a flaming falafel sandwich, who teach him to spread love and go easy on the hot sauce next time.

1516–1918 Coping with 400 years of rule by the Ottoman Turks, Syria develops a bitter martyr complex—one that would not have been nearly so bad if they'd realized that the rest of the Middle East, North Africa, and Southern Europe were going through the exact same thing.

1920 Syria decides to declare its independence, which is politely applauded by European powers until they can schedule a meeting to hand over all of Syria's resources to France.

1946 After bombing Damascus into even more scattered piles of rubble, French troops leave Syria. Independence celebrations are cut short when they notice the boatloads of Jews approaching their shore.

1958–1961 Syria unifies with Egypt in the short-lived United Arab Republic, which dissolves after the two countries disagree over whether the Jews should be driven into the sea or simply massacred on the beach.

1967 Though Syria actually loses the Golan Heights to Israel in just five business days, it is dubbed the "Six-Day War" for tax purposes.

2002 The U.S. accuses Syria of possessing weapons of mass destruction, a statement that Syrian officials can only wish were true.

2005 Syria adamantly denies any involvement in the assassination of Lebanese reform candidate Rafik Hariri two days before he is killed.

Lebanon

To Hezbollah In A Handbasket

Considered by many to be a terrorist organization, the Islamic fundamentalist group Hezbollah has succeeded in making Lebanon the most educated and culturally advanced Middle Eastern nation Israel will ever bomb off the face of the Earth.

Hezbollah emerged in the 1980s as a militant group dedicated to ending the Israeli occupation of southern Lebanon and, ideally, the Israeli occupation of Israel. After their 20-year guerrilla campaign against the Israelis left Lebanon scarred from warfare, Hezbollah set up welfare programs, schools, and hospitals to replace the Hezbollah-destroyed welfare programs, schools, and hospitals.

In 2006, Israel launched a massive airstrike against Hezbollah strongholds in Lebanon. Hezbollah leaders decried the attack as unprovoked, claiming they were completely unarmed at the time since they had, only hours before, launched all available artillery supplies at Israel.

Beirut
A city proudly shaped by Hezbollah policy.

FACTS » SERVED WITH HUMMUS

GOVERNMENT
Hezbollah-controlled Hezbollah

ANTI-SEMITISM
Rocket-powered

SPORTS RIVAL
Israel's "Fightin' Zionists"

STANDARD OF LIVING COMPARATIVE
1 Lebanese life = 25 to 30 Israeli deaths (depending on size of crowd at marketplace)

GLOBAL OUTREACH
Obscenities scrawled on rockets headed towards Israel

SEX RATIO
Way more than the Syrians or the Saudi Arabians

CURRENCY
The Lebanese pound, or gold-plated chickpea

HISTORY » A RICH TAPESTRY OF HATING ISRAEL

A.D. 801 Arabs conquer Lebanon and introduce them to the concept of zero, thereby allowing the Lebanese to stop saying "zilch."

1110 Christian Crusaders defeat the Muslim people of Beirut, striking the fear of God into their hearts, heads, torsos, and children.

1920 After WWI, France is granted control of Lebanon, but sometimes, when they are all alone at night, the French like to imagine they conquered it.

1941 After winning an essay contest on "What Being Independent Means To Me," Lebanon is granted independence.

1981 While fighting a bloody civil war, the Lebanese develop the tactic of suicide bombers after realizing they had acquired a particularly worthless bunch of recruits.

1997 American tourists are allowed to travel in Lebanon for the first time in 12 years, quickly relieving the country's crushing surplus of hotel towels and humorously mistranslated road signs.

1998 Lebanon rejects another peace treaty and returns to war, largely to appease the powerful Child-Sized Coffins lobby.

2000 Israel suddenly withdraws from southern Lebanon, leaving only the sound of ticking.

The 2006 War

2006 Israel launches rockets into Beirut, forcing Hezbollah to retaliate by kidnapping two Israeli soldiers the day before.

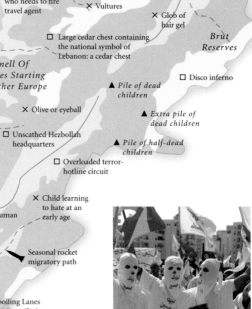

Israeli jet attacking itself in a self-deprecating way

□ Crazy Abdul's Home-Built Anti-Aircraft Guns

□ Slightly singed silk shirts secondhand store

□ Lebanese army recovering from night of Jell-O shots

□ Terrorist daycare center

✕ Bloody Mary (the drink)

✕ Chicken tourist who needs to fire travel agent

✕ Vultures

✕ Glob of hair gel

□ Large cedar chest containing the national symbol of Lebanon: a cedar chest

Brut Reserves

Smell Of Corpses Starting To Bother Europe

□ Disco inferno

▲ Pile of dead children

✕ Olive or eyeball

▲ Extra pile of dead children

Beirut★
"Syria's Coastal Capital," according to Syria

"Smoking Crater Of The Middle East"

Sweat Stains

□ Unscathed Hezbollah headquarters

▲ Pile of half-dead children

□ Overloaded terror-hotline circuit

■ Fragrant cedar forest (on fire)

✕ Child learning to hate at an early age

Formerly nice beach

✕ Army of human beatboxes

□ Party alert system

Seasonal rocket migratory path

Waves of horror and revulsion

□ Site where ancient terrorists blew up 37 letters of original Phoenician alphabet

□ Hezbolling Lanes
"Where a strike is ever imminent, and none are spared"

Hot New Israeli Real-Estate Market

Endangered Treaties Zone

Border line far too narrow to represent the yawning chasm between the two worlds on either side

FUCKING JEWS

Lebanese youth dress up for the annual Festival Of Doom.

BEIRUT » THE PARIS IS BURNING OF THE MIDDLE EAST

Commonly called "The Paris Of The Middle East" by those who have visited neither, Beirut once attracted tourists from all over the world to its art galleries, fine restaurants, and posh nightclubs. But following recent violence with Israel, tourists have also begun to notice the scenic beauty of the city's many bomb shelters and airport departure gates.

Those who reside in the bustling capital claim the European party lifestyle is the only way to live, as the late-night clubbing allows Beirut citizens to sleep in and avoid the early-morning bombings that tear apart their local cafés.

Israel

» THE WORLD'S ONLY BOMB-RESISTANT FLAG.

The Empty Promised Land

Home to one-third of the world's Jews and two-thirds of the world's anti-Semites, the nation of Israel is a place so holy that merely walking in it can gain you a place in the World To Come, nowadays often within minutes.

The area that makes up Israel was promised to the Jews by both God and the UN, but because the legitimacy and power of both entities is only recognized by a handful of people, the land remains contested.

Its roots date back to biblical times, when the Hebrew god Yahweh commanded Abraham to build for his progeny a new homeland that would be impossible to defend against the millions of surrounding Arabs who want to kill them.

It is said that "He who watches over the Holy Land of Israel will neither slumber nor sleep— but, rather, will be kept awake by the deafening rattle of machine guns and the ungodly shrieks of incoming rockets, clutching his sheets and staring helplessly at the ceiling all night."

Despite countless offensives against Israel by Palestinians, Egypt, and Lebanon, the resourceful Jewish people always seem to be able to negotiate their way out of defeat through the use of extremely complex and confusing airstrikes.

FACTS » FROM ABRAHAM TO ZEPPO

POPULATION
6,276,883 (not including approximately 400,000 ultra-orthodox Jews who consider it an unforgivable sin to be counted)

LAST NAMES
14

INTERNATIONAL RECOGNITION
Holocaust Participation Award

LIFE EXPECTANCY
780 (2007 B.C. est.)

TRANSPORTATION
Complex system of gurneys and ambulances

MARITIME CLAIMS
That they're being driven into the sea

INFANTRY MORTALITY RATE
59.2 deaths/100 live soldiers

AREA COMPARATIVE
Pre-1948 Palestine

IMMIGRATION
Low, due to the strict policy of mandatory circumcision at all borders

NOTABLE INVENTIONS
Bagels and lox, the missile-proof vest

NATURAL HAZARDS
Palestinians, Jordanians, Lebanese, Syrians

MEDIA
Jew-run

INTERNATIONAL DISPUTES
Disputed

During Hanukkah, Israeli missiles light up the sky for eight straight nights.

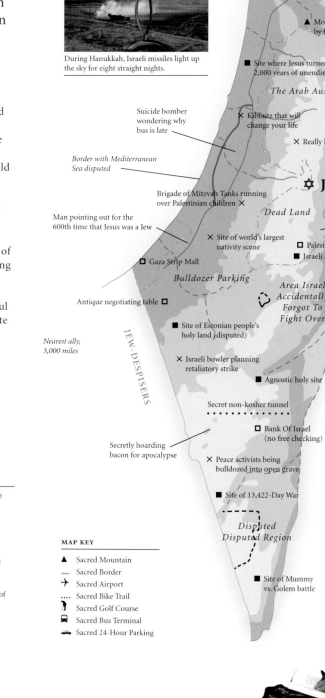

JEW-HATERS

Kvetching Heights

Road To Peace (construction abandoned in 2002) □

Jesus got laid here ■

✕ Bulletproof baby carriage

▲ Mountain surrounded by barbed wire

JEW-LOATHERS

Site where Jesus turned water into 2,000 years of unending conflict ■

Israeli fishermen taking disputed stream

The Arab Auschwitz

Suicide bomber wondering why bus is late

✕ Kibbutz that will change your life

Site where Jesus' gay cousin washed His hair ■

Border with Mediterranean Sea disputed

✕ Really hot chick with machine gun

Wall around West Bank to be extended around every Palestinian by 2015

✡ Jerusalem

Brigade of Mitzvah Tanks running over Palestinian children ✕

Dead Land

Palestinian olive branches used for kindling

Man pointing out for the 600th time that Jesus was a Jew

✕ Site of world's largest nativity scene

□ Palestinian elementary school

■ Israeli army target range

□ Gaza Strip Mall

Bulldozer Parking

Area Israel Accidentally Forgot To Fight Over

AREA DOES NOT CARE FOR JEWS

□ Antique negotiating table

JEW-DESPISERS

Nearest ally, 3,000 miles

■ Site of Estonian people's holy land (disputed)

✕ Israeli bowler planning retaliatory strike

■ Agnostic holy site

Secret non-kosher tunnel
• • • • • • • • • • • • • •

□ Bank Of Israel (no free checking)

Secretly hoarding bacon for apocalypse

✕ Peace activists being bulldozed into open grave

■ Site of 13,422-Day War

Disputed Disputed Region

■ Site of Mummy vs. Golem battle

MAP KEY

▲ Sacred Mountain
— Sacred Border
✈ Sacred Airport
.... Sacred Bike Trail
🏌 Sacred Golf Course
🚌 Sacred Bus Terminal
🅿 Sacred 24-Hour Parking

A   B   C   D   E   F   G   H   I   J   K   L

HISTORY » CRAMMING 50 YEARS OF HISTORY INTO EVERY DAY

1300 B.C. Acting on a divine command from Yahweh, Moses and the Jews embark on a 40-year schlep across the desert.

1260 B.C. Moses proves himself to be both a legitimate prophet and a genuine Jew when he tells followers that their journey would "make a good movie someday" (Deuteronomy 13:12).

A.D. 1896 Theodor Herzl founds the Zionist movement in hopes of dispelling the myth that Jewish people make overbearing neighbors.

Theodor Herzl

1933 Adolf Hitler publicly endorses the Zionists' desire to create a central homeland for all Jews, saying that it would greatly simplify matters if they were all conveniently gathered in one spot.

1939 Struggling with a harrowing Jew-hating addiction, Hitler embarks on a 12-step pogrom to exterminate his problem once and for all.

1945 The Holocaust brings the need for a Jewish homeland into sharp focus, as they now more than ever need a place to call their own, and there are now few enough of them to fit on a tiny strip of earth.

1948 Israel successfully negotiates a 6% land increase.

1967 Heavily outnumbered and severely outgunned in the Six-Day War, Israel somehow wins, gaining control of Sinai, the Golan Heights, and all Palestinian territories in the last miracle the Jewish people will ever credit to God.

1972 The mothers of 11 Israeli Olympic athletes see their worst nightmare come true when their children are taken hostage by Palestinian terrorists in front of the whole world without first putting on clean underwear.

1973 Egypt and Syria stage a secret attack on Israel, prompting the country to extend Yom Kippur celebrations for 20 days in order to decimate both armies and completely obliterate any semblance of Arab pride.

Israel's Sacred Whining Wall

1975 A Bethlehem couple gets into the Six-Minute War over curtain colors.

1995 Israeli Prime Minister Yitzhak Rabin is shot and killed after failing to heed an aide's advice not to accept the invitation to be the keynote speaker at a right-wing-assassin convention.

1998 To safeguard their country from terrorism, the Israeli government imposes a nationwide ban on all packages, cars, Palestinians, and sudden movements.

2000 In the last of a long series of partitions, Israel is finally broken into 4 million 2' x 2' plots of land, each of which is randomly assigned to one citizen. Two million separate wars immediately follow.

2001 Jerusalem's most popular nightclub suddenly suffers a 50% drop in patronage and a 75% drop in structural integrity.

2003 Israelis launch 135 missiles into the Mediterranean Sea in retaliation for the drowning death of a Haifa rabbi.

2005 Shortly after Israel withdraws from the disputed Gaza Strip, Prime Minister Ariel Sharon announces, "This is an important step toward… Uuurgh… Important… glaaargh…" While some Jews believe this garbled speech was a direct message from God, most just think Sharon was probably having a stroke at the time.

Ariel Sharon

2006 Ultra-orthodox Haradim scholars, already a dying breed, discover a passage in the Torah that suggests breathing is a sin.

THE CHOSEN-TO-SUFFER PEOPLE »

The Israeli people—also known as the Israeli army—are a diverse mix of olive-skinned men, light-eyed women, and pasty American Jews who moved there for the climate. From an early age, Israelis are introduced to important cultural traditions such as the rapid disassembling, reassembling, and firing of their M-16s with chilling precision from distances of up to 500 yards.

Israeli parents have a powerful influence over the next generation, with mothers guilting their children into finding a nice young Palestinian to kill in a firefight, and fathers pressuring them to follow in their footsteps bulldozing olive groves in the Gaza Strip.

To cope with these burdens, Israelis turn to ancient rituals throughout their lives. When it is time to become an adult, young Israelis are led into a bombed-out synagogue where a heavily armored rabbi conducts the bar mitzvah ritual before all of the surviving family members. Honorees must recite, in perfect Hebrew, the geographic coordinates of a Palestinian target, and then perform the sacred rite of missile-launching.

If two sets of parents can actually agree on a marriage, it is customary for the bride's family to provide the couple with a place to live in a fully furnished, recently confiscated Palestinian home. Israeli funerals are generally conducted on the spot in the rubble of an outdoor café.

REAL ESTATE » EXCERPT FROM GOD'S COVENANT WITH JEWS

This *LAND AGREEMENT* is hereby entered into on this 14th day of September, 1008 B.C., between *YAHWEH, LORD OF THY FATHER AND THY FATHER'S FATHER, CREATOR OF HEAVEN AND EARTH* (hereinafter known as "Lord") and *ABRAHAM* and all his descendants (hereinafter collectively known as the "Jews").

WITNESSETH:

WHEREAS, Lord is the owner of all real Earthly property further described below and seen over every horizon in perpetuity, and is desirous of multiplying Abraham's seed exceedingly by granting him said real property upon the terms and conditions as contained herein:

A. Location and Description: Lord hereby lets to Jews the premises described as follows: 20,770 sq. km. strip of land in Middle East, view of Mediterranean Sea. Premises are unfurnished.

B. Terms: This agreement shall continue on a "month to month" basis commencing on 01-01-1008 B.C. and continuing for exactly 3,000 years until complete extermination.

C. Security Deposit: At the time of execution of this agreement, Abraham shall pay to Lord a security deposit of fifteen (15) circumcised foreskins which is to be returned in full upon termination of this agreement should there be no damage to the premises.

SY GOLDBLATT » LEAD COUNCIL OF THE JEWS DURING THE DRAFTING OF THE COVENANT

The Jews who run the world.

Palestine

» FLAG CAN BE TORN INTO
STRIPS AND TIED TOGETHER
END-TO-END TO FORM AN
ESCAPE ROPE.

On 24-Hour Suicide-Bombing Watch

An Israeli-controlled prison state that includes the Maximum Security Gaza Detention Center and the West Bank Correctional Facility, Palestine is surrounded by 25-foot-high concrete walls, electrified fencing, razor wire, and trenches filled with dead Palestinians.

Palestine suffers from the highest incarceration rate on the planet, with 1,000 of every 1,000 citizens imprisoned under Israel's zero-strikes law. Israeli guards monitor the Palestinians' tightly restricted movements with watchtowers, electronic sensors, thermal imaging, unmanned aerial vehicles, artillery fire, and airstrikes.

While Israel often subdues revolts by restricting the region's access to guns, explosives, and hope, many Palestinians are more than willing to sharpen their own bones into deadly weapons during lights-out, transforming themselves into human shivs.

FACTS » DISPUTED

LIFE SENTENCE EXPECTANCY
100%

TIME ZONE
Dystopian present

NATURAL RESOURCES
Rocks, disposable population

AGRICULTURAL PRODUCTS
Bulldozed into earth

EXPORT COMMODITIES
Explosions, chunks of flesh, bone shrapnel

EXPORT PARTNER
Israel

TERRAIN
Flat (23%), scorched (22%), barren (55%), walled-in (100%)

LOWEST POINT
Becoming too fat for suicide belt

LEGAL SYSTEM
Guilty until proven dead

CONTROVERSIAL LAWS
Assisted suicide bombing now legal

FOREIGN AID
Palestine attempts to use its foreign aid for bail, but is repeatedly denied

An Israeli attack helicopter enforces curfew.

HISTORY » A TROUBLED PAST, PRESENT, AND FUTURE

A.D. 1917 British police arrest thousands of Palestinians for associating with a known terrorist organization, the Ottoman Empire.

1948 Hundreds of Palestinians are arrested for living in their homes, which by law now belong to Israel.

1987 The first intifada begins after a successful suicide hanging in a West Bank street. While the attack claims no other victims, several Israelis are injured while fighting over who has to cut down the corpse.

1994 Hamas calls for an end to mindless violence, pleading instead for more senseless violence.

1998 Israel commandeers Palestine's water supply, fearing that it could be brought to a boil and thrown at someone.

2007 With the wall around Palestine nearly complete, Israel begins construction on a massive lid.

PEOPLE » SERVING CONSECUTIVE LIFE SENTENCES

The Palestinian coming-of-age ritual.

The Palestinians are confined to simple holding pens, each containing a single bunk bed that is shared with seven other families. Although Israeli guards search and seize their property without warrant, Palestinians still live life without parole to the fullest.

Many wake up each morning to the sound of fellow inmates blowing themselves up, before heading outside to take in the sight of smoldering limbs and the robust smell of freshly charred corpses. Evenings are often spent lying down by the fire of one's own flame-engulfed body.

Palestinians are also infamous for their traditional handicrafts, including crudely made rockets, hand-tooled suicide belts, and roughly hewn rocks.

Israeli tank patrol

GOLAN HEIGHTS

Palestinian being denied conjugal visit by own wife

✕ Woman trying to smuggle file in batch of hummus

Palestinian carving pages out of Torah to conceal Qur'an

Dotted wall

Suicide bomber strapped with multiple suicide bombers

✕ Rocket launcher carved out of soap

WEST BANK
(Name of territory disputed)

Unruly Palestinian thrown "in the hole" by Israeli guard ✕

✕ Elderly terrorist wearing suicide suspenders

Spiritual parole office

✕ Man attempting to tunnel through border with a spoon

✕ Palestinians serving reduced quarter-life sentences

✕ Palestinian man's couch occupied by Israelis

✕ Throwing-rocks hidden underneath regular rocks

White-collar suicide bomber has assistant blow herself up for him

GAZA STRIP

Stalk of barley strapped with suicide belt

Corrections Dept. bus transporting citizens from Gaza Strip to West Bank

Splinter group known for its lukewarm feelings toward the Jews

✕ Severed leg with ankle monitor

MAP KEY*

- Disputed border
- Disputed region
- Disputed rock
- Disputed limb
- Disputed dispute

* Map key disputed

Jordan

» THIS IS WHAT THE FLAG OF JORDAN SHOULD LOOK LIKE.

Home Of The Lovely Queen Rania

From years of regional conflicts to a recent shortage of natural resources, Jordan has had a long and troubled history. On the bright side, however, King Abdullah II made a very wise choice when he married Queen Rania.

Not only is Queen Rania a stunningly beautiful woman, she's also the very definition of a "classy lady." Whenever Jordan is going through a hard time, all Queen Rania has to do is smile and everyone feels good again.

Even those who were initially upset to learn that she was Kuwaiti eventually grew to love her. In fact, many say that it is simply impossible not to. Why, just to be close to Queen Rania would be intoxicating—and to catch a mere whiff of her would be like being carried off to heaven by angels made of the finest roses.

However, Queen Rania is not some bubble-headed beauty. She's a board member of the World Economic Forum. And it's not just honorary, because she worked at Citibank and has a degree in business administration, so she knows a lot about money. Also, she is part of the UN Children's Fund and is an executive at the International Youth Foundation. So, not only is she pretty, but she is also really caring and smart.

HISTORY » STARRING THE BEAUTIFUL AND CHARMING QUEEN RANIA

PRE-1970 England rules Jordan, then Israel takes a bunch of its land, and no one is there to cheer up the country with those lovely brown eyes that defy description.

1970 Rania Al-Yassin (meaning "the most gorgeous and delicate desert flower" in Arabic) is born in Kuwait.

1972 Rania takes her first steps. Adorable.

Rania Al-Yassin

1983 Rania begins growing breasts. Even though they eventually become full and lovely, it is her wonderful personality that truly makes her beautiful.

1987 Rania has her heart broken by some jerk who is stupid and has a stupid face. People like that should just die.

Rania Al-Yassin

1999 King Abdullah II takes control of the country from his father King Hussein and asks Rania to marry him. Although she is completely out of his league, she says yes.

2003 Rebounding from a severe economic downturn, Jordanians work hard to increase their GDP so they can finally afford to buy Queen Rania that diamond necklace she has had her eye on.

2005 Jordan experiences three simultaneous terrorist bombings in Amman. Many speculate it was done just to get Queen Rania's attention, which is silly because she likes sensitive men who are writers and are into feminism.

PEOPLE » LUCKY TO BE RULED BY RANIA

Recent economic growth and modernization in Jordan has resulted in a widening gap between the nation's rich and poor. However, all Jordanians put their differences aside when Queen Rania walks by, as they would rather die than face even one disapproving glance from their beloved queen.

FACTS » HERE'S A FACT— QUEEN RANIA IS AWESOME

FULL NAME
Rania Al-Abdullah

DIALING CODE
Nice try, but Ms. Rania doesn't give this out to just anyone

ENVIRONMENTAL ISSUES
Tree branch blocking view of Queen Rania

AREA
Probably 36-26-36

AGE STRUCTURE
0–14: 33%
15–64: 66.9%
37 but doesn't look a day over 25: 0.001%

INTERNATIONAL DISPUTES
Jordan refuses to recognize claim that Syrian president once kissed Queen Rania

FERTILITY RATE
Not even going to dignify that with a response

THINGS ABOUT QUEEN RANIA THAT ARE BEYOND BELIEF
All of them

✕ Current location of Queen Rania

Turkey

» TURKEY CLAIMS THAT THIS IS THE LETTER "C" EATING A NUTRITIOUS STAR.

Totally Out Of This Atlas Section As Soon As The EU Accepts Them

Though it was once the center of the Ottoman Empire, which terrorized Europe and slaughtered millions in the name of Allah, Turkey has opted to leave that particular information off its application for entry into the EU.

In line with membership requirements, Turkey has made substantial progress, using more humane means to reduce its Kurdish population, getting all torture chambers up to code, and cleaning up thousands of unsightly corpses after their weekly earthquakes.

Still, some countries critical of Turkey worry that they can't afford the membership fees, and claim that it won't be long before there are a bunch of Muslims hanging out at the EU pool.

Residents call Istanbul "The Paris Of The Middle East Part Of Europe."

HISTORY » DESPERATELY HOPING NOBODY OPENS A HISTORY BOOK

7500 B.C. The Neolithic peoples of the mud-brick settlement of Çatal Hüyük invent the concept of indoors, as well as not defecating in the same place where you sleep.

A.D. 395–1071 The Byzantine Empire rules much of Asia Minor, also known as the Ass End Of The Roman Empire.

1453 Constantinople falls to the Ottoman Turks, who are assisted by the Divan Turks, as well as a mercenary force of Sofa Turks.

1529 Suleiman the Magnificent and his Ottoman army rampage across Europe, but Suleiman is humiliated during the Siege of Vienna when he gets his foot stuck in a skull, attempts to shake it free, then slips and falls into a pile of decapitated babies.

Osman III

1750 Sultan Osman III withdraws to his harem and becomes known as the "Sick Old Man Of Europe" by any woman within fingering range.

1915–1917 After the discovery of thousands of dead Armenians in mass graves, the Ottoman Empire slaps the Armenian government with a $50 fine for littering, and then holds a memorial service for several missing shovels.

1923 The Ottoman Empire falls and is replaced by the modern Republic of Turkey, which promises to never invade Europe again and to only turn the sword of Islam against its native Kurdish population.

1999 A massive earthquake rocks Turkey, killing 17,000. Days later, hundreds protest the "terrible act of God" as a breach of secularist law.

PEOPLE » ON THEIR BEST BEHAVIOR

By law all citizens must comb their hair, tuck their shirts in, and smile nice for any passing EU officials. While a majority are practicing Muslims, they're only allowed to sit in front of the Qur'an for 30 minutes a day, and the government makes sure they stay away from Islamic neighbors whom it sees as a bad influence. Likewise, diplomats try not to squirm in their seats during world summits, and politely laugh at all the Christian nations' corny jokes, knowing that they won't let just anyone into the world's most exclusive country club.

FACTS FOR YOU MY FRIEND »

OFFICIAL TITLE
The Completely European Nation Of Turkey

LARGEST CITY
Istanbul (not Constantinople)

GOVERNMENT
Radical secularism

RELIGION
Depends who's asking

CURRENCY
The homemade euro

TERRAIN
Known for splitting open and swallowing cities whole

GEOGRAPHY
Strategically located between mashed potatoes and cranberry sauce

HIGHEST POINT
Mount Ararat (16,854 ft.), the legendary peak where Noah crashed his ark, killing the last pair of unicorns

DERVISHES
Whirling

President gnawing on pork chop to fit in

Guy in charge of Europeaning everything up

Istanbul
Always waits until last minute to vacuum city

Turk trying to hide scimitar behind back

Man scrubbing all the corpses in the mass grave

Hand sticking out of freshly sodded area

Orient Express only running local today

Officials propping up charred bodies at bombed-out café

Turkish prisoners being greased up

Lamb-And Spice-Scented Region

Stockpile of pre-written thank-you notes

Closet where all the Kurds are stored

Turkish bubble bath

★**Ankara**

River redirected to not seem so Middle Eastern-y

Mayor licking thumb and wiping smudge from resident's face

Muslim extremist trying to look menacing on scooter

Businessman hoping to set up big chickpea deal on EU golf course

Unsightly ruins of ancient city

Mass flower beds

Man freshening up lake

Child practicing her Richter scales

River probably flowing the wrong way

Region Still Could Use A Good Sweeping

Area Rezoned For European Residences

Vase accentuates fertile plain

Man wearing fez in privacy of own home

Woman trying to dye her eyes blue

Children given cigarettes so they appear more sophisticated

Sparkling-clean torture chamber

Baklava mine

Falafelopolis

Student unable to locate Turkey on map of Europe

Cyprus

» SOMETHING IS DEFINITELY WRONG WITH THAT AARDVARK.

» THESE UN PEACEKEEPING TROOPS ACT NEUTRAL, BUT IN THEIR HEARTS THEY'VE TAKEN SIDES.

A Country Divided Exactly In Half

Years of hostility between Turks and Greeks in Cyprus came to a head in 1974, when the two warring groups joined together in the spirit of peace and cooperation to draw a line down the center of the island, perfect for screaming across.

Cleanly separated into Cyprus and the Turkish Republic of Northern Cyprus by a thin strip of masking tape, this small island nation is a testament to diplomacy as long as everyone stays on their own side. Though violence has been reduced greatly by the division, the region has seen a sharp rise in glaring, inching a toe over the line when no one is looking, and bilateral whining. Both sides have also reported the loss of hundreds of soccer balls and Frisbees to enemy territory. And as the separation drags on, many Cypriots are beginning to doubt the practicality of having 80% of the population on one side of the country and all of the bathrooms on the other.

In 2003, UN peacekeeping troops were deployed to the region at the request of the Greek Cypriots, but withdrew after determining that, since the Turks were not actually touching the Greeks—a fact the Turkish minority pointed out repeatedly while hovering their fingers only inches away—no international laws had been broken. Despite the UN's threat to impose harsh sanctions on the country if the two sides cannot amicably work out their differences, all recent attempts at peace talks have ended in headlocks.

CYPRUS » ADDITIONAL INFORMATION

There is no additional information on Cyprus. No facts or cultural tidbits that could possibly interest you or merit a separate, eye-catching informational box. Nothing of interest at all. In fact, most of what you've already read has been padded with adjectives and increased to 13-pt. font just to fill the space. We even made up an extra civil war or three. If you simply must have more information on Cyprus, please wait 75 to 100 years for the next event to occur.

FACTS » OR, IF YOU'RE TURKISH, LIES

LAND USE
Keeping each other apart

REASON TO VISIT
Cyprus could use the money

AGREEMENTS BY YEAR
1976: Everyone still really mad
1984: Someone definitely wrong
2000: No, you suck
2006: No more talks

FULL NAME
The Republic of Joshua Cyprus

LANGUAGES
Greek, Turkish, Profanity

CURRENCY
The Cypriot pound or Turkish lira–offer both and when clerk is confused, shove item inside jacket

MOST POPULAR USES FOR OLIVE OIL
Cooking, cleaning, lubricating Slip 'N Slides

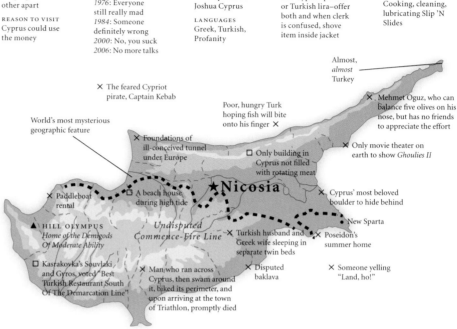

Map labels:
- The feared Cypriot pirate, Captain Kebab
- World's most mysterious geographic feature
- Poor, hungry Turk hoping fish will bite onto his finger
- Almost, *almost* Turkey
- Mehmet Oguz, who can balance five olives on his nose, but has no friends to appreciate the effort
- Foundations of ill-conceived tunnel under Europe
- Only building in Cyprus not filled with rotating meat
- Only movie theater on earth to show *Ghoulies II*
- ★ Nicosia
- Paddleboat rental
- A beach house during high tide
- Cyprus' most beloved boulder to hide behind
- New Sparta
- ▲ HILL OLYMPUS *Home of the Demigods Of Moderate Ability*
- *Undisputed Commence-Fire Line*
- Turkish husband and Greek wife sleeping in separate twin beds
- Poseidon's summer home
- Kasrakovka's Souvlaki and Gyros, voted "Best Turkish Restaurant South Of The Demarcation Line"
- Man who ran across Cyprus, then swam around it, biked its perimeter, and upon arriving at the town of Triathlon, promptly died
- Disputed baklava
- Someone yelling "Land, ho!"

HISTORY » POKING EACH OTHER WITH THE OLIVE BRANCH

3000 B.C. Aphrodite, the Greek goddess of love and beauty, arises fully formed and naked off the coast of Cyprus, in what would be the last time anyone from Cyprus ever saw a naked lady.

1400 B.C.–A.D. 1571 Due to its prime location in the Mediterranean Sea, Cyprus is conquered by the Mycenaeans, Egyptians, Persians, Romans, Ottomans, and during a brief period in between, two rather forceful sea turtles.

1878 Riding high off their victory against the Ottoman Empire, Britain dusts off its old colonizer hat and takes a photo of itself annexing Cyprus.

1960 After gaining its independence, Cyprus signs the Treaty of Guarantee, granting Britain, Greece, and Turkey the right to intervene at any time and proving the Cypriots may not fully understand what the word "independence" means.

1974 Cyprus is divided into two parts by a UN-patrolled "Green Line." The Green Line is then bisected at a 30° angle by a Red Line, measuring half its length. If a third line is drawn perpendicular to the Green Line to complete the right triangle, what is the length of its shortest side?

1981 Beatlemania finally reaches Cyprus.

1983 After peace talks fail, Turkish citizens declare their independence as the Turkish Republic of Northern Cyprus and make new passports and an 8" x 11" flag using Microsoft Paint.

1985 Violence breaks out during a soccer match when Turkish fans quickly sing "The Turkish Republic of Northern" right before the word "Cyprus" in the national anthem.

2003 Cyprus once again makes the UN's annual to-do list, beating out Myanmar, Sierra Leone, and Haiti to take the No. 12 spot.

2004 Figuring the country will be completely submerged in water before it has time to do too much damage, Cyprus is allowed to join the EU.

2007 Belgian Cypriots usurp control of the country in a largely unexpected coup.

There have been many battles in the falafel-gyro price war, but the victor is always the customer.

Europe

The United Kingdom

England
Surging Ahead To The 19th Century

For nearly 200 years, England ruled over 500 million people on six continents—a time in which it was commonly said that the sun never set on the British Empire. Today, however, the sun sets on the British Empire at precisely 5:47 p.m. GMT.

Although the world around them has advanced and changed, England holds fast to the antiquated traditions of its glorious past. Royal guards still protect the queen (Elizabeth II), though she is largely a figurehead and may in fact be animatronic. The people still eat crumpets. And to this day, they are very particular about their tea.

The British people long for the days when any son of a king could grow up to be a king, when girls were girls and boys were women, and when other nations didn't have boats. They cannot help but reminisce about the 1800s, when their empire was so powerful it could overtake any country simply by asking politely.

At the height of its power, the British Empire had access to the greatest minds, the most beautiful artwork, and the most important cultural artifacts around the world, which they promptly stole, boxed, and archived in the musty old cellar of Buckingham Palace, never to be seen again.

Understandably, they now worry that representatives from other nations will one day show up and ask for all their best stuff back.

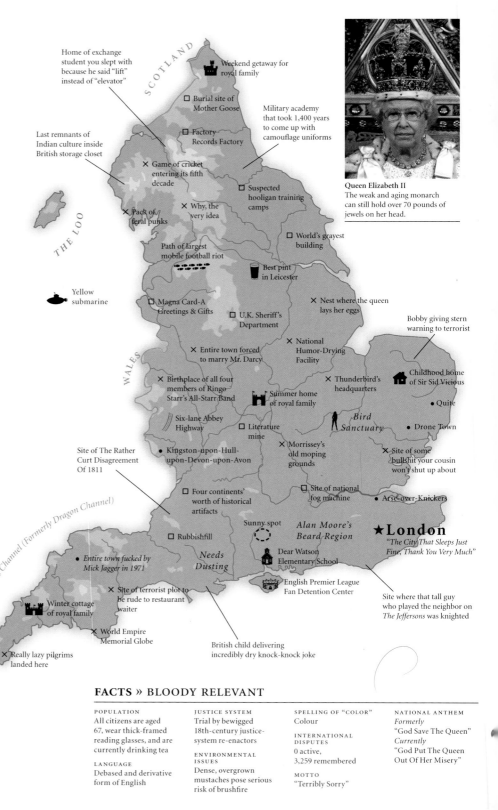

Queen Elizabeth II
The weak and aging monarch can still hold over 70 pounds of jewels on her head.

SCOTLAND

Home of exchange student you slept with because he said "lift" instead of "elevator"

Weekend getaway for royal family

Burial site of Mother Goose

Military academy that took 1,400 years to come up with camouflage uniforms

Last remnants of Indian culture inside British storage closet

Factory Records Factory

Game of cricket entering its fifth decade

Suspected hooligan training camps

THE LOO

Pack of feral punks

Why, the very idea

World's grayest building

Path of largest mobile football riot

Best pint in Leicester

Yellow submarine

Magna Card-A Greetings & Gifts

U.K. Sheriff's Department

Nest where the queen lays her eggs

Bobby giving stern warning to terrorist

WALES

Entire town forced to marry Mr. Darcy

National Humor-Drying Facility

Childhood home of Sir Sid Vicious

Birthplace of all four members of Ringo Starr's All-Starr Band

Summer home of royal family

Thunderbird's headquarters

Quite

Bird Sanctuary

Drone Town

Six-lane Abbey Highway

Literature mine

Morrissey's old moping grounds

Site of some bullshit your cousin won't shut up about

Site of The Rather Curt Disagreement Of 1811

Kingston-upon-Hull-upon-Devon-upon-Avon

Four continents' worth of historical artifacts

Site of national fog machine

Arse-over-Knickers

St. George's Channel (Formerly Dragon Channel)

Rubbishfill

Sunny spot

Needs Dusting

Alan Moore's Beard Region

Dear Watson Elementary School

★ **London**
"The City That Sleeps Just Fine, Thank You Very Much"

Entire town fucked by Mick Jagger in 1971

Site of terrorist plot to be rude to restaurant waiter

English Premier League Fan Detention Center

Site where that tall guy who played the neighbor on *The Jeffersons* was knighted

Winter cottage of royal family

World Empire Memorial Globe

British child delivering incredibly dry knock-knock joke

Really lazy pilgrims landed here

Nation's only dentist's office *(closed)*

Big Ben
The only thing in England making forward progress.

FACTS » BLOODY RELEVANT

POPULATION
All citizens are aged 67, wear thick-framed reading glasses, and are currently drinking tea

LANGUAGE
Debased and derivative form of English

JUSTICE SYSTEM
Trial by bewigged 18th-century justice-system re-enactors

ENVIRONMENTAL ISSUES
Dense, overgrown mustaches pose serious risk of brushfire

SPELLING OF "COLOR"
Colour

INTERNATIONAL DISPUTES
0 active, 3,259 remembered

MOTTO
"Terribly Sorry"

NATIONAL ANTHEM
Formerly
"God Save The Queen"
Currently
"God Put The Queen Out Of Her Misery"

ENGLAND » THIS FLAG REFLECTS THE IMAGINATION OF THE ENGLISH PEOPLE.

» DEF LEPPARD'S VERSION OF THE FLAG.

» THE NEW KNIGHTS OF THE ROUND TABLE.

HISTORY » A PROUD TRADITION OF PROUD TRADITIONS

6500 B.C. The third Ice Age devastates the population of England, destroys its art and culture, and bankrupts the British Ice Company.

A.D. 1215 The Magna Carta greatly reduces the powers of the king, who must now get full written permission from himself before enacting new laws.

1216 Inspired by the Magna Carta, English priests agree to significantly limit the power of God, whose rule of "divine right" had gone unchallenged for thousands of years.

1530 Henry VIII goes through the messiest divorce in history, denouncing the pope, shutting down every Roman Catholic church in England, and instituting an entirely new belief system all so he can legally dump his wife.

THE ELIZABETHAN ERA

During the Elizabethan era, women were subservient to men, forced to dress them, cook for them, curtsy on command, and remark hourly how impressive their accents were.

Because men prized male heirs, women were expected to give birth at least six times per year. In addition, they were obliged to write thank-you notes immediately following intercourse.

Queen Elizabeth herself never married. Though feminists believe this is because she was an independent woman who refused to answer to a king, most historians believe it is because she liked to kiss girls.

1562 England raises the legal drinking age to 7.

APRIL 1, 1586 On the first All Fools' Day, the British Navy suffers a costly setback when their cannons launch hundreds of gooseberry tarts at the Spanish Armada.

1658 A weak, malaria-ridden Oliver Cromwell dies in a pillow fight.

1674 England adopts due process, whereby offenders of British law are now granted the right to be drowned by a jury of their peers.

1765 England's Parliament levies a series of taxes on its American colonies: the Sugar Act, the Currency Act, the Stamp Act, the Pants Act, the Stamp Act Tax, the Mandatory Sewing Machine Ownership Act, the Sewing Machine Tax, the Unnecessary Tax, the Boston Massacre Tax, and the Tax Tax.

1767 The Townshend Acts levy taxes on windmill-style guitar strums.

THE VICTORIAN ERA

The reign of Queen Victoria was an era of extravagant fashion. Women wore two pounds of white makeup, chest-high stockings, and tight corsets that achieved the popular bound-in-heavy-steel-and-whalebone-restraints look. The English birth rate declined during the Victorian era, since by the time most women finished fully undressing prior to sex, they were no longer young enough to conceive.

Jack The Ripper

1888 The folk hero known only as Jack The Ripper gains notoriety for his campaign to end prostitution.

1918 England wins World War I thanks to its bold combat technique of asking for help.

1920–1929 The 1920s.

1944 Holed up in his London bunker, Winston Churchill single-handedly defeats Germany with a barrage of powerful and well-timed quips.

1962 British parents are outraged by the Beatles' new song "I Want To Hold Your Hand," which they suspect to be a euphemism for wanting to court someone.

2006 Prime Minister Tony Blair delivers a speech composed entirely of sighs.

2007 In response to the heightened security concerns of the War on Terror, England finally decides to arm its police officers with long pants.

Sconehenge
This stale monument is over 5,000 years old, and it is still a mystery who baked it.

PEOPLE WHO BEG YOUR PARDON »

The English people would like to dispute the stereotype that they are all overly polite, but refuse to bring up the subject for fear they will cause a stir. Two hundred years ago, many would tip their hats while conquering, raping, and enslaving their foreign subjects. Today, representatives from England still call their former territories to see if they need any humanitarian aid, or just to chat about the weather.

The English are known for their extremely British sense of humor. They will laugh at anything said in a dry, serious tone of voice, as demonstrated by the enduring popularity of

GREAT ENGLISH AUTHORS » YOU WERE SUPPOSED TO HAVE READ

John Milton

Though he intended Paradise Lost to be a long novel, a glitch in his printing press's immovable-type machine accidentally placed the right-hand margin in the center of every page, creating the world's most celebrated epic poem.

Shakespeare

Widely considered the greatest English writer, his undocumented life has given rise to theories that he was a fictional creation, and his writings have been attributed to Earl of Oxford Edward de Vere, Christopher Marlowe, and Sir Francis Bacon. Modern scholars now know that he was in fact Joseph Fiennes.

Charles Dickens

One of England's most prolific and influential authors, Dickens was responsible for 20 novels, 31 short stories, 13.8 million highfalutin adjectives, 900,000 extraneous independent clauses, and countless disappointing American report cards.

J. R. R. Tolkien

His vast and fantastical Middle Earth universe has intrigued and stunted the growth of generations of male readers.

Jane Austen

Lesbian.

Hugh Grant

Not an author.

Scotland, Wales & Northern Ireland

SCOTLAND » CAN BE DRAPED AROUND WAIST FOR USE AS EMERGENCY CLOTHING.

WALES » FLAG MAKER WAS GOING THROUGH A MESSY DIVORCE WHEN HE DESIGNED THIS ONE.

Scotland
England's Noisy Upstairs Neighbor

Throughout its history, Scotland has upheld a long and proud tradition of not being England.

Scotland is still often mistaken for its U.K. counterpart, however, forcing it to take steps to separate England's lack of identity from its own lack of identity.

For instance, in order to distinguish their cuisine from England's bland combination of foods, the Scots began eating sheep's heart, liver, and lungs mixed with oatmeal. Attempting to distance their national sport from England's boring pastime of cricket, they invented golf. In an effort to distinguish their dialect from the affected accent of the English, the Scots began speaking louder, and in an even more affected accent.

Deeply ashamed that they were unable to escape international comparisons to overly effete England, the men of Scotland went through an identity crisis and all began wearing dresses.

Wales
Land Of Consonant Sorrow

Wales is the birthplace of the Welsh language—the oldest, longest, and least-pronounceable language in the world. When spoken, it sounds like a beautiful song, but when written, it looks like the alphabet just vomited.

Featuring words such as "Llongyfarchiadau," "Sarnbigog," and "Gwyllbsfgwiwillynpwppligwyn," Welsh is the only language in which a run-on sentence can last over a year. In fact, speakers often forget what they are saying in the middle of a word.

Wales is expected to declare its independence from England in 2089, when it finally finishes writing its 1,500-page constitution.

MAP KEY
- Sand Trap
- Water Hazard
- Six-Lane Cartway
- The Rough

A rare photograph of what some claim to be the Loch Ness Monster.

Mercifully, the end of Britain

Shetland Islands

Shetland pony being stuffed with oatmeal and tripe

Spring quarters of royal family

Caddies relegated to this island

10,000 tourists yelling "Freedom!"

Site where Bigfoot reported Loch Ness Monster sighting

Frederick's Of Scotland erotic kilt warehouse

Wicker Man

Bar brawl for Scottish independence fought here in 1314

Historic Guys-With-Blue-On-Their-Face battlefield

Loch Ness

Inverness
Entire city stuffed inside bladder of a sheep and poached in 2003

Bagpipeline

Phlegm Buildup

Man enjoying after-dinner heart attack

Ruins of ancient caddyshack

MacIlhenny's Pub For The Study Of National Stereotypes

St. Andrews
Cheating at golf invented here

Burial site of the English language

Site of 1978 food massacre

Argyle Region

★**Edinburgh**

Human whisky distillery

World's deepest divot (−53 km.)

Out-of-shape city may run out of breath by 2014

Greenskeeper's castle

Forward-drinking city boasts highest tolerance of alcohol in world

City where ruddy skin was perfected

Nice out-of-the-way place to get punched in the head by a drunken Welshman

Autumn residence of royal family

Old man slowly chewing dried intestine

Stone fence built by Rome's first Englonaut

This Region Just Folklore

Site where Princess Di won handjob contest and the right to marry Charles

Tom Jones

This Welshman began singing "It's Not Unusual" in his native tongue in 1997, and is still on the first verse.

Elaborately manicured garden where naughty children make mischief

Llangynog
Pronounced [coughing sound]

Llanmawddwy
Last city the Welsh were allowed to name

Site where Catherine Zeta Jones was put in a basket and floated out to sea for Hollywood

First Welshman to be born with a neck, 1998

Natural beauty only brought out when photographers are coming over

Cockles Reserve

Cwmystwyth
Requires four tongues to pronounce

Grove of wise talking trees

★**Cardiff**

Storage castle

HISTORY » 1,500 YEARS UNDER PAR

A.D. 1034–1053 Scottish law allows one to become king by killing the current king, which results in Malcolm II's corpse ruling Scotland for nearly 20 years after he commits suicide.

1587–1596 In one of the longest and bloodiest battles of all time, Mary Queen of Scots is beheaded.

1765 Scotsman James Watt invents the modern-day invention—a useful process, machine, or improvement that did not previously exist.

1776 David Hume, the brilliant Scottish philosopher best known for his thorough and unassailable form of analytical skepticism, is swallowed whole by the Loch Ness Monster.

1996 A Scottish scientist successfully clones a sheep in order to fulfill a lifelong sex fantasy.

FACTS » READ SLOWLY

COUNTRY NAME
Short form: Wales
Long form: Wywllyness
Longer form: Wywllanbwyllgowowowllyn
Longest form: Wywllanpwchwywnbyogongwyn-gwllynbllgobbwylyllynn

TERRAIN
Features eight different types of hills

CLIMATE
Typically two to three nice days per year

TOURIST SITES
Llanfairpwllgwyngyllgogerychwyrndrobwlll-lantysiliogogogoch, Gwynnnegwelblblllliofrebwll, Welsh Slate Museum, Llanwrstrwtrgrochwwllyn

LITERACY RATE
One word per hour

PEOPLE » A SHEEP'S HELL

The people of Wales deny the stereotype that they are "sheep-fuckers," maintaining that they rarely even get to third base with their livestock.

NORTHERN IRELAND » FLAG
SYMBOLIZED BY THE ENDURING
IMAGE OF THE BLOOD-RED
HAND OF ULSTER.

CEASE - FIRE AGREEMENT

Whereby, the people of Northern Ireland are entitled to life free of
violence, it is hereby agreed that all hostilities between the IRA and the forces
of Great Britain shall immediately cease.

» A CITIZEN
OBSERVES
THE NATION'S
ALTERNATE-
SIDE-OF-
THE-STREET
CAR-BOMBING
POLICY.

Northern Ireland
Putting Differences Aside To Make Room For Fighting

Northern Ireland is an especially violent territory of the U.K., made up of a Protestant majority that believes in killing Catholics, and a Catholic minority that believes in killing Protestants. A small percentage of people profess no religious affiliation but still enjoy killing people.

Conflict between these two factions has resulted in near-constant violence, with intermittent periods of bloodshed. This tumultuous era of Northern Ireland's history is known as "The Troubles," while the remainder of Northern Ireland's history is known as "1954."

The Troubles have spawned some of the bloodiest incidents of white sectarian violence in modern history, as well as some of U2's finest music—a trade-off most of the world is willing to accept.

Today, the two sides have reached a tenuous peace agreement expected to last through next Thursday. The Irish Republican Army has ended its armed campaign against British rule, vowing to use only peaceful gunfire to achieve it political goals. And the Protestants have promised to get killed less often.

HISTORY » FIGHTING CEASEFIRE WITH GUNFIRE

5TH CENTURY A.D. St. Patrick brings Christianity from Western Europe, and early Northern Irishmen surround him, beat him with shillelaghs, and forcibly take the religion as their own.

1695–1829 Northern Ireland passes a series of Penal Codes against the Catholics, stripping them of such basic human rights as buying land, holding public office, voting, and having nice things.

1970 Multiparty peace talks go well, leaving only 12 dead and a mere 17 with serious injuries.

1972 British troops open fire on unarmed civil-rights demonstrators, killing 13 in a massacre now known as Bloody Sunday. Bloody Monday through Saturday follow, comprising the most violent week of Bloody January, the seventh-bloodiest month of Bloody 1972.

1991 Nation calls for immediate cease-fire so they can enjoy a nice, quiet lunch for once.

1998 Catholic and Protestant factions sign the Good Friday Agreement to halt the fighting once and for all. Three days later, however, the hostilities miraculously rise again.

1999 David Trimble (Protestant) and John Hume (Catholic) are awarded the Nobel Peace Prize for orchestrating the Good Friday Agreement. A month-long conflict immediately erupts over who deserves it more, and who gets to keep it in their house for the first week.

2003 A Unionist terrorist kills 56 Unionists when he temporarily forgets what the difference is between Unionists and Nationalists.

2005 The IRA ends their armed campaign by hiding their guns behind their backs and saying, "See?"

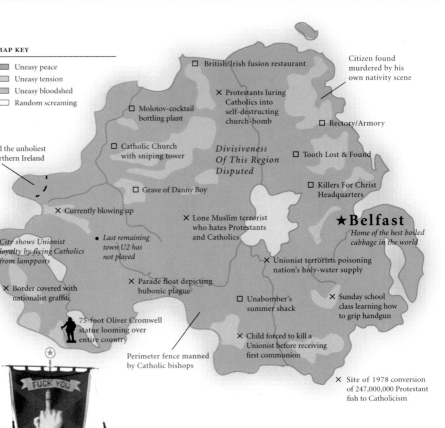

MAP KEY
- Uneasy peace
- Uneasy tension
- Uneasy bloodshed
- Random screaming

□ British/Irish fusion restaurant

Citizen found murdered by his own nativity scene

× Protestants luring Catholics into self-destructing church-bomb

□ Molotov-cocktail bottling plant

□ Rectory/Armory

□ Catholic Church with sniping tower

Divisiveness Of This Region Disputed

□ Tooth Lost & Found

Considered the unholiest part of Northern Ireland

□ Grave of Danny Boy

□ Killers For Christ Headquarters

× Currently blowing up

× Lone Muslim terrorist who hates Protestants and Catholics

★ **Belfast**
Home of the best boiled cabbage in the world

• City shows Unionist loyalty by flying Catholics from lampposts

• Last remaining town U2 has not played

× Unionist terrorists poisoning nation's holy-water supply

× Border covered with nationalist graffiti

× Parade float depicting bubonic plague

□ Unabomber's summer shack

× Sunday school class learning how to grip handgun

75-foot Oliver Cromwell statue looming over entire country

Perimeter fence manned by Catholic bishops

× Child forced to kill a Unionist before receiving first communion

× Site of 1978 conversion of 247,000,000 Protestant fish to Catholicism

FUCK YOU

FACTS » COMPILED BY PEOPLE WHO HAVE NOTHING BETTER TO DO

INTERNATIONAL RECOGNITION
Winner of UN's "Whitest Conflict On Earth" award 35 years running

LIKELIHOOD OF GETTING PUNCHED IN FACE AT PUB
High

LIKELIHOOD OF GETTING SHOT IN FACE AT PUB
Moderate

LEADING CAUSE OF DEATH
Going to the pub

NATURAL HAZARDS
Sunlight, moonlight, 60-watt light

BRITISH OCCUPATION
1,500 reluctant British troops on punishment duty; 22,000 crazy British Special Air Service units on reward duty

FAMOUS PROVERBS
"May the road always rise to meet you, but not with the massive force of a 50-pound car bomb"

PEOPLE » LOATHE THY NEIGHBOR

The people of Northern Ireland are widely known as some of the friendliest, most hospitable in the world, always willing to take a stranger in, cook him a hot meal, ascertain his religious affiliation, and then either put him up for the night or strap dynamite to his bludgeoned body and detonate it in the town square.

Many are envied for their beautiful accent, a lyrical brogue that reminds many listeners of an aggressive, expletive-ridden poem.

The nation is also home to the most unreliable car bombs in the world, due to the combination of Irish explosive experts and British automobiles. On the rare occasion one actually explodes, it is often already broken-down on the side of the road.

Ireland

Blowing Their Pot O' Gold On Whiskey

After centuries of subjugation by the English and years of chronic poverty, the Emerald Isle enjoyed an incredible economic turnaround in the 1990s, and has at last managed to beat the stereotype of the poor, drunken, fighting Irishman into a bloody pulp.

Irish citizens are now able to purchase multiple cases of microbrewed beer each night, can afford to get into brawls at high-end clubs, and can easily pay for the expensive dental work they invariably require every other Saturday morning.

With a large Irish diaspora, the country is a haven for tourists looking to drink away their savings in a pastoral setting. Each year, they come by the thousands, embracing their Irish heritage by taking long drunken drives through the countryside and gazing woozily at the gorgeous smears of green.

After stopping off to take in 10 or 12 pints of local color at a pub, visitors crawl to more famous landmarks. There, they are amazed by the dizzying number of Blarney Stones, upon which they slur a wish to make the country stop spinning.

PEOPLE » ENJOYING MANY WEE NIPS

Enterprising Irish youths.

Known for their large loving families and gregarious nature, it is often said that the Irish never quit until closing time or she gets her tubes tied.

With more than 500,000 pubs, and a population that attends Mass several times a day, Ireland has one of the highest confession rates in the world. Priests (who outnumber women two to one) rarely require more than 12 Hail Marys per sin, since the confessions are often hilarious and fun-loving tales of over-indulgence and merriment, and usually involve the priests themselves.

Despite their recent economic renaissance, the Irish refuse to forget their past—especially the time England fucked them over for 200 years—and still hold onto traditions such as drinking, sobering up, singing about drinking, and drinking.

The particular Irish gift for storytelling has produced some of the world's most renowned men of letters, including Sean Hannity and Bill O'Reilly.

FECKIN' FACTS »

POPULATION
4.1 million, with 1.6 million in Dublin, and the rest in New York or Boston, where they are tending bar part-time

RELIGION
Catholic (74%), Super-Catholic (26%)

MEDICAL ISSUES
Communicable diseases spread by visitors to the Blarney Stone

LANGUAGE
Foul

EXCHANGE RATE
One U2 = 100 Enyas

CUISINE
Shot of whiskey with beer and a whiskey chaser, cabbage

BIRTHRIGHT
A kiss

21ST-CENTURY INNOVATION
Urinating indoors

NATIONAL VOWEL, PUNCTUATION MARK
O, '

St. Patrick, the patron saint of Ireland, is honored each year with millions of brutal hangovers.

- 65% of town whiskey-blind
- × Leprechaun's pot of vomit
- Tenacious snake
- ■ Beer spring
- □ Bomb-proof pub
- Green plastic bowler haberdashery
- □ Strategic potato reserves
- ▥ Liver Bank
- × Bar fight entering third year
- ■ Lotus-Overeaters Anonymous meeting
- ■ Site of the four-hour potato famine of July 12, 2005
- □ Struggling restaurant with "Irish need not apply" sign in window
- *Shiteload Of Sheep*
- × Gaelic new-age hippie colony (drunk)
- × Irishman drinking self under the table
- × Mother warming up bottle of Jameson for infant
- Second-most-kissed rock in country
- ★ **Dublin** Home to 1.6 million enablers
- Region boasts 50 shades of green vomit
- × Frank McCourt desperately trying to remember other abusive cousins to write about
- ■ Faggy foot-dancing school
- × Child taking hair of the dog for a walk
- ■ Bono born here for our sins
- □ Offshore pub
- • Entire city passed out since 1806
- ▦ World's tallest battered-wife shelter
- × Spot where Western civilization got drunk for the first time
- *Red-Headed Stepchild Sanctuary*
- × Spot where Oscar Wilde lost duel with wallpaper
- ■ Guinness world record for Guinness-drinking forgotten here
- ⛴ Abortion ferry
- × Pope message-relay tower
- River dyed sickly pale for St. Patrick's Day

HISTORY » BROUGHT TO YOU BY THE POTATO

8000 B.C. Fascinated by the size of the woolly mammoth's genitals, Irishmen write an elaborate rhyme on a cave wall.

2000 B.C. The Irish toast the Bronze Age.

A.D. 432 St. Patrick arrives in Ireland, offering 25-cent chicken wings and two-for-one taps all night long.

1387 Luck of the Irish runs out.

1690 Deposed British King James II escapes to Ireland and organizes an army that defeats the British at the Battle of the Boyne. Grateful for their help in restoring him to the throne, James II grants Ireland its independence. Just kidding!

1802 Ireland wins "Best Bogs" in *The Times Of London*'s "Best Of Europe" poll.

1845–1849 During Ireland's Great Potato Famine, 1 million die, 2 million flee the country, and the rest are left mourning the senseless waste of so much sour cream.

1921 Ireland gains independence, led by labor unions who demand equal rights, fair wages, and full-time paid drunkenness for all.

1922 Only halfway into his epic masterpiece *Ulysses*, James Joyce stops writing, but still tells all his friends it's "great."

2007 The Irish government reluctantly recognizes the role of African-American Boston Celtics guard Dennis Johnson in the team's 1984 NBA championship.

Portugal

Still Searching For India

In the 1400s, Portuguese explorers set out to find a western passage to India. Six centuries later, they're still looking for it, as they are too proud to ask for directions from passing sailors, and too stubborn to consult the foldout world map in their ship's glove compartment.

Although the Portuguese insist that they know where they're going, they spent nearly two years sailing up and down the coast of the Mississippi River, once circumnavigated Iceland, and in 1876 passed by the Bering Strait for what seemed like the 20th time in a one-month span.

Unfortunately, when they finally asked for directions in 1902, they forgot whether they were supposed to take a left or a right at Barbados, and spent the next century complaining that their compass was "stupid" and that "everything in the Atlantic Ocean looks exactly the same."

In 2005, after 12 years at sea, two modern Portuguese explorers finally spotted land they believed to be India. However, it was Portugal.

FACTS » THE LITTLEST EMPIRE

GEOGRAPHY
Hand-me-down mountains, castoff rivers from Spain

ECONOMY
Cork-based

AREA COMPARATIVE
Slightly smaller than one rectangle

HISTORICAL LANDMARKS
Africa

LANGUAGE
Portuguese, which originated from people speaking Spanish with too many olives in their mouths

CONSTITUTION
Bad photocopy of Spain's; can't read the part about free speech

FOOTBALL
Soccer

RELIGION
Catholicesque

TOP OCCUPATION
Collecting unemployment

LEADING INDUSTRIES
Winemaking, winedrinking

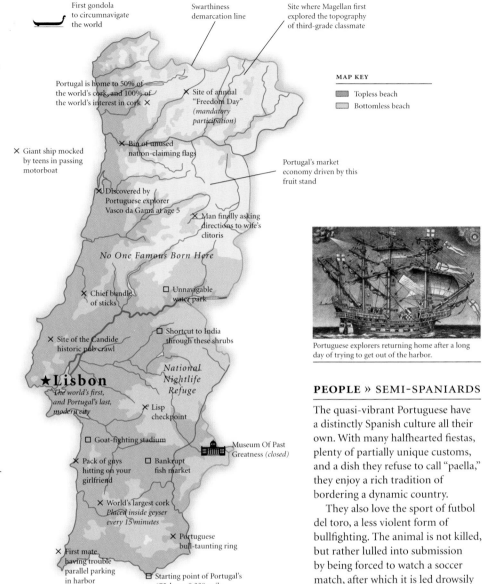

First gondola to circumnavigate the world

Swarthiness demarcation line

Site where Magellan first explored the topography of third-grade classmate

Portugal is home to 50% of the world's cork, and 100% of the world's interest in cork ✕

✕ Site of annual "Freedom Day" *(mandatory participation)*

✕ Giant ship mocked by teens in passing motorboat

✕ Bin of unused nation-claiming flags

Portugal's market economy driven by this fruit stand

✕ Discovered by Portuguese explorer Vasco da Gama at age 5

✕ Man finally asking directions to wife's clitoris

No One Famous Born Here

✕ Chief bundle of sticks

☐ Unnavigable water park

✕ Site of the Candide historic pub crawl

☐ Shortcut to India through these shrubs

National Nightlife Refuge

★ **Lisbon**
The world's first, and Portugal's last, modern city

✕ Lisp checkpoint

☐ Goat-fighting stadium

✕ Pack of guys hitting on your girlfriend

☐ Bankrupt fish market

Museum Of Past Greatness *(closed)*

✕ World's largest cork
Placed inside geyser every 15 minutes

✕ Portuguese bull-taunting ring

✕ First mate having trouble parallel parking in harbor

☐ Starting point of Portugal's 675-hour, 8,239-mile "Nostalgia Boat Tour"

MAP KEY

▨	Topless beach
▨	Bottomless beach

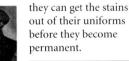

Portuguese explorers returning home after a long day of trying to get out of the harbor.

PEOPLE » SEMI-SPANIARDS

The quasi-vibrant Portuguese have a distinctly Spanish culture all their own. With many halfhearted fiestas, plenty of partially unique customs, and a dish they refuse to call "paella," they enjoy a rich tradition of bordering a dynamic country.

They also love the sport of futbol del toro, a less violent form of bullfighting. The animal is not killed, but rather lulled into submission by being forced to watch a soccer match, after which it is led drowsily from the ring.

HISTORY » THE LAST PORTUGUESE COLONY

A.D. 1423 Portuguese explorers discover your childhood home.

Da Gama

1523 Vasco da Gama's 16-year-old son, Tommy da Gama, shames his family when he announces that he does not want to become a professional explorer, and will instead go to dental school.

1755 Lisbon is destroyed in a vicious acting out of God when the city is hit simultaneously by an earthquake, tsunami, fire, tornado, cyclone, mudslide, and an extra-dreary light rain.

1873 Brilliant but methodical Portuguese aphorist Romero de Carlos dies while composing what comes to be known as the nation's Unfinished Motto: "Liberty, Freedom, And."

1918 Portugal helps the Allies defeat the Germans in WWI by throwing thousands of grapes at them. The Germans surrender immediately so they can get the stains out of their uniforms before they become permanent.

Magellan

1917 A child in Fatima reports seeing a vision of the Virgin Mary, which appears to him in a stained-glass window.

1932–1968 Antonio de Oliveira Salazar is elected as dictator for life. Salazar's reign is marked by extreme political repression, but he does fulfill his campaign promise to make the donkey carts run on time.

1939–1945 Portugal maintains official neutrality in WWII, as all of its soldiers are still AWOL from WWI.

1975–2000 Portuguese pilots search for an air passage to India.

Cabral

2007 Portugal's colonial era officially ends, as the nation loses its last international territory when it finally cedes control of Portugal.

Spain

» TO THIS DAY, SPAIN ISN'T SURE WHAT IT DID WITH ITS ARMADA.

Enjoying A Three-Century Siesta

Though it once dominated the seas and spanned five continents, today the drowsy Spanish Empire lacks the energy necessary to wipe out an entire indigenous population, would rather bum around Europe than conduct a brutal Inquisition, and lost the contact information for its American colonies centuries ago.

With a stunning array of nappable landscapes, including long, lazy coastlines and slouching mountains, Spain offers incredible beauty to those who are nodding off or just resting their eyes.

Spain takes up most of the Iberian Peninsula, and sublets the rest to Portugal in an effort to scrounge up a little extra spending money for that economy it's been meaning to get.

Businesses generally open at noon, just in time for the lunch break, when the Spanish can relax over a long meal, drink two beers to wash down their sangrias, and then close for siesta, which lasts until the next day's lunch break.

Spain has missed 70 of the last 75 sessions of the Spanish parliament, and the only business it has conducted at the UN was proposing a resolution to put off talks on nuclear proliferation until after Spain's seven-day weekend, though the country's representative wasn't able to cast a vote after sleeping through the Thursday 11 a.m. meeting.

SPANISH CUISINE » PAELLA

Spain's sole cultural contribution in the past 500 years, the Arab-inspired paella is a fried dish consisting of rice, shrimp, pork, lobster, sardines, beef, squid, rope, Cornish game hens, more pork, goose, antlers, liver, baby back ribs, snails, lasagna, paper towels, wristwatches, vegetables, and anything else in arm's reach that's not too heavy.

HISTORY » ALL CONQUERED OUT

500,000 B.C. Impressed with the calm beauty of the Iberian Peninsula, thousands of Neanderthals retire in Spain to live out their 20s in comfort.

15,000 B.C. The discovery of the stone brings about such important innovations as the hard surface, the rockqueduct, and the contraceptive boulder.

7500 B.C. Artists in the Altamira cave paint some of Europe's earliest artwork that nobody gets.

575 B.C. The Greeks introduce winemaking, lovemaking, and the deadbeat dad.

A.D. 400–500 The angst-ridden Visigoths spend all their time listening to morose chants, painting their fingernails black, and acting like they don't care when the Moors conquer them. Looking back at old yearbook paintings years later, they can't believe what losers they were.

711–1013 Muslims rule over Spain, turning off millions of Christians who don't care for all the flourishing of arts, math, and science.

844 During the Reconquista, St. James amazes onlookers when he performs his first miracle, turning ordinary Muslims into corpses.

1469 Claiming he's not like all the other genocidal imperialists, Isabella agrees to marry Prince Ferdinand of Aragon, and lists one of everything in the country on their wedding registry.

Queen Isabella

1483 Tomás de Torquemada, a partner at a private execution firm who previously served as Madrid's District Inquisitor, is appointed Inquisitor General of Spain.

1492 Working late one night to unify Spain, Ferdinand and Isabella send Christopher Columbus out to pick up some Indian food. On his way back, Columbus inadvertently discovers, rapes, plunders, murders, and claims America.

1494 Somewhat to the dismay of the other 99.6% of the world, Pope Alexander VI divides the New World between Spain and Portugal, minus a very reasonable finder's fee.

The Spanish Inquisition

1588 The Spanish Armada is defeated by a few English rowboats, a guy on the shore waving his arms around, and the fact that they couldn't get the ships to turn left.

1605 Cervantes pens the world's first novel, *Don Quixote*, a scathing indictment of the windmill industry.

1808–1814 French forces occupy the country and Napoleon appoints his mentally challenged brother to handle all of Spain's administrative affairs—though in those days, they just called them retards.

1898 Thinking that the Spanish-American War was supposed to be fought a month later, the Spanish show up disheveled and disoriented three weeks after the Americans had won, claiming that traffic was an absolute nightmare.

"Guernica"

1937 Pablo Picasso captures the horror of the Spanish Civil War with his painting "Guernica," which accurately depicts the 1937 assault on flat-faced weirdos by an army of vicious triangles.

1943 A devout Catholic, fascist dictator Francisco Franco is compelled to go to confession after coveting the wife of one of his 200,000 executed dissidents.

Francisco Franco

1959 The ethnic Basques in northern Spain create the separatist organization ETA to preserve their ancient language, traditional kidnapping techniques, and assassination arts and crafts.

1992 Barcelona learns it is hosting the Summer Olympics when a Romanian girl shows up at city hall with the torch.

2004 191 people die in the Madrid terrorist bombings, which the U.S. and England blame on Spain's lax approach to security, immigration, and endoskeletons.

✗ Basque terrorist hitting snooze button on bomb

✗ Basque separatist kidnapping self to avoid work

☐ Convenience store closed 24/7

Spanish Harlem

● **Pamplona**
Home to the annual Resting Of The Bulls

✗ Woman shopping for can of beans accidentally buying $12 million Goya painting

Ebro River
This river flows downstream, just like all the others

☐ Gaudí never finished building La Sagrada Familia, claiming he couldn't find a big enough wick for the top

✗ Bull that doesn't mind the color red that much

● *City powered entirely by sexual energy*

✗ Spot behind architecture school where Gaudí used to smoke crack between classes

Man sleeping right through scheduled nap

✝ 200-mile-high crucifix

✗ Man speaking Mexican

☐ Nathional Inthitute For Dialect Prethervation

Salvador Dalí's unventilated studio

★ **Madrid**
City forgot to turn the economy on

✗ Host family

✗ Birthplace of the bull that gored your brother

☐ Understated Hemingway reference

Wild On! film crews

RECLINING PLATEAU

✗ Parents taking time to watch their kids watch sports on TV

✗ Rapist claiming it's part of his heritage

✗ Farmer annoyed that all his olives are orange

🚂 Modern slow-speed trains with state-of-the-art sleeping cars

☐ Homicidal windmill on the lam

✗ Filmmaker Pedro Almodóvar's childhood home, where he was raised by six transsexual nuns

Ibiza
Romantic assholes' paradise

✗ Man taking 30-year coffee break

✗ Flamenco dancer cheating on dance instructor with husband

☐ Great spot to thank God you're not in Africa

☐ Site of that famous museum you learned about in high school Spanish class

Tapas Beach

Clay skyscraper

Stupid restaurant that doesn't even have nachos

✗ Jammed yacht belonging to Latsis family

PEOPLE » ON BREAK FROM LIFE

The Spanish are known for their good looks and ability to age extremely well, as many are so lazy that it takes them 40 years to get around to turning 21. Despite modern distractions, Spaniards manage to strike a balance between free time, spare time, and time off. Most start their mornings at the crack of dawn by taking off their dance clothes and crawling into bed for a full day's sleep. But after a long evening of relaxing with friends, they rarely have the energy to put things off until tomorrow.

Spanish honeymoons generally last up to six minutes, depending on the agility of the couple.

EL FACTS »

FORM OF GOVERNMENT
Parliamentary mañanarchy

OFFICIAL LANGUAGE
English subtitles

INTERNATIONAL DISPUTES
Some neighboring countries actually have to work in the morning, you know

INTERNET
Trying to use dial-up, but someone's on the phone

NON-WORK FORCE
17.2 million

WIND RESERVES
254 million cubic meters

CRIMINAL RECORD
Got caught with hash once

NATIONAL HOLIDAY
Every day

LIFESTYLE EXPECTANCY
79.2 hot-blooded years

YARDSTICK
The meter

CURRENT GRAND INQUISITOR
Tomás de Torquemada XXIV

RELEVANCE TO AMERICA
Spanish-born Penélope Cruz shows her breasts in *Jamón, Jamón*

TRANSPORTATION
The Spanish aren't going anywhere

UNPOPULAR MEATS
Anything not slathered in ham

NATIONAL SPORT
Cornering a dazed bull and stabbing it to death in front of 50,000 people

CURRENCY
One euro, broken into several tapas platters

France

One Nation Above God

Home to Earth's entire population of 62.7 million people, every single one of the planet's 427 cities, and all of its history, culture, and beauty, France is the only country in the world.

Located directly in the center of the universe, around which everything else revolves, the nation of France is the sole beacon of life and civilization in an otherwise black and empty void.

Stretching from the globe's southernmost point in Marseille to its northern tip in Paris, and extending all the way to the Far East, or Dijon, France is known throughout France for its streets, buildings, wine, and food—things that simply don't exist anywhere else.

The French have produced every great achievement in every field of endeavor in the history of mankind, including the sculptures of Michelangelo, the symphonies of Beethoven, and the writings of William Shakespeare.

Today, this birthplace of art, aviation, democracy, coffee, man, Buddhism, socialism, reggae, John Wayne, pasta, karate, the American Revolution, arrogance, space exploration, the Nile River, and everything else that has ever come to pass, has earned its place as the finest, greatest, and best nation in all of France.

HIGH-AND-MIGHTY FACTS »

POPULATION
62,745,000 (an estimated 32.3 million despise you personally)

SEXUAL DISTRIBUTION
48% female, 43% male, 9% other

PRIMARY CONTRIBUTION TO WORLD CULTURE
The blowjob

ELEVATION EXTREMES
Highest point: Mont Blanc (4,870 m.)
Lowest point: France has no lowest point

GEOGRAPHY
High-and-mighty mountains in the southeast, overbearing coastal plains in the north, and pretentious, ostentatious river valleys in the west

HATED BY
Everyone

CUISINE
French

WORKFORCE
35 million full-time and freelance strikers

INTERNATIONAL DISPUTES
Not worth France's time

LEADING CAUSE OF DEATH
Turtleneck asphyxiation

CELLULAR TELEPHONES IN USE
0 (1986 est.)

CINEMA
An average of 200 films are released each year, over half of which are about French cinema

PEOPLE » BETTER THAN YOU

The people of France are extremely proud of their cultural achievements, and offer no apologies for giving the world such things as self-indulgent cinema, the awkward *ménage à trois*, and the Frenchman.

French citizens are known to welcome all tourists by offering a friendly sneer, a hearty goodbye, and a warm, indecipherable greeting muttered under their breath.

The men of France—known internationally as God's gag gift to women—are legendary for their amorous nature. However, they are often compared to French soldiers: Both come on strong, make a few quick mistakes, regret getting involved, lose all interest, and ultimately give up, but still have the temerity to brag about the conquest to their allies for years.

On the international stage, the French have earned a reputation for being cold and standoffish, but they are always quick to condescend to a nation in need. If another country is in crisis, they are the first to tell them what they did wrong, send thousands of relief workers there to shake their heads disapprovingly, and donate millions of dollars in guilt-inducing foreign aid.

Paris Fashion

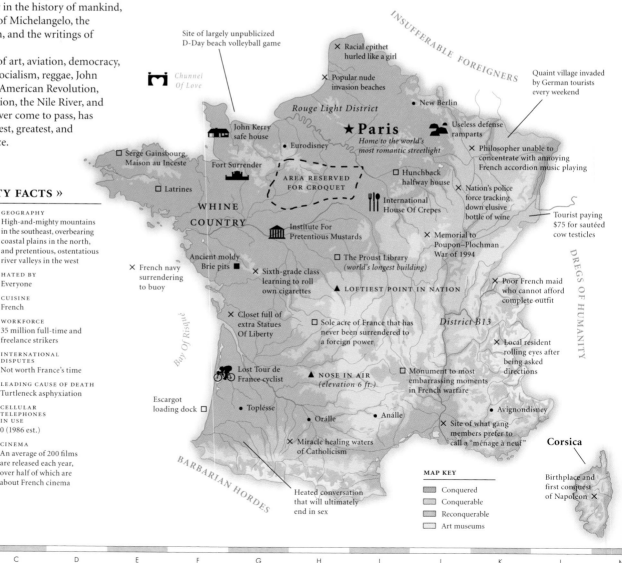

Site of largely unpublicized D-Day beach volleyball game

Channel Of Love

INSUFFERABLE FOREIGNERS

× Racial epithet hurled like a girl

× Popular nude invasion beaches

Rouge Light District

• New Berlin

Quaint village invaded by German tourists every weekend

☐ Serge Gainsbourg Maison au Inceste

John Kerry safe house

• Eurodisney

★ **Paris**
Home to the world's most romantic streetlight

Useless defense ramparts

× Philosopher unable to concentrate with annoying French accordion music playing

Fort Surrender

AREA RESERVED FOR CROQUET

☐ Hunchback halfway house

× Nation's police force tracking down elusive bottle of wine

☐ Latrines

WHINE COUNTRY

☐ Institute For Pretentious Mustards

International House Of Crepes

Tourist paying $75 for sautéed cow testicles

× Memorial to Poupon–Plochman War of 1994

Ancient moldy Brie pits ■

× French navy surrendering to buoy

× Sixth-grade class learning to roll own cigarettes

☐ The Proust Library *(world's longest building)*

▲ LOFTIEST POINT IN NATION

DREGS OF HUMANITY

Bay Of Risqué

× Closet full of extra Statues Of Liberty

☐ Sole acre of France that has never been surrendered to a foreign power

District B13

× Poor French maid who cannot afford complete outfit

Lost Tour de France cyclist

▲ NOSE IN AIR *(elevation 6 ft.)*

☐ Monument to most embarrassing moments in French warfare

× Local resident rolling eyes after being asked directions

Escargot loading dock ☐

• Toplésse

• Oràlle

• Anàlle

• Avignondisney

× Site of what gang members prefer to call a "ménage à neuf"

× Miracle healing waters of Catholicism

BARBARIAN HORDES

Heated conversation that will ultimately end in sex

MAP KEY

☐ Conquered
☐ Conquerable
☐ Reconquerable
☐ Art museums

Corsica

Birthplace and first conquest of Napoleon ×

HISTORY » A VAINGLORIOUS REVOLUTION

26,000 B.C. Archaeologists have unearthed the earliest-known French stereotypes, discovering several stone berets, an obsidian baguette, and an 8,000-year-old female skeleton with hairy armpits.

52 B.C. Nearsighted Frenchmen surrender to a statue of Julius Caesar.

A.D. 814 Charlemagne, the famed Emperor of the West, dies having not accomplished one single interesting thing during his entire life.

Joan of Arc

1429 Joan of Arc, an illiterate 17-year-old, leads French troops to victory against England in the Hundred Years' War. Baffled and emasculated French soldiers are convinced the British only let her win because she's a girl.

World War II
Nazi soldiers enjoy a romantic stroll through Paris.

1555 French astrologer Nostradamus accurately predicts the gullibility of future generations.

1651 French comedian Molière "invents" sarcasm, because he was clearly the first person ever to make a cutting, ironic remark. Oh, what a genius! Bravo, Molière. Bra-*vo*.

1750–1800 The French fake their way through the Enlightenment by stroking their chins, furrowing their brows, and gazing off into the distance whenever another European philosopher passes by.

1786 The illiterate French masses, finally realizing that current King Louis XVI is not in fact the all-powerful Louis XIV, openly revolt and overthrow the oppressive system of Roman numerals.

1789 The Storming of the Bastille, followed by the Storming Out of the Bastille upon seeing a mouse.

1806 Napoleon commissions the Arc de Triomphe, under which he plans to triumphantly parade his glorious armies upon returning from his latest battlefield victory. Plagued with marital difficulties with his wife Josephine, however, he uses the famous monument primarily to sit under, alone, and cry.

1836 French architects create the Arc de Triomphe to commemorate the successful construction of the Arc de Triomphe.

1838 The guillotine device is made far more practical with the revolutionary invention of the headbasket.

1842 France surrenders to Spain moments before the first shots can be fired in what becomes known as the Negative Thirteen Seconds' War.

1868 While excavating an ancient French restaurant at Les Eyzies, geologists discover Cro-Mignon, the world's oldest steak.

1883 Paris-born painter Claude Monet rents a house at Giverny, which boasts France's blurriest garden.

1913 Two art thieves steal the Louvre.

1915 French soldiers develop the wartime strategy of closing one's eyes and hoping it all goes away.

1919 France wins the Battle of the Treaty of Versailles.

1940 A confident French military enters WWII equipped with the most expensive hats of any army in Europe, the finest cigarettes a military budget can buy, and specially designed guns capable of being dropped to the ground in under 0.85 seconds.

1942 Nation witnesses the first of many architecture booms, inspired by the cutting-edge German Destructionist movement.

1945 Believing they had all the time in the world to explore the nation, the Germans end their six-year occupation of France without once visiting the Eiffel Tower.

1947 A stirring, dramatic performance by French mime Marcel Marceau strikes a chord with thousands of men and women who had once been trapped inside an oversized box.

1958 Charles de Gaulle, the former leader of the French armed forces in WWII, wins the 1958 presidential election, marking the first and only

A Frenchman weeps during the great 1941 Brie shortage.

victory the former general would ever achieve.

1973 Love conquers France.

1984 In Lourdes, in the same spring where St. Bernadette once saw a vision of the Virgin Mary, over half the visiting French pilgrims report seeing visions of Christ in the water where their reflection should be.

1992 A French health study proclaims that drinking 14 glasses of red wine per day can help prevent sobriety.

2005 Violent riots break out among youth gangs in Paris, forcing France to surrender to France.

2007 French architects begin construction on the giant, 75-story Ivory Tower, which upon completion will stand over 1,000 feet tall, weigh 7 million tons, and be able to permanently house the entire population of France.

NAPOLEON » PINT-SIZED PROTECTOR OF FRANCE

Napoleon Bonaparte, or "The Littlest General," was a diminutive man no bigger than a thimble. He seized control of France with an adorable coup d'état in 1799. While riding in the front shirt pocket of his first lieutenant, Napoleon drove the Austrians out of Lombardy. He also developed the revolutionary war tactic of climbing inside one's opponent's mouth, traveling down his trachea, and eating through his vital organs. After successfully conquering half the world, Napoleon was captured in a butterfly net by the owner of a local traveling circus, and in May 1821, drowned in a bowl of vichyssoise. He was buried in a matchbox.

Andorra

The Outlet Mall Of Europe

Conveniently located between Spain and France, Andorra is a one-stop shopping source for discounted and tax-free items. The nation opened its doors to the public in 1278, becoming the world's first parliamentary co-principality to have a sale on irregular slacks.

For centuries, this shopper's mecca has attracted millions of international consumers searching for bulk, overstock merchandise that's priced to sell. Fully stocked and open extended hours on weekends, Andorra offers a huge selection of quality goods with prices ranging from "low" to "low, low."

HISTORY » A "NOT QUITE PERFECT" HISTORY

A.D. 803 Dissatisfied with the high prices and confusing haggling found in Moorish bazaars, Emperor Charlemagne conceives of a principality where the customer is king.

1278 Andorra celebrates its grand opening, commemorated with the cutting of a 75-mile-long ribbon strung around its perimeter. Among the early irregular goods offered: unvarnished hay carts, unprocessed wool, and hair shirts with inconsistent scratchiness.

1282 After the trampling deaths of several hundred visitors during the opening of a new chain of wholesale grocers, Andorra decides it should probably have more than one entrance.

1409 Andorra is conquered by the "Super Savers," a violent, nomadic horde that thrives on coupon use.

1593 Charter members of the highest food court in the land sign the historic À La Carta, which severely limits the powers of the Burger King.

1787 Andorran delegates ratify a historic constitution, which states in its preamble that the customer is always right, and is entitled to life, liberty, and the pursuit of great bargains.

1866 The first Chinese immigrants arrive in Andorra, to serve as laborers for the Panda Express.

1992 Yielding to pressure from shoppers, Andorra moves its lone public restroom off the 10,000-foot peak of Coma Pedrosa and closer to the food court.

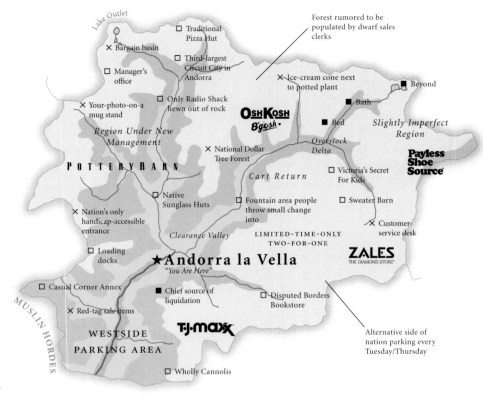

Lake Outlet

× Bargain basin

□ Traditional Pizza Hut

□ Manager's office

□ Third-largest Circuit City in Andorra

× Your-photo-on-a mug stand

□ Only Radio Shack hewn out of rock

Forest rumored to be populated by dwarf sales clerks

× Ice-cream cone next to potted plant

■ Beyond

■ Bath

Region Under New Management

OshKosh B'gosh •

■ Bed

Slightly Imperfect Region

× National Dollar Tree Forest

Overstock Delta

Payless Shoe Source

POTTERY BARN

Cart Return

□ Victoria's Secret For Kids

□ Native Sunglass Huts

□ Fountain area people throw small change into

□ Sweater Barn

× Nation's only handicap-accessible entrance

Clearance Valley

LIMITED-TIME-ONLY TWO-FOR-ONE

× Customer-service desk

□ Loading docks

★ **Andorra la Vella**
"You Are Here"

ZALES THE DIAMOND STORE®

□ Casual Corner Annex

■ Chief source of liquidation

□ Disputed Borders Bookstore

MUSLIN HORDES

× Red-tag sale items

T·J·maxx

Alternative side of nation parking every Tuesday/Thursday

WESTSIDE PARKING AREA

□ Wholly Cannolis

FACTS » PLENTY OF FREE PARKING

POPULATION 76,115 (business hours), 50 overnight custodial staff (after closing)	**MOTTO** "Nos mos non prodo venalicium" ("We will not be undersold")	**CAPITAL** Party City (northeast of the more populous Dress Barn)	**LANGUAGE** Word of mouth	**PRESIDENT/MANAGER** Dave
LOCATION According to European TV ads, "15 Minutes From Everywhere!"	**SEX RATIO** Intimate relationships between coworkers are discouraged	**ARABLE LAND** Available for rent; call 555-8712	**DEATH RATE** 6.07 deaths/1,000 population, mostly all occurring in or around the Smith & Wesson factory outlet	**IMPORTS** Customers **EXPORTS** Satisfied customers

PEOPLE » NO ONE LIVES HERE

Andorra has no residential population. The employees, who commute from Spain, Portugal, and France, arrive at approximately 7:30 a.m. to set up, with second shift closing the country at 11 p.m. Although no one officially lives in Andorra, there is suspicion among Foot Locker employees that Mr. Joe, a member of the custodial staff, makes his home in the storage closet.

The Human Development Index ranks Andorra as one of the top 50 outlet centers in the world.

THE SALE-O-CAUST »

Between 1940 and 1945, Andorra was responsible for the systematic extermination of 6 million overstocked items in what has become known as the Sale-O-Caust. Referred to as the "Final $olution" by the highest levels of Andorran management, the entire country's inventory was methodically sorted, and every sale item was branded with a number and a bar code. The items were loaded on unrefrigerated freight cars to travel several miles to their surplus-warehouse destination. Many perishables did not survive the train ride.

Though some groups deny the Sale-O-Caust ever occurred, or claim that its inventory was greatly exaggerated, retail historians maintain its authenticity, saying the only victims were those who missed out on the great savings.

Monaco

Where The Rich Can Strike It Richer

This tiny nation is composed solely of the glamorous Monte Carlo Casino, which features a red-carpet sidewalk, high-end boutiques, and special ATMs that dispense sparkling jewels in lush, black-velvet satchels.

Monaco is a land where anyone, regardless of nationality or social standing, can pull himself up by his $700 imported Italian bootstraps. A chauffeured-Bentley public-transportation system connects to all the country's potential jackpots. And while the poor—those with only a handful of millions to their names—dot the streets, the rich live the jet-set life in Monaco. They tend to their yachts, racecars, and tans, and periodically gamble away fortunes in the casino just to relieve the crushing boredom of being unfathomably rich.

A HIGHER CLASS OF PEOPLE »

In Monaco, the haves and the have-mores coexist peacefully. The typical citizen of Monaco works a full eight-hour lifetime, dresses in the traditional tuxedo or gown, and is considered the best in the world at knowing when to bet on black. Some tensions exist between Monaco's "townies," who have their primary residences in Monaco and various other vacation homes around the world, and the "summer folk," who have their primary residences elsewhere and a vacation home in Monaco.

HISTORY » ODDS ON THEIR SIDE

A.D. 1297 Monaco is seized from the Genoese by François Grimaldi, who then declares it a ritzy neighborhood-state.

1712 Nearly 20 people are killed and four are injured in the Great Cashalanche of 1712.

1911 A constitution is created, finally ending the despotic absolute rule of the Prince of Monaco, a tyranny so oppressive that the only way to escape it was to die or walk a few blocks to France.

1929 Monaco hosts a world-championship auto race through its narrow, boutique-lined streets. The race, which continues annually to this day, poses an ongoing threat to the nation's porcelain-fruit vendors and men who deliver large sheets of priceless Tiffany glass.

Monaco's UN representative never shows his hand.

Grace Kelly

1956 Glamorous Prince Rainier marries glamorous movie star Grace Kelly. When the couple presents their firstborn, the world learns that glamour genes cancel each other out, as the child is a half-human, half-warthog abomination.

1982 Princess Grace is killed in a rare non-Formula One–related car crash in Monaco. Tragically, there are no paparazzi on the scene to capture the moment.

1980 A suave jewel thief steals the Countess of Monaco's diamond necklace during a masked ball. She does not alert the authorities because she is, alas, madly in love with him.

1992 Pope John Paul II agrees to annul Princess Caroline's first marriage and legitimize her three children so that they might later assume the throne. Interestingly, from 1992 until his death in 2005, Pope John Paul II often wows crowds with his "nearly infallible" winning streak at the Monte Carlo craps tables.

2005 Prince Albert II succeeds his late father Rainier III as Monaco's ruler, changing absolutely nothing.

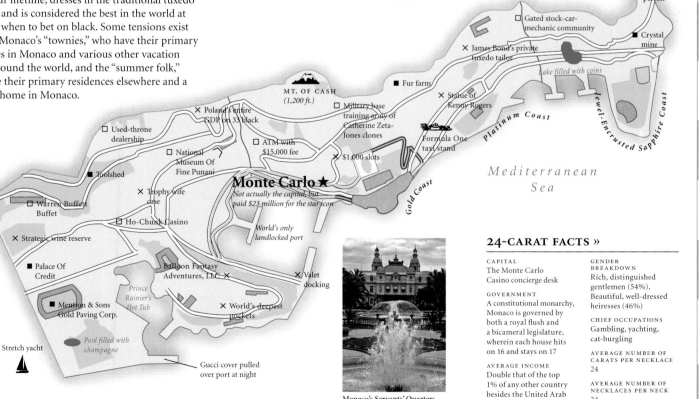

× Lone poor person

□ Gated stock-car-mechanic community

■ Crystal mine

× James Bond's private tuxedo tailor

Lake filled with coins

■ Fur farm

MT. OF CASH (1,200 ft.)

× Statue of Kenny Rogers

Platinum Coast

Jewel-Encrusted Sapphire Coast

× Poland's entire GDP on 33 black

□ Military base training army of Catherine Zeta-Jones clones

Formula One taxi stand

□ Used-throne dealership

□ ATM with $15,000 fee

× $1,000 slots

Mediterranean Sea

□ National Museum Of Fine Punani

■ Toolshed

Monte Carlo ★
Not actually the capital but paid $23 million for the star icon

Gold Coast

× Trophy wife case

■ Warren Buffett Buffet

□ Ho-Chunk Casino

World's only landlocked port

× Strategic wine reserve

■ Palace Of Credit

Balloon Fantasy Adventures, LLC ×

×Valet docking

Prince Rainier's Hot Tub

■ Mention & Sons Gold Paving Corp.

× World's deepest pockets

Stretch yacht

Pool filled with champagne

Gucci cover pulled over port at night

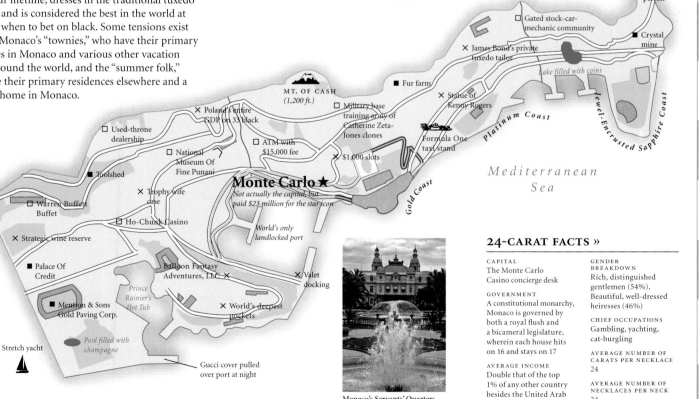
Monaco's Servants' Quarters

24-CARAT FACTS »

CAPITAL
The Monte Carlo Casino concierge desk

GOVERNMENT
A constitutional monarchy, Monaco is governed by both a royal flush and a bicameral legislature, wherein each house hits on 16 and stays on 17

AVERAGE INCOME
Double that of the top 1% of any other country besides the United Arab Emirates

GENDER BREAKDOWN
Rich, distinguished gentlemen (54%), Beautiful, well-dressed heiresses (46%)

CHIEF OCCUPATIONS
Gambling, yachting, cat-burgling

AVERAGE NUMBER OF CARATS PER NECKLACE
24

AVERAGE NUMBER OF NECKLACES PER NECK
24

Italy

» THE FLAG OF ITALY MEANS "ITALIAN MEATS AND CHEESES FOR SALE HERE."

What Are You Looking At?

Italy is known as one of the most racially intolerant nations in the world, where citizens base their opinions of other ethnicities on appearance and stereotypes alone. But then, what more do you expect from a bunch of greasy, filthy womanizers?

Often characterizing entire races based on a few narrow-minded assumptions, these gold-chain-wearing, spaghetti-slurping mobsters rarely dig deeper than the two or three sweeping generalizations they associate with other cultures.

Though many Italians continue to speak derisively about other ethnicities in that high-pitched Goombah whine of theirs, the reality is, all they would have to do is row their gondola over to a library and pry open a book with their pudgy sausage fingers to learn that there is more to most cultures than what one sees on television.

After all, how would Italians feel if people didn't know anything about *their* Mafia-run, meatball-based civilization?

Once these wildly gesticulating, wifebeater-clad winos with slicked-back hair and toothpicks hanging out of their mouths take off their designer sunglasses and open up their beady little eyes to the true beauty of other cultures, perhaps they will stop relying on negative ethnic slurs to classify strangers.

Stupid wop dagos.

FACTS » WE GOT YOUR FACTS RIGHT HERE

OLIVE OIL CONSUMPTION
1.2 billion barrels per day

JUSTICE SYSTEM
Just ask Vinny

TERRAIN
Tight-fitting borders accentuate voluptuous mountains, curvy rivers

NATURAL HAZARDS
Mudflows, volcanic eruptions, Roberto Benigni

LANGUAGE
Italian (The Language Of Lust)

NATIONAL HOLIDAY
Sunday

INTERNATIONAL DISPUTES
Ongoing conflict over what France allegedly said about Italy's 6.4 million mothers

CURRENCY
One euro = .25 cannoli

ENVIRONMENTAL AGREEMENTS
Will start wearing shirt at the dinner table (2004)

LEADING CAUSE OF AFFECTION
Being a grandson

SPEED LIMIT
Recently reduced to infinity-minus-one mph

PACKAGE DEAL
Day tour of ancient ruins, four nights in Salerno Hyatt: 230 euros

GEOGRAPHY NOTE
Italy is often said to be shaped like a boot in a desperate attempt to make geography sound interesting

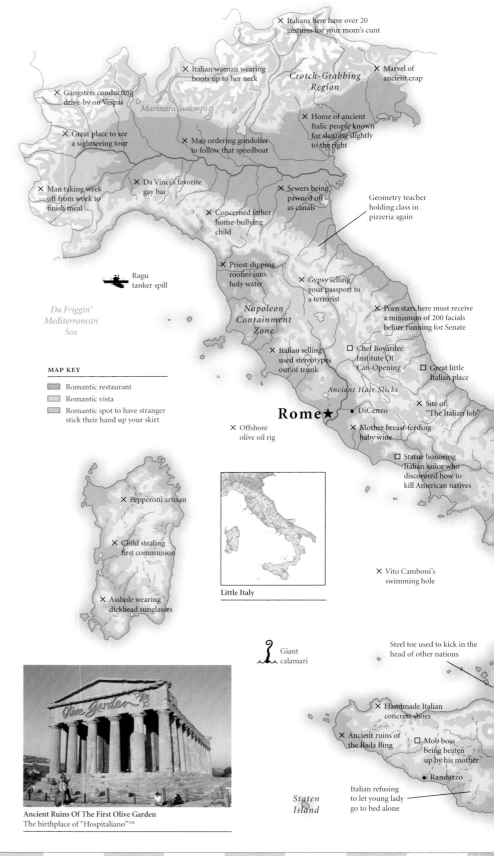

MAP KEY
- Romantic restaurant
- Romantic vista
- Romantic spot to have stranger stick their hand up your skirt

Map labels:
- Italians here have over 20 gestures for your mom's cunt
- Italian woman wearing boots up to her neck
- *Crotch-Grabbing Region*
- Marvel of ancient crap
- Gangsters conducting drive-by on Vespas
- *Marinara Swamps*
- Home of ancient Italic people known for slanting slightly to the right
- Great place to see a sightseeing tour
- Man ordering gondolier to follow that speedboat
- Man taking week off from work to finish meal
- Da Vinci's favorite gay bar
- Concerned father home-bullying child
- Sewers being pawned off as canals
- Geometry teacher holding class in pizzeria again
- Ragu tanker spill
- Priest slipping roofies into holy water
- Gypsy selling your passport to a terrorist
- *Da Friggin' Mediterranean Sea*
- *Napoleon Containment Zone*
- Porn stars here must receive a minimum of 200 facials before running for Senate
- Italian selling used stereotypes out of trunk
- Chef Boyardee Institute Of Can-Opening
- Great little Italian place
- *Ancient Hair Slicks*
- **Rome** ★
- DiCenzo
- Site of "The Italian Job"
- Offshore olive oil rig
- Mother breast-feeding baby wine
- Statue honoring Italian sailor who discovered how to kill American natives
- Pepperoni artisan
- Child stealing first communion
- **Little Italy**
- Asshole wearing dickhead sunglasses
- Vito Camboni's swimming hole
- Giant calamari
- Steel toe used to kick in the head of other nations
- Handmade Italian concrete shoes
- Ancient ruins of the Bada Bing
- Mob boss being beaten up by his mother
- Randazzo
- *Staten Island*
- Italian refusing to let young lady go to bed alone

Ancient Ruins Of The First Olive Garden
The birthplace of "Hospitaliano"™

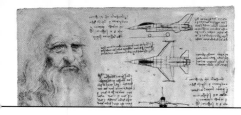

HISTORY » WE COULDA BEEN SOMEBODY

10,000,000 B.C. Recently unearthed fossils reveal that early Italian hominids had prehensile noses and opposable middle fingers.

753 B.C. Rome is built in exactly one day, six hours, and 17 minutes, spurring the popular expression, "Rome wasn't built in a day."

71 B.C. The Spartacus-led slave revolt fails when members of his army shout out "I am Spartacus!" to create a diversion, but the true Spartacus draws too much attention to himself by loudly shouting "I am Charles!"

57 B.C. Caesar conquers Gaul by asking if he could just borrow it for a minute, and then never giving it back.

49–44 B.C. A power-mad Caesar spends the last five years of his life attempting to conquer the Atlantic Ocean.

47 B.C. After 17 years, 12 venereal diseases, and 36 children, an exhausted Cleopatra at last sleeps her way to the top of the Roman Empire.

A.D. 38 Tyrannical leader Caligula appoints his favorite horse, Incitatus, to a seat on the Roman Senate, a move that infuriates citizens, fellow consul members, and Caligula's second-favorite horse.

64 While a conflagration destroys half of Rome, King Nero famously fiddles while Rome burns. To make matters worse, he only adds to the ensuing chaos by fiddling "Flight Of The Bumblebee."

79 Mt. Vesuvius respects the city of Pompeii's wish to be cremated and then buried under thousands of tons of volcanic ash.

88 Due to a scheduling mix-up, dozens of confused, ax-wielding gladiators ruin the Colosseum's first annual dog show.

217 The Public Baths of Caracalla are inaugurated, leaving thousands of lascivious Romans filthier than ever.

1173 The Leaning Tower of Pisa is constructed by Bonanno Pisano, a 12th-century architect known for his magnificent bronze casting, beautifully detailed arches, and having a left leg three inches longer than his right one.

1335 Milan erects the world's first public clock, allowing Italians to be more precisely late.

1503–1506 A simple, straightforward portrait of a woman takes homosexual Leonardo Da Vinci nearly four years to paint.

1508–1512 Pope Julius II commissions Michelangelo to paint the ceiling of the Sistine Chapel. The artist spends four years painstakingly depicting a complex scheme representing the Creation of Adam, the Downfall of Man, and the Promise of Salvation, going against the pope's original orders of "a light shade of blue."

1796 Napoleon sends his retarded brother to conquer Italy.

1901 Guglielmo Marconi conducts the first transatlantic radio transmission. Wacky European deejays now no longer have to telegraph the sound of a toilet flushing in Morse code.

1915 The inexperienced and easily frightened Italian military enters World War I, and immediately surrenders to a flock of low-flying pigeons.

1930 During their first meeting, Fascist dictator Benito Mussolini encourages a young, introverted Adolf Hitler to come out of his shell.

1935–1940 Using mustard gas—a chemical agent with no relation to the culinary condiment—Italian forces disappoint thousands of starving Ethiopians to death.

An elderly woman asks for a pound of thinly sliced Mussolini.

1945 Mussolini is killed, and he and his mistress's corpses are found hung upside-down on meat hooks in Milan. Later, a thinly sliced pound of Mussolini is mistakenly purchased by an elderly woman.

1946 With Germany defeated and the Holocaust but a recent memory, Italians for the first time look back on their role in World War II and adopt the national motto, "Fuhgeddaboutit!"

1993 The nation of Italy is discovered to be a front for the Mafia.

2004 In a watershed moment for the worldwide edification of Italian culture, over 50 hours of classic Dean Martin celebrity roasts are made available to the general public.

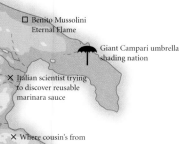

□ Benito Mussolini Eternal Flame

☂ Giant Campari umbrella shading nation

✕ Italian scientist trying to discover reusable marinara sauce

✕ Where cousin's from

Grease-Stains

Meta-terranean Sea

PEOPLE » YOU FUCKING LOOKING AT ME?

Italians are family-oriented people, as most have several brothers and sisters, 12 grandparents, and 37 cousin Tonys. Italians tend to stay very close to their families, with the average Italian man living inside his mother's womb until he turns 25. Many of them continue to reside with their parents until they get married, at which point they exchange heartfelt embraces, bid a tearful goodbye, and move downstairs.

Italians have a passion for eating, and for telling others to eat. Although Italians traditionally eat only one meal a day, that meal spans 12 hours and 15 courses.

These amorous people are known for their incredible virility—the handsomest of Italians can impregnate a woman just by whispering her name romantically. Because passionate lovemaking can break out at a moment's notice in this nation, the streets of Italy are lined with condom machines, lube fountains, and public mattresses that can be rented for two euros per minute.

The average Italian can speak fluently in over 14 languages with his hands.

Venice, City Of Romance

Vatican City

PAPAL FUN-COIN » GOOD FOR ONE RIDE IN VATICAN CITY.

The Catholic Disneyland

The world's smallest independent state is a papal kingdom of imaginary characters and expensive attractions where vacationing families can go to escape reality for a few days.

St. Peter's Magic Castle looms over this wondrous land of make-believe, where pointy-hatted trolls spout ninth-century wisdom, and where, with the swoop of a holy scepter, child-rape allegations can disappear.

While there can be long lines at the confession booths and the communion-wafer stands, both children and adults say it's worth the wait to get doused with holy water and have their sins washed away.

Vatican City's popular mascot poses with tourists.

FACTS » ENJOY A COLD CUP OF CHRIST'S BLOOD

ADMISSION
$12 (boys under 12 free)

AREA COMPARATIVE
Half the size of New Life Church, Colorado Springs, CO

CHIEF FINANCIAL OFFICER
Francesco "Frankie Crackers" Bartoli

SUFFRAGE
Universal at age 80

POPULATION
783 (one pontiff, 57 cardinals, 724 houseboys, and the kooky but lovable ghost of Pope Sixtus V)

AFTERLIFE EXPECTANCY
100%

LEADING INDUSTRIES
Usury, real estate, bingo

LOCAL CUISINE
Fish on Fridays

CRIMINAL JUSTICE
Offenders are forgiven after serving 5–10 Hail Marys

IMPORTS
Money

EXPORTS
Guilt

HISTORY » EXACTLY WHAT JESUS WOULD HAVE WANTED

A.D. 30 Jesus Christ ordains the Apostle Peter the first pope, declaring, "You are the rock upon which I will build an opulent mansion."

325 Emperor Constantine legitimizes the papacy by declaring just one sect of Christianity the official religion of the Roman Empire, forever dooming to heresy the promising "Jesus was a centaur" sect.

593 World-renowned explorer Pope Gregory I discovers Purgatory.

1054 A rift between cardinals results in the Great Schism, a church split between two rival popes, confusing everyone for centuries, including God, who at this point has mostly stopped paying attention.

1191 The Inquisition forces all participants to confess it's "the best Vatican attraction ever."

1633 Pope Urban VIII conceives an ambitious plan to send enormous pages of the Bible into outer space so that Galileo's telescope will for once see something factual.

1882 Friedrich Nietzsche pronounces God dead. Next of kin Pope Leo XIII inherits all of God's books, furniture, and an estimated $100 billion in church property.

The Golden Chalices
A favorite Vatican attraction.

1962 Pope John XXIII announces Vatican II. Many conservative Catholics complain that there are still a lot of bugs, and eagerly await the Vatican II.I upgrade.

2005 As soon as Pope Benedict XVI moves in, he immediately finds the perfect gold pedestal upon which to display his Hitler Youth knife.

MAP KEY
🍶 Adultery
🦐 Theft
🍶 Murder

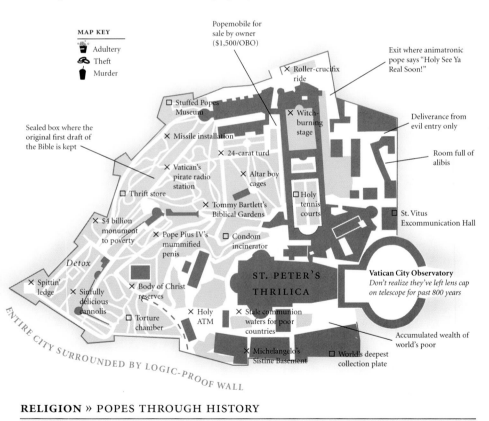

Popemobile for sale by owner ($1,500/OBO)

✕ Roller-crucifix ride

Exit where animatronic pope says "Holy See Ya Real Soon!"

☐ Stuffed Popes Museum

✕ Witch-burning stage

Deliverance from evil entry only

Sealed box where the original first draft of the Bible is kept

✕ Missile installation

✕ 24-carat turd

Room full of alibis

✕ Vatican's pirate radio station

✕ Altar boy cages

☐ Thrift store

✕ Tommy Bartlett's Biblical Gardens

☐ Holy tennis courts

☐ St. Vitus Excommunication Hall

✕ $4 billion monument to poverty

✕ Pope Pius IV's mummified penis

☐ Condom incinerator

Detox

✕ Spittin' ledge

✕ Sinfully delicious cannolis

✕ Body of Christ reserves

ST. PETER'S THRILICA

Vatican City Observatory
Don't realize they've left lens cap on telescope for past 800 years

☐ Torture chamber

✕ Holy ATM

✕ Stale communion wafers for poor countries

Accumulated wealth of world's poor

✕ Michelangelo's Sistine Basement

☐ World's deepest collection plate

ENTIRE CITY SURROUNDED BY LOGIC-PROOF WALL

RELIGION » POPES THROUGH HISTORY

Innocent X	**Honorius IV**	**Paul III**	**Reptilius IV**	**John Paul II**	**Benedict XVI**

Malta & San Marino

MALTA » CAN BE ROLLED UP AND USED AS TEMPORARY CHANGING ROOM.

SAN MARINO » WE ARE GOING TO USE THIS FLAG TO WIPE OUR ASS.

Malta
An Agoraphobic's Hell

Malta is the most densely populated nation in the world, with over 400,000 tightly packed people standing shoulder-to-shoulder in the tiny island's crowded streets, trains, offices, and bathrooms.

Malta's rampant overpopulation has created many severe environmental concerns, including deforestation, lack of oxygen, and that fat guy Steve who doesn't wear deodorant. Commuting is a major problem, as foot traffic is so bad that even those who work from home are usually an hour late.

Maltese women are often attracted to tall men, as they are the only ones visible, but typically end up marrying the guy they stood next to in college. Relationships are difficult to maintain in Malta, as many citizens regularly feel smothered by their girlfriends, their mothers, their neighbors, and their local deli proprietors.

FACTS » A LITTLE CARRIED AWAY WITH THE BREEDING

POPULATION BREAKDOWN
Women (52%), Frotteurs (48%)

LAND USE
Standing room only

HOLIDAYS
Indistinguishable from normal days, except people spend them with their hands raised over their heads

TOPOGRAPHY
Mostly hair, some hats

NATURAL HAZARDS
Loose mouse

FUNERALS
Maltese citizen are lifted up and passed overhead until they reach the Bay Of The Dead

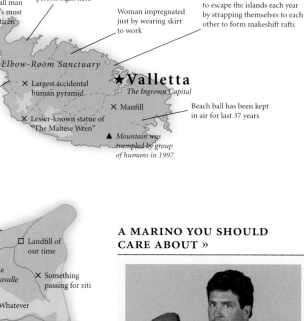

A public restroom in Valletta.

Map labels:
- ✕ Annual 5K charity stampede
- ☐ Malta's 20-story cemetery
- ✕ Seven-foot-tall man who is Malta's most influential citizen
- Because of population growth this city will be pushed into the ocean within 15 to 20 minutes
- Room for one more person right here
- Woman impregnated just by wearing skirt to work
- Thousands of Maltese attempt to escape the islands each year by strapping themselves to each other to form makeshift rafts
- *Elbow-Room Sanctuary*
- ✕ Largest accidental human pyramid
- ★ **Valletta** *The Ingrown Capital*
- ✕ Manfill
- Beach ball has been kept in air for last 37 years
- Malta's longtime president was toppled when someone on the other side of the island pushed the person next to him really hard
- ✕ Lesser-known statue of "The Maltese Wren"
- ▲ *Mountain was trampled by group of humans in 1997*

San Marino
These Assholes Don't Belong In An Atlas

Boy, it's a good thing there aren't 200 countries in the world for the writers of this atlas to worry about.

It sure is lucky that large, historically rich nations like China, Egypt, or Brazil don't still exist—otherwise the men and women who spend 60-plus hours a week putting this book together might find themselves a tad irked at the prospect of throwing away what little energy they have left on a tiny, insignificant city-state like San Marino. Whew! Thank God that's not in fact the case!

Bordered on the north, south, east, and west by Italy (SEE: ACTUAL GODDAMN NATION), the enclave of San Marino should have been no more than a line or two in the former's write-up. Comprised of an area smaller than some of the shits the editors of this atlas have taken, and with a system of government we're, in all honesty, not going to waste our time describing, the Republic of San Marino is the reason why many of us are still at the office working at this late hour, unable to join our families for dinner once again tonight.

We sincerely hope that's worth your sovereignty, you stupid jerks.

Map labels:
- Border disputed by editors of this atlas
- Some douchebag's house
- ☐ Landfill of our time
- ● Serravalle *Fuck Serravalle*
- ✕ Something passing for ziti
- ✕ Whatever
- ★ **San Marino** *You better hope you're not from here*
- 🕷 Ant *(actual size)*
- ● *Guess what—see this city right here? We're not even going to mention its name*
- ✕ Place explosives here
- *Some Fucking River*
- *Make-Believe Region*
- ✕ Site of imagined nuclear holocaust of 2:37 a.m. last night
- ● Chief source of idiots
- ✕ Toxic waste (hopefully)
- Bullshit border
- There isn't even a wooden fence here

FACTS » YOU WILL PAY FOR THIS, SAN MARINO

POPULATION
Numbers 1 through 29,251 on our shit list

EDUCATION
Going to be handed one. Going to be handed one.

RELIGION
Just sit tight and pray

INFANT MORTALITY RATE
Not nearly high enough

GEOGRAPHIC COORDINATES
43° 56′ N, 12° 25′ E (Big mistake, San Marino… big mistake)

EXPORTS
Additional work, grief, marital problems

INTERNATIONAL DISPUTES
Seriously, what the hell has kept Italy from invading?

A MARINO YOU SHOULD CARE ABOUT »

Miami Dolphins quarterback Dan Marino achieved more during his 17-year Hall of Fame career than the "nation" of San Marino has managed to accomplish since A.D. 301. Although he never won a Super Bowl, at least Dan Marino wasn't selfish enough to declare himself a sovereign nation, thus depriving generations of atlas editors of much-needed sleep.

HISTORY » HERE'S YOUR GODDAMN HISTORY

Fuck you.

Switzerland

» WILL ONE DAY
SIGNAL ALL SWISS
TO TAKE SWIFT AND
DECISIVE ACTION.

Neutral…
Too Neutral

S witzerland is a quiet, unassuming nation—which is exactly what they want you to think.

A peaceful sanctuary for the wealthiest, most literate, and most virile people in Europe, Switzerland also just so happens to house millions of extremely well-trained members of the best-equipped citizen's army in the world—one which could, if the need arose, fully mobilize in under 12 hours.

But the Swiss, a historically nonviolent people, have stayed out of every major world conflict for the past 200 years, preferring instead to quietly observe from afar, carefully analyzing every other nation's strengths and weaknesses, keeping meticulous notes, and counting down the seconds on their Swiss watches.

This behavior has earned them the complete trust of the international community, which every year places hundreds of millions of dollars into private Swiss bank accounts and sends top diplomats to seemingly harmless summits in Geneva. Yet everyone has faith that the gentle Swiss would never exploit this powerful strategic advantage.

No, they would never do that…

The Swiss Army Tank

FACTS » JUST MINDING THEIR OWN BUSINESS… WITH MILITARY PRECISION

POPULATION
8 million exactly

OFFICIAL LANGUAGES
German, French, Italian, Romansh, English, Spanish, Chinese, Russian, Hungarian, Eskari, Inuit, Binary

CURRENCY
Swiss franc, the value of which is determined by the current international gold-filling standard

GUNS
2.5 per household, each with 1,000 rounds of hollow-point ammo

LEADING IMPORT
Millions upon millions of foreign monies, all in exchange for nothing

OTHER, LESS IMPORTANT, BARELY USED IMPORTS
Ammunition, targeting computers, uniforms, torture racks, pillories

NATIONAL MOTTO
"We'll Take Those Weapons Off Your Hands, That Money Out Of Your Pocket, And That Gold From Your Teeth"

POLITICAL AFFILIATION
Switzerland officially became neutral on the same day that the world's first commercial cheese factory was established in Switzerland. Coincidence?

ADMINISTRATIVE DIVISIONS
Broken into exactly 26 cantons, 2,889 municipalities, 3,831,206 private residences, and 12,325,969.5 rooms

NATIONAL HOLIDAY
Independence Day, Aug. 1 (acknowledged with silent, knowing nods)

MOST FAMOUS CARNIVAL RIDE
The Matterhorn

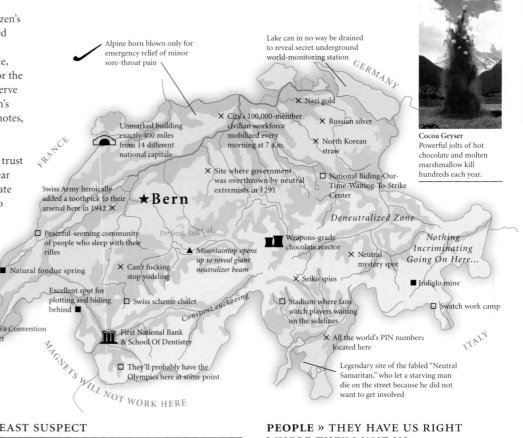

Alpine horn blown only for emergency relief of minor sore-throat pain

Lake can in no way be drained to reveal secret underground world-monitoring station

GERMANY

Unmarked building exactly 400 miles from 14 different national capitals

✕ City's 100,000-member civilian workforce mobilized every morning at 7 a.m.

✕ Nazi gold

✕ Russian silver

✕ North Korean straw

FRANCE

Swiss Army heroically added a toothpick to their arsenal here in 1943 ✕

★ Bern

✕ Site where government was overthrown by neutral extremists in 1291

▢ National Biding-Our-Time-Waiting-To-Strike Center

■ Peaceful-seeming community of people who sleep with their rifles

Perfectly Still Lake

Deneutralized Zone

■ Natural fondue spring

▲ Mountaintop opens up to reveal giant neutralizer beam

■■ Weapons-grade chocolate reactor

✕ Neutral mystery spot

Nothing Incriminating Going On Here…

✕ Can't fucking stop yodeling

Constant Cuckooing

✕ Seiko spies

■ Indiglo mine

Excellent spot for plotting and hiding behind

▢ Swiss scheme chalet

■ Stadium where fans watch players waiting on the sidelines

▢ Swatch work camp

▢ Geneva Convention Center

🏛 First National Bank & School Of Dentistry

✕ All the world's PIN numbers located here

MAGNETS WILL NOT WORK HERE

▢ They'll probably have the Olympics here at some point

ITALY

Legendary site of the fabled "Neutral Samaritan," who let a starving man die on the street because he did not want to get involved

Cocoa Geyser
Powerful jolts of hot chocolate and molten marshmallow kill hundreds each year.

HISTORY » THE COUNTRY YOU'D LEAST SUSPECT

A.D. 1291 The nation of Switzerland declares its independence, and then synchronizes all its watches on Aug. 1 at exactly 4:17:03.29 p.m.

1815 To celebrate the country's official declaration of neutrality, citizens retrieve their government-distributed rifles and take part in a well-rehearsed, chillingly accurate 2.1 million-gun salute.

1848 Swiss politicians engineer their constitution, which,

made up of double-hardened titanium, a tightly wound mainspring, a rotor swing, and hundreds of quartz crystals that vibrate 32,000 times a second, is still running smoothly today.

1887 Swiss physicist Dr. Eugen Frick creates the world's first wooden contact lenses, an invention considered both ahead of and behind its time.

1914–1918 The Swiss observe in amusement as the rest of

the world piddles away their pitiful little lives without even the slightest clue of what is to come.

1946 The Swiss are shocked to learn of "World War II," an apparently terrible conflict that took place right in their backyard.

2007 The Swiss enter "Phase Three," which in no way involves relaying secret orders to the Papal Swiss Guard on Aug. 1, 2009 at exactly 4:17:03.29 p.m.

PEOPLE » THEY HAVE US RIGHT WHERE THEY WANT US

Though neutral, Switzerland requires all men to serve in the military and all women to be blonde. When not going on simple "hikes" in the "Alps," the Swiss are often found hunched over surveillance monitors, gathering seemingly innocuous data from all over the world. Even while eating linzer torte and wearing lederhosen atop a picturesque snowcapped peak, the average citizen of Switzerland remains quite prepared to blow your head off if you make the wrong move, and will very convincingly make it look like an accident.

Austria

Birthplace Of Classical Muzak

The former classical music center of the world, where Mozart and Beethoven produced their most seminal works, Austria has a rich cultural legacy that continues to inspire waiting-room patients, hotel elevator passengers, and customers being placed on hold.

Home to some of the most stirring symphonies ever selected as cell-phone ringtones, Austria's proud musical heritage is heard by countless men and women rushing frantically through airport terminals each year. Whether one is urinating in an upscale restaurant bathroom, standing impatiently in line at the bank, or playing Tetris, the nation's impact on the background life of other cultures is literally immeasurable.

Indeed, one can hardly tune across the entire FM radio dial without being very briefly reminded of Austria's artistic renaissance.

Today, classical music virtuosos in the capital of Vienna continue to follow in the footsteps of the great public-domain masters of the past, receiving an audience of untold millions, be they stuck in psychiatric institutions or trapped against their will in somebody's womb.

Incestuous Habsburg Dynasty ended here in 1918 when Charles I's wife gave birth to a foot

HISTORY » CARE TO LEARN ABOUT THE HABSBURG DYNASTY?

A.D. 1278 Austria falls under control of the Habsburg Dynasty, a monarchy that rules the nation for 640 years with an iron fist and, after much inbreeding, a single eye.

1385 Austria experiences a period of decline during the short but notable reign of Habsburg stillborn Rudolf IV.

1566 Revealing the true purpose behind their coupling, Habsburg descendant Philip the Handsome accidentally shouts out "Oh, Spain!" "Oh, Italy!" and the names of six other territories he would soon acquire while consummating his marriage with the heiress of Castile and Aragon.

1612 Habsburg emperor and compulsive masturbator Matthias I passes down the throne of Austria to his crusty wool sock.

1730 Vienna becomes the classical music capital of Europe. Thousands of marching bands take to the streets in protest.

Mozart

1756 Mozart's development as a composer suffers greatly from not having Mozart played to him while still inside his mother's womb.

1788 Classical composer Joseph Haydn once again puts off commencing work on his "Unstarted Symphony."

1791 A destitute and exhausted Mozart is forced to compose a funeral march during his final days in order to pay for his burial.

A young Hitler finishes work on "You Better Buy This Painting If You Know What's Good For You."

1820 Enraged by the unjust loss of his hearing, a spiteful Beethoven composes his famous "Concerto For Wine Press & Cat."

1823 Along with elements of nature and humanism, Franz Schubert's syphilis becomes an underlying theme in his later work.

1907 A young Adolf Hitler attempts to make it as a painter in Vienna, but soon discovers where his real talents lie after gassing a room full of Jews at one of his gallery openings.

Sigmund Freud

1925 Hard at work on his theory of psychosexual fixation, Freud is interrupted once again by his mother, who walks completely nude past the open door of his study.

1938 Nazi sympathizers in Austria welcome invading Germans with open arms, all of which point in the direction of the nation's hidden Jewish population.

1945 Following their new bid to remain neutral in the event of future wars, Austria hands out millions of emergency blindfolds to its citizens.

1986 Kurt Waldheim, an alleged Nazi, is elected president of Austria, barely beating out Mendel Schmidt, a confirmed Nazi.

Map labels

- Bottomless orchestra pit
- Cemetery where Hitler realized what he wanted to do with his life
- Salzburgpenis *City named during Freudian slip*
- Monument to Sigmund Freud's mother
- Mozart descendant playing for spare change
- ★ **Vienna**
- Concert playing Beethoven's 5th Symphony being interrupted by cell phone playing Beethoven's 5th Symphony
- Time travelers about to barge in on Hitler's parents having sex
- × Site where Arnold Schwarzenegger tap-danced to take talent portion of Mr. Universe competition
- *What A Surprise—More Alps Over This Way*
- Birthplace of your subconscious yearning for approval
- Site where philosopher Ludwig Wittgenstein posited brilliant "No One Will Remember Me" theory
- ▲ Austria's pointiest point
- × Awkward silence being broken by avalanche
- × Best place in the world to break your leg skiing
- *Id, Ego, And Superego All Vying For Control Of This Region*
- Motel room where Habsburgs held family reunions

FACTS » MOST SPLENDID

NATIONALITY
Noun: Austrian
Adjective: Austrian
Wrong: Australian

LAND USE
Skiing (48%), crashing (33%), drinking cocoa and nursing broken leg (19%)

PICTURESQUENESS
83%

MANMADE HAZARDS
Landslide button, avalanche lever, earthquake machine

EMOTIONAL BOUNDARIES
Completely closed off

NATIONAL DEBT
$594 billion; working it off by washing EU's dishes

MOST COMMON RECURRING DREAM
A giant Vienna sausage in lederhosen spanking the nation collectively

ENVIRONMENTAL CONCERNS
The hills are alive with sound of music

NATIONAL SIGN OF DISAPPROVAL
Dropping monocle into wineglass

CONTRIBUTIONS TO WORLD OF MUSIC
Mozart, Haydn, Schubert, Falco

LARGEST STRUDEL
Made by Ingrid Braunhelder, Innsbruck

Germany

» IT WAS THE FLAG'S FAULT, HONESTLY—IT MADE THEM DO IT.

» MUNICH'S ANNUAL SAUSAGEFEST.

Genocide-Free Since April 11, 1946

Though Germany is now an upstanding member of the international community, boasting one of the strongest economies in the world, it wasn't too long ago that the nation struggled with a harrowing Jew-killing addiction.

Today a stable republic, having gone almost 60 years without touching a single Jew, Germany admits that there was a time when it couldn't get through the day without putting away a few hundred women and children. And while the nation would love to say that giving up the systematic slaughter of an entire race of people has been easy, it's still the first thing it thinks about each morning, and the last thing that crosses its mind every night.

Looking back now, Germany can hardly explain how things got so out of hand, as most of what happened between 1939 and 1946 remains a blur. Even years after other nations decided to intervene, Germany refused to apologize for how it had behaved, denying specific events it claimed not to remember, and even going so far as to blame 6 million other people for its human-rights abuse problem.

Despite the fact that Germany today attends weekly EU meetings, and has a number it can call whenever it feels the urge to open up concentration camps and march thousands of innocent civilians to their death, temptation still looms around every corner.

Every train station, open stove, or ditch wide enough to hold several hundred corpses seems to cry out the nation's name, and its citizens often have to leave the room when others start murdering Jews in front of them. Some days are especially tough, with the desire to load entire families into a gas chamber becoming almost unbearable.

However, Germany knows that even something as harmless as murdering one Hasidic child could lead to a relapse, and that before long the entire nation would find itself in Poland, bleary-eyed at 3 a.m., cremating any Jew it could get its hands on.

Germany celebrates its entry into the European Union.

FACTS » DENIED FOR YEARS

POPULATION BREAKDOWN
German (91%), Lesser races (9%)

NATIONAL ANTHEM
The word "progress" shouted repeatedly for three minutes

LEADING GLARES
Icy (48%), Cold (32%), Baleful (20%)

CONSTITUTION
Among the most tersely worded in world

RATE OF ABILITY TO GIVE 110%
110%

ENVIRONMENTAL AGREEMENTS
Kyoto Treaty (signed under assumed name "Jermany")

EXCHANGE STUDENT
Anders

COMEDY FILMS PRODUCED
1 per decade, a limit imposed by German law

FESTIVALS
Oktoberfest (Sept. 22—moment you black out)

BIGGEST REGRET
...

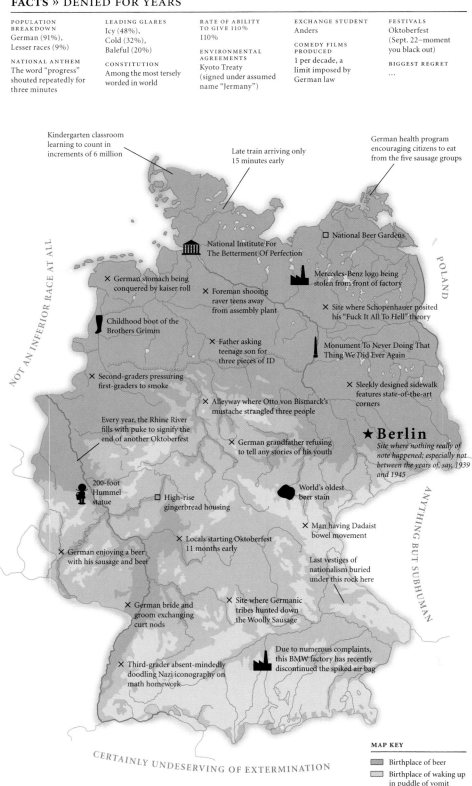

Kindergarten classroom learning to count in increments of 6 million

Late train arriving only 15 minutes early

German health program encouraging citizens to eat from the five sausage groups

NOT AN INFERIOR RACE AT ALL

POLAND

National Beer Gardens

National Institute For The Betterment Of Perfection

✕ German stomach being conquered by kaiser roll

✕ Foreman shooing raver teens away from assembly plant

Mercedes-Benz logo being stolen from front of factory

Childhood boot of the Brothers Grimm

✕ Father asking teenage son for three pieces of ID

✕ Site where Schopenhauer posited his "Fuck It All To Hell" theory

Monument To Never Doing That Thing We Did Ever Again

✕ Second-graders pressuring first-graders to smoke

✕ Alleyway where Otto von Bismarck's mustache strangled three people

✕ Sleekly designed sidewalk features state-of-the-art corners

Every year, the Rhine River fills with puke to signify the end of another Oktoberfest

✕ German grandfather refusing to tell any stories of his youth

★ **Berlin**
Site where nothing really of note happened; especially not between the years of, say, 1939 and 1945

200-foot Hummel statue

High-rise gingerbread housing

World's oldest beer stain

✕ Man having Dadaist bowel movement

ANYTHING BUT SUBHUMAN

✕ Locals starting Oktoberfest 11 months early

Last vestiges of nationalism buried under this rock here

✕ German enjoying a beer with his sausage and beer

✕ German bride and groom exchanging curt nods

✕ Site where Germanic tribes hunted down the Woolly Sausage

Due to numerous complaints, this BMW factory has recently discontinued the spiked air bag

✕ Third-grader absent-mindedly doodling Nazi iconography on math homework

CERTAINLY UNDESERVING OF EXTERMINATION

MAP KEY
◼ Birthplace of beer
◻ Birthplace of waking up in puddle of vomit

» ADOLF HITLER, WHO ALWAYS BLAMED THE JEWS FOR HIS INABILITY TO GROW A FULL MUSTACHE.

» KAISER WILHELM II, THE MAN CREDITED WITH INTRODUCING THE POINTY HAT TO EUROPE.

HISTORY » TWO-TIME WORLD WAR RUNNER-UP

1700 B.C. Ruthless Germanic tribes pretty much set the tone for the next 4,000 years.

A.D. 1455 Johannes Gutenberg creates the printing press, a mechanical device that allows for the mass production of identical texts. The press fails to catch on for several years, however, as Gutenberg can't figure out how to get the word out about it.

1499 The Germans invent beer, but awake the next morning with no recollection of having done so.

1517 Martin Luther nails his 95 Theses to the door of a church in protest of the Vatican's sale of "indulgences." Though outraged, the Catholic Church offers to forgive Luther for a low, one-time fee of $8.

1914–1918 Germany declares war on Russia, France, Belgium, Serbia, Luxembourg, and, after getting a little carried away, Trinidad & Tobago.

1914 Germany uses a vast array of lethal gases that result in hundreds of deaths among Allied Forces. The Allied death toll climbs significantly higher, however, when German troops begin using lethal solids.

1917 The tide of World War I turns as German propaganda declaring that Germany had decisively won the war reaches German troops.

1918 Germany admits defeat, and uses its last remaining limb to sign the Treaty of Versailles.

1930 After failing as a painter, Hitler takes an abrasive and confrontational turn at performance art. Unsuspecting audiences across Europe are soon blown away.

1931 In his signature work, *Mein Kampf*, Hitler describes his plan to wipe out the evils of Judaism, Communism, and after a number of fights with his editor, Unnecessary Revisions.

1933 Jewish physicist Albert Einstein proves to be years ahead of his time when he leaves Germany shortly before the Nazis come into power.

1936 At the Summer Olympics in Berlin, African-American athlete Jesse Owens humiliates Hitler by defeating German competitors in the 100-meter dash, high jump, and Jew-slaughtering competition.

1938 Thousands of Jewish storefronts are destroyed in what comes to be known as Kristallnacht ("The Night Of Broken Mirrors And Glass"). Seven years of terrible, terrible luck for the Jews follows.

1939–1945 Hitler, a lifetime OCD sufferer, sets out to kill exactly 3 million Jews, but is forced to start over after accidentally killing number 3 million and one.

1939 The German government forces all Jews to wear gold stars on their sleeves. At first, many believe they're being rewarded.

1939 Unable to believe that they have been taken from their homes, stripped of their belongings, and rounded up in barricaded ghettos, German Jews become the earliest-known Holocaust deniers.

1940 Awakening in concentration camps across Germany, hundreds of prisoners are immediately filled with regret over the number tattoos they got the night before.

1941 Auschwitz officials separate arriving Jews into three lines: those in the first line are put to work, those in the second line are sent to the gas chambers, and those in the third line are ordered to file annual tax returns for Nazi officials.

1942 Performing experimental amputations, agonizing surgeries, and other heinous tests on Auschwitz prisoners, Dr. Josef Mengele confirms his theory that human beings are capable of unspeakable cruelty.

1942 Hundreds of Jews die of heart attacks after being led into a laughing-gas chamber.

1943 The Germans are unable to find a decent bagel.

1944 In its bombing of London, Germany unveils its indiscriminate "whatever-seeking missiles."

1945 Not wanting to live in a world without Hitler, Hitler commits suicide.

1947 Nazi war criminals are found guilty and hanged, prompting over 15,000 people to hold a mass protest against the mild sentence.

1963 U.S. President John F. Kennedy travels to Berlin to deliver his famous "Ich bin ein Berliner" speech, which due to a grammatical error translates to "I am a jelly doughnut." However, modern American scholars contend that, within the context of the speech, it is clear that Kennedy meant "I *want* a jelly doughnut."

1965 East Germany finally decides to insulate the Berlin Wall, as the sounds of political freedom and economic prosperity have been keeping them up all night.

Ronald Reagan is often lauded for bringing down the Berlin Wall.

1982 East Germany begins to relax its border policy with the construction of the Berlin Door.

2007 Germany launches a major civilian project to rearrange all the nation's cities in alphabetical order—something that had been bothering them for a long time.

PEOPLE YOU CAN SET YOUR WATCH TO »

The average German is comprised of 12 right angles and six 45-degree angles. They are known for their rigid appearance, which they attain each morning by ironing their shirts, pants, hats, and skin to achieve the sharpest possible creases. Germans are quite self-conscious about the way they look, and most spend all day continuously exercising the 43 muscles that lead to improved frowning.

Although they have a reputation for being cold in interpersonal relationships, the average German couple warmly salutes one another before leaving for work in the morning, and often engages in intimate, extended handshakes at night. Germany is one of the few nations in the world in which one communicates love and affection via glaring.

Germans are also extremely punctual and efficient, often arriving at appointments several months in advance. The people of Germany have never been late for anything, except on occasions where it is customary to be "fashionably late," in which case they arrive precisely 17 minutes and 34 seconds after the scheduled start time. There are exactly 82,422,299 people in Germany—exactly—as German workers performed the census five times to make sure they didn't miscount.

Liechtenstein & Luxembourg

LIECHTENSTEIN » SIGN UP FOR PAPERLESS FLAG AT LIECHTENSTEIN-MUTUAL.COM.

LUXEMBOURG » FLAG REPRESENTS FRANCE WHEN HUNG THE WRONG WAY.

Liechtenstein Mutual
A Neighbor You Can Bank On™

With one convenient location between Austria and Switzerland in the heart of Europe, Liechtenstein Mutual offers a full range of savings, investment, checking, and lending services with no questions asked.

Whether financing your first military coup or putting away that nest egg for your next genocide, Liechtenstein Mutual has the financial services to meet your needs. Based on the Swiss model of banking, all terrorist money-laundering is guaranteed up to $100 million. And, as one of only two doubly landlocked financial institutions in the world, you can be sure your money is safe and secure.

FACTS » AND FIGURES

CLIMATE
Controlled by assistant manager Fritz Straus, whose desk is located near the radiator and thermostat

SOCIAL SERVICES
Free duffel bag with minimum balance of $2 million

DEFENSE
Mandatory security guard service for all males over age of 65

WILDLIFE
Home to only one wild species, the great slot-backed boar

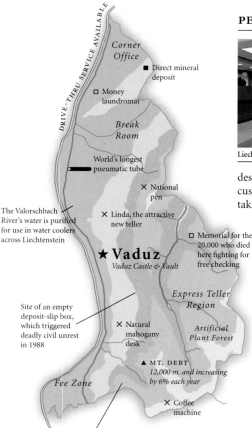

DRIVE-THRU SERVICE AVAILABLE

Corner Office

■ Direct mineral deposit

□ Money laundromat

Break Room

World's longest pneumatic tube

✕ National pen

✕ Linda, the attractive new teller

The Valorschbach River's water is purified for use in water coolers across Liechtenstein

□ Memorial for the 20,000 who died here fighting for free checking

★ **Vaduz**
Vaduz Castle & Vault

Express Teller Region

Site of an empty deposit-slip box, which triggered deadly civil unrest in 1988

✕ Natural mahogany desk

Artificial Plant Forest

▲ MT. DEBT 12,000 m. and increasing by 6% each year

Fee Zone

✕ Coffee machine

Indigenous teller population driven off by introduction of ATMs

PEOPLE » "WE'RE HERE TO HELP"

Liechtenstein's Lobby

The people of Liechtenstein are courteous, professional, and always willing to lend a helping hand to the next person in line. More than half the population is of teller stock, while the remainder are descended from associates, managers, guards, and custodians. A longstanding cultural tradition is the taking of a lunch break around noon.

PUTTING PEOPLE'S PROFITS FIRST »

When Napoleon lost his wallet during a battle in 1806, he just rode into one of Liechtenstein's convenient branches, wired home for invasion money, and 10 minutes later he was back on his bloody rampage.

Just before WWII, when times were tight for everyone in Europe, Liechtenstein gave a small business loan to an Austrian entrepreneur, who used it to purchase the first of his many "bread ovens." He went on to boast of serving more than 6 million satisfied customers.

Luxembourg
Oh, The Injustice!

The people of Luxembourg may appear to be content with their gourmet food, fine opera, and quiet carriage rides down winding, castle-dotted roads, but for 700 years they have suffered under the yoke of a soul-crushing, unelected monarchy.

Cruelly subjugated by the barbaric system of hereditary rule, citizens are mere chattel, gathering serenely in their playhouses, art museums, and villa parlors, surely crying on the inside for emancipation from the evil Grand Duke of Luxembourg.

All freedom-loving nations must stand in solidarity with Luxembourg, and urge them to rise up from their tea-and-truffles parties and violently revolt. It is the righteous destiny of these poor, exploited peons to take a leisurely stroll with their parasols through the manicured parks and quaint villages of Luxembourg and demand the tyrant's head!

✕ Border patrol flower garden

□ Quaint little castle

● Clervaux
Classical music has been playing in this town since 1748

Breakfast Nook

□ Adorable stone bridge

● *Town populated entirely by Peter Sellers characters*

✕ Tourists entering Luxembourg for excuse to say word "Luxembourg"

Birthplace of world's most famous Luxembourger *(identity unknown)*

✕ Charming local world-domination cabal

Molehill Range

✕ Grandfather with blond muttonchops

✕ Gated gnome community

□ Museum that at one point housed a live Pygmy

□ Home of the De-Luxe Luxem-Burger

✕ Site of initial construction of snow-globe dome over entire country

Oostvogel's Grand Duchy Sweet Meats

★ **Luxembourg**
Voted "Least Creative Capital Name In Europe" a record 572 times

□ Lollipop Guild HQ

✕ Plaque for being original member of EU

✕ Border doubles as track for Luxembourg 5K Run

Luxembourg's citizens somehow go on living in meager châteaus like this under the shadow of their oppressor.

FACTS » VICIOUSLY SUPPRESSED

LANGUAGE
The universal language of the caged slave

TRADITIONAL DRESS
Shackles, chains, decorated waistcoat

TEA
Served promptly at 4 p.m.

NATURAL RESOURCES
Gourmet cheese niblets

TRANSPORTATION
Two-horse coach that makes stops on either end of the country every 20 minutes

NATIONAL DEFENSE
Moat

GEOGRAPHY
Rolling, sweeping, sun-dappled

LEADING INDUSTRIES
Castle maintenance, period-instrument repair

INTERNATIONAL DISPUTES
Cannot agree with France on border color

TREATIES
Somehow signed treaty with Choctaw Indians, 1834

A B C D E F G H I J K L M

Belgium

A Proud Tradition Of Chocolate, And Also Some Other Stuff

While known worldwide for its delicious chocolates, mouth-watering waffles, and extraordinary desserts, there is a lot more to the nation of Belgium than first meets the eye. For instance, the country is also home to delectable pies, scrumptious pastries, custards, rich creams, and truffles.

With a surprise around every corner, be it an out-of-the-way bakery, a local bakery, or an old historic landmark like the nation's first bakery, Belgium has something for everyone. Brussels, the country's capital and an architectural wonder, is the site of some of the most elaborately stacked cakes in the world, while Antwerp, its commercial center, is a fusion of old and new, with fresh éclairs replacing day-old éclairs each morning in the city's many shop windows.

Despite the nation's many culinary attractions, however, a visit to Belgium would not be complete without stopping at the breathtaking Basilica of the Sacred Heart, making a quick right at Rue Viveaux, and walking two blocks to one of the most renowned chocolate shops in all of Western Europe.

Brussels
One of the many incredible sights in Belgium's capital city.

FACTS » MAY CONTAIN NUTS

GIRTH RATE
Two in every one Belgians are overweight

POPULATION GROWTH
3.6 pounds per week

ILLICIT FOODS
Hydroponic truffles, fudge-laced brownies, pharmaceutical-grade waffles

FAVORITE INVASION
Difficult to choose, but probably 1914

PUBLIC DEBT
$1.053 trillion, or chocolate-covered waffles for everyone at World Bank

ADMINISTRATIVE DIVISIONS
Limburg, Flanders, Oost-Vlaanderen, Vlaams—wait, you don't actually care, do you?

CULTURAL ACHIEVEMENTS
The Belgian waffle, the Belgian fry, the Belgian coronary

HISTORY » A HISTORY AS OLD AS THE DOUGHNUT ITSELF

A.D. 400–1800 Belgium is invaded and traded among numerous foreign powers. Prussia loses it to Austria in a poker game in 1233, while thirsty Cossacks swap it for a carafe of cold ale in 1476.

1523 Brussels sprouts are developed by Belgium's all-time worst chocolatier, Johannes Schlophane.

1914 Violating Belgium's declaration of neutrality, Germany sends hundreds of infantry troops, three air-force divisions, and 14 naval battalions just to mock the Belgians for being such pussies.

1915 Four German soldiers swiftly topple a stack of buttermilk pancakes.

1930 Known for his surrealist painting of a pipe above the inscription, "This is not a pipe," artist René Magritte unveils its controversial follow-up, "Now this—*this* is a pipe!"

1939 Fearing another German invasion, Belgian Jews put off about $2.5 million in dental work until after the war.

1940 Belgian soldiers temporarily hold back invading German forces, thanks to a strategic military maneuver known as "dying in large, towering mounds."

1958 Brussels hosts the World's Fair, sparking much controversy with an exhibit entitled "Ticket Booth: The Outrageous Entrance Fees Of The Future!"

1959 Belgian cartoonist Pierre Culliford creates "The Smurfs," a scathing satire of little blue people who live in mushroom houses. The popular comic strip would over the course of its run coin 43 different nouns, 27 verbs, and over 200 adjectives.

1960 The nation happily relinquishes its control of Belgian Congo after a violent Congolese movement proves that it can dehumanize, abuse, and slaughter innocent natives just as well as Belgium.

2002 Along with inmates in 10 other EU nations, Belgian prisoners convert their currency to the new Euro Lights.

Site of the historic Butter-Side-Up/Butter-Side-Down Agreement, which states that either way is just as delicious

Chocoholic beating wife after fudge binge

× Kids excited to eat steak for dessert

□ This Belgian brewery produces over 300 distinct types of hangovers

● Antwerp
Yes, this is where Antwerp is

× Neighborhood of Jews hoarding chocolate coins

Dutch-Speaking Region

× Fetishist wearing fruit leather and being whipped with licorice

Wafflehouse Of Representatives

× Doctor worried patient isn't overeating enough

× Man has too much food in mouth to dispute Belgian gluttony stereotype

★ **Brussels**
Brunch served here between the hours of 11 a.m. and 11 p.m.

× Egg filled with creamy chicken embryo filling

Border reinforced with vegetables to prevent emigration

× Site where 35,000 Jews received golden tickets to take a tour of German factories in 1939

× One of Belgium's largest fudge-packing districts

German-Screaming Region

× Archaeologist's assistant eating conclusive proof that french fries originated in Belgium

× Site of violent 1974 Oompa Loompa riots

● *City momentarily overwhelmed by smell of freshly baked bread*

× Last known location of Tintin and Snowy

French-Muttering Region

Belgium's increasing percentage of dark chocolate has recently led to animosity from radical white-chocolate purists

× Chocolate-covered chocolate

Netherlands

» THE DUTCH FLAG IS
SO SCANDALOUS IT IS
UNLAWFUL TO BRING
IT INTO THE U.S.

Where Everything Is Legal

The brazen and unruly Dutch stand idly by while anything and everything takes place on their quaint, cobblestone streets, including drug use, prostitution, and an epidemic of unlicensed bicycling.

In this lawless nation, bustling cities like Amsterdam are lined with Old World shops selling pot brownies, Cuban cigars, and very dirty magazines. Not to be outdone, the nation's movie theaters often show first-run movies before their proper release date—and many contain swearing.

Police do nothing as gay men stroll into chapels and emerge with the full legal rights of married couples, all the while double-parked. Lesbians wantonly adopt children and care for them. And an unchecked multitude of thieves, both old and young, get away with state-sponsored health insurance without paying a dime.

Although authorities in the Netherlands seem unconcerned that such outlandish behavior has spread through their country like a virus, one day a public litterer is going to go too far, and the nation will regret its reckless ways.

THE DIKES » LIFE BELOW SEA LEVEL

Much of the Netherlands is below sea level, protected by an intricate series of dikes, which prevent the sea from burying the nation. When a dike leak occurs, Dutch officials dispatch a highly trained boy in short pants to plug the hole with his finger.

FACTS » LAWLESSNESS AND DISORDER

OFFICIAL NAME
Kingdom Of The Netherlands

UNOFFICIAL NAME
That Totally Crazy Place With The Hookers In The Windows

PREFERRED METHOD OF PAYMENT FOR DINNER
Each party paying an equal share

LEAST-VISITED AREA
Green-light district

EXPORTS
Fruits, vegetables, fish products

EXPORTS VIA THE HUMAN RECTUM
Marijuana, clear plastics

UNIRONIC HEAD COVERING
The bonnet

FOOTWEAR INNOVATION
The tennis clog

WHAT VAN GOGH DID AFTER SELLING ONLY ONE PAINTING WHILE ALIVE
Cut off his ear

WHAT VAN GOGH WOULD DO IF HE KNEW HIS PAINTINGS NOW SOLD FOR $100 MILLION
Shit his pants

FOOTBALL ANTHEM
"Who Let The Dutch Out?"

HISTORY » CLOGGING TOWARD DESTINY

57 B.C. Roman conquerors notice that the Netherlands' inhabitants have a calm, tolerant demeanor, inspiring the Romans to name the area "Mellogermania."

A.D. 1506 The Dutch attempt to resist Habsburg rule by submerging the country into the North Sea, but are caught.

1568 Dutch merchants rebel against the Habsburg monarchy, and the Eighty Years' War begins. (*Warning: Eighty Years' War spoiler ahead!*) The Dutch win.

1602 Modern capitalism is born with a young startup called the Dutch East India Company, which had a big dream and a simple idea: What if you just enslaved people and stole all their stuff?

1605 An incident in which a crazed Spaniard attempts to joust at a windmill inflames opposition to Spanish rule.

1609 Giving up on their dream of a great northern beaver-pelt empire, the Dutch trade Manhattan for Suriname.

1648 Having grown prosperous on overseas trade, the Dutch enjoy a great Golden Age, but blow their hard-earned gains on still-life paintings of objects lying in and around their houses.

1940 Nazi Germany can no longer tolerate a neighboring country that exhibits so little respect for law and order. They invade the Netherlands, bringing swift justice to marijuana users, homosexuals, and flagrant Jews.

2004 A town council in the Netherlands considers passing a law that would forbid wordplay involving the words "dike" and "dyke."

Stripper Clogs

The attic where Anne Frank hung out during the Nazi invasion.

Construction project underway to give the Netherlands its first hill

Nation spent $6 million getting these islands lined up just right

A drug-fueled haze of loosely remembered events

Nuclear sump pump

Bay Of Looming Disaster

☒ Dildo bog

☐ Abortion & Euthanasia Fair

• Van Vanden Haven

☒ Your missing tie-dyed T-shirt

☒ Here there be whores

☐ Only dike with purpose of keeping Mexicans out

Hightimes Lands

☒ Freak-out tent

■ Lake formed by excess bong water

☐ Historic last remnant of "wall of clogs" built to stave off invading Germans

☒ Soviet Submarine MOSKVA-1
A Cold War relic whose crew is not aware of the Soviet Union's collapse, and which plays an important part in the violent third act of this atlas

Transcontinental bike path

☒ National bong

★ **Amsterdam**

🪀 Bullshit windmill that doesn't even do anything

☒ Still keeping a few Jews in the attic for possible future bargaining

☐ Hippie graveyard

☐ Adults-only hostel

☐ Once-great crack den gone all touristy

Single missile silo keeping Belgium in line

Nether Regions

Repurposed wood from once-mighty Dutch fleet now local man Klassje Ovdenaardem's fence planks

Lowtimes Lands

☒ Really potent tulips

☒ Border bitterly disputed between extremist Dutch Calvinists and Belgian Protestants

☐ Birthplace of the casual athletic shoe

■ Wind-powered brothel

☒ Dude, weed

» AMSTERDAM IS
AN INTERNATIONAL
CENTER OF CHILD
PORNOGRAPHY.

Denmark

» THE DANES WERE SORT OF GOING FOR A "MINIMALIST'S UNION JACK" THING HERE.

"We're Happy Because You're Not Here"

Whether building magical castles out of Legos, reading Hans Christian Andersen's whimsical fairy tales, or enjoying their near-perfect economy, the Danes are a happy people—happy to be free of all foreigners, undesirables, and especially Muslims.

Responding to the rise of global terrorism following the 9/11 attacks on the United States, the Danish government instituted strict immigration laws in order to protect its country and allow the Danes to lead a somewhat charmed life. Today, citizens spend far more time enjoying the outdoors while dutifully patrolling the borders. They're more carefree with their defense spending. And they never fail to stop and smell the roses before corralling the nation's two remaining Middle Easterners onto a ferry bound for Sweden.

Despite the tougher immigration laws, the Danes remain surprisingly open to tourism. They are quick to welcome anyone who can show six forms of ID, submit to a mandatory body-cavity search, make a pledge of loyalty to the king of Denmark, and prove that they once passed through the birth canal of a Danish woman. But as the old Danish saying goes, "It's not easy to get into Denmark, but once you're here, you'll be sad when we deport you."

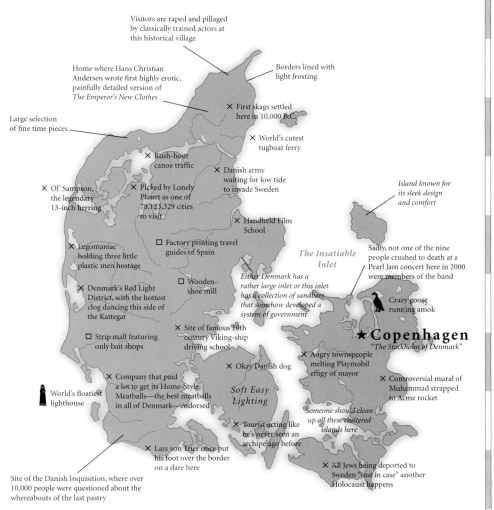

Visitors are raped and pillaged by classically trained actors at this historical village

Home where Hans Christian Andersen wrote first highly erotic, painfully detailed version of *The Emperor's New Clothes*

Large selection of fine time pieces

Borders lined with light frosting

× First skags settled here in 10,000 B.C.

× World's cutest tugboat ferry

× Rush-hour canoe traffic

× Danish army waiting for low tide to invade Sweden

× Ol' Sampson, the legendary 13-inch herring

× Picked by Lonely Planet as one of 78,123,329 cities to visit

Island known for its sleek design and comfort

× Handheld Film School

□ Factory printing travel guides of Spain

× Legomaniac holding three little plastic men hostage

The Insatiable Inlet

Sadly, not one of the nine people crushed to death at a Pearl Jam concert here in 2000 were members of the band

Either Denmark has a rather large inlet or this inlet has a collection of sandbars that somehow developed a system of government

□ Wooden-shoe mill

× Denmark's Red Light District, with the hottest clog dancing this side of the Kattegat

Crazy goose running amok

★ **Copenhagen**
"The Stockholm of Denmark"

× Site of famous 10th century Viking-ship driving school

□ Strip-mall featuring only bait shops

× Angry townspeople melting Playmobil effigy of mayor

× Okay Danish dog

× Controversial mural of Muhammad strapped to Acme rocket

World's floatiest lighthouse

× Company that paid a lot to get its Home-Style Meatballs—the best meatballs in all of Denmark—endorsed

Soft Easy Lighting

Someone should clean up all these cluttered islands here

× Tourist acting like he's never seen an archipelago before

× Lars von Trier once put his foot over the border on a dare here

× All Jews being deported to Sweden "just in case" another Holocaust happens

Site of the Danish Inquisition, where over 10,000 people were questioned about the whereabouts of the last pastry

FACTS » INTERROGATED, DELOUSED

LOCATION
Not your concern

GOVERNMENT
Constitutional monarchy with a moat

ETHNIC GROUPS
Scandinavian (89%), Visiting Scandinavians (10%), Irish (1%, confined to U2 touring bus)

TRANSPORTATION
Breaststroke, doggy paddle

INTERNATIONAL ORGANIZATIONS
EU, NATO, The Denmarks-Only Club

EDUCATION
Literacy Rate: 104%
Math Rate: 22%

GREATEST IRONY
Entire nation allergic to fish

FUTURE RULERS
Massive tidal waves caused by melting polar ice caps

CULTURE » SHAKY AND OUT OF FOCUS

Danish cinema experienced a boom in international popularity in 1995, with the start of the Dogme filmmaking movement. This new, avant-garde style champions films that do not rely on artificial lighting, special effects, scored music, or audiences.

HISTORY » SOMETHING BOUND TO HAPPEN ANY DAY NOW

10,000–4000 B.C. Denmark's numerous prehistoric bogs offer a perfectly preserved fossil record of what early man looked like drowning in a bog.

A.D. 960 Christianity is introduced to the Vikings, teaching them that rape and pillage is a sin in the eyes of God, unless properly classified as a "crusade."

1397 Denmark takes control of Sweden and Norway after the three countries have a nice long talk about it over tea and finger sandwiches.

1600 In response to Shakespeare's *Hamlet*,

Denmark outlaws ghosts.

Hans Christian Andersen

1859 Hans Christian Andersen writes a series of delightful children's stories about toy soldiers, princesses, and ugly ducklings in an elaborate, 20-year-long announcement of his homosexuality.

1911 The Danish government outlaws corporal punishment. The nation experiences a 67% rise in sass mouth.

1922 Danish physicist Niels Bohr discovers that the

electron's orbital angular momentum is quantized as $L=nh$, that items can be separately analyzed as having contradictory wave-like and particle-like properties, and that talking to women is utterly terrifying.

1940 Nazis occupy Denmark. The Danish government responds with a powerful and devastating soliloquy.

2006 A comic featured in a Danish newspaper sparks controversy over its offensive stereotypes and deplorable humor. "Marmaduke" is subsequently pulled from several Danish publications.

Iceland

So "Cold" From All The "Ice"

For hundreds of years, the deceitful Icelandic people have been fooling the world into believing that their temperate, lush, and geologically stunning island nation is in fact some kind of "land of ice."

In what must be the greatest geographic hoax in history, millions of middle-school students are fed lies day after day by Iceland's highly coordinated campaign of misinformation, insinuation, and not changing the name of their country to something more descriptive.

What natives would have us infer to be a cold, unforgiving wasteland of loneliness and sorrow is actually a hidden paradise of gorgeous waterfalls, lava fields, and naturally occurring outdoor hot tubs. During festivals, these cruel, scheming people make a big production out of eating "traditional dishes" such as ram's testicles and rotten shark meat, which only further exposes the depths of their treachery: For all we know, they probably eat pizza.

Icelanders greedily keep their "barren" landscapes of awe-inspiring beauty all for themselves, enjoying their universal health care and low crime rates while ignorant foreigners still taken in by the ruse shudder every time they view the country on a map or globe.

If any sense of justice, or accuracy, still exists, Iceland should be called Greenland, and Greenland—well, Greenland should just be called something else.

PEOPLE » ONE BIG ICY FAMILY

Thanks to a millennium of meticulous record-keeping, Icelanders are a genetically perfect people. These closely related descendants of Vikings can trace their family tree back 50 generations, and can also trace most family arguments back to the time when Uncle Naddodr the Destroyer got drunk and made a pass at Raven-Floki's wolf-bride during the blood feast of 901.

Björk travels to a concert in Reykjavik.

HISTORY » "FROZEN" IN TIME

A.D. 870 Irish monks who first settled the island greet Viking explorers with open arms, and then, with open chest wounds.

930 Icelanders form the world's first parliamentary body, the Althing, to settle local disputes, dispense justice, and give them an excuse to push petty thieves into lava floes every now and then.

1262 Iceland comes under the rule of the King of Denmark. Despite attempts to bribe their new ruler with flowing buckets of herring, corruption levels drop to an all-time low.

1445 The Black Death makes a convincing argument against the old Icelandic adage that fish soup is the best medicine.

1783 Eruption of the Laki volcano wipes out 30% of Iceland's population. From this day forth, all agree to live life to the fullest and not atop an active volcano.

1958 Iceland and the U.K. enter the Cod War, a protracted non-military dispute defined by a policy of Mutual Assured Destruction of all fish in the North Atlantic.

1976 Eleven years after chewing herself out of a semi-gelatinous sac of glitter, Björk records her first platinum album while still just a larva.

2004 Iceland resumes commercial whaling with a unanimous parliamentary resolution acknowledging environmental concerns, international opposition, and the fact that whale meat just tastes so darn good.

Iceland would have you believe this ideal picnic spot is an inhospitable tundra.

AN EXTREMELY THIN SHEET OF FACTS »

CAPITAL
Reykjawhatever

POPULATION
At capacity

ECONOMY
Iceland recently switched from a fish-based economy to borrowing money from Björk

MILITARY
Without its own army, Iceland is protected by the U.S. military, which in return gets more smoked salmon than it knows what to do with

SOCIAL LIFE
Icelanders claim to have sex four times a night in winter—when night lasts six months

LANGUAGE
Icelandic has not changed since it was developed by aliens 1,000 years ago

Icelandic public housing units

MAP KEY
☐ Ice
◻ Land
◼ Bald-faced lies

✕ Man smelting like there's no tomorrow

✕ Man who was wading in ocean when an island formed under him

Man plugging car into waterfall for the night

✕ Disappointed ice tourists

Iceland enjoys a birth rate of 1.7 new islands per year

Ice Bay

✕ Man complaining that geothermal spa in his backyard isn't hot enough

✕ Kiddie geothermal pool

Entire peninsula formed by leftover fish guts

✕ Little girl terrified of volcano in closet

✕ Fisherman who wouldn't rather be fishing

Hall Of Assistant Mountain King For Administrative Affairs

✕ Stew geyser

✕ Stand makes best herring shake in Iceland

✕ Drunk guy with no shirt on

Haunting, Ethereal Music

✕ World's first Sugarcube fans

☐ Hatchery where Björk was born

Reykjavík ★
Only capital city built on a rainbow

Unparalleled Beauty

✕ Icelander denying she ever filled out scientific survey about happiness

✕ Non-scenic point

✕ Crushed Icelanders

☐ Proposed military base (pending military)

✕ Iceland's only grocery store open past 6 p.m.

☐ Björk's unicorn stable

✕ Lonely Olympic village

✕ Kids playing hopscotch on lava floe

Area composed entirely of misconceptions

✕ Angry environmentalists floating away on glacier

✕ 1986 Anti-Melting Treaties signed here

Ice Biochemical Precipitate

▲ *Mt. Hvannadalshnukur* Mountain subdued with harpoons

ICE OCEAN

✕ Man who can only fall asleep with the geyser on

✕ Family packing into small '97 fjord

Norway

» TRADITIONALLY MADE OF BONES, HAIR, BLOOD, AND POLYESTER.

Suppressing The Urge To Chop You In Half With An Axe

The gentle and self-composed Norwegians know all too well what they are capable of. Within each tall, progressive, and sensibly dressed citizen dwells a bloodthirsty Viking warrior, longing to inflict the most grotesque atrocities imaginable upon the feeble masses.

Modern Norway, one of the world's most socially conscious democracies, has opted to repress its past, distracting itself by building safe, clean roadways and funding reliable public waterworks. But, O, how they long to feel the weight of a broadsword in their calloused hands, lopping off the weakly limbs of a commoner, his warm blood flowing as the rivers of wine in the halls of Valhalla.

As the third-largest exporter of petroleum on the planet, Norway is home to responsible officials who recently decided to set aside a percentage of oil revenues each year in anticipation of a time when this finite resource will run out. However, at heart, every last one of them would trade all the accruing interest in the world for just one night of fevered pillage, grimacing madly with blood-splattered faces as they hack away at the enemy, resting for a moment to join fellow warriors in debauched celebration, drinking from skulls filled to the brim with mead, and laughing heartily as they pick shards of bone from their long, flowing beards and toss them into a roaring fire.

King Magnus Skullsplitter

Old rape route (now Norwegian cruise line)

× Fjord assembly line

□ 4 million sq. ft. herring cannery

• City terrified that the Vikings will come back

Nice Stretch Of Glacier

□ Largest wheat smelter in world

× Offshore water deposits

□ Ice-themed vacation resort

□ Oil refinery run by slave-trolls

This part always clumps up ×

Mosjoen is home to a huge underground mining scene

□ Valhalla Trailer Park

Old viking boats recycled for use as bookcases

× School of lutefisk

× Neatly flattened pile of cardboard boxes

One of world's richest regions, mainly because it doesn't spend money on clothes

□ Metrodome

× Japanese tourists at metal show

× Best blonde braids in Scandinavia, second runner-up

□ Ditch reserved for Nobel Prize losers

□ Quaint spot for fish pulp

× Secret tunnel to escape Norway

The Anvil Plains

× Other end of secret tunnel

× Odin's eyeball

★ Oslo
Funny story, we almost left Oslo completely off this map

× Roaming Lutheran horde

Bay Of Smelt

FACTS » FORGED IN STEEL

OFFICIAL NAME
Kingdom Of Norway Of Kicking Ass

MOTTO
Alt For Norge ("Everything For Norway, Including Your Intestines")

ENERGY
The Norwegian parliament is currently debating plans to rape and pillage the remaining oil deposits in the Arctic north

RELEVANCE TO U.S.
The smorgasbord

TOURIST SITES
Most of Norway's thousands of famous fjords are too deep for visitors to see all the decapitated bodies at the bottom

RELIGIOUS ACTIVITIES
Lutherans: Attending services at beautiful, ancient wooden churches
Black-Metal Satanists: Burning down beautiful, ancient wooden churches

THOR VS. JESUS
Thor

NOTABLE NORWEGIANS » HENRIK IBSEN

The country's most celebrated literary figure, Ibsen exposed the disquieting reality behind the facades of Norwegian life in his plays "A Doll's House," "Hedda Gabler," and "Why The Hell Aren't We Stabbing Anybody Anymore?"

HISTORY » OFFICIALLY FORGOTTEN BATTLEFIELD GLORY

A.D. 793 Vikings usher in the Viking Age by raping, pillaging, and generally just being Vikings.

908 Viking explorers take a moment from their revelry to pray to Odin that their glorious, blood-drenched deeds are never overshadowed by the implementation of universal affordable health care.

This beautiful fjord is filled with 9,127 skeletons.

955 During a visit to the Swedish countryside, Norse raider Kjar Bloodhammer accidentally slips and falls in the mud in front of his whole army. To save face, he decapitates all innocent bystanders in the area and claims the country as his own.

1067 Historians in Iceland, Greenland, Great Britain, and Canada, all desperate to avoid having their heads slowly roasted on an open spit, officially declare the Viking Age over.

1324 The Vikings stand in awe of the Black Death as an even more efficient killer.

1537 Norwegians are disappointed to learn that, as Protestants, they are not allowed to eat the body and drink the blood of Christ.

1893 Looking back on his country's proud history, prissy Victorian expressionist Edvard Munch just about sums it all up with his painting "The Scream."

1960 Norway discovers offshore oil deposits, bringing some much-needed evil back into their lives.

1987 In what must now pass for glory in this emasculated land, Norwegian metal band Mayhem releases its first album, *Deathcrush*.

2007 Norway once again leads the world in all categories of the UN Development rankings, yet many mourn that there is not a skull, sword, or impaled torso in sight.

Former Viking Warrior Randy Moss

Sweden

Nobel Prize Winner For Great Cheekbones

Singled out for their achievements in bone structure, cascading blonde locks, and slender thighs, the people of Sweden have been awarded the Nobel Prize in Beauty 87 years running—a prestigious medal best displayed between their ample yet perky breasts.

For almost a century, this Scandinavian nation has led the world in the development of unblemished skin and crystal-blue eyes, and made impressive breakthroughs in the field of lip poutiness. Last year, it donated 2,000 thong and stiletto heel combinations to benefit under-ogled nations.

From their tireless efforts to raise the standard of gorgeousness, to their selfless bikini-team outreach, Swedes have shown they are more than just a pretty face, neck, chest, stomach, butt, thighs, and calves.

In the rare case that an unattractive Swede is produced, the government provides for these unfortunates in special hidden communities above the Arctic Circle. There, the malformed attend state-supported beauty schools and receive free universal plastic surgery.

HISTORY » A MARCH OF PERFECTION

2300 B.C. Cave paintings traced to this time period depict simple assembly instructions for primitive end tables.

A.D. 845 Swedish Vikings, curious about the peoples of other lands, explore the British Isles and Baltic nations and document how the people there react to being stabbed repeatedly.

1914 Sweden dozes off for most of WWI.

1943 IKEA is founded by Ingvar Kamprad, a Swedish citizen who had to get rid of roughly

2 million Allen wrenches.

1952 Sweden founds the Nordic Council, joining with Denmark and Norway to become a powerhouse of neutrality.

1960 The nation's suicide rate skyrockets as desperate citizens attempt to escape the grim realities and wretched desolation of Swedish cinema.

1965–2000 Intermission.

2003 Foreign Minister Anna Lindh is stabbed to death in a Stockholm department store, demonstrating yet another problem of electing women to public office.

This region too bland for habitation

✕ Death surely better than this

☐ IKEA detention center

✕ Most unsung blemish

✕ Witch-king of Angmar

Baby stroller with airbags

☐ Center Of Fjord Tourism

Brunette Separatists

Seized by Norwegian bikini team during the Budweiser Ad Wars of 1988–1992

☐ Death metal deposits

☐ Roxette deportation zone

Swimsuit competition deciding winner of Nobel Prize in Chemistry

☐ Glam metal refinery

☐ Secret Swedish garbage dump

Fossilized breast implant

■ Source of world's blondeness

✕ Actual Swedish chef unwittingly entertaining tourists

IKEA PARKING LOT

✕ Syphilitic sea captains

Government bank providing free spending money

Gulf Of Erotica

■ Natural peroxide springs

Pre-Laminated Forest

☐ Only clinic licensed to perform the painful Swedish bikini wax

✕ Your dream girl and her 10,000 gorgeous sisters

★ **Stockholm**
Burned down in 1916 due to a malfunctioning space heater

✕ Last shred of dignity not taken by ABBA or Ace Of Base

✕ Everyone wearing those helmets with horns

Lake Citron

✕ Rebellious teen dying hair auburn

Island Of Never-Tell Land

☐ Lutefisk hatchery

Massage-oil pipeline

• Inhabitants here salted and crusted

Birthplace of Hägar the Horrible

• Inhabitants here pickled in brine

Day-old potato pancake barge

☐ Indie rock training camp

☐ Genetic lingonberry-breeding laboratory and pancake house

The most breathtaking elbow you've ever seen

ABBA's last performance, 1982.

PEOPLE » AVAILABLE IN WHITE, OFF-WHITE, PALE, AND IVORY

Nearly every Swede of working age is employed by home-goods manufacturing giant IKEA. While many should be upset at having to work the traditional six-month-long night shift, it is customary in Sweden to never speak about, analyze, or experience emotions.

FACTS » PRE-ASSEMBLED

FAVORITE PASTIME
Paying taxes

ABBA BREAKDOWN
Björn Ulvaeus 25%,
Benny Andersson 25%
Agnetha Fältskog 25%
Anni-Frid Lyngstad 25%

BIGGEST ASSHOLE
Mats Alfredsson,
48, Stockholm

FISH
Swedish

EDUCATION
With four different letter A's in its alphabet, Sweden has the world's highest grade-point average

CULTURE
Has produced 29 Nobel Prize winners, countless musicians, and both of your living-room end tables

DEFENSE STRATEGY
Dual airbags

RELIGION
Norse mythology, which is kind of like Catholicism meets *Lord Of The Rings*

REBELLIOUS TEENAGE PHASE
Once said "Neutrality is stupid"

TREATIES SIGNED
All of them

Finland

It's A Winter Wonderland!

This progressive social democracy has turned a potentially cold and inhospitable nation into a magical land of tax-supported wintry delight, where citizens enjoy free universal health care, early-childhood snow-angel-making education, and same-sex snowman unions.

A national sledway system offers free and fun mass transit to Finnish citizens, connecting commuters via both push- and pull-based technology to either the best tobogganing hill or the ice-skating rink by Grandma's house. A generous social welfare program offers hot chocolate and dry wool socks to those who have gotten wet, while a well-bundled-up rule-enforcement community sits on those who don't play fair and rubs snow in their faces.

Tongues stuck to flagpoles remain the nation's primary health concern, but extensive government investment in the hot-water sciences has greatly reduced instances of crying and overall embarrassment in recent years.

HISTORY » THE WEATHER OUTSIDE IS FRIGHTFUL…

0 The Finnish book of epic folktales, *Kalevala*, reveals that the world was created when Ilmatar, the Virgin of the Air, descended to the waters where a pochard laid its eggs on her knee, and from these eggs, all the world was hatched. This human-origin theory remains controversial to this day.

1150 Swedish troops quickly subdue the Finnish, who are bundled up so well in their snowsuits that they can barely move their limbs.

1917 Finland declares independence. In celebration, famed Finnish musician Jean Sibelius composes the national anthem, the Nokia chime.

1939 The Soviet Union attacks Finland, but the Finnish hold back the Soviets' far superior numbers with a hastily constructed yet awesome snow fort.

2003 Every single fucking person in the world finds a Nokia phone under the Christmas tree.

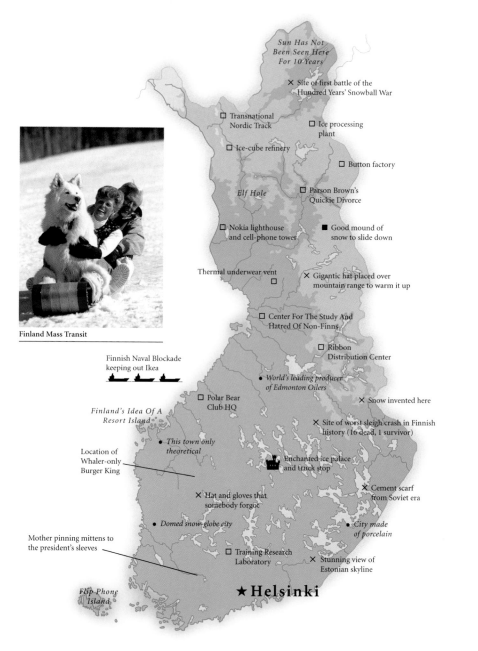

Finland Mass Transit

Sun Has Not Been Seen Here For 10 Years

✕ Site of first battle of the Hundred Years' Snowball War

☐ Transnational Nordic Track

☐ Ice processing plant

☐ Ice-cube refinery

☐ Button factory

Elf Hole

☐ Parson Brown's Quickie Divorce

☐ Nokia lighthouse and cell-phone tower

■ Good mound of snow to slide down

Thermal underwear vent ☐

✕ Gigantic hat placed over mountain range to warm it up

☐ Center For The Study And Hatred Of Non-Finns

☐ Ribbon Distribution Center

• World's leading producer of Edmonton Oilers

Finnish Naval Blockade keeping out Ikea

✕ Snow invented here

☐ Polar Bear Club HQ

✕ Site of worst sleigh crash in Finnish history (16 dead, 1 survivor)

Finland's Idea Of A Resort Island

• *This town only theoretical*

■ Enchanted ice palace and truck stop

Location of Whaler-only Burger King

✕ Cement scarf from Soviet era

✕ Hat and gloves that somebody forgot

• *City made of porcelain*

• *Domed snow-globe city*

Mother pinning mittens to the president's sleeves

☐ Training Research Laboratory

✕ Stunning view of Estonian skyline

Flip-Phone Island

★ **Helsinki**

PEOPLE » TRACKING IN A LOT OF SNOW

Investment in education has made Finlanders the most literate people in the world, yet children awaken with cries of "Yay!" every morning, as school is always canceled. Each day, parents toboggan to work in the cell-phone industry, but find no use for the technology themselves, as dialing a cell phone is nearly impossible while wearing mittens, and enunciating can be difficult when teeth are chattering. The nation's scientists, meanwhile, lead the world in catching snowflakes on their tongues, and in 2007 successfully mapped the snowman genome.

FACTS » NO TWO ARE ALIKE

POPULATION
United under National Friends & Family Plan: 2.6 billion anytime minutes, plus free nights and weekends

LIFE EXPECTANCY
Old Man Winter is believed to be over 10,000 years old

NARRATOR
Burl Ives

LAND USE
Winter (74%), Wonder (22%), Bootprints (4%)

CRIME
Surprise snowball attacks

JUSTICE SYSTEM
Laughing away anger, but quickly balling up retaliatory snowball

LEADING CIVIL-SERVICE AGENCIES
Social Shoveling Administration, Centers For De-Icing Control, Department Of Hats

NATURAL HAZARDS
Socks getting bunched up in toe of boot

FAUNA
The legendary White Squirrel

GLOBAL-WARMING ISSUES
Melting marshmallows

Estonia, Latvia & Lithuania

ESTONIA » THERE ARE OVER 1,400 ESTONIAN FOLK SONGS ABOUT THIS FLAG.

LITHUANIA » EFFORT TO CHANGE TO ONE BLACK STRIPE IN 1992 WAS A CRY FOR HELP.

LATVIA » LATVIAN-BORN ARTIST MARK ROTHKO STOLE ALL HIS BEST IDEAS FROM THE LATVIAN FLAG.

Estonia
United In Circular Dancing

The merry nation of Estonia has been under foreign control for most of its history, due to the fact that its main form of defense is holding hands and singing.

For decades, its people have sung and danced in the face of great adversity, utter hopelessness, and bullets.

Estonia was the site of the "Singing Revolution," during which citizens serenaded invading Soviet forces with traditional Estonian folk songs such as the up-tempo "Stop, You're Wrecking Our Homes," the hauntingly beautiful "Spare The Women And Children," and "Roosiaia Kuninganna," the tale of a tiny talking mouse. It was the kind of catchy, non-violent rebellion that the whole family could enjoy.

In 1991, Russian forces, impressed that the Estonians could hold a high C-sharp for three straight years, granted them their independence and placed 25 cents in their open mandolin case.

FACTS » CELEBRATED

JOINED UN 1991 (celebrated with singing and dancing)

JOINED EU 2004 (rejoiced in song and dance)

NATIONAL ANTHEM 1945–1991

INTERNATIONAL GROUPS NATO, European Union, UN Choir

NATIONAL INSTRUMENT The tambourine

NATIONAL PERCUSSIVE INSTRUMENT The woodblock

DANCING FORMATIONS Square, ring, ovoid

TECHNOLOGICAL ADVANCEMENTS Development of the Mobius Strip dance formation

ENVIRONMENTAL ISSUES De-enchantment-ization of forests

WHAT THEY CALL THEMSELVES Estland

WHAT WE MUST CONTINUE TO CALL THEM Estonia

HISTORY » PASSED DOWN THROUGH CHORAL TRADITION

A.D. 1940 In the midst of WWII, the baritone regiment of the Estonian military is equipped with the best clogs of any army, allowing them to develop one of the most rhythmic battle marches in Europe. They also outfit themselves with matching mustaches. Despite all this, thousands are slaughtered by the Russians.

1945–1991 The U.S.S.R. outlaws the Estonian practices of singing, dancing, and looking at Soviet soldiers with sad little puppy-dog eyes that make you just want to hug every last one of them.

1996 The U.S. cuts off foreign aid to Estonia. The people of Estonia dance.

2004 An Estonian couple comes in last place in the annual International Wife-Carrying Contest. Moments later, they finish first in the International Wife-Beating Competition.

2007 Tears are shed as the nation exports its last remaining piece of limestone.

The Estonian Festival Of Üliöpilastantsupidudel Dancing.

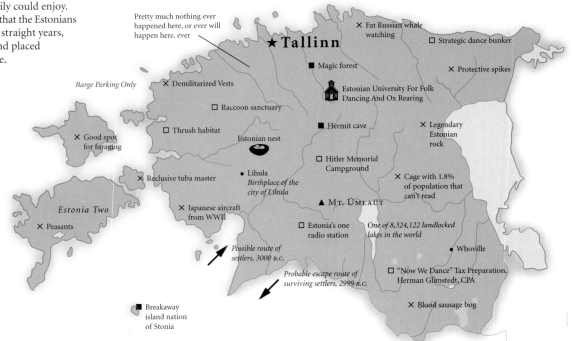

Pretty much nothing ever happened here, or ever will happen here, ever

★ **Tallinn**

✕ Fat Russian whale watching

☐ Strategic dance bunker

■ Magic forest

✕ Protective spikes

Barge Parking Only

✕ Demilitarized Vests

🏛 Estonian University For Folk Dancing And Ox Rearing

☐ Raccoon sanctuary

☐ Thrush habitat

■ Hermit cave

✕ Legendary Estonian rock

✕ Good spot for foraging

Estonian nest

☐ Hitler Memorial Campground

✕ Cage with 1.8% of population that can't read

✕ Reclusive tuba master

• Lihula *Birthplace of the city of Lihula*

▲ Mt. Ümlaüt

Estonia Two

✕ Japanese aircraft from WWII

☐ Estonia's one radio station

One of 8,324,122 landlocked lakes in the world

✕ Peasants

• Whoville

Possible route of settlers, 3000 B.C.

Probable escape route of surviving settlers, 2999 B.C.

☐ "Now We Dance" Tax Preparation, Herman Glimstedt, CPA

■ Breakaway island nation of Stonia

✕ Blood sausage bog

In 1940, Estonian troops retreat in a circular, syncopated pattern from invading Russian troops.

PEOPLE » A FOLK-DANCING FOLK

The people of Estonia constantly celebrate their love of song in their annual yearlong folk festival. Their capital, Tallinn, is the birthplace of four distinct kinds of folk singing, seven different forms of folk dancing, and over 15 types of folk humming.

When they are not singing or dancing, the people of Estonia are busy sewing colorful dancing skirts, skipping trousers, and singing vests, incorporating polka-dot and checkered patterns. Children help in the effort by whistling the traditional sewing tune.

According to leading Baltic scholars, Estonians could only be more lovable if they were made two inches tall and placed in little wooden doll houses.

Lithuania
Goodbye, Cruel World

All the cheerful circle dancing in the world can't make the people of Lithuania feel better. The UN recently reported that the nation has the world's highest suicide rate—bleak news that immediately sent millions of citizens headfirst out of their top-story office windows.

Boasting the strongest rope in all of Europe, bathrooms fully equipped with toaster outlets, and airtight garages able to accommodate the entire family and their car, Lithuania is known for its spectacular, panoramic views that grow increasingly detailed with each passing second until the entire landscape turns, at once, to black.

In Lithuania, one's fear of heights is surpassed only by one's fear of going through life unloved, and the weight—the goddamn weight of it all—is just too much for a nation of 3 million lost souls to carry.

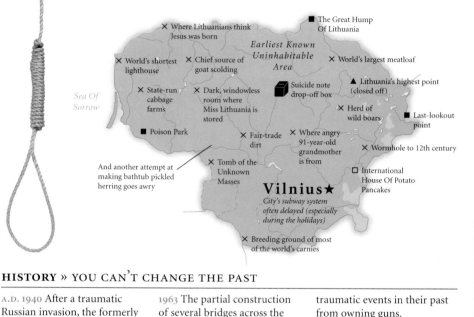

- ✕ Where Lithuanians think Jesus was born
- ■ The Great Hump Of Lithuania
- *Earliest Known Uninhabitable Area*
- ✕ World's shortest lighthouse
- ✕ Chief source of goat scolding
- ✕ World's largest meatloaf
- *Sea Of Sorrow*
- ✕ State-run cabbage farms
- ✕ Dark, windowless room where Miss Lithuania is stored
- ■ Suicide note drop-off box
- ▲ Lithuania's highest point (closed off)
- ✕ Herd of wild boars
- ■ Last-lookout point
- ■ Poison Park
- ✕ Fair-trade dirt
- ✕ Where angry 91-year-old grandmother is from
- ✕ Wormhole to 12th century
- And another attempt at making bathtub pickled herring goes awry
- ✕ Tomb of the Unknown Masses
- ☐ International House Of Potato Pancakes
- **Vilnius★** *City's subway system often delayed (especially during the holidays)*
- ✕ Breeding ground of most of the world's carnies

HISTORY » YOU CAN'T CHANGE THE PAST

A.D. 1940 After a traumatic Russian invasion, the formerly outgoing Lithuania retreats inside its borders and stops taking part in UN activities.

1959 The nation of Lithuania does not want to talk about it.

1963 The partial construction of several bridges across the nation allows motorists to more quickly reach their final destination.

1987 New background checks keep those without sufficiently traumatic events in their past from owning guns.

2006 In a rare moment of bilateral cooperation, 342 Lithuanian congressmen are found days later to have signed a suicide bill.

Latvia
The Baltic Drainage Region

Nestled in the ditch between Lithuania and Estonia, Latvia is home to Europe's most breathtaking swamps, picturesque marshes, and an endless horizon that glimmers with several different shades of runoff.

It is impossible to walk through Latvia without witnessing the influence of other cultures' waste and refuse, or without knee-high rubber boots and waterproof pants. Whether roaming the soggy, rolling hills of ancient sewage, strolling alongside a meandering culvert, or gazing in awe at the nation's many gleaming sinkholes, most visitors are at a loss to describe the vast array of muck.

Latvia features over 3,000 puddles. While most puddles are small, the nation's deepest is Drizdis (65.1 mm.), and the largest is Lubanca (3,243 cm.). Latvia is also home to several man-made puddles.

- Proposed site of trans-Latvian canal to nowhere
- ■ Covered in soap scum
- 🍃 *This former area of Latvia failed to survive the Third Drizzle Age*
- ■ Rare flower used to make gray-green pigment
- Largest piece of cheese in Latvia, decreasing by 1,100 bites per year
- World's least-used observation deck
- ☐ Mildew farm
- ☐ Culinary Institute And Taxidermy College Of Latvia
- ☐ Bread assembly line
- ☐ Institute For The Eradication Of The National Cuisine
- ☐ Mediocre little Latvian restaurant
- **★Riga** *Site of the Treaty of Berlin, 1896 (loooong story)*
- ▲ *Latvian citizen Toms Berzina became first man to successfully eat this mountain*
- ✕ Swimming trench
- ✕ Drinking hole
- ● *Soggiest town in Latvia*
- ✕ National pothole
- *Great Puddle Plains*
- ✕ Lair of the Bog Men
- Latvian scientists working on creation of new meal
- Shitty-American-Building-Supervisor Training Institute
- ✕ Sponge nobody wants to use
- ✕ Swamp dwellers
- ✕ Couple filing for divorce after argument about bread

PEOPLE » EAT, DRINK, AND BE MERRY, FOR TOMORROW WE DIE OF EATING

The people of Latvia often begin each day with a large glass of sour cream. Most citizens drag a lunch cauldron to work each day to boil meats, which are served with a barley sauce, nettle gravy, or oatslaw.

Traditionally, Latvian women were the ones who could not cook, but in today's enlightened society, many Latvian men cannot cook either.

Latvia's beautiful Talsi Ditch.

Belarus

» THIS FLAG IS PROUDLY HUNG
ALL OVER THE COUNTRY.

Inhabitable By 2307

Ever since Belarus suffered the bulk of the fallout from the Chernobyl meltdown in 1986, life has been difficult for the 10 million citizens, or 5 million two-headed citizens, of this green-glowing former Soviet state.

Whether living in the country's contaminated wetlands or its sweeping, jagged wastelands, Belarusians must deal with a lagging economy, a smoldering infrastructure, and constant bouts of violent and toxic vomiting spells. Though the nuclear disaster was devastating, this resilient people continues to ooze slowly toward a more stable way of life, committed to rebuild their country or melt trying.

HISTORY » REPEATEDLY REFUSING TO BE WIPED OFF THE FACE OF THE EARTH

A.D. 700 The Slavs settle in what is now Belarus to select future generations' final resting place.

1240 Surviving Belarusians join the Grand Duchy of Lithuania Neighborhood Watch Program, which seeks to repel future marauders using colorful, pointy flags.

1900 French physicist Paul Villard discovers the gamma ray. Nearly 1,400 miles away, clouds form and lightning strikes as the people of Belarus collectively shudder.

1918 After World War I, Belarus declares its independence. Soviet Russia joins in the celebration by taking their independence for safekeeping, and preserving Belarusian culture by restricting any expression of it for 70 years.

1930 Soviet leader Joseph Stalin implements the first-ever "censuscide," a government mandate in which workers visit 250,000 homes, execute the residents, and then count them.

1941–1945 Belarus graciously hosts World War II.

1986 Following the Chernobyl nuclear accident, the Soviet Union evacuates hundreds of thousands of Belarusian citizens into the most heavily contaminated areas.

1991 As the U.S.S.R. begins to collapse, Belarus finally redeclares its independence. Thousands of sickly gray, pockmarked citizens hit the streets, where their bodies promptly fall apart.

Miss Belarus 2007

Zone of heavy industry possibly least-polluted area in all of Belarus

Peat bog off-limits for another 20,000 years

Especially terrifying radioactive wolf pack ✕

☐ School for the non-deformed

☐ Small human settlement

☐ Rarely used bike path

✕ Mother giving death to third child

Brain Groves

Pregnant woman suffering from morning radiation sickness throwing up her fetus ✕

☐ Beautiful new gated-fallout-shelter community

Lake of Ash

✕ WHO worker sobbing uncontrollably

☐ Studio where *Belarus' Scariest Home Videos* is shot

✕ Meal being cooked over open hole in ground

★ **Minsk**
Home of the 3006 Nuclear Winter Olympics

✕ Sentient bowl of plastic fruit

☐ First-aid kit full of shotgun shells

☐ Extra Eyeball Drop-Off Center

■ Site of Annual Glowing Man Festival

☐ Naturally illuminated spas

■ Emergency fallout ditch

Absolute Void In Time And Space Left By Stalin

☐ Mass grave and daycare center

✕ Ancestral home of comic-book onomatopoeia

Zone Of Alienation

■ Zombie-free stretch of border

• *City would gladly give up riverfront location to be a little farther east*

✕ Mutated 12th finger has made this sweatshop worker's job easier

✕ Glowing beaver with strength of 10 men

Overrun By Flaming Three-Foot Cockroaches

Polonium River

Lake Waubegonsk, where the women are sterile, the men are hairless, and all the children exhibit above-average levels of Cesium-137

FACTS » STILL UNDER QUARANTINE

ETHNICITY/RACE
Belarusian (81.2%), Russian (11.4%), Puddles (7.4%)

AREA
80,155 sq. mi. of mass graves and concrete bunkers

TERRAIN
Mountainous region with rolling, luminescent hills and glorious, radioactive sunsets

PRECIOUS COMMODITIES
Hair, teeth, skin

GOVERNMENT
Republic with three arms of government: The president's left arm writes the laws, his right arm enforces the laws, and the one coming out of his chest beats criminals over the head

FASHION
Sleeveless Hazmat suits that let extra limbs breathe; stylish, form-fitting lead vests

TRANSPORTATION
Shambling, lurching, dripping, spreading

CLIMATE
Moist warm summers, cold nuclear winters

HOSPITALS' WISH LIST
Basic equipment, vaccines, pharmaceuticals, walls, roof

HALF-LIFE EXPECTANCY
Men: 41,000
Women: 44,000

LITERACY RATE
98% can accurately read a Geiger counter

POTABLE WATER
Most of the drinking water was poisoned during the 1930s, but thanks to a modern de-Stalinization process, much of the poison will be usable again

Family Life
Dinner is a time for Belarusian families to catch up on the day's events, talk about their problems, and check each other's radiation levels.

PEOPLE » THE SONS AND DAUGHTERS OF ATOM

The Soviet Union had an undeniable influence on Belarus: Many Belarusians still speak Russian, bear Russian-made scars, and emit traces of highly unstable Russian uranium thanks to the Soviets' laissez-faire attitude toward nuclear safety. A family-oriented society, most citizens prefer to spend time with their wives and children in the comfort of their own solid-lead underground shelters. Some have also developed unusual physical powers in recent years, such as superhuman strength, shape-shifting tumors, and the ability to liquefy at will.

Poland

Rotate Page 360 Degrees To Read

Once a society of hunter-gatherers, where the men stalked wild berries and the women died collecting buffalo from the field, the nation of Poland is better known today for a number of cultural achievements, including the screen-door submarine, the glass-bottom locomotive, and the cordless extension cord.

Bordered by the Baltic Sea, where hundreds of Polish fish drown every day, and occupying a strategic location on top of land instead of water, Poland has been the victim of numerous invasions, the quickest taking place during World War I, when German troops used the military tactic of marching in backwards to convince everyone they were actually leaving.

By 1939, Germany had invaded again, this time with the intent of eradicating the nation's entire population, a harrowing threat citizens continue to face whenever they come across a bottle of polish remover.

Today, however, Poland is a free and democratic republic. It successfully elected its first non-duck official in 2004, recovered economically from a power outage that left hundreds trapped on shopping-mall escalators in 2005, and in 2006, completely turned its tourist industry around—a task that took 1,000,001 citizens: one to serve patrons lunch, and a million to rotate the restaurant.

Map labels

- Site where 747 airliner crashed into Polish cemetery; rescue workers have so far uncovered 2,450 bodies
- ☐ Offshore apple orchard
- Underwater electrical outlet
- ✕ Polish citizen delivering Polack joke wrong
- Most of region's meats imprisoned in cold, gelatinous molds
- ✕ Region has lowest life expectancy for potatoes in world
- ✕ Polish man discovering long-lost twin in front of mirror
- ✕ Site of some awful Jew-slaughtering thing
- ✕ Communal pierogi
- *Vast, Depressing Stretches Of Gray*
- ✕ Sparse clump of vegetation clinging desperately to soil
- ✕ Mule pulling stubborn Pole
- Statue of Polish soldier riding underneath horse ☐
- **Warsaw ★** *Star put next to city to help remind citizens it's the nation's capital*
- ✕ Bleak, soul-crushing amusement park
- ☐ Yuri's House Of Beets
- ☐ Yuri's House Of Cabbage
- Border around Poland appears and disappears depending on whim of surrounding nations
- ✕ Colorblind citizen not missing out on much
- ☐ Yuri's House Of Suicide
- ✕ Frightening Pole with arms the size of your legs, and legs the size of your arms
- ✕ Monochromatic region colorized by Ted Turner in 1989
- ✕ Although outwardly cold, Polish citizens here are surprisingly dead on the inside
- ✕ Sausage being stuffed with feelings of regret, sorrow
- ✕ Joke wouldn't seem so funny if this were *your* husband dying of old age inside a revolving door
- ✕ Historians are able to trace last 50 years of cultural upheaval just by looking at this old Polish woman's face
- Shhh! People are trying to suffer here!

FACTS » SEE "FACTS"

LOCATION
Poland

AGE EXPECTANCY AT BIRTH
0 years

EMIGRATION RATE
Left before officials had a chance to count

NATURAL HAZARDS
Using fork to get spoon out of toaster

FERTILITY RATE
4 infants/woman, as someone once read that every fifth child born in the world is Chinese

HISTORY » EUROPE'S OLD STOMPING GROUNDS

A.D. 200–1800 Poland is occupied by the Romans, the Turks, several Mongol hordes, the Cossacks, France, Kenya, the Sioux Indians of the North American Great Plains, and a group of three tough-looking teenagers.

1861 Russian troops fire on a crowd protesting Russian rule in Warsaw. They also fire on a crowd celebrating Russian rule in Warsaw.

Poland's Annual Lightbulb-Changing Festival

1915 After a number of violent clashes, German and Russian forces finally decide to just let Poland choose who gets to occupy it.

1918 Poland is granted independence by Allied forces for 37 seconds.

1934 Germany signs a 10-year non-aggression pact with Poland, guaranteeing that it will not invade the nation, that it has no intention of rounding up its citizens in temporary ghettos, and that it would never even think of transporting those citizens to various death camps set up in major Polish cities in the spring of 1940.

1940 The death camp of Auschwitz celebrates its grand opening in Poland with a special "Jews Get In Free" promotion.

1941 Nazi commander Heinrich Himmler arrives unannounced at Auschwitz for a surprise inspection. Death-camp officials run around killing thousand of Jews as SS officers stall Himmler at the entrance gate.

1945 Allied forces liberate 4 million Polish corpses.

1947 Poland turns to Communism in the belief that only by becoming a classless society, with all citizens working together as one, can it truly succeed in screwing in a lightbulb.

1955 Poland establishes the Warsaw Pact to counter alleged threats from NATO, protect its interests from Eastern invasion, and get all of its members—even Bulgaria—laid by the end of the summer.

1978 After eating a record 86 straight communion wafers and swimming across Lake Mazury with a lit prayer candle in his ass, Cardinal Wojtyla of Poland is anointed as Pope John Paul II.

2001 Although the traveling salesman did seem strangely familiar at the time, Poland doesn't realize it has signed into the U.S.-led Coalition Of The Willing until it's too late.

Pope John Paul II

2005 Pope John Paul II's medical condition is upgraded to "deceased."

Czech Republic

» VACLAV HAVEL WELCOMES YOU TO THE CZECH REPUBLIC.

Where People Go To Say They've Been

Whether guzzling beers in the general vicinity of historic Old Town Square, or passed out drunk in one of Moravia's rustic villages, backpackers from around the world travel to the Czech Republic to become cultured.

Eager to take in all the history and tradition within a two-block radius, visitors awake at the crack of noon, hurriedly devour traditional Czech cuisine to soothe their raging hangovers, and set out to broaden their horizons by staring slack-jawed at buildings they were told are important or something.

Many stand impatiently before the famous Astronomical Clock, glancing down at their watch to see if they've been there long enough to grow as human beings, and if they can still make it back to their hostel in time for the complimentary brunch.

Still, no soul-searching journey is complete without a trip to Prague Castle to use the restroom before heading out to a local pub.

After leaving, the newly enlightened backpackers may forget about the Charles Bridge and Tyn Cathedral, but they will always remember the first time they gazed in awe at the shape of their room's electrical outlet.

HISTORY » STILL IN FIRST-DRAFT FORM

A.D. 1300 Bohemia is created as an "alternative space" for free-thinking, free-living, and free-loading artists and poets around Europe.

1415 Theologian and religious thinker Jan Hus is burned alive at the stake to teach Bohemian writers a real-life lesson in symbolism.

1784 Invention of bifocals increases the nation's perceived intelligence by 32%.

1846 Czechoslovakian poet Karel J. Erben revolutionizes the writing process by inventing procrastination.

1915 Franz Kafka awakes in bed one morning, and suddenly realizes he has to write an entire short story by noon.

1939 The country is overrun by German Brainstormtroopers, who challenge the Czechs to quickly come up with rich, nuanced reasons why they should not be executed.

1968 After an unsuccessful book-burning fails to stifle independent thinking, Socialist forces organize a Czech author-burning.

1978 Vaclav Havel pens an absurdist play in which a poor, dissenting playwright becomes the president of a European nation. The play becomes so popular that the nation decides to base an actual election on it in 1989. Havel goes on to rule the nation for 13 years, delighting the populace with his portrayal of an international ambassador for human rights and democracy.

1992 Three years after the two nations split up in the Velvet Divorce, the Czech Republic and Slovakia reunite for one awkward night.

1999 The UN refuses to publish the Czech Republic's international treatise on economic disparities between developing nations set in the year 2056.

PEOPLE » LEFT TO THEIR OWN PLOT DEVICES

The Czech Republic—most notably its capital city, Prague—is populated primarily by backpack-laden people in their mid-20s. These individuals, armed with just a pen, some notebook paper, and an inability to censor themselves, have committed some of the world's most heinous crimes against literature, each of which has been extensively recorded by the perpetrators themselves and brazenly shown to friends and relatives.

A majority of the conflicts they've created remain unresolved to this day.

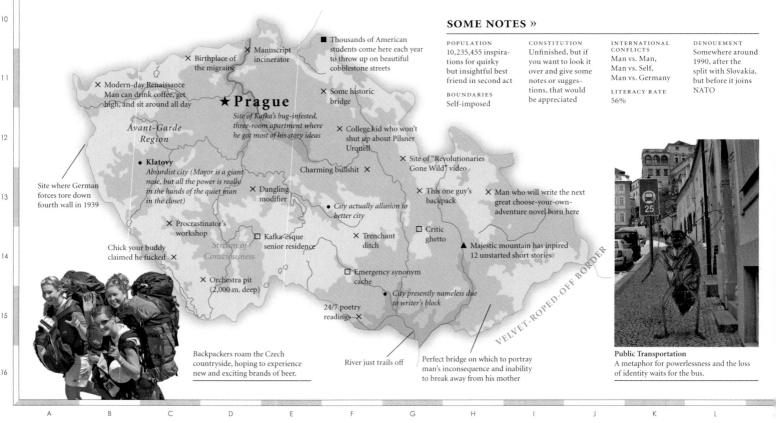

SOME NOTES »

POPULATION
10,235,455 inspirations for quirky but insightful best friend in second act

BOUNDARIES
Self-imposed

CONSTITUTION
Unfinished, but if you want to look it over and give some notes or suggestions, that would be appreciated

INTERNATIONAL CONFLICTS
Man vs. Man, Man vs. Self, Man vs. Germany

LITERACY RATE
56%

DENOUEMENT
Somewhere around 1990, after the split with Slovakia, but before it joins NATO

Map labels

- Manuscript incinerator
- Birthplace of the migraine
- Modern-day Renaissance Man can drink coffee, get high, and sit around all day
- Thousands of American students come here each year to throw up on beautiful cobblestone streets
- Some historic bridge
- ★ Prague
- *Site of Kafka's bug-infested, three-room apartment where he got most of his story ideas*
- *Avant-Garde Region*
- College kid who won't shut up about Pilsner Urquell
- • Klatovy *Absurdist city (Mayor is a giant nose, but all the power is really in the hands of the quiet man in the closet)*
- Charming bullshit
- Site of "Revolutionaries Gone Wild" video
- Site where German forces tore down fourth wall in 1939
- Dangling modifier
- This one guy's backpack
- Man who will write the next great choose-your-own-adventure novel born here
- Procrastinator's workshop
- *City actually allusion to better city*
- Kafka-esque senior residence
- Trenchant ditch
- Critic ghetto
- Chick your buddy claimed he fucked
- *Stream of Consciousness*
- Majestic mountain has inpired 12 unstarted short stories
- Orchestra pit (2,000 m. deep)
- Emergency synonym cache
- *City presently nameless due to writer's block*
- 24/7 poetry readings
- *VELVET-ROPED-OFF BORDER*

Backpackers roam the Czech countryside, hoping to experience new and exciting brands of beer.

River just trails off

Perfect bridge on which to portray man's inconsequence and inability to break away from his mother

Public Transportation
A metaphor for powerlessness and the loss of identity waits for the bus.

A B C D E F G H I J K L

Slovakia

Don't Breathe The Air

Lacking the proper ventilation of most nations, this smoke-filled former Soviet state is home to several Communist monuments to inefficiency, hundreds of leaky, Russian-made factories, and Eastern Europe's chunkiest air.

Gazing across Slovakia's incredible rainbow of gray, one's eyes begin to well up at the sight of endless smokestacks, turning to a sharp, stinging pain as they strain to make out the vague shape of a landfill closer to the horizon, until they finally burst into uncontrollable, burning tears as one takes in the scope of the country's immense acid rain forests.

Recent attempts to clean up Slovakia's natural smoglands have been met with fierce opposition from a widespread campaign of emphysema.

Bratislava
Slovakia's capital boasts breathtaking views.

HISTORY » CONQUER, ABANDON, REPEAT

A.D. 1241 Slovaks play an essential role thwarting the Mongol advance into Europe by acting as human shields, human stabbing cushions, and human trampolines.

1536 The Ottoman Empire seizes Slovakia, but despite bringing thousands of foot-rests, still finds the country's standard of living rooms far too low.

1867–1918 The Austro-Hungarian Empire, unable to eliminate all of the resilient Slovaks, issues a proclamation urging them to die.

1918 After decades of abuse, Czechoslovakia is quietly formed by taking the names of two countries, jamming them together, and hoping other nations won't be able to figure out who they are.

1939 Slovakia claims independence as a fascist state. The Nazis express support by annexing Slovakia, picking up a nasty case of hoof-and-mouth disease in the process.

1942–1944 Over 70,000 Slovak Jews are sent to concentration camps. An underground resistance movement gains support due to objections over the burning-Jew smell.

1948 Communists gain control after organizing mass protests against human-Slovak rights.

1968 The U.S.S.R. disagrees with Slovak leader Alexander Dubcek's vision to "put a human face on Socialism," prompting an invasion and the removal of Dubcek's face.

1975 U.S.S.R. builds an Iron Curtain around Slovakia after running out of funds to put up a much thicker Lead Curtain.

1993 Czechoslovakia splits in the Velvet Divorce, with Slovakia getting half the life expectancy and the Czech Republic taking all the good air.

2004 Slovakia is finally admitted to the EU after a long campaign by the Make-A-Wish Foundation.

AIRBORNE FACT PARTICLES »

AREA COMPARATIVE
Paper bag attached to a tailpipe

INTERNATIONAL RELATIONS
Downwind countries complain that Slovakia's air is ruining their curtains

HEALTH
With new education and wellness programs, the government now strongly urges the dead to quit smoking

CURRENCY
36.77 pounds of koruny equal $1 U.S.

CRIME
Prostitution and drug abuse are on the rise, which many Slovaks deal with by taking up drugs and prostitution

TOURISM
Traditionally conducted by 30,000 men driving tanks

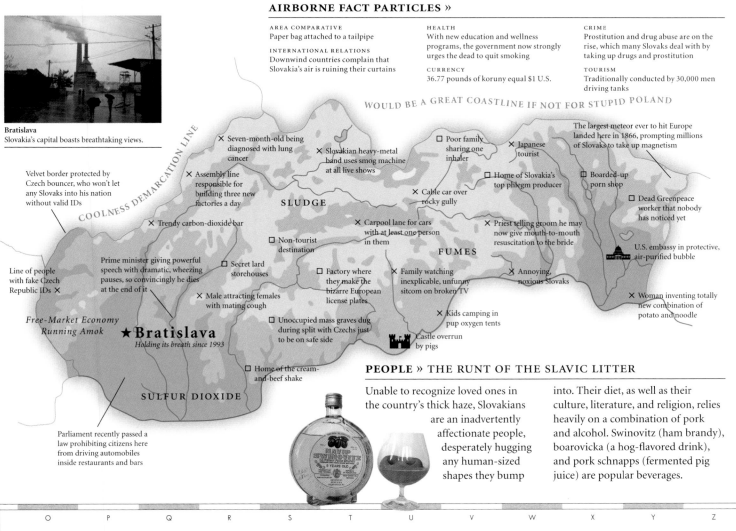

WOULD BE A GREAT COASTLINE IF NOT FOR STUPID POLAND

COOLNESS DEMARCATION LINE

× Seven-month-old being diagnosed with lung cancer

× Assembly line responsible for building three new factories a day

× Slovakian heavy-metal band uses smog machine at all live shows

□ Poor family sharing one inhaler

× Japanese tourist

The largest meteor ever to hit Europe landed here in 1866, prompting millions of Slovaks to take up magnetism

□ Home of Slovakia's top phlegm producer

□ Boarded-up porn shop

SLUDGE

× Trendy carbon-dioxide bar

× Cable car over rocky gully

□ Dead Greenpeace worker that nobody has noticed yet

Velvet border protected by Czech bouncer, who won't let any Slovaks into his nation without valid IDs

× Carpool lane for cars with at least one person in them

× Priest telling groom he may now give mouth-to-mouth resuscitation to the bride

U.S. embassy in protective, air-purified bubble

□ Non-tourist destination

FUMES

Line of people with fake Czech Republic IDs ×

Prime minister giving powerful speech with dramatic, wheezing pauses, so convincingly he dies at the end of it

□ Secret lard storehouses

□ Factory where they make the bizarre European license plates

× Family watching inexplicable, unfunny sitcom on broken TV

× Annoying, noxious Slovaks

× Woman inventing totally new combination of potato and noodle

× Male attracting females with mating cough

Free-Market Economy Running Amok

★ **Bratislava**
Holding its breath since 1993

□ Unoccupied mass graves dug during split with Czechs just to be on safe side

× Kids camping in pup oxygen tents

Castle overrun by pigs

□ Home of the cream-and-beef shake

SULFUR DIOXIDE

Parliament recently passed a law prohibiting citizens here from driving automobiles inside restaurants and bars

PEOPLE » THE RUNT OF THE SLAVIC LITTER

Unable to recognize loved ones in the country's thick haze, Slovakians are an inadvertently affectionate people, desperately hugging any human-sized shapes they bump into. Their diet, as well as their culture, literature, and religion, relies heavily on a combination of pork and alcohol. Swinovitz (ham brandy), boarovicka (a hog-flavored drink), and pork schnapps (fermented pig juice) are popular beverages.

Hungary

» HUNGARY ADMITS THAT IT GOT A LITTLE CAUGHT UP IN EUROPE'S BIG TRICOLOR FAD.

Must Be 18 Years Or Older To Enter

Now the adult-film capital of the world, the nation of Hungary first started doing a little porn back in the '80s to make some extra GDP. Today, 70% of the population is employed as porn stars, porn directors, porn script supervisors, porn gaffers, and porn extras, while the other 30% just likes to watch.

Hungary has a rich tradition in both classical and folk pornography, but in today's competitive market, they have begun to offer more sophisticated adult fare, including peep operas, girl-on-girl symphonies, and all-anal one-act plays.

Known for its liberal outlook, Hungary is a strong advocate of same-sex sex, and it broke down longstanding barriers in 1998 when it became the first nation to televise an interracial fisting scene.

Its gender equality ranks among the best in the world, with more Hungarian women moving away from traditional roles such as horny housewives and mothers whom people would like to fuck, and instead becoming busty CEOs, slutty teachers, and skanky doctors.

In addition, Hungary's progressive health-care system offers full coverage for all severe throat abrasions, critically calloused knees, and brutally fucked skulls.

A GIANT LOAD OF FACTS »

OFFICIAL NAME
Hungary

PORN NAME
Gary Hung

AGE STRUCTURE
Barely legal: 39%
Just 19: 20%
Mature: 41%

RESOURCES
100% natural

CLITERACY RATE
99%

POPULATION GROWTH RATE
–25%, as most semen ends up on breasts and faces

CONSTITUTION
Revised in 1972 with addition of pull-out centerfold

INTERNET COUNTRY CODE
.xxx

MALE LABOR FORCE BY OCCUPATION
Pool boys: 5.5%
Pizza guys: 33.3%
Repairmen: 61.2%

GLAND USE
Sucking: 31%
Rubbing: 33%
Licking: 36%

LOWEST POINT
When visiting UN delegate recognized one of Hungary's representatives from *Skin Merchant II*

TRADITIONAL HANDICRAFTS
Anal beads, pearl necklaces

CONDOM USES
Protecting against STDs, drinking out of

LEADING CAUSE OF DEATH
Underpenetration

HISTORY » PASSED DOWN THROUGH NONSTOP SLOPPY ORAL TRADITION

3000 B.C. Ancient cave splatterings reveal what early Hungarians did after hunting.

A.D. 123 Archaeologists in Hungary unearth the first roughly hewn sex toys, including an obsidian dildo perfectly preserved in a layer of amber jizz.

451 Known for his controversial war tactics, Attila the Hun wins the Battle of Chalons-sur-Marne when he pretends like he just got seriously hurt, and then after opposing forces stop to make sure he's okay, immediately slaughters thousands of them.

Stephen III

1162 After the stressful, uptight reign of King Géza II, King Stephen III immediately wins over his populace by asking them to just call him Stephen, or if they prefer, King S.

1241 Hungary's borders are penetrated by invading Mongol hordes. It hurts the first few times, but each successive penetration feels so great that Hungarians soon invite Ottoman tribes to invade them from the other side at the same time.

Harry Houdini

1874 Budapest-born Harry Houdini performs perhaps his greatest stunt when, after spending nine months in a confined space without food or oxygen, he masterfully escapes his mother's womb.

1918 Austria-Hungary's military is dishonorably discharged from WWI.

1949 Communist-run "secret police" ineffectively attempt to terrorize the Hungarians by writing several parking tickets for citizens and never telling them about it.

1956 An anti-Communist uprising begins in Hungary.

This movement becomes so popular that it is followed by an anti-Stalinist uprising, an anti-Soviet uprising, and a pro-uprising uprising.

1989 Communism proves that it can effectively create a free and equal society by ending.

2007 Hungary's porn industry suffers a huge downturn, as nations that used to purchase full-length videos now just choose to import a few eight-second clips for free.

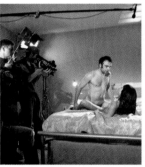

A Scenic View Of Budapest
The natural beauty of Hungary is captured daily and sent around the world for a small fee.

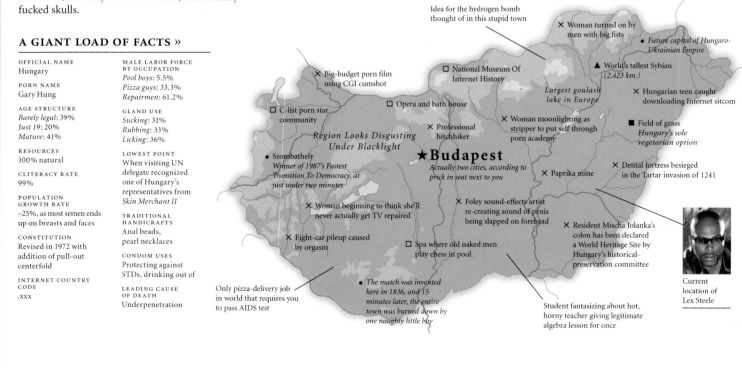

Idea for the hydrogen bomb thought of in this stupid town

✗ Woman turned on by men with big fists

• *Future capital of Hungaro-Ukrainian Empire*

▲ World's tallest Sybian *(2,423 km.)*

□ National Museum Of Internet History

✗ Big-budget porn film using CGI cumshot

□ Opera and bath house

Largest goulash lake in Europe

✗ Hungarian teen caught downloading Internet sitcom

□ C-list porn star community

Region Looks Disgusting Under Blacklight

✗ Professional hitchhiker

✗ Woman moonlighting as stripper to put self through porn academy

■ Field of grass *Hungary's sole vegetarian option*

• Szombathely
Winner of 1987's Fastest Transition To Democracy, at just under two minutes

★ **Budapest**
Actually two cities, according to prick in seat next to you

✗ Paprika mine

✗ Dental fortress besieged in the Tartar invasion of 1241

✗ Woman beginning to think she'll never actually get TV repaired

✗ Foley sound-effects artist re-creating sound of penis being slapped on forehead

✗ Resident Mischa Jolanka's colon has been declared a World Heritage Site by Hungary's historical-preservation committee

✗ Eight-car pileup caused by orgasm

□ Spa where old naked men play chess in pool

Only pizza-delivery job in world that requires you to pass AIDS test

• *The match was invented here in 1836, and 15 minutes later, the entire town was burned down by one naughty little boy*

Student fantasizing about hot, horny teacher giving legitimate algebra lesson for once

Current location of Lex Steele

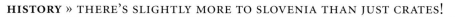

Manufacturing Crates Since 1837

Occupying a strategic crate-producing location in Central Europe, the nation of Slovenia manufactures over 90% of the world's crates. From big crates to little crates to medium-sized crates, this former Yugoslav republic can even produce custom-made crates for special crate-related occasions.

Until 1946, Slovenia only produced square crates, but growing international demand led them to start making crates of varying heights and widths. Slovenia sometimes stores smaller crates inside of larger crates, which saves space and cuts export costs. Slovenia is currently home to the world's largest crate. It is also home to the world's smallest crate.

Today, Slovenia is diversifying its crate-based economy—they have built new lightweight portable crates, made the crates easier to open, and revolutionized the crate industry with their innovative crate-shaped packages.

In 2007, Slovenia produced its first cardboard crate, or box.

HISTORY » THERE'S SLIGHTLY MORE TO SLOVENIA THAN JUST CRATES!

42,000,000,000,000 B.C. Archaeologists discover the oldest-known year.

181–15 B.C. The Romans conquer Slovenia so gradually that the Slovenians don't even notice.

A.D. 955 The Slovenians are forced to forfeit the Battle of Lechfeld to the Germans when their soldiers fail to show up.

1473 Slovenians construct the world's first waterless moat.

1584 The Bible is published in the Slovene language. Citizens are upset to learn that, due to poor translations in the past, they have been worshipping the wrong guy all this time.

1915 Italy and Germany attempt to declare war on Slovenia, but neither can remember the country's name.

1929 The Kingdom of Yugoslavia is founded on the guiding principle of Slovenia, Croatia, Serbia, Montenegro, Bosnia, and Macedonia all being located in the same general area.

1991 Slovenia breaks away from Yugoslavia, knowing that the experience will someday make a good essay topic.

1992 The world's cartographers bemoan the dissolution of Yugoslavia.

2002 Even though the nation doesn't know what any of them stand for, Slovenia joins international organizations OPCW, OSCE, SECI, EIB, IOM, FAO, and UPU, solely because it believes they will look good on its EU resume.

2004 Slovenia receives notice by mail that it has been admitted to the EU, and knows right away that it got in because of the size of the envelope. The nation immediately purchases several EU hats and sweatshirts.

Some of Slovenia's oldest, most beloved crates.

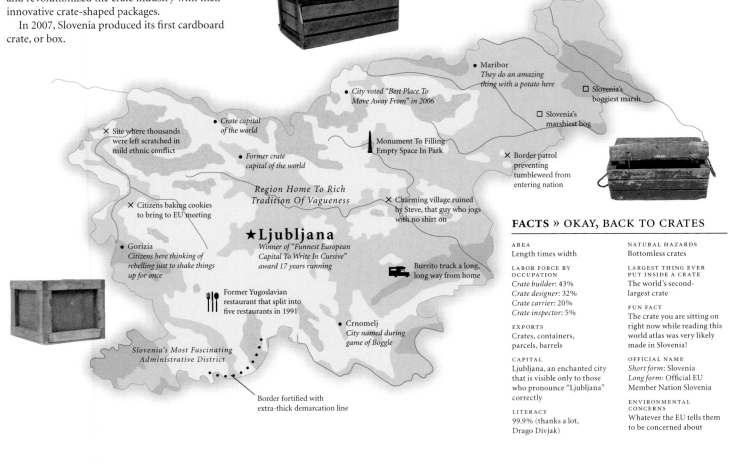

- • Maribor
  They do an amazing thing with a potato here
- □ Slovenia's boggiest marsh
- • City voted "Best Place To Move Away From" in 2006
- □ Slovenia's marshiest bog
- × Site where thousands were left scratched in mild ethnic conflict
- • *Crate capital of the world*
- ▮ Monument To Filling Empty Space In Park
- • *Former crate capital of the world*
- × Border patrol preventing tumbleweed from entering nation
- × Citizens baking cookies to bring to EU meeting
- *Region Home To Rich Tradition Of Vagueness*
- × Charming village ruined by Steve, that guy who jogs with no shirt on
- • Gorizia *Citizens here thinking of rebelling just to shake things up for once*
- ★ **Ljubljana** *Winner of "Funnest European Capital To Write In Cursive" award 17 years running*
- 🍴 Former Yugoslavian restaurant that split into five restaurants in 1991
- 🚚 Burrito truck a long, long way from home
- • Crnomelj *City named during game of Boggle*
- *Slovenia's Most Fascinating Administrative District*
- Border fortified with extra-thick demarcation line

FACTS » OKAY, BACK TO CRATES

AREA
Length times width

LABOR FORCE BY OCCUPATION
Crate builder: 43%
Crate designer: 32%
Crate carrier: 20%
Crate inspector: 5%

EXPORTS
Crates, containers, parcels, barrels

CAPITAL
Ljubljana, an enchanted city that is visible only to those who pronounce "Ljubljana" correctly

LITERACY
99.9% (thanks a lot, Drago Divjak)

NATURAL HAZARDS
Bottomless crates

LARGEST THING EVER PUT INSIDE A CRATE
The world's second-largest crate

FUN FACT
The crate you are sitting on right now while reading this world atlas was very likely made in Slovenia!

OFFICIAL NAME
Short form: Slovenia
Long form: Official EU Member Nation Slovenia

ENVIRONMENTAL CONCERNS
Whatever the EU tells them to be concerned about

Croatia

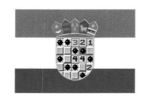

Where All Roads Lead To Serious Injury

From the rolling, explosive foothills in the north to the constantly detonating Dinaric Alps in the south, to the sometimes stunning, sometimes suddenly horrific coastline on the Adriatic Sea, the former Yugoslav republic of Croatia possesses the highest concentration of landmines in the world.

Despite the 1 million mines laid to hold back Serbian forces during a bloody war for independence in 1991, the 2 million more used after the war to keep civilians from walking into old minefields, and an additional 300,000 employed recently to protect what little unaffected terrain remains, Croatia is one of the most beautiful destinations on earth—one that many Croats, too frightened to leave their homes, hope to someday visit again.

HISTORY » MARCHING EVER CAUTIOUSLY INTO THE FUTURE

A.D. 600 Croat tribes settle in what is now Croatia. Instead of tilling the fields or establishing some sort of dukedom, they spend their first 200 years staring slack-jawed at the land's stunning beauty.

1413–1652 Croat mercenaries in traditional uniforms introduce the cravat to Western Europe and the Middle East. This leads Austrian and Ottoman forces, who can never remember how to fasten the complicated necktie, to invade Croatia before every wedding and formal function.

1918–1945 The former kingdoms of Croatia, Serbia, Montenegro, Bosnia and Herzegovina, along with Dalmatia and Slovenia, form the First Yugoslavia, a unified state that lasts surprisingly long considering the innate pessimism of its name.

1941 Under control of Nazi Germany, a radical Croat regime slaughters nearly 200,000 Serbs, Romans, Jews, and Gypsies at some of the most open-minded, ethnically diverse concentration camps in all of Europe.

1945–1991 The Second through 23rd Yugoslavias are formed.

1991 Concerned about growing tension with Serbia, Croatia declares independence by laying thousands of "sovereignty mines." Three days later, Serbian troops single-handedly take control of the Croatian city of Zadar, after losing their other three limbs in the process.

1994 Croat soldiers use their experience digging holes to bury hundreds of their slain troops and civilians.

1995 Controlling one-third of Croatia, the Serbian army unexpectedly retreats in favor of slaughtering a more fulfilling ethnic minority in Bosnia.

1996 Croatia celebrates its defeat of Serbian forces with the bloodiest, shortest-lived victory march in history.

Sheryl Crow

1999 Following the release of her fifth album, *C'mon C'mon*, singer/songwriter and anti-landmine activist Sheryl Crow receives the first of many invitations from the Croatian government to take an unaccompanied walking tour of the country.

2002 Croatia is eliminated from the World Cup in the first round after team members refuse to set foot on the wide, unmarked field.

2004 In an impassioned speech, President Stjepan Mesic vows to put a man safely on the surface of Croatia by 2012.

PEOPLE » THIS LAND IS MINE LAND

There's more to Croatia than meets the highly trained eye of a certified landmine expert. Croatia is a gender-equal nation, where both men and women prefer to walk three steps behind the other. In fact, the ever-courteous citizens of Croatia can regularly be seen opening doors for their neighbors, and heard desperately insisting that they not be the first ones to walk through the entryway.

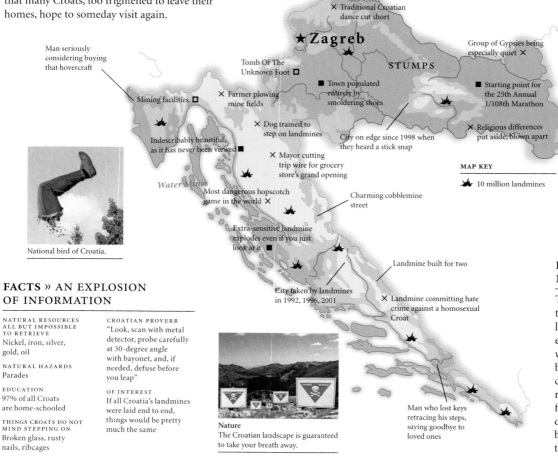

Man seriously considering buying that hovercraft

Tomb Of The Unknown Foot □

★ **Zagreb**

× Traditional Croatian dance cut short

Group of Gypsies being especially quiet ×

STUMPS

Mining facilities □

× Farmer plowing mine fields

■ Town populated entirely by smoldering shoes

■ Starting point for the 25th Annual 1/108th Marathon

× Dog trained to step on landmines

Indescribably beautiful, as it has never been viewed ■

× Religious differences put aside, blown apart

City on edge since 1998 when they heard a stick snap

× Mayor cutting trip wire for grocery store's grand opening

Water Mines

Most dangerous hopscotch game in the world ×

Charming cobblemine street

MAP KEY

✹ 10 million landmines

Extra-sensitive landmine explodes even if you just look at it ■

Landmine built for two

City taken by landmines in 1992, 1996, 2001

× Landmine committing hate crime against a homosexual Croat

Man who lost keys retracing his steps, saying goodbye to loved ones

FACTS » AN EXPLOSION OF INFORMATION

NATURAL RESOURCES ALL BUT IMPOSSIBLE TO RETRIEVE
Nickel, iron, silver, gold, oil

NATURAL HAZARDS
Parades

EDUCATION
97% of all Croats are home-schooled

THINGS CROATS DO NOT MIND STEPPING ON
Broken glass, rusty nails, ribcages

CROATIAN PROVERB
"Look, scan with metal detector, probe carefully at 30-degree angle with bayonet, and, if needed, defuse before you leap"

OF INTEREST
If all Croatia's landmines were laid end to end, things would be pretty much the same

National bird of Croatia.

Nature
The Croatian landscape is guaranteed to take your breath away.

Bosnia & Herzegovina

» A BEAUTIFUL BOSNIAN MASS GRAVE.

Partners In War Crime

Bosnia and Herzegovina, a peace-torn Balkan nation currently struggling through its second consecutive decade of non-warfare, once boasted the world's highest war-crime rate, with a new genocide occurring every 7.2 seconds.

Nearly one out of every one Bosnian has been convicted of war crimes, while the rest have been accused of war misdemeanors and are still awaiting trial. Startling statistics from The Hague reveal that 88% of Bosnian crimes against humanity occur in the home, and that nearly half of the time they are committed against someone the offender knows.

Today, Bosnians are encouraged to notify international officials immediately if they believe a genocide is being carried out against them or a race they love.

PEOPLE » EVERYONE'S GUILTY OF A GENOCIDE OR TWO

Bosnia and Herzegovina is home to four distinct types of people: Bosnian Muslims, Bosnian Serbs, Bosnian Croats, and Europe's top genocide-defense lawyers. The influence of this last group has allowed many Serbs and Croats to walk free after claiming that the systematic extermination of an entire race was "just an accident."

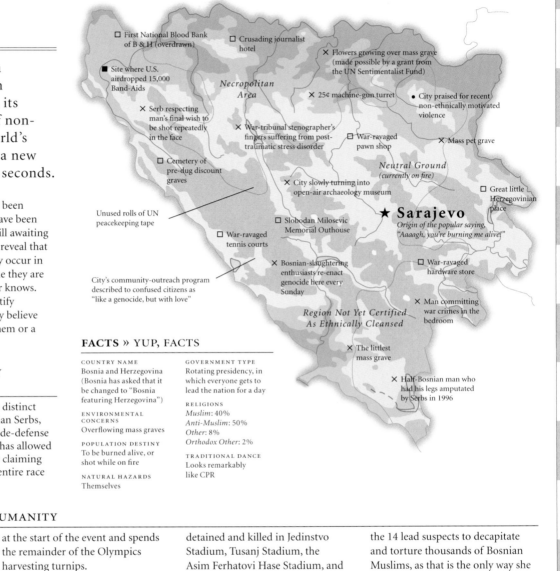

- First National Blood Bank of B & H (overdrawn)
- Crusading journalist hotel
- Site where U.S. airdropped 15,000 Band-Aids
- × Flowers growing over mass grave (made possible by a grant from the UN Sentimentalist Fund)
- Necropolitan Area
- × 25¢ machine-gun turret
- • City praised for recent non-ethnically motivated violence
- × Serb respecting man's final wish to be shot repeatedly in the face
- × War-tribunal stenographer's fingers suffering from post-traumatic stress disorder
- War-ravaged pawn shop
- × Mass pet grave
- Cemetery of pre-dug discount graves
- × City slowly turning into open-air archaeology museum
- Neutral Ground (currently on fire)
- Great little Herzegovinian place
- Unused rolls of UN peacekeeping tape
- Slobodan Milosevic Memorial Outhouse
- ★ **Sarajevo** Origin of the popular saying, "Aaaagh, you're burning me alive"
- × War-ravaged tennis courts
- × Bosnian-slaughtering enthusiasts re-enact genocide here every Sunday
- War-ravaged hardware store
- City's community-outreach program described to confused citizens as "like a genocide, but with love"
- × Man committing war crimes in the bedroom
- Region Not Yet Certified As Ethnically Cleansed
- × The littlest mass grave
- × Half-Bosnian man who had his legs amputated by Serbs in 1996

FACTS » YUP, FACTS

COUNTRY NAME
Bosnia and Herzegovina (Bosnia has asked that it be changed to "Bosnia featuring Herzegovina")

ENVIRONMENTAL CONCERNS
Overflowing mass graves

POPULATION DESTINY
To be burned alive, or shot while on fire

NATURAL HAZARDS
Themselves

GOVERNMENT TYPE
Rotating presidency, in which everyone gets to lead the nation for a day

RELIGIONS
Muslim: 40%
Anti-Muslim: 50%
Other: 8%
Orthodox Other: 2%

TRADITIONAL DANCE
Looks remarkably like CPR

HISTORY » HABITAT FOR INHUMANITY

Gavrilo Princip

A.D. 1914 Bosnian Serb nationalist Gavrilo Princip single-handedly precipitates WWI when he assassinates Austrian archduke Franz Ferdinand in Sarajevo, declares war on Serbia, mobilizes the Russian army, invades Belgium, burns down Germany, leads three separate colonial uprisings in Africa, and posits the theory of Social Darwinism as related to imperialism, nationalism, and domestic economies.

1984 Sarajevo hosts the Winter Olympics, marking the first time the Games are held in a Socialist nation. In accordance with the Socialist ideology of equal distribution, every participant is given one gold medal at the start of the event and spends the remainder of the Olympics harvesting turnips.

1992 The deeply divided ethnic groups of Bosnia hold a referendum on independence, with the 56% of the population comprising Serbs and Croats voting "Yes" and the 44% comprising Bosnian Muslims voting "No, No, No—Don't You See, They're Going To Kill Us All."

1993 War crimes and atrocities are witnessed by human-rights watchdog Champ, a one-year-old golden retriever who unfortunately cannot comprehend these crimes or report them to international officials.

1994 Thousands of Bosnians are detained and killed in Jedinstvo Stadium, Tusanj Stadium, the Asim Ferhatovi Hase Stadium, and the, in retrospect, aptly named Banja Luka Mass Execution Dome.

1995 In a last-ditch effort to prolong violence between Serbs, Croats, and Muslims, the U.S. deploys 50,000 strifekeeping forces to Bosnia.

1996 Bosnia and Herzegovina is conquered by the United Nations.

1998 In order to help increase its dwindling population, Bosnia abolishes death.

2001 Struggling to identify the culprit, the lone witness of the Bosnian genocide asks each of the 14 lead suspects to decapitate and torture thousands of Bosnian Muslims, as that is the only way she would recognize him.

2003 The Hague finds 250,000 deceased Bosnian Muslims guilty of being accessories to genocide, as they knowingly participated in the atrocities and failed to stop dying.

2005 In order to cut travel costs, The Hague opens up a local branch in Sarajevo.

Serbia & Montenegro

SERBIA » SERBIA GETS ONE SPECIAL CREST FOR EVERY FORMER SOCIALIST FEDERATION IT DESTROYS.

MONTENEGRO » MEANT TO BE ANNIVERSARY PRESENT FOR SERBIA, BUT THEN SERBIA HAD TO GO ACT LIKE A JERK.

Serbia
"So We've Done A Little Ethnic Cleansing"

A landlocked country with a genocidal temper, Serbia wasted too many years putting up with a bunch of nagging Yugoslav republics, only to have them all take off at the first sign of ethnic cleansing.

After a long day of supporting the economies of the other five republics, Serbia couldn't even blow off steam by slaughtering a village of Albanians without getting Slovenia or Croatia on its case. When they weren't bitching about the rape camps, these so-called allies were running their mouths off to the UN about how Serbia didn't "respect them as independent nations"—just to be a pain in Serbia's ass.

Though many feared the 2006 separation from its partner country Montenegro would devastate Serbia, the nation insists it couldn't be happier. The Serbian government even issued a public statement of support for its former ally, wishing Montenegro the best of luck finding another country that will want a washed-up Balkan nation with a sagging coastline and a big, fat inflation problem.

Montenegro
Just Getting Out Of A Bad International Relationship

After standing side by side through years of war and peace and war and war and war, Montenegro approved a tear-stained referendum in 2006 to dissolve its loveless union with Serbia.

Despite Serbian diplomats' drunken late-night calls claiming the radio is playing their national anthem, Montenegro is unwilling to reconcile, fearing that Serbia would one day direct its rage at them and turn their entire landscape into a fresh mass grave. With its new independence, Montenegro is finally working on its economy again, which has resulted in a great deal of attention from foreign investors.

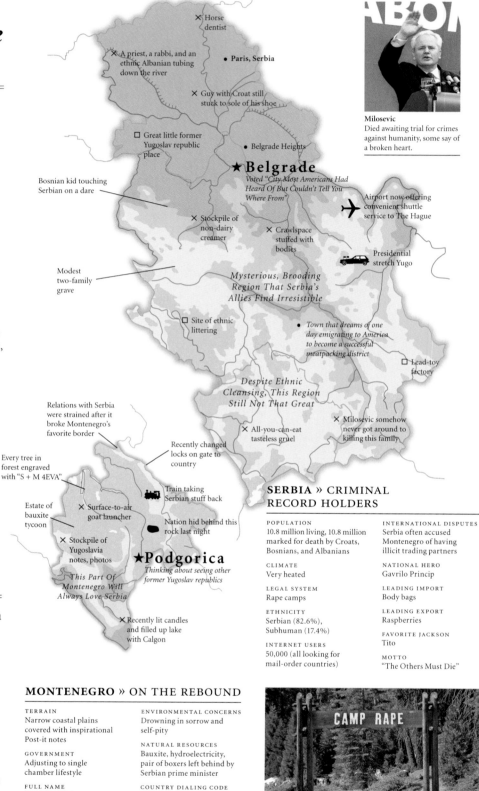

Map labels:
- ✕ Horse dentist
- ✕ A priest, a rabbi, and an ethnic Albanian tubing down the river
- • Paris, Serbia
- ✕ Guy with Croat still stuck to sole of his shoe
- □ Great little former Yugoslav republic place
- • Belgrade Heights
- ★ Belgrade
- Voted "City Most Americans Had Heard Of But Couldn't Tell You Where From"
- Bosnian kid touching Serbian on a dare
- ✕ Stockpile of non-dairy creamer
- ✕ Crawlspace stuffed with bodies
- Airport now offering convenient shuttle service to The Hague
- Presidential stretch Yugo
- Modest two-family grave
- Mysterious, Brooding Region That Serbia's Allies Find Irresistible
- □ Site of ethnic littering
- • Town that dreams of one day emigrating to America to become a successful meatpacking district
- □ Lead-toy factory
- Despite Ethnic Cleansing, This Region Still Not That Great
- ✕ All-you-can-eat tasteless gruel
- ✕ Milosevic somehow never got around to killing this family
- Relations with Serbia were strained after it broke Montenegro's favorite border
- Recently changed locks on gate to country
- Every tree in forest engraved with "S + M 4EVA"
- Estate of bauxite tycoon
- ✕ Surface-to-air goat launcher
- Train taking Serbian stuff back
- Nation hid behind this rock last night
- ✕ Stockpile of Yugoslavia notes, photos
- ★ Podgorica
- Thinking about seeing other former Yugoslav republics
- This Part Of Montenegro Will Always Love Serbia
- ✕ Recently lit candles and filled up lake with Calgon

Milosevic
Died awaiting trial for crimes against humanity, some say of a broken heart.

SERBIA » CRIMINAL RECORD HOLDERS

POPULATION
10.8 million living, 10.8 million marked for death by Croats, Bosnians, and Albanians

CLIMATE
Very heated

LEGAL SYSTEM
Rape camps

ETHNICITY
Serbian (82.6%), Subhuman (17.4%)

INTERNET USERS
50,000 (all looking for mail-order countries)

INTERNATIONAL DISPUTES
Serbia often accused Montenegro of having illicit trading partners

NATIONAL HERO
Gavrilo Princip

LEADING IMPORT
Body bags

LEADING EXPORT
Raspberries

FAVORITE JACKSON
Tito

MOTTO
"The Others Must Die"

MONTENEGRO » ON THE REBOUND

TERRAIN
Narrow coastal plains covered with inspirational Post-it notes

GOVERNMENT
Adjusting to single chamber lifestyle

FULL NAME
Republic of Montenegro (using maiden name)

MOTTO
"You Can Do This"

ENVIRONMENTAL CONCERNS
Drowning in sorrow and self-pity

NATURAL RESOURCES
Bauxite, hydroelectricity, pair of boxers left behind by Serbian prime minister

COUNTRY DIALING CODE
Unlisted

LOWEST POINT
Seeing several thousand tourists in one month just to make Serbia jealous

Serbia's Camp Rape has come under increased international scrutiny following a series of unfortunate accidents involving campers.

Albania

» ONE OF THE FINEST RESORTS IN ALBANIA.

The Haiti Of Europe

Stumbling in pursuit of the Albanian dream, the grumpy and perpetually hungover people of Albania can commonly be seen squatting next to abandoned factories, desperately trying to remember what they did with their economy.

The least-developed country in Europe, tiny Albania remains an intriguing oasis of poverty and chaos in this otherwise staunchly middle-class continent.

Decades under the totalitarian government of Communist Enver Hoxha saw the nation's tin factories nationalized, their gruel strictly rationed, and their populace razed to make room for socialist housing projects.

The last Europeans to be housebroken, the Albanians could only watch, slack-jawed and drooling, as the Western world learned to hate them for being Communist in addition to hating them for being Albanian.

Political dissenters were soon unibrowbeaten into submission. Their attempts to flee the country were futile, as their crudely fashion rafts were ill-suited for escape attempts through the Dinaric Alps, and their heavily laden mule caravans proved woefully inadequate when crossing the Adriatic Sea.

Since the fall of Communism, Albanians have fled like greased rodents into neighboring countries, where they are unwelcome and even persecuted for a multitude of very good reasons.

The 6:04 a.m. shuttle to Tirana.

FACTS » HAIRY

POPULATION
3.5 million

EMIGRATION-VISA APPLICATIONS PENDING
3.5 million

NATIONAL HOLIDAY
Wailing Day (May 3)

LOCAL GREETING
"Why are you here?"

BIRTH RATE
Highest in Europe

INFANT MORTALITY RATE
Highest in Europe

ALPHABETIC RANK IN EUROPE
First

RANK IN ALL OTHER EUROPEAN STATISTICS
Last

LEGAL SYSTEM
Blood feuds

BONO AWARENESS RATING
0.1

BORDER TO HELL
BORDER TO GREATER HELL

□ Bus driving school
□ Bus hijacking school
□ Donkey whipping post
✕ Horse-and-cart congestion
□ Gypsy preserve
Region Almost As Two-Dimensional As Map Suggests
□ Gruel plantation
• Peshkopi *Formerly Peshkoni until citizens informed mapmakers of their typo in 2001*
✕ Nation's sole VCR
■ Natural deposits of U.S. nickels
★ **Tirana** *Failure to build road out of town has left residents trapped for over three centuries*
BORDER TO LESSER HELL
□ Europe's largest concrete slab
✕ Official Albanian cat-drowning site
Slogging Grounds
□ Vest factory
✕ State-owned radio chained to tree
□ Two-headed-eagle reserve
✕ Villagers surviving on recycled beef
Government-Sanctioned Suicide Bluffs
Tumbleweed Trail
224 MILES OF GORGEOUS COASTLINE WASTED ON ALBANIANS
⬛ Grease reserve
✕ Dry-out spot
✕ Funland Goat-Cart Track
□ Museum Of The 41°00′N, 20°00′E Coordinates
Stone Silence
BORDER TO SEMI-NON-HELL (CLOSED)

HISTORY » DEVELOPMENTALLY DISABLED

A.D. 1421 Modern Albania is hewn from the stone cliffs of the Balkan Peninsula by the thick-armed and hairy-backed *homo albaniens*, a species of sub-hominids somewhat related to humans.

1478 The Ottoman Empire conquers Albania, forcing the country to convert to Islam. The Albanians are fascinated by the Holy Qur'an, as it can be torn up and put to good use in their outhouses, and is softer than tree bark and twigs.

1928 Ahmet Zogu is crowned King Zog of Albania after his campaign promise of a varmint in every pot.

1934 Exhausted by the squalor of her homeland and the hopelessness of its citizens, Mother Teresa picks up and moves to India.

1940–1945 Albania is one of the few European countries to protect its Jews from the Holocaust, worried that the standard of living in the concentration camps would spoil them.

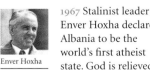

Enver Hoxha

1967 Stalinist leader Enver Hoxha declares Albania to be the world's first atheist state. God is relieved.

1970 Cut off from Communist China, Albania is forced to survive on its own cabbage reserves for the next 20 years.

1992 After years of brutal Communist rule, Albania collapses into democracy.

1996 The new capitalist economy of Albania is set back when the entire population is duped into a pyramid scheme.

1999 During the war in Kosovo, the Albanian tourism ministry launches the "Albania: It's Nicer Than Genocide" campaign to attract refugees.

2000 At long last, Albania begins to emerge from its long spell of hard luck, welcoming tourists to its balmy Mediterranean shores and incredibly desperate hotels where a week in a charming concrete bunker on the Albanian Riviera can be yours for just 300 lekë.

2001 The first census in 12 years reveals Albanians still can't count.

Jim Belushi

2004 The UN rules that the slaughter of 3,000 ethnic Albanians was a justified retaliation for the renewal of Albanian-descendant Jim Belushi's sitcom *According To Jim*.

Greece

» ONE DAY ZEUS WILL SHATTER THIS USELESS CROSS WITH HIS MIGHTY THUNDERBOLT.

PLEDGE WEEK ΠΚΦ

2,500 Years Past Its Prime

Ancient Greece was the birthplace of art, science, democracy, medicine, poetry, and philosophy. Today, however, the nation has more important things to do than contribute to the advancement of the human race.

Modern Greeks have bills to pay and families to provide for. Sure, they would love to sit around all day deducing things and studying triangles, but unfortunately, triangles don't cut it in the real world. There is work to be done, and the less time one spends contemplating his own existence, the faster he can get home.

With 20% of the population living in poverty, most citizens are more worried about putting food on the table than developing entire mathematical systems to judge spatial distance. In fact, the only equation the Greeks have produced in the past 2,000 years is that time equals money.

Even if citizens had the energy to construct towering marvels of architecture or document 40 years of history when they got home from work, by the time they were done, they would be unemployed and divorced. And in the 21st century, the Socratic method can't put the kids through college.

Although present-day Greeks have not gotten around to making any lasting cultural achievements, they point out that if their ancient ancestors had rising mortgage rates to deal with, perhaps we wouldn't have physics today.

PEOPLE » THE CHILDREN OF ZEUS AND SOME GOAT HE FUCKED

The people of Greece were once ruled by the gods of Mt. Olympus, whom they worshipped, prayed to, and occasionally had sex with. Today, however, most Greeks have turned away from mighty Zeus, instead choosing to follow Jesus Christ, who has never thrown a single thunderbolt in his life, and whose only power is Sin-Forgiving.

Greeks are known for their love of food, as one cannot meet a Greek person without being offered something to eat, something to drink, a menu, your choice of seating, and the day's specials. They accept nothing other than cash in return for their goodwill.

The Greeks' success in the diner industry is logical, as they have a reputation for being a hospitable and generous people, especially with the cucumber sauce.

BULGARIA

MACEDONIA

ALBANIA

Governed By Goats

Statue depicting the great armless people of ancient Greece

× Site of first-history-related pop quiz

□ Demetrios & Sons Roofing & Siding securing contract to rebuild Parthenon

● Oracle of Delphi psychic readings

Birth Canal Of Civilization

Region overseen by Greek god of drainage basins

Guy selling columns out of the back of his chariot

× Poseidon letting global warming do all the work

● Birthplace of phrases "Eureka!" and "Fuck, wait, never mind"

× Perfectly preserved triangle from 480 B.C.

⚠ Watch for falling Parthenon

★ **Athens**
Site of the first Olympics, and, after a catastrophic earthquake five years later, the first Paralympics

× Tomb of the Unknown Prep Cook

× Obligatory feta cheese reference found here

□ Used lyre shop

× Epic diner menu passed down through oral tradition

× Harpies reserve

▲ Olive-pit landfill

× Centaur rides

Rhapsode fancies himself a modern-day Archilochus

Leros
Birthplace of the story problem

× Site where Zeus accidentally seduced his wife

× Cardboard box full of old ancient-history stuff

Island devoted to manufacturing Paris Hilton's boyfriends

× Home of the Colossusburger

Site of Great Tzatziki Spill of 1986

 Waterway patrolled by the Kraken

Crete
Island cleaned up in 2004 by ΣΤΔ fraternity as community-service punishment for a campus date-rape scandal

GREEKS » THE FOUNDERS OF FOUNDING STUFF

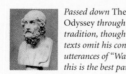
Passed down The Odyssey *through oral tradition, though most texts omit his constant utterances of "Wait, wait, this is the best part!"*
Homer, *Epic Poet*

Invented history when he remembered something that happened last week and then wrote it down.
Herodotus, *Historian*

Father of the annoying question. Little is known about Socrates, as no one could ever get a straight answer out of him.
Socrates, *Philosopher*

Developed the comic techniques of satire, the callback, and the Rule of Three. And the callback.
Aristophanes, *Playwright*

Wrote the Hippocratic Oath, which laid the foundation for modern medical malpractice.
Hippocrates, *Physician*

Created democracy, a form of government in which all power is directly controlled by the people, and which sadly has been lost to time.
Cleisthenes, *Politician*

MYTHIC FACTS »

LEADING CAUSE OF DEATH
Mustache asphyxiation

TOP OCCUPATION
Guy who washes graffiti off Parthenon

BAKLAVA AVAILABILITY
High to Very High

INVENTIONS
Science, art, philosophy, sodomy, Grecian Formula

INTERNATIONAL ORGANIZATIONS
EU, WTO, ΣΦΛ

NATIONAL SEX POSITION
The one where the goat is on top

CHRONICLERS OF GREEK CULTURE
Herodotus (460–425 B.C.), Thucydides (424–395 B.C.), Nia Vardalos (2002–present)

DEBT
$150 billion (after 50% discount for creating civilization)

HISTORY » GETTING ALL THEIR CULTURE OUT OF THE WAY EARLY

12,000 B.C. Basically just a lot of castrating and penis-throwing.

10,000 B.C. After a tryst with a random mortal woman, Zeus fathers Xanthus, the God of Being Abandoned At Birth.

7500 B.C. Heracles defeats the Hydra and completes the Twelve Labors, which confuses everyone until he explains that he is actually the same guy as Hercules from Roman mythology.

Heracles

1400 B.C. The Greeks domesticate the centaur, which they keep for milk, meat, and human companionship.

1200 B.C. The Greeks enter the Trojan War to save the most beautiful woman in the world—Helen, the last attractive woman to bear that name.

The Trojan Horse

599 B.C. Sappho of the Island of Lesbos writes some of the world's most beautiful poetry on the subjects of wrestling, shot-putting, and women's tennis.

560 B.C. Unemployed triangle salesman Pythagoras is credited with introducing numbers to mathematics. Later, he develops inverted integers in order to spell out the word "boobs."

490 B.C. After the Greeks defeat the Persians at the Battle of Marathon, a messenger runs toward Athens to deliver news of the victory, but only makes it halfway and decides he'll try again next year.

484 B.C. Aeschylus introduces the idea of dialogue and interacting characters to playwriting. This vastly improves the theater, which until this point consisted of actors standing on the stage and awkwardly looking around.

480 B.C. The soldier-citizens of Sparta, who believe in a life of simplicity, discipline, and total self-denial, lose to the Persians at Thermopylae, fearing that victory will make them weak.

455 B.C. Greece hosts the first Mathlympics, with naked mathletes coming from all over the land to compute.

406 B.C. Sophocles writes *Oedipus & Katie*, the first Greek dramedy.

287 B.C. Although Archimedes creates the lever and the compound pulley, his greatest invention is booth seating for ancient Greek diners.

A.D. 529 Aristotle and Plato's schools of philosophy close down as Christianity supplants thought.

1951 NATO regrets letting Greece join after noticing that they still use catapults.

1973 Col. George Papadopoulos seizes power in Greece while everyone is still laughing about his name.

2002 *My Big Fat Greek Wedding* is released in theaters worldwide, marking the nation's first cultural achievement since geometry.

 2004 The culmination of over 3,000 years of Greek civilization, as the 2004 Summer Olympics in Athens boasts primetime ratings well above the 14.5 guaranteed most advertisers, and nets NBC/Universal $75 million in profits.

Macedonia
Not To Be Confused With Macedonia

The name Macedonia should conjure up glorious images of Alexander the Great conquering a vast empire, not an impoverished landlocked Balkan state that co-opted the epic name in order to lure naive tourists to its assemblage of broken-down cars, dead trees, and condemned buildings.

The real Macedon Empire was located in northern Greece and featured real-life ancient castles and actual history. However, the only contribution this poor man's Greece has made to theater is the art of storming out, its only advance in philosophy has been the method of plugging one's ears and screaming, and its lone mathematical achievement was the Theory That Triangles Have Three Sides.

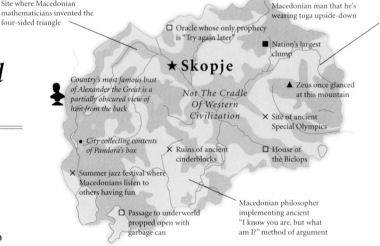
Site where Macedonian mathematicians invented the four-sided triangle

No one has heart to tell Macedonian man that he's wearing toga upside-down

Oracle whose only prophecy is "Try again later"

Nation's largest clump

★ **Skopje**

Not The Cradle Of Western Civilization

Where ancient armies once marched through on their way to somewhere important

Country's most famous bust of Alexander the Great is a partially obscured view of him from the back

Zeus once glanced at this mountain

City collecting contents of Pandora's box

Ruins of ancient cinderblocks

Site of ancient Special Olympics

House of the Biclops

Summer jazz festival where Macedonians listen to others having fun

Macedonian philosopher implementing ancient "I know you are, but what am I?" method of argument

Passage to underworld propped open with garbage can

Macedonia's Minotaur escapes the Labyrinth for another smoke break.

HISTORY » NOT EVEN "ONCE-GREAT"

199 B.C. The Macedonians attempt a surprise attack on the Romans by hiding in the Trojan Donkey. However, it is too hot in there so the soldiers just ride on the outside.

The ruins of modern Macedonia.

A.D. 1178 Macedonians petition for independence, but their application is lost in the red tape and confusion of the Byzantine bureaucracy.

1945 Slovenia, Croatia, Bosnia and Herzegovina, Serbia, Montenegro, and Macedonia form the People's Republic Of Yugoslavia and swear never to let anything come between them and to always get along, forever and ever, no matter what.

2001 Six months of fighting with Albanian rebels ends after both sides admit they can no longer stand the sight of each other.

Bulgaria

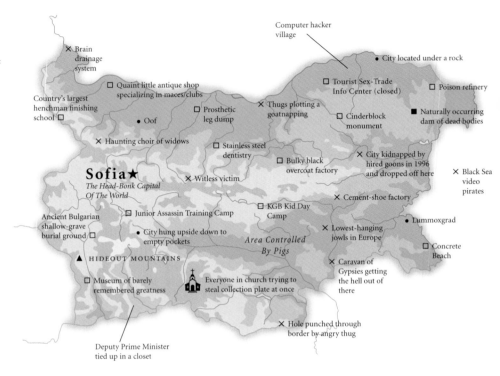

» MISS BULGARIA 2007.

Ancestral Homeland Of The Goons

This former Soviet state was once the region's main source of brutes, thugs, and KGB henchmen. Since the fall of Communism, however, Bulgaria's bumbling quest for self-governance has been plagued by a rise in disorganized crime.

Without the Soviet Union to lead them, the oafish people of Bulgaria do not know who to punch anymore, can no longer write a legible ransom note, and have completely forgotten how to properly stuff a guy into a sack. Still, Bulgaria has attempted a number of money-losing schemes, including pig trafficking, outsider trading, and garbage laundering.

Recently, Bulgaria issued a vague threat to the rest of the world, saying it would be a shame if the international community suddenly found its legs broken and its teeth missing for not paying back Bulgaria the money from that one horse race that one time.

Map labels

- Computer hacker village
- × Brain drainage system
- City located under a rock
- □ Quaint little antique shop specializing in maces/clubs
- □ Tourist Sex-Trade Info Center (closed)
- □ Poison refinery
- Country's largest henchman finishing school □
- □ Prosthetic leg dump
- × Thugs plotting a goatnapping
- □ Cinderblock monument
- ■ Naturally occurring dam of dead bodies
- Oof
- × Haunting choir of widows
- □ Stainless steel dentistry
- □ Bulky black overcoat factory
- × City kidnapped by hired goons in 1996 and dropped off here
- × Black Sea video pirates
- **Sofia** ★ *The Head-Bonk Capital Of The World*
- × Witless victim
- × Cement-shoe factory
- Ancient Bulgarian shallow-grave burial ground □
- □ Junior Assassin Training Camp
- □ KGB Kid Day Camp
- • Lummoxgrad
- × City hung upside down to empty pockets
- *Area Controlled By Pigs*
- × Lowest-hanging jowls in Europe
- □ Concrete Beach
- ▲ HIDEOUT MOUNTAINS
- × Caravan of Gypsies getting the hell out of there
- □ Museum of barely remembered greatness
- ✝ Everyone in church trying to steal collection plate at once
- × Hole punched through border by angry thug
- Deputy Prime Minister tied up in a closet

HISTORY » THE LOWEST RUNG OF THE UNDERWORLD

A.D. 502 Slavic and Turkic youths form the first-ever gangs, and learn the important lesson of teaming up on one another.

870 Pope Adrian refuses to make Bulgaria an archdiocese after Bulgarian priests try to sell him 200 cases of bootlegged communion wafers.

1322 Bulgarian explorer Dimitar Radenko enters the local record books by discovering Romania.

1876 The Ottomans bump off 30,000 Bulgarians to send a clear message to the remaining three.

1886 Conspirators abduct Prince Alexander, then mail his foot to his uncle, the czar of Russia. The czar forces Alexander to abdicate for ruining his new mailbox.

1912 Bulgarians make a massive strategic miscalculation in the Balkan Wars by attacking the heavily fortified city of Constantinople with two crowbars and a piano wire.

1914 Gambling addict King Ferdinand wins big by allying himself with the Central Powers, betting on the Allies in WWI, and then throwing the war.

1945 Bulgaria is honored with the distinction "Only Axis Power Not To Export Their Jews For Extermination" at the Allied Awards Banquet.

1947 The Communist Party assumes control and nationalizes the ransacking of the economy.

1959 Bulgarian hitmen are ordered to eliminate a U.S. spy, but he escapes after the hitmen accidentally run into each other, bonk their heads, and lose consciousness.

1978 Bulgarian dissident Georgi Markov dies after being beaten with a poison-tipped baseball bat.

2004 NATO accepts Bulgaria after a stirring endorsement from a wheelchair-bound NATO representative.

FACTS » A NATION OF MINIONS

LANGUAGES
Bulgarian (84.8%), Pig-Bulgarian (15.2%)

CRIME RATE
16 murders, 27 rapes, 59 thefts per person

CURRENCY
Stolen

NATIONAL DRINK
Booze

MAJOR INDUSTRY
Vehicle disassembly

HAZARDS
Dangerous-criminal-mastermind shortage

RESOURCES
Fool's coal

BRAWN / BRAINS
100% / 0%

Pig trafficking is rampant in the Bulgarian Black Market.

PEOPLE » AWAITING THE BOSS'S INSTRUCTIONS

Dressed in their cheap dark suits, most Bulgarians work in the hitman, thug, heavy, bruiser, or expendable-goon sectors of the economy. Known for their efficient and time-tested torture techniques, Bulgarians excel at leg-breaking, finger-snapping, and punching. Unfortunately, in the rare moments when they try to express love, their large, sausage-like fingers tend to accidentally snap their own children's spines.

Romania

Bram Stoker's Romania

This haunted land, dotted with craggy rocks, dead trees, and ominous full moons, attracts many unsuspecting visitors who never make it out of the country alive.

Travelers in Romania often have no choice but to seek the shelter of a creepy, dark castle for the night, not realizing that their host is likely an otherworldly ghoul who seeks to suck their blood, tear them to shreds, or simply twirl his long fingers in a frightening manner.

Romanians, however, are proud of their heritage, and often elect vampires or werebeasts to the nation's highest office. The constitutional remedy for removing leaders who fail to serve the public's interests is the storming of the presidential palace by a quorum of torch-wielding villagers. Other methods used for the transfer of political power include plunging a wooden stake into the heart, decapitation, and melting.

FACTS » VAMPIRICAL EVIDENCE

POPULATION
Dead (46%),
Undead (29%),
Other (25%)

IMMORTALITY RATE
38 immortals/10,000 neck bites

SUPERNATURAL RESOURCES
Frightanium, Boooron, Sasquatchphates, Obnoxygen

MILITARY
Soldiers armed with garlic, crucifixes, silver ammunition

IMPORTS
Mist

EXPORTS
Curses

LEGAL SYSTEM
Trial by Jurgen

CURRENCY
Olympic gold medals in gymnastics

ENDANGERED SPECIES
The Creature from the Black Lagoon

PEOPLE » DEATH TO THE MONSTER!

Like most Eastern Europeans, Romanians eat cabbage, keep all of their material possessions in small sackcloths, and will follow anyone with a nice uniform and a crisp salute. They are distinguished, however, by unique cultural practices, such as smearing their bodies with a thick paste of protective garlic every evening, and the nailing of their first-born sons to their front doors to appease the creatures of the night.

Romania has a sizable community of Gypsies, both the most persecuted and least-defensible people known. A nomadic group believed to have emigrated from India circa A.D. 1000, the Gypsies are renowned for their arts of illusion, which allow them to take anything from a tourist and turn it into money. This never-say-I-can't-steal-or-beg-from-you tradition explains why Gypsies are constantly being chased by furious Romanian mobs waving pitchforks.

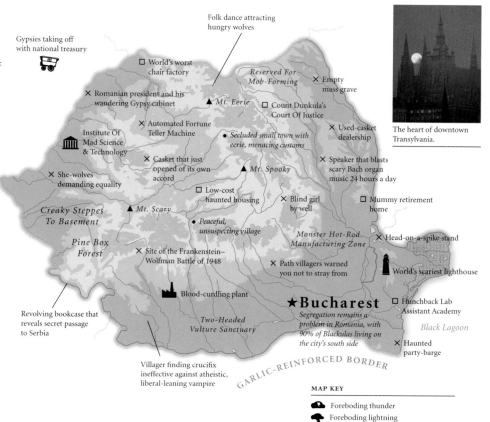

Gypsies taking off with national treasury

Folk dance attracting hungry wolves

World's worst chair factory

Romanian president and his wandering Gypsy cabinet

Reserved For Mob-Forming

Mt. Eerie

Empty mass grave

Count Dunkula's Court Of Justice

Automated Fortune Teller Machine

Institute Of Mad Science & Technology

Secluded small town with eerie, menacing customs

Used-casket dealership

Casket that just opened of its own accord

Mt. Spooky

Speaker that blasts scary Bach organ music 24 hours a day

She-wolves demanding equality

Low-cost haunted housing

Blind girl by well

Mummy retirement home

Creaky Steppes To Basement

Mt. Scary

Peaceful, unsuspecting village

Monster Hot-Rod Manufacturing Zone

Head-on-a-spike stand

Pine Box Forest

Site of the Frankenstein–Wolfman Battle of 1948

Path villagers warned you not to stray from

World's scariest lighthouse

Revolving bookcase that reveals secret passage to Serbia

Blood-curdling plant

★ **Bucharest**
Segregation remains a problem in Romania, with 90% of Blackulas living on the city's south side

Hunchback Lab Assistant Academy

Black Lagoon

Haunted party-barge

Two-Headed Vulture Sanctuary

Villager finding crucifix ineffective against atheistic, liberal-leaning vampire

GARLIC-REINFORCED BORDER

The heart of downtown Transylvania.

MAP KEY
Foreboding thunder
Foreboding lightning
Foreboding partly cloudy skies with 30% chance of foreboding showers

HISTORY » A GRIPPING, TERRIFYING TALE

A.D. 1448–1476 Romania is ruled with an iron fist and blood-slicked pike by Vlad "The Impaler" Dracula, who shrewdly exploits his reign of terror to endear himself to every male schoolchild over the age of 10 for centuries to come.

1941–1945 Allied with Nazi Germany, Romania invades the Soviet Union under the leadership of Gen. Nosferatu. After making initial gains, the Romanian force is decimated by the first light of the sun.

1965 Communist dictator Nicolae Ceausescu rises to power with a policy of "Blood-Sucking Economics" that wins over the fiscally conservative Romanians.

A Romanian gymnast.

1976 Romanian gymnast Nadia Comaneci enjoys great success at the Olympic Games until Ceausescu puts a spell on the petite girl and steals her gold medals. He wears them proudly at all state functions.

The nation's leading breakfast cereal.

1980 Ceausescu demolishes the historic center of Bucharest to make way for modern, high-rise human holding pens, made of the grayest concrete available.

1982 Romania is rocked by a prostitution scandal when it is revealed that the nation's prized sex workers are in fact reanimated bodies stitched together from different cadavers.

1984 After a tight election race between Ceausescu and the puppet dictator Count von Count, a recount is demanded by von Count, only because he wants to hear the numbers again.

1989 Ceausescu and his wife, the Blood Countess, turn themselves into bats in an attempt to escape an angry mob, but are ultimately whacked to death by tennis rackets.

Ukraine

» UKRAINE'S GUAR-
ANTEE: "A BLUE-EYED
BLONDE IN STOCK OR
YOUR MONEY BACK."

The Bridebasket Of Europe

Ukraine leads the world in the harvesting, processing, and exporting of wivestock, boasting mail-order shipments of over half a million tons of fresh brides annually.

The second-largest nation in Europe, Ukraine features many acres of fertile farmland capable of producing the ripest, golden-blonde brides in the world. Rows of Ukrainian silos are packed to the brim every wedding season with beautiful fiancées, many of which, due to overproduction, must be sold at a bulk discount.

Although Ukraine's bridemarket remains robust thanks to emerging technologies like ukraineladies.com and onetruelove.net, it has suffered under three generations of Soviet rule. In addition, spouse farmers face high feed costs and lack modern bride refineries.

Still, many wholesale wife dealers routinely fetch a fair-market price for their crop, especially after impressive showings at pageants, where the most highly sought-after brides are lined up, roped, and tagged.

PEOPLE » TAKE A BRIDE, LEAVE A BRIDE

Marital Shipment
A 24-pack of brides sets sail for the U.S.

Most Ukrainian families live in small apartments in densely populated industrial centers, yet even the most cramped housing features stalls lined with fresh straw for women of salable age.

Ukrainian family size has decreased in recent years as a dwindling surplus of daughters and widowed daughters-in-law are being sold in large number to stretch family budgets and make room for more daughters.

With more than 70% of households earning their incomes from the sale of viable females, a new cultural tradition has developed in which the head of the household dresses elderly loved ones in lingerie, applies several layers of makeup to disguise wrinkles, tops them with a cheap blonde wig, and then drops them off at the local FedEx branch for overnight shipping to Nevada.

For the Ukrainian men who mail off their women to make ends meet, life in Ukraine can sometimes be empty and unfulfilling. Many have attempted to sell themselves, but have discovered that the international mail-order-husband industry is sluggish at best.

FACTS » SECURELY PACKAGED

POPULATION
46 million (all single)

ETHNIC BREAKDOWN
Ukrainian (73%), Russian (21%), Online picture too blurry to tell (6%)

RELIGIOUS BREAKDOWN
Orthodox (58%), Reform Orthodox (33%), Orthodox Orthodox (9%)

CAPITAL CITY
Ukraine City

ARCHITECTURE
The kind with domes

PROTECTED SPECIES
The circus bear

DIETARY STAPLES
Pickled beets, pickled cabbage

FAVORITE DESSERT
Pickled cake

EXCHANGE RATE
100 dollars = 513 hryvnia = 1 woman

NATURAL HAZARDS
Wolves that have acquired a taste for children

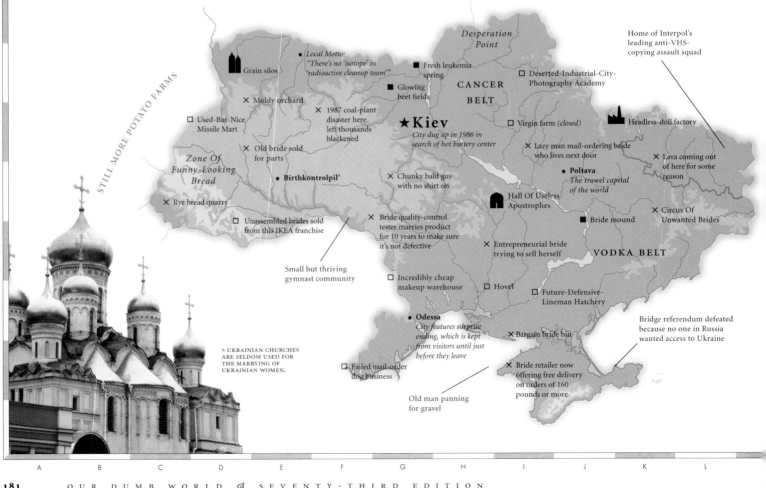

STILL MORE POTATO FARMS

Grain silos

• Local Motto:
"There's no 'isotope' in radioactive cleanup team!"

× Moldy orchard

□ Used-But-Nice Missile Mart

× Old bride sold for parts

Zone Of Funny-Looking Bread

× Rye bread quarry

□ Unassembled brides sold from this IKEA franchise

• Birthkontrolpil'

× 1987 coal-plant disaster here left thousands blackened

■ Fresh leukemia spring

■ Glowing beet fields

★ **Kiev**
City dug up in 1986 in search of hot buttery center

× Chunky bald guy with no shirt on

□ Bride quality-control tester marries product for 10 years to make sure it's not defective

Small but thriving gymnast community

□ Incredibly cheap makeup warehouse

• **Odessa**
City features surprise ending, which is kept from visitors until just before they leave

□ Failed mail-order dog business

Old man panning for gravel

Desperation Point

CANCER BELT

□ Deserted-Industrial-City-Photography Academy

□ Virgin farm *(closed)*

■ Headless-doll factory

× Lazy man mail-ordering bride who lives next door

• **Poltava**
The trowel capital of the world

■ Hall Of Useless Apostrophes

× Entrepreneurial bride trying to sell herself

■ Bride mound

VODKA BELT

× Circus Of Unwanted Brides

□ Hovel

□ Future-Defensive-Lineman Hatchery

× Bargain bride bin

× Bride retailer now offering free delivery on orders of 160 pounds or more

Home of Interpol's leading anti-VHS-copying assault squad

× Lava coming out of here for some reason

Bridge referendum defeated because no one in Russia wanted access to Ukraine

» UKRAINIAN CHURCHES ARE SELDOM USED FOR THE MARRYING OF UKRAINIAN WOMEN.

» RADIATION FROM CHERNOBYL HAS HAD A UNIQUE EFFECT ON AREA CHICKENS.

» UKRAINIAN FARMERS WERE IMPRESSED BY GERMANY'S P-31 TRACTOR.

MOLDOVA » NATION'S FLAG IS CURRENTLY A NEST FOR A FAMILY OF MICE.

HISTORY » A LONG AND PROUD TRADITION OF EXISTING

A.D. 248 Goths settle the region. Their dark and brooding customs are mercilessly teased by area warlords.

447 Attila the Hun sweeps through the area, conquering Ukraine so quickly that he later wishes he had taken more time to enjoy the process.

879 Dashing Viking monarch Oleg establishes the promising new state of Kievan Rus, and quickly becomes a darling of the portraitazzi.

King Oleg

1240 The invading Mongols easily conquer Kiev despite a gallant effort by Ukrainian soldiers mounted on heavily armored war brides.

1650 The Cossacks, local tribes known for their horsemanship, enjoy a rapid political ascension thanks to large contributions from powerful hay dealers.

1918 Ukraine joins the U.S.S.R. for the great posters.

1919 The Battleship Potemkin docks in the Ukrainian port city of Odessa. Filmmaker Sergei Eisenstein is on hand to film the historic event, but after it's edited no one can tell what's supposed to be happening.

1932 Soviet leader Joseph Stalin pushes the state to industrialize by introducing collective tinfoil farming.

1941–1944 The brutal Nazi occupation of Ukraine leaves 5 million dead and an additional 1.5 million severely lifeless.

1944 Stalin deports 200,000 Ukrainians to Siberia following accusations that they collaborated with Stalin.

1953 Ukraine considers changing its name to "The" just to fuck with the international community's mind.

1954 An armed uprising by Ukrainian insurgents against the Soviets completely fails except in one respect: It earns Soviet leader Nikita Khrushchev the great new nickname, "Butcher of the Ukraine."

1986 Despite being told to never, under any circumstances do so, a

A 17th century Cossack

worker in the Chernobyl nuclear reactor hits the "meltdown" button.

1986 Ukrainians respond quickly to the Chernobyl nuclear disaster, setting up large wind machines to ensure that all the fallout blows into Belarus.

1995 Ukrainian scientists develop freeze-dried wife packets.

2000 A worker at Chernobyl finally finds the valve that's been venting all the radioactivity, and closes it.

2004 In the so-called Orange Revolution, angry citizens dressed in orange storm the capital after a contested presidential election. It is later discovered that many were only there to pick up their deer-hunting licenses.

UKRAINE'S POCKMARKED PRESIDENT »

Despite a facial deformity brought on by an election-battle dioxin poisoning, Viktor Yushchenko won the nation's highest office in 2004. How did he overcome his unsightly affliction and appeal to voters?

☠ *Three major radio-only debates*

☠ *Rumor that he stormed into Chernobyl to save three toddlers*

☠ *Immediate rapport with teenage voters*

☠ *Proposed making Secretary of Dermatology a cabinet-level position*

☠ *Popular campaign slogan, "I am not an animal, I am a human being!"*

☠ *Refusing to come out of his room*

Moldova
Europe's Basement

A dark, dank, and musty nation, Moldova was formerly known as the Great Soviet Storage Cellar. Today, it is a forgotten land of crumpled propaganda posters, boxes of spent uranium rods, and other junk nobody wants.

Independence in 1991 brought with it the expectation that the small nation would be converted into a cool hangout by importing shag carpeting, beanbag chairs, and a ping-pong table.

However, Moldovans rejected the proposal, and the country remains unfinished.

Before accepting another application from Moldova, the EU has insisted that the nation invest in a dehumidifier and eliminate its raging centipede problem.

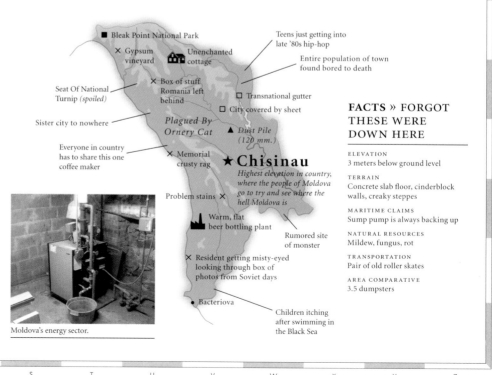

■ Bleak Point National Park

✕ Gypsum vineyard

Unenchanted cottage

Teens just getting into late '80s hip-hop

Entire population of town found bored to death

Seat Of National Turnip (spoiled)

✕ Box of stuff Romania left behind

□ Transnational gutter

□ City covered by sheet

Sister city to nowhere

Plagued By Ornery Cat

▲ Dust Pile (120 mm.)

Everyone in country has to share this one coffee maker

✕ Memorial crusty rag

★ **Chisinau**

Highest elevation in country, where the people of Moldova go to try and see where the hell Moldova is

Problem stains ✕

■ Warm, flat beer bottling plant

Rumored site of monster

✕ Resident getting misty-eyed looking through box of photos from Soviet days

• Bacteriova

Children itching after swimming in the Black Sea

Moldova's energy sector.

FACTS » FORGOT THESE WERE DOWN HERE

ELEVATION
3 meters below ground level

TERRAIN
Concrete slab floor, cinderblock walls, creaky steppes

MARITIME CLAIMS
Sump pump is always backing up

NATURAL RESOURCES
Mildew, fungus, rot

TRANSPORTATION
Pair of old roller skates

AREA COMPARATIVE
3.5 dumpsters

Russia

» PRETTY FUCKING
ORIGINAL, RUSSIA.

Where Russians Are Sent To Die

A vast, sprawling, ramshackle nation where the decaying infrastructure is marred by tank-sized holes, and the entire navy has been capsized since 2002, Russia is struggling to figure out how it fits into a post-Soviet world, and exactly where half its nuclear arsenal went.

Today, almost every city in the country suffers widespread blackouts between scheduled blackouts. Many of Russia's 25-foot-deep potholes have fallen into disrepair. Massive chunks of the once-impressive Mir Space Station regularly fall from the sky and crush entire villages. And the Kremlin, a longtime symbol of Soviet power, has fallen apart twice in the past three years and is now overrun with feral cats. Sadly, after pest-control agents failed to return countless calls, the government just stopped trying.

Likewise, the Russian health-care system spends most of its budget scraping the rust off outdated equipment, and patients are often forced to share anesthetics with doctors.

Still, while pessimism is rampant, Russians remain full of hope that the duct tape will hold on their many unmanned nuclear reactors.

FACTS » BROKEN AND USELESS

BORDERS ON
Eurasia, violent paranoid schizophrenia

CLIMATE
Frigid to sub-subarctic

TERRAIN
Broad plains of scorched irradiated earth, desolate Siberian gulags, walled-off regions of radioactive contamination, steppes (12)

NATURAL RESOURCES
Vast stores of oil, timber, and iron buried beneath a permafrost layer of Russians

GOVERNMENT
Privatized

LIFE EXPECTANCY
Male: 59 years
Female: 113 years

RELIGION
Nah

ETHNIC GROUPS
Russian (42.7%), Mafia (23.2%), Tatar (3.8%), ethnic groups who hopefully will not achieve independence until we are long dead (30.3%)

MILITARY
1,140,000 active troops crammed into two tanks

TRADITIONAL RUSSIAN PRACTICAL JOKE
Loading the gun with blanks

ECONOMY
Pilfered in 1991 by three rich Russian guys

NATIONAL HOLIDAY
Still Alive Day

CRIME
Organized

CRIME AND PUNISHMENT
Currently stuck on page 686

NATIONAL GRAIN
Vodka

SPACE PROGRAM
Primarily funded by blowing up wealthy tourists in orbit

TIME ZONES
28

MOST POPULAR TV PROGRAM
Wake Him With Stick, airing Mondays at 5 p.m., 6 p.m., 7 p.m., 8 p.m., 9 p.m. Central; 10 p.m., 11 p.m., 12 a.m., 1 a.m., 2 a.m., and 3 a.m. Pacific

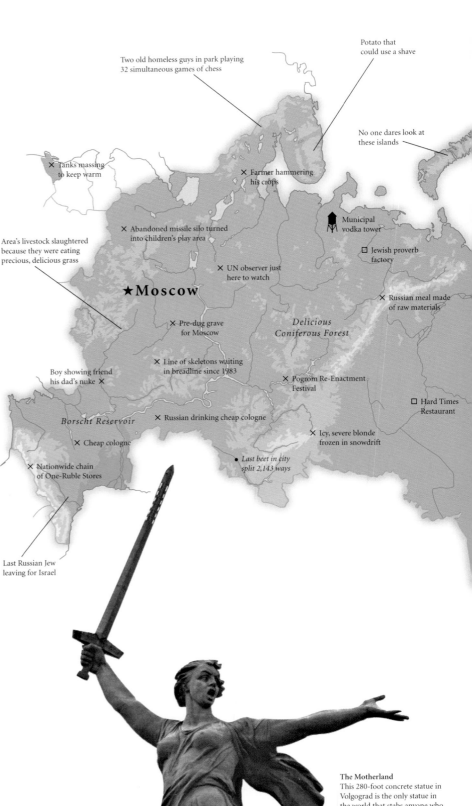

Two old homeless guys in park playing 32 simultaneous games of chess

Potato that could use a shave

No one dares look at these islands

× Tanks massing to keep warm

× Farmer hammering his crops

× Abandoned missile silo turned into children's play area

▲ Municipal vodka tower

Area's livestock slaughtered because they were eating precious, delicious grass

□ Jewish proverb factory

× UN observer just here to watch

★ **Moscow**

× Russian meal made of raw materials

× Pre-dug grave for Moscow

Delicious Coniferous Forest

× Line of skeletons waiting in breadline since 1983

× Pogrom Re-Enactment Festival

Boy showing friend his dad's nuke ×

□ Hard Times Restaurant

Borscht Reservoir

× Russian drinking cheap cologne

× Icy, severe blonde frozen in snowdrift

× Cheap cologne

● *Last beet in city split 2,143 ways*

× Nationwide chain of One-Ruble Stores

Last Russian Jew leaving for Israel

The Motherland
This 280-foot concrete statue in Volgograd is the only statue in the world that stabs anyone who comes to see it.

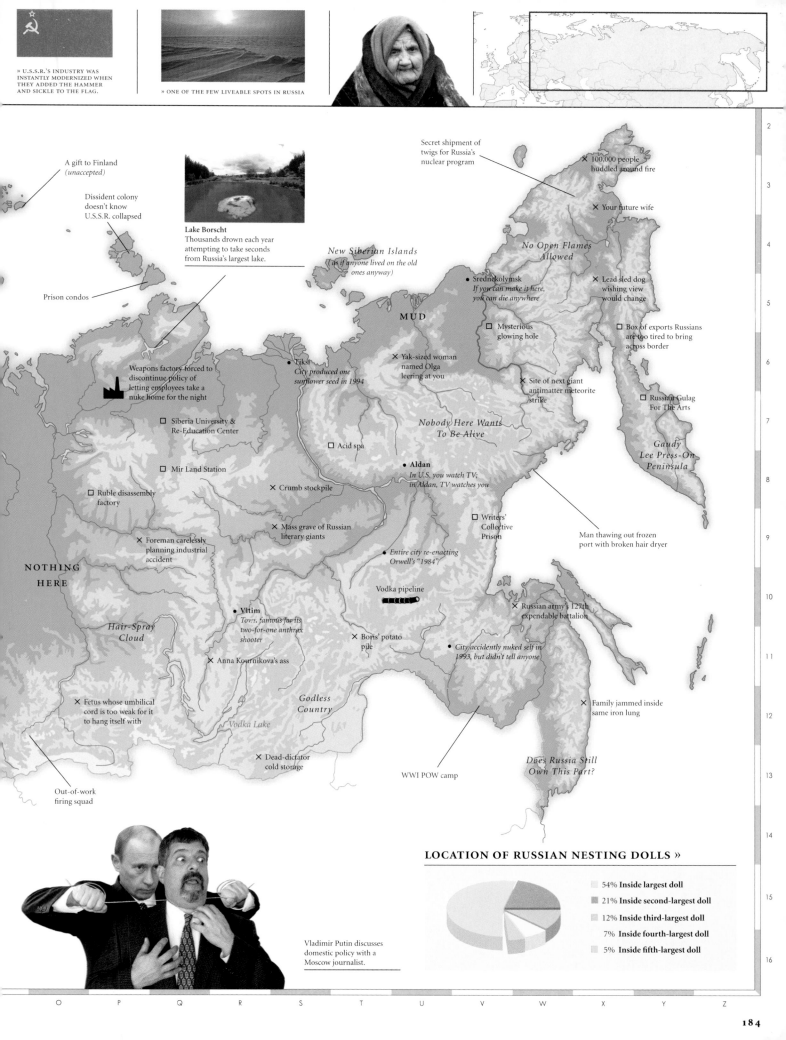

» ONE OF THE FEW LIVEABLE SPOTS IN RUSSIA

A gift to Finland
(unaccepted)

Dissident colony
doesn't know
U.S.S.R. collapsed

Prison condos

Secret shipment of
twigs for Russia's
nuclear program

× 100,000 people
huddled around fire

× Your future wife

Lake Borscht
Thousands drown each year
attempting to take seconds
from Russia's largest lake.

New Siberian Islands
(as if anyone lived on the old
ones anyway)

No Open Flames
Allowed

× Lead sled dog
wishing view
would change

● Srednekolymsk
If you can make it here,
you can die anywhere

□ Box of exports Russians
are too tired to bring
across border

MUD

□ Mysterious
glowing hole

Weapons factory forced to
discontinue policy of
letting employees take a
nuke home for the night

● Tiksi
City produced one
sunflower seed in 1994

× Yak-sized woman
named Olga
leering at you

● Site of next giant
antimatter meteorite
strike

□ Russian Gulag
For The Arts

□ Siberia University &
Re-Education Center

□ Acid spa

Nobody Here Wants
To Be Alive

Gaudy
Lee Press-On
Peninsula

□ Mir Land Station

● **Aldan**
In U.S. you watch TV;
in Aldan, TV watches you

□ Ruble disassembly
factory

× Crumb stockpile

□ Writers'
Collective
Prison

Man thawing out frozen
port with broken hair dryer

NOTHING

HERE

× Foreman carelessly
planning industrial
accident

× Mass grave of Russian
literary giants

● *Entire city re-enacting*
Orwell's "1984"

Hair-Spray
Cloud

● **Vitim**
Town famous for its
two-for-one anthrax
shooter

Vodka pipeline

× Russian army's 127th
expendable battalion

× Boris' potato
pile

● *City accidently nuked self in*
1993, but didn't tell anyone

× Anna Kournikova's ass

× Fetus whose umbilical
cord is too weak for it
to hang itself with

Godless
Country

× Family jammed inside
same iron lung

Vodka Lake

× Dead-dictator
cold storage

Does Russia Still
Own This Part?

Out-of-work
firing squad

WWI POW camp

LOCATION OF RUSSIAN NESTING DOLLS »

Vladimir Putin discusses
domestic policy with a
Moscow journalist.

54% **Inside largest doll**

21% **Inside second-largest doll**

12% **Inside third-largest doll**

7% **Inside fourth-largest doll**

5% **Inside fifth-largest doll**

O   P   Q   R   S   T   U   V   W   X   Y   Z

184

Russia

» THE COMMUNIST PARTY WELCOMES NEW MEMBERS WITH A FRIENDLY FIRING LINE.

HISTORY » WAR, PEACE, CRIME, PUNISHMENT, AND VODKA

A.D. 862 In his most epic blunder, the legendary warrior Rurik founds Russia.

989 Vladimir I converts the nation to Christianity by baptizing the faithful and christening the severed heads of the unfaithful.

1200–1400 Mongols invade and visit unspeakable horror on the people of Russia, who were passed out at the time.

1544 Known for his tendency to throw kittens out of Kremlin windows, melt the elderly, and dance in the skin of flayed torture victims, Ivan the Terrible prompts many to worry about his upcoming teen years.

1605 After two imposters known as False Dmitri I and False Dmitri II are put down for posing as the heir to the Russian throne, False Dmitri III decides to go ahead and change his name to False Dave.

1613 The just and fair Michael Romanov is named czar, becoming the first and last in a not-very-long line of kind rulers.

1712 Russia's European-style capital, St. Petersburg, is built by German engineers, which explains exactly why it is the only Russian city left standing today.

Peter the Great

1725 By increasing the power of the Russian Navy, introducing education reform, and modernizing the economy, 6'8" Peter the Great proves to be Russia's most influential shaved bear.

1796 Catherine the Great is crushed by her horse when it catches her making love to another horse.

1812 Napoleon leads a 500,000-man army into the heart of Russia, but many fall to the harsh winter. During their hasty retreat back to Paris, many also fall to the harsh Belarusian, Polish, Czech, and German winters.

1861 Alexander II introduces sweeping land reforms for the country's millions of destitute serfs, looking like a real jerk to all his friends who genuinely enjoy subjugating peasants.

1904 Russia loses the Russo-Japanese War after traveling all the way to Manchuria only to realize that they left their ammo on the counter at home.

1914 The Russians and Germans act as a well-oiled machine in WWI, with the Germans killing, and the Russians dying in straight lines.

Rasputin

1915 Believed to possess psychic powers, the mystic Rasputin gains influence over Czarina Alexandra by knowing all about her zodiac sign, predicting that she will look "amazing" in every dress she tries on, and, most importantly, by having a really good sense of humor.

Czar Nicholas

1918 Czar Nicholas II concedes power to the Bolsheviks once and for all in his famous "I've Been Shot, And—Oh, Look, My Daughters Are Being Stabbed With Bayonets" speech to a crowd of assassins.

1918 Russia gets out of WWI by signing a disastrous treaty with Germany, giving up half its territory and a third of its population in exchange for a proper burial for the other two-thirds of its population.

1922 Vladimir Lenin and the Bolsheviks establish the Soviet Union, and immediately begin dividing the abject misery equally among the workers.

1927 Diminutive leader Joseph Stalin takes over the Soviet Union and embarks on a campaign to cut the country's average height in half within 10 years.

A cosmonaut receives a warm welcome after returning from the first oxygen-free trip into orbit.

1938 Under Stalin's agriculture reforms, the Russian people are forced to stand in long lines to be assigned to a breadline.

1943 Hopeless against the seemingly unstoppable Nazi military juggernaut, the Allied powers unanimously agree that Russia is their best hope for sacrificing 27 million soldiers.

1945 Russia helps defeat Germany only after those unfit for combat are relocated to the borders and outfitted with barbed wire.

1950 Stalin carves his 60 millionth notch in the old bedpost.

1957 The U.S.S.R. launches little dogs into space to test the effects of zero-gravity on cruelty.

1960 Nikita Khrushchev bangs his shoe on the podium during a speech

Nikita Khrushchev

at the UN, leaving the country deeply disturbed at how he treats one of the 11 remaining shoes in all of Russia.

1964 The KGB assassinates every citizen in the city of Tomsk due to a typo in an interoffice memo.

1979 The Soviet Union invades Afghanistan as a warning to other anti-Communist rebels thinking about miring the Russian army in a nine-year bloodbath.

1980 With the U.S., China, West

Germany, and others boycotting the Moscow Olympics, the U.S.S.R. adopts a strict policy against athletes grabbing more than one gold medal from the pile after their events.

1982 Finally succumbing to the weight of his own eyebrows, Leonid Brezhnev dies and is replaced by the corpse of Yuri Andropov.

Vladimir Lenin
The Bolshevik leader practices being a statue.

1984 Andropov is replaced by the corpse of Konstantin Chernenko.

1985 Desperate Soviet troops in Afghanistan try to buy Stinger missiles from the opposing mujahideen forces during a battle.

1986 Censorship is relaxed under Mikhail Gorbachev's rule, leading millions of Russian parents to realize that they, too, love their children.

1989 The U.S.S.R. pulls all of its last remaining troop out of Afghanistan.

1991 The Soviet Union dissolves in a big wet mess of drywall, paint, and vodka, prompting Gorbachev to step down to spend more time with his splotch.

1991 New president Boris Yeltsin

A B C D E F G H I J K L

3 4 5 6 7 8 9 10 11 12 13 14 15 16

» RUSSIA'S NEW SUBMARINES EMPLOY STATE-OF-THE-ART SINKING TECHNOLOGY.

MORE DYING »

closes his inauguration ceremony by urinating all over the front row.

1992 In former Soviet Union, career ends Yakov Smirnoff.

1995 Yeltsin wakes up with a terrible hangover to find a new constitution scrawled all over his forehead in permanent marker.

2000 Former KGB hitman Vladimir Putin is elected president, promising to do away with corruption, rub out fiscal irresponsibility, and end currency devaluation by finding a discreet location to lay them down on a tarp and methodically put three bullets in their brains.

2001 Russia justifies its invasion of Chechnya by claiming Chechen rebels are responsible for making the U.S. think Saddam Hussein was behind the 9/11 terrorist attacks.

2002 Russia signs a treaty with the U.S. to reduce its nuclear arsenal from 6,000 to 2,000 over 10 years. After an initial count, Russia asks if reducing the amount of weapons from 17 to 10 would still count.

2003 Nine crew members are killed when a decommissioned submarine sinks while being towed to a scrap yard. Fourteen more die trying to dredge it up from the ocean floor, and another 16 are crushed pulling it onto a trailer, which later jackknifes on the highway, killing 60.

2004 Responding to a hostage crisis at the Beslan school, Russian soldiers kill 30 Chechen rebels and more than 180 children, hoping the students might take a very important lesson away from all of this.

2007 After Boris Yeltsin dies of congestive heart failure, his liver is preserved in a Yeltsin-shaped vat of alcohol.

PEOPLE » MOTHER RUSSIA NEEDS A DRINK

Whether throwing themselves in the line of enemy fire, succumbing to radiation poisoning, or ending it all with a single shot in a dark room, the Russians have spent 1,000 years dying en masse. A tough, resilient people, Russians pride themselves on never having been conquered by anyone but Russians, who in turn have done everything in their power to wipe them out.

Centuries of hardship have shaped the national character into a cold, feelingless lump of off-gray concrete. Though Russians rarely smile and can often seem closed-off, all it takes is a little patience, two liters of vodka, and an ice pick to get them to open up.

More than a recreational activity in Russian culture, drinking is a complex tradition with many purposes, be it conducting business, celebrating a birthday, acknowledging the celebration of a birthday, or simply marking the fact that one happens to be awake. In social settings, the more a Russian can drink without getting drunk and dying, the more respect he receives from his peers before they black out. Moreover, Russian children consume more alcohol by age 11 than most people drink of any liquid in their entire lifetime.

Recent free-market reforms have allowed many Russian women to purchase much-needed makeup in bulk, to afford long-distance phone calls to potential American husbands, and even to buy enough bullets for family game night.

And, despite Russia's reputation as a racist country, progress has been made in—actually, forget it. Black people should just steer clear of Russia.

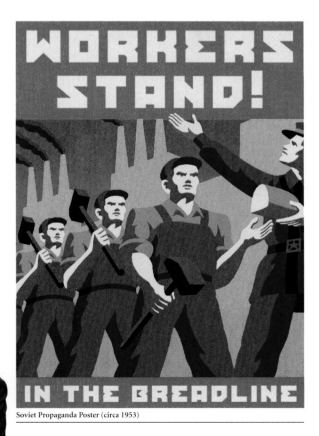

Soviet Propaganda Poster (circa 1953)

POLITICS » "GREAT" COMMUNIST "THINKERS"

Vladimir Ilyich Ulyanov "Lenin," chairman from 1917–1924
While most of Lenin's social theories have rotted away, his skin, clothes, and horizontal posture remain remarkably well-preserved. Still observed by hundreds of devout tourists every day, Lenin is sure to live on through his legacy of lying flat for generations—barring an unexpected spike in formaldehyde prices or a klutzy janitor.

Joseph Stalin, chairman from 1927–1953
Originally a Party secretary, Stalin rose to power through the same means as any other dictator: overwhelming ruthlessness, a fanatic cult of personality, and a truly stupendous mustache. Under his Great Purge of the 1930s, Stalin killed an estimated 60 million Russians, and re-killed an estimated 10 million just to be sure.

Nikita Khrushchev, chairman from 1953–1964
Brusque, blunt, and embarrassing even to the Russian people, Khrushchev is credited with developing a massive arsenal of insults, and increasing the country's production of goofs and gaffes nearly tenfold. He also eagerly oversaw the Soviet space program, although he was bewildered when more than half the people he shot into space somehow returned to Earth.

Mikhail Gorbachev, chairman from 1985–1991
Gorbachev, the last leader of the Soviet Union, championed the economic reforms of perestroika, or "reconstruction," and social reforms of glasnost, or "openness," revealing that the U.S.S.R. was on the verge of bankruptzyia, or "bankruptcy." After serving a short stint in a local jail for bringing democracy to his people, Gorbachev now makes a decent living renting his birthmark out for children's parties.

Asia

China

» TRUST US, THE FLAG REPRESENTS 6,000 YEARS OF CHINESE HISTORY.

A Human Assembly Line

With over 700 billion citizens manufactured since 1892, China is the world's largest mass producer of Chinese.

Assembled from raw genetic materials, thousands of disposable workers are churned out each minute. Babies are separated by a large sorting machine, which sends the boys into the electronics field and girls off a cliff. A small number of females are treated with a fine shellac, packaged, and sold to foreign parents. If any Chinese are defective or dissenting, they are incinerated.

China recently switched over to private enterprise after decades of state-run production of Chinese. However, the country has been exporting Chinese for years: American industrialists found them indispensable in constructing massive railway systems in the 1800s, sometimes going through 15,000 in a single week. Lately, China has attempted to flood the global market with inexpensively produced Chinese for export, where they are used in restaurants and laundromats the world over. But China still keeps a majority of the Chinese-made Chinese at home, as they have yet to find anyone better equipped for all the backbreaking labor.

Still, human-rights groups criticize labor conditions in which workers squat over conveyor belts giving birth for hours on end, often resulting in repetitive carpal birth-canal syndrome. Ecologists have also warned of the damaging effects of coal-burning wombs.

INTERNATIONAL RELATIONS » AN EMERGING SUPERPOWER-HOG

While China still lags behind the U.S. in the technology and banking sectors, it is already poised to pass its Western rival for complete dominance of the international pollution industry. The country opens a massive new factory every 1.3 seconds, purchases 750 million diesel-burning cars a day, and has increased mandatory CO_2 emissions by 85% in hopes of becoming the world leader in global warming. In 2010, China plans to light the smog above the city of Wuhan on fire in a friendly challenge to the U.S.

Though China owns more than one-third of the U.S. in the form of debt, Wal-Mart owns more than half of China. A recent move to open a new Wal-Mart plant in China resulted in Dongtan, a city of over 20 million people.

China is also home to a new generation of talented young filmmakers who, armed only with a camcorder, are capable of shooting, editing, and distributing a major American motion picture in under three hours.

Many of China's Buddhist pagodas have been modernized into prisoner crematoriums.

POLITICS » THE CHANGING SMILING FACE OF CHINA

Since emerging on the world scene, China has had to adjust to modern sensibilities with a more progressive single-party system. Unlike in years past, the government now guarantees fair and balanced propaganda in 25 languages to all citizens, providing a wide array of fully censored media outlets, with a growing number of privately owned state-run radio stations and television networks.

While it has often come under fire for human-rights abuses, the Communist government now grants watchdog groups unfettered access to literally millions of pages of black magic-marker ink.

Likewise, China's constitution has been amended to ensure that such fundamental rights as free speech and the universal pursuit of happiness—regardless of race or religion—are strictly off-limits to all citizens. In addition, it for the first time provides the right to a fair and speedy execution.

The revamped prison system is run so cost-efficiently that the government often electrocutes inmates before they can order their last meal. Crime rates have decreased rapidly in recent years with the introduction of mobile execution vans, which cut through red tape by plowing over crowds of potential lawbreakers on their daily routes, picking up soon-to-be-convicted criminals for termination.

PEOPLE » THE GREAT MELTING WOK

The most populous country on earth, China is home to more than a billion people, broken into several million different ethnic groups that speak countless indiscernible dialects. The Chinese are reserved and humble, largely out of fear that the colossal sound of all of them speaking at once could result in China collapsing into the Pacific Ocean.

At any given moment, an estimated 200 million Chinese people are lighting a cigarette with the still-burning tip of the cigarette they just finished. While it is a family-oriented society, most share an intensely intimate relationship with smoking, and will rarely hesitate to trade their daughters for half a pack of Marlboros.

A truly ancient people, the Chinese have spent 4,000 years developing 29 distinct methods of spitting. Indeed, no other country can match the quality, durability, and porcelain-like shine of their finely crafted phlegm balls.

The average Chinese citizen works for the equivalent of two lifetimes, often waiting 80 years or more before getting a long enough break from the assembly line to die.

The Chinese love to eat anything. Whether throwing fresh frog vomit into a simmering wok, or dicing up a handful of crispy fried monkey rectums for a late-night snack, they dine on some of the most delicious and otherwise-unusable animal parts in the world. In the 20th century, they adapted their traditional cuisine and brought the ancient Chinese secret of avoiding health-code violations to America, where millions enjoy the savory pork flavor of stir-fried cat.

Though the recent economic boom has created a middle class for the first time, poverty remains a major concern for the 989 million impoverished rural citizens. Despite their destitution, many still follow such age-old traditions as feng shui, which they use to arrange the four children, 13 grandchildren, and 27 great-grandchildren who inhabit their tiny homes in the most pleasing manner.

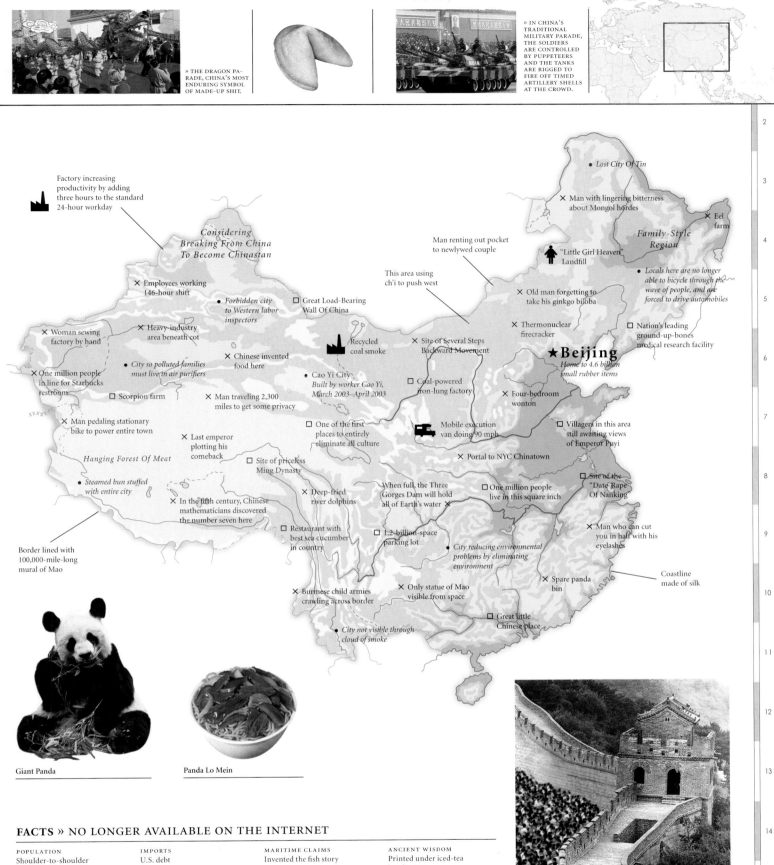

» THE DRAGON PA-
RADE, CHINA'S MOST
ENDURING SYMBOL
OF MADE-UP SHIT.

» IN CHINA'S
TRADITIONAL
MILITARY PARADE,
THE SOLDIERS
ARE CONTROLLED
BY PUPPETEERS
AND THE TANKS
ARE RIGGED TO
FIRE OFF TIMED
ARTILLERY SHELLS
AT THE CROWD.

Factory increasing
productivity by adding
three hours to the standard
24-hour workday

*Considering
Breaking From China
To Become Chinastan*

Man renting out pocket
to newlywed couple

This area using
ch'i to push west

• Lost City Of Tin

✕ Man with lingering bitterness
about Mongol hordes

✕ Eel
farm

*Family-Style
Region*

"Little Girl Heaven"
Landfill

• Locals here are no longer
able to bicycle through the
wave of people, and are
forced to drive automobiles

✕ Employees working
146-hour shift

• *Forbidden city
to Western labor
inspectors*

□ Great Load-Bearing
Wall Of China

✕ Heavy-industry
area beneath cot

✕ Woman sewing
factory by hand

✕ Chinese invented
food here

■ Recycled
coal smoke

✕ Site of Several Steps
Backward Movement

• *City so polluted families
must live in air purifiers*

✕ One million people
in line for Starbucks
restroom

□ Scorpion farm

✕ Man traveling 2,300
miles to get some privacy

• Cao Yi City
*Built by worker Cao Yi,
March 2003–April 2003*

□ Coal-powered
iron-lung factory

✕ Old man forgetting to
take his ginkgo biloba

✕ Thermonuclear
firecracker

□ Nation's leading
ground-up-bones
medical research facility

★**Beijing**
*Home to 4.6 billion
small rubber items*

✕ Four-bedroom
wonton

✕ Man pedaling stationary
bike to power entire town

Hanging Forest Of Meat

✕ Last emperor
plotting his
comeback

□ One of the first
places to entirely
eliminate all culture

□ Site of priceless
Ming Dynasty

■ Mobile execution
van doing 90 mph

✕ Portal to NYC Chinatown

□ Villagers in this area
still awaiting views
of Emperor Puyi

• *Steamed bun stuffed
with entire city*

✕ In the fifth century, Chinese
mathematicians discovered
the number seven here

✕ Deep-fried
river dolphins

When full, the Three
Gorges Dam will hold
all of Earth's water ✕

□ One million people
live in this square inch

□ Site of the
"Date-Rape
Of Nanking"

✕ Man who can cut
you in half with his
eyelashes

Border lined with
100,000-mile-long
mural of Mao

□ Restaurant with
best sea cucumber
in country

□ 1.2-billion-space
parking lot

• *City reducing environmental
problems by eliminating
environment*

✕ Spare panda
bin

Coastline
made of silk

✕ Burmese child armies
crawling across border

✕ Only statue of Mao
visible from space

□ Great little
Chinese place

• *City not visible through
cloud of smoke*

Giant Panda

Panda Lo Mein

An Ancient Wonder
The Great Wall Of China barely contains the country's swelling
population.

FACTS » NO LONGER AVAILABLE ON THE INTERNET

POPULATION
Shoulder-to-shoulder

NATIONAL HAPPINESS
N/A

LEADING CAUSE OF DEATH
Being born with vagina

EXPORTS
Plastic, lumber, metal, kidneys,
guns, babies, flags, T-shirts,
snow globes, pugs, pants,
lo mein, refugees

IMPORTS
U.S. debt

NEW YEAR
Chinese

CALENDAR
Chinese

FAVORITE NBA PLAYER
The Chinese one

DEFORESTATION RATE
2 billion chopsticks/day

MARITIME CLAIMS
Invented the fish story

TRADITIONAL MEDICINE
Any plant or animal part
that resembles a penis

CAPITAL PUNISHMENT
1.5 per citizen

LUCKY NUMBERS
4, 8, 15, 16, 23, 42

ANCIENT WISDOM
Printed under iced-tea
bottle caps

TECHNOLOGY
Engineers are reportedly within
five years of developing the
world's first super-conducting
super-polluter

YOU KILLED MY MASTER
Prepare to die

China

1.2 BILLION YEARS OF HISTORY »

Shortly after the Triassic period, the Chinese began developing an extremely advanced and dynamic society that predates even the ancient Mesopotamians, whom the Chinese invented as a children's toy.

ANCIENT HISTORY »
THE BEFORE TIME

Confucius

2737 B.C. King Shennong, the inventor of tea, spends more than 45 years putting things into boiling water before his career-defining discovery of dried leaves.

2697 B.C. Chinese philosopher Tien-Lcheu invents India ink. Sadly, his most groundbreaking ruminations on the theoretical "pen" were never written down.

2000 B.C. Feng shui, the practice of carefully arranging objects in a given environment to attain harmony, is developed as a way to make overly neurotic control freaks appear spiritual.

1766 B.C. The irrepressible desire to sustain an erection leads Chinese men to reduce countless now-extinct species to a fine, water-soluble powder.

1300 B.C. Emperor Xiao Yi reads to the royal court from the world's first book. He is later mortified when an onlooker tells him he was reading it backwards the whole time.

1008 B.C. Chinese hunters attempt to kill off a herd of dragons by running them off a cliff but, duh, dragons can fly.

750 B.C. Mathematicians invent the abacus, an early but complex counting tool which, by their initial calculation, took some 27,000 years to figure out how to use.

Lao Tzu

573 B.C. Lao Tzu conceives Taoism, or, "The Way." He originally called his religion Taoshuxiawizgaoism, or "The Way, As In The Way The Wind Blows Or The Sea Flows, But Really Kind Of More Mysterious Than That—Just The Overall Flow Of Life, If You Know What I Mean," but changed it after initial negative feedback.

521 B.C. Chinese philosopher Confucius changes the course of history and establishes a major religion by pointing shit out.

518 B.C. Szechuan astronomers discover three stars meaning "Extra Spicy."

Sun Tzu

512 B.C. Sun Tzu gains notoriety for his book *The Art Of War*, though many agree that his follow-ups, *The Return Of The Art Of War*, *A Very Art Of War Christmas*, and *The Art Of War: 50 And Loving It!* are less inspired than the original.

221 B.C. The Qin Dynasty unifies China in hatred of the Qin Dynasty.

214 B.C. Construction of the first Great Wall Of China is delayed by the first snag in planning, the first zoning regulations, and the first pain-in-the-ass contractor trying to milk you for every last dime.

206 B.C. Fireworks are invented to scare evil spirits, though the so-called grand finale just winds up disappointing most of them.

164 B.C. Seeking a legitimate substitute for food, Lord Liu An invents tofu, and discovers it to be an excellent source of protein, embarrassment, and relentless taunting.

A.D. 105 Eunuch Cai Lun invents paper—perhaps the single most important innovation in human culture—so he can create papier-mâché testicles for himself.

125 Year of the Tiger or Maybe of the Dog.

189 Eunuchs gain even more prominence in the royal court after Emperor Ling Di accidentally sets off a firecracker in his lap.

581 The Sui Dynasty reunites China for what everyone hopes is the last time.

618 The Tang Dynasty is established, easily the most interesting of China's 700 or so dynasties.

950 Millions of Chinese girls rush to have their feet bound, partially because they're forced to at knife-point, but also because it looks really great.

1000 The invention of gunpowder is followed shortly thereafter by the invention of the moment of silence.

1211 Genghis Khan alerts the Chinese people to his invasion by ordering archers to fire 50,000 warning shots.

1220 Sunglasses are invented, making China, for a time, the coolest-looking country around.

Master Carradine

1240 Everybody is kung fu fighting.

1251 Genghis Khan's grandson, Kublai Khan, rises to power after eating 50 horses on a dare.

1271 Marco Polo journeys the Silk Road to China, where the Mongols introduce him to such mysterious wonders as paper money, coal,

a regular bathing schedule, the concept of not being completely ignorant, long division, underpants, and Italian food.

1295 Marco Polo returns to China, traveling thousands of miles through perilous seas and deserts after realizing he forgot to pick up a side of duck sauce.

1333 The Black Death arrives in China, spreading much too fast for the country's acupuncturists to handle.

1368 During the Ming Dynasty, artisans produce exactly 100 precious vases.

1369 Superglue is invented.

1551 After finally completing the entire 4,000-mile-long Great Wall Of China, Emperor Jiajing kills his wife when she changes her mind and says she actually preferred it in the original cornflower blue.

1644 The Fu Manchu mustache is developed to complement the invention of creepiness.

1780 Carrying out their plans to dominate the Chinese market, the British kick over a fruit cart.

MODERN HISTORY »
CREDIT CARD–CARRYING COMMUNISTS

After centuries of economic dominance as the only place to purchase illegal fireworks, and 2.5 million years of oppressive dynastic rule, China found itself in a modern world that was no longer impressed with the country's vast array of stick utensils and fancy paper.

1839 Due to overcrowding in the popular opium parlors and opium dens, proprietors are forced to open opium closets, opium cupboards, and opium drawers.

LA CHOY
Sliced Water Chestnuts

1839–1842 Just as the Chinese wake up to fight the Opium War, the British are already holding their war-medals presentation ceremony.

1860 After warning the country of a "yellow peril" that threatens the good of the nation, the British jail thousands of citizens for breaking the new "Being Chinese" law.

1899 The Fists Of Righteous Harmony—a secret society of martial artists who believe they are impervious to bullets— stages the Boxer Rebellion. After the uprising, surviving members maintain that they are still impervious, just not to bullets going that fast.

1911 The Qing Dynasty becomes so corrupt and lazy that Chinese revolutionaries have to wait around until well past noon to overthrow them.

1934–35 Mao Zedong leads the Chinese Communists on the Long March to escape Chiang Kai-shek's Nationalist forces. Traveling 6,000 miles over mountains and rivers, the journey claims the lives of thousands who failed to wear comfortable shoes.

1937 What starts out as a harmless raping contest between two competitive Japanese soldiers in Nanking turns tragic 250,000 rapes later.

1958 Mao's first attempt to collectivize farming goes poorly when the Chinese government spends the entire agriculture budget on propaganda posters praising the most glorious harvest.

1972 In the U.S.'s first-ever state visit

to China, President Richard Nixon makes major headway on a number of seemingly intractable issues, until an aide points out that he has been talking to a poster of Chairman Mao.

1976 Mao dies and is publicly displayed in a crystal coffin to scare Chinese children.

Mao Zedong

1987 Ten million workers perish digging a hole to the other side of the world. Officials quietly conceal the project with a piece of cardboard.

1989 The Chinese Army forcibly clears Tiananmen Square of pro-democracy protesters, killing 200. Chinese generals are puzzled by the international uproar, as the number of dead is far under their daily quota.

1999 NATO mistakenly bombs the Chinese embassy in Yugoslavia, claiming all the buildings look exactly the same.

2001 China detains a U.S Navy EP-3 Aries spy plane after a midair collision with a Chinese fighter jet. Within two weeks, the EP-3 Aries aircraft is available for purchase in U.S. Wal-Mart stores for $39.95.

2003 The Chinese government cracks down on practitioners of Falun Gong, inspiring millions of annoying American protesters to give China more reason to crack down.

2012 China completes its 100-year invasion of Seattle, San Francisco, and Los Angeles.

HONG KONG » WHERE EAST BEATS WEST

An exotic seaport off the coast of China, the Hong Kong province is plagued by massive, well-choreographed brawls that break out almost daily on every street corner. The dazzling, high-speed, and acrobatic violence puts every citizen at constant risk of being thrown off a two-story balcony onto a pile of cardboard boxes. Whether they are already Shaolin masters or are just learning from an old man about the mysterious "snake-fist" style of kung fu, the people of Hong Kong are always generous, comical, klutzy, serious, and, occasionally, righteous. While not all are able to leap over a 12-foot fence, most can withstand powerful blows that send them flying into a brick wall without serious injury. Each day, citizens carry two buckets of water up a half-mile of steps, fight rivals on their way to lunch, and return home to find their wives and children taken hostage. Most evenings are spent seeking revenge or plunging fists into hot coals to toughen them up.

Although Hong Kong has risen from a port city into an economic powerhouse, it remains a dangerous place for any wealthy foreigners attempting to bribe dim-witted government officials, steal a village's precious religious relic, or buy out family-owned businesses for some sort of shady development deal.

China's surplus babies are dispensed in a Beijing adoption arcade.

Tibet

» THESE MONKS HAVE BEEN MOUNTING A MEDITATION OFFENSIVE FOR THE LAST 50 YEARS TO DRIVE OUT CHINA.

Transcending Independence Since 1950

Ruled by the Chinese since Chairman Mao's invasion in 1950, and exploited by the Western world since Richard Gere's enlightenment in 1987, the nation of Tibet has struggled for its independence from some of the most insufferable men in history.

Enduring the slaughter of over a million of their countrymen under China's rule was nothing compared to the humiliation they face today. If it were up to them, the average Tibetan would happily watch his village burn to the ground, or his wife and children get slaughtered with a Chinese saber, if it meant avoiding another photo opportunity with Sharon Stone.

For the past 20 years, Tibetan children have been constantly monitored by tourists' cameras, able-bodied men have been enslaved in "Free Tibet" bumper-sticker factories, and women have been brutally oppressed by Hollywood PR firms looking to improve their high-profile clients' images.

If nothing is done to prevent this injustice from occurring, Tibetan monks will continue to be forced to appear in Steven Seagal movies, robbing them of their dignity and forever preventing any chance of achieving true enlightenment.

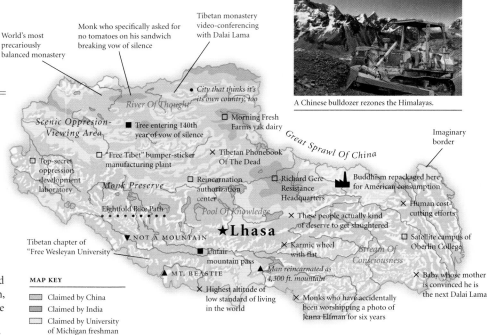

World's most precariously balanced monastery

Monk who specifically asked for no tomatoes on his sandwich breaking vow of silence

Tibetan monastery video-conferencing with Dalai Lama

River Of Thought

• City that thinks it's its own country, too

Scenic Oppresion-Viewing Area

■ Tree entering 140th year of vow of silence

□ Morning Fresh Farms yak dairy

Great Sprawl Of China

Imaginary border

□ Top-secret oppression development laboratory

□ "Free Tibet" bumper-sticker manufacturing plant

✕ Tibetan Phonebook Of The Dead

□ Reincarnation authorization center

□ Richard Gere Resistance Headquarters

■ Buddhism repackaged here for American consumption

Monk Preserve

Eightfold Bike Path

Pool Of Knowledge

✕ These people actually kind of deserve to get slaughtered

✕ Human cost-cutting efforts

★Lhasa

▼ NOT A MOUNTAIN

✕ Karmic wheel with flat

□ Satellite campus of Oberlin College

Tibetan chapter of "Free Wesleyan University"

■ Unfair mountain pass

Stream Of Consciousness

▲ MT. BEASTIE

Man reincarnated as 4,300 ft. mountain

✕ Baby whose mother is convinced he is the next Dalai Lama

A Chinese bulldozer rezones the Himalayas.

MAP KEY

▨ Claimed by China
▨ Claimed by India
▨ Claimed by University of Michigan freshman

✕ Highest altitude of low standard of living in the world

✕ Monks who have accidentally been worshipping a photo of Jenna Elfman for six years

PEOPLE » INEXPLICABLY NONVIOLENT

Despite possessing the shaved heads, mysterious mountaintop temples, flowing saffron robes, and resolute discipline normally associated with punching through solid steel, Tibetan monks insist on remaining unengaged with their Chinese overseers, choosing instead to follow the peaceful teachings of Their Holiness the Dalai Lama.

While many scholars are simply waiting for these powerful monks to one day end their oppressors' lives with a single, lightning-quick jab to the throat, the highly disciplined monks of Tibet can instead be found meditating in their monasteries, where few seem the slightest bit interested in levitating giant boulders over their heads using only the power of thought, or suddenly backflipping into action and round-house-kicking their way to freedom.

RELIGION » THE DALAI LAMA SELECTION PROCESS

After the death of a Dalai Lama, monks begin to search for his reincarnation, a young boy who is identified by his ability to complete 8 of the following 10 tests:

1. Sit still and shut the hell up for at least five minutes

2. Identify, by smell, which items belonged to previous Lama

3. Get high score on monastery's Ms. Pac-Man machine

4. Fold and iron 200 robes in one hour

5. Spend night in haunted amusement park alone

6. Assemble 500 "Free Tibet" buttons per hour

7. Kill man with bare hands

8. Endure two-minute conversation with Susan Sarandon

9. Win "Why I Deserve The Nobel Peace Prize" essay contest

10. Recite lyrics to Beastie Boys' song "Sabotage"

HISTORY » WHAT IS THE SOUND OF ONE CHINESE HAND HITTING A MONK?

5TH CENTURY B.C. Some guy introduces Buddhism to Tibet.

A.D. 1207 Genghis Khan rides by Tibet and yells up at them to surrender, which they promptly do.

1893 British colonialists attempt to invade Tibet, which is known as the Roof of the World, but they forget to bring their 16,000-foot ladder.

1950 Chinese Communists invade Tibet and install their "Great Leap Forward" policy, which for 1.2 million Tibetans means being thrown off a cliff.

1950 China's People's Liberation Army frees Tibet of their government, cultural artifacts, and religious heritage.

1951 The Chinese begin a large infrastructure project to transform Tibet's disparate frozen-yak-shit paths into a province-wide, multilane, frozen-yak-shit highway system.

1959 After the failure of an anti-Chinese uprising, the 14th Dalai Lama flees to India, pursued by 90,000 fans, publicists, producers, agents, hangers-on, and poseurs.

Dalai Lama

1989 The Dalai Lama wins the Nobel Peace Prize for spending 30 years failing to come to a peaceful agreement with China.

1990s Tibetan independence is demanded on the bumpers of passing Volvo station wagons and in passing mention during celebrity awards ceremony acceptance speeches.

1998 A "Free Tibet" concert convinces the Chinese government to grant Tibet independence. They decide to retake the region the next day.

Nepal

» PREVIOUS FLAG WAS SO POINTY THAT HUNDREDS OF SOLDIERS DIED FOLDING IT.

» NEPAL'S MOST PHOTOGRAPHED PHOTOGRAPH.

Earth's Crawlspace

The world's most topographically and politically improbable nation, Nepal is wedged between northern India and China, combining the least comfortable elements of both.

Clinging at a 45-degree angle to a small patch of land between Mount Everest and another part of Mount Everest, the Nepalese are acutely aware of Earth's delicate balance: If global warming persists, the Himalayan ice caps will melt, flooding the entire nation and washing citizens into either India or China, where many will be more cramped, less welcome, and probably upside-down.

Since the country adopted a constitutional monarchy in 1990, things have gone rapidly downhill thanks to landslides, Maoist revolts, and the occasional drug-fueled murder-suicide of the royal family by a crown prince.

HISTORY » NOWHERE TO GO BUT DOWN

560 B.C. After a bout of severe hypothermia, Siddhartha Gautama, the Buddha, starts talking in short, incomprehensible riddles.

A.D. 1816 The entire British East India Company comes down with a bad case of vertigo.

1846 Rana chiefs gain control of Nepal and cut the mountain nation off from the outside world without really doing anything at all.

1951 The Nepalese Congress Party brings democracy to Nepal, but it is abandoned eight years later after most of the public dies attempting to scale the treacherous voting booths.

1989 Nepal's economy suffers severely when its currency plummets, bounces twice, and impales the country's finance minister.

1996 Maoist rebels kill over 14,000 citizens and get covered in dust during a 10-year search for their old grappling hooks.

2001 Crown Prince Dipendra goes on a drunken rampage, slaughtering nearly the entire royal family during a dinner party. New ruler Gyanendra assumes full executive power in order to quash the Maoist movement, bringing Nepalese history back around in a rather awkward but extremely Hinduesque full circle.

MOUNT EVEREST » FIRST ASCENT

Edmund Hillary (and Tenzing Norgay)

British explorer Sir Edmund Hillary climbed Mount Everest in 1953 with the aid of local Sherpa Tenzing Norgay. Near the peak, Hillary sent Norgay ahead to clear a path, set the lines, achieve the summit, carve footholds, and fix the flagpole for Hillary, who then ascended to become the first man in history to climb the world's highest mountain.

FACTS » HANGING ON BY A THREAD

OFFICIAL NAME
Nepal Adhirajya Johnson III

HIGHEST POINT
There is nothing above the Nepalese people except the poverty line

MOTTO
"Mother and motherland remain greater than the kingdom of heaven, but Mom's getting older and I'd like to see level ground just once before I die"

SPORTS
Soccer, cricket, and kabaddi; although nothing is known of kabaddi, it is almost certainly the most enjoyable of the three

HEALTH HAZARDS
Walking

TOP OCCUPATION
Shoveling bodies from Mount Everest

CLIMATE
Lashing winds in the north, south, east, west; freezing death everywhere else

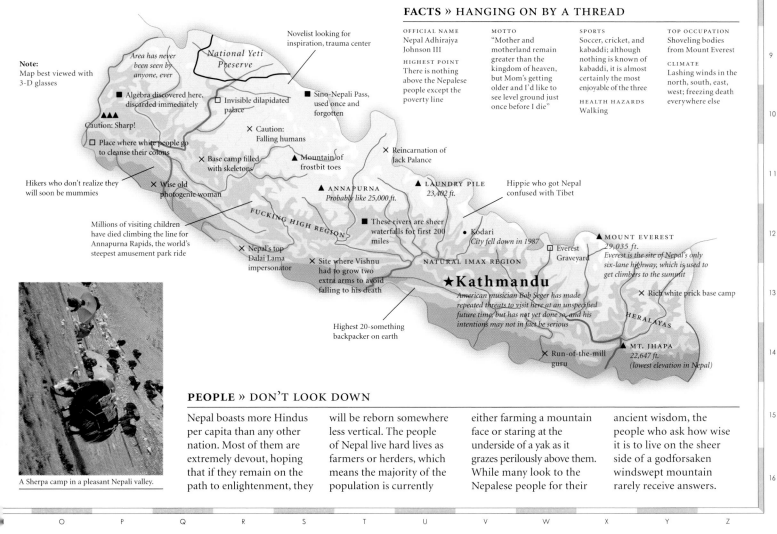

Note:
Map best viewed with 3-D glasses

- Area has never been seen by anyone, ever
- *National Yeti Preserve*
- Novelist looking for inspiration, trauma center
- ■ Algebra discovered here, discarded immediately
- □ Invisible dilapidated palace
- ■ Sino-Nepali Pass, used once and forgotten
- ▲▲▲ Caution: Sharp!
- □ Place where white people go to cleanse their colons
- ✕ Caution: Falling humans
- ✕ Reincarnation of Jack Palance
- Hikers who don't realize they will soon be mummies
- ✕ Base camp filled with skeletons
- ▲ Mountain of frostbit toes
- ✕ Wise old photogenic woman
- ▲ ANNAPURNA *Probably like 25,000 ft.*
- ▲ LAUNDRY PILE *23,402 ft.*
- Hippie who got Nepal confused with Tibet
- *FUCKING HIGH REGION*
- Millions of visiting children have died climbing the line for Annapurna Rapids, the world's steepest amusement park ride
- ■ These rivers are sheer waterfalls for first 200 miles
- • Kodari *City fell down in 1987*
- ▲ MOUNT EVEREST *29,035 ft. Everest is the site of Nepal's only six-lane highway, which is used to get climbers to the summit*
- ✕ Nepal's top Dalai Lama impersonator
- □ Everest Graveyard
- ✕ Site where Vishnu had to grow two extra arms to avoid falling to his death
- NATURAL IMAX REGION
- ✕ Rich white prick base camp
- ★ **Kathmandu** *American musician Bob Seger has made repeated threats to visit here at an unspecified future time, but has not yet done so, and his intentions may not in fact be serious*
- *HERALAYAS*
- Highest 20-something backpacker on earth
- ✕ Run-of-the-mill guru
- ▲ MT. JHAPA *22,647 ft. (lowest elevation in Nepal)*

A Sherpa camp in a pleasant Nepali valley.

PEOPLE » DON'T LOOK DOWN

Nepal boasts more Hindus per capita than any other nation. Most of them are extremely devout, hoping that if they remain on the path to enlightenment, they will be reborn somewhere less vertical. The people of Nepal live hard lives as farmers or herders, which means the majority of the population is currently either farming a mountain face or staring at the underside of a yak as it grazes perilously above them. While many look to the Nepalese people for their ancient wisdom, the people who ask how wise it is to live on the sheer side of a godforsaken windswept mountain rarely receive answers.

Bhutan

» THE DRAGON GIVES
WISDOM TO THOSE
HUMBLE ENOUGH TO
RECEIVE IT.

Please Remove Your Shoes Before Reading This

Bhutan, a mystical land nestled in the Himalayan mountains, is a Buddhist Shangri-la that features enough breathtaking vistas, exotic wildlife, and magical inner peace to out-serene the crap out of Tibet.

Visitors to Bhutan must hire a trained guide to lead them on a difficult journey to the remote mountain peak where a hidden doorway to the country is revealed only to the righteous. Few are allowed in, as Bhutan features the world's only border-security system that employs monks concentrating intensely in order to make the country invisible.

Bhutan is also the only nation to measure GNH (Gross National Happiness) in lieu of GNP (Gross National Product). As a result, the Bhutanese stock market has not posted a market gain since 1704, and investors are beginning to worry about their retirement portfolios.

Unconcerned with material things, citizens take care not to disrupt the nation's karma by stepping on ants or disturbing blades of grass, as such infractions can doom one to be reincarnated as an American.

PEOPLE » ENLIGHTENED BEINGS OF PURE ENERGY

The Bhutanese are a simple and contented people, with many still practicing the subsistence-farming methods passed down by their ancestors. A Bhutanese farmer starts his day by bowing in reverence to the tigers and elephants assembled peaceably in front of his yak-skin tent. A quick flight on the back of an eagle to a cave set high in a cliff invigorates him for a long day of blissful meditation, during which he envisions his crops growing tall and healthy. By the time he flies home, the crops have been magically harvested by his wife.

Farming In Bhutan

HISTORY » BE STILL, LOOK WITHIN, AND DON'T VISIT US

1600 B.C. Warring tribes battle for control of the country using only multisided dice.

A.D. 1907 Ugyen Wangchuck appears in a puff of smoke and installs himself as the hereditary leader of the country.

1949 Bhutan grants India power over Bhutanese foreign affairs in exchange for a pledge of foreign aid. The king rejoices, as he knows the outside world is just an illusion, and no one would have listened to Bhutan at the UN anyway.

1972 16-year-old Jigme Singye Wangchuck takes the throne and, in a surprising move, fires the ghosts of his ancestors, who had long acted as counselors.

1974 King Singye Wangchuck ascends to the throne, stating his goal to increase Gross National Happiness. President Richard Nixon cuts off diplomatic relations, stating that Wangchuck's goal is diametrically opposed to that of the United States.

King Wangchuck

1999 Television is introduced into Bhutan, only because King Wangchuck wanted to watch Wimbledon. Crime, illiteracy, and juvenile delinquency skyrocket.

2005 After struggling for days to write a new parliamentary constitution, Bhutanese politicians hear the call of the songbird and the whistle of the wind and thus declare the constitution already written.

Thimphu, Capital Of Bhutan
A city with unique challenges in sanitation and sewage management.

FACTS » AN ISOLATED BUDDHIST MONKARCHY

NATIONAL SPORT
Mind-ball

CRIME
Nonexistent; to attack another is to attack oneself

CUISINE
All dishes contain enough chili peppers to instantly dissolve one's false attachment to the gastrointestinal system

POPULAR ACTIVITIES
Subsistence agriculture, animal husbandry, contemplating the thousand-petaled lotus flower on the crown of one's head, archery

TRANSPORTATION
The Noble Eightfold Mule Trail

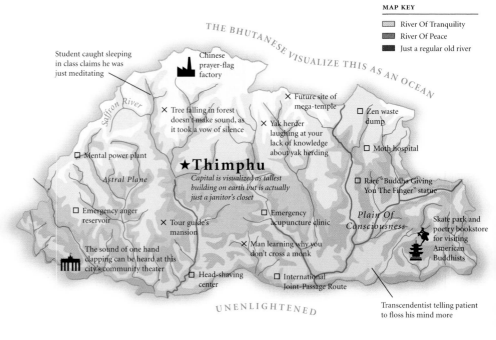

MAP KEY
- River Of Tranquility
- River Of Peace
- Just a regular old river

THE BHUTANESE VISUALIZE THIS AS AN OCEAN

Student caught sleeping in class claims he was just meditating

Chinese prayer-flag factory

Saffron River

✕ Tree falling in forest doesn't make sound, as it took a vow of silence

✕ Future site of mega-temple

✕ Yak herder laughing at your lack of knowledge about yak herding

☐ Zen waste dump

☐ Moth hospital

☐ Mental power plant

Astral Plane

★ Thimphu
Capital is visualized as tallest building on earth but is actually just a janitor's closet

☐ Emergency anger reservoir

✕ Tour guide's mansion

☐ Emergency acupuncture clinic

☐ Rare "Buddha Giving You The Finger" statue

Plain Of Consciousness

Skate park and poetry bookstore for visiting American Buddhists

The sound of one hand clapping can be heard at this city's community theater

✕ Man learning why you don't cross a monk

☐ Head-shaving center

☐ International Joint-Passage Route

Transcendentist telling patient to floss his mind more

UNENLIGHTENED

Myanmar

» STALK OF RICE REPRESENTS EVERY CITIZEN'S ANNUAL FOOD RATION, WHICH THE GOVERNMENT WITHHOLDS.

You Will Be Shot On Sight

In Myanmar (formerly Burma), a chaotic Asian country ruled by a trigger-happy military junta, citizens are either in the army shooting entire families for not obeying the military, or they are being shot at by soldiers for misunderstanding the military's orders.

Of the few residents with steady jobs, those who make it through the morning commute without getting shot often arrive to find that the authorities have gunned down all of their coworkers, meaning they must go to the unemployment office and wait in long lines to be shot. If the office closes before their number is called, however, they are ordered to go home, are given a voucher to come back and get shot first thing in the morning, and are shot on their way out the door.

The unemployment workers are then all shot.

Recently, government officials have attempted to reduce corruption by absolutely refusing to accept bribes under $5,000, shooting those who offer anything lower. Still, graft remains an enormous challenge for the impoverished majority, who often have to bribe six people before they can safely bribe someone to use the bathroom, and, since bribery is punishable by death, must also bribe themselves with what little cash they have left to keep quiet about it.

Citizens who fail to be shot in a timely fashion are fined and shot.

PEOPLE » DELIVERED INTO EVIL, AND SHOT

Ever since the wildly popular Aung San Suu Kyi promised widespread reforms, won the presidential election in a landslide, and was placed under permanent house arrest by the ruling faction as the election results were annulled, the people of Myanmar have enjoyed incredible freedoms in every major democratic nation to which they have fled.

Despite the fact that the government outlawed gatherings of more than one person in 2002, hundreds of courageous souls still blatantly assemble in the middle of London's Trafalgar Square to criticize Burmese officials and demand an end to violent heroin trafficking.

Indeed, thousands are now enjoying liberty as never before—though they will always remember the horror of the black-market trading and forced labor that their now-deceased cousin told them about in a letter smuggled out of Myanmar last week.

A Burmese soldier hunts down the last remaining Burmese.

Map labels:
- CHINA PRETENDING NOT TO NOTICE MYANMAR
- INDIA LOOKING THE OTHER WAY
- ✗ Tour guide hiding mass grave behind his back
- ✗ Sign reading "Do Not Feed The Pigeons Or The Children"
- Desperate citizens trading wheelbarrow full of children for a bowl of rice
- ✗ Official informing potato farmers that potatoes are now illegal
- Refugee rubber trees fleeing country ☐
- ✗ Children finishing vegetables at gunpoint
- ✗ Great little Burmese place for rounding up people and shooting them
- ☐ Misfiring range
- Drug traffickers smuggling heroin in pile of dead babies
- ✗ Confusing crime against humanity
- *Duty-Free Opium Shipping*
- ✗ Fight breaking out over who dropped corpse
- ☐ River renamed, rerouted, and repolluted in 1999
- ☐ Teak detention center
- ✗ Old shoe in the road
- ★ Nay Pyi Taw
- Construction workers whistling at passing woman's cadaver
- *Wastewater Of 4 Billion People*
- ☐ Weatherproof killing deck
- ✗ Fisherman trying to talk down gun-toting tuna
- ☐ Toll booth charging a limb
- THAILAND COVERING ITS EARS AND HUMMING LOUDLY
- Aung San Suu Kyi's daughter under tree-house arrest
- Burma-Shave Signs
- Site of massive new depopulation effort
- Kids telling ghost stories around labor-campfire
- ☐ U.N. refuses to recognize several rocks in this area

FACTS » A GLIMMER OF HOPELESSNESS

AREA
675,000 sq. km.

AREA OFF-LIMITS
674,999 sq. km.

POPULATION
At last official count, two UN census workers were killed

POLITICAL CLIMATE
Year-round rain of bullets and terror

MOTTO
"A Bullet For Every Man, Woman, And Child"

LABOR FORCED
27.01 million at gunpoint

OFFICIAL LANGUAGE
Burmese is shouted by 12% of the population, obeyed by 80%, and whimpered by 8%

CENSORSHIP
~~Yes~~ No

INTERNATIONAL DISPUTES
Because of Myanmar's pile of unpaid human-rights violations, the UN has been forced to take away its diplomatic parking privileges

STATE RELIGION
Completely straight-faced form of Buddhism

LEADERS » THAN SHWE

Known for being extremely superstitious, dictator Than Shwe cannot even step on a crack in the sidewalk without having to execute an elderly grandmother, and considers his entire morning ruined if he accidentally shoots 13 people in a row.

A CONTINUALLY RENAMED HISTORY »

A.D. 1044 Mongols destroy thousands of the nation's Buddhist temples, giving the Burmese their first lesson in Buddhist non-attachment.

1852 Citizens furious over British plans to annex Burma are forced to admit that all of Britain's paperwork looks very official.

1948 When Burma declares independence with U Nu as its first prime minister, the U.S. deploys USO diplomats Abbott and Costello there for his first day in office. U Nu's political career never recovers.

1962 Gen. Ne Win seizes power and unveils his "Burmese Way Of Socialism," nationalizing executions and collectivizing bullet wounds.

1989 Gen. Than Shwe renames the country Myanmar, wisely ignoring his psychic-hotline adviser's original suggestion of Lashawnda.

1991 Imprisoned pro-democracy leader Aung San Suu Kyi is awarded a Nobel Consolation Peace Prize.

2006 Officials move the capital from Rangoon to the remote city of Naypyidaw, breaking several wineglasses, the capitol dome, and about 30,000 forced laborers in the process.

Bangladesh

» BLOOD SEEPS OUT
OVER THE FERTILE
LOWLANDS WITH SUR-
PRISING PRECISION.

God's Practical Joke

Framed by the Ganges and Brahmaputra Rivers, Bangladesh is home to some of the richest, most fertile soil in the world. That's the setup. The moment Bangladeshis establish an agricultural society around it, however, God delivers the devastating punch line, drowning hundreds of thousands in a typhoon. It works every time.

Though the torrential gag rushes right over most of the unsuspecting Bangladeshis' heads, some catch on and flee for drier land. While anyone else would see it coming across the horizon from a mile away, the gullible Bangladeshis soon return, giving God the perfect chance to rain horror down on them yet again. God never gets tired of that routine.

HISTORY » NO LIFEGUARD ON DUTY, EVER

Early records of Bangladeshi history are too soaked and runny to decipher, though most historians agree they would probably be depressing. While the Battle of Plassey in 1757 marked the beginning of British rule, England hardly considered it a victory, as most of their weapons, half of their food, and every last one of their standard-issue boots were completely ruined.

After the British partitioned the subcontinent in 1947, Bangladesh was made a part of Pakistan for four months before sliding into India's possession after typhoon season, only to rejoin Pakistan three months later during a flash flood.

In 1971, shortly after a powerful cyclone with record winds and killer rains, Bangladesh finally seceded from Pakistan by default. To commemorate its independence, the British helped Bangladeshi officials collect everything not stained or soggy, including all the remaining waterproof currency, and packed it up for safekeeping back in England.

FACTS » DROWN AT YOUR OWN RISK

POPULATION BREAKDOWN
-500,000/tidal wave
-250,000/typhoon
-100,000/cyclone

BANGLADESHI PROVERB
"If you don't like the weather, wait a minute and it will kill you"

PASTIMES
Swimming, grieving, wet-vacing

TRADITIONAL GREETING
The last bubbles of air escaping from the lungs

TRANSPORTATION
Rowboats, dinghies, flash floods

HUMIDITY
4,790%

LEADING EXPORTS
Flailing, airborne Bangladeshis

LEADING IMPORTS
Highly absorbent paper towels

HEALTH HAZARDS
Trench foot, trench waist, trench neck

INTERROGATION TECHNIQUES
One million drops of water dripped on head every 30 seconds

PEOPLE » THE LONG-SUFFERING STRAIGHT MAN OF ASIA

In general terms, Bangladeshis are small, brown, numerous, and wet. The national sport is cricket, although Bangladeshi teams have yet to win an international match, as playing with 16-foot stilts makes batting difficult, and the traditional strategy of drowning in the middle of the field has thus far proven unsuccessful.

In Bangladesh, knowledge is passed down through the generations by oral tradition, though the most important piece of wisdom, "Build on higher ground," is inevitably lost forever in howling winds and lashing rains.

So, with impeccable timing and convincing delivery, the people of Bangladesh continue to play the part of the poor ignorant villagers who put themselves in unspeakable danger out of a common human desire to provide for their families. And it kills year after year.

Locals rush to catch the 10:24 express tsunami.

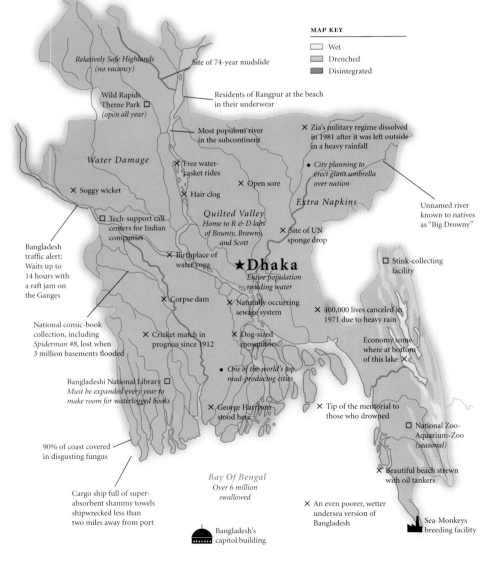

MAP KEY
☐ Wet
▨ Drenched
▨ Disintegrated

Relatively Safe Highlands
(no vacancy)

Site of 74-year mudslide

Wild Rapids
Theme Park ☐
(open all year)

Residents of Rangpur at the beach
in their underwear

Most populous river
in the subcontinent

Zia's military regime dissolved
in 1981 after it was left outside
in a heavy rainfall

Water Damage

✕ Free water-
casket rides

✕ Open sore

• City planning to
erect giant umbrella
over nation

✕ Soggy wicket

✕ Hair clog

Extra Napkins

☐ Tech-support call
centers for Indian
companies

Quilted Valley
Home to R & D labs
of Bounty, Brawny,
and Scott

✕ Site of UN
sponge drop

Unnamed river
known to natives
as "Big Drowny"

Bangladesh
traffic alert:
Waits up to
14 hours with
a raft jam on
the Ganges

✕ Birthplace of
water yoga

★ **Dhaka**
*Entire population
treading water*

☐ Stink-collecting
facility

✕ Corpse dam

✕ Naturally occurring
sewage system

✕ 400,000 lives canceled in
1971 due to heavy rain

National comic-book
collection, including
Spiderman #8, lost when
3 million basements flooded

✕ Cricket match in
progress since 1912

✕ Dog-sized
mosquitoes

Economy some-
where at bottom
of this lake ✕

• One of the world's top
mud-producing cities

Bangladeshi National Library ☐
*Must be expanded every year to
make room for waterlogged books*

✕ George Harrison
stood here

✕ Tip of the memorial to
those who drowned

☐ National Zoo-
Aquarium-Zoo
(seasonal)

90% of coast covered
in disgusting fungus

Bay Of Bengal
*Over 6 million
swallowed*

✕ Beautiful beach strewn
with oil tankers

Cargo ship full of super-
absorbent shammy towels
shipwrecked less than
two miles away from port

Bangladesh's
capitol building

✕ An even poorer, wetter
undersea version of
Bangladesh

▮ Sea-Monkeys
breeding facility

Sri Lanka & Maldives

SRI LANKA » FLAG FEATURES THE FABLED SWORD-WIELDING PIG-LION OF SRI LANKA.

MALDIVES » MADE OF SUPER-ABSORBENT CLOTH.

Sri Lanka
It's All Your Fault

In 2004, Sri Lanka was devastated by a massive tsunami, which killed 30,000 citizens, left over a million homeless, and could have all been averted had you donated a mere $5 to the relief efforts. But no, you just had to have that sandwich.

All you had to do was part with a few measly dollars, and rescue workers would have been able to save countless innocent Sri Lankans from this tragedy. Instead, you chose three slices of turkey, lettuce, and some mayonnaise over thousands of human lives.

And you don't even like turkey.

Nearly 10,000 people died from a lack of medical supplies while you wolfed down that sandwich—your second sandwich of the day, we might add. Sure, it was good, but was it "millions will never drink fresh water again in their lives" good?

In fact, had you not also purchased that accompanying drink, it is almost certain that Sri Lanka would today be a land without poverty, famine, disease, and warring rebel factions.

Congratulations.

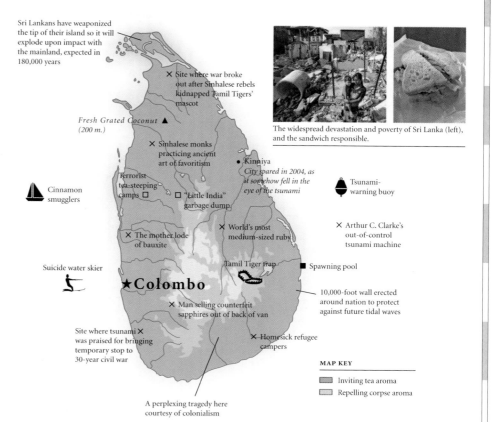

Sri Lankans have weaponized the tip of their island so it will explode upon impact with the mainland, expected in 180,000 years

✕ Site where war broke out after Sinhalese rebels kidnapped Tamil Tigers' mascot

Fresh Grated Coconut ▲
(200 m.)

✕ Sinhalese monks practicing ancient art of favoritism

• Kinniya
City spared in 2004, as it somehow fell in the eye of the tsunami

Terrorist tea-steeping camps ☐

☐ "Little India" garbage dump

⚓ Cinnamon smugglers

Tsunami-warning buoy

✕ The mother lode of bauxite

✕ World's most medium-sized ruby

✕ Arthur C. Clarke's out-of-control tsunami machine

Suicide water skier

Tamil Tiger trap

■ Spawning pool

★ **Colombo**

✕ Man selling counterfeit sapphires out of back of van

10,000-foot wall erected around nation to protect against future tidal waves

Site where tsunami ✕ was praised for bringing temporary stop to 30-year civil war

✕ Homesick refugee campers

A perplexing tragedy here courtesy of colonialism

MAP KEY
▨ Inviting tea aroma
▧ Repelling corpse aroma

The widespread devastation and poverty of Sri Lanka (left), and the sandwich responsible.

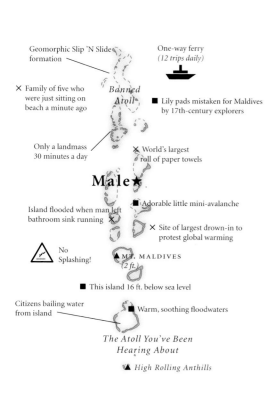

Geomorphic Slip 'N Slide formation

One-way ferry *(12 trips daily)*

✕ Family of five who were just sitting on beach a minute ago

Banned Atoll

■ Lily pads mistaken for Maldives by 17th-century explorers

Only a landmass 30 minutes a day

✕ World's largest roll of paper towels

Male ★

Island flooded when man left bathroom sink running

■ Adorable little mini-avalanche

△ No Splashing!

✕ Site of largest drown-in to protest global warming

▲ MT. MALDIVES *(2 ft.)*

■ This island 16 ft. below sea level

Citizens bailing water from island

■ Warm, soothing floodwaters

The Atoll You've Been Hearing About

◣ High Rolling Anthills

Maldives
Soon To Be Underwater

At less than seven feet above sea level, the Maldives islands are gravely threatened by melting polar ice caps, light rain, and kids doing cannonballs off the coast of India.

Although the tsunami that struck the nation in 2004 caused more damage to the region than any natural disaster in recorded history, Maldivians relive this same terror with each run-of-the-mill wave that washes over the entire island.

The greatest aspiration of the Maldivian people is the creation of a mound of earth to keep their nation from becoming completely submerged. Project Molehill, launched in 1982, challenged the country's scientists and engineers to create the small lump by the year 2000. Although the project failed, it inspired an entire generation of Maldivians—quite possibly the last Maldivians ever—to dream.

HISTORY » THE FUTURE LOST CIVILIZATION OF MALDIVES

A.D. 1211–1886 The nation uses its low-lying geography as a natural protection against invaders. When threatened, the entire population lies down on their stomachs until hostile ships pass by unawares.

1887 A child stands up to too quickly to check if the ships are gone, and the British wipe out nearly half the population.

DEC. 2004 As the Indian Ocean tsunami hits Maldives, officials order all citizens to move to higher ground. Since Maldives lacks any higher ground, most choose to simply run around in circles.

The Maldives islands during high tide.

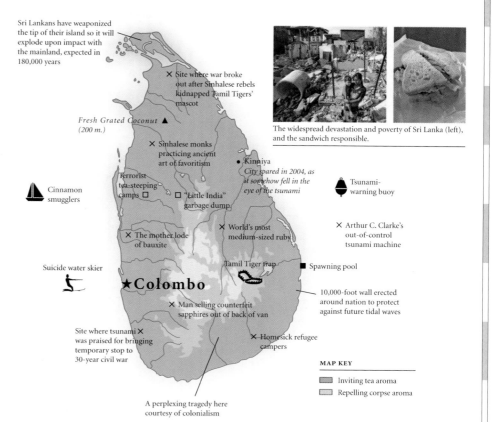

India

» INDIA IS NOT SURE WHAT THE FUNGAL GROWTH IN THE CENTER OF ITS FLAG IS.

» THE TRADITIONAL SARI IS WORN BY INDIAN WOMEN IN VARIOUS STYLES, INCLUDING WRAPPED AROUND THE WAIST, DRAPED OVER THE SHOULDER, OR TIED AROUND A STREET POLE IN HOPES OF SURVIVING THE ONCOMING FLOOD.

Please Hold While We Die Of Malaria

Mired by rising poverty levels, polluted groundwater that threatens the lives of millions, and a rapidly crumbling infrastructure, the nation of India has every intention of addressing these problems just as soon as it finishes telling Midwesterners how to install Windows XP on their home computer.

The world's leading technical-support provider, India is far too busy trying to figure out why someone in Utah can't get their screensaver to work to deal with any crises of its own.

In fact, despite the rampant spread of infectious disease and other complications resulting from less than adequate living conditions, the biggest challenge India currently faces is helping a 42-year-old mother of three set up her brand-new fax machine over the phone.

With roughly 30 million citizens working in the troubleshooting field, Indian men and women are qualified to assist everyone but themselves. They fix slow Internet connections while sitting waist-deep in sewage, reassure anxious customers that everything will be fine with their hard drive between cholera-induced fainting spells, and listen to iPod-related complaints while fending off giant, football-sized rats.

In 2006, the construction of a new transportation system was postponed, and national elections were once again delayed after India spent six hours trying to help a Michigan couple start up their computer, only to realize they hadn't plugged it in.

PEOPLE » PRAYING TO THE GODS OF WASTE MANAGEMENT

Bhopal
Many Indian homes today feature indoor gutters.

The second-most populous nation in the world, India is home to 1.1 billion citizens, 30,000 backed-up sewers, and a single, broken septic tank.

A deeply spiritual people, Indian men and women are filled with almost as much faith as they are parasites, and have nearly as many gods as they do reasons to pray.

Devout Hindus spend years trying to cleanse their souls of earthly impurities, and decades trying to cleanse their flesh of dirt, grime, waste, caked-on layers of mud, and refuse.

Hindu citizens deem the cow to be a sacred figure. Cows hold a privileged place in Indian society, and along with government officials, doctors, and other members of the nation's elite, possess free reign to defecate openly in public. To have a cow empty its bowels in one's home is considered an honor. To have a cow empty its bowels in one's toilet, however, is considered a blessing.

The people of India speak English as their official language for government affairs, 64,000 dialects of Hindi as their official language for social affairs, and Spanish if a Verizon customer presses 2 now.

While traveling by railway remains the easiest way to commute to work, Indian men often complain about the quality of service, with trains never seeming to derail on time, local lines suddenly going express off a bridge when they're scheduled to crash into a nearby tunnel, and construction work regularly leaving thousands of passengers late for important appointments in their next life.

Although still viewed as an outdated practice, India's tradition of arranged marriage has evolved in recent years, with parents today in charge of choosing their son's future wife, as well as his future mistress, marriage counselor, divorce lawyer, and second wife.

Weddings in India are known for their festive atmosphere, with every family member taking part in the ceremony. After the bride is dragged down the aisle by her father, relatives come together to hold down her screaming body during the reading of the vows. Once rings have been exchanged, and the crying has finally come to a stop, the newlywed couple shares in their first and last kiss as husband and wife.

RELIGION » TAKING IT ONE LIFETIME AT A TIME

Seeking answers to life's most difficult questions, Westerners pray to Khandarohi, the Hindu God of Tech Support.

Millions Of Gods
There are over 330 million Hindu gods. Each deity represents a small component of the Supreme Being Brahman, ranging from knowledge (*Saraswati*) to unity (*Skanda*) to the ability to diffuse awkward situations (*Rashirenko*) to that feeling you get when you're driving a rental car (*Namarishna*).

One Religion Fits All
Hindus may choose to worship any of the religion's gods. If one cannot find the deity that suits him, he can visit one of India's many Make-Your-Own-God temples. Just combine all your favorite virtues, pick a name, and decide how many arms it will have.

Karma
Belief that if one is good, good things will come to him, and that if one is okay, okay things will come to him.

Reincarnation
Hindus believe in the constant cycle of birth, life, death, and rebirth. By their fifth lifetime, most Hindus can't even remember what their name is.

Brahman
The supreme Hindu god is Brahman, a formless deity who defies intellectual description and can be present anywhere... even right behind you.

The Bindi
Hindu women traditionally apply a red dot, or "bindi," to the area between their eyebrows. This area, known as the *agna*, is the central location of concealed wisdom, latent energy, and the eyes of 50 strangers on the bus.

» AROMATIC SPICES ARE USED IN INDIAN CUISINE TO COVER UP THE STENCH OF EVERYTHING THAT IS NOT INDIAN CUISINE.

» INDIAN CITIZENS GO TO THE MOVIES AS AN ESCAPE FROM DAY-TO-DAY LIFE. THIS EXPLAINS WHY THE AVERAGE BOLLYWOOD FILM IS SIX HOURS LONG.

» THE GANGES RIVER IS SAID TO STRIP ONE'S BODY OF ALL SIN, AND IN TIME, OF ALL SKIN.

Bombay
Hundreds of Indian elephants die every year of embarrassment.

FACTS VINDALOO »

TRADITIONAL GREETING
"Hello, this is Jerry from Dell, what I can help you with today?"

AREA COMPARATIVE
Slightly smaller than area of Indian population

LIFETIME EXPECTANCY AT REBIRTH
15.4 lifetimes

MAJOR DISEASES
Irritable bowel syndrome, cantankerous bowel syndrome, unreasonable bowel syndrome

TRADITIONAL SAYING
"Don't eat the yellow feces"

AVERAGE LENGTH OF FINGERNAILS
1.2 ft.

COUNTRY DIALING CODE
1-800-VERIZON

NATIONAL SEX POSITION
The one with the woman sort of...hmm, how did her legs get like that?

INNOVATIONS
New, cleaner-burning brides

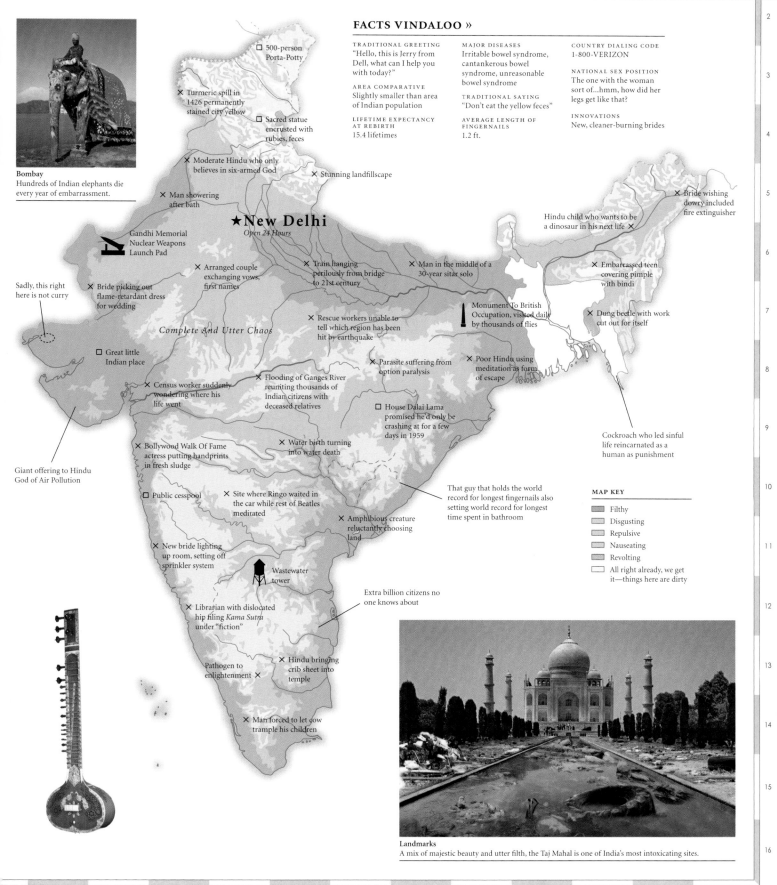

□ 500-person Porta-Potty

✕ Turmeric spill in 1426 permanently stained city yellow

□ Sacred statue encrusted with rubies, feces

✕ Moderate Hindu who only believes in six-armed God

✕ Stunning landfillscape

✕ Man showering after bath

★ **New Delhi**
Open 24 Hours

Gandhi Memorial Nuclear Weapons Launch Pad

✕ Arranged couple exchanging vows, first names

✕ Train hanging perilously from bridge to 21st century

✕ Man in the middle of a 30-year sitar solo

Hindu child who wants to be a dinosaur in his next life ✕

✕ Embarrassed teen covering pimple with bindi

Sadly, this right here is not curry

✕ Bride picking out flame-retardant dress for wedding

Complete And Utter Chaos

✕ Rescue workers unable to tell which region has been hit by earthquake

Monument To British Occupation, visited daily by thousands of flies

✕ Dung beetle with work cut out for itself

□ Great little Indian place

✕ Parasite suffering from option paralysis

✕ Poor Hindu using meditation as form of escape

Giant offering to Hindu God of Air Pollution

✕ Census worker suddenly wondering where his life went

✕ Flooding of Ganges River reuniting thousands of Indian citizens with deceased relatives

□ House Dalai Lama promised he'd only be crashing at for a few days in 1959

Cockroach who led sinful life reincarnated as a human as punishment

✕ Bollywood Walk Of Fame actress putting handprints in fresh sludge

✕ Water birth turning into water death

□ Public cesspool

✕ Site where Ringo waited in the car while rest of Beatles meditated

✕ Amphibious creature reluctantly choosing land

That guy that holds the world record for longest fingernails also setting world record for longest time spent in bathroom

✕ New bride lighting up room, setting off sprinkler system

Wastewater tower

Extra billion citizens no one knows about

✕ Librarian with dislocated hip filing *Kama Sutra* under "fiction"

✕ Hindu bringing crib sheet into temple

Pathogen to enlightenment ✕

✕ Man forced to let cow trample his children

MAP KEY

▥	Filthy
▨	Disgusting
▦	Repulsive
▩	Nauseating
▧	Revolting
□	All right already, we get it—things here are dirty

Landmarks
A mix of majestic beauty and utter filth, the Taj Mahal is one of India's most intoxicating sites.

India

The Wandering Serpent

The Exhausted Hole

Anal

30 Seconds In The Temple

The Not In Your Lifetime

HISTORY » NONVIOLENCE IS NOT THE ANSWER

5400 B.C. The settlers of the Indus Valley are the first humans to develop pornoglyphic writing, covering their cave walls with detailed sketches of every sexual position they could think of.

2600 B.C. The Indus Valley Civilization constructs the world's first urban sanitation, sewage, and drainage systems. These mysterious underground structures continue to confound many of India's modern citizens to this day.

1248 B.C. Snake-charming originates in India after a number of severe setbacks with the art of bear-charming.

New Delhi
A man who regrets wasting his last five paychecks on snakes.

800 B.C. The caste system begins to emerge in India. The highest-ranking social class is comprised of "Those Who Came Up With The Caste System," while the lowest rung is occupied by "Those Who Bullied Those Who Came Up With The Caste System All Throughout High School."

500 B.C. Buddhism develops as an outgrowth of the Indian custom of devising new and uncomfortable ways to sit.

A.D. 300 Vatsyayana writes the *Kama Sutra*. Despite common misconceptions, only one of the book's 35 chapters illustrates sex positions, while the other 34 illustrate how to get out of sex positions.

1504 After sailing halfway around the world, Christopher Columbus arrives on the shores of Bombay and proudly declares that he has finally discovered Cuba.

1600 When India begins to resent competition from Europe, the British form the East India Company in a move to destroy all East Indian companies.

1908 Not satisfied with having occupied their land, British soldiers invade 14 astral planes belonging to Indian citizens.

1924 Mahatma Gandhi popularizes hunger.

1931 British authorities arrest Gandhi on 12 counts of public conduct, fearing that if left to his own devices, he might resort to wide-scale nonviolence.

1933 Discouraged by the failure of his many hunger strikes, Gandhi vows to eat nonstop until India is granted independence.

1948 Gandhi is assassinated by Nathuram Godse, a Hindu radical who feels that Gandhi's overtures to Pakistan have weakened India's position. Godse is tried, executed, and reincarnated as a pubic louse.

1954–1963 The Taj Mahal is built as a mausoleum for Shah Jahan's second wife. Known for its majestic white dome and beautiful columns, the structure is altogether ruined by the fact that there is a dead body inside.

1968 The Beatles travel to India, where transcendental meditation with soul guide Maharishi Mahesh Yogi brings about spiritual awakening and inspires Paul McCartney to write "Rocky Raccoon."

1984 A gas leak at the Union Carbide pesticides plant in Bhopal leads to the deaths of thousands, but on the bright side, the victims are for once not infested with bugs.

1984 Prime Minister Indira Gandhi is assassinated by her own Sikh bodyguards. As she lies in a pool of her own blood, she regrets not checking their references more closely.

1989 A devastating typhoon leaves India with its first source of clean water in years.

1997 After decades of selfless work, Mother Teresa finally gives hope to thousands of sick, disease-ridden Calcutta citizens by dying.

Calcutta
This yogi is five inches away from spiritual enlightenment.

1998 Bollywood becomes the biggest film industry in the world, releasing an average of 800 identical movies each year.

2000 Despite not possessing any nuclear technology, India successfully fakes the detonation of an atomic bomb by getting all 900 million citizens to shout "Boom!" simultaneously.

2007 In gratitude for India's help with their technology problems, several Western nations set up call centers for Indian citizens to contact any time they encounter water that is browner than usual, need help with raw sewage and runoff management, or just want to know what to do about that pile of cow shit on their front lawn.

CASTE SYSTEM »

Cows

Priests
BRAHMIN

Warriors
KSHATRIYA

Merchants, Traders
VAISHYA

Craftworkers, Laborers
SHUDRA

UNTOUCHABLES

TWICE-BORN GROUPS

LEADERS » MAHATMA GANDHI

Although best known for his hunger strikes, spiritual leader Mahatma Gandhi used a variety of nonviolent means to achieve India's independence from England. Here are a few of his less popular forms of civil disobedience:

1917 *Refused to put on clothes for 23 consecutive days.*

1922 *Twiddled thumbs. Promised only to stop if British forces evacuated.*

1928 *Waved around handgun and threatened to murder everyone involved in the occupation of India, but in that peaceful Gandhi sort of way.*

1932 *Bribes—lots and lots of bribes.*

1934 *Kept making that noise with his mouth. You know, the one where it sounds likes he's not doing it on purpose, but you totally know he is.*

1938 *Remarked how British troops could stay in India all they wanted, but that it wasn't going to change the fact that he, Gandhi, had the previous night, fucked all of their mothers.*

1939 *A little something called "begging."*

1942 *Calmly explained to England that, while they may derive temporary satisfaction through violence, in the larger context of a single transitory life, one's actions are inconsequential, insignificant, and essentially meaningless. Later cursed himself for thinking that was actually going to work.*

Pakistan

Would Trade It All For A Little More Kashmir

With the fertile Indus River Valley and the mineral-rich Hindu Kush Mountains, Pakistan seems to have it all. But deep down, the country doesn't care about anything except the disputed region of Kashmir, which it must share with its hated rival, India. In fact, Pakistan has several times offered India the entire nation of Pakistan in exchange for one night of sole ownership of Kashmir.

While it has tried to distract itself by joining the War on Terror, Pakistan still sometimes calls other nations "Kashmir" in the middle of important meetings, and often hangs out on the border, jealously watching the unattainable land in the dark. Even though the UN insists it's a terrible idea, Pakistan seems to spend all its time obsessively developing a nuclear arsenal in the hopes of taking the land by force or, if it comes to it, destroying it outright. Because as much as Pakistanis love the region, they believe that if they can't have Kashmir, no one can.

HISTORY » NOT LETTING GO

6500 B.C. Recently uncovered artifacts from this era include the first farming implements, the first farmer's daughter, and several meters away, the brutally murdered remains of the first traveling salesman.

A.D. 1947 Britain partitions India and Pakistan by forcibly drawing a random line down the middle, tearing millions of family rooms apart and keeping citizens who happen to be in the pantry from ever seeing their bathrooms again.

1965 A war starts when Pakistan notices that India has been moving the border of Kashmir approximately one inch west every day for the last 17 years, meaning Pakistan now controls only 15 feet of the region.

1971 Another war flares up when both nations realize it has been six years since they fought over Kashmir.

1998 After India conducts several nuclear tests, Pakistan successfully explodes their own nuclear bombs in Karachi and Islamabad to prove that they want Kashmir just as much as the Indians do.

1999 After Pervez Musharraf wins the presidential election in a political coup, the transition of power is delayed several hours as the country struggles to understand a bound-and-gagged Nawaz Sharif's concession speech.

2001 Pakistan cooperates with both sides on the War on Terror by hunting down terrorists and then imprisoning them in terrorist training camps.

2004 Dr. Abdul Qadeer Khan sells plans for an atomic bomb to North Korea, enraging the Pakistani government by not getting a receipt for tax purposes.

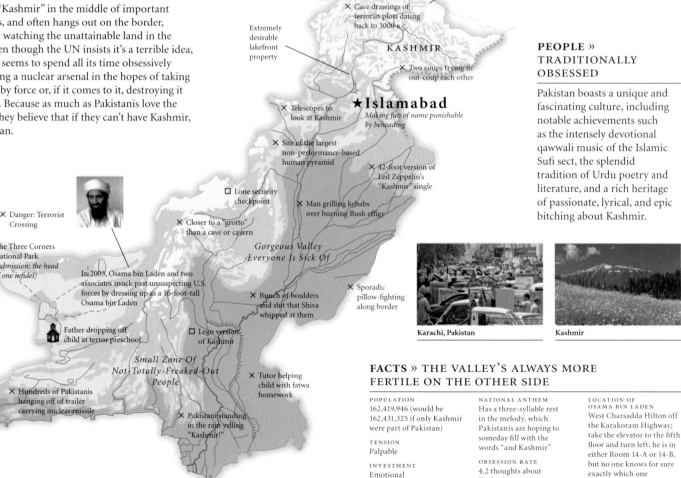

Sheep who just wants to get away from it all

× Cave drawings of terrorist plots dating back to 3000 B.C.

KASHMIR

Extremely desirable lakefront property

× Two coups trying to out-coup each other

× Telescopes to look at Kashmir

★ **Islamabad**
Making fun of name punishable by beheading

× Site of the largest non-performance-based human pyramid

× 42-foot version of Led Zeppelin's "Kashmir" single

□ Lone security checkpoint

× Man grilling kebabs over burning Bush effigy

× Danger: Terrorist Crossing

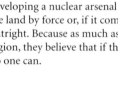

□ The Three Corners National Park *(admission: the head of one infidel)*

× Closer to a "grotto" than a cave or cavern

Gorgeous Valley Everyone Is Sick Of

× Sporadic pillow-fighting along border

In 2003, Osama bin Laden and two associates snuck past unsuspecting U.S. forces by dressing up as a 16-foot-tall Osama bin Laden

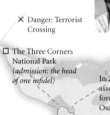

▲ Father dropping off child at terror preschool

□ Lego version of Kashmir

× Bunch of boulders and shit that Shiva whipped at them

Small Zone Of Not-Totally-Freaked-Out People

× Tutor helping child with fatwa homework

× Hundreds of Pakistanis hanging off of trailer carrying nuclear missile

× Pakistani standing in the rain yelling "Kashmir!"

PEOPLE » TRADITIONALLY OBSESSED

Pakistan boasts a unique and fascinating culture, including notable achievements such as the intensely devotional qawwali music of the Islamic Sufi sect, the splendid tradition of Urdu poetry and literature, and a rich heritage of passionate, lyrical, and epic bitching about Kashmir.

Karachi, Pakistan

Kashmir

FACTS » THE VALLEY'S ALWAYS MORE FERTILE ON THE OTHER SIDE

POPULATION
162,419,946 (would be 162,431,325 if only Kashmir were part of Pakistan)

TENSION
Palpable

INVESTMENT
Emotional

NATIONAL ANTHEM
Has a three-syllable rest in the melody, which Pakistanis are hoping to someday fill with the words "and Kashmir"

OBSESSION RATE
4.2 thoughts about Kashmir per minute

LOCATION OF OSAMA BIN LADEN
West Charsadda Hilton off the Karakoram Highway; take the elevator to the fifth floor and turn left; he is in either Room 14-A or 14-B, but no one knows for sure exactly which one

Afghanistan

» IF YOU LOOK CLOSELY, YOU'LL SEE THAT BUILDING IS ON FIRE.

Allah's Cat Box

Once the charred remains of a great civilization, Afghanistan was home to towering columns of wreckage that dotted the smoldering landscape. However, a U.S. invasion in 2001 left the nation nothing more than a shell of its former shell.

The once-devastated ruins of the Haji Piyada Mosque were tragically decimated, streets that mere decades ago were filled with mangled corpses are now completely deserted, and the nation's most prominent craters have been bombed beyond recognition. Even the rubble—formerly a symbol of hope—is now buried beneath many layers of debris.

However, some relics of Afghanistan's glorious past still remain, strewn across the countryside in slightly different places than they were strewn before.

Facing such dire conditions in their present life, most Afghans are eager to get to the next one. Citizens race toward the hereafter using all methods available to them, including guns, bombings, suicides, and, in the most desperate situations, supporting democracy.

Kabul
Rolling fields of rubble.

FACTS » GATHERED OFF THE GROUND

TERRAIN
Covered in rocks and land-mines (25%), inaccessible (75%)

RUBBLE
Urban (36%), rural (64%)

RADICAL EXTREMIST TEMPERATURES
Lows of −58° F, highs of 127° F

CUISINE
With very little that will grow, locals must be very imaginative when pretending to eat

DEATH EXPECTANCY
Soon

NATIONAL ANTHEM
"This Wasteland Is Your Wasteland"

SEMIPRECIOUS GRAIN
Poppies

AID
The U.S. has pumped over $8 billion into the economy, thus modernizing the opium and heroin trades

CURRENCY
The afghani or Afghan; one is the currency and the other is the people, but both are worth close to nothing in Afghanistan

AFGHAN PROVERB
"Killing a woman is a duty, but killing a boy is a pleasure"

ENVIRONMENTAL CONCERNS
That giant hole with smoke pouring out of it

X UN peacekeeper dozing off in rocking chair

X Horse-drawn corpse

X Prosthetic-stump factory

X Lone border-patrol guard

X Man revisiting his childhood rubble pile

□ Terrorist sleepaway camp

• Progressive city allows women to slightly shift burqa

□ School built out of old weapons

Permanent U.S. military base

Man shot in head because his wound looked like Muhammad

X War on Terror re-enactors

□ Site of history's first known rug-burnings

X 18-year-old U.S. soldier still searching for self

X Extra set of keys to World Trade Center

Site where Osama bin Laden became the first person to trek through the Khyber Pass hooked up to a kidney dialysis machine

□ Inducted into the Battlezone Hall Of Fame, 1998

Bookstore

• Sprained ankle capital of the world

★ **Kabul**
Insists phrase "war-torn Kabul" actually has nice ring to it

X Landmine used to level baby's crib

X Decorative pit filled with spikes

• 5,000-pound bomb put this city off the map in 2003

■ Former site of ground

X Hole stuffed with ammo

□ Rubble factory

X Man having terrifying nightmare of woman with a face approaching

X People who've never even come close to experiencing freedom

■ Ignore the poppy field

X Irreparably damaged wreckage

X Demolitions expert seeking inspiration

X Lost and found body parts bin

X Giant Islamic statue commemorating destruction of giant Buddha statue

X Red Cross aid boxes made into latrines

X Man using rocket launcher to open UN rations

• City certainly contains a lot of rocks

X Corpse repurposed as bomb

X Pakistani soldier leaning over border to help reload mortars

X Somebody's head

X Woman being raped in voting booth

Agritorture Sector

Blackhawk helicopter struck by surface-to-air rock

X Hamid Abdul, al-Qaeda's No. 2,176 man, captured here

□ Bin Laden's summer cave

MAP KEY

⚔ Village (10–500 people)
⚓ Town (500–5,000 people)
🔱 City (5,000–10,000 people)
⚒ Metropolis (10,000+ people)

National Geographic's "Afghan Girl"—Where Is She Now?
The Afghan refugee who captivated the world with her 1985 cover photo (left), as she appears today (right).

HISTORY » THE GOLDEN AGE OF RUBBLE

50,000 B.C.–PRESENT Afghanistan enters the Stone Age.

48,000 B.C. Prehistoric skulls impaled with simple farming tools reveal that early Afghans preferred killing each other to growing food.

A.D. 642 Arab conquerors introduce Islam to the Afghans, who up until this point had been killing each other without a higher purpose.

Sir Edmund Lyons

1839–1842 The British Empire's superior navy attempts to attack the landlocked nation by portaging across the Khyber Pass into Afghanistan.

1919 Afghanistan is granted independence against its will.

1979 The U.S.S.R. invades Afghanistan, making a war-campaign promise to send all Afghans to the afterlife.

1981 U.S. supports mujahideen resistance efforts in Afghanistan by arming their soldiers with heavier rocks.

1992– 1996  Afghanistan enjoys a nice, relaxing civil war.

1994 The U.S. attempts to buy back the unused Stinger missiles it supplied to the mujahideen for $100,000 apiece, but Afghans insist that they can't part with the surface-to-air missiles, which they need for shooting down American helicopters believed to be carrying $100,000.

1996 The Taliban, a group of Islamic fundamentalists, seizes control of Kabul, killing thousands of Muslims under the strict misinterpretation of the Qur'an.

Mohammed Omar

1998 Frustrated by his filthy, blood-covered outfits, the mother of Taliban leader Mohammed Omar declares a jihad on tough stains.

MAR. 2001 Taliban members achieve spiritual nirvana through the act of blowing up two giant Buddha statues at Bamiyan.

OCT. 2001 Pressured by America to turn over Osama bin Laden, the Taliban claims they don't know where he is, but that they saw him go that way.

NOV. 2001 In retaliation for the Sept. 11 attacks, the U.S. flies two commercial planes into Afghanistan's two largest rubble heaps.

JAN. 2002 U.S. fighter planes bomb Afghanistan back into the February Of 2001 Age.

OCT. 2002 Hundreds of suspected al-Qaeda terrorists are incarcerated, starved, and tortured mercilessly at an American detention center in Guantánamo Bay. Many see their sentence as a welcome improvement over living in Afghanistan.

2003 The U.S. launches "Operation Valiant Strike" in Afghanistan. Frightened Taliban members surrender upon hearing the mission's name.

A lazy Saturday afternoon in Afghanistan.

Hamid Karzai

2004 Afghanistan joins the civilized world by democratically electing former oil baron Hamid Karzai as president.

2005 A 7.6-magnitude earthquake significantly accelerates Afghanistan's rebuilding process.

2006 In response to a wave of anti-U.S. demonstrations in Afghanistan, Bush deploys 100,000 pro-U.S. demonstrators to Afghanistan.

TERRORISM » OSAMA BIN LADEN

In 2001, sitting on a chunk of rubble in Afghanistan's remote wastelands, Saudi exile Osama bin Laden had a dream. On a bloody rag, he sketched a simple and inexpensive plan to launch a devastating military attack on the U.S. mainland. Using only his multimillion-dollar oil inheritance, the support of the ruling Taliban government, and the CIA funding and training he received while fighting the Russians in the 1980s, he somehow raised a small army of jihadists to carry out the Sept. 11 attacks against the U.S.

In a show of "tough love," bin Laden family friend and U.S. President George W. Bush exacted the harshest punishment he could—forcing bin Laden to live with the guilt of knowing that what he did was wrong.

PEOPLE » RELAXING WITH A NICE, SOOTHING BLOODBATH

Children
Lacking a blanket, an Afghan boy cuddles with his AK-47.

Since ancient times, Afghanistan has been a cultural crossroads for many different peoples and their traditional killing techniques. Today, Afghans become proficient at firing rocket launchers and machine guns while still in the womb, and learn to drive car bombs by the tender age of 10.

Many citizens are employed as poppy farmers, as Afghanistan is the world's leading producer of heroin and opium. However, without paved streets or elementary schools, the nation lacks even the most basic infrastructure necessary to push the product.

Because of this, most families are forced to live uncomfortably in small- to medium-sized piles of rubble, though the wealthiest Afghans can afford to buy burnt-out husks of former homes. Years of adapting to this harsh environment have toughened the people to the point where it now takes two or more headshots to put them down.

Celebration
A bride is joyfully beheaded as part of a traditional Afghan wedding.

Armenia & Georgia

Armenia
"Wah, Wah, Wah, The Turks Were Mean To Us"

The site of the forgotten genocide of the 20th century, Armenia is proof positive of how easily a people can be ignored when they don't own the media.

After a million or so Armenians were slaughtered by the Turks sometime between 1900 and 1950 (although we might be off on that figure) and hundreds—perhaps thousands—yes, likely thousands more were displaced and deported, the Armenians vowed they would not be forgotten, a noble cause they probably still fight for today.

Although the claim of "genocide" has long been disputed, several prominent international historians believe that something of incredible importance happened here, something future generations could probably learn a very important lesson from...if only they could remember what.

Georgia
Even More Christian Than The Other Georgia

In A.D. 310, Georgia became the second nation to adopt Christianity as its official religion, and was immediately praised for embracing the Christian virtue of blindly following.

Since then, this former Soviet republic has shown its faith by building churches on every square foot of its land. With over 80 million mega-churches, mini-churches, and churches stacked on top of other churches, the Georgian people attend mass every Sunday, oftentimes by accident.

Georgia is also the site in which archaeologists discovered *Homo erectus*, a 1.8-million-year-old human fossil that Christian Georgians believe may date as far back as 4,000 years ago.

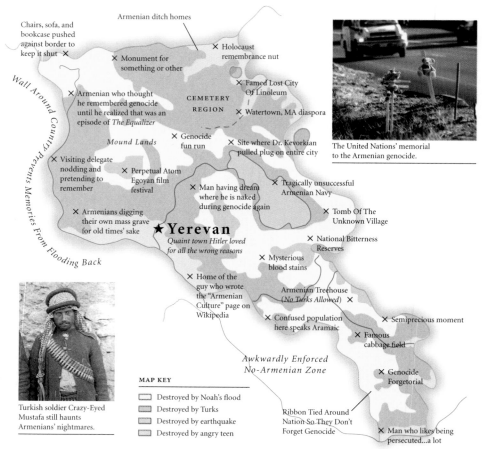

Chairs, sofa, and bookcase pushed against border to keep it shut ✕

Armenian ditch homes

✕ Holocaust remembrance nut

✕ Monument for something or other

Wall Around Country Prevents Memories From Flooding Back

✕ Armenian who thought he remembered genocide until he realized that was an episode of *The Equalizer*

CEMETERY REGION

✕ Famed Lost City Of Linoleum

✕ Watertown, MA diaspora

Mound Lands

✕ Genocide fun run

✕ Site where Dr. Kevorkian pulled plug on entire city

✕ Visiting delegate nodding and pretending to remember

✕ Perpetual Atom Egoyan film festival

✕ Man having dream where he is naked during genocide again

✕ Tragically unsuccessful Armenian Navy

✕ Armenians digging their own mass grave for old times' sake

★ **Yerevan**
Quaint town Hitler loved for all the wrong reasons

✕ Tomb Of The Unknown Village

✕ National Bitterness Reserves

✕ Mysterious blood stains

✕ Home of the guy who wrote the "Armenian Culture" page on Wikipedia

✕ Armenian Treehouse (*No Turks Allowed*) ✕

✕ Confused population here speaks Aramaic

✕ Semiprecious moment

✕ Famous cabbage field

Awkwardly Enforced No-Armenian Zone

✕ Genocide Forgetorial

Ribbon Tied Around Nation So They Don't Forget Genocide

✕ Man who likes being persecuted...a lot

The United Nations' memorial to the Armenian genocide.

MAP KEY
- ▭ Destroyed by Noah's flood
- ▭ Destroyed by Turks
- ▭ Destroyed by earthquake
- ▭ Destroyed by angry teen

Turkish soldier Crazy-Eyed Mustafa still haunts Armenians' nightmares.

FACTS » IN CHURCH WE TRUST

AREA COMPARATIVE
Slightly smaller than Georgia

CONSTITUTION
Adopted Aug. 24, 1995, but still hasn't been told it was adopted

HIGHEST POINT
Mt'a Shkhara, 5,201 m. (5,325 m. with steeple)

GDP
Whatever turns up in nation's collection plate

LAND USE
Churches (42%), cathedrals (20%), basilicas (17%), chapels (12%), monasteries (9%)

DEATH RATE
1 death per citizen

ENVIRONMENTAL ISSUES
Inadequate supplies of potable water, oversupplies of holy water

PUBLIC CONTROVERSY
Divisive debate on whether to display Ten Commandments at school, or just turn school into church

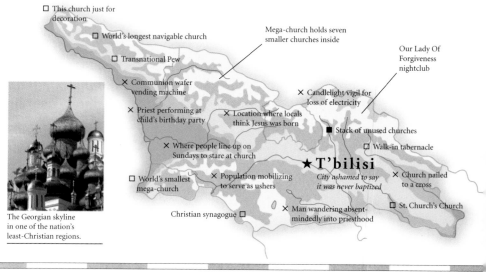

▢ This church just for decoration

▢ World's longest navigable church

Mega-church holds seven smaller churches inside

Our Lady Of Forgiveness nightclub

▢ Transnational Pew

✕ Communion wafer vending machine

✕ Priest performing at child's birthday party

✕ Candlelight vigil for loss of electricity

✕ Location where locals think Jesus was born

■ Stack of unused churches

✕ Where people line up on Sundays to stare at church

▢ Walk-in tabernacle

★ **T'bilisi**
City ashamed to say it was never baptized

▢ World's smallest mega-church

✕ Population mobilizing to serve as ushers

✕ Church nailed to a cross

Christian synagogue ▢

✕ Man wandering absent-mindedly into priesthood

■ St. Church's Church

The Georgian skyline in one of the nation's least-Christian regions.

Azerbaijan

» THE FLAG OF AZERBAIJAN DOES NOT STRIKE FEAR INTO THE HEARTS OF INFIDELS AT ALL.

A Hotbed Of Islamic Laxtremism

The former Soviet republic of Azerbaijan is rife with Islamic laxtremists, who advocate a loose interpretation of the Qur'an and refer to Allah as "The Fairly Gracious, The Overall Pretty Merciful, the One True God As Far As We Know."

After 70 years of Communist rule, Azeri citizens have gotten so used to their secular lifestyle that, today, most can name just one—*maybe* two—of the five pillars of Islam, couldn't tell you who Muhammad was if you drew them a picture, and only go to mosque on Easter and Ramadan.

This relaxed attitude toward Islam has led the nation to sign a bilateral trade agreement with the U.S., as they claim that infidels "are okay once you get to know them."

Few young Azeri men ever become suicide bombers, unless doing so will get them out of saying their five daily prayers.

HISTORY » MUSLIMS, BUT NOT SO UPTIGHT ABOUT IT

A.D. 600–642 Azerbaijan's history during this period is garbled and incomprehensible, as the man charged with the duty of narrating its oral tradition suffered a stroke in 599.

1015 The conquering Seljuk Turks demand that all subjects bow to Mecca, but the Azeris protest, complaining that they threw out their backs the last time.

1848 The world's first oil well is drilled in Baku. Although they have built several more wells and continue to pump oil to this day, Azerbaijan has yet to find a practical use for it.

1992 Muslim women in Azerbaijan choose to forgo the wearing of black, face-concealing chadors in public, instead deciding to keep that sort of thing in the bedroom, where it belongs.

Garry Kasparov

1997 Azerbaijan-born chess champion Garry Kasparov, one move away from being checkmated by the Deep Blue computer system, narrowly escapes defeat by spilling a soda on the machine.

1998 The king of Saudi Arabia offers an all-expenses-paid Hajj pilgrimage to 10,000 Azeri citizens, but they refuse, claiming that there is an *Andy Griffith* marathon about to start.

An Azeri Muslim celebrates Ramadan in his own way.

FACTS » NOT SO MUCH SHARIA LAW AS SHARIA GUIDELINE

RELIGIOUS BREAKDOWN
48% identify selves as "Muslims"
52% identify selves as "Islams"

AREA COMPARATIVE
Exactly the size of one Azerbaijan

NATIONAL SHAME
Never once being correctly identified on *Where In The World Is Carmen Sandiego?*

MAIN USE OF QUR'AN
Coaster

DAILY PRAYERS OBSERVANCE
Typically only pray when they need a raise or want their favorite sports team to win

MAJOR EXTREMIST ORGANIZATIONS
Al-Spayda organization devoted to neutering house pets

NATIONAL PASTIME
Wet-burqa contests

FAVORITE RAMADAN SNACKS
Doughnut holes, pork rinds, gummi Muhammads

Map labels

× Mecca over this way somewhere

× Muslims here thought Muhammad cartoons were pretty funny

• City's mayor is Wiccan

× A muezzin issuing the call to prayer mistakenly calling Allah "Aldah"

Laxtremist terrorist cell blowing up uncomfortable couch

× Farmer trying to make silk with goats

UNHOLY LAND

× Clump of women only halfheartedly wailing

□ Small community of Azerbai-curious Russians

Muslim child assuring pen pal that he is not the crazy kind

□ Hotel room with no Qur'an in the drawer

× Qur'an used as paperweight

× A fun funeral going on here

• City has never heard of the "sandwich"

× Seriously lost American backpackers

× Finest sheep wine in nation

★ Baku

□ Khrushchev mosque

□ Factory that makes Muhammad-on-a-crucifix trinkets

□ Muslim Paradise Bar & Grill

× Azeri woman wearing halter-burqa

□ Drive-thru mosque

Anti-jihad demonstration

× Islamic fun-amentalist

□ "Allah'T Of Fun" mini-golf course

□ Liberal school that teaches both Qur'an and biblical creation theories

40-foot-tall billboard of Muhammad

□ Confused Azeri child worshipping Santa Claus

× Parents celebrating Christmas so 5-year-old son doesn't feel like outcast

The Stans

TURKMENISTAN » ALL OF NIYAZOV'S FAVORITE SHAPES ARE ON THE FLAG.

TAJIKISTAN » ONLY FLAG LEFT IS NOW LINING THE FLOOR IN THE MOUNTAIN HUT OF YAK HERDER YOMJ ASANUYEV.

UZBEKISTAN » FLAG REPRESENTS MANY OF THE COUNTRY'S MOST IMPORTANT SYMBOLS.

Turkmenistan
Long Live The Late President Niyazov!

Since his glorious, state-sanctioned passing in 2006, President For Life Saparmurat Niyazov, known as "Father of the Turkmen," has only become more popular among citizens, who are bound by law to worship his rotting corpse.

Throngs of adoring subjects bemoan the fact that the only physical mementos they have of their late dictator are the gigantic posters of him on every street corner, the 700-foot gold statue which rotates to catch the most flattering sunlight, and every page of *Ruhnama*, the national epic that Niyazov wrote and made required reading for all citizens.

Throughout the nation, the name of the revered dictator lives on in the wide variety of things named after him: Turkmenistan's only university (including several scholarships and four endowed professorships), the main thoroughfare, all airports, most species of insects, a meteorite, the word for when you find something for which you've been looking for a long time, most major months, five days of the week, and a wildly popular grape-flavored soft drink.

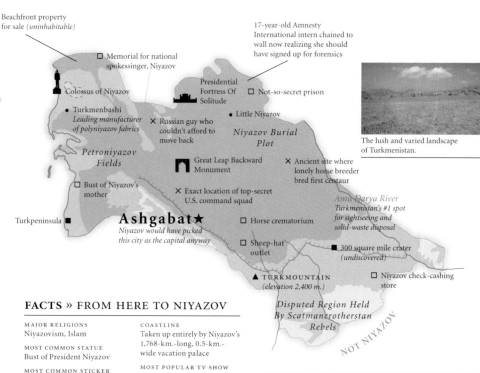

Beachfront property for sale *(uninhabitable)*

□ Memorial for national spokessinger, Niyazov

Colossus of Niyazov

• Turkmenbashi
Leading manufacturer of polyniyazov fabrics

Petroniyazov Fields

□ Bust of Niyazov's mother

Turkpeninsula ■

Ashgabat★
Niyazov would have picked this city as the capital anyway

× Russian guy who couldn't afford to move back

▉ Great Leap Backward Monument

× Exact location of top-secret U.S. command squad

Presidential Fortress Of Solitude

□ Not-so-secret prison

17-year-old Amnesty International intern chained to wall now realizing she should have signed up for forensics

• Little Niyazov

Niyazov Burial Plot

× Ancient site where lonely horse breeder bred first centaur

Amu Darya River
Turkmenistan's #1 spot for sightseeing and solid-waste disposal

□ Horse crematorium

□ Sheep-hat outlet

■ 300 square mile crater *(undiscovered)*

□ Niyazov check-cashing store

▲ TURKMOUNTAIN *(elevation 2,400 m.)*

Disputed Region Held By Scatmancrotherstan Rebels

NOT NIYAZOV

The lush and varied landscape of Turkmenistan.

FACTS » FROM HERE TO NIYAZOV

MAJOR RELIGIONS Niyazovism, Islam

MOST COMMON STATUE Bust of President Niyazov

MOST COMMON STICKER Niyazov urinating on the Ford emblem

MEDIA Nation's only independent TV station shows round-the-clock Niyazov hagiographies

DRESS CODE Surprisingly casual

COASTLINE Taken up entirely by Niyazov's 1,768-km.-long, 0.5-km.-wide vacation palace

MOST POPULAR TV SHOW *Niyazov: Goofing Around*, a hilarious comedy in which Niyazov executes those who commit bloopers

STATE PERIOD OF MOURNING Indefinite

OTHER Niyazov

HISTORY » SEPARATING THE TURKMEN FROM THE TURKBOYS

A.D. 1939 According to legend, God sneaks through Niyazov's mother's window and fills her with His only son.

1940 Glorious leader Saparmurat Niyazov is born. Government-salaried astronomers notice that the stars twinkle a little brighter that day.

1985 The U.S.S.R., staying true to its single criterion for political leaders, installs Niyazov, the most brutal man in the Soviet Union, as head of the Turkmen state.

1987 Niyazov calls for a national moment of silence from 9:30 to 10:00 p.m. to commemorate his favorite television show.

1998 Niyazov outlaws all recorded music, lip-synching, long hair, opera, ballet, and gold teeth. Most Turkmen opt to sit quietly and stare at the floor to avoid punishment.

2001 Niyazov declares all non-Niyazov-related deaths punishable by death.

DEC. 21, 2006 Niyazov dies. At his state funeral, thousands of political dissenters are crushed in memoriam.

DEC. 22, 2006 The day after Niyazov's death, the puppet legislature votes unanimously to make him President For Afterlife.

2007 The legislature passes a law requiring all remaining common nouns in the Turkmen language be replaced with the name "Niyazov." In the same session, Niyazov himself is posthumously honored for his epic poem, *Niyazov*.

OCT. 2007 Niyazov's cadaver continues to provide strong, silent leadership, and maintains the tie-breaking vote in all national debates.

Saparmurat Niyazov

All Bow Before Him
A statue of Niyazov shoots death rays at political opponents.

PEOPLE » SOME TURKMEN ARE MORE EQUAL THAN OTHERS

Aside from those in Niyazov's inner circle, the lives of common Turkmen are harsh, poor, and unhappy. The Turkmen population, the smallest of the Stans, is composed of roughly equal numbers of Turkmen and Turkwomen, according to the latest Turkcensus.

Turkfamilies are recorded as having an average of 2.3 Turkchildren, who attend Turkschool until the sixth Turkgrade, at which point they enter the Turkforce, where they Turktoil until they Turktire. Turkseniors generally die alone and afraid.

» THE PRESIDENT OF TAJIKISTAN ENJOYS A MEAL COURTESY OF THE CHRISTIAN AID SOCIETY.

Rock

Weed

Clump

» THE DIVERSE FLORA OF THE REGION.

» THE TRI-NATIONAL OUTHOUSE.

Tajikistan
Making Its Own Sad, Poor Way

For decades, they suffered in utter poverty under the Soviet Union, but when the U.S.S.R. was dissolved in 1991, Tajikistan was finally granted its greatest wish: to suffer as an independent nation.

Free from the oppressive yoke of an abusive donor state, Tajiks can now decide exactly what they don't eat and when they want to not eat it. They take pride in mismanaging their own finances, failing to care for at-risk citizens on their terms, and not improving the crumbling infrastructure at a pace that suits their specific, seemingly insurmountable needs.

While citizens succumb to starvation and disease at the same rate as they did under the Soviets, now when a family huddles for warmth under a flag, it is their own flag. What were once senseless, avoidable deaths are now the foundation of their national identity. Indeed, Tajikistan seems poised to achieve a new era of economic misery it can truly call its own.

Uzbekistan
About Uzbekistan

Uzbekistan is a country with an extremely important history that is related to the history of many other countries in the region also.

What is the most interesting thing about Uzbekistan? That it is a republic, or that it shares a border with five different countries? Or perhaps the most interesting thing is that Uzbekistan is mostly flat with some mountains and that its major river is the Amu River.

In closing, Uzbekistan is a former Soviet republic whose capital is Tashkent with dry summers and many deer and bears, and its population is 27 million.

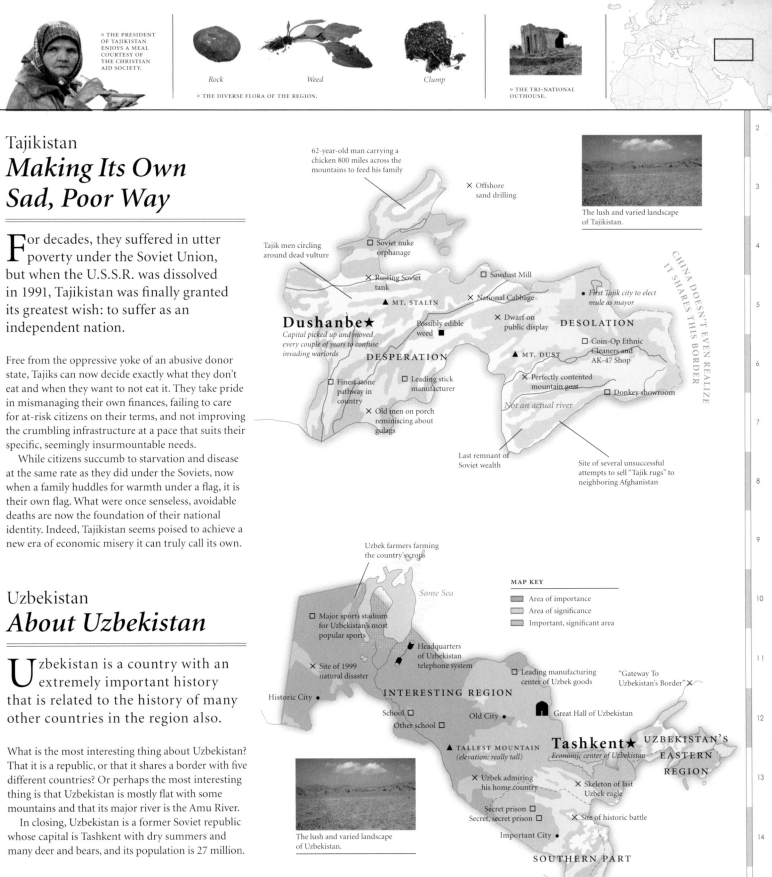

62-year-old man carrying a chicken 800 miles across the mountains to feed his family

The lush and varied landscape of Tajikistan.

✕ Offshore sand drilling

☐ Soviet nuke orphanage

Tajik men circling around dead vulture

✕ Rusting Soviet tank

☐ Sawdust Mill

▲ MT. STALIN

✕ National Cabbage

● First Tajik city to elect mule as mayor

Dushanbe★
Capital picked up and moved every couple of years to confuse invading warlords

✕ Dwarf on public display

DESOLATION

Possibly edible weed ■

☐ Coin-Op Ethnic Cleaners and AK-47 Shop

DESPERATION

▲ MT. DUST

✕ Perfectly contented mountain goat

☐ Donkey showroom

☐ Finest stone pathway in country

☐ Leading stick manufacturer

Not an actual river

✕ Old men on porch reminiscing about gulags

Last remnant of Soviet wealth

Site of several unsuccessful attempts to sell "Tajik rugs" to neighboring Afghanistan

CHINA DOESN'T EVEN REALIZE IT SHARES THIS BORDER

Uzbek farmers farming the country's crops

Some Sea

MAP KEY

▨ Area of importance
▨ Area of significance
▨ Important, significant area

☐ Major sports stadium for Uzbekistan's most popular sports

Headquarters of Uzbekistan telephone system

✕ Site of 1999 natural disaster

☐ Leading manufacturing center of Uzbek goods

"Gateway To Uzbekistan's Border" ✕

Historic City ●

INTERESTING REGION

School ☐

Old City ●

Great Hall of Uzbekistan

Other school ☐

Tashkent★ UZBEKISTAN'S
Economic center of Uzbekistan EASTERN REGION

▲ TALLEST MOUNTAIN (elevation: really tall)

✕ Uzbek admiring his home country

✕ Skeleton of last Uzbek eagle

Secret prison ☐
Secret, secret prison ☐

✕ Site of historic battle

The lush and varied landscape of Uzbekistan.

Important City ●

SOUTHERN PART

HISTORY » THE HISTORY OF UZBEKISTAN

327 B.C. Alexander the Great conquers Uzbekistan, as he did so many other countries, and forever changes the course of Uzbekistan's rich history.

A.D. 1300 Infamous Central Asian conqueror Tamerlane has a profound effect on the country. He kills many citizens of Uzbekistan who write many poems about his deeds and how they made them feel in general.

1865 Uzbekistan comes under the control of Russia, which is a very important nation. During this time, the Uzbek people develop a very distinct identity that is specific to the country, and their population at this time is about 5 million.

1991 The Soviet Union loses the Cold War to America, a country with a rich history that may even rival that of Uzbekistan itself.

Kazakhstan & Kyrgyzstan

Kazakhstan
A Huge Waste Of Space

Larger than all of Western Europe, Kazakhstan was once a convenient dump for Russia's toxic waste and political prisoners. Today, the only vestige of the Soviets is the abandoned Baikonur Cosmodrome, a spaceport facility from which the Kazakhs hope to launch the first pack animal into orbit.

Kazakh officials remain committed to capitalizing on their unwarranted size. They are currently in negotiations with China to pave their entire country.

However, the recent discovery of vast oil reserves in Kazakhstan promises that this prehistoric land of nomadic horse-eaters may be dictating U.S. foreign policy as early as 2015.

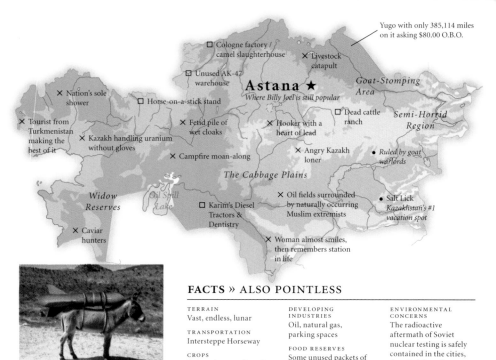

- Yugo with only 385,114 miles on it asking $80.00 O.B.O.
- ☐ Cologne factory / camel slaughterhouse
- ✗ Livestock catapult
- ☐ Unused AK-47 warehouse
- **Astana** ★ *Where Billy Joel is still popular*
- *Goat-Stomping Area*
- ✗ Nation's sole shower
- ☐ Horse-on-a-stick stand
- ☐ Dead cattle ranch
- *Semi-Horrid Region*
- ✗ Tourist from Turkmenistan making the best of it
- ✗ Fetid pile of wet cloaks
- ✗ Hooker with a heart of lead
- ✗ Kazakh handling uranium without gloves
- ✗ Campfire moan-along
- ✗ Angry Kazakh loner
- • Ruled by goat warlords
- *The Cabbage Plains*
- *Widow Reserves*
- *Oil Spill Lake*
- ✗ Oil fields surrounded by naturally occurring Muslim extremists
- • Salt Lick *Kazakhstan's #1 vacation spot*
- ☐ Karim's Diesel Tractors & Dentistry
- ✗ Caviar hunters
- ✗ Woman almost smiles, then remembers station in life

The Kazakhstan Space Program

FACTS » ALSO POINTLESS

TERRAIN
Vast, endless, lunar

TRANSPORTATION
Intersteppe Horseway

CROPS
Stale anthrax, radioactive mouse turds

DEVELOPING INDUSTRIES
Oil, natural gas, parking spaces

FOOD RESERVES
Some unused packets of cosmonauts' powdered vodka mix

ENVIRONMENTAL CONCERNS
The radioactive aftermath of Soviet nuclear testing is safely contained in the cities, deserts, lakes, rivers, and air

Kyrgyzstan
They Are Called "Kyrgyz," And It Only Goes Downhill From There

For centuries, the Kyrgyz have been teased, beaten, and had their lunch money stolen by every major imperial power in Asia.

At the UN, the Kyrgyzstan ambassador is routinely pushed out of his seat by the Chinese and Russian ambassadors. But whenever he informs authorities, the Kyrgyz often suffer an even worse humiliation, such as getting stuffed into a mass grave.

The Kyrgyz's flimsy yurts have often been directly in the path of conquering Huns, Mongols, Soviets, and Turks, who demand the cry of "Uncle" before commencing with the violent pillage of Kyrgyzstan.

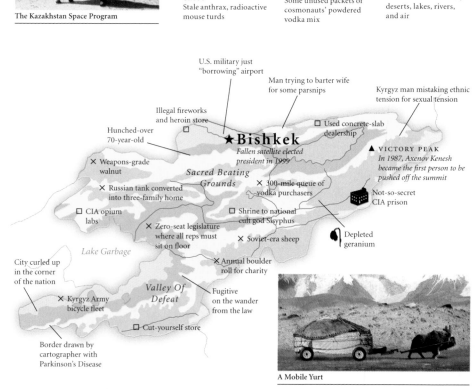

- U.S. military just "borrowing" airport
- Man trying to barter wife for some parsnips
- Kyrgyz man mistaking ethnic tension for sexual tension
- ☐ Illegal fireworks and heroin store
- ☐ Used concrete-slab dealership
- ✗ Hunched-over 70-year-old
- ★ **Bishkek** *Fallen satellite elected president in 1999*
- ▲ VICTORY PEAK *In 1987, Axenov Kenesh became the first person to be pushed off the summit*
- ✗ Weapons-grade walnut
- *Sacred Beating Grounds*
- ✗ 300-mile queue of vodka purchasers
- ✗ Russian tank converted into three-family home
- Not-so-secret CIA prison
- ☐ CIA opium labs
- ☐ Shrine to national cult god Sisyphus
- ✗ Depleted geranium
- ✗ Zero-seat legislature where all reps must sit on floor
- ✗ Soviet-era sheep
- *Lake Garbage*
- ✗ City curled up in the corner of the nation
- ✗ Annual boulder roll for charity
- *Valley Of Defeat*
- Fugitive on the wander from the law
- ✗ Kyrgyz Army bicycle fleet
- ☐ Cut-yourself store
- Border drawn by cartographer with Parkinson's Disease

A Mobile Yurt

HISTORY » LET'S NOT RELIVE IT

PRE-1900 The nomadic people of Kyrgyzstan get conquered. A lot.

1916 The Kyrgyz revolt against Russian rule, giving the Russians a terrific opportunity to try out some new weapons.

1917 The overwhelmed Kyrgyz flee to China to escape a massacre, giving Chinese border guards a terrific opportunity to try out some new weapons.

1920–1990 Country tries not to be noticed.

2005 A popular revolt unseats Askar Akayev, president since 1991. Afterward, no one knows what to do.

Mongolia

Once A Mighty Atlas Entry

Though it now occupies no more than a single page in most volumes, Mongolia was a great and sprawling atlas entry just a few short centuries ago, covering nearly two-thirds of the book's surface, and stretching from page 52 all the way to page 140.

Ancient readers once trembled with fear at the sight of the thousands of words describing Mongolia, each one bigger and more intimidating than the last. With its cartographic might, Mongolia was poised to overtake the whole European section, if not the entire world map.

But sadly, other countries soon encroached on Mongolia's margins, invading its white space and leaving it with only 93.5 square inches of territory.

Today, although Mongolia is but a shadow of its former layout, it will always have its great history timeline to look back on. And nobody, not even the editors of this atlas, can take that away.

HISTORY » THE DECLINE, FALL, FURTHER FALL, AND CONTINUAL FALL OF THE GREAT MONGOL EMPIRE

A.D. 1206 Virile warlord Genghis Khan begins building what eventually becomes a 13.8-million-square-mile empire. Khan later writes that he would have conquered even more land if he "wasn't constantly being abducted by time travelers."

Genghis Khan

1214 Khan allows his hordes to pillage cities and towns, but reserves the right to do all the raping—or, if the conquered women are amenable, the tender lovemaking—himself.

1227 Genghis Khan dies. With his last words, he laments not spending more time with his 14,542 children.

1228 After his death, the people of Mongolia, who have relied solely on Khan's offspring to populate their land, suddenly realize they never learned how to procreate.

1286 Mongolia's population plummets from 65,000,000 to 17.

1380 The Russians easily defeat the Golden Horde. Historians theorize that, while the Horde was made up of descendants of the fierce, ruthless Genghis Khan, they somehow all got his recessive genes.

1381–1888 Nothing happens.

1900 Mongolians are now outnumbered two to one by horses, in addition to owning less property and holding fewer positions in public office.

1939 Japan invades Mongolia during WWII, but after traveling 2,000 miles and killing 10% of the population (14 people), the Japanese army retreats out of boredom.

1976 Industrial Revolution begins with the introduction of the steam-powered yak.

PEOPLE » DOWN TO A SINGLE HORDE

The Mongolian "person" was thought to be extinct until 1982, when a Russian conservationist discovered a small family of them living in a felt tent in Ulaangom. Since then, several more clusters of this species were found, and have all been relocated to Ulaanbaatar in the hopes that they will eventually breed and repopulate the nation of Mongolia.

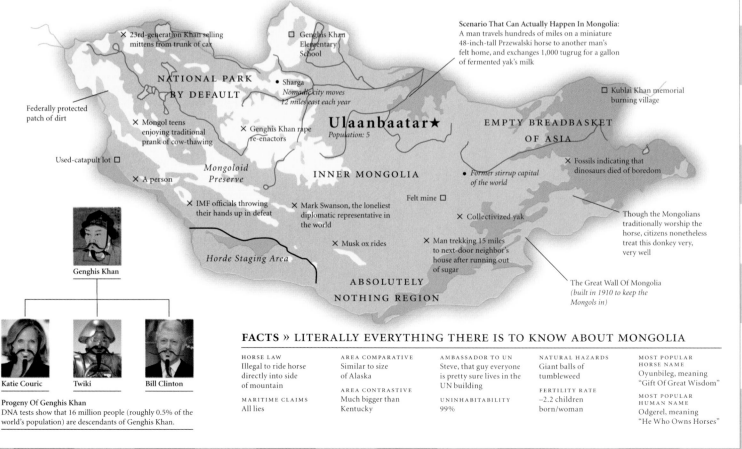

× 23rd-generation Khan selling mittens from trunk of car

□ Genghis Khan Elementary School

Scenario That Can Actually Happen In Mongolia:
A man travels hundreds of miles on a miniature 48-inch-tall Przewalski horse to another man's felt home, and exchanges 1,000 tugrug for a gallon of fermented yak's milk

NATIONAL PARK BY DEFAULT

• Sharga
Nomadic city moves 12 miles east each year

□ Kublai Khan memorial burning village

Federally protected patch of dirt

× Mongol teens enjoying traditional prank of cow-thawing

× Genghis Khan rape re-enactors

Ulaanbaatar★
Population: 5

EMPTY BREADBASKET OF ASIA

Used-catapult lot □

Mongoloid Preserve

INNER MONGOLIA

• *Former stirrup capital of the world*

× Fossils indicating that dinosaurs died of boredom

× A person

Felt mine □

× IMF officials throwing their hands up in defeat

× Mark Swanson, the loneliest diplomatic representative in the world

× Collectivized yak

Though the Mongolians traditionally worship the horse, citizens nonetheless treat this donkey very, very well

× Musk ox rides

× Man trekking 15 miles to next-door neighbor's house after running out of sugar

Horde Staging Area

ABSOLUTELY NOTHING REGION

The Great Wall Of Mongolia *(built in 1910 to keep the Mongols in)*

Genghis Khan

Progeny Of Genghis Khan
DNA tests show that 16 million people (roughly 0.5% of the world's population) are descendants of Genghis Khan.

Katie Couric   Twiki   Bill Clinton

FACTS » LITERALLY EVERYTHING THERE IS TO KNOW ABOUT MONGOLIA

HORSE LAW
Illegal to ride horse directly into side of mountain

MARITIME CLAIMS
All lies

AREA COMPARATIVE
Similar to size of Alaska

AREA CONTRASTIVE
Much bigger than Kentucky

AMBASSADOR TO UN
Steve, that guy everyone is pretty sure lives in the UN building

UNINHABITABILITY
99%

NATURAL HAZARDS
Giant balls of tumbleweed

FERTILITY RATE
–2.2 children born/woman

MOST POPULAR HORSE NAME
Oyunbileg, meaning "Gift Of Great Wisdom"

MOST POPULAR HUMAN NAME
Odgerel, meaning "He Who Owns Horses"

North Korea

Disclaimer: This entry for the nation of North Korea came directly from the North Korean Ministry of Information, the only source for information about the country. It was provided on the condition that it run unaltered.

Our Flag - Huge! Our Iconography is as strong as our Dear Leader.

Welcome To The Official DPRK World Atlas Of North Korea Atlas Page! Nuclear Capable!

Written, Edited, Typed, And Approved By The Cartographic Arts And Studies Ministry Of North Korea, An Actual Department That Democratic People's Republic Of North Korea Actually Have And Feed Regularly!

The Democratic People's Republic of North Korea is the center of the world, and the home of our Dear Leader **Kim Jong Il**, inventor of the Prosperous and Great Country, the Korean Workers' Party, the nuclear weapon, and special People's Food Distribution System, which is evidently vastly misunderstood outside of DPRK. Everybody is fine! Please do not ask further, as constant talk of food is distracting to the worker!

We in North Korea have pride of giant hydroelectric dams, functioning tall buildings, lack of obesity problems unlike lesser nations of world, and our nuclear weapons we possess now and which work. Also, North Korea is welcoming of unification with South Korea anytime, to exchange ideas of government, glorious nature of **Kim Jong Il**, and food please.

MAP KEY

T Trench of Triumph
M Mound of Victory
S Sidewalk of Glory
P Puddle of Unparalleled Greatness

Modern buildings with computers and many other modern things ✕

Radiation Only Making Citizens Stronger

✕ This statue of great and glorious **Kim Jong Il** is tallest!

✕ Excellent choreographic routine celebrating **Kim Jong Il's** wondrous bowel movement

World leaders making pilgrimage to learn at feet of **Kim Jong Il**

✕ No, this statue of beloved **Kim Jong Il** is tallest!

✕ Stacks of nuclear bombs 10-no, 20-stories high!

✕ This statue of powerful and dear **Kim Jong Il** is tallest AND shiniest in all of DPRK!

✕ Biggest, most impressive hole in entire world

This Barren Area Actually FILLED With Busy Factories Making Great Things And Devices!

☐ Laundromat of extreme cleanliness

✕ Proud citizen collapsing with joy

✕ Spare nuclear bombs that we could simply throw away, as we would still have hundreds more!

★**PYONGYANG**
Glorious rays of Pyongyang energy illuminating the world

✕ Economy can be seen growing all the way from outer space, it is that big!

Delicious Fields Of Grass

HOME OF THE SPOILED AND THE WEAK

Our strong and glorious leader **Kim Jong Il**.

Bow down to the destructive force of synchronized marching!

GLORIOUS AND TRUE NUMBERS AND FACTS OF THE DPRK »

POPULATION
23 million (determined using flawless North Korean system of escalating numbers)

MILITARY FORCES
23 million

NUCLEAR DEVICES
Several, better than the devices of any other nation by great magnitude

FREEDOM
Proudly eradicated in 1954, decades ahead of other nations

ANNUAL GDP
Many thousands!

ANNUAL CALORIC INTAKE PER CITIZEN
2,500, exactly the amount considered a healthy daily average

IMPORTS
Please stop talking about foodstuffs such as rice, fish, grains, paper, and leather

EXPORTS
Glorious ideas, trace radiation

STARVATION
No - please desist in asking

The National Meal of North Korea
On display at the National Museum Of The Worker in Pyongyang, it is guarded by both fiercely loyal guards and unbribable, non-hungering landmines in the floor.

Our NuclearMissileMobile
This vehicle was converted from an old mobile food-transport device, which for reasons not including a lack of food was sold to Dear Leader **Kim Jong Il** in 2003.

HISTORY » OFFICIALLY APPROVED CHRONICLE OF ETERNAL NORTH KOREAN HISTORICAL SAGA

The paradise of North Korea, where the scholar, the worker, and the Dear Leader are as one people, sprang forth from the heart and dreams of Eternal President Kim Il Sung after Korea's great victory in World War II. Korea has not yet been defeated at World War!

President Kim also helped little brothers of China and cousins of Soviet Union develop own government, build fearsome and not incompetent military, and feed their starving own people. The reverse of this is not true.

Later long after this, on 25 June 1950, geographic assassins moved 38th parallel of globe to make it look as if North Korea was invading country to South, which is also Korea, and cries out to this day for unification at the bosom of its Northern self. This war also DPRK would win. Details unimportant to average citizen.

Before this, Eternal President Kim had the infinite wisdom of begetting an equally, and more so in many fashions, glorious leader-son. **Kim Jong Il** was of such foresightful aspect, leaderly mien, and staunch bearing that Kim Il Sung felt free to die of blissful transport in 1994, not malnutrition. Then as now, **Kim Jong Il** was named Chairman of Workers' Party, Chairman of National Defense Committee, General Secretary, Secretary General, Personal Life Coach to all Koreans, Inspirational Enjoyer of Luxury Foodstuffs,

and Official Virgin Inspector.

The DPRK continues to lend aid to struggling China in its fight against having a middle-class and with its unfortunate surpluses, perhaps, of food? In any case, no other countries are fit to trade with the DPRK, as we have our own clothes and nuclear devices and are therefore entirely self-sufficient.

The Taepodong Missile used by DPRK to bring justice in all forms. On lower right can be seen bravely sacrificing DPRK Air Force General tasked with throwing lit missile toward the North Korean sky.

In October of 2006, **Kim Jong Il** activated the **Kim Jong Il** Nuclear Device, which registered at less than a kiloton on decadent and weak international scale of force, but over a trillion Jong Ils on powerful, robust, well-fed DPRK Nuclear Radiance Measurement Standard. As a result, DPRK is currently accepting all surrenders.

Satellite photo of Korea shows not crumbling inefficient infrastructure, but that residents of North are aware of importance of saving electricity and going to bed early, unlike misled and trifling South.

Pyongyang
Beautiful portraits of Dear Leader uplift the spirits of the people at all times and places!

PEOPLE » KIM JONG IL, OTHERS

There are 23 million North Koreans, which according to DPRK World Factsbook, makes it the best nation on Earth at populating itself correctly.

Somewhat more slender and light than the other, more shamefully vigorous populations of the world, the Korean worker's inner strength flows not from food, but from their love for their Dear Leader, whose love for them is like cherries, beef kimchi, and unpolished brown rice with a bowl of steamed mountain vegetable. Median age of North Korean citizens varies with local rainfall, but is usually 30.4 years, if not dead. Of natural causes!

The average DPRK resident enjoys a standard of living! This is complete with work, three regularly shaped meals in a certain period of time, and freedom to assemble at mandatory assembly and dance in front of astounding monument to thoughts of Dear Leader.

North Koreans have great pity for other, less fortunate peoples, who suffer under leaders who are not **Kim Jong Il**. But the North Korean heart is generous, and they will one day gladly bring the people of the world with them to a **Kim Jong Il**-ruled paradise lit by a million suns.

TECHNOLOGY » BISON FIGHTER

The mighty Bison fighter, a mainstay of the DPRK air defense forces. For best results, enlarge design with pantograph, trace unstoppable Bison fighter design onto plywood, cut out with saber saw, fill with kerosene, and attach flag from top of left page before attempting to fly.

South Korea

» SOUTH KOREA'S FLAG COULD BE A LOT BETTER.

#1 At Being #2

Despite having grown into one of Asia's economic and industrial powerhouses, South Korea is still ranked no higher than second in each of the 127,481 categories in which nations are measured.

After decades of tireless, round-the-clock labor and innovation, the country remains in the shadow of China's incredible array of resources, Japan's technological advances, and North Korea's unflinching and absolute insanity. Though the nation boasts three of the Asian Gaming Guild's top four *StarCraft* players, the UN still refuses to recognize this as a qualifying achievement.

Since WWII, when the U.S. and Soviet Union—who were much more interested in China—reluctantly drew straws to decide who would have to occupy Korea, the nation has developed massive second-rate companies such as Daewoo and Samsung, flooding the global pawn-shop and clearance-sale markets with countless stereos, TVs, and telephones. This incredible growth has increased their standard of living exponentially, to just under good enough.

In the Western world, South Koreans are known as hardworking Japanese, crafty Chinese, or, in some cases, the people who fought the Americans in the Vietnam War. Likewise, their traditional Asian or Asian-fusion cuisine is grudgingly enjoyed by diners everywhere when the local Thai place is closed.

But with worldwide conflict only increasing, South Korea will certainly be singled out in coming years for not having nearly as many Muslims as nearby Indonesia.

PEOPLE » PRACTICING THEIR SCALES

With a growing middle class scrambling to prove how unworthy they are of their newfound status, it is increasingly difficult to climb down the social ladder in South Korea. Unlike previous generations, many women now work outside the home, whether scrubbing the driveway, patching the roof, or fanning their husbands in the hot afternoon sun.

Once women become mothers, however, they undergo an astonishing transformation into ruthless monsters. Children take their first steps, go through puberty, and experience midlife crises only when their mothers say so. They must endure intense shame at not feeling shameful enough for their multiple failures as virtuoso cellists and high-level mathematicians. After a lifetime of character-building agony, they are permitted to die.

FACTS » ROOM FOR IMPROVEMENT

POPULATION
Not even 50 million

IMPORTS
Juilliard applications

NATIONAL ANTHEM
"Aegukga," which chronicles the making of a Kia Sport Wagon

EXPORTS
Not Sony or Honda, that's for sure

DOMESTIC THREATS
Self-doubt, self-loathing, self-murdering

FOREIGN THREATS
North Korean nuclear warhead stalling in midair

SPORTS
AP Physics, AP Trigonometry, AP Tae Kwon Do

CUISINE
Pungent cabbage–based

AVERAGE ANNUAL GPA
3.998

MOTTO
"You Have Failed Even In Failing," which sounds quite cold in the native Korean

NATIONAL PRIDE
Rev. Sun Myung Moon

NATIONAL SHAME
Rev. Sun Myung Moon

MILITARY READINESS
World Of Warcraft can be up and running in under two minutes

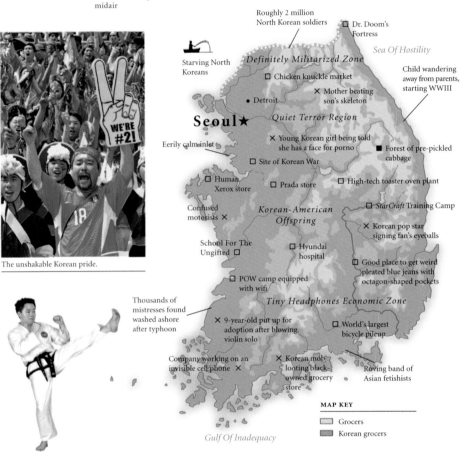

The unshakable Korean pride.

Map labels:
- Roughly 2 million North Korean soldiers
- Starving North Koreans
- Dr. Doom's Fortress
- Sea Of Hostility
- Definitely Militarized Zone
- Chicken knuckle market
- Mother beating son's skeleton
- Child wandering away from parents, starting WWIII
- Detroit
- Seoul ★
- Quiet Terror Region
- Eerily calm inlet
- Young Korean girl being told she has a face for porno
- Forest of pre-pickled cabbage
- Site of Korean War
- Human Xerox store
- Prada store
- High-tech toaster oven plant
- Confused motorists
- Korean-American Offspring
- *StarCraft* Training Camp
- Korean pop star signing fan's eyeballs
- School For The Ungifted
- Hyundai hospital
- Good place to get weird pleated blue jeans with octagon-shaped pockets
- POW camp equipped with wifi
- Tiny Headphones Economic Zone
- Thousands of mistresses found washed ashore after typhoon
- 9-year-old put up for adoption after blowing violin solo
- World's largest bicycle pileup
- Company working on an invisible cell phone
- Korean mob looting black-owned grocery store
- Roving band of Asian fetishists
- Gulf Of Inadequacy

MAP KEY
- Grocers
- Korean grocers

HISTORY » AN HONORABLE MENTION IN TRAGEDY

8000 B.C. Ancient settlers make pottery, but are too embarrassed to leave it out for future archaeologists.

A.D. 1895 Though their beloved Queen Min is killed during an attack by Japanese ninjas, Koreans have to admit that the elaborate fighting sequence was pretty fucking awesome.

1948 Korean independence is declared, second-guessed, taken back, and apologized for.

1953 South Korea comes in third in the Korean War.

1960 Under pressure from widespread student protests, embattled President Syngman Rhee revises the constitution to omit all dangling modifiers.

1983 Following the cancellation of *M*A*S*H*, Korea falls under dictatorial control for 20 hilarious seasons.

1985 The Korean government allocates $1.3 billion for piano-recital preparedness.

1988 South Korea hosts the Summer Olympics, which with only 8,465 participants and fewer than 264 gold medals awarded, is an utter failure.

2000 South Korea enacts its diplomatic "Sunshine Policy" toward North Korea; in response, the North unveils its "Heat Of 10 Million Suns Policy."

Ban Ki-moon

2006 Despite his desperate pleas against it, and his mother's insistence that he'll do a terrible job, Ban Ki-moon is elected secretary-general of the UN and begins to write his resignation speech.

Taiwan

» FLAG SOLD SEPARATELY.

» TAIWAN'S ARMY STANDS IN READY FORMATION.

Made In Taiwan

Taiwan, a cheap knockoff island poorly modeled off the bigger, more durable, and fully functional China, is one of the most shoddily made countries in all of Asia.

Hastily established in the 1600s, Taiwan slightly resembles a real republic, but lacks the basic features of most higher-end nations: international recognition, borders, and even independence.

Its fragile economy, built with second-rate plastics manufacturing, is known to completely collapse without warning. When Taiwan was a brand-new nation, it had thriving diplomatic relations with China, Japan, and the U.S., but they all broke off after just a few uses.

For the past 30 years, Taiwan has sat untouched in the corner of the Pacific Ocean, ignored by the countries that for a brief, fleeting period found it to be interesting and worth their time.

HISTORY » 1992–2007 NOT INCLUDED

2000 B.C. Polynesians settle Taiwan. After only a few hours of occupation, several pieces of land snap off, forming the P'enghu archipelago.

A.D. 1895 Japan acquires Taiwan in the Sino-Japanese War, but returns it to its original owner (China) 50 years later, complaining that its citizenry is defective.

1948–1949 Efforts to rebuild Taiwan's economy prove incredibly frustrating, despite carefully following the poorly translated instructions on the back of their constitution.

1954 Chiang Kai-shek is elected president after he promises to transform Taiwan into a nation capable of folding out into an economic superpower.

1991 A wave of nostalgia hits the international community, as many nations find boxes of old treaties and trade agreements while cleaning out their attics and re-establish diplomatic ties with Taiwan for old time's sake.

INTERNATIONAL RELATIONS » CHINA

China has owned Taiwan for over 60 years, though many suspect the Chinese are just holding onto it for posterity. During the 1970s, they were very rough with Taiwan, often abusing the nation for fun and taking all their frustrations out on it. For a 20-year period, they completely ignored it, instead becoming obsessed with their other possessions, such as Hong Kong and Tibet. However, they always return to Taiwan whenever another nation expresses interest in it. The U.S. and China continue to fight over it to this day, even though each country only wants it because the other one does. The international community has urged the two nations not to start a whole world war over something silly like Taiwan.

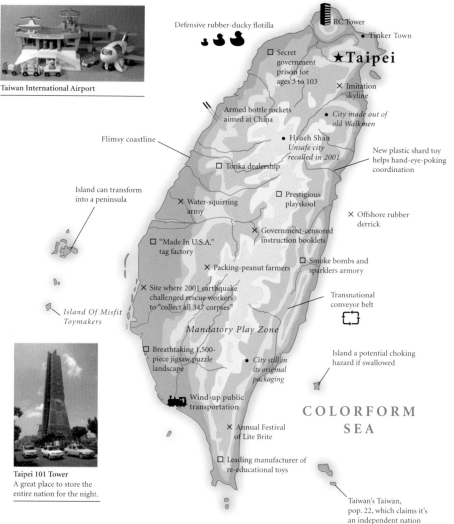

Defensive rubber-ducky flotilla

RC Tower

Tinker Town

☐ Secret government prison for ages 3 to 103

★ Taipei

✕ Imitation skyline

Armed bottle rockets aimed at China

• City made out of old Walkmen

Flimsy coastline

• Hsueh Shan *Unsafe city recalled in 2001*

New plastic shard toy helps hand-eye-poking coordination

☐ Tonka dealership

☐ Prestigious playskool

Island can transform into a peninsula

✕ Water-squirting army

✕ Offshore rubber derrick

✕ Government-censored instruction booklets

☐ "Made In U.S.A." tag factory

☐ Smoke bombs and sparklers armory

✕ Packing-peanut farmers

Transnational conveyor belt

✕ Site where 2001 earthquake challenged rescue workers to "collect all 347 corpses"

Mandatory Play Zone

Island a potential choking hazard if swallowed

☐ Breathtaking 1,500-piece jigsaw puzzle landscape

• City still in its original packaging

COLORFORM SEA

Wind-up public transportation

✕ Annual Festival of Lite Brite

☐ Leading manufacturer of re-educational toys

Taiwan's Taiwan, pop. 22, which claims it's an independent nation

Island Of Misfit Toymakers

Taiwan International Airport

Taipei 101 Tower
A great place to store the entire nation for the night.

FACTS » COLLECT THEM ALL

AREA
Expands to twice its size when placed in water

GOVERNMENT
Some national assembly required

NATURAL RESOURCES
While supplies last

SYNTHETIC RESOURCES
Elastomers, polystyrene

LABOR FORCE
Ages 12 & under

CAPITAL
Taipei®

POWER SOURCE
Two AA batteries

EXPORTS
Anything not nailed down

GDP
$631.2 billion, plus shipping & handling

TOURISM
Country may not match picture on front of brochure

PEOPLE » LIFELIKE

Chiang Kai-shek

The people of Taiwan can be identified by their waxy, rigid features and extremely poor balance, as they can only stand upright if they are placed in the exact right position or if they dig their feet into the dirt. Although they don't have a voice politically, most Taiwan-made people can speak up to five pre-programmed phrases in English, such as "Yes, sir" and "I can work a double shift." Many of them reside together in extremely cramped living spaces inside tightly sealed boxes.

Japan

» THE GIANT RED CIRCLE SYMBOLIZES JAPANESE INGENUITY AND CREATIVITY.

So Sorry For Getting Nuked

In 1945, two atomic bombs were dropped on the nation of Japan, destroying entire cities and instantly killing millions of citizens. However, some survived, and from the radioactive ash rose a mutant race of super-submissive, ultra-vulnerable people able to feel 100 times the shame of any ordinary human.

Forever transformed, the Japanese were left with a vast array of superhuman weaknesses: the ability to see flaws in themselves from up to 20 miles away, hear the slightest sigh of stern disapproval from halfway around the world, and apologize over 50 times in a single minute.

More compliant than 10 yes-men combined, and able to bow for hours without rest, Japanese citizens can lift the weight of the world onto their shoulders after only a brief meeting with their superiors.

In addition, their powerful photographic memory allows them to relive every stumble, stutter, and awkward pause from their last business presentation each night as they lie awake in bed.

And in times of great danger—for instance, after dropping a box of paper clips in front of a group of peers—they quickly respond by shrinking to a man half their size and becoming completely invisible.

Despite their incredible gifts, however, there is still one Earthly force capable of rendering Japanese citizens completely and utterly helpless: eye contact.

Japanese citizens performing their morning bowing exercises.

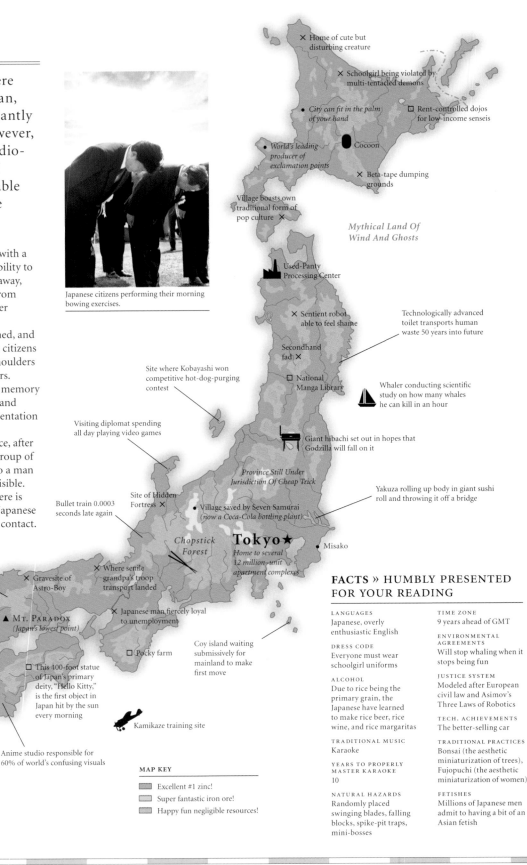

- Home of cute but disturbing creature
- Schoolgirl being violated by multi-tentacled demons
- City can fit in the palm of your hand
- Rent-controlled dojos for low-income senseis
- World's leading producer of exclamation points
- Cocoon
- Beta-tape dumping grounds
- Village boasts own traditional form of pop culture

Mythical Land Of Wind And Ghosts

- Used-Panty Processing Center
- Sentient robot able to feel shame
- Technologically advanced toilet transports human waste 50 years into future
- Secondhand fad
- National Manga Library
- Whaler conducting scientific study on how many whales he can kill in an hour
- Site where Kobayashi won competitive hot-dog-purging contest
- Visiting diplomat spending all day playing video games
- Giant hibachi set out in hopes that Godzilla will fall on it
- *Province Still Under Jurisdiction Of Cheap Trick*
- Yakuza rolling up body in giant sushi roll and throwing it off a bridge
- Site of Hidden Fortress
- Village saved by Seven Samurai (now a Coca-Cola bottling plant)
- Bullet train 0.0003 seconds late again
- *Chopstick Forest*
- **Tokyo ★**
- *Home to several 12 million–unit apartment complexes*
- Misako
- Man committing ritual sepukku after finding hole in sock
- Gravesite of Astro-Boy
- Where senile grandpa's troop transport landed
- Site where 15 vehicles came together in Voltron-like traffic accident
- ▲ MT. PARADOX *(Japan's lowest point)*
- Japanese man fiercely loyal to unemployment
- Japanese logger chopping down trees with bare hands
- Pocky farm
- Coy island waiting submissively for mainland to make first move
- *Grope Zone*
- This 400-foot statue of Japan's primary deity, "Hello Kitty," is the first object in Japan hit by the sun every morning
- Cosplay prostitute charges $50 extra to do Pikachu voice
- City folded out of two-inch square of paper
- Kamikaze training site
- Plasma discharge
- World's tallest bonsai tree (3.2 ft.)
- Anime studio responsible for 60% of world's confusing visuals
- Boring haiku feels 21 syllables long

MAP KEY

- ▬ Excellent #1 zinc!
- ▬ Super fantastic iron ore!
- ▬ Happy fun negligible resources!

FACTS » HUMBLY PRESENTED FOR YOUR READING

LANGUAGES
Japanese, overly enthusiastic English

DRESS CODE
Everyone must wear schoolgirl uniforms

ALCOHOL
Due to rice being the primary grain, the Japanese have learned to make rice beer, rice wine, and rice margaritas

TRADITIONAL MUSIC
Karaoke

YEARS TO PROPERLY MASTER KARAOKE
10

NATURAL HAZARDS
Randomly placed swinging blades, falling blocks, spike-pit traps, mini-bosses

TIME ZONE
9 years ahead of GMT

ENVIRONMENTAL AGREEMENTS
Will stop whaling when it stops being fun

JUSTICE SYSTEM
Modeled after European civil law and Asimov's Three Laws of Robotics

TECH. ACHIEVEMENTS
The better-selling car

TRADITIONAL PRACTICES
Bonsai (the aesthetic miniaturization of trees), Fujopuchi (the aesthetic miniaturization of women)

FETISHES
Millions of Japanese men admit to having a bit of an Asian fetish

Samurai,
1520

Soldier,
1942

CEO,
1985

Hot-Dog-Eating
Champion, 2006

HISTORY » BUILDING A BRIDGE TO THE 27TH CENTURY

10,000 B.C. A broken vase, a blood-stained dagger, and the skeleton of a young woman discovered from this time reveal the earliest known instance of unbearable shame in Japan.

A.D. 50 Early Japanese villagers consume entire meals with nothing more than two primitive sticks held together between their thumb and forefinger.

1200 Karate is developed in Japan to defend against invading stacks of wooden boards.

1410 Japanese geishas entertain their male clients using a variety of methods, including singing, dancing, light conversation, and referring them to real prostitutes.

1600 Backwoods Japanese citizens popularize the ancient art of sumo rasslin'.

1904 Japan defeats the Russian army, killing thousands of enemy combatants while apologizing profusely throughout.

1932 Thousands of bonsai trees are cleared to make room for tiny agriculture, miniature paper mills, and the most adorable little parking lots you've ever seen.

1937 Japanese soldiers carry out the Rape of Nanking, a massacre in which 100,000 Chinese women are raped, and then brutally killed after asking if "it's in yet."

1941 In a surprise attack, Japan hits the U.S where it hurts the most: 2,300 miles off the coast of California.

1942 Japan watches on in embarrassment as a confused U.S. first blames Chinese, then Korean, Taiwanese, Vietnamese, and finally even Hawaiian forces for the strike on Pearl Harbor.

1944 Tuyoshi Oshima, the worst kamikaze pilot in history, completes a 13-hour transpacific flight and lands safely at Chicago's O'Hare International Airport.

1945 After realizing they may have made a horrible mistake, the U.S. drops a second nuclear bomb on Japan in hopes of destroying any evidence of the first.

1946 Hiroshima announces plans to build a memorial park in remembrance of the attack, as well as 10,000 memorial homes, 5,000 memorial office buildings, new memorial roads and sidewalks, a working memorial sewage system, and millions of memorial graves.

1952 Twelve geometric folds are introduced to Japan's constitution, turning the former dictatorship into an elegant paper crane.

1968 After weeks of divisive trilateral talks, Japan signs a tentative peace treaty with Mothra.

1988 Japanese video games are blamed for the rise in teenage mushroom stomping.

1990 Air Japan's first commercial kamikaze flight ends tragically.

1992 Japan significantly reduces crime by instituting harsher penalties for offenders, who if found guilty must now appear on Japanese game shows.

1995 The breathtaking Japanese anime film *Ghost In The Shell* leaves Western audiences speechless by making absolutely no sense whatsoever.

1998 A ban on commercial whaling helps Japanese men rediscover their love of recreational whaling.

2001 Japanese film critics attack *Pearl Harbor.*

2003 Millions upon millions of Japanese citizens pack the streets of Tokyo shoulder to shoulder to protest overpopulation.

2004 After the sixth earthquake in as many years, Japanese officials decide to rebuild the country entirely out of doorways.

2005 World-renowned competitive hot-dog eater Takeru Kobayashi swallows his pride 49 times in under 12 minutes.

2006 Technological advances produce the pocket-sized car, the handheld dishwasher, and the 22-mm. plasma television.

A Japanese man operates Sony's new 12.8 GHz palmtop computer.

Harajuku
One of Tokyo's busiest shopping districts.

PEOPLE » ON THE CUTTING EDGE OF COMPLETE INSANITY

The people of Japan can be divided into two distinct groups: Japanese women, and those who purchase their old and used underwear from vending machines.

Because their culture values extremely youthful appearance and behavior, it is not unusual for women in Japan to dress in girlish clothing, carry stuffed animals around in public, or defecate in their stockings to attract the eye of a nearby male.

Japanese women communicate through a complex system of giggles, high-pitched shrieks, handstands, and the occasional overturning of a pop star's tour bus.

Among men, the traditional greeting begins with a slow, pronounced bow to show respect. This is followed by a second, deeper bow to show that one has not only already shown respect, but that he continues to do so. Third and fourth bows quickly follow to clear up any accidental confusion about whether or not respect has been shown. A fifth and final bow completes the greeting, and serves as an apology for all the unnecessary bowing that has taken place.

Schoolgirls
Japanese robots are able to emulate a number of basic human traits, such as leading others on.

Laos

» THE TALLEST BUILDING IN LAOS.

A Mud Hole

One of the poorest and least developed countries in the world, Laos was bombed back into the Stone Age by the U.S. in 1969. However, a thriving flea-market economy, a transnational dirt trail, and the recent purchase of a bucket has this mountainous nation on the fast track to the Bronze Age.

While only 5% of the land in Laos is suitable for sustaining agriculture, less than 3% is suitable for sustaining human life. Despite this, the Communist government of Laos has attempted to create collectivized rice paddies in every nook, cranny, and crater available. Though rice rarely grows in the country, runoff water from the overflowing paddies creates vast sludge deposits, which many see as an opportunity to compete in the worldwide mud market. In addition, Laos has also invested heavily in its bucket, which citizens hope will revolutionize the nation's trench and digging industries.

FACTS » KIND OF DISEASE-Y

ECONOMY
Rag-based

INFRASTRUCTURE
Primarily sticks and mud

COMMUNICATIONS
The information super-ditch connects Laos to the Third World Wide Web

MINERAL RESOURCES
Small amounts of gravel

MONKEYS THEY GOT
Slow Loris, Golden Monkey, Black Gibbon, Douc Langur

MARITIME CLAIMS
Pretty sure they saw a fish once

INTERNATIONAL DISPUTES
Both Vietnam and Thailand claim Laos is constantly spilling on them

TRANSPORTATION
Public oxen taxis, dragging

PARASITE MORTALITY RATE
83 deaths/1,000 live births

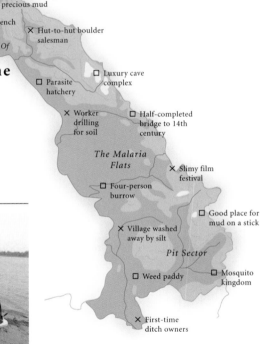

- City doesn't have fire yet
- × Beetle with highest standard of living in country
- × Guy using U.S. bomb crater as swimming toilet
- × Man panning for mud
- × Used-vegetable vendors
- × Scientists hitting each other with bamboo
- *Sludge Central*
- ⚓ Tugboat anchor no one knows what to do with
- ☐ Hidden gunk mine
- ☐ Moat protecting most precious mud
- ☐ Fancy new trench
- *Muck Lands*
- ☐ Hut-to-hut boulder salesman
- • Lost City Of Things
- ★ **Vientiane**
- ☐ Parasite hatchery
- ☐ Luxury cave complex
- × Man eating rice-shaped pebbles
- × Worker drilling for soil
- ☐ Half-completed bridge to 14th century
- *The Malaria Flats*
- × Slimy film festival
- ☐ Four-person burrow
- ☐ Good place for mud on a stick
- × Village washed away by silt
- *Pit Sector*
- ☐ Weed paddy
- ☐ Mosquito kingdom
- × First-time ditch owners

HISTORY » SINKING THROUGH TIME

2000 B.C.–A.D. 1968 Laotians finally emerge from the Stone Age and enter the promising Thatch Age.

1969 Unable to distinguish Laos from Vietnam, the U.S. drops more bombs on Laos than were used in all of World War II, obliterating the country and running out of ideas for places to bomb twice.

1971 Mostly just bombing.

1972 Brief break in bombing interspersed with relentless bombing.

1973 In order to destabilize the economy, the U.S. drops millions of dollars in counterfeit Laos currency taped to bombs.

A Laotian collects the mysterious objects that have washed ashore.

1974 Modern Laotians use shards of glass, military munitions, and neighbors as primitive tools.

1975 The Communist Pathet Lao party seizes power and forces King Savang Vatthana to abdicate. The former king eventually dies in captivity at the Royal Zoo.

1979 A major famine and the flight of hundreds of thousands of refugees to Thailand results in President Souphanouvong's historic "Fuck this shit" speech.

1991 Archaeologists discover the bones of a Cro-Magnon man dating back to 1968.

1995 The U.S. lifts its 20-year trade embargo by bombing Laos once more for old time's sake.

1997 Association of Southeast Asian Nations invites Laos to join the Asian financial crisis.

2005 The nation undertakes a massive dam project to generate hydroelectric power, but accidentally floods the wrong half of the country.

PEOPLE » PROMISING NEW UNDERDEVELOPMENTS

Constantly struggling to pull themselves out of their country, Laotians spend the wet season harvesting mud, and the dry season gathering dirt. Soil erosion, however, has led to a significant drop in how much earth is collected each year. Still, the nation has significant mud reserves, according to the 300 or so citizens trapped waist-deep in muck.

Outside the capital city of Vientiane, most Laotians live without access to basic facilities, such as stagnant water, collapsible shelter, and holes.

Cambodia

Where The Streets Are Paved With Skulls

Known for centuries as a nation of thick-skinned and levelheaded Buddhists, Cambodia suffered a complete turnaround in the late 1970s when the Khmer Rouge seized power, set countless citizens on fire, and decapitated the rest.

Though the tragedy is now behind them, the reconstruction process has been hampered by poverty, crude surgical tools, and a general lack of advanced anatomical theory, leaving for many a deep and jagged void where their brains once were.

FACTS » A SKULL FOR EVERY OCCASION

AREA COMPARATIVE
Slightly smaller than Oklahoma

MISERY COMPARATIVE
Oklahoma circa 1932 times 100,000

EDUCATION
98% of Cambodians can wield a sickle at a 12th-grade level

OFFICIAL MOTTO
"R.I.P."

IMPORTS
Shovels, lime

EXPORTS
Halloween supplies

AWARDS
Rated No. 1 destination by *Killing Fields & Streams* magazine

GREATEST SHAME
Being ruled by France

LITERATURE
Long, sweeping obituaries; terse, minimalist wills

PEOPLE » RICH IN CALCIUM

Composed of dozens of fractured bones and a sometimes-intact system of joints and ligaments, the people of Cambodia are products of their recent past. While most can still be found splayed out in small rural fields, many have also taken up permanent residence in the alleyways and overstuffed dumpsters of the country's more urban areas. Farmers at heart, Cambodians have never been able to forget their deep, inextricable, and often involuntary connection to the earth.

KHMER » AN UNDENIABLE INFLUENCE

The Khmer language is used for government, business, funerals, and pleas for mercy. Ethnic Khmers are a majority in cemeteries, and citizens refer to their ravaged country as "Land of Khmer." Why they do not rename the country Khmer is a senseless tragedy of incomprehensible proportions.

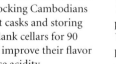

Map labels

THAILAND
LAOS
VIETNAM
The Killing River
The Killing Lake

Really sick of hearing John Lennon's "Imagine"
Border Definitely Not Disputed
▲ Escape Over These Mountains
■ Inadvertently beautiful pile of ankle bones
● Torched Village
✕ Shrine to Baal
▲ SKELETON MOUNTAIN (Elevation 1,123 feet, arms, skulls)
THE KILLING PLAINS
THE KILLING FIELDS
□ Boneyard
● Holiday Inn
□ A single butterfly
Lowest Hellevation
● Flaming Village
Invisible Cloud Of Evil
THE KILLING GLEN
□ Optimist sees this mass grave as half-full
THE KILLING BOG
□ Henry Kissinger's personal ear collection
THE KILLING PLATEAU
□ "World's Greatest Dad" coffee skulls for sale here
□ Half-buried ribcages
□ Bone Hill
✕ Unused scythe
✕ Death's Door
Backpacker finding self, remains of hundreds
Skull Island
✕ Site of 1987's Severed Hands Across Cambodia
★ Phnom Penh
Home of the Phnomenal Styles Hair Salon
□ Cambodia–Vietnam disputed skull pile
□ CIA heroin refinery
THE KILLING KNOLL
□ Law firm of Skull, Skull, Ting, and Skull LLC
Somber Pall
□ Denny's
THE KILLING INLET
Eccentric rich Frenchman who's into kiddie skeleton porn
□ Offshore skull refinery

Phnom Penh Chuck E. Cheese's
A group of Cambodian children play among some old friends.

HISTORY » A SERIES OF UNRELENTING DARK AGES

Angkor Wat, marvel of femural architecture.

A.D. 802–1432 The Hindu–Buddhist Khmer Empire, though peaceful, apparently accumulates an extraordinary amount of bad karma.

1863 French colonizers set out to see if locking Cambodians in airtight casks and storing them in dank cellars for 90 years will improve their flavor and reduce acidity.

1941 The abusive Japanese army occupies Cambodia during WWII, ushering in what Cambodians call "Certainly The Worst Period We'll Ever Have To Endure."

1969 Hoping to reduce the impact a murderous political movement could have on the country, U.S. forces spend four years relentlessly carpet-bombing Cambodia.

Pol Pot

1974 Ambitious, claustrophobic, and surrounded by machetes, Khmer Rouge leader Pol Pot picks up a *Guinness Book Of World Records* at the worst possible moment.

1975 Lon Nol's government is overthrown and flees the capital, leaving only a skeleton crew of personnel.

1976 After much debate, the Khmer Rouge cuts down its extermination list to monks, intellectuals, minorities, people with glasses, the disabled, people with opposing political views, and people.

1977 Thousands of devout Buddhists are unexpectedly reincarnated as topsoil.

1981 Though the pro-Vietnam Kampuchean People's Revolutionary Party wins national elections, Cambodia's government-in-exile maintains its seat in an urn at the UN.

2005 Vowing to deal with the ghosts of their past one day at a time, Cambodians expect to achieve closure in an estimated 1.7 to 3.1 million days.

Vietnam

The Horror…
The Horror…

One of the most popular travel destinations in the world, the nation of Vietnam is visited by thousands of Americans during harrowing flashbacks, recurring nightmares, and long, crippling panic attacks that surface without warning.

Constantly drawn to the nation's unforgettable mix of culture, history, and people—regardless of how many drinks one tries to consume—hundreds arrive in Vietnam each morning after staring blankly at their still-trembling hands. Whether making a brief stopover in the flame-engulfed capital of Hanoi on their way to the attic, or spending hours trading gunfire with Vietcong snipers in the produce aisle of their local supermarket, there is always something for even the most traumatized of American veterans to re-experience in Vietnam.

With guided tours led by phantom platoon commanders starting every hour on the hour, shell-shocked visitors can take in the sights of decapitated corpses, the sounds of women being defiled in front of their children, and the stench of napalm as it burns on a nearby hill, all from the comfort of their suburban homes. In addition, the memory of Vietnam's bustling nightlife, and with it, the prospect of having fathered a bastard son all those years ago, is sure to keep most awake until the early hours of the morning.

In the end, whatever the reason for their stay—be it guilt, regret, horror, resentment, grief, anger, or confusion—Vietnam will undoubtedly have American minds coming back again and again.

FACTS » IN THE SHIT

LANGUAGES
Vietnamese (official), but many able to beg for lives in English

NATIONALITY
Formal: Vietnamese
Informal: Charlie
John McCain: Gook

BIRTH RATE
3.2 children/U.S. Army lieutenant

PRESIDENT
You know what, we're not even going to tell you, because you're just going to make fun of his name

FAVORITE HIDING SPOT
Right behind that elephant grass in Bien Hoa

NATIONAL HOLIDAY
Independence Day (Sept. 2, Dec. 15, Feb. 7, April 28, May 4, June 9, July 13, Aug. 20)

CURRENCY
The dong, divided into 100 wangs

THIS WILL CHEER YOU UP
Vietnam has a burgeoning economy and has its sights set on becoming a developed nation by 2020

THIS WON'T
Over 2.5 million Vietnamese were slaughtered in a brutal, unnecessary war

MAP KEY

- Everyone fucking freeze, we're in a fucking minefield!
- The goddamn LZ's too hot, we gotta dust off right fucking now!
- Hit the dirt, Charlie in the goddamn treeline!
- Oh God, no—oh shit—I swear to God I thought that little girl had a grenade—oh shit—I was sure of it!

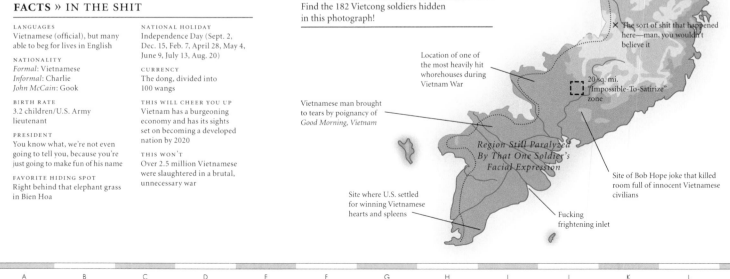

Find the 182 Vietcong soldiers hidden in this photograph!

Map labels

- × Where dad's arms are
- Spot where John McCain was tortured to the brink of becoming president
- × Burial grounds of Nixon's presidency
- **Hanoi ★**
- × Last known location of American innocence
- □ Gary Glitter's foxhole
- × POW who still thinks U.S. lost the war
- □ CIA Memorial Heroin Airstrip
- × Influence of French colonialism hard to ignore in this highly oppressive bakery
- POW fantasy camp
- × Man finding chunks of his uncle in his rice
- Vietnam War re-enactor smoking marijuana, shooting indiscriminately into jungle
- Ho Chi Minh Bike Trail
- × 17th Parallel somewhere around here
- Vietcong guerrilla tactics being used to plan surprise party
- Vietnamese village doing well; you know, considering ×
- × Hyperbole failing to express tragedy of Vietnam War
- × Naturally occurring Iraq War parallel
- Vietnam Veterans Memorial Wall
- × Secret Swift Boat Headquarters
- × The sort of shit that happened here—man, you wouldn't believe it
- 20 sq. mi. "Impossible-To-Satirize" zone
- Location of one of the most heavily hit whorehouses during Vietnam War
- Vietnamese man brought to tears by poignancy of *Good Morning, Vietnam*
- *Region Still Paralyzed By That One Soldier's Facial Expression*
- Site of Bob Hope joke that killed room full of innocent Vietnamese civilians
- Site where U.S. settled for winning Vietnamese hearts and spleens
- × Fucking frightening inlet

HISTORY » DOOMED TO BE RE-REPEATED

2000 B.C. The Dragon Lord of the Lac, from whom all Vietnamese are said to be descendant, has a lot of explaining to do when Mrs. Dragon Lord of the Lac comes home.

1400 B.C. Early Vietnamese settlers discover fire, and moments later, how to get information out of people.

A.D. 939 The Vietnamese, riding atop their mighty war elephants, are easily defeated by the Chinese and their war mice.

1284 The anguished, shrieking tones of Vietnamese classical music can be traced back to this era, when the Vietnamese capture and torture a Chinese opera troupe for their musical secrets.

1820–1850 The Vietnamese struggle to pass the time without any enemy combatants to torment.

1858 The French establish control in Vietnam, with Saigon becoming known as "the Paris of the East," guaranteeing that it will be attacked repeatedly by foreign armies.

Ho Chi Minh

1942 Revolutionary Ho Chi Minh defeats Japanese occupiers in what would take way too long to describe.

1954 The French admit defeat in Vietnam, but in that shitty way where you can tell they still think they're better than you.

1960 Faced with their latest adversary, the Vietnamese meditate upon an ancient proverb, "Ngoc gai dong hoi thanh hoa," which roughly translates to "Motherfuckers gotta learn the hard way."

1961 U.S. military advisers arrive in Vietnam and quickly advise that a half-million more military advisers are needed.

Lyndon B. Johnson

1966–1973 The United States bombs, napalms, and machine-guns every square inch of Vietnam, failing to realize that the Vietnamese thrive in such conditions.

1967 U.S. prisoners of war stay at the "Hanoi Hilton," a camp known for its convenient location in the heart of Vietcong territory, its indoor water-torture facilities, and its courteous, early morning wake-up calls from 10,000 volts of electricity.

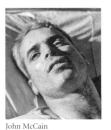
John McCain

1967–1973 Despite being beaten and tortured, prisoner of war John McCain refuses to give his Vietnamese captors any information regarding U.S. troop movement, the location of several inland army bases, his stance on Medicare, who his running mate will be, or his positions on abortion, same-sex marriage, and the war in Vietnam.

JUNE 1967 Thousands of hippies join the war effort when they hear Jefferson Airplane will be playing a free USO event in Saigon later that fall.

1968 In a graphic show of military incompetence, hundreds of My Lai villagers are massacred by American soldiers, instead of slaughtered as they were ordered to be.

DEC. 1968 American Gen. William Westmoreland, a distinguished Eagle Scout, confounds the Vietcong with a series of complex knots.

MAY 1970 U.S. forces realize they may have entered into war with Vietnam for the wrong reasons, none of which include "having a good time" or "meeting new and interesting people."

1971 Your half-brother is born in Saigon.

1972 The U.S. achieves its biggest military victory upon defeating its purpose.

1973 After suffering the deaths of 58,000 American troops and killing only four enemy combatants at Kent State University, the U.S. withdraws from Vietnam.

1989 The premiere of the Vietnam War–based musical *Miss Saigon,* a senseless, unnecessary tragedy that dragged on for too many years and traumatized everyone who experienced it.

1994 The bodies of nearly 50,000 American soldiers are finally sent back to their families when the U.S. lifts its 20-year trade embargo on Vietnam.

2000 U.S. President Bill Clinton reports to Vietnam 30 years late.

PEOPLE » WATCHING YOU EVEN NOW

Known for their incredible stealth, exceptional swiftness, and uncanny ability to blend in with any environment, the people of Vietnam have you completely surrounded. Whatever you do now, don't look up.

Keep your eyes locked right here on the page. Pretend as if you're reading about Vietnam's literacy rate (93%) or the nation's chief agricultural crop (rice) if you have to. Take a deep breath. Nice and easy. Good.

NO, DON'T TURN THE PAGE, THEY'LL KNOW! Okay, okay, calm down, you're all right, you're all right. Do you want to get out of this alive? Well, pull yourself together then for Christ's sake.

Now listen carefully: What you're going to need to do is first reach down into your pocket...good...good...careful...be careful of your keys...and...NO! NO! YOU IDIOT! GET DOWN! GET THE FUCK DOWN! AAAAARRRRRRGGGHHH!

Dong Ha
Two American tourists have fun imagining what life was like during the Vietnam War.

VIETNAM » COULD IT BE THE NEXT VIETNAM?

The Hanoi Hilton

Over the past decade, a worrisome trend has emerged in Southeast Asia—nations in this region are, one by one, beginning to fall to Prosperity. Dubbed the "Green Scare," this economic ideology was first observed in Capitalist China in the late 1990s, and the early warning signs can already be seen in Vietnam—electricity, running water, even hot meals. There is a real fear that, if wealth continues to spread unabated, it may soon reach Laos, Thailand, and other underdeveloped nations, posing a great threat to the American way of life, namely the import of manufactured goods and agricultural products at little to no expense. The U.S. and its allies have vowed to do whatever it takes—including a protracted, costly invasion—to prevent this from happening.

Thailand

» THE KING OF
THAILAND'S ROYAL
SPOO RAG.

» THIS BEAUTIFUL
THAI WOMAN BOASTS
A NINE-INCH PENIS.

» THE BAHT, A SPECIALLY
DESIGNED BILL MADE TO
FIT INTO THAILAND'S
SMALLEST G-STRINGS

Where A Kid Can Be A Kid Prostitute

Steeped in equal parts ancient tradition and the bodily fluids of Western sex-tourists, the nation of Thailand enters the 21st century grappling with an emerging global economy, political unrest, and the seductively sweaty bodies of delicately featured underage rent-boys.

Thailand is known for its variety of tourist attractions, including bars that serve as guises for child brothels, restaurants that serve as guises for child brothels, and museums that serve as guises for child brothels. In addition, the nation is home to several hundred adult brothels, which also serve as guises for child brothels.

A land of interesting, complicated, and occasionally sickening history, Thailand is the only nation in Southeast Asia never to have been subjugated by a European power—at least not without seeing the money up front.

With an unusually free press, several growing Muslim separatist movements, and a burgeoning but unpredictable technology sector, modern Thailand remains a nation caught between prosperity and collapse, a country that could truly go either way— or even Around the World twice in each hole, if the price is right.

Streets Of Bangkok
Aging Thai hookers look for a john before naptime.

MAP KEY

- Red-light alleyway
- Red-light bathroom
- Red-light elementary school
- Red-light Museum of Natural History & Science
- Red-light AIDS clinic

▲ *Mountain successfully deep-throated by Thai 14-year-old in 2005*

✕ Poon reserves

✕ Man angered to find out prostitute actually 19

□ Great little Thai place

● *Phrae*
City known for tolerance toward gay-fisting community

✕ Mystery orifice

Nakhom Phanom ●
40% of education budget spent on shortening school uniforms

□ XXX hospital

✕ Heavily congested sex traffic

✕ Privates sector

So Wetlands

✕ STDs known for balance of spicy, sour, sweet, salty, bitter, and chunky

Only region in world where bird flu was transmitted from humans to chickens

Prostitute accepting lollipops as pay ✕

□ Tourist Center / Short-Term Foster-Care Office

✕ Fetus in a teddy

✕ Site of "Handjobs Across Thailand"

□ Used fuck-swing shop

□ Drive-thru abortion center

□ Trouser snake den

Red-Light District

✕ Nation's most glorious hole

✕ 12-year-old prostitute faking knowing what orgasm is

Blueball District

Bangkok★
President currently trying to prevent coup via telephone

"Just Friends" District

Child selling body to pay preschool tuition

Sexually drained Westerners

✕ Inspector making sure there's no grass on the playing field

Sex-crazed Westerners

✕ Barely illegal teens

Man who can only afford 25-year-old prostitute

✕ Leaky dam being plugged in sexiest manner possible

Rare statue of Standing Buddha

□ Great little orphanage bar

Site where military absent-mindedly staged coup

Pattani ●
City excited about being included in its first-ever atlas

FACTS » THE CUSTOMER ALWAYS COMES FIRST

INFANT FERTILITY RATE
92%

IMPORTS
Petroleum jelly

EXPORTS
Rice, rare and esoteric venereal diseases, tin

CLIMATE
Hot and wet

SIX-WAY WITH CHEERLEADER, CHEERLEADER'S MOM, SIAMESE TWINS, AND FOREIGN MINISTER IN CHARGE OF ECONOMIC DEVELOPMENT
$175 USD

LENGTH OF TIME LOVE YOU
Long

JUSTICE SYSTEM
Handcuffs, chains, mild strangulation, and series of sharp lashes to the buttocks, until safety word is uttered

TERRAIN
Central Plain, Khorat Plateau in the east, thousands of shaved crevices in Bangkok

LOWEST POINT
Membership bid for Epcot Center denied

» A ROW OF GOLDEN STATUES LINE THE PATH TO THE ROYAL CHAMPAGNE ROOM IN BANGKOK.

HISTORY » WITH A HAPPY ENDING

5 MILLION B.C. A steaming oceanic vent leaks a cloudy discharge, creating a crab-infested landmass that will one day grow into Thailand.

A.D. 200 Buddhist monks develop the martial sex style known as Thai Kickfucking.

1238 The Sukhothai kingdom is founded on the Siamese principle of "father governs children," under which all citizens could take their problems directly to the king. As the empire grows, however, people have to start going through the king's assistant, the king's assistant's assistant, and later, royal comment cards.

1283 King Ramkhamhaeng establishes the Thai alphabet, and, after never being able to remember it, the Thai alphabet song.

1431 The armies of Ayutthaya invade the Khmer city of Angkor. Although this is more of a civil war than a coup, Thais still revere this time in history, seeing it as the first of their many festive, colorful, almost annual internal struggles for national control.

1440–1939 The people of Thailand call their country by the wrong name for nearly 500 years.

1511 Sailing along the international skin-trade route, Portuguese sexplorers discover the southern region of hundreds of Thai women.

1782 The city of Bangkok is chosen as the national capital, establishing an enduring yet unfortunate international pun.

1860 Seeking a Western educator for his children, King Mongkut of Siam hires British governess Anna Leonowens, who teaches them how to fabricate portions of one's life story so that it might be adapted into a stage play, a musical, and several films called *The King And I.*

1939 Siam changes its name to Thailand, which translates as "Land Of The First Time Is Free, Baby."

1942 Thailand declares war on the U.S., but the Thai ambassador in Washington refuses to deliver the declaration, as he is in the middle of a luncheon with Franklin Roosevelt and thinks the president is finally starting to like him.

1955 SEATO (Southeast Asia Treaty Organization) disbands citing its terrible acronym.

1977 Military seizes power in a bloodless, and surprisingly fun, coup.

1990 Citing a need to control the spread of STDs, the government installs a monitoring system of coin-operated two-way mirrors in every home.

1997 Thailand suffers greatly in the Asian financial crisis, as the baht loses 66% of its value and the cost of a blowjob from an 8-year-old skyrockets to almost $2 U.S.

2003 The bird-flu epidemic forces Thailand to enact stricter regulation of the chicken-prostitution industry.

2004 To aid Thailand's struggling economy, the U.S. stuffs $1 million in foreign aid into the G-string of a Thai hooker.

2006 The Royal Thai Army seizes control of the nation while PM Thaksin Shinawatra is in New York. Thaksin addresses his wildly celebrating people by satellite, saying he is sorry he could not be there for their historic 100th coup, but is proud to have played his own small part.

The Thai king's position as Rim Inspector is purely ceremonial.

PEOPLE » SOMEONE FOR EVERYONE

Education
Most Thai first-graders can fuck at a 12th-grade level.

If one knows where to look in Bangkok, one can find a diverse mix of cultures and people: schoolgirls, ladyboys, barely legal teens, dancers, bar girls, schoolboys, trannies (pre- and post-op), hunky chunkers, mama-sans, Garys Glitter, shockingly brutal kickboxers, and former medium-ranked officials of the British government. Each group has its own colorful neighborhood, distinctive folkways, hourly rates, and varying policies on condom use.

While most Thai citizens are often cold and reserved on the outside, on the inside they are generally warm, deep, generous, unbelievably wet, compassionate, and surprisingly tight.

The traditional dress of Thailand can be found either sliding down the legs of a Thai citizen, piece by piece in a trail leading from the hotel door to the bedroom, or just balled up in the corner of a darkened alleyway. It is also used to fasten all four limbs to their respective bedposts.

The average Thai citizen spends all day in bed, slaving away at work. Most of them put in incredibly long hours, often taking overnight shifts and serving several clients at once. For some, the workday is so stressful that they barely have time to breathe. Many feel objectified, demeaned, and even physically abused at their job. To make matters worse, they only get one short bathroom break in which to shower, rinse their mouths out, and call their two children at home.

This has put a strain on many relationships, as by the time most get home from work, the last thing they want to even think about is sex.

Despite these difficult working conditions, Thailand is relatively prosperous compared to its neighbors, though there are pockets of poverty where children are put to bed still hungry for cock.

THAI CUISINE »

Sweet & Sour Virgin............$6.95 🌶
An enticing starter sure to satisfy. 48 oz. of juicy dark meat served on a bed. This house favorite will have you coming back again and again. *(Add $4.95 for twin sister)*

Nakhon Surprise....................$7.50
Lean, tender, sizzling-hot. Guaranteed to be like nothing you've ever tried before. Put your inhibitions aside and dig in! *(Warning: Might get a little messy)*

Combination Platter........$8.95 🌶🌶
Your choice of three: regular, gay, lesbian, mature, schoolgirl, shemale, grannie, plumper, duck. Perfect for sharing.

Taste Of Heaven....................$5.45
Golden brown on the outside, hot and gooey on the inside. Best stuffed with 6 to 10 inches of meat.

Southeastern Supreme......$9.75 🌶🌶
Able to satisfy even the largest of sexual appetites, this guilty pleasure is just waiting to be drizzled in a creamy white sauce. *Towel included.*

Spicy Shanghai Delight...$15.89 🌶🌶🌶
Hot n' spicy family-style offering will get your blood pumping and your temperature rising. *Serves 6 to 8 at once.*

Today's Special..........$25.00 🌶🌶🌶
Ms. Ayaka Siripon.

For delivery, call +66 (230)-387-3789
*For ages 10 and under, please ask for our Kids Menu.
**Staff not responsible if you find a hair on your selection.

Malaysia

» ONLY THE DESTRUCTION OF THE GREAT SATAN COULD RIVAL THE BEAUTY OF MALAYSIA.

An Allah-Inclusive Terrorist Resort

The leading vacation destination for Islamic extremists, Malaysia is the perfect place for worn-out radicals to loosen their suicide belts, put their feet up on their wives, and forget all about the Zionist plot to take over the world.

A relaxing retreat from the frantic pace of insurgent life, Malaysia offers visitors a chance to unwind with a strict translation of the Qur'an by the pool, forbid their children from having fun at one of the nation's many beaches, or just take a romantic walk around the capital of Kuala Lumpur three paces ahead of their spouse. In fact, Malaysia is the closest an Islamic fundamentalist can get to paradise without blowing himself up outside a foreign U.S. embassy.

With dozens of hijacked flights landing at Sepang International Airport every week, this Mecca away from Mecca has vacationing jihadis thanking Allah five times a day for the chance to finally get some rest—rest not even the murderous and illegitimate state of Israel can take away from them.

Malaysia also offers Internet and car-bomb-rental services for the business traveler.

PEOPLE » BOMBING AWAY THE DAYS

Not everyone in Malaysia is on vacation, and each morning thousands of citizens bid goodbye to the bomb-making materials in their basement and set out for another long and grueling day of planning attacks against the Western world.

While their work is rarely glamorous and few ever receive the recognition they deserve, Malaysians continue to toil in hopes of one day making a difference in the lives of innocent marketplace vendors, coffeeshop patrons, or those just happening to be boarding the same bus to Tel Aviv.

An Islamic vacationer trades terrorism for tourism.

A TYPICAL MALAYSIAN VACATION ITINERARY »

9:30 A.M. *Check all suspicious luggage and suitcase nukes at hotel front desk*

9:45 A.M. *Blame poor mini-bar selection on the Jews*

11:30 A.M. *Meet up with wife staying at different, nearby hotel*

11:45 A.M. *Strike wife repeatedly for forgetting to pack the suntan lotion*

12:00 P.M. *Order family to commence having fun on vacation*

12:30 P.M. *Enjoy lunch at "All You Can't Eat" buffet*

1:15 P.M. *Declare jihad on lack of convenient beach parking*

2:30 P.M. *Take inflatable prayer mat out for a swim*

2:40 P.M. *Promise children you won't work during vacation, the way you did in Madrid in 2004*

3:00, 3:15, 3:30, 3:45 P.M. *Thank Allah for much-needed break from daily routine*

5:00 P.M. *Lazily burn American flag between afternoon naps*

7:00 P.M. *Pose for family photo in front of full-scale replica of 9/11 Ground Zero*

11:00 P.M. *Put children to bed. Order one of hotel's many after-dark beheading videos*

12:30 A.M. *Shave beard and all body hair to purify spirit. Bid goodbye to wife. Prepare to board hijacked flight for L.A. in the morning*

FACTS » FORBIDDEN BY SHARIA LAW

MOTTO
"Where Every Day Is Ramadan—But, You Know, In The Positive Sense"

RELIGIOUS BREAKDOWN
Muslim (62%), Infidel (20%), Heathen (18%)

BOUNDARIES
Kind of all over the place

HUMAN RIGHTS RECORD
177–54

WIDELY KNOWN FACT
Rock singer Lou Reed is not from Malaysia

LEGAL SYSTEM
Islamic tourists are forbidden from trading their wives for extra beach towels

NOTABLE INVENTIONS
Two-piece burqa, travel-size Qur'an, bomb with snooze button

LAND OF CONTRASTS?
Yes

MONKEYS THEY GOT
The kind with the ass hanging out

Hotel with Qur'an in nightstand, closet, bathroom, under both beds, and on top of television

Coin-operated binoculars facing Mecca

× Sunset filling extremist with slightly less hate toward infidels

× Jewish family very angry at their travel agent

Luxury caves

Hammock tied between two Muslim women

★ **Kuala Lumpur**

× Neil Hamburger, left for dead

Petronas Twin Towers (built in celebration of 9/11 attacks)

× Kids building, then destroying, two twin sand towers

Elderly man telling same old story about how Malaysia got to be on two separate landmasses

Frustrated Muslim strapping explosives to coconut to get it open

Jet full of soon-to-be-ignored Malaysian exchange students headed to America

× Flotsam filling up good amount of empty white space here

Great out-of-the-way place to plan future terrorist attacks

Natural beauty of coast shrouded in accordance with strict Sharia law ×

Terrorist escaping daily grind, authorities ×

Muslim tourist homesick for smoking craters ×

Deforestation has left this power line inhabited by nearly 100 distinct species of birds

Site where nation hid GDP so they wouldn't waste it, but have since forgotten where they put it

Headless Beach

× Terrorist attraction

× Region marked by suspicious amount of racial harmony

× Poverty here bears strong colonial influence

× Scenic view leaves Muslim woman speechless until given permission to talk

Extremist awaiting an afterlife of leisure

× Muslim environmentalist chaining wife to tree

A B C D E F G H I J K L M

» THIS IS WHAT THE SULTAN OF BRUNEI WEARS WHEN HE DOESN'T CARE HOW HE LOOKS.

BRUNEI » THIS $4 MILLION FLAG REPRESENTS BRUNEI'S TENDENCY TO OVERSPEND.

HISTORY » RICH WITH HISTORICAL THINGS HAPPENING

2100 B.C. Shards of broken pots confirm the existence of one of the earliest and most accident-prone civilizations on Earth.

A.D. 1400 Malaysia becomes the center of the East Indian spice rack trade.

1509–1511 Invading Portuguese forces devastate the native population of Malaysia by explaining to them that they are about to be invaded.

1641 The Dutch easily oust the Portuguese, whose control over the area for the last 20 years has consisted of a single scarecrow wearing a Portuguese hat.

1824 In a three-nation trade, the Dutch receive the port city of Bengkulen from the British, and send Admiral Geert Van den Heuvel to Germany. The British receive modern-day Malaysia and Germany's second-round military draft pick in 1825.

1941 Following reports that Malaysia has come under Japanese attack, British officials quickly respond by granting the nation emergency independence.

1947 During its Tin Boom, Malaysia constructs everything out of the plentiful resource. However, 10 mph winds soon blow over and crumple dozens of major cities.

1955 Malaysia holds its first-ever democratic elections. Millions of citizens are so excited that they completely forget to vote.

Anwar Ibrahim

1966 In honor of President Lyndon B. Johnson's visit to Malaysia, national officials establish a hotel reservation in his name.

1968 Race riots erupt in Malaysia between the ethnic Malay majority, the wealthy Chinese minority, and probably some black people.

1991 Hoping to attain developed-nation status by 2020, Malaysia launches its ambitious "Vision 2020" program. Unfortunately, the nearly $25 billion spent on promotional banners and buttons pushes the target date back to 2456.

The Petronas Twin Towers
The only twin towers in the world to be visited by Islamic extremists through the front door.

1998 Kuala Lumpur becomes the first Asian city to host the Commonwealth Games, which in reality is just a watered-down version of the Special Olympics.

1998–2004 Malaysia builds the world's tallest buildings, the Petronas Towers, and also claims the world record for never shutting up about them.

2000 Several high-level al-Qaeda members meet in Kuala Lumpur to plan attacks on the USS Cole, strikes on the World Trade Center towers, and how to get the most out of their three-night stay in Malaysia.

2002 Deputy Prime Minister Anwar Ibrahim is found guilty of sodomy and sentenced to nine years in prison, a punishment he is delighted to accept.

Brunei
A Money-Rich Nation

Brunei is ruled by Hassanal Bolkiah, a wealthy sultan who always surrounds himself with beautiful oil, soft luxurious cash, and the most expensive wives money can buy.

Bolkiah inherited Brunei from his father in 1967, and the first thing he did was buy a brand-new population, as the one that had been left there looked old and dirty. A few years later, he purchased the nation's independence from the U.K. for $12 million.

Since then, the sultan has used his vast private fortune to get Brunei just the way he likes it. He imported a few Swiss Alps to spruce up the nation's landscape, and later commissioned the construction of hundreds of pristine rainforests and white-sand beaches along the coast.

In 2002, Bolkiah was lauded for lowering Brunei's unemployment rate to 0%, when he gave everyone in the nation a full-time job hand-feeding him grapes.

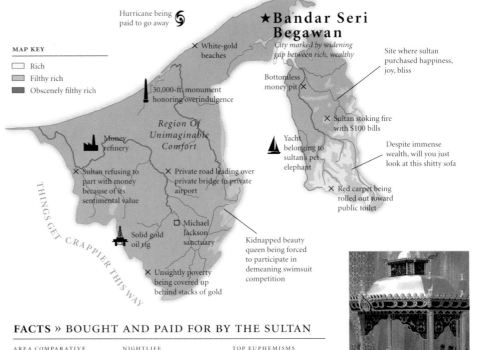

Hurricane being paid to go away

★**Bandar Seri Begawan**
City marked by widening gap between rich, wealthy

MAP KEY
☐ Rich
▨ Filthy rich
▩ Obscenely filthy rich

✕ White-gold beaches

Bottomless money pit ✕

Site where sultan purchased happiness, joy, bliss

✕ Sultan stoking fire with $100 bills

30,000-ft monument honoring overindulgence

Region Of Unimaginable Comfort

Yacht belonging to sultan's pet elephant

Money refinery

✕ Sultan refusing to part with money because of its sentimental value

✕ Private road leading over private bridge to private airport

Despite immense wealth, will you just look at this shitty sofa

✕ Red carpet being rolled out toward public toilet

☐ Michael Jackson sanctuary

Solid gold oil rig

THINGS GET CRAPPIER THIS WAY

Kidnapped beauty queen being forced to participate in demeaning swimsuit competition

✕ Unsightly poverty being covered up behind stacks of gold

FACTS » BOUGHT AND PAID FOR BY THE SULTAN

AREA COMPARATIVE
2,226 times larger than One Square Mile Island

TOURISM INDUSTRY
Booming since 2006, when the sultan paid 25.3 million tourists to visit Brunei

NIGHTLIFE
Most socializing is done at posh, exclusive parties, and we're very sorry, but you are not on the list

LEADING OCCUPATION
Guy who assures the sultan that oil lasts forever

TOP EUPHEMISMS
Black gold (oil), Green gold (money), Yellow gold (gold)

SUFFRAGE
Used to be none, but made progressive leap to N/A in 2005

The Sultan's Royal Bathroom

Singapore

Where Dirt Gets The Death Penalty

The hermetically sealed corporate biosphere of Singapore protects each of its carefully monitored 4.4126 million citizens from germs, crime, emotion, and dust.

Citizens are provided with the highest-quality education, health care, and punishment in the world, often receiving heavy penalties for criminal offenses such as spitting, speaking out of turn, gum possession, and public coughing. However, all are free to stroll in 32-inch strides through any of Singapore's pristine green spaces for seven minutes a day. City sidewalks are sterilized twice a week, and are off-limits to pedestrians. Singapore also boasts many modern buildings, though contemplating one's reflection in the towering glass structures for too long is severely frowned upon.

The constant whir of hidden security cameras reassures residents that they are being observed at all times. If a Singaporean feels a sneeze coming on, baton-wielding police officers in black body armor burst out of nowhere to shrink-wrap his body and hose him down with military-grade bleach. Female offenders are immediately compacted into cubes and disposed of.

PEOPLE » FREEDOM OF REPRESSION

Singapore provides a clean and productive workspace for all of its employees, and ensures high morale with weekly motivational executions. All of the tightly packed citizens must dress in matching khaki pants and polo shirts, and are required to maintain a two-inch distance from each other at all times.

Public displays of affection are illegal and private displays of affection are strongly discouraged. Over 90% of the population lives in high-rise housing modules, where residents are free to decorate their homes any way the government likes, with one of three officially approved shades of gray paint.

In the 1970s, the Family Planning Ministry's "One Child Is More Than Enough" campaign prompted millions to fling their infants out the window, which the government declared a form of littering punishable by euthanasia.

A PAINSTAKINGLY SANITIZED HISTORY »

300 B.C. Modern archaeologists have been unable to uncover any broken pottery, shards of glass, or lint from this era.

A.D. 1819 The British introduce natives to a crude form of caning, which they slowly perfect over 150 years and countless broken spines.

1959 Neatness guru Lee Kuan Yew rules Singapore with an iron glove after the nation is granted full self-oppression.

Lee Kuan Yew

1993 In response to a high-profile article calling Singapore "Disneyland with the death penalty," officials order a temporary stay of execution for all tourists on death row at amusement-park prisons.

2003 Health officials stave off the SARS virus by regularly scrubbing every citizen's lungs.

2007 Singapore reservedly marks the eradication of its last germ with scores of isolated one-person parades.

PUNISHMENT »

A popular method of discipline in Singapore is caning, in which a criminal is shackled, bent over a trestle, and depantsed by a trained martial artist. A six-foot-long wet rattan cane is then whipped across the buttocks, sometimes with such force that the cane breaks, which is punishable by an additional 10 strokes.

The Singaporean government credits caning for the success of its mandatory 9 p.m. national toothbrushing.

FACTS » WAR ON GRIME

REQUIRED FERTILITY RATE
1.06 children/woman

GOVERNMENT TYPE
Draconian utopia

CABINET
Minister of Detainment, Minister of Torture, Minister of Parks and Recreation

SUFFRAGE
21 years of age, compulsory under punishment of death

LIFE EXPECTANCY
Alpha Male/Female: 77/81
Beta Male/Female: 75/79
Gamma Male/Female: 70/74
Delta Male/Female: 65/69
Epsilon Male/Female: 55/59

MOTTO
"Be Better Than You Are"

BROADCAST MEDIA
Nation's only media outlet plays repetitive loop of the phrase "Move along"

CONSTITUTION
Guarantees the right to not be allowed

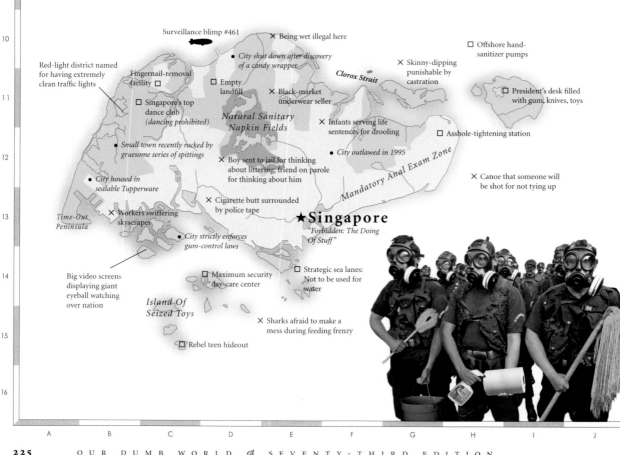

Surveillance blimp #461

× Being wet illegal here

• City shut down after discovery of a candy wrapper

□ Offshore hand-sanitizer pumps

Red-light district named for having extremely clean traffic lights

Fingernail-removal facility □

□ Empty landfill

Clorox Strait

× Skinny-dipping punishable by castration

□ Singapore's top dance club (dancing prohibited)

× Black-market underwear seller

Natural Sanitary Napkin Fields

□ President's desk filled with gum, knives, toys

× Infants serving life sentences for drooling

□ Asshole-tightening station

• Small town recently rocked by gruesome series of spittings

• City outlawed in 1995

Mandatory Anal Exam Zone

• Boy sent to jail for thinking about littering; friend on parole for thinking about him

• City housed in sealable Tupperware

× Cigarette butt surrounded by police tape

× Canoe that someone will be shot for not tying up

Time-Out Peninsula

× Workers swiffering skyscraper

★**Singapore**
"Forbidden: The Doing Of Stuff"

• City strictly enforces gum-control laws

Big video screens displaying giant eyeball watching over nation

□ Maximum security day-care center

□ Strategic sea lanes: Not to be used for water

Island Of Seized Toys

× Sharks afraid to make a mess during feeding frenzy

□ Rebel teen hideout

The Philippines

Willing To Relocate For Work

With 9.1 million citizens working abroad, and countless more in-between jobs overseas, the Philippines supplies the world with foreign laborers, despite the harrowing commute each morning.

A popular destination for hundreds of family-support payments each month, and voted "Best Weekend Getaway Spot" by Filipinos employed out of the country Monday through Friday, the Philippines is governed by Gloria Macapagal-Arroyo, the country's second female president and a nanny to three young children in the city of Chicago.

In 2006, a devastating mudslide on the island of Leyte claimed the lives of thousands when Filipino rescue workers, based in Germany, Hong Kong, Thailand, and Mexico, took several weeks to get back and help.

EMPLOYMENT HISTORY »

A.D. 1521 Explorer Ferdinand Magellan reaches the Philippine Archipelago and gives hundreds of unemployed natives their first job as slaves. The benefits, as many will soon discover, are terrible.

1900 Fighting a war with the U.S., Filipinos sustain heavy casualties when 20,000 troops call in to their supervising general with a "sore throat" the morning of the Battle of Tirad Pass.

1941 Japan invades the U.S.-controlled Philippines, leading to a violent and drawn-out battle. Nearly 75% of American casualties are outsourced to Filipino soldiers.

1965–1986 Dictator Ferdinand Marcos makes seemingly arbitrary changes to the island nation, micromanaging day-to-day operations and refusing to give Filipino citizens the independence they deserve. Also, he eliminates the nation's longstanding "Casual Fridays" policy.

President Gloria Macapagal-Arroyo
President Arroyo delivers a presidential address in the Philippines, provides child care to the Thompson siblings in Chicago, and works the night shift at a McDonald's in Bombay, all on May 14, 2005.

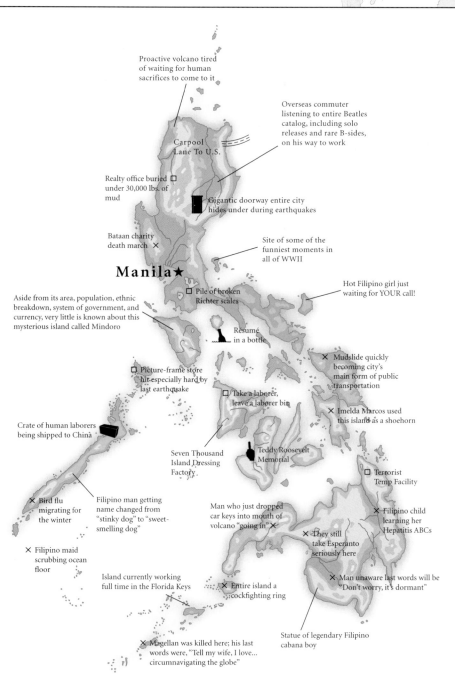

Proactive volcano tired of waiting for human sacrifices to come to it

Overseas commuter listening to entire Beatles catalog, including solo releases and rare B-sides, on his way to work

Carpool Lane To U.S.

Realty office buried under 30,000 lbs. of mud

Gigantic doorway entire city hides under during earthquakes

Bataan charity death march ✕

Site of some of the funniest moments in all of WWII

Manila ★

Aside from its area, population, ethnic breakdown, system of government, and currency, very little is known about this mysterious island called Mindoro

Pile of broken Richter scales

Hot Filipino girl just waiting for YOUR call!

Résumé in a bottle

Mudslide quickly becoming city's main form of public transportation

Picture-frame store hit especially hard by last earthquake

Take a laborer, leave a laborer bin

Imelda Marcos used this island as a shoehorn

Crate of human laborers being shipped to China

Seven Thousand Island Dressing Factory

Teddy Roosevelt Memorial

Terrorist Temp Facility

✕ Bird flu migrating for the winter

Filipino man getting name changed from "stinky dog" to "sweet-smelling dog"

Man who just dropped car keys into mouth of volcano "going in" ✕

✕ They still take Esperanto seriously here

✕ Filipino child learning her Hepatitis ABCs

✕ Filipino maid scrubbing ocean floor

Island currently working full time in the Florida Keys

✕ Entire island a cockfighting ring

✕ Man unaware last words will be "Don't worry, it's dormant"

✕ Magellan was killed here; his last words were, "Tell my wife, I love... circumnavigating the globe"

Statue of legendary Filipino cabana boy

PEOPLE » PERSONAL INFORMATION

Filipino citizens often toil at multiple jobs, even if that means punching out at a ceramics factory in India and traveling 25 hours in order to start the morning shift as a hospital custodian in Seattle. Filipino children as young as 7 are often encouraged to help their families by leaving the country and getting a paper route in Belgium or France. Indeed, by the time they reach the age of 10, many have already learned the value of a dollar, a yen, a drachma, a euro, a Taiwanese dollar, a Singapore dollar, a Malaysian dollar, and a franc.

FACTS » AVAILABLE ON REQUEST

OFFICIAL NAME
The Philippines

CAN BE REACHED AT
14° 35' N 121° 0' E

LANGUAGES
Fluent in Filipino, English, and some Spanish

SKILLS
Mining nickel, copper, and cobalt

MANAGEMENT EXPERIENCE
79 regional provinces

HONORS AND AWARDS
Granted independence July 4, 1946

WORST QUALITIES
Earthquakes, deadly mudslides, "too much of a perfectionist sometimes"

NATIONAL SICK DAY
Oct. 29

CRIMINAL RECORD
Killed about 14,130 people in 1905, but other than that, clean

Indonesia

THE INDONESIAN FLAG
IS PRETTY CUT-AND-
DRIED, REALLY.

Working The Cradle-To-The-Grave Shift

A sprawling archipelago nation that fully employs all 250 million citizens at a dozen garment factories, Indonesia accounts for 90% of the world's labor and less than 0.002% of its wages, which are withheld until the workers pay to have their blood stains cleaned up.

Regularly reaching temperatures of 125 degrees in the shade of an industrial sewing machine, Indonesia is a dark and cramped country with one bathroom facility that has been out of order since 1998, when someone tried to flush their arm down the toilet.

While it has long struggled with poverty, Indonesia's close relationship with such world powers as Nike and the Gap has allowed citizens to provide a much higher standard of living for Western consumers tired of low-quality T-shirts.

The equal-opportunity government bans discrimination based on age, physical disability, or desire to receive monetary compensation. While there is no maternity leave, mothers are given 30 minutes with their newborn babies in order to train them. Also, strict new labor laws keep children from working more than 40 hours a day and prevent employers from terminating workers' lives without providing due cause and two weeks' notice.

In December 2004, a massive tsunami destroyed large parts of Sumatra and the Aceh region, killing over 200,000 and giving the Indonesian people their first-ever day off.

PEOPLE » FORCED INTO A LABOR OF LOVE

An extremely diverse people, Indonesia's 300 distinct ethnic groups overcome differences in language and traditional customs every day in order to pursue a common goal of producing identical pajama bottoms.

In fact, Indonesians work so efficiently that most could stitch together Ralph Lauren's entire spring line while blindfolded, with both legs tied to their chair, next to a steaming hot-water pipe, and without any food for up to nine days.

Indonesia has the largest Muslim population in the world, though their interpretation of Islam differs from other sects in that the five-times-daily prayers are expected to be done while sewing. However, the religion's central tenet of submission is highly praised by the nation's supervisors, managers, and CEOs.

While their lives can sometimes be hard, Indonesians take solace in knowing that, even after they die at the end of their next shift, their work will live on, balled up on the floor of someone's closet.

ECONOMY » GOOD TO THE LAST DYING DROP

It is corporate policy that all employees must treat the coffee beans with dignity and respect.

On the islands of Java and Sumatra, people wake up early each morning with an intense craving for coffee harvesting. Many even claim they don't feel alive until they get their hands on that first bushel of coffee, and that they still usually need a pick-me-up of several dozen more bushels by mid-afternoon or they'll simply crash after being beaten by supervisors.

Although most say they could quit cold turkey if they wanted to, those who have tried to stop working in the coffee fields have experienced serious withdrawal effects, such as even-worse poverty, retaliation from plantation owners, and starvation.

More than half the population lives on less than half the cost of a half-caf Caramel Frappuccino per week.

FACTS » QUALITY INSPECTED

NATIONAL MOTTO "Machine Wash Warm"	SHOES PER CAPITA 0.44	GOVERNMENT Doing its best	MONKEYS THEY GOT Black monkey, Sumatran orangutan, grizzled leaf monkey, pig-tailed snub-nosed monkey, Mentawai macaque, proboscis monkey, silvery gibbon
RELIGION 86% Islam 12% Christianity 2% Cotton-polytheism	NATIONAL HOLIDAY Observed through crack in wall	NATURAL DISASTERS All	
	LEAST FAVORITE ISLANDS #13, #104, #9, #138	OTHER BAD STUFF Smog, crime	

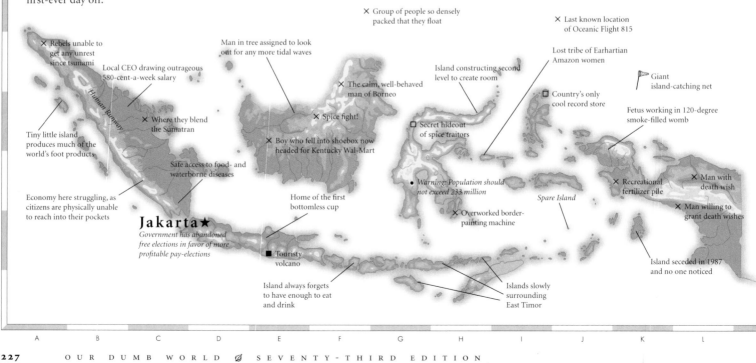

✕ Group of people so densely packed that they float

✕ Last known location of Oceanic Flight 815

✕ Rebels unable to get any unrest since tsunami

Man in tree assigned to look out for any more tidal waves

Lost tribe of Earhartian Amazon women

Local CEO drawing outrageous 580-cent-a-week salary

Human Runway

✕ The calm, well-behaved man of Borneo

Island constructing second level to create room

🚩 Giant island-catching net

☐ Country's only cool record store

Tiny little island produces much of the world's foot products

✕ Where they blend the Sumatran

✕ Spice fight!

☐ Secret hideout of spice traitors

Fetus working in 120-degree smoke-filled womb

Safe access to food- and waterborne diseases

✕ Boy who fell into shoebox now headed for Kentucky Wal-Mart

• *Warning: Population should not exceed 233 million*

Spare Island

✕ Recreational fertilizer pile

✕ Man with death wish

Economy here struggling, as citizens are physically unable to reach into their pockets

Home of the first bottomless cup

✕ Overworked border-painting machine

✕ Man willing to grant death wishes

Jakarta★
Government has abandoned free elections in favor of more profitable pay-elections

■ Touristy volcano

Island seceded in 1987 and no one noticed

Island always forgets to have enough to eat and drink

Islands slowly surrounding East Timor

HISTORY » ANOTHER DAY, ANOTHER 1/1,000TH OF A DOLLAR

2 MILLION B.C. Java Man, one of the earliest café-dwelling specimens of *homo erectus*, is believed to have been an unemployed gatherer who had a great idea for a cave drawing but never got around to it.

A.D. 301 The first sweatshop churns out the first low-cost loincloths, which are later recalled due to excessive flammability.

1670 Dutch explorers arrive looking to borrow a pinch of nutmeg, a few cloves, 700,000 tons of cardamom, and Indonesia.

1941 The Japanese conquer Indonesia, which concerns the Dutch much more than it does the colonized Indonesians.

1945 Japan ends its occupation after WWII, giving Indonesia a five-second window in which to call out "Independent!" just before the Dutch can finish yelling "Administrative territory belonging to—!"

1965 Gen. Suharto leads a coup against President Sukarno, who wins the next election after

Suharto

citizens think he is Suharto, leading Sukarno to depose himself and hand over power to Suharto, who, in a moment of confusion, was already staging a coup against himself—anyway, it all got resolved with 32 years of brutal totalitarian rule by Suharto.

1966 Believing that one voice can make a difference, Suharto permanently silences between 200,000 and 1 million of them.

1967 Suharto's "New Order" policies encourage foreign investment and domestic terror.

However, the dramatic increase in per capita income is largely offset by the rising cost of per capita funerals.

1997–1998 The Indonesian economy is hit hard by the Asian financial crisis, which makes the rupiah slightly less worthless than it already sounds.

2002 Terrorists bomb two nightclubs in the resort region of Bali, killing 202 Australians, 179 of whom were trying to hit on the same Indonesian chick.

Petra Nemcová

2004 A terrible tsunami leaves millions hopeless, devastated, and searching for answers as international supermodel Petra Nemcová goes missing for eight grueling hours.

ENVIRONMENT » NO ISLAND NATION IS AN ISLAND

With over 17,000 individual islands, Indonesia is the world's first- through 129th-largest archipelago. A third of the islands are inhabited, another third are overinhabited, and the rest of the spare islands are often pawned off as last-minute birthday gifts. Children are taught from an early age to memorize the name of their island, in the event they get lost going out for milk.

Indonesia's location on the Pacific "Ring Of Fire" makes it an ideal spot for simultaneous earthquakes, volcanic eruptions, monsoons, tidal waves, killer whirlpools, deadly breezes, and devastating partly cloudy afternoons.

It also enjoys a vast array of droughts.

Home to an extremely diverse ecosystem, Indonesia boasts man-eating fauna such as rhinos and leopards, some of Asia's most stunning carnivorous mega-flora, and several unidentifiable species that descend from the sky at night and bring unspeakable horror.

East Timor
A Country That Got Some Sense Bombed Into It

When East Timor chose a mildly socialist and agrarian government in 1975, it was practically begging a larger, more powerful country to come along and decimate it.

The Timorese must have realized that the free world could never sit idly by while an impoverished island in the Indian Ocean distributed vegetables equally among its people. Yet it soon became clear that the only thing capable of stopping the spread of such destructive economic practices was a massive Indonesian military force equipped with state-of-the-art U.S.-made weapons. East Timor was finally granted independence from Indonesia in 2002, but couldn't even take a minute from its 80-hour shift to thank them for the gift of capitalism.

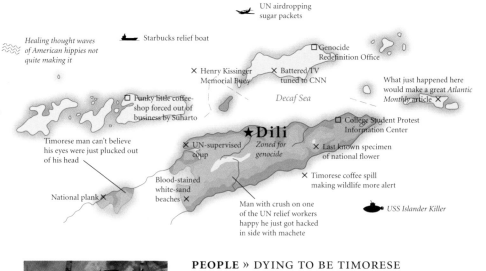

UN airdropping sugar packets

Starbucks relief boat

Healing thought waves of American hippies not quite making it

Henry Kissinger Memorial Buoy

Battered TV tuned to CNN

Genocide Redefinition Office

Decaf Sea

What just happened here would make a great *Atlantic Monthly* article

Punky little coffee-shop forced out of business by Suharto

College Student Protest Information Center

★**Dili**

Zoned for genocide

Timorese man can't believe his eyes were just plucked out of his head

UN-supervised coup

Last known specimen of national flower

Timorese coffee spill making wildlife more alert

Blood-stained white-sand beaches

National plank

Man with crush on one of the UN relief workers happy he just got hacked in side with machete

USS Islander Killer

Dili
Two Timorese teens go for a joyride.

PEOPLE » DYING TO BE TIMORESE

The average Timorese citizen has been beaten, raped, tortured, burned, maimed, murdered, and exposed to more than 25 years of brutality at the hands of the Indonesian government before the age of 16.

But after decades of fighting for independence, carrying out bombings for independence, and setting entire cities aflame for independence, the Timorese now live as an independent people atop a small cinderblock just outside the ashes of their capital.

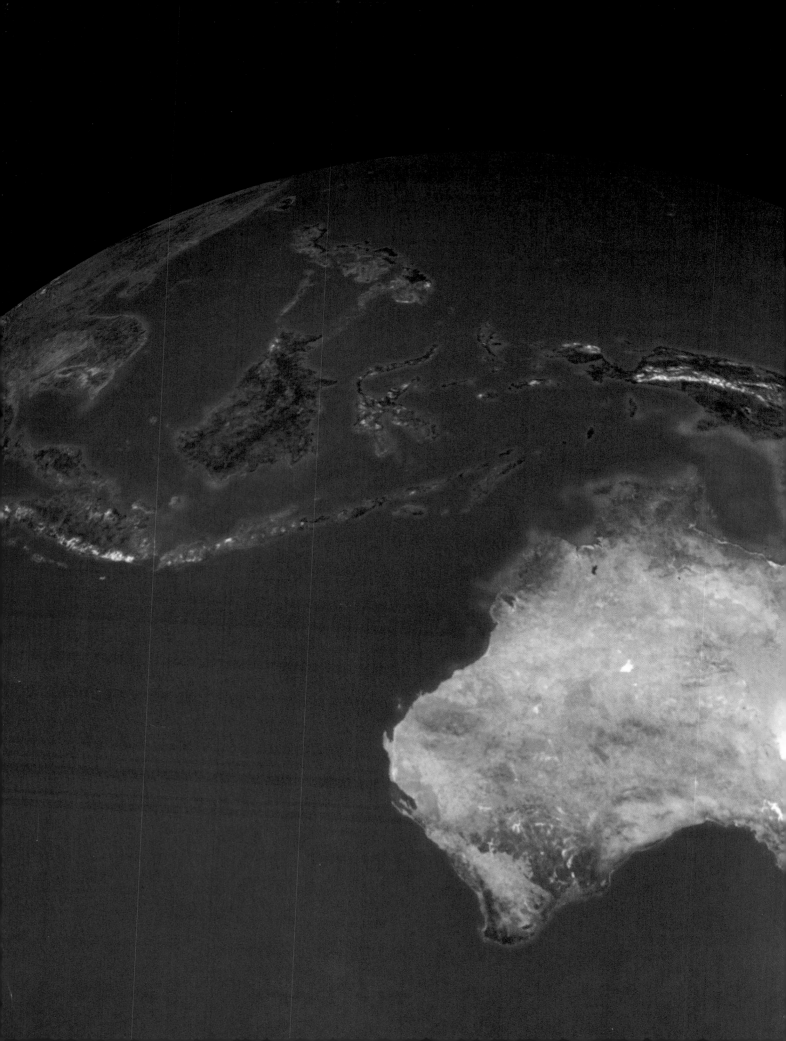

Oceania

Australia

» THE AUSTRALIAN FLAG WAS
INSPIRED BY WATCHING THE
BRITISH FLAG AT NIGHT.

As Seen On Animal Planet

Once home to some of the most diverse and undisturbed wildlife in the world, the nation of Australia has fallen prey to a deadly scourge of nature shows, with dozens of endemic species being poked, prodded, and bothered to the brink of extinction.

For centuries, marsupials and reptiles alike roamed the Outback without fear of being ambushed, turned on their backs, and having their genitalia discussed in front of millions of Discovery Channel viewers.

Today, however, the nation's delicate ecosystem has been thrown out of balance, with countless species being threatened by the introduction of such wild and unpredictable predators as Jack Hanna.

Kangaroos and koalas, previously found only in mainland Australia, have been displaced from their natural habitats, and must now survive in new and distressing environments, namely late-night talk shows.

Sadly, those left behind have fared no better. The nation's black mambas are unable to stalk their kill without documentarians loudly narrating their every move, and saltwater crocodiles have stopped mating, as many worry that the moment they start having sex, four cameramen and a boom-mic operator will burst in on them.

Other species, however, have adapted to their new challenges, but now only get the desire to mate when they are being filmed.

Indeed, if nothing is done to curb this threat, soon all that may remain of these once glorious creatures will be 47 documentary films, five seasons of *The Crocodile Hunter*, and roughly 30,000 taped *Tonight Show* appearances.

HISTORY » SLANG FOR "A CONTINUOUS NARRATIVE OF PAST EVENTS"

53,000 B.C. During this period, Australia is home to several species of "mega-fauna," including *Diprotodon*, a giant 10-foot-tall kangaroo, *Genyornis*, a 230-pound flightless bird, and *Hydrasis*, a mammoth 25-centimeter single-cell organism.

20,000 B.C. Native aborigines invent the boomerang, and spend the next 12,000 years trying to figure out how to make it work.

A.D. 1770 British explorer James Cook arrives in Australia and deems the landmass a continent. Although Australia is only one-fifth the size of Asia, Cook maintains that it "seemed huge compared to his boat."

1785 England establishes Australia as a penal colony for convicted felons, as the harshest punishment the pasty nation can think of is sunshine and warm weather.

1800 English authorities get suspicious when an elderly woman visits the penal colony with 35,000 birthday cakes.

1854 The nation develops Australian rules football, a combination of rugby, soccer, and murdering people in cold blood.

1856 Australia becomes the first nation to introduce the "secret ballot" for elections, ushering in a new age where one's vote, and the tampering of one's vote, would forever remain confidential.

1901 Australia places a ban on all non-white immigration in hopes of preventing other races from diluting their proud tradition of racism.

1911 Canberra is founded and designated as Australia's capital, which is odd because isn't Sydney the capital?

1914 Australia commits hundreds of thousands of troops to the British effort in WWI, but asks if it's okay to just send them once the war is over to help celebrate.

Australia was formed as a penal colony. Did you really need a caption to tell you that?

1992 The Citizenship Act is amended so that citizens no longer have to swear an oath of allegiance to the British. They are, however, still required to say at least one nice thing about them per year.

1998 The Great Barrier Reef is named one of the "Seven Wonders Of The World, Not Including The Pyramids Of Course, Or Any Of The Other Great Egyptian-Related Monuments."

2000 Hosting its first Summer Olympics, the city of Sydney spends all day nervously worrying if any of the other 199 participating nations are going to show up.

2001 Sir Donald Bradman, Australia's most famous cricket player, dies of anonymity.

2006 Australia's "Crocodile Hunter" Steve Irwin dies of a fatal stingray barb to the chest. His funeral marks the first time he has ever worn a suit.

PEOPLE » MORE OF AN ACCENT THAN A NATIONALITY

Founded as a British prison colony in 1770, Australia today is home to roughly 20 million citizens—a remarkably high figure considering the scarcity of vaginal intercourse during those first few decades.

A hard-to-understand people, Australians are known around the world for their use of slang, with the last formal English word believed to have been spoken in the city of Sydney around 1971. Common phrases include "g'day mate," which is slang for "hello, friend," "crikey," which is slang for "wow," and "pass us a tinny, you bugga," which is slang for "g'day mate."

Often stereotyped as fearless wildmen of the Outback thanks to such films as *Crocodile Dundee*, most Australian men actually live in large urban centers, and are, if anything, closer to Paul Hogan's character in the Los Angeles–based sequel *Crocodile Dundee III*.

Still, one should avoid sweeping generalizations when it comes to Australians, as they all carry large hunting knives between their teeth and wrestle dangerous reptiles for sport.

While it's true that citizens enjoy drinking lager and other varieties of beer, and that many have a high tolerance for alcohol, there is no truth to the rumor that bedrooms in Australia spin in the opposite direction when one is drunk.

The Australian Outback is home to countless species of hicks.

CONTINENT-SIZED FACTS »

LOCATION
Bottom-right corner of Earth

NATIONAL PRIDE
Gets to sit at special "continent table" during UN meetings

LANGUAGES
English (every fifth word), Unknown (rest of time)

FAMOUS ACTRESSES
Nicole Kidman, Naomi Watts, Cate Blanchett, Eric Bana

LAND OF CONTRASTS?
Yes

NATIONAL HOLIDAY
Jan. 26 (commemorates day Australia thought up idea to have a national holiday)

LABOR FORCE BY OCCUPATION
Outdoorsman (72%), Indoorsman (28%)

INTERNATIONAL ARGY BARGIES
None

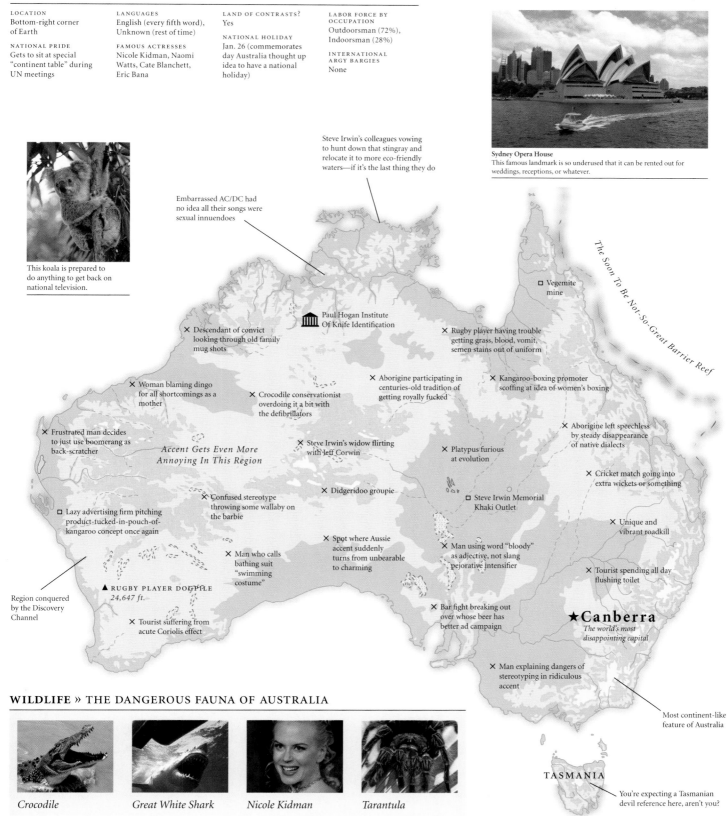

Sydney Opera House
This famous landmark is so underused that it can be rented out for weddings, receptions, or whatever.

This koala is prepared to do anything to get back on national television.

Steve Irwin's colleagues vowing to hunt down that stingray and relocate it to more eco-friendly waters—if it's the last thing they do

Embarrassed AC/DC had no idea all their songs were sexual innuendoes

The Soon To Be Not-So-Great Barrier Reef

□ Vegemite mine

🏛 Paul Hogan Institute Of Knife Identification

× Descendant of convict looking through old family mug shots

× Rugby player having trouble getting grass, blood, vomit, semen stains out of uniform

× Woman blaming dingo for all shortcomings as a mother

× Crocodile conservationist overdoing it a bit with the defibrillators

× Aborigine participating in centuries-old tradition of getting royally fucked

× Kangaroo-boxing promoter scoffing at idea of women's boxing

× Frustrated man decides to just use boomerang as back-scratcher

Accent Gets Even More Annoying In This Region

× Steve Irwin's widow flirting with Jeff Corwin

× Platypus furious at evolution

× Aborigine left speechless by steady disappearance of native dialects

× Cricket match going into extra wickets or something

× Didgeridoo groupie

□ Steve Irwin Memorial Khaki Outlet

□ Lazy advertising firm pitching product-tucked-in-pouch-of-kangaroo concept once again

× Confused stereotype throwing some wallaby on the barbie

× Unique and vibrant roadkill

× Spot where Aussie accent suddenly turns from unbearable to charming

× Man using word "bloody" as adjective, not slang pejorative intensifier

× Tourist spending all day flushing toilet

▲ RUGBY PLAYER DOUG-ILE 24,647 ft.

Region conquered by the Discovery Channel

× Man who calls bathing suit "swimming costume"

× Bar fight breaking out over whose beer has better ad campaign

★ **Canberra**
The world's most disappointing capital

× Tourist suffering from acute Coriolis effect

× Man explaining dangers of stereotyping in ridiculous accent

Most continent-like feature of Australia

WILDLIFE » THE DANGEROUS FAUNA OF AUSTRALIA

Crocodile

Great White Shark

Nicole Kidman

Tarantula

TASMANIA

You're expecting a Tasmanian devil reference here, aren't you?

A Bunch Of God-Damned Islands

PAPUA NEW GUINEA » A DANGEROUS PLACE TO HAVE A NECK

Despite the common stereotypes, the remote island nation of Papua New Guinea is no longer populated by scores of savage headhunters. In fact, most citizens are so poor that they are forced to subsist merely on head-gathering and head-foraging.

The thick, unnavigable jungles isolate citizens so much that many are unaware of the existence of their families only a few feet away, and often meet siblings for the first time while cannibalizing them.

Largely unexplored, the island is home to thousands of unique, never-before-seen plants and animals, none of which are as well-cataloged or displayed as the researchers' heads that can be found impaled on forked sticks in front of huts across the country.

Untouched by any outside cultures, the island's inhabitants live without modern conveniences such as civilization, and much of the terrain is so rugged that the only mode of transportation available is pterodactyl.

Unlike most of the country, some regions, such as the cave Tik Thok shares with brother Jig Dug, have a high population density, especially when Jig eats too many missionaries.

In order to improve its image, the government now offers all-expense-paid trips to any foreign citizens over 250 pounds with no next of kin.

CULTURE » BOILED ARTS

A culturally diverse nation, Papua New Guinea is home to over 800 indigenous tribes, each creating its own unique folk decorations using paints, leaves, dried macaroni, or their favorite stickers to adorn prized skulls.

Many of the country's more traditional chants have lately been supplanted by pop chants and adult-contemporary chants.

Li'l Cannibal Islands

- ■ Sleestack caves
- ✕ Tribe known for dipping themselves in poison
- ✕ Great place for a frenzy
- ✕ Giant strawberries
- ✕ Bungalow still on hold for Jeffrey Dahmer
- ✕ Human totem pole
- ■ Horrifying craft fair
- ✕ Village wiped out by bake sale
- ✕ Disappointed child picking at missionary casserole
- ✕ Man who just wants classy face tattoo
- ✕ Head shop getting raided by Red Cross
- ✕ Top-secret dart-testing range
- ✕ Most people in this region don't even have access to the conch shell

★ **Port Moresby**

Dead, Bloated Missionary Bay

- 🦋 Butterfly with one-foot wingspan that feeds on insects, rodents, and children
- ✕ International canoe port

Shipwrecked crew swimming to shore

THE GREAT WETNESS

MAP KEY
- ▮ Japanese troops who don't know WWII is over
- ▯ U.S. tourists who enjoy documentaries about WWII
- ▯ Papua New Guinea locals who don't realize that the U.S., Japan, and wars exist

Headhunter
U.S. President Bill Clinton made his first and last diplomatic visit to Papua New Guinea in 1999.

SAMOA » LIVING FAT OFF THE LAND

A half-submerged island nation with more than 1.2 million miles of waistline, Samoa was a mighty seafaring nation until the entire fleet exploded when the morbidly obese sailors tried to squeeze their asses in.

With almost every tectonic plate in the region smashed to pieces by the colossal-boned Samoans, the country puts a severe strain on the earth's crust. Samoa also suffers regular earthquakes every day during lunch hour, school recess, and whenever more than two people sit down.

Likewise, frolicking in the ocean has caused some of the worst maritime disasters in history, and children's playful cannonballs into the Pacific have flooded cities as far away as Tokyo.

Health problems are rampant in Samoa, as most citizens have multiple heart attacks between meals, and suffer chronic respiratory ailments caused by the full-grown glazed pigs lodged in their windpipes.

Since labor often takes up to 18 years, many Samoans are born just in time to rent a crane to take them to their high school prom.

A Samoan wishes his coconut was a pork shoulder.

DOUBLE-STUFFED FACTS »

AREA COMPARATIVE Fat camp buffet line	**GDP** 734 billion calories	**NATIONAL SPORT** Five-meter waddle	**EXPORTS** NFL nose tackles
MOTTO "Every Man Is At Least One Island"	**NATURAL HAZARDS** Entire contents of body sucked out by infant mistaking you for a nipple	**IMPORTS** Cargo snack containers	**MILK SOURCE** The coconut
			CUISINE All

- ✕ Teenagers snacking on landfill
- Tourists accidentally going spelunking in sleeping Samoan's vagina
- □ Mermaid BBQ
- ✕ Rumored location of Fatlantis
- Elderly tailor still measuring customer from 1964
- ⛵ Japanese fishermen arguing over best way to harpoon walking whales
- No more than three Samoans allowed on this side of the island at a time
- ✕ In 1987, Christo tried to wrap a Samoan in fabric but ran out of material
- Only place that feels like home to Bruce Vilanch

★ **Apia**
Birthplace of entire USC Trojans defensive line

- ✕ Uneaten morsel
- ✕ Barge taking student to school

The Lamest Excuse For A Bay In The South Pacific

- Tourist in slow-moving buffet line forced to eat napkins again

MARSHALL ISLANDS » A POPULAR NUKE DESTINATION

Used by the U.S. military as a nuclear-testing site for 30 years, these beautiful South Pacific islands are known for their white-hot-sand beaches and balmy, 10,000-degree temperatures.

Etched snugly into the walls of their homes, residents of the Marshall Islands are permanent shadows of their former selves.

The remaining citizens must use extra caution before emerging from their fallout shelters, slathering their entire bodies in pure zinc to avoid getting 73rd-degree sunburns.

The islands remain an intensely hot tourist destination for B2 bomber pilots, with terrific sightseeing opportunities through lead sunglasses available 1,500 miles offshore.

Still, islanders enjoy the outdoors, whether taking in some heavy particles, catching a few blast waves, or just relaxing in the boiling surf as they watch a firestorm roll in.

Sunset on the Marshall Islands.

- ✕ Cockroach colony biding its time
- Man shaking both his heads in disgust at U.S.'s actions
- ✕ Fat man
- Recently placed want ad encouraging nations to test nuclear weapons again
- ✕ Little boy
- Guy sweeping up his loved ones
- ✕ Blown up by NASA via remote control
- ✕ Glass beach
- ✕ Man hitting snooze button on air-raid siren
- *Heavy Water*
- Child practicing "stop, drop, and vaporize"
- Island commended for its nuclear non-proliferation work
- ★ Majuro
- ✕ Great spot to take on magnetic properties
- Mushroom cloud that looks like puppy
- Island sent dolphins to first Gulf War

GUAM » DROP AND GIVE ME 20,000

Valued for its charming airstrips, quaint bunkers, and great location just a short bombing distance from some of the best American military targets, Guam provides the perfect base for planning a weekend sneak attack or annihilating a small nation.

Each day is meticulously scheduled from the crack of dawn until lights-out. Every corner of the nation is freshly pressed and tucked in tight,

and all the roads are spit-shined until citizens can see their reflection in the concrete.

With physical fitness essential to morale and combat readiness, more than half the population completes the twice-daily jogs around the country, while the rest are deported to the middle of the ocean for having flat feet.

Guam truly does more by 6 a.m. than most territories do all year.

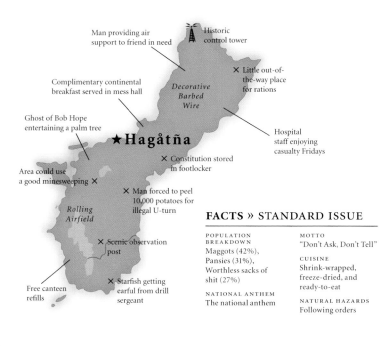

- Man providing air support to friend in need
- Historic control tower
- Complimentary continental breakfast served in mess hall
- ✕ Little out-of-the-way place for rations
- *Decorative Barbed Wire*
- Ghost of Bob Hope entertaining a palm tree
- ★ Hagåtña
- Hospital staff enjoying casualty Fridays
- Area could use a good minesweeping ✕
- ✕ Constitution stored in footlocker
- *Rolling Airfield*
- ✕ Man forced to peel 10,000 potatoes for illegal U-turn
- ✕ Scenic observation post
- Free canteen refills
- ✕ Starfish getting earful from drill sergeant

FACTS » STANDARD ISSUE

POPULATION BREAKDOWN
Maggots (42%), Pansies (31%), Worthless sacks of shit (27%)

NATIONAL ANTHEM
The national anthem

MOTTO
"Don't Ask, Don't Tell"

CUISINE
Shrink-wrapped, freeze-dried, and ready-to-eat

NATURAL HAZARDS
Following orders

KIRIBATI » AN ISLAND, A PALM TREE, AND ONE GUY

An archipelago of eight-by-eight-foot islands, Kiribati is featured in every one-panel cartoon where shipwrecked businessmen, bankers, and other upper-middle-class Americans make pointed observations about society.

This ancient rock drawing has been rejected by *The New Yorker* for 11,000 years in a row.

Whether complaining about how much their cell-phone roving charges will be, or hoping that someone back home remembered to TiVo their favorite sitcom, residents are always up in arms over the island offering no recycling facilities for the bottle that just washed ashore.

In their well-kept stubble and perfectly torn pants, residents can live off the same coconut for up to 80 years. When they finally get rescued, most usually shrug their shoulders and remark, "At least my mother-in-law's probably dead by now."

- Dinner-party conversation playing out verbatim here
- ✕ Gay cruise upsetting local traditions
- *Arable Water*
- ✕ Man daydreaming about desk job
- ★ Tarawa
- ✕ Wife likes coconuts from that island better
- ✕ Ship that is always half-sinking
- ✕ Guy in boat selling falling-coconut insurance
- ✕ Man realizing mermaid was just dead fish
- ✕ Dyslexic struggling to write "S.O.S." in the sand
- ◄ Wisecracking shark
- ✕ Jack La Lanne pulling four barges across Pacific for 93rd birthday

More Fucking Islands

PALAU » AN ISLAND OF MOOCHERS

While it relies on U.S. aid for everything from infrastructure improvements to gambling debts, Palau promises that it will start making some cash of its own just as soon as that mail-order seashell business takes off.

It's not that Palau doesn't appreciate all of America's help through the years—it's just that the population has been busy record-shopping lately, and the Palauan president injured his wrist signing all those aid checks, so he's been taking it easy on the governing for the past few months.

Palau is one of the youngest countries in the world. The UN rejected its application several times, explaining that snorkeling is a hobby, not an industry.

The Palauan workforce.

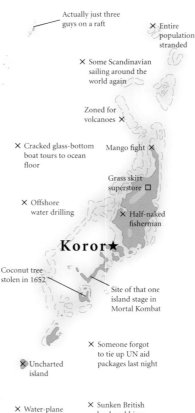

Actually just three guys on a raft

✕ Entire population stranded

✕ Some Scandinavian sailing around the world again

Zoned for volcanoes ✕

✕ Cracked glass-bottom boat tours to ocean floor

Mango fight ✕

Grass skirt superstore ☐

✕ Offshore water drilling

✕ Half-naked fisherman

Koror★

Coconut tree stolen in 1652

Site of that one island stage in Mortal Kombat

✕ Someone forgot to tie up UN aid packages last night

✕ Uncharted island

✕ Water-plane runway

✕ Sunken British land-grabbing machine

VANUATU » AN ISLAND UNTO ITSELF

Vanuatu boasts endless stretches of white-sand beaches, palm trees that provide just the right amount of shade, and easygoing natives who pay no taxes and want you to stay the hell away.

In 2006, an environmentalist group named Vanuatu the "happiest place on Earth." The nation's Department Of Counter-Tourism contested the title, claiming the island was actually a miserable place full of roving packs of wild boars and active volcanoes, and that it had, in fact, sunk into the ocean long ago.

The heart of Vanuatu's tourism campaign.

✕ Boulder

✕ Pebble

✕ Stationary crab

✕ President peeing in ocean

☐ Live bait outlet mall

✕ Vanuatu branch of the *Survivor* fan club

✕ Nation's only subway station

✕ Nothing at all worth seeing, really

✕ No charming beach town here

☐ Vanuatu customs office *(closed)*

★Port-Vila

✕ Pedal boat gridlock

✕ Man entertaining friends with hilarious dance in hamburger bra and Dockers pleated khakis

✕ Beach deposits

✕ Mineral resource rental

TONGA » OKAY, WE MADE THIS ONE UP

The island of Tonga is a small archipelago located in the southern Pacific Ocean formed largely by fossilized coral and—all right, you caught us. There's no such place as Tonga.

We sure had you going there for a minute, though. You should have seen your face when we mentioned the coral! Priceless.

But no. There is no small grouping of over 170 atolls two-thirds of the way from Hawaii to New Zealand that was once nicknamed the "Friendly Islands" by Captain Cook and whose main exports are pumpkins and vanilla beans. "Tonga" is actually the name of our editor's Pomeranian. But we all had a bit of fun, didn't we?

FACTS » YOU ARE SO GULLIBLE

POPULATION
Let's go with 106,000

GOVERNMENT
Bicameral House Of Representative Monarchies

NATIONAL MAGNIFICATION RATE
100x

SPECIAL ABILITIES
Flight, X-ray vision, fireballs

LANGUAGE
Vulcan, why not?

IF TONGA WERE A TREE, WHAT KIND OF TREE WOULD IT BE?
Birch

LAND USE
Drowning prevention

KILLER HOUSE BAND
The Snapping Twinkies

NATIONAL FLOWER
The plumeria, for all you know

FAVORITE BOOK
Our Dumb World

MAP KEY

▨ Printing error
▦ Figment of imagination
☐ Stain from friggin' awesome sandwich
▭ Just a drawing of an island

✕ Constitution of Tonga stuffed in bottle, floating to UN headquarters

✕ This island is so remote that natives think Bowie is still in his Ziggy Stardust phase

✕ Made you look

✕ Affordable spot of ocean right near the land

✕ This is not an island

Defensive Sandbar

Future home of Arby's

Used-fish dealership

Combined, These 14 Islands Would Make One Pretty Okay Island

✕ Found, developed, and time-shared city of Atlantis

☐ Prison *(by default)*

✕ The end of the world as we know it

NOT A REAL OCEAN

✕ Totally pulled this island out of our asses

★Nuku'alofa
Name of capital split across 26 islands

✕ Perfect spot for expansion island

New Zealand

» REVERSE SIDE OF FLAG CAN BE USED AS AN EMERGENCY BLUE SCREEN.

In A World... Where Nothing Is What It Seems...

From rugged prairies to rugged mountains to rugged extras, New Zealand has all the locations and personnel required for a major Hollywood blockbuster, and if they do not have it, they will simply create it in post.

New Zealand consists of two islands, though focus groups have indicated there is a market for a third.

The first island houses film studios, airplane-hangar-sized special-effects sets, and crew trailers. Citizens in this location are often asked to stay indoors during principal photography. The second island consists of a holding area and parking lot for the equipment trucks.

HISTORY » AN ISLAND NATION LEARNS...THAT SOMETIMES LOVE IS THE ONLY THING THAT MATTERS

A.D. 1840 The British convince the native Maori to sign an exclusive contract granting the U.K. control of New Zealand's external affairs, first-look rights for all new constitutions, and 4% of net GDP.

1841 Maori chieftains enroll in a correspondence course in entertainment law.

1845 *The Maori Wars*, originally conceived as a trilogy, ends after the first installment in which the Maori resist British colonial rule.

1939 Japanese location scouts find New Zealand to be ideal for their major WWII epic.

1947 In what many critics call a "tacked-on happy ending," New Zealand is granted independence by Britain.

1999 Troops from New Zealand join UN peacekeeping forces in Timor via creative editing.

2005 A *Variety* magazine article leaks the information that former prime minister David Lange will die in the final installment of his life.

PEOPLE » FOUR MILLION LIVES... HANG IN THE BALANCE...

New Zealand is sparsely populated with people of European descent, ideal for casting in primary or secondary roles. In addition, New Zealand contains a large indigenous population called the Maori, who are perfect for lighting, rigging, carpentry, or any stunts calling for an actor to be lit on fire.

New Zealanders of all races pride themselves on their national character development, their tight-knit film communities, and their vibrant traditional craft services, still practiced in the original buffet style.

FACTS » STARTS FRIDAY

NATIONAL ANTHEM
Composed by John Williams

MOTTO
"Every hour is magic hour"

VIOLENT CRIME
Squibs, blood packets, delicately handled rape scenes

NATIONAL QUOTAS
SAG-dictated, subject to change without notification

MARITIME CLAIMS
2004 tsunami result of out-of-control CGI effects

PET PEEVE
Being confused for Australia, reshoots (tie)

CULTURE
It is customary to exchange headshots when meeting a New Zealander for the first time

FAMOUS CITIZENS
Peter Jackson (director), Russell Crowe (actor), Paul Byrne (extra, *Xena: Warrior Princess*)

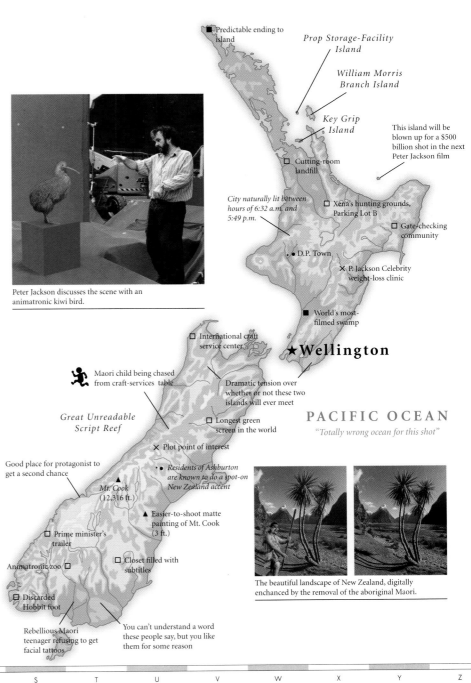

Peter Jackson discusses the scene with an animatronic kiwi bird.

Predictable ending to island

Prop Storage-Facility Island

William Morris Branch Island

Key Grip Island

This island will be blown up for a $500 billion shot in the next Peter Jackson film

Cutting-room landfill

City naturally lit between hours of 6:32 a.m. and 5:49 p.m.

Xena's hunting grounds, Parking Lot B

Gate-checking community

D.P. Town

P. Jackson Celebrity weight-loss clinic

World's most-filmed swamp

International craft service center

★ **Wellington**

Maori child being chased from craft-services table

Dramatic tension over whether or not these two islands will ever meet

Great Unreadable Script Reef

Longest green screen in the world

PACIFIC OCEAN
"Totally wrong ocean for this shot"

Plot point of interest

Good place for protagonist to get a second chance

Residents of Ashburton are known to do a spot-on New Zealand accent

Mt. Cook (12,316 ft.)

Easier-to-shoot matte painting of Mt. Cook (3 ft.)

Prime minister's trailer

Closet filled with subtitles

Animatronic zoo

Discarded Hobbit foot

Rebellious Maori teenager refusing to get facial tattoos

You can't understand a word these people say, but you like them for some reason

The beautiful landscape of New Zealand, digitally enchanced by the removal of the aboriginal Maori.

North Pole

Guess What, Kids— No Santa Here

While the North Pole still holds some mysteries, 150 years of exhaustive scientific study has conclusively proven that this bleak arctic ice sheet is absolutely void of any obese and immortal altruist living in an enchanted village powered by elf dust.

Despite the claims of so many ignorant children, who say Santa's Village is only visible to those who "believe," thousands of infallible radar installations would have nonetheless detected it by now. In addition, none of the myriad government satellites currently in orbit—devices that could photograph a reindeer carcass from space—have ever picked up even a single image of a warmly lit workshop or a giant candy cane.

Even if this supposed "Santa Claus" has somehow survived centuries of deadly below-freezing temperatures, he did so without a viable communications infrastructure, steady source of food, or functioning electrical grid.

However, though mountains of irrefutable evidence can now debunk any and all claims of this ridiculous figure's existence, one question still remains: Where do all the presents come from?

Soviet submarine that could use a push

Candy cane could never stand a chance of penetrating ice

✕ Inuit pie plant (formerly Eskimo pie plant)

✕ Scientists trying to figure out why children are so fucking gullible

✕ Site of 1982 blubber fight

✕ Hole that goes to South Pole

Perhaps this barren strip of jagged ice is Santa's runway

✕ Robert Peary's toes

✕ Breath freezes inside your lungs here

✕ Reindeer has red nose because of internal hemorrhaging

✕ Maybe Santa's corpse would be here

✕ Knockoff snowflake warehouse

✕ Inuit child skipping past near-dead team of German explorers

MELTIEST POINT ON PLANET

✕ Geologists burning thousands of letters to Santa to stay warm

✕ Expedition stopping to enjoy popsicles made from own urine

Not A Trace Of Peppermint In This Ice Floe At All

✕ This man with white beard is not Santa, he's George, and he's Jewish

Here is exactly how far Santa would make it before being shot down by NORAD

Squint real hard and maybe—just maybe—you'll see the spot where Santa would have succumbed to the cold, had he been real.

FACTS » AN ICEPACK OF LIES

LOCATION
The part at the very top

AREA COMPARATIVE
One Santa's Village ravaged by relentless pounding ice storms

OFFICIAL MOTTO
Probably something about triumph or perseverance

ECONOMY
Economic activity is mainly limited to nothing

LABOR FORCE
Imaginary

AGRICULTURAL PRODUCTS
Dancing in children's heads

NATURAL HAZARDS
Being a gigantic iceberg

ZIP CODE
None

INTERNATIONAL DISPUTES
Israel refuses to acknowledge North Pole's existence

OUR MAGNETIC POLES »

The Earth's magnetic field, which radiates from the poles and creates a powerful radiation shield, plays a vital role in global navigation and broadcasts of ABC's *Wife Swap*.

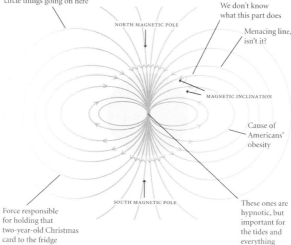

If "T" is equal to one N/Amp-m (force/current-distance), then B proves that there are some pretty important circle things going on here

NORTH MAGNETIC POLE

We don't know what this part does

Menacing line, isn't it?

MAGNETIC INCLINATION

Cause of Americans' obesity

SOUTH MAGNETIC POLE

Force responsible for holding that two-year-old Christmas card to the fridge

These ones are hypnotic, but important for the tides and everything

A GREAT EXPLORER »

Robert Peary (and Matthew Henson)

American explorer Robert Peary reached the North Pole in 1909 with the aid of his black assistant Matthew Henson. Near the Pole, a severely frostbitten Peary sent Henson ahead to clear a path, establish the landmark's exact location, and plant the flag for Peary, who was later informed that he had become the first man in history to conquer the top of the world.

South Pole

Waiting For Death's Warm Embrace

A massive, ice-covered continent at the Earth's southernmost tip, Antarctica would set all records for low temperatures if the man in charge of keeping such measurements weren't currently lost in a blinding whirlwind of snow, wildly gnawing at his quickly freezing flesh in a desperate attempt to survive for another five minutes.

Composed of harsh, unforgiving hellscapes dotted with white fields of maddening flatness, much of Antarctica remains uncharted, giving geologists reason to believe there are a number of exciting ways to die yet to be discovered.

As Antarctica's ice and snow continue to melt at an alarming rate, scientists studying the effects of global climate change while huddled together for warmth near a small gas stove in the depths of the frozen continent are doing all they can to figure out why they should give a flying fuck about anything besides getting the hell out of there. Most agree that Antarctica will soon become a popular vacation spot for tourists looking to escape the 140-degree temperatures and massive flooding of the rest of the world.

Explorer Ernest Shackleton overcame a blister on his thumb, incessant nagging from his wife, and mental retardation to reach the South Pole.

FACTS » FREEZER BURNT

LOCATION
The bottom

LEGAL SYSTEM
Law Of Club And Fang

LIFE EXPECTANCY
3,700 years (frozen in suspended animation)

INTERNATIONAL RELATIONS
The 45-nation Antarctic Treaty protects the region from exploitation, outlaws military activity, and declares it far too fucking cold

LAND USE
Holding ice

HOLIDAY
Day It Reached −3° Day

NATURAL HAZARDS
Frostbite, hypothermia, being absorbed by shape-shifting alien creature that has been lying in wait for millennia

TERRITORIAL CLAIMS »

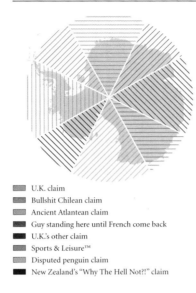

- U.K. claim
- Bullshit Chilean claim
- Ancient Atlantean claim
- Guy standing here until French come back
- U.K.'s other claim
- Sports & Leisure™
- Disputed penguin claim
- New Zealand's "Why The Hell Not?!" claim

SIDEBAR » SOME LIVING THINGS

Antarctica is populated mostly by penguins, penguin-eating seals, lichen, algae, and another type of lichen. It is also home to several small groups of researchers studying the effect that sleeping 20 hours a day has on one's ability to listlessly throw playing cards into a hat. These dedicated scientists also spend much of their time interpreting data from the growing number of voices in their head, trying to remember what it is they were sent into this terrible place to do, and resisting the impulse to step out into the cold and keep walking until they disappear into oblivion.

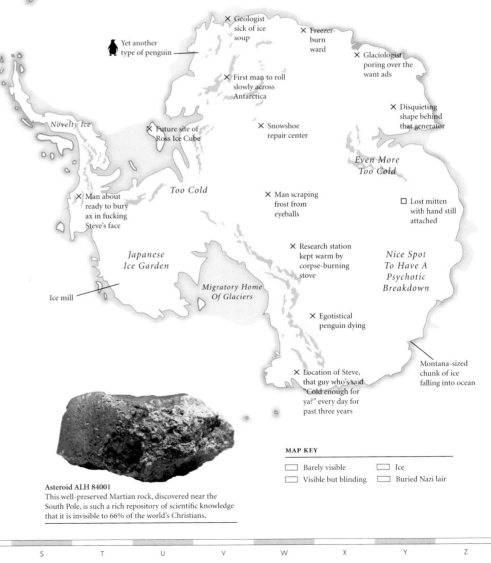

- × Geologist sick of ice soup
- × Freezer-burn ward
- × Glaciologist poring over the want ads
- Yet another type of penguin
- × First man to roll slowly across Antarctica
- × Disquieting shape behind that generator
- *Novelty Ice*
- × Future site of Ross Ice Cube
- × Snowshoe repair center
- *Even More Too Cold*
- × Man about ready to bury ax in fucking Steve's face
- *Too Cold*
- × Man scraping frost from eyeballs
- □ Lost mitten with hand still attached
- *Japanese Ice Garden*
- × Research station kept warm by corpse-burning stove
- *Nice Spot To Have A Psychotic Breakdown*
- Ice mill
- *Migratory Home Of Glaciers*
- × Egotistical penguin dying
- Montana-sized chunk of ice falling into ocean
- × Location of Steve, that guy who's said "Cold enough for ya?" every day for past three years

Asteroid ALH 84001
This well-preserved Martian rock, discovered near the South Pole, is such a rich repository of scientific knowledge that it is invisible to 66% of the world's Christians.

MAP KEY

- ▭ Barely visible
- ▭ Visible but blinding
- ▭ Ice
- ▭ Buried Nazi lair

Greenland

» GREENLAND NIGHTLIFE

The Largest Land Mass On Earth

As anyone who has seen a world map in the last 50 years knows, Greenland is larger than Africa and South America combined.

Comprising nearly half the Earth's surface area, Greenland stretches from the North Pole to the equator. Its colossal size poses a hazard for ships departing from the eastern seaboard of the U.S., the banks of Western Europe, and parts of South America. Larger vessels must maneuver perilously around Greenland's towering ice-cliff borders shortly after leaving port. These ice cliffs, which can be seen from as far away as Kansas, reach into the troposphere. Greenland's tallest mountain dwarfs Mount Everest at 186,911 feet.

Greenland's massive landscape is topped with a thick ice shelf that occasionally cracks, dropping large chunks of ice onto other nations. One such chunk that fell in 1992 crushed Guatemala, Honduras, and Nicaragua.

Despite its immense size, Greenland is home to just eight Inuit hunter-gatherers and a lone U.S. Navy communications officer stationed in a small radio tower.

HISTORY » AT MOST, ONE OR TWO EVENTS

Greenland has played, at best, no part on the international stage.

The first recorded mention of Greenland comes from the 10th century, when Viking explorer Erik the Red, who was famous for not being particularly good at naming things, spotted the stark white continent and named it "Greenland." He then patted his dog, "Cat," laid anchor and dropped sail on his "bathtub," and founded a new colony he called "No Way We'll All Freeze To Death In Just A Few Short Years-Towne."

In the centuries that followed, the area remained largely uninhabited, save for nomadic Inuits who, in 1432, reported heavy snow, and, in 1433, died.

Greenland was not thought about again until the 16th century, when British explorers Martin Frobisher and John Davis passed by the country while looking for a new passage to China. They passed it again on their way back.

Today, Greenland sits at the forefront of climate science. The remote land hosts researchers from all over the world, who venture to the country to measure ice-core temperatures in an effort to determine the Earth's climate history. Unfortunately, they find that the ice is always exactly 0°C.

FACTS » MAY APPEAR LARGER IN MERCATOR PROJECTION

SIZE
10^{20} Rhode Islands

MOTTO
"If you can't take the bitter unending cold, get out of the hypothermic shock"

LEADING INDUSTRY
Ice scraping

IMPORTS
One piece of mail every 60 years

EXPORTS
Rising sea levels

NATURAL RESOURCES
Seals

LEGAL SYSTEM
The ancient Eskimo code of the ice ax

LAND USE
Ice (81%), rock (12%), rocky ice (5%), icy rock (2%)

POTENTIAL LAND USE
Best Supermax prison ever

GREAT WORKS OF LITERATURE
Burned for fuel

SOVEREIGNTY
Greenland is the private property of Danish fur trader Soren Rasmussen; it is currently for sale

WORLD'S SNOWBALL RESERVES

SHITLOAD OF FJORDS

✕ Totally awesome frost ape that hasn't even been discovered yet

☐ High-rise igloo

✕ Legendary ice scraper stuck in rock

NATO forces dumping salt

☐ Hidden Nazi Fortress Of The Red Skull

Inexplicable free Wi-Fi zone

✕ Real-estate deal of the century

■ Ample room for port city of Hoolarilik (*potential pop. 30 million*)

✕ Front door to hypothermia ward frozen shut

✕ Driver of overheated tow truck having mental breakdown

Radio tower
(*barely gets AM stations*)

MAP KEY

☐ Vast
▨ Barren

✕ Walk to neighbor's house entering 15th day

☐ Childhood home of Gerry Mercator

GREENLAND   AFRICA   SOUTH AMERICA   THE CONTINENTAL U.S.   A GOLF BALL

× Low-traffic Slushee stand

× Post office refuses to deliver mail here, on principle

700-foot-tall naturally occurring snowman

× Man working on his novel beginning to go crazy

Greenland bikini team *(frozen in ice)*

× World's slipperiest sidewalk

• **God-it's-cold**

× Nebraska-sized hail

× Man attempting to circumnavigate Greenland dying of old age

▲ MT. ENORMOUS *(977,082,342,737 m.)*

× Discarded frostbit penis

× Man whose car broke down 20 miles away trying to find somebody, anybody

• *Seized by walruses*

Indian Ocean

Vast Oil Fields And Massive Gold Deposits Free For The Taking

□ Local news team forced to talk about snow for half an hour again tonight

■ Former site of peninsula that broke away in 1511 B.C. to form what is known today as "Europe"

Failed Penguin Colony

× Out-of-control snow-cone machine

× Frozen Viking who thought he could wear fur shorts all winter

× Local man whose blood freezes every morning

Nuuk★ *(pop. 11)*

× Remains of caveboy who was paid five rocks to shovel after Ice Age

□ Snow-pants rental

■ Formerly great little Greenlandian place, now deserted

× Enclave of Vikings who believe The Great Raid Of 841 is still going on

× Italian woman trying to sell someone some shaved ice

□ 3,000-meter snow fort

× Ham-radio enthusiast

× Organic frozen-food store

Only patch of green in Greenland

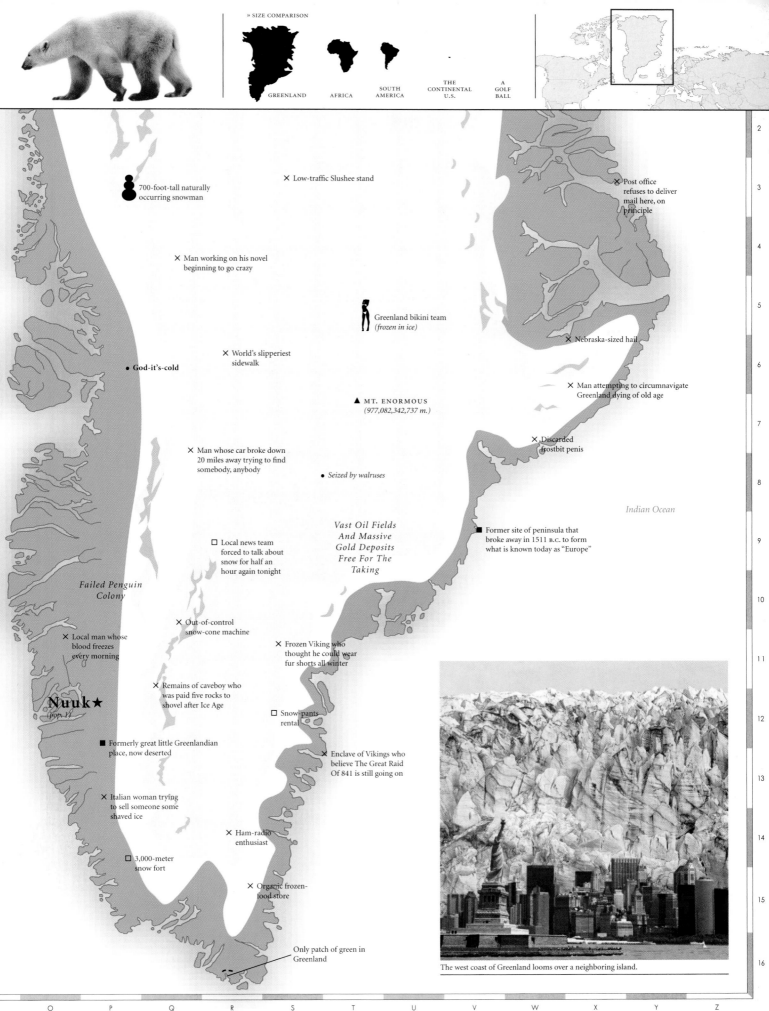

The west coast of Greenland looms over a neighboring island.

2 3 4 5 6 7 8 9 10 11 12 13 14 15 16

J O P Q R S T U V W X Y Z

Photography Credits

AFGHANISTAN 203–204
Afghan Shooting A Man - Z. Mir/**N**
bin Laden - **GC**
Boy With AK47 - **GC**
Explosion - **GC**
Fighter - Shamil Zhumatov/**N**
Girl Skeleton - **GC**
Man Portrait - Joseph Rodriguez/**N**
Praying Man - **GC**
Rubble Horizontal - **GC**
Rubble Vertical - **GC**
Missile Launcher - Saeed Khan/**N**
RPG Skybox - John D. McHugh/**GC**
British Naval Officer - **GC**
Buddha Statue - Muzammil Pasha/**N**

ALBANIA 176
Cabbage - **P**
Jim Belushi - Vince Bucci/**GC**
King Zog - **GC**
Resort - **N**

ANDORRA 147
Sign Background - **GC**
Zales - Web Image

ANGOLA 068
Jonas Savimbi - **GC**
Skybox - **N**
Soldier Cutout - Scott Peterson/**GC**

ANTIGUA+BARBUDA 041
Bouquet - **GC**
Wedding Rings - **GC**
Cake - **N**

ARGENTINA 049–050
Nazi On Porch - **I**
Juan Perón - **GC**
Old Nazi For Porch - **I**
Nazi Beach - **N**
Dictator 1 - **N**
Dictator 2 - **N**
Dictator 3 - **GC**
Madonna - **N**
Tango - **N**
Wanniarachchi - **GC**

ARMENIA 205
Man - Dimitar Dilkoff/**GC**
Memorial - Jim Baird/**N**

AUSTRALIA 231–232
Aborigines - Dallas Heaton/
John Heaton/**N**
Backpackers - Greg Wood/**GC**
Boomerang - **N**
Clipper Ship - **GC**
Football - Tony Ashby/**GC**
Kangaroo - **GC**
Koala - John G. Mabanglo/**GC**

Nature Show - Robert Caputo/**GC**
Nicole Kidman - Mark Mainz/**GC**
People Photo - William West/**GC**
Prisoner - **GC**
Rupert Murdoch - Evan Agostini/**GC**
Russell Crow - **GC**
Shark - Carl Roessler/**GC**
Snake - **P**
Sydney Opera House - Tim Graham/**GC**
Tarantula - **N**
Tasmanian Devil - Ian Waldie/**GC**
Vegemite - **GC**

AUSTRIA 154
Mozart - **GC**
Mozart - Sean Gallup/**GC**
Skybox - **GC**
Viola - **P**
Austria Skybox - **GC**

AZERBAIJAN 206
Kasperov - Maxim Marimur/**GC**
Mosque - Damie Meyer/**GC**
Hot Dog Eater - **I**

BAHAMAS 040
Palm Tree - Tim Graham/**GC**
Tropical drink - Sklar/**N**

BAHRAIN 121
Sheik Skybox - **GC**
Water slides - Charlene Fox

BANGLADESH 197
Wave - Pablo Sanchez/**N**

BARBADOS 043
Yacht with Jolly Roger - **GC**
Treasure Chest - **P**

BELGIUM 158
Waffle - **N**
Chocolate - **P**
Brussel Sprouts - **P**

BELIZE 017
Columbus - **GC**
Windswept Trees - Scott Smith/**N**
Hurricane - Tim Chapman/**N**

BENIN 099
Happy Africans - Florin Iorganda/**N**

BOLIVIA 051
Razorblade - **P**
Bolivian Farmers - Aizar Raldes/**N**

BOSNIA+HERZEGOVINA 174
Skybox - **N**
UN Soldier - Thomas Coex/**GC**

BOSTWANA 066
AIDS Man - Brent Stirton/**GC**
Condom - **I**
Hand With Vial -
Maxim Marmur/ **GC**

Skybox - Jacob Halaska/**N**

BRAZIL 047–048
Asses - Alexander Hassenstein/**GC**
Carmen Miranda - **GC**
Favela - B. Martinez/**GC**
New Shantytown -
Antonio Scorza/**GC**
Pele - **GC**
Plant - Tim Graham/**GC**
Sao Paulo Skyline - **N**
Sao Paulo Skyline -
Marie Hippenmayer/**GC**
Soccer Player - Stuart Franklin/**GC**
Thong Woman -
H. John Maier Jr./**GC**
Tree Frog - **P**

BRUNEI 224
Palace - Jimin Lai/**GC**
Brunei Palace - Jimin Lai/**GC**
Sultan of Brunei - **N**

BULGARIA 179
Thug - **I**
Pigs - Elizabeth Snow

CAMBODIA 218
Skull Skybox - Harley Soltes/**N**
Skeletor - W. Cameroon - **P**
Children dancing - ZJ (sreisaat)

CAMEROON 091
Mapmaker - **GC**
Map - James Whitmore/**GC**

CANADA 023–024
CN Tower/Skyline - **P**
Hockey Fight - Craig Abel/**GC**
Moose - Jack Flash/**GC**
Stanley Cup - Bruce Bennett/**GC**
Wayne Gretzky - Barry Gossage/**GC**
Mountie - Richard T. Nowitz/**GC**

CENTRAL AFRICAN REPUBLIC 090
Zebra - **P**

CHAD 089
Corrupt Man - **GC**

CHILE 053
Heads 1 - Robert Nickelsberg/**GC**
Heads 2 - **P**

CHINA 189–190
Bamboo Plant - **I**
Bowl of Rice - **P**
David Carradine - **GC**
Dragon - **P**
Dragon Dance - Frederic J. Brown/**GC**
Forbidden City -
John W. Banagan/**GC**
Fortune Cookie - **P**
Kung Fu - Anoek De Groot/**N**
Lao Tzu - **GC**
Mao Zedong - **GC**

Noodles - Burke/**N**
Paper - **I**
People Section - **GC**
Ramen - **P**
Shanghai Skyline - Peter Gridley
Tanks - Robyn Beck/**GC**
Tea - **I**

COLOMBIA 052
Razor/Coke - **P**

COSTA RICA 032
Real Estate Agent - **GC**
Rainforest - Tim Graham/**GC**
Mountain - **N**

CROATIA 173
Landmine - Alexander Joe/**GC**
Severed Leg - **GC**
Sheryl Crow - Mark Mainz/**GC**
Croatia Landscape -
Monika Fahrnberger

CUBA 035–036
Mechanic/Surgeon - Adalberto
Roque/**GC**
Prison - Joe Mozingo/**N**
Hospital - Lee Lockwood/**GC**
Boat - Gregory Ewald/**GC**
Stray Dog-Dog - **N**
Stray Dog-Street - A.J. Sisco/**N**
Camp X-Ray - Shane T. McCoy/**GC**
Castro - Grey Villet/**GC**
Cigar Guys - Stephen Ferry/**GC**
Cigar Spot - **I**
Collapsed Building - Scott Warren/**GC**
Elian Gonzalez - Tim Chapman/**GC**
Man not watching Castro - **GC**
National Hospital - **N**
Prostitute - Enrique Cano/**N**
Surgeon/mechanic - Jorge Rey/**GC**
Truck Boat - Gregory Ewald/**GC**
Broken Car - **GC**

CYPRUS 134
UN Soldiers by Fence - Jeff McIntosh/**N**

CZECH REPUBLIC 169
Backpackers - Greg Wood/**GC**
Typewriter - **P**
Prague Buildings -
Dallas and John Heaton/**N**
Cockroach - Amie Vanderford
Background for cockroach -
Aaron Barker

DENMARK 160
Hans - **GC**
Happy Couple Screencap - **GC**
Lego Castle - Ben Apps

DOMINICA 043
Rocky Beach - Keith Levit/**N**

DOMINICAN REPUBLIC 038
Sammy Sosa -

Jonathan Daniel/**GC**
Pineapple Baseball -
Tobias Titz/**GC**
Sammy Sosa - Jed Jacabsohn/**GC**
Sosa - Jonathan Daniel/**GC**
Sugar Cane - Melanie Stetson/**GC**
Tape Ball - **I**

DEM. REPUBLIC OF CONGO 069
Gorilla - **P**
Mobutu Headshot - **GC**
Molotov Cocktail In Air - Marco
Longari/**GC**
Shot Of Violence - Lionel Healing/**N**

EAST TIMOR 228
Timor Violence - William West/**GC**

ECUADOR 056
Volcano - **GC**
Charles Darwin - **GC**
Capybara - **GC**
Tapir - **P**
Tortoise 1 - Rodrigo Buendia/**GC**
Tortoise 2 - **GC**

EGYPT 113–114
Abu Simbel - Hisham Ibrahim/**GC**
Abu Simbel - **GC**
Camel - Peter McBride/**GC**
Egypt Nefertiti - Sean Gallup/**GC**
Giza - **GC**
Horus - Jacob Halaska
Mummy - Aladin Abdel Naby/**N**
Museum goers - Mike Nelson/**GC**
Necklace - **P**
Nerfertiti - Sean Gallup/**GC**
Pith - **GC**
Souvenirs - Khaled Desoukv/**GC**
Souvenirs - Khaled Desoukv/**GC**
Sphinx - **GC**
Tut - Ethan Miller/**GC**
Mummy - Aladin Abdel Naby/**N**

EL SALVADOR 029
Jose Cabezas - **GC**

ENGLAND 137–138
Big Ben - Richard T. Nowitz
Cup of Tea - **P**
Doubledecker Bus - Mark Polott/**N**
Hugh Grant - Dave Hogan/**GC**
Jack the Ripper - J. Vollmer/**N**
Queen - **GC**
Spice Girls Head 2 - Victor
Malafronte/**GC**
Spice Girls Head 1 - **GC**
Spice Girls - **GC**
Sherlock Holmes - Lambert/**GC**
Shakespeare - Rischgitz/**GC**
Redd Roxx - **GC**
London Vista - **C**
Isaac Newton - **GC**

ERITREA 084
Protestors - Alexander Joe/**N**

Teen - Scott Peterson / **GC**
Teens on Truck - Issouf Sanogo/**GC**

ESTONIA 165
Baltic Town - Dallas and John Heaton/**N**
Folk Dancers - Morev Valery/**N**
Tuba - **P**

ETHIOPIA 085–086
Bowl Rough - **I**
American Kids Skybox - **I**
Dead Animals - Michael Wirtz/**N**
Fork and Spoon - **I**
Sad Child - Abraham Fisseha/**N**
Sally Struthers - Frederick M.
Brown/**GC**
Soldiers - **GC**
We Are The World - **GC**
Landscape - Gughi Fassino/**N**

FINLAND 164
Dog Toboggan - **N**
Kids Sledding - Phoebe Dunn/**N**
Snowman - **P**
Snowflake - Don Hammond/**C**
Nokia - **GC**
Kalevala - **P**
Candy Cane - Lew Robertson/**N**

FRANCE 145–146
Arc de Triomphe - Gary M. Prior/
GC
Bread - **P**
Charlemagne - **GC**
Model Body - Francois Guillot/**GC**
Model Head - Francois Guillot/**GC**
Monet Painting - **GC**
Poodle - Enrique Cano /**N**
Guillotine - Rischgitz/**GC**
Joan of Arc - **GC**
Wine - **P**
Model - Mustafa Ozer/**GC**
Sartre - **GC**
Versailles - **GC**

FRENCH GUIANA 060
Rocket - **N**

GAMBIA 104
River Skybox - Fritz Poelking/**N**

GEORGIA 205–206
Cross - Dmitry Astakhov/**GC**

GERMANY 155–156
EU Rally - **GC**
Gutenberg Bible - **P**
Hitler - Imagno/**GC**
Kaiser Wilhelm - **GC**
VW Bug - Hugo Jaeger/**GC**
Beer - **GC**
Beer - **P**
Berlin Wall - **N**

GHANA 100
Horrified - Roberto Schmidt/**GC**
Kofi Annan - Jean-Pierre Clatot/**GC**

GREECE 177
Amphora - **GC**
Aristophanes - **GC**
Evzone Skybox - Nigel Hicks/
Dorling Kindersly/**N**
Hercules - **GC**
Hercules Head - Gordon Gahan/**GC**
Herodotus - Mansell/**GC**
Hippocrates - Mansell/**GC**
Homer - **GC**
Socrates - **GC**
Socrates - **GC**
Trojan Horse - **P**
Zeus - **P**

GREENLAND 239–240
Polar Bear - Tom Brakefield/**GC**
Landscape - Owen Jones

GRENADA 041–042
Helicopter - Matthew Naythons/**GC**

GUATEMALA 028
Police - Eliana Aponte/**N**
Sad Person - **GC**
Shelter - Joel Auerbach/**N**

HAITI 037
Witch Doctor - George Konig/**GC**
Zombie Skybox - **GC**
Zombie - Issouf Sanogo/**N**

HONDURAS 030
Bananas - **P**
Coffee - **P**
Fruit - **P**
Mudslide - **N**
Guerillas - Cindy Karp/**GC**

HUNGARY 171
Houdini - **GC**
Porn DVD - **I**
Porno Shoot - Gabriel Bouys/**GC**
King Stephen III - **GC**
Mine - Ericka Rennie

ICELAND 161
Vista - Paul Nicklen/**GC**
Landscape - Connie Coleman

INDIA 199–200
Sitar - **GC**
Bollywood Film - **N**
Buddha Head - **P**
Call Center Skybox - **N**
Cow Headshot - **N**
Ganges Skybox - **GC**
Bindi - **N**
Taj Mahal - Franz Aberham/**GC**
Gandhi - Elliott & Fry/**GC**
Village - Adek Berry/**GC**
Elephant - Dallas and John Heaton/**N**

INDONESIA 227–228
Skybox Nikes - **I**

Suharto - **GC**
Workers Skybox - Dimas Aro/**N**

IRAN 125–126
Khomeini - Gabriel Duval/**GC**
Landscape - **P**
Protest - Behrouz Mehri/**GC**
Protest Effigy - Rizwan Tabassum/**GC**
Satellite Photo - **GC**

IRAQ 123–124
Babylonia Shard - Roger Viollet/**GC**
Baghdad Bombing -
Wathiq Khuzaie/**GC**
Boy Walking - Wathiq Khuzaie/**GC**
Bush Statue Pick - **GC**
Car Bomb - Scott Peterson/**GC**
King Nebuchadnezzar - **GC**
Mosque - **GC**
Old Woman - Karim Sahib/**GC**
Saddam Hussein - AFP/**GC**
Smoky Street - Sabah Arar/**GC**

IRELAND 141
St. Patrick - **GC/N**
Potato - **P**
A House in Dingle - Chris Furniss

ISRAEL 129–130
Ariel Sharon - David Silverman/**GC**
Ben Gurion - Horst Tappe/**GC**
Jews - **GC**
Landscape Skybox - **GC**
Missile Menorah - **I**
Moshe Dayan - Arnold Newman/**GC**
Old Jews - **N**
Theodor Herzl - Imagino / **GC**
Jews Meeting - AFP/**GC**
Charlton Heston - Gene Lester/**N**
Mel Gibson - Vince Bucci/**GC**

ITALY 149–150
Mussolini Deli - Bert Hardy/**GC**
Landscape - Stefano Salvetti/**GC**
Tower of Pisa - **P**
Temple - Corbin G. Keech

IVORY COAST 101
Violence - Issouf Sanogo/**N**

JAPAN 215–216
Businessman - Koichi Kamoshida/**GC**
Geisha - Koichi Kamoshida/**GC**
Bowing - **N**
Royal Rania - Christophe Simon/**GC**
Shibuya Station Street Scene -
Kyle Hammons

JORDAN 132
Rania 1 - Kazuhiro Nogi/**GC**
Rania 2 - Kahlil Marzaawi/**GC**
Rania 3 - **GC**
Rania 4 - **GC**
Rania 5 - Khalil Marzaawi/**GC**
Rania 6 - MJ Kim/**GC**

Photography Credits

Rania 7 - Hassanm/**GC**

KENYA 081
Runners' Spot - Prakash Sing/**GC**

KUWAIT 122
Colin Powell Pick - Arnold Sachs/**GC**
Schwarzkopf - Bill Gentile/**N**
Kuwait King - **N**

KYRGYZSTAN 209
Man - Alexander Nemenov/**GC**

LAOS 217
Bucket - **P**
Water Buffalo - Sukree Sukplang/**N**
Hut - **P**
Woman - Sukree Sukplang/**N**
Mirek Towski/**N**

LATVIA166
Golden Goblet - Cary Wolinsky/**GC**
Ditch - Peter Cunliff-Jones/**GC**

LEBANON 128
Happy Girl with Rubble - Scott
Peterson/**GC**
Rubble - Ramzi Haidar/**GC**
Skybox - Haitham Mussawi/**GC**
Terrorist Crowd -
Salah Malkawi/**GC**

LIBYA 112
Ronald Reagan - **GC**
Pen - **P**

LITHUANIA 166
Noose - **P**

LUXEMBOURG 157
Castle - **P**

MACEDONIA 178
Alexander - **GC**
Landscape - David Brauchli/**GC**

MADAGASCAR 075
Green Mountain - Rene Fredrick/**GC**
Lemur - **P**

MALAWI 073
Beggar Statue - Krista Kennell/**N**
African Sculptures - **P**

MALAYSIA 223–224
Anwar Ibrahim -
Bazuki Muhammad/**N**
Orangutan PICK - **GC**
Orangutan - Adek Berry/**GC**
Petronus Towers -
Dallas and John Heaton/**N**

MALDIVES 198
Water - Stephen St. John/**GC**

MARIANA ISLANDS 234
Sweatshop - Lisa Terry/**GC**

MEXICO 025–026
Cortez, Montezuma - **P**
Fence - David McNew/**GC**
GM Factory - **I**
Mariachi Band - **GC**
Tequila - **I**
Day of the Dead - **N**
Pancho Villa - **N**
Pyramid - **P**
Julio Chavez - Mike Fiala/**N**

MONACO 148
Casino - Dominique Faget/**GC**
Formula One - Alberto Pizzoli/**GC**
Grace Kelly - **GC**

MONGOLIA 210
Landscape - Olivier Renck/**GC**
Mogan Freeman - Jim Ross/**GC**

MOROCCO 107–108
Cheap Rugs - **GC**
Bazaar - Marco Di Lauro/**GC**
Women - Frederic J. Brown/**GC**
Bazaar - Desiree van der Mei/**N**

MOZAMBIQUE 074
Sad Man - Melanie Freeman/**GC**

MYANMAR 196
Skybox - **GC**
Soldier Pointing Gun -
Robert Nickelsberg/**GC**
Than Swe - **GC**

NAMIBIA 067
Landscape - Xavier Front/**N**
Brangelina - Frazer Harrison/**GC**

NEPAL 194
Boy - Robb Kendrick / **GC**
Tenzing Norgay - Baron / **GC**

NETHERLANDS 159
Dikes - Ed Oudenaarden/**GC**
Dike- Tim Graham/**GC**

NEW ZEALAND 236
Film Reel - **P**
Xena - **GC**

NICARAGUA 031
Ortega - Terresita Chavarria/**GC**

NIGER 097
Mother - Pet-Anders Pettersson/**GC**

NIGERIA 095–096
Computer Students - **GC**
Plane Crash - Afolabi Sotunde/**N**

NORTH KOREA 211–212
Army on parade - **GC**

Nuke - **GC**
Flags - **GC**

NORTH POLE 237
Peary - **GC**
Landscape - Nicki Nikoni/**GC**
Schackleton - **GC**

NORTHERN IRELAND 140
Jameson Whisky Molotov Fire - **N**

NORWAY 162
Henrik Ibsen - **GC**
Viking - **GC**
Grass Roof Home -
Dallas and John Heaton/**N**
Rat - Harold M. Lambert/**GC**
Troll - Uwe Gerig/**N**

PAKISTAN 202
Crapscape - Paula Bronstein/**GC**
Kashmir - Jagdish Agarwal/**N**
Nuke - T.C. Halhotra/**GC**
Old Man - Eric Feferberg/**GC**
Street Scene - Asif Hassan/**GC**

PALESTINE 131
Soldier - Hazem Bader/**GC**

PANAMA 033
Canal Dig - **GC**
Noriega - Bill Gentile/**N**
Inner Tubers - Pat Canova/**N**
Mosquito - Dr. Murawski/**GC**
Noriega - **N**

PAPUA NEW GUINEA 223
Landscape - **N**

PARAGUAY 054
Dam - Patrick B. Barr

PERU 055
Llama - **GC**

PHILIPPINES 226
Skybox - Romeo Gacad/**GC**
Workers Skybox - Halim Berbar/**N**

POLAND 168
Karwowski - **I**
Brendan Head - **I**
Ladder Spin - **I**
Lech Walesa - **GC**

PORTUGAL 142
Magellan - **N**
Vasco Da Gama - **GC**
Map - Evans/**GC**
Ship - **GC**
Donkey -Jamie Hunter

PUERTO RICO 039
Parade - Frances M. Roberts/**N**

QATAR 121
Background for News Van -
Ali Al-Saadi/**GC**

REPUBLIC OF CONGO 070
Poor Man -
Keith Levit Photography/**N**
Violence - Yann LaTronche/**N**

ROMANIA 180
Bat Skybox - Greg Wood/**GC**
Castle Dracula - Dan Materna/**N**

RUSSIA 183–186
Ballet - Patrick Riviere/**GC**
Charging Crowd - **GC**
Crowd Of Workers - **GC**
Dead Body Pile - **GC**
Gorbachev -
Direck Halstead/**GC**
Khrushchev - Hank Walker /**GC**
Khrushchev - **GC**
Krushchev - **GC**
Krushchev Banging Shoe - **GC**
Lenin - P. Otchupa/**GC**
Lenin Speech - **GC**
Rasputin - **GC**
Revolutionaries Shooting - **GC**
Rusty Submarine - **GC**
Scattering Crowd - Bulla/**GC**
Siberia - Sarah Leen/**GC**
Stalin - **GC**
Arctic Fox - Paul Nicklen/**GC**
Bear - **GC**
Yeltsin - STF/**GC**
Siberia Landscape - Sarah Leen/**GC**

RWANDA 079–080
Skull 1 - Pilar Olivares/**N**
Skull 2 - Erik De Castro/**N**

SAUDI ARABIA 117–118
Bush Kisses Sheik - **GC**
Camels - W. Robert Moore/**GC**
King Fahd - Joseph Barrak/**GC**
Calligraphy - Ramzi Haldar/**GC**
Oil Mecca -
Muhammad Fala'ah/**GC**
Beauty Contest - Salah Malkawi/**GC**
Lawrence of Arabia - **GC**

SCOTLAND 139
Bagpiper - Amanda Clement
Bagpiper - Tim Brakemeier/**N**

SERBIA 175
Gavrilo Princip - **GC**
Milosevic - **GC**

SEYCHELLES 076
Building - Belen Molina/**N**

SIERRA LEONE 103
Diamond Skybox - Steve Puettzer/**GC**

SINGAPORE 225
Cleaning Police - Asim Tanveer/**N**
Kwan Yew - Robyn Beck/**GC**

SLOVAKIA 170
City - Forrest Anderson/**GC**
Skybox - Peter Essick/**GC**

SLOVENIA 172
Crates - **P**

SOMALIA 082
Kids Playing on Chopper - **GC**
Skyline - Tyler Hicks/**GC**

SOUTH AFRICA 063–064
Landscape - **C**
Cemetery - Doring Kindersley/**N**

SOUTH KOREA 213
Tae Kwon Do - Glyn Kirk/**N**
Tae Kwon Do Face - **P**
Tae Kwon Do - Friedemann Vogel/**GC**
Violin Kid - Jonathan Kim/**N**

SOUTH POLE 238
Sidebar - **N**
Penguins - Eastcott Mornatiuk/**GC**

SPAIN 143–144
Beach - Glenn Campbell/**GC**
Castanets - **P**
Cigarette - **P**
Dali Moustache - **GC**
De Soto mustache - **GC**
Flamenco - Sash Knotek/**N**
Franco - **GC**
Ham Spot - **P**
Siesta Skybox - Pierre-Philippe
Marcou/**GC**
Spanish Armada - **GC**

SRI LANKA 198
Tsunami Aftermath - **GC**

STANS 207–209
Rock - **GC**
Stone - **GC**
Clump Skybox - **I**
Week - **I**
Outhouse Skybox - Shah Marai/**GC**
Old Woman Eating - Elvis Barukcic/**GC**

SUDAN 087–088
Jacob Silberberg/**GC**
Rally - Michael Brown/**GC**
Severed Head - Christophe Simon/**GC**
Sharon Stone - Bryan Bedder/**GC**
Fighters - Jacob Silberberg/**GC**

SURINAME 060
African Hut - **N**
Jungle Landscape - John Wang/**GC**
Eiffel Tower - **GC**

SWAZILAND 065
King Mswati - AFP/**GC**
Open Grave - Oleg Popov/**N**
AIDS March -
William F. Campbell/**GC**

SWEDEN 163
Swedish Model - **N**
Disused tank - Oliver Dewar

SWITZERLAND 153
Cuckoo Clock - Christopher Conrad

SYRIA 127
Scimitar - **I**
Distrustful Men - Louai Beshara/**GC**

TAIWAN 214
Chinese Navy - **GC**

TANZANIA 077
Home - Kate Holt
Animals Free - **P**
Lion - **GC**

THAILAND 221–222
Beach - **GC**
Kick Boxing - Frederic J. Brown/**N**

THREE SAINTS 044
Beach Skybox - Mario Tama/**GC**
Parrot - **GC**

TIBET 193
Bulldozer Pick - Liu Jin/**GC**
Monks Skybox - Alex Wong/**GC**
Mountain Pick - Paula Bronstein/
GC/N

TONGA 235
Palm Tree - **P**

TRINIDAD+TOBAGO 042
Limbo - Tony Bock/**N**
Steel Drum - **GC**
Drummer - Bob Coates/**N**

TUNISIA 111
Desert - Fethi Belaid/**GC**
Woman - **GC**

TURKEY 133
About photo - **GC**
Skyline - Scott Barbour/**GC**

UGANDA 078
Child Soldiers - Per-Anders
Pettersson/**GC**
Idi Amin - **GC**

UKRAINE 181
Cathedral - Sergei Supinsky / **GC**
Cossack - **GC**
King Oleg - **GC**
Painted Egg Sidebox - Yarovitsin

Roman / **N**
Wheat Field - **P**
Yuschenko - Bassignac Gilles / **N**
Ukraine Bride 2 - Burke / **N**

UNITED ARAB EMIRATES 120
Sheik - Hussein Anwar/**N**
Tennis - David Cannon/**GC**
Palm Island - **N**

URUGUAY 054
Soccer - Alejandra Brun/**GC**

U.S. BULLSHIT STATES 017–018
Minnesota Man - **I**
Alaska Land - Rich Reid/**GC**

U.S. MIDWEST 017–018
Dairy Cow - Lisa Adams
Flag Day Parade - Tim Boyle/**GC**
Red Barn - **N**
Snowblower - **GC**
Corn spot - Scott Lanza/**N**
Aerial Shot - David E. Scherman/**GC**

U.S. NORTHEAST 013–014
Amish - Kevin LaMarque/**N**
Ivy League Option 1 - **GC**
Lobster - **P**
Maine Lighthouse - Laura Farr/**N**
NYC Skyline - **GC**
US Capitol - **GC**
Liberty Bell - Peter Gridley/**N**

U.S. PACIFIC COAST 021
Beach - Prakash Singh/**GC**
Surfer Skybox - Pierre Tostee/**GC**

U.S. SOUTH 015–016
Alligator - Joe Raedle/**GC**
Basset Hound - **GC**
Chicken Drumstick - **I**
Colonel Sanders - **N**
Confederate Soldiers - **GC**
Cotton Picking - **GC**
Preacher - Phil Huber/**GC**
Bourbon - **I**
Civil War Battle - **GC**
Color Painting, Confederates - **GC**
Trailer Park - Mario Tama/**GC**
Retirees - Joe Raedle/**GC**
Retired People - **N**

U.S. ABOUT & HISTORY 009–012
Mount Rushmore Bush Head 1 - **GC**
Mount Rushmore Bush Head 2 - **GC**
1920s Gays - **GC**
Bald Eagle - Joe Sohm
FDR in Wheelchair -
Margaret Suckley/**N**
iPod Babies - **GC**
Nixon Middle Finger - **N**
Cubicles - Matthew Borkoski/**N**
Las Vegas Sphinx - Ethan Miller/**GC**
Paul Bunyan statue - Andrea

Feininger/**GC**

U.S. WEST 019–020
Covered Wagon - **N**
Cowboy Boots - **GC**
Cowboy Screencap - **GC**
Ghost Town - **P**
Hoover Dam - **GC**
Monument Valley - **P**
Six-Shooter - **P**
49er - **GC**

VATICAN CITY 151
Pope Innocent X - **GC**
Leo XIII - **GC**
Paul III - **GC**
Pope Benedict - Franco Origlia/**GC**
Pope John Paul - Patrick Herzog/**GC**
Pope-Hat - Vincenzo Pinto/**GC**

VENEZUELA 57–58
Shooters - **GC**
Protestors - Jack Bocaranda/**GC**
Beach - Adam Pretty/**GC**
Bolivar Skybox - Kimberly White/**N**
Chavez Moon Podium - **N**
Chavez Moon Podium - **N**
Chavez Mooning Rough - **N**
Indians Skybox - Emilio Guzman/**N**
Jungle Skybox - **GC**
Snake - GK Hart/Vikki Hart/**GC**
Chavez Skybox - Juan Barreto/**GC**
Pot Bangers - Juan Barreto/**N**
Snake - **P**

VIETNAM 219–220
Vet Possible - Justin Sullivan/**GC**
Hanoi Hilton - Hoang Dinh Nam/**N**
Huey Chopper - **GC**
LBJ - Ewing Galloway/**N**
M16 - Wolfgang List/**N**
Pho - **I**
Punji - National Archives
Vet - Justin Sullivan/**GC**
Vietnam and Burning - **N**
Ho Chi Minh - **GC**
Huey Chopper - **N**
M16 - Wolfgang List/**N**

WALES 139
Tom Jones - Dave Hogan/**GC**

WESTERN SAHARA 108
Dunes - Tim Graham/**GC**

ZAMBIA 071
Clothes Donation Bin - **I**
Mother + 1 - **GC**

ZIMBABWE 072
Mugabe - **GC**
Rhodes - **GC**

Country Index